THE MMPI MMPI-2 & MMPI-A IN COURT

THE MMPI, MMPI-2 & MMPI-A IN COURT

A PRACTICAL GUIDE FOR EXPERT WITNESSES AND ATTORNEYS

KENNETH S. POPE ▪ JAMES N. BUTCHER ▪ JOYCE SEELEN

AMERICAN PSYCHOLOGICAL ASSOCIATION
WASHINGTON, DC

Published by the
American Psychological Association
750 First Street, NE
Washington, DC 20002

Copies may be ordered from
APA Order Department
P.O. Box 2710
Hyattsville, MD 20784

Typeset in Berkeley by York Graphic Services, Inc., York, PA

Printer: Braun-Brumfield, Inc., Ann Arbor, MI
Jacket and text designer: Grafik Communications Ltd., Alexandria, VA
Technical/Production editors: Valerie Montenegro and Peggy Schlegel

Library of Congress Cataloging-in-Publication Data

Pope, Kenneth S.
The MMPI, MMPI-2, and MMPI-A in court: a practical guide for expert witnesses and attorneys / Kenneth S. Pope, James N. Butcher, and Joyce Seelen.
p. cm.
Includes bibliographical references and index.
ISBN 1-55798-182-5 (acid-free paper: casebound)
1. Psychology, Forensic. 2. Evidence, Expert—United States. 3. Psychological tests—Law and legislation—United States. 4. Minnesota Multiphasic Personality Inventory. I. Butcher, James Neal, 1933– II. Seelen, Joyce. III. Title.
KF8965.P66 1993
347.73'67—dc20 92-35352
[347.30767] CIP

Printed in the United States of America
First edition

Contents

continued

Exhibits and Tables

Figures

Preface

As the following biographical sketches indicate, the three of us come from diverse professional backgrounds. Yet all three have come to find the Minnesota Multiphasic Personality Inventory (MMPI) and its use and abuse in court central to our professional concerns.

In 1965, James Butcher, a new faculty member of the University of Minnesota and just out of graduate school at the University of North Carolina, organized the Symposium on Recent Developments in the Use of the MMPI to provide a forum for researchers to discuss current and proposed research on the MMPI. Over the 27 years of its existence, the annual symposium has served as a vehicle for many important new developments with the MMPI and generated numerous research investigations that have opened new research directions for the instrument. A year after the MMPI symposium began, the need for practical training in the use of the test became apparent because many psychologists were not receiving assessment training in their graduate programs. The MMPI symposium was expanded to include practical workshops on the clinical application of the MMPI. Since its inception, the MMPI Workshop Series has provided professional training on the MMPI and MMPI-2 to thousands of psychologists in the United States.

Throughout his career in psychology, Butcher has been involved in studying the use of the MMPI in intercultural contexts. He has conducted research on psychopathology among different ethnic groups in the United States and has extensively explored the use of the MMPI in other cultures. Over the years he has conducted professional training programs in many other countries, including Belgium, China, Chile, Denmark, Egypt, Italy, Israel, Iran, Japan, Hong Kong, Mexico, and Norway. In 1970, he founded the International Conference on Personality Assessment, which has been held every 2 years. The International Conference provides the opportunity for scholars from a wide range of countries to discuss their research and to exchange views on issues and techniques in personality assessment with professionals from other countries.

Butcher has conducted extensive research on the MMPI for over 30 years in a broad range of contexts. His publications include basic research works in abnormal psychology, personality assessment, and the MMPI—including research methodology and computer applications of psychological tests. Most recently he has been a central figure in the revision of the MMPI and development of the MMPI-2 and MMPI-A. Butcher's contribution to the MMPI revision began in 1969 when he organized a national symposium to address the question of whether the MMPI needed to be revised and, if so, how. During the 1970s, he published articles and held additional meetings to keep alive the possibility of an MMPI revision. Finally, in 1982 the test publisher initiated a revision with a team composed of Jim Butcher, Grant Dahlstrom, Jack R. Graham, and Auke Tellegen (who participated in the later stages of the project). The MMPI revision effort spanned 10 years and included scores of empirical studies with a broad range of normal and clinical populations. This revision effort culminated in the publication of MMPI-2 in 1989 and the MMPI-A in 1992.

Butcher has authored a number of books on the MMPI and abnormal psychology. His published books include *Use of the MMPI-2 in Treatment Planning* (Oxford University Press, 1990); *A Practitioner's Guide to Computerized Psychological Assessment* (Basic Books, 1987); *Essentials of MMPI-2 and MMPI-A Interpretation* (with Carolyn L. Williams; University of Minnesota Press, 1992); *Abnormal Psychology and Modern Life* (9th ed., with Robert C. Carson; HarperCollins, 1992); and *Handbook of Research Methods in Clinical Psychology* (with Philip C. Kendall; John Wiley & Sons, 1982).

Butcher's forensic testimony, the source of much material included in this book, has been extensive and covers many types of legal cases. As might be expected, his testimony almost always centers around the interpretation of MMPI scores. Issues concerning technical aspects of the test or the likely meaning of a particular MMPI configuration are common themes in his court testimony. His forensic experience includes personal injury, criminal, family custody, and medical malpractice.

Joyce Seelen began working as an attorney in 1980 when she joined the Colorado State Public Defender's system. Learning how to examine and cross-examine psychological and psychiatric experts and how to understand psychological test results was a necessary part of representing poor persons accused of committing crimes. On an almost daily basis, psychological assessment issues arose in connection with testimony about competency, sanity, and mental culpability.

In 1982, Seelen represented a patient who had been confined to the state psychiatric hospital for many years after having been found not guilty of murder by reason of insanity. The patient maintained that he was sane. However, none of the doctors agreed. The heart of the subsequent trial was the cross-examination of the prosecution's doctors. A jury of six disregarded the stated opinions of the experts and decided that the patient was ready, with professional help, to begin life outside the hospital. (Colorado law has since been changed to limit a patient's opportunity to request release from a psychiatric hospitalization through a sanity trial.) That case provided a valuable lesson in the power of understanding and using psychological information.

When she left the public defender's office in 1983, she began a private civil practice that emphasized representation of people exploited by those in positions of trust. In most exploitation and abuse litigations, the primary damages are psychological. The initial hurdle in emotional damages cases involved how to communicate the emotional injury to the jury as effectively as an X ray or photograph could depict physical injury. Testimony based on standardized psychological tests—particularly the MMPI—and other methods of psychological assessment have provided that method of communication.

Ken Pope has found the MMPI useful in his clinical practice; has discovered—while serving on various hospital and professional ethics committees—an amazing range of ways that tests can be misused; and finds issues regarding the administration, scoring, and interpretation of the MMPI arising in many if not most of the civil and administrative law cases in which he consults or testifies as an expert witness. Unlike his two co-authors, he lacks any of the interesting personal anecdotes about how he became involved with the MMPI, and will leave it at that.

The three of us joined together to write this book because we could not find anything like it in the available literature. Each of us wanted a single volume that we could use in preparing for trials and could take to court with us. We wanted an up-to-date overview of the relevant issues and research. We wanted a single volume in which we could find information on all three versions of the MMPI, *Ethical Principles of Psychologists and Code of Conduct* of the American Psychological Association (APA), the validity and reliability data, the guidelines for forensic psychologists, and related information. We also wanted a single volume that could serve as sort of a checklist during preparation, something that could help to ensure that we did not overlook any crucial steps or resources during preparation. Finally, we wanted to assemble the basic deposition and cross-examination questions that are so central to expert testimony regarding psychological assessment.

Although the book focuses on the MMPI, we decided to include a variety of contextual, peripheral, and collateral information and issues (such as establishing fee arrangements and a written agreement between attorney and expert witness, examining complex theory and research in specific topic areas, and presenting the results of neuropsychological tests) that, although not inherently related to the MMPI, nevertheless tend to be important to trials involving the MMPI. We tried to include the kind of information we find useful and about which we and so many of our colleagues have questions as we prepare to go to court. We have tried to create a book that would be helpful not only to seasoned experts but also to those who have never previously been near an MMPI or a courtroom.

Five general areas of terminology and format seemed especially problematic. First, for the sake of brevity and convenience, we did not want to refer constantly to "the MMPI, the MMPI-2, and the MMPI-A." Therefore, we have often shortened this cumbersome phrase to "the MMPI." Although this choice to use "the MMPI" in a generic sense to refer to all three versions of the test risks some confusion, we have tried to ensure that the context (and, in some cases, explicit qualifiers such as "the original MMPI") will make it clear whether we are referring specifically to the original test (as distinct from the MMPI-2 and MMPI-A) or to the test as it appears in all three versions.

Second, it was relatively easy to refer to attorneys. But what words would we use to refer to psychologists and other professionals who might be called to present testimony on the MMPI? (Using the term "professional," unless the context happened to make it very clear, made it unclear whether we might be referring to attorneys, as they too are professionals.) To refer always to "expert witnesses" would unintentionally exclude some to whom this book is addressed. Clinical, counseling, and industrial-organizational psychologists as well as a variety of nonpsychologist therapists, counselors, and other professionals might have administered the MMPI to clients, patients, job applicants, students, and others. In a subsequent legal action, they might be subpoenaed to testify as percipient or fact witnesses (simply describing the results of the MMPI assessment and their sessions with the individual who was assessed without qualifying as an expert witness or offering professional opinions) rather than expert witnesses. Moreover, attorneys may retain an "expert" on the MMPI to help prepare a case (e.g., help the attorney to learn about the MMPI, help formulate deposition and cross-examination questions) while not designating the expert as a witness who would offer testimony. Coming up with no adequate, all-purpose term that did not seem bizarre, cumbersome, or confusing, we have used such terms as "expert witness," "expert," "psychologist," and so on, with the clear understanding that some of these terms may not fit all readers or even a particular reader in all cases.

Third, what should we term the individual who takes the MMPI? This individual might be a defendant, plaintiff, client, patient, research participant, job applicant, student, or a variety of other designations. In constructing case examples and discussing issues related to the MMPI, we have used whatever designation seemed to make or clarify the point at hand. We hope, however, that the reader will be able to generalize and adapt from our specific examples to those that will be most relevant to him or her. Although the examples in almost any book will tend to reflect, at least to some degree, the experiences and concerns of its authors, we have tried to provide a variety of situations illustrating issues involving forensic uses of the MMPI. Finally, some forensic testimony focuses on individuals who have taken the MMPI in what might be called a mental health context. Some readers may have a preference for the term "patients" to refer to such individuals; others may prefer the term "clients." However, in this book we have used those terms interchangeably. Similarly, individual readers may prefer the term "therapy" or "counseling" in such contexts; again, we have used those terms interchangeably in this volume.

Fourth, although we have attempted to provide adequate explanations for each of the terms and concepts in the book, these explanations are not repeated throughout the volume. If the reader does not find the definition of a term in a particular chapter, the Glossary may provide a quicker, more convenient route to clarification than using the index. Finally, the reader who is unfamiliar with mathematical notation may come across symbols such as "≤" or ">." These symbols have the following meanings: "<" means "less than" as in "$a < b$" or "a is less than b"; "≤" means "less than or equal to"; ">" means "greater than" as in "$x > y$" or "x is greater than y"; and "≥" means "is greater than or equal to."

Fifth, we have departed from strict adherence to the format followed in most journals and books published by the American Psychological Association (1983). For readers who are unfamiliar with the customary format, the authors' last names are listed in the text along with the dates of publication or presentation; the work may be looked up in the alphabetized reference section for a more complete citation. For convenience, we have provided the legal citation for each case as we mention it in the text (rather than providing such information in the reference section). We have also frequently referred to individuals by using their first and last name, as well as other identifying information, in the text (rather than providing only the last name in the text and initials in the reference section).

Acknowledgments

We received an enormous amount of help in putting this book together. We would particularly like to acknowledge the following individuals who offered useful comments, suggestions, and other help regarding this book: Nancy Adel, Esq., partner, Law Firm of Adel & Pollack, Los Angeles; Cheri Adrian, PhD, clinical psychologist, UCLA Neuropsychiatric Institute and Hospital, and independent practice; Robert McKim Bell, Esq., deputy attorney general, California Department of Justice, Los Angeles area; Yossef S. Ben-Porath, PhD, Department of Psychology, Kent State University; Bruce Bongar, PhD, diplomate in family psychology, Department of Psychology, Pacifica Graduate Institute, Palo Alto, CA; Margaret Bragg, Esq., appellate attorney, Denver, CO; Laura S. Brown, PhD, clinical diplomate in independent practice, Seattle, WA; Kathleen Callanan, PhD, executive officer, Board of Behavioral Science Examiners, California Department of Consumer Affairs, Sacramento; Brandt Caudill, Esq., partner, Law Firm of Callahan, McCune & Willis, Tustin, CA; Benjamin I. Collins, PhD, independent geologist, Denver, CO; Steven Edelstein, Esq., Miami, FL; Philip Erdberg, PhD, clinical diplomate in independent practice, Corte Madera, CA; James Eyman, PhD, The Menninger Clinic; Jesse D. Geller, PhD, Yale University; Joe George, PhD, Esq., attorney and psychologist in independent practice, Sacramento, CA; William T. Gibson, PhD, University Counseling Center, University of Idaho; Jack Graham, PhD, professor of psychology, Kent State University; Roy Hewitt, Esq., deputy attorney general, California Department of Justice, San Diego area; Sheila Jensen, enforcement coordinator, California Board of Behavioral Science Examiners, Sacramento; Alan Kaplan, Esq., Law Firm of Herzfeld & Rubin, Los Angeles; Lawrence Majovski, PhD, neuropsychologist in independent practice, Los Angeles; the late Alan K. Malyon, clinical diplomate in independent practice, Los Angeles; Mark G. Ohnstad, Esq., Law Firm of Thomsen & Nybeck, P.A., Minneapolis, MN; Thomas S. O'Connor, Executive Officer, California State Board of Psychology, Sacramento; Robert Pelc, PhD, clinical psychologist and forensic diplomate in independent practice, Denver, CO; Carlos Ramirez, Esq., deputy attorney general, California Department of Justice; Los Angeles area; Sherry Skidmore, PhD, forensic diplomate in independent practice, Riverside, CA; Gary L. Sampley, La Jolla, CA; David Shapiro, PhD, diplomate in forensic psychology, Timonium, MD; Janet L. Sonne, PhD, clinical psychologist, Department of Psychiatry, Loma Linda University Medical Center, Loma Linda, CA; Sharyn Wilson, Bakersfield, CA; and Karen Zager, PhD, clinical psychologist in independent practice in New York, NY, and former editor of *The Independent Practitioner*, in which some segments of chapter 8 were previously published.

We would also like to thank Jack Graham for providing some case material presented in this book.

Finally, we owe a huge debt of gratitude to Theodore J. Baroody, Julia Frank-McNeil, Valerie Montenegro, Peggy Schlegel, W. Ralph Eubanks, and Susan Bedford of APA Books; Gary R. VandenBos of Publications and Communications; and Devona Marinich of Marketing Services for their exceptional generosity, skill, and support.

The authors would like to thank the following publishers for their kind permission to quote from the following copyrighted material:

THE AMERICAN PSYCHOLOGICAL ASSOCIATION for authorization to quote from *Casebook on Ethical Principles of Psychologists* (copyright 1987 by the American Psychological Association), *Ethical Principles of Psychologists and Code of Conduct* (copyright 1992 by the American Psychological Association), *General Guidelines for Providers of Psychological Services* (copyright 1987 by the American Psychological Association), *Guidelines for Computer-Based Tests and Interpretations* (copyright 1986 by the American Psychological Association), *Model Act for State Licensure of Psychologists* (copyright 1987 by the American Psychological Association), Policy on Training for Psychologists Wishing to Change Their Specialty (see appendix C-2; copyright 1976 and 1982 by the American Psychological Association), *Publication Manual of the American Psychological Association* (copyright 1983 by the American Psychological Association), *Standards for Educational and Psychological Testing* (copyright 1985 by the American Psychological Association).

THE BOARD OF BAR COMMISSIONERS OF THE STATE BAR OF NEW MEXICO and WILLIAM E. FOOTE, PHD of the NEW MEXICO PSYCHOLOGICAL ASSOCIATION for allowing us to reprint the *Statement of Principles Relating to the Responsibilities of Attorneys and Psychologists in Their Interprofessional Relations: An Interdisciplinary Agreement Between the New Mexico Bar Association and the New Mexico Psychological Association* as appendix D. Copyright 1986 by State Bar of New Mexico.

JOSSEY-BASS INC., PUBLISHERS, for permission to quote from K. S. Pope and M. J. T. Vasquez's *Ethics in Psychotherapy and Counseling: A Practical Guide for Psychologists*. Copyright 1991 by Jossey-Bass Inc., Publishers.

LOUIS NIZER, ESQ., for permission to quote from L. Nizer's *My Life in Court* (Garden City, NY: Doubleday). Copyright 1961 by Louis Nizer.

PLENUM PUBLISHING COMPANY for permission to reprint the "Specialty Guidelines for Forensic Psychologists" as appendix C-1. These guidelines were published in volume 15 (pp. 655–665) of the journal *Law and Human Behavior*. Copyright 1991 by Plenum Publishing Company.

UNIVERSITY OF MINNESOTA PRESS for permission to reprint items on the MMPI, MMPI-2, and MMPI-A, to incorporate profiles into the figures and transparencies, and to reproduce other materials.

CHAPTER 1

A BRIEF OVERVIEW

We wrote this book to help those who testify about the Minnesota Multiphasic Personality Inventory (MMPI) and attorneys who encounter their testimony.

Clinicians, counselors, therapists, and others can be invited or compelled to discuss the MMPI—under oath—from a variety of perspectives (see, e.g., Saks, 1990). Some may be subpoenaed to testify as a percipient or fact witness about a therapy client who terminated years before. The former client may be suing for custody of children, for mental and emotional damages from an accident, for damages from malpractice by a surgeon, or for damages from malpractice by the former therapist. Some may be appointed by the court to conduct an independent psychological evaluation (e.g., of a defendant's competence to stand trial or of a workers' compensation claim). Others may be contacted by a potential assessment client or the client's attorney to administer standardized psychological tests as part of preparation for a court action. Still others may be asked to evaluate individuals involved in violence and other forms of abuse and discrimination (e.g., victims or perpetrators of rape, incest, battering, sexual harassment, racial discrimination in hiring, or "hate crimes," such as attacks on gays and lesbians). Whatever the path leading to the civil, criminal, or administrative courts, those who testify can profoundly affect the lives of the others involved in the case.

Likewise, attorneys may encounter testimony about the MMPI that appears in a variety of guises. The MMPI may be presented as an objective test far more reliable than the subjective impressions, experience-based hunches, dogmatic assertions, and questionable opinions of a so-called expert. It may be described as a psychometric oracle, whose Delphic powers enable omniscient understandings of the human mind and infallible predictions about future behavior. It may emerge in court proceedings as a key piece of evidence, illuminating a complex pattern of symptoms, etiology, and likely prognosis. It may strike the judge and jury as yet another source of pseudoscientific hokum, its findings expressed in an impenetrable shroud of multisyllabic professional jargon.

PROBLEMS WITH EXPERT TESTIMONY

Why is expert testimony—about the MMPI, about other psychological tests, and about other clinical and professional issues—so often a painfully frustrating (or simply painful) experience for expert and attorney alike? Why are experts and attorneys so often wary of each other? Why does the introduction of psychological testimony often seem to obscure and distort the issues rather than help the triers of fact to understand the matters at hand?

Perhaps part of the problem is that some of the testimony is bogus and that opposing attorneys and other experts are unprepared to encounter and counter fraudulent hucksterism. Some experts are in the business of selling opinions-to-order, and some attorneys are looking to buy. In a recent national survey of the ethical dilemmas faced by psychologists, the participants' most contemptuous language (e.g., "whores") was used in describing these so-called experts, as in the following examples:

> *There are psychologists who are "hired" guns who testify for whoever pays them. (Pope & Vetter, 1992, p. 402)*
>
> ◆ ◆ ◆
>
> *A psychologist in my area is widely known, to clients, psychologists, and the legal community to give whatever testimony is requested in court. He has a very commanding "presence" and it works. He will say anything, adamantly, for pay. Clients/lawyers continue to use him because if the other side uses him, that side will probably win the case (because he's so persuasive, though lying). (Pope & Vetter, 1992, p. 402)*

In some cases, it is not overt greed and lack of integrity but rather seemingly altruistic impulses that motivate false or distorted testimony. Judge David Bazelon (1974), for example, observed that "psychiatrists have justified fudging their testimony on 'dangerousness'—a ground for involuntary confinement—when they were convinced that an individual was too sick to seek help voluntarily" (p. 22).

All too often in such instances, opposing attorneys (and other experts) have simply been unprepared to challenge on an adequately informed basis the premises, inferences, databases, decision rules, and other aspects of the expert's misleading testimony. This book is based on and will repeatedly emphasize trial attorney Louis Nizer's (1961) fundamental rule that "as any trial lawyer will admit, proper preparation is the be all and end all of trial success" (p. 8).

Perhaps another part of the problem is that those who testify about the MMPI are too often unprepared to provide a coherent, well-informed description of how the MMPI works, why it works, and what it means in the case at hand. Even when they can provide such clear and compelling testimony during direct examination, they may be unprepared to face a skilled, carefully planned, fully informed cross-examination. Particularly those clinicians entering the courtroom or facing informed, effective cross-examination for the first time may have no real idea of what to expect in this unfamiliar environment with its special customs and detailed rules. In his classic textbook *The Art of Cross-Examination*, Francis Wellman quoted an apt statement about the plight of the witness:

> *Of all unfortunate people in this world, none are more entitled to sympathy and commiseration than those whom circumstances oblige to appear upon the witness stand in court. . . . You are then arraigned before two legal gentlemen [sic], one of whom smiles at you blandly because you are on his side, the other eying you savagely for the opposite reason. The gentleman who smiles, proceeds to pump you of all you know; and having squeezed all he wants out of you, hands you over to the other, who proceeds to show you that you are entirely mistaken in all your supposition; that you never saw anything you have sworn to . . .; in short, that you have committed direct perjury. He wants to know if you have ever been in state prison, and takes your denial with the air of a man who thinks you ought to have been there, asking all the questions over again in different ways; and tells you with an awe inspiring severity, to be very careful what you say. He wants to know if he understood you to say so and so, and also wants to know whether you meant something else. Having bullied and scared you out of your wits, and convicted you in the eye of the jury of prevarication, he lets you go. (Wellman, 1903/1936, pp. 194–195)*

Even professionals who have a basic knowledge of the MMPI and experience testifying in a variety of forensic settings may be unprepared for cross-examination by the attorney who has taken the time to prepare properly, who has mastered the intricacies of the MMPI, who knows the normative sample, the psychometric structure, the validity and reliability statistics, the common interpretive errors, and so on. The intensity and intricacy with which such thoroughly prepared attorneys can completely dismantle an expert can stun the judge, jury, and the expert. One trial attorney vividly described expert witness behaviors indicating that it is time for "the cross-examiner to uncoil and strike":

> *Have you ever seen a "treed" witness? Have you ever had the experience of watching a witness's posterior involuntarily twitch?*

Have you ever seen them wiggle in their chairs? Have you ever seen their mouths go dry? Have you seen the beads of perspiration form on their foreheads? Have you ever been close enough to watch their ancestral eyes dilating the pupil so that they would have adequate tunnel vision of the target that was attacking? (Burgess, 1984, p. 252)

Louis Nizer (1961) wrote that the old process by which a person who testified was forced to "walk barefoot and blindfolded over red-hot plowshares laid lengthwise at unequal distances has been replaced by a stream of burning questions which a cross-examiner may hurl at the witness to drag from him the concealed truth" (p. 14).

Perhaps yet another part of the problem is that what seems to be perhaps the most widely known and used standardized test of personality[1]—the MMPI—has been revised. As the following chapters document, the original MMPI was in many ways a powerful instrument yet a heavy burden for an expert witness to bring into court. For example, the norms, established in the 1930s, were based on an exclusively White sample; Black, Asian American, Hispanic, American Indian,[2] and other ethnic groups were not included in the attempt to define "normal" responses. The normative group came from one limited geographic locale in Minnesota; most had been visitors (not patients) to the University of Minnesota hospital, and a much smaller group were airline workers and Civilian Conservation Corps (CCC) workers. The typical Minnesotan from this supposedly normative sample was in his or her mid-30s, resided in a rural or small town, had 8 years of formal education, and "worked at a skilled or semi-skilled trade (or was married to a man with such an occupational level)" (Dahlstrom, Welsch, & Dahlstrom, 1972, p. 8). A review by Colligan, Osborne, Swenson, and Offord (1983) found the original norms to be so dated that they were misleadingly inappropriate for contemporary assessment: "These MMPI changes [in norms] are not only statistically significant but are also of clinical importance" (p. xv).

Failure to include any minorities in the sample in which test developers were attempting to define "normality" caused additional problems. In one MMPI study of a rural population, one MMPI item alone perfectly discriminated all Black test takers from all White test takers. A prominent computerized MMPI scoring and interpretation service, using data from this rural population, incorrectly classified 90% of the apparently normal Black test takers as showing profiles characteristic of psychiatric patients (Erdberg, 1970, 1988; Gynther, Fowler, & Erdberg, 1971; see also Hutton, Miner, Blades, & Langfeldt, 1992).[3]

Faschingbauer (1979) vividly underscored some of the difficulties facing the clinician attempting contemporary use of the original MMPI:

The original Minnesota group . . . seems to be an inappropriate reference group for the 1980s. The median individual in that group had an eighth-grade education, was married, lived in a small town or on a farm, and was employed as a lower level clerk or skilled tradesman. None was under 16 or over 65 years of age, and all were white. As a clinician I find it difficult to justify comparing anyone to such a dated group. When the person is 14 years old, Chicano, and lives in Houston's poor fifth ward, use of the original norms seems sinful. (p. 375)

Skillful, informed cross-examination on such aspects can increase the judge's and the jury's hesitance to rely on such a dated and seemingly biased instrument. The revisions—the MMPI-2 (for adults) and the MMPI-A (for adolescents)—were developed to eliminate, or at least to minimize, such flaws and to create new strengths. But new versions bring new questions,

[1] See, for example, Anastasi, 1988; Carson & Butcher, 1992; Davison & Neale, 1990; Goldstein, Baker, & Jamison, 1980; Kimble, Garmezy, & Zigler, 1974; Lees-Haley, 1992; Lubin, Larsen, & Matarazzo, 1984; McConnell, 1974; Waskow & Parloff, 1975.

[2] As with some other terms used in this book, *American Indian* may be controversial. Currently, there is a lack of consensus among those who refer to themselves as American Indian, Native American, and so on, as to which term, if any, appropriately characterizes this population.

[3] For additional considerations regarding race, ethnicity, and assessment, see the chapters "Assessment, Testing, and Diagnosis" and "Cultural, Contextual, and Individual Differences" in Pope & Vasquez, 1991 (pp. 87–100 & 130–138).

new issues, and new difficulties. Effective cross-examination can underscore the inherent doubts about using an instrument that may seem new and relatively untried.

ORGANIZATION OF THIS BOOK

In the pages ahead, we provide a detailed guide for the expert witness and attorney to the strengths and weaknesses of the MMPI, the MMPI-2, and the MMPI-A. We hope that it will serve as a primary or secondary text in formal courses in assessment, forensic practice, and trial preparation. Because this book is intended to be helpful not only to seasoned attorneys and expert witnesses but also to clinicians who may never have set foot in a courtroom and to attorneys who have never heard of the MMPI, *The MMPI, MMPI-2, and MMPI-A in Court* includes general information in such areas as testing and assessment (e.g., understanding the validity and reliability of a test and recognizing responsibilities when test results indicate a risk of suicide or homicide), legal proceedings (e.g., subpoenas and depositions), witness–attorney interactions (e.g., handling initial contacts and setting fees), and discovery and cross-examination strategies (e.g., examination of an expert's assertions regarding prior research and generally accepted theory; patterns of questions regarding assessment of harm, rehabilitation, or prognosis) that may not be inherently related to the MMPI but can play an important role in providing the proper foundation and context for MMPI-based assessment, testimony, and cross-examination.

Chapter 2 presents a discussion of the MMPI, the MMPI-2, and the MMPI-A: their development; the validity, clinical, and content scales and their psychometric properties; and their applicability to forensic issues. Chapter 3 presents a discussion of case law defining the scope and limits of MMPI-based testimony. Chapter 4 presents a guide to preparation, procedures, and issues for the psychologist, expert witness, or other professional who offers MMPI-based testimony. As mentioned at the beginning of the current chapter, such professionals may appear in a variety of roles (e.g., a therapist who has administered an MMPI and is appearing as a percipient witness, a professional retained by an attorney to offer expert testimony on the MMPI, or a court-appointed expert). Chapter 5 presents a guide to preparation, procedures, and issues for the attorney who retains an expert to testify on the MMPI or who encounters such testimony from an opposing witness. The middle chapters of the book examine special topics relevant to forensic settings: assessing credibility (chapter 6) and the forensic assessment report (chapter 7). Chapter 8 presents a detailed guide to deposing and cross-examining the expert who is offering MMPI-based testimony. This chapter is intended to be helpful not only to the attorney conducting the deposition and cross-examination but also to the expert preparing for this usually bracing experience. Chapter 9, the final chapter in the book, offers a few final thoughts.

This book is also intended to serve expert witnesses and attorneys as a convenient source of basic numerical, research, and reference data about the MMPI. Therefore, a number of appendixes have been included to present a sample agreement between an expert witness and attorney; a sample informed consent form for forensic assessment; a comparative listing of original MMPI, MMPI-2, and MMPI-A items; a description of the scales for all three versions; the reliability, validity, and congruence data; a listing of relevant case law, and so on.

The first step in proper preparation for expert witnesses and attorneys is learning, updating, or reviewing information about the three versions of the MMPI, which is the topic of the next chapter.

Chapter 2

THE MMPI, MMPI-2, AND MMPI-A IN COURT TESTIMONY

For many reasons, the MMPI, the most widely used test in clinical practice in the United States (Lubin et al., 1984), has apparently become the favored personality assessment instrument for evaluating individuals in forensic settings. This chapter summarizes the use of the MMPI, and its revised forms MMPI-2 and MMPI-A, in forensic settings and highlights the psychometric features that support its use in forensic evaluations. We examine the similarities and differences among the different forms of the MMPI to compare their relative merits and limitations in forensic assessment. We explore the reasons for the MMPI's broad application in forensic assessment and discuss the potential vulnerabilities an expert witness might experience using the MMPI in court testimony. We describe possible areas of MMPI-related testimony that might be challenged in cross-examination and address several issues involved in using the instrument as a basis of forensic testimony. Finally, we cover a number of different forensic applications and provide information relevant for use in personal injury and family custody cases, insanity assessments, and evaluations of convicted felons.

THE MMPI

The original MMPI is a 566-item true–false personality questionnaire developed in the 1930s and early 1940s as a diagnostic aid for psychiatric and medical screening (Dahlstrom, Welsh, & Dahlstrom, 1972, 1975; Graham, 1977; Greene, 1980). The test originators, Starke Hathaway and J. C. McKinley, developed the personality questionnaire using empirical scale construction methods. The scales, which focus on abnormal behavior and symptoms such as depression and schizophrenia, were constructed by contrasting item responses of various patient groups with those of a sample of nonpsychiatric ("normal" or "normative") individuals.

The MMPI provides several sources of behavioral and symptomatic hypotheses about the person who takes the test. First, there are the validity scales, which yield information about how the individual approached the test (e.g., test-taking attitudes) and about whether the responses form a sufficient basis for further inferences. In some instances, the pattern of validity scales may indicate that the profile is invalid and that no inferences may be drawn from the other scales or indexes. As chapter 6 emphasizes, the validity of the individual's self-report is one of the most important determinations addressed by the MMPI in forensic evaluations. Chapter 6 focuses exclusively on exploring the credibility of self-report in forensic settings.

Second, the MMPI contains a number of objectively derived, scored, and interpreted scales that are associated with well-established behavioral correlates (see appendix G). These scales, and the patterns which they form, provide hypotheses about personality and, if relevant and appropriate, diagnosis and prognosis. They provide descriptive information that can aid understanding of a wide range of personality traits and symptom patterns.

Third, the MMPI provides other useful scales and indices developed to identify or clarify specific problem areas, including important content themes. A number of focused scales, such as those designed to assess alcohol or drug abuse problems (MacAndrew [MAC] Scale on the original and revised version; Addiction Proneness Scale [APS] and Addiction Acknowledgment Scale [AAS] on the MMPI-2) or emotional control problems (Overcontrolled Hostility [O-H] scale), have been developed for appraising specific behavior problems.

In spite of the MMPI's broad use and recognized effectiveness in clinical and forensic assessment, a number of problems emerged with the original MMPI that brought its use into question. For example, as discussed elsewhere in this volume, serious questions have been raised about the relevance and appropriateness of the items, the nature of the normative sample, and the contemporary usefulness of its dated norms. The problems and limitations of the original MMPI have been carefully evaluated (see, e.g., Butcher, 1972; Butcher & Owen, 1978).

In 1982, the MMPI copyright holder, the University of Minnesota Press, initiated an extensive revision of the MMPI item pool and launched an extensive study to collect new norms (see Preface and chapter 1). The MMPI revision for use with adults (MMPI-2) was completed in 1989. A number of articles have subsequently appeared detailing issues of reliability and validity.[1] The revised version for adolescents (MMPI-A) was published in 1992 (Butcher et al., 1992).

THE MMPI-2

The MMPI-2 is the revised form of the MMPI designed for use with adults aged 18 or older. Although the item pool was revised and expanded, continuity with the original instrument was assured by keeping virtually intact the original clinical and validity scales (Butcher, Dahlstrom, Graham, Tellegen, & Kaemmer, 1989). The expanded, modified item pool provided opportunity for new scale development (see appendix F).

A large, contemporary normative sample (1,462 women and 1,138 men), generally representative of the national population, was obtained. The normative sample was a randomly solicited group from California, Minnesota, North Carolina, Ohio, Pennsylvania, Virginia, and Washington state.

The contemporary normative sample of individuals yielded new norms for the widely used validity and clinical scales. These norms were constructed following a strategy to eliminate psychometric problems plaguing the original *T* scores (i.e., the fact that the percentile values were not consistent and uniform for given levels of *T* scores). *T* scores, which are discussed in a subsequent section of this book (see also Glossary), fall in a distribution in which the mean (or average) is 50 and the standard deviation (a statistical measure of the degree to which the individual scores are spread out from or are "bunched up" around the mean) is 10.

An additional set of personality and symptom scales was constructed to assess content dimensions by drawing from items in the expanded item pool (Butcher, Graham, Williams, & Ben-Porath, 1990). Several new symptom-oriented scales, such as Bizarre Mentation (BIZ) and Depression (DEP), focus directly on symptom themes presented by individuals during the evaluation. Other scales were developed to assess important clinical problems, such as Antisocial Practices (ASP) and Type A Behavior (TPA), and clinical problem areas, such as Work Interference (WRK) and Negative Treatment Indicators (TRT).

In addition to the MMPI-2 content scales, a number of specific problem scales were retained from the original MMPI; for example, O-H, Anxiety (A), and Repression (R). Other specific problem scales were developed with the new item pool, such as the APS and the AAS. (See appendix G for specific descriptions of the MMPI-2 content scales and supplemental scales. Additional interpretive information is presented in Butcher & Williams's [1992a] textbook on the MMPI-2 and MMPI-A.)

THE MMPI-A

The MMPI Restandardization Committee recognized that adolescents cannot adequately be assessed by the same diagnostic measure as adults. Consequently, they

[1] Ben-Porath & Butcher, 1989a, 1989b; Ben-Porath, Butcher, & Graham, 1991; Butcher, Aldwin, Levenson, Ben-Porath, Spiro, & Bosse', 1991; Butcher, Graham, Dahlstrom, & Bowman, 1990; Butcher, Jeffrey, et al., 1990; Butcher & Pope, 1992; Egeland, Erickson, Butcher, & Ben-Porath, 1991; Hjemboe & Butcher, 1991; Keller & Butcher, 1991.

developed a separate form of the MMPI (MMPI-A) for people between the ages of 14 and 18. This revised version of the MMPI for adolescents differs from both the original MMPI and the MMPI-2 in several respects.

First, although the items necessary for scoring the traditional validity and clinical scales were retained in the MMPI-A, a number of new items addressing specific adolescent problems and issues were added. Minor changes were made in the wording of several items to make them more readable for adolescents.

Second, data from a new adolescent normative sample were collected for the development of specific nationally based norms for adolescents. The adolescent normative sample, obtained from public and private schools in California, Minnesota, North Carolina, Ohio, Virginia, Pennsylvania, New York, and Washington state, was balanced for important background variables such as age, gender, and ethnicity. New adolescent-specific norms were derived for the traditional validity and clinical scales.

Third, a number of new adolescent-specific scales were developed, using both original MMPI items as well as newer items. A new set of adolescent-specific content scales assessing important problem themes such as School Problems (a-sch), Low Aspirations (a-las), Conduct Disorder (a-con), and Alienation (a-aln) was developed. Two new scales to assess the possibility of alcohol or drug problems were constructed: the Alcohol or Drug Problem (PRO) scale and the Alcohol or Drug Problem Acknowledgment (ACK) scale. (See appendix G for a description of the MMPI-A content and supplementary scales.)

Fourth, the traditional MMPI clinical and validity scales and the new MMPI-A scales were validated in an extensive clinical study incorporating adolescents in mental health, special school, and alcohol and drug treatment settings.

The MMPI-A contains 478 items and typically requires about an hour to an hour and a half to administer. The MMPI-A scales and their uses have been described in detail in several publications (Butcher & Williams, 1992a, 1992b; Butcher et al., 1992; C. L. Williams, Butcher, Ben-Porath, & Graham, 1992).

Although in this book we focus primarily on assessments of adults using the MMPI and MMPI-2, the forensic psychologist should also be aware of the MMPI-A because this version is recommended for individuals between the ages of 14 and 18.

SIMILARITIES AND DIFFERENCES AMONG THE ORIGINAL MMPI, THE MMPI-2, AND THE MMPI-A

In this section we compare and contrast the psychometric properties of the MMPI, MMPI-2, and MMPI-A to clarify the relationships among the different versions. (Please refer to the information presented in appendix H for a comparative summary of the relevant features of the MMPI, MMPI-2, and MMPI-A.)

Relationship Between the MMPI and MMPI-2

The MMPI-2 contains less objectionable and more contemporary item content than is available in the now very dated original MMPI. A number of new items were incorporated into the MMPI-2 to address clinical problem areas and symptoms not covered by the original instrument. As noted previously, the clinical and validity scales on the original MMPI and MMPI-2 are virtually identical in terms of item composition, reliability, and validity.

The MMPI Restandardization Committee used a research protocol that would maximize the continuity between the original MMPI and the revised version in terms of the traditional validity and clinical scales. With a few minor exceptions, the MMPI-2 item content is identical (a few items were deleted from a few scales: 4 on *F* [Infrequency], 1 on *Hs* [Hypochondriasis], 2 on *D* [Depression], 4 on *Mf* [Masculinity–Feminity], and 1 on *Si* [Social Introversion]; no additional items were incorporated into the traditional scales). In the development of the MMPI-A, a few more objectionable items were dropped from the clinical scales (see appendix F).

As shown by subsequent research, these minor modifications did not lower the reliability of the traditional validity and clinical scales (Ben-Porath & Butcher, 1989a). Therefore, most of the validity and clinical scales are unchanged in their measurement focus or have been shown to be psychometrically comparable. Ben-Porath and Butcher (1989a) conducted an empirical comparison of the MMPI and MMPI-2. They used a test–retest research design. Half of the participants took the original version of the MMPI twice, and the other half took the MMPI on one occasion and the MMPI-2 on another occasion. Test administration was counterbalanced. Appendix F shows that the test–retest correlations between separate administrations of the original and revised versions are comparable to correlations between the different administrations of the original MMPI.

The congruence between the MMPI and MMPI-2 is evident in the comparability of the high point scores and profile codes (Graham et al., 1991). Generally, when well-defined profile types are studied, an individual's profile types are similar when tested with either the MMPI or the MMPI-2 (Graham et al., 1991).

Although many of the items and scales in the MMPI-2 are the same as in the original MMPI, the norms of the MMPI-2 are based on a more contemporary, representative sample of individuals. One of the most important reasons for revising the MMPI was that the original norms are inappropriate for evaluating contemporary individuals. Test takers who are evaluated according to the original norms tend to show considerably more psychological problems than they actually have. The original norms tend to *overpathologize* test takers, as shown in Figures 2-1 and 2-2.

The profiles shown in Figures 2-1 and 2-2 represent a number of "normal" groups that had been administered the original MMPI. Results are plotted on original norms (see also Figure 2-6 presented later in this chapter). In all cases, the mean profile of the "normal" or "normative" group (even those taking the test in situations such as personnel selection in which people tend to try to "look good" on the test) shows moderate to high scale elevation when using the original norms.

The MMPI-2 norms provide a more relevant and appropriate basis than the original norms for evaluating contemporary individuals, as shown in Figures 2-3 and 2-4. These "normal" individuals tend to score near the MMPI-2 mean of 50 on the test. Individuals taking the test in employment selection tend to produce, as expected, even below average ($T < 50$) scores on the clinical scales (see also Figure 2-7 presented later in this chapter).

The MMPI-2 versions of the validity and clinical scales are essentially the same as the original MMPI versions in terms of the item composition (e.g., only five scales lost any items), scale reliabilities, and external correlates. These scales in the MMPI and MMPI-2 function in a similar manner psychometrically (Ben-Porath & Butcher, 1989a, 1989b; Chojenackie & Walsh, 1992; Graham, Watts, & Timbrook, 1991). In a recent article, Dahlstrom (1992) raised a question about the congruence of MMPI and MMPI-2 codes, basing his concerns on a large sample of normal profiles available from the MMPI restandardization study. Difficulties with this conceptualization have been described by Tellegen and Ben-Porath (1992a), who noted that Dahlstrom's conclusions about congruence (that differ somewhat from those of Graham, Timbrook, Ben-Porath, and Butcher, 1991) are limited because he incorporated only normal-range profiles in his analysis. These "normal" profiles have a very constricted range and would not be recommended for clinical interpretation because, in over two thirds of the cases, *T* scores are below 60, and in many, *T* scores are below 50.

Appendix F shows the continuity of the traditional scales. Psychometric characteristics, such as test–retest stability and factor structure, of the MMPI and MMPI-2 indicate that the revised version can be considered to be a similar (and in some aspects equivalent) form of the test.

But there are also significant differences between the MMPI and MMPI-2. The expanded item pool in the MMPI-2 allowed for the development of newer, more relevant clinical measures than are available in the original MMPI item pool (see appendix G).

Relationship Between the MMPI and MMPI-A

The 478 items of the MMPI-A contain the relevant items for scoring the traditional validity and clinical scales. As previously noted, additional adolescent-specific items were included to address more directly the problems and attitudes experienced by younger people. The MMPI Restandardization Committee assured continuity between the two forms by keeping relatively intact the standard validity and clinical scales. The exception was Scale *F*, which was reconstructed to make it more appropriate for assessing adolescents.

The traditional MMPI clinical scales have been cross-validated in adolescent clinical settings (Butcher et al., 1992; C. L. Williams & Butcher, 1989). As

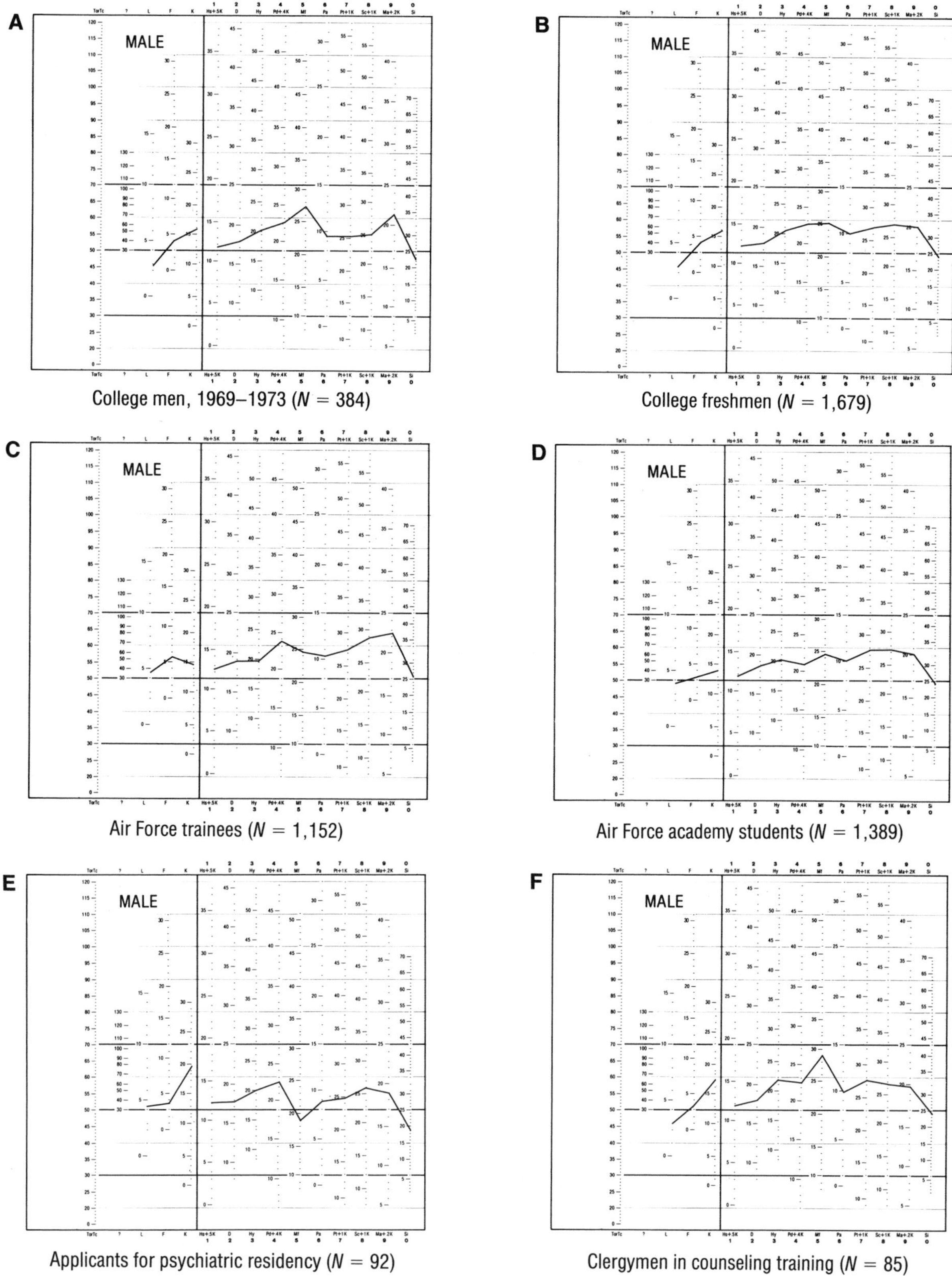

FIGURE 2-1. Group mean profiles for several samples of "normal" men, illustrating the inaccuracy of the original MMPI in characterizing "normal" individuals. (Sources: *A*, Schneider & Cherry, 1976; *B*, Loper, Robertson, & Swanson, 1968; *C*, Bloom, 1977; *D*, Lachar, 1974; *E*, Garetz & Anderson, 1973; *F*, Jansen & Bonk, 1973. Reprinted by permission.)

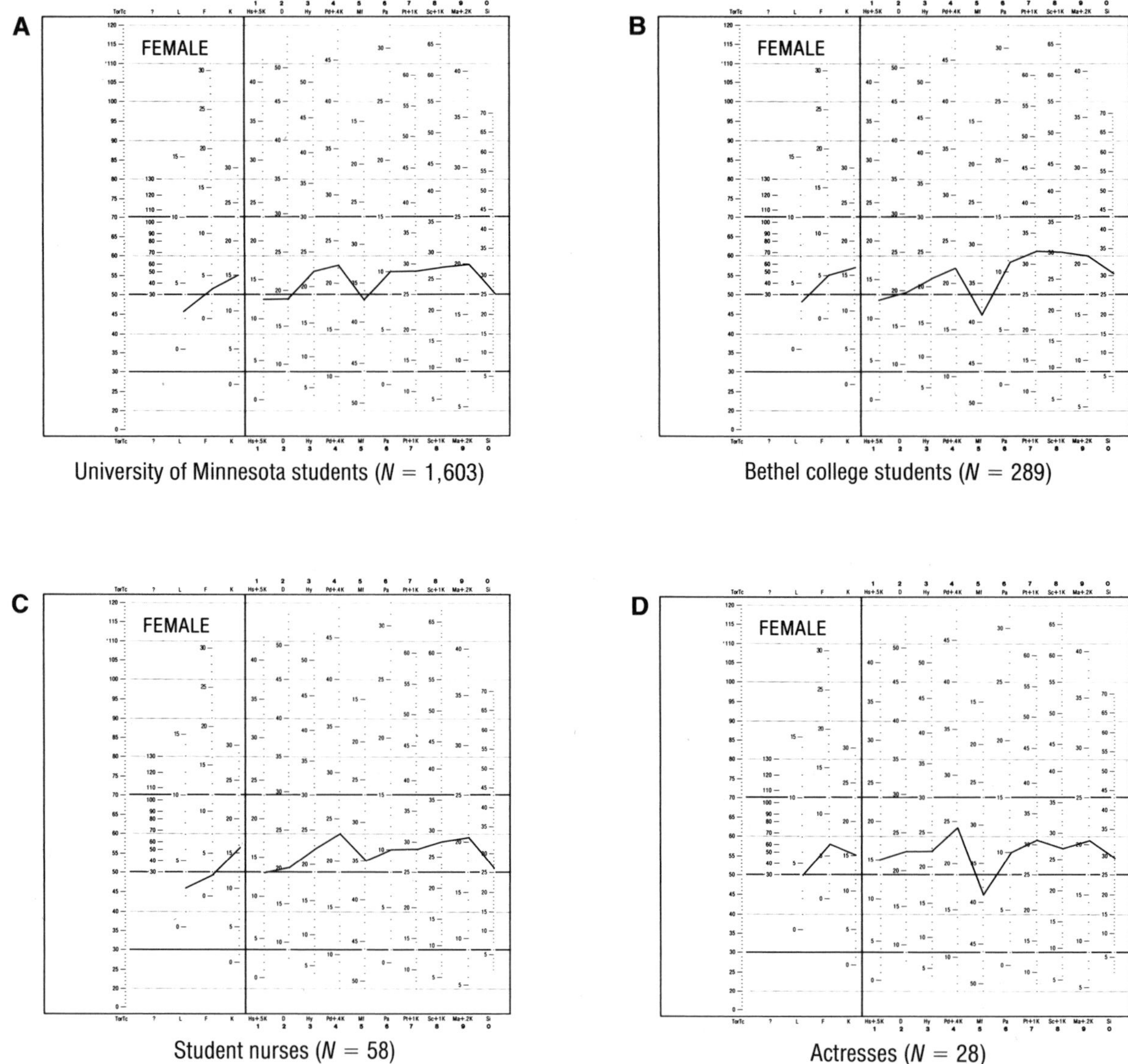

FIGURE 2-2. Group mean profiles for several samples of "normal" women, illustrating the inaccuracy of the original MMPI in characterizing "normal" individuals. (Sources: *A*, Loper, Robinson, & Swanson, 1968; *B*, Butcher & Pancheri, 1976; *C*, Wolf, Freinck, & Shaffer, 1964; *D*, Taft, 1961. Reprinted by permission.)

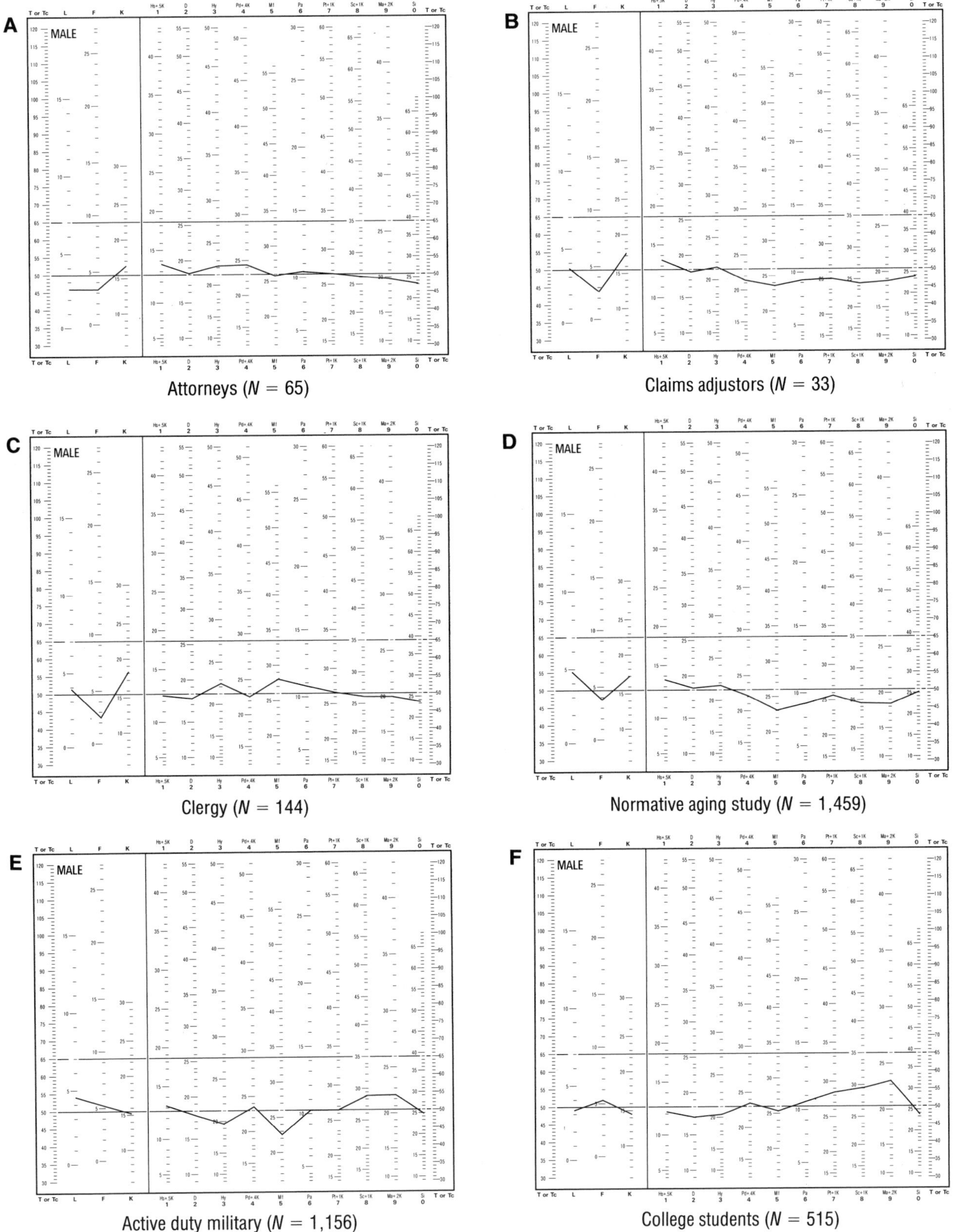

FIGURE 2-3. Group mean MMPI-2 profiles of several groups of "normal" men, illustrating how contemporary "normal" samples are characterized by the new norms. (Sources: *A*, *B*, *C*, Putnam, Adams, & Butcher, 1992; *D*, Butcher et al., 1991; *E*, Butcher, Jeffrey, et al., 1990; *F*, Butcher, Graham, et al., 1990. Reprinted by permission.)

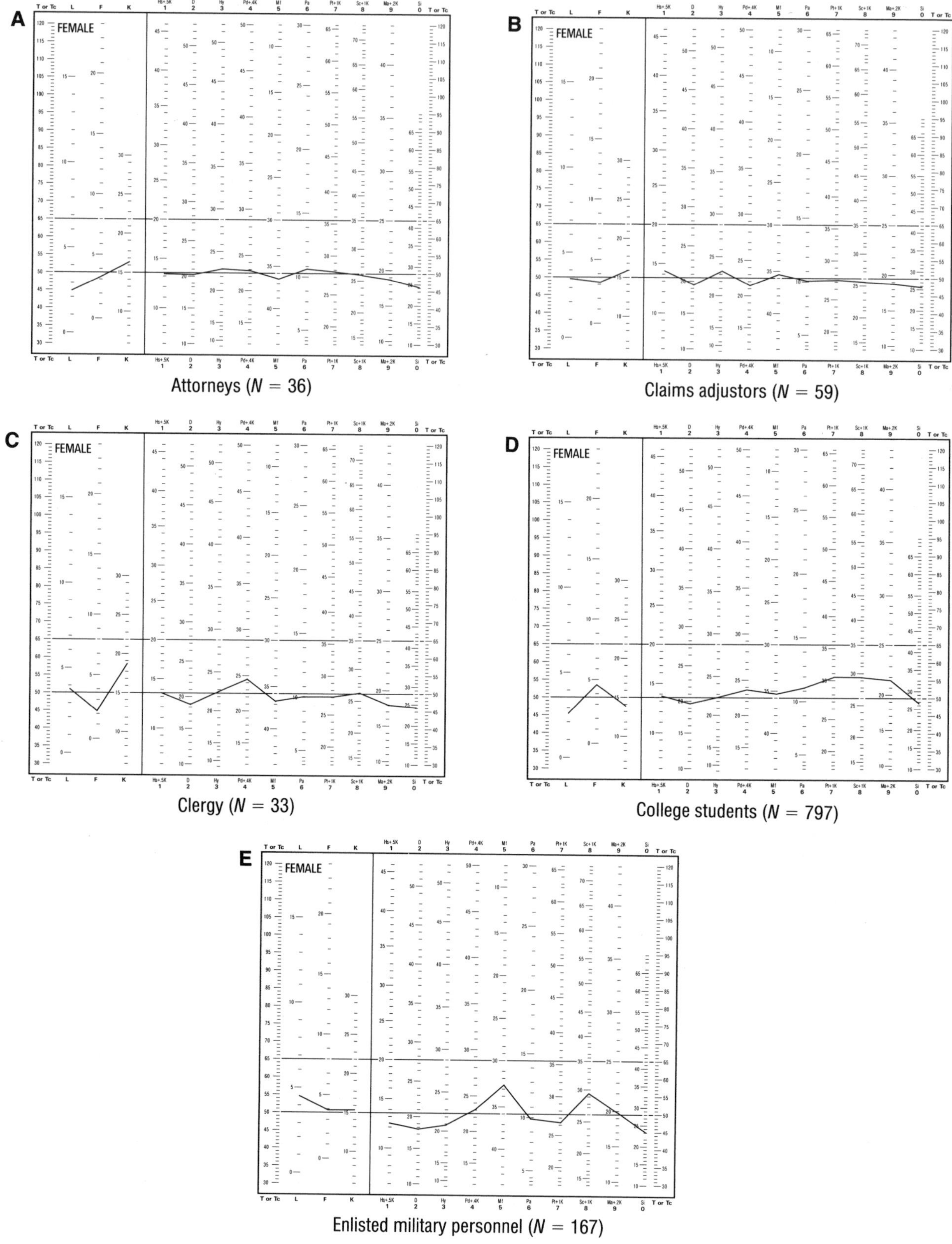

FIGURE 2-4. Group mean MMPI-2 profiles of several groups of "normal" women, illustrating how contemporary "normal" samples are characterized by the new norms. (Sources: *A*, *B*, *C*, Putnam, Adams, & Butcher, 1992; *D*, Butcher, Graham, et al., 1990; *E*, Egeland, Erickson, Butcher, & Ben-Porath, 1991. Reprinted by permission.)

appendix F shows, correlation coefficients between the MMPI-A and the original MMPI for the validity and clinical scales are quite high, indicating that the MMPI-A validity and clinical scales are alternate measures of the original MMPI versions of those scales. Many of the traditional correlates established for the *Hs* (Hypochondriasis), *D* (Depression), *Hy* (Hysteria), *Pd* (Psychopathic Deviate), *Pa* (Paranoia), *Pt* (Psychasthenia), *Sc* (Schizophrenia), *Ma* (Hypomania), and *Si* (Social Introversion) scales have been found to apply to adolescents in mental health, drug and alcohol, and special school settings (see Butcher et al., 1992).

VALUE OF USING THE MMPI, MMPI-2, OR MMPI-A IN FORENSIC TESTIMONY

The MMPI has become one of the most widely used instruments in the objective assessment of personality for forensic testimony (Lees-Haley, 1992). Several reasons, highlighted in Exhibit 2-1, account for the MMPI's wide applicability in forensic evaluations. First, there are a number of measures that address the credibility of the individual's responses; some new measures of validity were added to the revised versions. For a discussion of these measures, see chapter 6.

Second, the instrument can be interpreted in an objective manner through reference to external, empirically based correlates. The MMPI provides an objective portrayal of mental health symptoms that is less dependent on subjective impressions than are a variety of other procedures. Use of the MMPI helps to counteract the old nemesis of mental health professionals who, testifying in court, are vulnerable to the criticism that their interpretations are subjective (Ziskin, 1981b; see also chapter 4 of this volume).

Third, the MMPI has generally strong scale reliability (Dahlstrom et al., 1972; Leon, Gillum, Gillum, & Gouze, 1979). Test–retest studies show that constructs measured by the scales tend to be consistent on retesting because many of the scales assess fairly stable traits or personality features. In a recent study of test–retest reliability scores obtained from felony offenders during the first few weeks of incarceration, Jemelka, Wiegand, Walker, and Trupin (1992; see also Van Cleve, Jemelka, & Trupin, 1991) found that test scores of incoming state prisoners are stable, at least during the first month of incarceration. A recent test–retest study of 1,050 "normal" men who were administered the MMPI-2 on two occasions 5 years apart revealed that the clinical scale scores were quite stable over time, with stability coefficients ranging from .56 to .86, with a median stability index of .68 (Spiro, 1992).

Fourth, reliability of the measures is supported and enhanced by the general agreement regarding the meaning of scale scores among those adequately trained in the use of the instrument. Unlike some assessment techniques in which different, sometimes conflicting methods can be used to score the results, MMPI scale scores are statistically computed. Moreover, there are "standard" interpretations for various MMPI scores and score ranges that are based on empirical research. Consequently, interpreters who possess adequate education, training, and experience with the instrument tend to be consistent in interpreting particular score patterns.

Fifth, the clinical scales have well-established correlates for describing aspects of personality. There is an extensive body of research published in peer-reviewed scientific and professional journals that supports MMPI use in assessment of personality characteristics (for reviews, see, e.g., Graham, 1990; Greene, 1991; Keller & Butcher, 1991).

Sixth, the MMPI is used extensively in forensic settings because it is relatively easy to communicate results to nonpsychologists. The MMPI can be easily explained to lay audiences because very few theoretical assumptions are required and little psychological training is needed to understand the nature, rationale, and workings of the test. A guide to presenting MMPI and MMPI-2 data in court is given in appendix I.

POTENTIAL PROBLEMS TO ANTICIPATE IN TESTIMONY REGARDING THE MMPI OR MMPI-2

In this section, we discuss some of the possible questions or difficulties that psychologists might encounter (particularly in cross-examination) when presenting MMPI- or MMPI-2-based testimony. First, we examine some issues specific to using the different versions of the inventory; then we explore questions that might apply regardless of which version is used.

EXHIBIT 2-1

Reasons for Using the MMPI/MMPI-2/MMPI-A in Court

- The MMPI is the most frequently used clinical test (Lubin, Larsen, & Matarazzo, 1984). It is employed in many court cases to provide personality information on defendants or litigants in which psychological adjustment factors are pertinent to resolution of the case.
- The inventory is relatively easy to administer, available in a printed booklet, on cassette tapes, and on computer. It usually takes between 1–1½ hours for adults to complete and 1 hour for adolescents.
- Individuals self-administer the test, under carefully monitored conditions, by simply responding "T" (true) or "F" (false) to each item on the basis of whether the statement applies to them. The items are written so that individuals with a sixth-grade reading level can understand them.
- The MMPI, MMPI-2, and MMPI-A are relatively easy to score. The item responses for each scale are tallied and recorded on a profile sheet. Scoring is simple and can be delegated to clerical staff to conserve more costly professional time. Computerized scoring programs are available and enhance the scoring process (i.e., reduce errors and score the numerous available scales quickly). The objective scoring assures reliability in the processing of the test protocol, which is a critical determination in forensic cases.
- Forensic assessments involving people from different language or cultural backgrounds are often difficult to conduct due to the lack of appropriate, relevant assessment instruments. The MMPI and MMPI-2 have been extensively used in other countries, and there are many foreign-language versions of the MMPI and MMPI-2 available, such as Spanish, Thai, Vietnamese, Chinese, Norwegian, Japanese, Dutch, Hebrew, and Italian. In cases where the person being evaluated does not speak or read English, a foreign-language version of the instrument can be administered. In many cases, appropriate national norms can also be obtained.
- The MMPI-2 and MMPI-A possess a number of response attitude measures, in addition to those that appear on the original MMPI, that appraise the test-taking attitudes of the test taker. Any self-report instrument is susceptible to manipulation, either conscious or unconscious; thus, it is imperative to have means to assess the person's test-taking attitudes at the time he or she completed the test.
- The MMPI, MMPI-2, and MMPI-A are objectively interpreted instruments. Empirically validated scales possess clearly established meanings. A high score on a particular clinical scale is statistically associated with behavioral characteristics. These scale "meanings" are easily taught and are objectively applied to test takers. Clinical interpretation strategies are very easily learned. The established correlates for the scales allow them to be interpreted objectively—even by computer.
- MMPI, MMPI-2, and MMPI-A scales possess high reliability (i.e., are quite stable over time). This well-established scale reliability is especially important in forensic applications.
- The MMPI, MMPI-2, and MMPI-A provide clear, valid descriptions of people's problems, symptoms, and characteristics in a broadly accepted clinical language. Scale elevations and code type descriptions provide a terminology that enables clinicians to describe test takers clearly. To say that a person possesses "high 4 characteristics" or exhibits features of a "2-7" communicates very specific information to other psychologists. This clinical language can easily be translated into everyday language that makes sense to the lay public (Finn & Butcher, 1990).
- MMPI-2 and MMPI-A scores enable the practitioner to predict future behaviors and responses to different treatment or rehabilitation approaches as was the case for the MMPI.
- MMPI, MMPI-2, and MMPI-A profiles are easy to explain in court. The variables and the means of score comparison are relatively easy for people to understand.

Vulnerabilities in Testimony Regarding the Original MMPI

A number of problems have been cited as limiting or detracting from application of the original MMPI in forensic settings. These include outmoded items, narrow normative sample, and antiquated, inexact norms. We examine each of these criticisms in more detail.

Item-level problems

(Possible cross-examination question: ***Isn't it true that the items in the MMPI are questionable because they are objectionable and antiquated?***)

The objectionable item content of the original MMPI has been the source of criticism (Butcher & Tellegen, 1966) and litigation (*McKenna v. Fargo*, 451 F. Supp. 1355 [1978]). Lawsuits over MMPI items have focused on items containing religious or gender preference content. In these cases, the test was being used to screen individuals for high stress positions, such as air traffic controllers, or positions involving a high degree of public responsibility and emotional stability, such as police officers or nuclear power plant operators. Most recently, in *Soroka v. Dayton Hudson Corp.*, 735 Cal.App.3d 654, 1 Cal.Rptr.2d 77 (Cal.App. 1 Dist. 1991),[2] use of the original MMPI was questioned because the objectionable religious and gender preference questions in the inventory were considered inappropriate in the selection of security personnel. Because of the objectionable item content, the MMPI was questioned on grounds that the test invaded privacy and discriminated on the basis of race, religion, and physical handicap.

The objectionable item content in the original MMPI may also be viewed as producing negative effects in other respects. Having a large number of awkward, antiquated, or objectionable items in the inventory may lower the motivation of individuals to answer the items appropriately. The case of a woman who was being evaluated in a family court context before her custody hearing provides an example. She complained that "these items are stupid! I don't know what relevance my bowel movements being black or tarry could possibly have to keeping custody of my child."

Nonrepresentative standardization sample

(Possible cross-examination questions: ***Isn't it true that the MMPI normative data were collected in the 1940s? Isn't it true that these data are inappropriate for use with people today?***)

The original normative sample was composed of a relatively small number of mostly rural, middle-aged White visitors to the University of Minnesota Hospital (and a much smaller group of airline workers and Civilian Conservation Corps workers) in the 1930s and 1940s who were selected for their notable lack of physical or mental health problems. The sample does not meet expectations of representativeness. Several researchers have noted this weakness when the MMPI is used to evaluate individuals whose demographics (e.g., ethnicity) are missing from the "normative" sample (e.g., Butcher & Owen, 1978; Colligan, Osborne, Swenson, & Offord, 1983; Parkison & Fishburne, 1984; Pancoast & Archer, 1989).

Antiquated and inexact norms

(Possible cross-examination questions: ***Isn't it true that the original MMPI norms are too inexact for use today? Isn't it true that the original MMPI tends to show more psychological problems than the individual really has?***)

Even individuals without problems, when evaluated using the original norms, may appear to be disturbed. The use of old norms in evaluating an individual in forensic assessments could lead an opposing attorney to make a motion to strike any MMPI-based testimony because an incorrect (and dated) normative standard was used in assessing the person.

One of the reasons the MMPI revision was required was that the original MMPI norms appeared to many to be overpathologizing contemporary individuals. The research articles cited in Figures 2-1 and 2-2 show that samples of "normal" or nonclinical individuals were depicted by the original norms as having elevations on the clinical scales that are significantly above the *T*-scale mean of 50.

The problem of the inaccuracy of the original norms is further shown in the profiles reported in Figure 2-5 in which the raw scores for the normative

[2] On January 31, 1992, the California Supreme Court agreed to review the *Soroka* decision. The court had not yet issued its opinion when this book went to press.

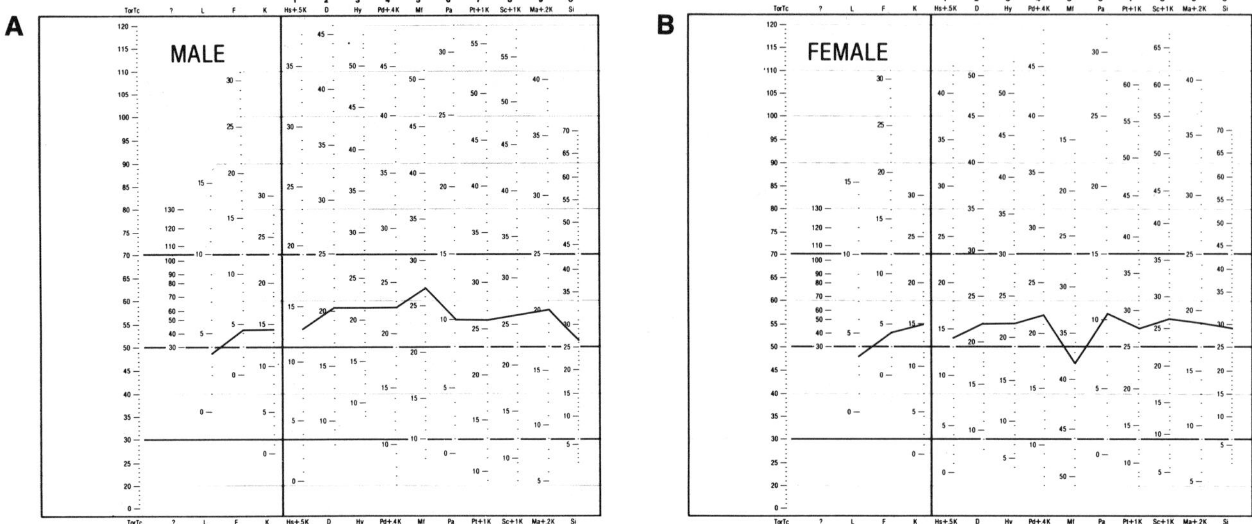

FIGURE 2-5. Group mean profiles of the MMPI-2 restandardization samples (*A*: men, *N* = 1,138; *B*: women, *N* = 1,462) plotted on the original MMPI norms to illustrate the inaccuracy of the original inventory to characterize "normal" individuals. (Source: Butcher, Dahlstrom, Graham, Tellegen, & Kaemmer, 1989. Reprinted by permission.)

sample (1,462 women and 1,238 men) collected in the 1980s for the MMPI-2 are plotted on the original MMPI norms. The differences shown in the profiles (i.e., the elevations of the clinical scales above the *T*-scale mean of 50) indicate that the original MMPI norms tend to be inadequate for characterizing contemporary individuals. The original norms misleadingly characterize even "normal" individuals as having more psychological problems than they actually have.

Several reasons have been noted for the increased elevation of "normal" samples on the traditional MMPI norms, the most important of which is the fact that psychologists administering the MMPI today generally use a different set of instructions than Hathaway and McKinley used in the original MMPI norm data collection. In clinical practice today, item omissions are usually discouraged, and individuals are asked to answer all of the items. However, in the original test construction, individuals in the normative sample were allowed to leave out items they considered irrelevant. The original normative individuals omitted many items; consequently, the norms were set artificially low for evaluating profiles produced by test takers who have been encouraged to answer all items. Because individuals today are encouraged to respond to all of the items in the booklet, they are being inappropriately compared with those who were tacitly encouraged to omit items. Consequently, contemporary individuals may misleadingly appear more pathological.

Vulnerabilities in Testimony Regarding the MMPI-2

Item changes

(Possible cross-examination question: ***Is the MMPI-2 measuring the same things as the original validated MMPI scales?***)

Because much of the established MMPI research was based on responses to the old item wordings, does the meaning of the items for the new inventory still apply?

The MMPI and MMPI-2 have clear continuity at the item level. Although a few of the original items were changed slightly to improve wording and clarity, most items are worded exactly the same in the MMPI-2 as in the original instrument. Research has provided evidence that item wording changes have not altered the meaning or the psychological equivalence of an item. The MMPI profiles presented in Figure 2-6 show clearly that airline pilot applicants produced essentially the same clinical profile (plotted on the original MMPI norms) whether the original item wordings or the MMPI-2 wordings were used.

Moreover, the comparability of the original MMPI items with the rewritten MMPI items has been empiri-

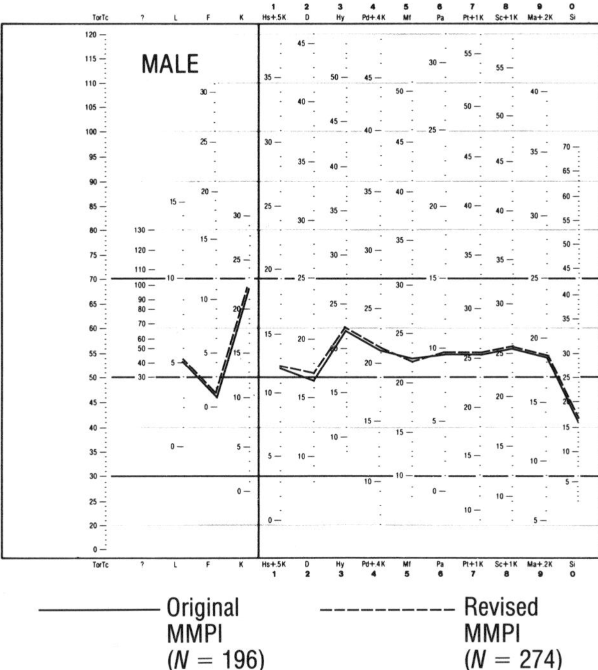

FIGURE 2-6. Basic profiles of two groups of airline pilot applicants who had been administered either the original MMPI or the MMPI-2, with both profiles plotted on the original MMPI norms. (Source: Butcher, 1992c. Reprinted by permission.)

cally evaluated by Ben-Porath and Butcher (1989b). These authors showed that individuals who were initially administered the MMPI and a week later administered the revised items responded in a manner that was comparable with other individuals who were initially administered the MMPI and retested a week later with the same original items. The authors concluded that the items rewritten for the MMPI-2 are psychometrically comparable to their MMPI counterparts (Ben-Porath & Butcher, 1989a); see appendix F.

Normative sample

(Possible cross-examination question: ***Does the MMPI-2 normative sample reflect the contemporary population of the United States?***)

Of course, any normative group can be questioned as being truly representative of the population. Even the federal government's census has been suspect. Following the 1990 census, a great deal of criticism ensued over the lack of thoroughness with which the people in the United States were counted. A number of groups and even entire cities were apparently missed in the count.

The MMPI-2 normative sample is a generally representative sample that is superior, for comparative purposes, to the narrow-based sample of the original MMPI. Great care was taken in selecting the MMPI-2 normative sample. Individuals were randomly solicited from seven regions of the United States, and regions were chosen to ensure that the sample would reflect ethnic diversity. This large, general sample (Butcher et al., 1989) serves as a more appropriate and diverse comparison group than was available for the original MMPI (Hathaway & McKinley, 1943).

Impact of changes in clinical and validity scales

(Possible cross-examination question: ***Are the traditional validity and clinical scales different in the MMPI-2 as compared with the original MMPI?***)

Have there been any changes in the item composition of the clinical and validity scales that would inherently weaken the validity of the MMPI-2 as compared with the original instrument? The short answer to this question is no. The MMPI Revision Committee conducted the restandardization in a manner that would maintain continuity between the MMPI-2 and the original MMPI. The reason for desiring continuity with the traditional scales is so that the previous research on the instrument would remain relevant.

Initially, the goal was to keep the full validity and clinical scale items intact. However, the desire to further reduce the objectionable nature of some test items resulted in some slight change. A few items deemed objectionable (Butcher & Tellegen, 1966) were deleted from four scales (see appendix F). The deletion of these items, although lowering objectionability, did not reduce the scale reliabilities. Correlates for the clinical scales have been shown to be continued for the MMPI-2 (Graham, 1988). Consequently, the revised scales operate in a way that is comparable to those of the original MMPI.

Comparability of *T* scores

(Possible cross-examination question: ***Are the* T *scores in MMPI-2 comparable to the* T *scores in the original MMPI?***)

The issue of comparability of *T* scores requires some explanation. Two factors account for the slight shift in *T* scores between the two versions of the MMPI. First, there are average raw score differences between the two normative samples resulting in large part from the fact that Cannot Say scores were allowed on the original test, somewhat deflating scores. As noted earlier, the fact that many individuals in the original MMPI normative group omitted large numbers of items artificially lowered the raw scores and the *T*-score distribution for the scales. This resulted in artificially inflating the *T* scores for contemporary individuals tested with the original MMPI.

Second, the original *T* scores were not uniform with respect to the percentile rank across the clinical scales. This lack of uniformity was undesirable in that a *T* score of 70 on one scale might be at a percentile rank of 91 on another clinical scale and a percentile rank of 97 on still another. To make the *T* scores comparable across percentile values of the clinical scales, a new set of *uniform* *T* scores was derived (Tellegen & Ben-Porath, 1992b).

There are, as a result, small differences between *T* scores. However, it is important to realize that the relationship between the uniform *T*-score distribution and the original MMPI distribution is very strong; both are based on a linear *T*-score transformation for the raw scores. Correlations between linear *T* scores and uniform *T* scores are in the range of .99.

The MMPI-2 norms are more appropriate for use with contemporary people than are the original MMPI norms. This is clearly demonstrated by contrasting the airline pilot applicant profiles presented in Figure 2-6 (presented earlier) and Figure 2-7. In comparing these profiles, keep in mind that the individuals being evaluated are not clinical patients but are "normal" individuals who are applying for positions as airline pilots with a major air carrier. In general, typical airline pilot applicants tend to be well adjusted. They have usually been prescreened or preselected (most have come through rigorous military screening programs). Finally, most are extremely defensive and take the MMPI with a response set to present a nonpathological pattern. Yet, when we plot their MMPI scores using the original MMPI norms (see Figure 2-3), we find that most of their clinical scores are *elevated* at about one-half to nearly a full standard deviation above the mean. However, when their clinical scale scores are plotted using the MMPI-2 norms (see Figure 2-4), their scores fall, as they should given

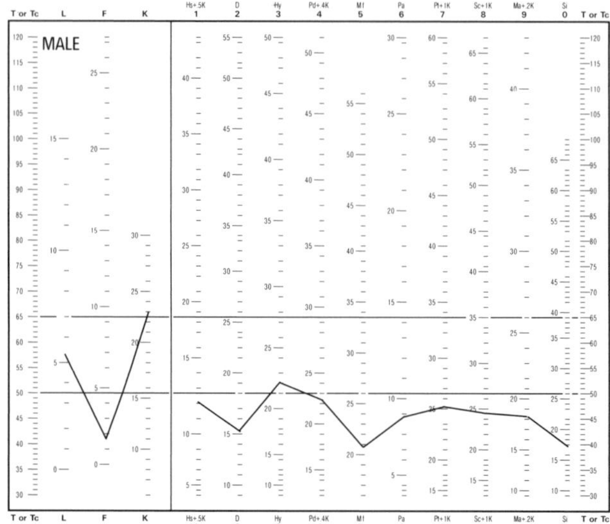

FIGURE 2-7. MMPI-2 basic profile of airline pilot applicants ($N = 437$), illustrating how well-adjusted individuals who present themselves in a positive light score on the MMPI-2 norms. (Source: Butcher, 1992c. Reprinted by permission.)

their virtuous self-presentation, *below* the mean on all but one of the scales (Butcher, 1992c).

Validity considerations

(Possible cross-examination question: ***Has the MMPI-2 been validated to a reasonable degree of medical certainty?***)

Because the validity and clinical scales of the original MMPI were retained in the MMPI-2 and MMPI-A, there is continuity of validity. That is, the validity research on the original scales has been shown to apply equally well to the MMPI-2 (Graham, 1988) and the MMPI-A (C. L. Williams & Butcher, 1989). In addition, several studies have documented the validity of the traditional validity and clinical scales on the MMPI-2.[3] Several studies have also reported extensive validity with the MMPI-A (Butcher & Williams, 1992a; Butcher et al., 1992; Williams et al., 1992).

Recent research has supported the continuity of the original MMPI and MMPI-2 scores in samples of psychiatric patients. Blake et al. (1992), for example, conducted research showing "that all scales on the two forms were highly correlated. Discriminant function analyses show that there were essentially no dif-

[3] Ben-Porath & Butcher, 1989a, 1989b; Ben-Porath et al., 1991; Butcher et al., 1991; Butcher, Graham, Dahlstrom, & Bowman, 1990; Butcher, Jeffrey, et al., 1990; Egeland et al., 1991; Hjemboe & Butcher, 1991; Keller & Butcher, 1991; Strassberg, Clutton, & Korboot, 1991.

ferences between the two forms in the accurate classification of clinical and nonclinical groups" (p. 323).

General Criticisms of the Empirical Approach to Personality Assessment

The issue of whether response sets invalidate empirical scales

(Possible cross-examination question: ***Hasn't research shown that people do not answer each item in a completely truthful way but simply answer in a socially desirable way or acquiesce to the demands of the situation?***)

Some researchers have contended that personality questionnaires are susceptible to response sets and thus are not thought to present valid sources of personality information (Edwards, 1957; Jackson & Messick, 1962). However, J. Block (1965) showed that when response sets are controlled, valid personality prediction could be obtained from MMPI items across a wide variety of samples.

Psychometric weakness: low internal consistency of empirical scales

(Possible cross-examination question: ***Isn't it true that the MMPI scales suffer from low internal consistencies and are therefore not reliable measures?***)

Internal consistency is one form of scale reliability. This statistic reflects the degree to which a scale measures a unitary construct as opposed to multiple characteristics. The higher the scale's internal consistency, the more likely it measures a single dimension or trait.

The internal consistencies of MMPI and MMPI-2 empirical scales differ widely. Some are relatively low (e.g., Scale 3), whereas others are typically quite high (e.g., Scale 7). However, the internal consistencies of homogeneous content scales (such as the original MMPI's Wiggins content scales and the MMPI-2's content scales) are typically quite high because internal consistency was incorporated in the scale construction approach.

The important thing to remember about internal consistency is that it is considered to be a less important scale property for empirical scales than for homogeneous or content scales. External validity, the degree to which a scale measures behavior, is the empirical scale's ultimate criterion of worth. How the items of a scale relate to each other is relatively less important than that they, as a group, predict a particular criterion reliably. The MMPI clinical scales were developed by assuring that the scale measured or predicted behavior or characteristics.

Psychometric weakness: overlapping items on the scales

(Possible cross-examination question: ***Isn't it true that the MMPI is a weak measure of personality because its different scales contain overlapping items?***)

One important reason that item overlap occurs in omnibus-type personality scales is that psychological phenomena are not independent of each other. Clinical behaviors of interest to the practitioner are seldom isolated problems that are unrelated to other characteristics or traits. Depression as a symptomatic behavior is highly correlated with anxiety, social introversion, and low self-esteem. Any attempt to measure any one of these characteristics will result in an encounter with the others. It is difficult to measure depression in the absence of assessing (at least to some extent) these other qualities. In fact, an artificial elimination of item overlap may result in an incomplete assessment of psychological variables.

With regard to empirical scales, such as the MMPI clinical scales, external validity is the ultimate criterion, and item overlap is of secondary importance. In the development of the MMPI-2 content scales, efforts were made to minimize item overlap in order to produce relatively pure content dimensions. Even in these instances, however, some item overlap was allowed because a particular item theoretically "belonged" on more than one scale. For example, the item "I have difficulty keeping my mind on a task or job" is clearly a strong anxiety-type item and is a marker for the MMPI-2 Anxiety (ANX) content scale. However, it is also a very strong component of the WRK content scale, in which it appears to assess an inability to work effectively. The item has content relevance and predictive validity for both scales.

Psychometric weakness: test–retest reliability

(Possible cross-examination question: ***Isn't it true that you get different scale scores on the MMPI scales when you retest people at a later date?***)

Most MMPI scales have moderate to high test–retest reliabilities depending on the length of the scale

(Scale 1 usually has a somewhat lower reliability coefficient than Scale 8, which is longer) or the degree to which it measures "traits" in contrast to factors that are caused or evoked more by specific situations (see appendix F).

Some MMPI scales have exceptionally high test–retest stability. For example, the long-range test–retest stability for the *Si* scale was found to be .734 for a sample of "normal" men over a 30-year test–retest period (Leon et al., 1979). Spiro (1992) found that the stability index for *Si* was .86 in a test–retest study of the MMPI-2 spanning 5 years. Matz, Altepeter, and Perlman (1992) found moderate to high stability coefficients (.60–.90) for the MMPI-2 validity scales in a sample of college students.

Item responses out of context
(Possible cross-examination question: ***Doesn't MMPI Item ___ actually measure something different from the scale it appears on?***)

It is generally not a good idea for expert witnesses who are testifying about the MMPI to introduce individual items, out of their scale context, in support of the interpretation. The MMPI is most valuable as an assessment instrument if the scale level rather than individual item level is the basis for interpretation. This is true for several reasons. First, items tend to be less reliable than groups of items or scales. Second, at least in the case of empirically derived measures, some items on the scale might have lower content relevance and validity than other items on the scale, and their inclusion as a focus in the testimony might detract from the overall value of the scale in assessing the personality features in question.

Ziskin (1981b) pointed out that

> *there is a need to look at the subject's responses to individual items on the test. This statement may be objectionable to many psychologists who insist that evaluation should not be on the basis of the individual responses to items but rather on scale scores and configurations of scores. I am aware that is the way the test is used by most psychologists. However, neither lawyers nor jurors are bound to that approach. (p. 8)*

The following scenario illustrates possible problems psychologists might encounter when items are taken out of scale context:

Attorney: Tell me, Doctor, do you think most people inwardly dislike putting themselves out to help other people?

Psychologist: Er . . . no, I think most people would like to be helpful to others.

Attorney: That's interesting, Doctor. A "false" response to that item measures a point on the Paranoia scale, doesn't it, Doctor?

Psychologist: I don't remember the way particular items are scored.

Attorney: You don't know whether an item on a scale measures the characteristics of the scale, Doctor?

Psychologist: I only go by the total score of the scale.

Attorney: [Showing the items to the psychologist, having first asked the judge's permission to approach the witness] As you look at the items on the scale and the scoring key, is it your opinion that the item is scored on the Paranoia scale if it is answered "false"? . . .

Attorney: Now, Doctor, doesn't it seem a bit strange to you that a "false" response to that item would measure paranoid thinking?

Psychologist: Could you repeat the question?

Attorney: Wouldn't you agree that a cynical, paranoid, mistrustful person would actually inwardly dislike putting themselves out to help other people, Doctor?

Psychologist: Er . . . yes, that would seem to be the case. But, you said that it was scored the other way.

Attorney: Wouldn't you agree then, Doctor, that the item is scored in the wrong direction on the Paranoia scale to actually measure paranoid thinking?

Psychologist: Intuitively, it would seem that more cynical people would answer the other way, but . . . .

Attorney: Now, Doctor, are you aware of other items on the test that are incorrectly scored as this one is?

As indicated in this example, the attorney was able to get the psychologist to question the accuracy of the test by reference to individual items.

It is often easy for an attorney, in cross-examination, to obfuscate issues and "prove" incorrect or misleading points by examining individual item responses. The knowledgeable psychologist, as much as possible, can stay on much safer ground by referring to the full scale scores. He or she can do this by stating that items should not be considered individually. Interpreting at the scale level is more typical and psychometrically appropriate than taking items out of context.

A recent personal injury case highlighted the relative power of using scale-level interpretations rather than item descriptions. The litigant, a 32-year-old woman, was allegedly injured in an automobile accident (although she was not hospitalized nor had she sought treatment for the injury for a period of time following the accident). She claimed to have disabling physical and psychological symptoms (headaches, double vision, and troubling nightmares) and sued the car rental company for a considerable sum of money to compensate for her injury.

On the psychological evaluation, her MMPI-2 clinical profile showed some Scale 1 and Scale 2 elevation, indicating that she was presenting herself as having mood and somatic complaints. However, her validity configuration showed a clear pattern of response defensiveness often seen among personal injury claimants who are presenting unrealistic complaints (Butcher & Harlow, 1987). Her *L* (Lie) scale elevation (62 *T*) and *K* (Defensiveness) scale score ($T = 70$) showed a clear pattern of evasiveness. The expert witness testifying on behalf of the insurance carrier presented the MMPI-2 validity pattern as reflecting a conscious response attitude, with the litigant claiming excessive virtue and distorting self-presentation in an attempt to make her somatic complaints more believable. The presence of conscious defensive responding and lack of frankness on the MMPI-2 profile called into question the truthfulness of her claims (for a discussion of this interpretive strategy, see chapter 6).

During the cross-examination, the woman's attorney attempted to get the psychologist to establish the woman's disability by examining her responses to a few single items that stated her symptoms. For example, at one point the attorney attempted to get the psychologist to acknowledge that his client's response of "true" to the MMPI item acknowledging having nightmares actually showed that she was having residual problems from the accident. Rather than acknowledging that the response to a single item showed any lingering disability, the psychologist called attention to the fact that her full scale score on the Keane PTSD (Posttraumatic Stress Disorder Scale; Butcher et al., 1989; Fairbank, McCaffrey, & Keane, 1985; Keane, Malloy, & Fairbank, 1984; Keane, Wolfe, & Taylor, 1987; Lyons & Keane, 1992), which contained the item, was actually low. Thus, she did not appear to have problems of a posttraumatic nature because her scores on the MMPI-2 PTSD scale were actually well within the normal range, despite her response to the one item.

At another point, the attorney attempted to get the psychologist to acknowledge his client's inability to work by her response to a single item:

Attorney: Doctor, I want to talk about individual questions. Wouldn't my client's responding "false" to the item "I am about as able to work as I ever was" indicate that she was disabled?

Psychologist: No. You are moving away from the reliability and validity of the scale when you interpret at the item level. . . . The way the MMPI-2 is actually used is by interpreting scales. Her low score on the Work Interference scale shows that she actually reports few problems in this area.

The psychologist testified that the item in question actually appeared on the WRK scale, which addresses the general problem of low functioning in a work context. Her total score on that scale placed her in the normal range, indicating that she reported no more work adaptation difficulties than most people do.

In both of these instances in the testimony, the attorney's efforts to prove his case at the item level were frustrated by the fact that the client's total score on those scales actually showed her *not* to report many problems in those areas compared with most people. By focusing on individual items, the attorney was attempting to force the psychologist to understate the cumulative effect of the individual items and the overall comparative nature of the instrument.

TABLE 2-1

Means and Standard Deviations by Ethnic Origin for 1,138 Community Adult Males

Scale	White (N = 933)		Black (N = 126)		American Indian (N = 38)		Hispanic (N = 35)		Asian (N = 6)	
	M	*SD*	*M*	*SD*	*M*	*SD*	*M*	*SD*	*M*	*SD*
L	3.36	2.13	4.26	2.77	4.26	2.78	4.51	2.63	4.50	3.27
F	4.29	2.98	5.18	3.76	6.42	4.46	6.17	4.07	7.33	5.61
K	15.45	4.74	15.08	4.88	13.55	4.64	14.29	4.50	13.83	5.08
Hs	4.69	3.78	5.58	3.91	6.92	4.48	6.17	4.11	6.50	5.28
D	18.16	4.59	19.02	4.24	19.08	4.98	19.06	5.00	16.83	3.97
Hy	21.06	4.60	20.03	5.06	20.42	5.49	19.77	5.56	17.50	4.89
Pd	16.25	4.49	17.57	4.40	19.50	5.23	18.29	5.62	16.67	4.13
Mf	26.21	5.13	25.84	4.20	23.39	6.07	24.43	4.60	24.17	6.18
Pa	10.09	2.82	9.87	3.09	10.70	3.21	10.51	3.07	10.33	2.16
Pt	11.04	6.53	11.60	6.75	12.79	7.34	13.00	6.81	14.33	7.15
Sc	10.75	6.86	12.79	7.38	13.82	9.01	13.89	8.20	16.50	10.05
Ma	16.58	4.46	18.33	4.31	17.84	4.59	18.77	4.88	15.83	5.98
Si	25.80	8.70	25.56	7.43	28.32	8.63	24.77	8.26	32.17	9.45

Note: From Butcher, Dahlstrom, Graham, Tellegen, & Kaemmer (1989). Reprinted by permission.

READING LEVEL

Forensic assessments may be complicated by the fact that the individual who is being assessed cannot adequately read or comprehend English. The MMPI-2 items were written in relatively simple English. It takes only about a fifth-grade reading level to understand the item content (Paolo, Ryan, & Smith, 1991).

Individuals with even lower reading skills can be tested by using a tape-recorded version of the instrument available through the test publisher. Tape-recorded administration has been found to be a comparable form of test administration producing results equivalent to the written format (Dahlstrom et al., 1972).

If the individual is able to read and understand the items at a fifth-grade level, he or she can likely respond to the items well enough to produce a valid, interpretable record. However, the validity scales *F*, *F(B)* (Back Side *F*), and *VRIN* (Variable Response Inconsistency) should be carefully evaluated to assure that the person has responded appropriately to the content of the test items.

CULTURAL DIVERSITY AND MMPI RESPONSES

As noted in chapter 1, the original MMPI was criticized because only Whites were included in the normative sample, and the test seemed, at least in some instances, to produce misleading results for minorities. Chapter 4 presents a more detailed discussion of such difficulties.[4] At this point, we touch on only two aspects.

First, if language is the significant issue, it may be possible to obtain an appropriate foreign language version of the test. The original MMPI has been widely translated and adapted in other languages and cultures.[5] In many cases, it is possible to obtain a translated version of the MMPI that has been

[4] See Thinking About Tests in Context; see also *Standards for Educational and Psychological Testing* (APA, 1985), Standard 7.6, p. 47; and Pope & Vasquez's (1991) chapters "Assessment, Testing, and Diagnosis" (pp. 87–100) and "Cultural, Contextual, and Individual Differences" (pp. 130–138).

[5] See, for example, Butcher, 1985; Butcher & Pancheri, 1976; Cheung & Song, 1989; Cheung, Zhao, & Wu, 1992; Clark, 1985; Hess, 1992; Lee, Cheung, Man, & Hsu, 1992; Rissetti & Maltes, 1985; Manos, 1985; Manos & Butcher, 1982; Savasir & Erol, 1990.

TABLE 2-2

Means and Standard Deviations by Ethnic Origin for 1,462 Community Adult Females

	White (*N* = 1184)		Black (*N* = 188)		American Indian (*N* = 39)		Hispanic (*N* = 38)		Asian (*N* = 13)	
Scale	***M***	***SD***	***M***	***SD***	***M***	***SD***	***M***	***SD***	***M***	***SD***
L	3.47	1.98	3.95	2.32	4.64	2.68	2.92	2.16	4.85	3.31
F	3.39	2.64	4.43	3.38	5.69	3.99	6.32	4.35	3.54	2.07
K	15.34	4.47	14.13	4.56	12.41	5.67	12.37	4.88	14.85	4.04
Hs	5.49	4.24	7.50	5.16	8.74	4.63	8.92	5.50	6.38	2.84
D	19.93	4.97	21.00	4.99	21.33	4.84	21.55	4.69	19.23	4.28
Hy	22.05	4.55	22.17	5.38	22.59	5.39	22.53	6.00	20.62	4.09
Pd	15.68	4.48	18.30	4.42	19.08	4.74	19.89	5.34	14.31	4.89
Mf	36.31	3.91	34.60	4.22	33.23	4.85	34.05	4.76	35.62	4.39
Pa	10.13	2.91	10.40	3.11	11.51	3.62	11.34	3.15	9.54	2.88
Pt	12.27	6.89	13.55	7.68	17.64	8.76	17.21	8.92	10.00	5.03
Sc	10.39	6.88	14.10	8.63	17.00	9.93	18.42	10.63	8.92	4.01
Ma	15.61	4.29	17.85	4.62	17.90	5.29	20.00	4.91	15.31	3.84
Si	27.78	9.36	28.37	8.54	32.26	7.25	27.45	7.79	28.77	7.67

Note: From Butcher, Dahlstrom, Graham, Tellegen, & Kaemmer (1989). Reprinted by permission.

renormed for the appropriate culture (e.g., Chile, China, Italy, Israel, Norway, Russia, Japan, Korea, and Thailand). The MMPI-2 has also been adapted for use with a variety of languages and cultures. Research also supports the use of MMPI items presented, using American Sign Language, to hearing-impaired individuals (Brauer, 1992).

Second, in the MMPI-2 normative study, an effort was made to increase the relevance of the revised norms for minorities by including individuals from different regional and ethnic backgrounds in the normative sample. Consequently, the instrument is based on a normative group that is more appropriate for testing a broad range of ethnically diverse people. The relative performance on MMPI-2 scores for different ethnic groups is presented in Table 2-1 and Table 2-2.

A recent study of men undergoing court-ordered evaluations provided an empirical evaluation of the relative unimportance of ethnic group differences on the MMPI-2, at least for certain groups under certain circumstances. Shondrick, Ben-Porath, and Stafford (1992) compared Black and White men who had been ordered by the court to take the MMPI as part of their pretrial evaluation. The group mean profiles of Black and White defendants are shown in Figures 2-8 and 2-9. The authors found relatively few scale-level differences between the two groups, indicating that the MMPI-2 normative sample is appropriate to use for Blacks as well as for majority individuals. Only Scale 9 on the clinical and validity profile and CYN (Cynicism) and ASP (Antisocial Practices) on the content scale profile were significantly different; these differences were slight, although statistically significant.

POTENTIAL PROBLEMS WITH SHORTENED AND OTHER ALTERED FORMS

Because of the time it takes to complete the MMPI (about 1 or 2 hours), some researchers have recommended using shortened versions of the MMPI to reduce the testing time. The use of an abbreviated or short form of the MMPI is predicated on the belief that shortened scales of the MMPI provide adequate measures of the variables assessed by the full form of the test. Using an incomplete or partial form of the

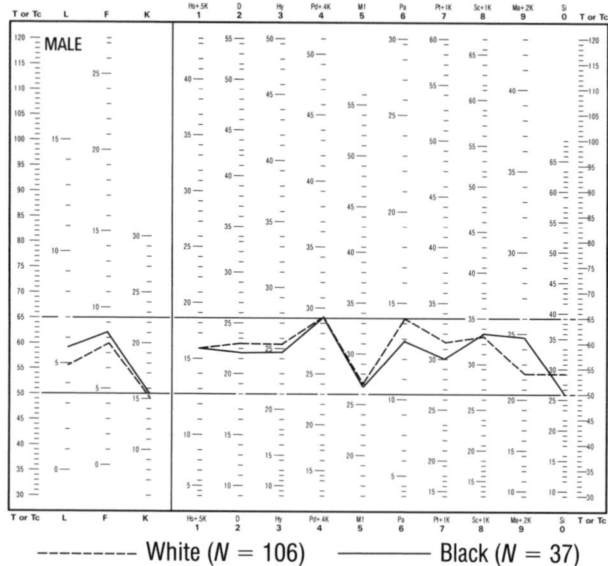

FIGURE 2-8. Group mean MMPI-2 clinical scale profile of White and Black men who had been court-ordered to take the MMPI-2. (Source: Shondrick, Ben-Porath, & Stafford, 1992. Adapted by permission.)

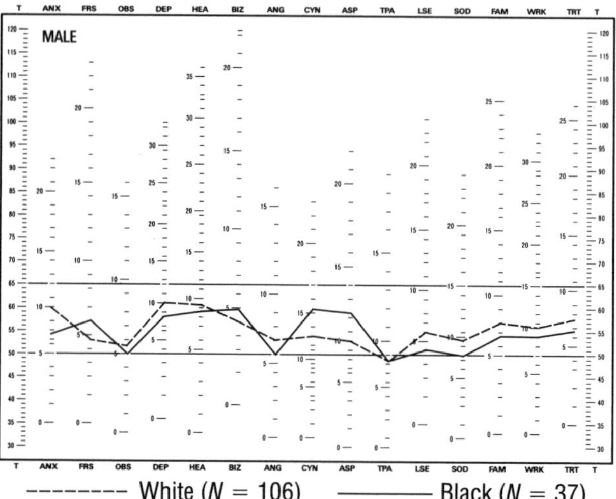

FIGURE 2-9. Group mean MMPI-2 content scale profile of White and Black men who had been court-ordered to take the MMPI-2. (Source: Shondrick, Ben-Porath, & Stafford, 1992. Adapted by permission.)

MMPI in forensic assessment can, however, lead to considerable difficulty for the psychologist in court. Results that are based on incomplete administration may differ significantly from those that are based on the full form administered according to standardized instructions under standardized conditions.

Abbreviated Forms

An important distinction needs to be made between an *abbreviated form* of the MMPI and a *short form* of the instrument. The abbreviated form is created by reducing the number of items by presenting only the items contained on desired scales. For example, scores for the complete validity and clinical scales can be obtained by administering only the first 370 items of the MMPI-2 or the first 350 items of the MMPI-A. Reduced-item administration is relatively easy because all the items composing the original clinical and validity scales are included in the first part of the test booklet. The actual number of items administered for each scale (e.g., the Depression scale) remains the same as when the full test is administered. An abbreviated form of the MMPI allows the psychologist to administer and score specific scales; the reliability and validity of these scales is *not* reduced by this procedure. However, the scales containing items in the back of the booklet, for example, the MAC-R (MacAndrew Scale-Revised) Scale or the MMPI-2 content scales, are not scorable.

Short Forms

The so-called short forms, however, are a very different matter. Shortened versions are sets of scales that have been decreased in length from the standard MMPI form; thus, fewer items from each scale are administered. The MMPI test publisher, the University of Minnesota Press, does not recognize an official MMPI short form.

The reliability and validity of MMPI short forms are questionable (Butcher & Hostetler, 1990). A review of the evidence published in peer-reviewed scientific and professional journals suggests that the ability of MMPI short forms to predict the full scale score is equivocal at best. Most researchers have concluded that the limitations of MMPI short forms are too great to use them for clinical prediction.[6]

Shortened scales are also less reliable than the full versions of the MMPI-2 scales. The decreased reliabil-

[6] For example, Graham, 1987; Greene, 1982; Hart, McNeill, Lutz, & Atkins, 1986; Helmes & McLaughlin, 1983; Hoffmann & Butcher, 1975; Streiner & Miller, 1986; Willcockson, Bolton, & Dana, 1983.

ity of shortened scales is likely to lessen the validity of the scales (Butcher & Hostetler, 1990), in part because the reliability of a test puts a limit on its validity. Shortened MMPI scales have been considered to be too inaccurate to use in clinical evaluations (Dahlstrom, 1980; Graham, 1987; Greene, 1982; Hoffman & Butcher, 1975; Lachar, 1979). Roger Greene (1982), professor at Pacific Graduate School of Psychology, recommends that users of short forms of the MMPI should consider it a new test and employ an "honesty in labeling" approach because shortened scales are not equivalent measures to the full form (see also appendix J).

Valuable clinical information is lost when a short form is used in lieu of the full MMPI. Short forms have been developed only for the clinical and validity scales and do not allow for the assessment of other supplementary measures. In light of the research showing the lowered predictive efficiency of many shortened forms, expert witnesses presenting assessment results that are based on shortened forms run the risk of vigorous challenge on cross-examination.

Responsibilities When Using Shortened and Other Altered Forms and Scoring Systems

The topic of altered forms of a test raises an important issue for forensic practitioners, although this may not apply to all altered forms. The publisher of the MMPI seeks to ensure that no infringement of copyright occurs through the creation, marketing, and use of "new" tests that are based on improperly derived copyrighted items. Thus, it is important, whenever an expert witness encounters a new test that is based on a current, copyrighted instrument, that he or she ensure that the authors have obtained whatever relevant, necessary authorization that may be legally required to use licensed or copyrighted items before the expert includes it in a forensic test battery.

Similarly, when the MMPI or other psychological tests are computer scored (see following sections), there may be important issues regarding licensing and copyright applicable to the scoring keys and resulting printout. (The issues tend to be significantly different for computer-based *scoring* [because the copyright holders of standardized tests often tend to hold rights to the scoring key; e.g., it would be rare that an individual would try to develop a "new" scoring key to a test of arithmetic ability by changing the "correct" answers to problems in addition, subtraction, multiplication, and division] in contrast to computer-based *interpretation* systems [assuming that the provider of the service has developed a significantly original, empirically based, and adequately validated interpretative system that would not inappropriately "borrow" from the copyrighted decision rules of interpretive programs owned by the copyright holder to the test itself].)

Shortened and otherwise altered (e.g., translations into other languages; forms that are administered by computer) versions of valid, reliable, and standardized psychological tests may be both useful and legitimate. However, it is the expert witness's responsibility to ensure that a test is both useful (e.g., is valid and reliable for the purposes to which it will be put; see chapter 4) and legitimate (e.g., that it does not violate copyright or other laws). If an expert witness is discovered to have used a modified test that violates copyright (and perhaps other) laws, it is obvious that a skilled cross-examination may call the integrity, carefulness, and credibility of the expert witness as well as of the expert witness's testimony (e.g., the results and interpretations of the testing) into serious question.

Forensic practitioners must also use exceptional care in regard to direct use of copyrighted test materials. Both stimulus materials (i.e., lists, figures, or other printed matter that are shown to the person taking a test either to explain the test or to form the basis for the person's response) and answer sheets (the printed forms on which either the person taking the test or the person administering the test records the test taker's responses) may be copyrighted. For example, the answer sheets for the Wechsler Adult Intelligence Scale—Revised (WAIS–R) are copyrighted. If the expert witness works in an institution (e.g., a large hospital or clinic offering extensive test services conducted by both senior staff and psychology interns) that conducts a high volume of assessments using such materials, it may be very tempting (because it is less expensive), when the stock of response sheets it running low, to reproduce them through photocopying or offset printing rather than ordering them from the test publisher. Again, in addition to whatever ethical and related issues may be involved, forensic practitioners making use of materials that may violate copyright laws seem to invite, if the behavior is discovered, a cross-examination focusing on integrity, carefulness, and credibility of both the expert witness and his or her testimony.

COMPUTER-BASED MMPI INTERPRETATION AND FORENSIC TESTIMONY

National survey research suggests that computer-based test scoring and interpretation services have been accepted and are widely used by psychologists: Less than 40% report that they have never used a computerized test interpretation service (Pope, Tabachnick, & Keith-Spiegel, 1987, 1988). In his review of computerized psychological assessment programs, Bloom (1992) concluded that "the very high level of professional vigilance over test administration and interpretation software undoubtedly accounts for the fact that computerized assessment programs have received such high marks" (p. 172; see also Zachary & Pope, 1984). These automated services have also gained increased acceptance in forensic settings, even though there is debate about how computer-based reports are to be incorporated in the clinical assessment (Fowler & Butcher, 1986; Garb, 1992; Matarazzo, 1986; Rubenzer, 1991). Psychologist and attorney Jay Ziskin (1981b), for example, stated that he "would recommend for forensic purposes the utilization of one of the automated MMPI services" (p. 9). According to Ziskin, the advantages include the reduced possibility of scoring or transposition errors, the capacity of computers to store and use more quickly vast amounts of actuarial information, and the reduced likelihood that personal (i.e., examiner) biases will intrude on the process of gathering, scoring, and interpreting the test data.

As noted in Exhibit 2-1 (presented earlier), one of the important reasons for the broad acceptance of the MMPI in forensic settings is that the profiles, being objectively and externally validated scales and indices, can be interpreted with a great deal of objectivity. Any interpreter (or computer interpretation system developer) relying closely on the external empirical correlates of the scales and indices would produce highly similar interpretations, eliminating or at least reducing the subjective sources of error (see chapter 4). The MMPI scale scores can be interpreted from an actuarial perspective (Butcher, 1987a; Fowler, 1987; Gilberstadt, 1969) by referring to the established correlates for given scale elevations and profile types.

Although most computer-based psychological test interpretation programs are not full actuarially derived systems (they have been referred to as *automated clinicians* by Fowler, 1969, 1987), they nevertheless can be viewed as objective interpretation systems when they provide hypotheses and personality descriptions in an automatic, consistent manner for the scores incorporated in the system.

It is important to emphasize again at this point that the MMPI, even when scored and interpreted by a computer, produces *hypotheses* that must be considered in light of other sources of information. Almost anyone—including judges and juries—may tend to overlook this point when encountering an impressive computer printout of results from a scientifically based test (e.g., O'Dell, 1972).

Advantages of Using Computer-Based Psychological Tests in Forensic Testimony

The value of using a computer-based interpretation system for MMPI interpretation can be summarized as follows: (a) Their use avoids or minimizes subjectivity in selecting and emphasizing interpretive material; (b) the reliability of the output can be assured because the same interpretations will always be printed for particular scores or patterns; (c) the interpretations for a test provided by a computer (assuming that the empirical base and decision-making rules of the interpretive program meet the criteria set forth in the American Psychological Association's [APA] *Guidelines for Computer-Based Tests and Interpretations* [1986b]) are usually more thorough and better documented than those derived from a clinical or impressionistic assessment (depending, of course, on the knowledge, skill, and experience of the clinician); (d) biasing factors, such as halo effects, that can influence more subjective procedures such as clinical interviewing are usually avoided; and (e) computer-based reports can usually be explained and described clearly to a jury or judge, assuming that the expert witness is adequately familiar with database and inference rules on which the report is based.

Cautions or Questions in Using Computerized Reports

A number of factors need to be taken into consideration in using computer-based personality test evaluations in forensic assessments.

When computer-processed test interpretation is included in a forensic case, it is important to establish the chain of custody involved in the processing of the protocol (i.e., the record of the individual's responses). The expert witness must be able to document that the computer-based report is actually the report for the client in the case. For example, in cross-examination, an attorney might ask, "How do you know that the report actually matches the answer sheet filled in the individual you assessed?" (see also chapter 8). The psychologist should be prepared to explain how the answer sheet was provided and to discuss how he or she knows that the computer-based results are actually those for the individual's answer sheet. There have been cases in which the chain of custody was weakened by the fact that the psychologist was unable to assure that the test protocol provided for the person who was assessed was the correct one.

Similarly, there is an important need to assure that the particular interpretation in the computer-based report is an appropriate prototypal match between the person's scores on the test and the statements generated by the computer. An attorney, in cross-examination, might ask, "How do you know that the computer report actually fits the person?" (see chapter 8).

Computer-based psychological tests are usually prototypes and are generally actuarially based. Some—perhaps many—of the statements in a report may not be descriptive of a particular person. As emphasized repeatedly in this book, the MMPI, whether scored and interpreted by an individual or a computer, produces *hypotheses*.

The psychologist should be prepared in direct or cross-examination to discuss computer-generated statements that do *not* fit the client. Typical questions to which the expert may be asked to respond include, "Do all of the computer-generated descriptions apply in this particular case? If not, how did you determine *which* ones would be used in this case?" and "What is there about the particular person in question that makes you conclude that the prototype does not fit?"

Direct and cross-examination questions may focus on the issue of whether the computer output can "stand alone" as a report. The issue of whether a psychologist needs to personally interview the client depends on the nature of testimony. As noted in chapter 1, some expert witnesses may be called to testify only about the nature of the MMPI; whether a particular profile, taken as a whole, is valid (i.e., whether the pattern of validity scores would preclude other inferences from being drawn on the basis of the test); and what hypotheses are produced, in light of the empirical research, by a particular profile. If, however, a psychologist is asked to testify about the psychological status or adjustment of a person, it is important to incorporate as much information as possible into the clinical evaluation (see, for example, the explicit qualifications regarding validity in the forensic assessment report for Ms. Jones in chapter 7). The use of a computer-based report in isolation from other important information such as personal history, biographical data, interview observations, previous records, and so forth, is *not* appropriate. (See APA [1986b] for a discussion of the *Guidelines for Computer-Based Tests and Interpretations*.) However, as mentioned above, there are instances in which testimony that is based on the computer-generated MMPI report alone is appropriate and useful (e.g., if the issue of testimony involves a technical point concerning the use of the test itself or when the computer-generated report is used to cross-check an interpretation of a psychologist who perhaps also testified on the basis of the MMPI).

Another consideration in using computer-based test interpretations as part of a forensic evaluation and testimony centers around the possible lack of acceptance of high technology and fear of computers among some people in today's society. Some people mistrust automation and have a bias against mechanization of human affairs. There is always the possibility that a member of the jury or even the judge may have a bias against any mechanization when it comes to human personality. This possibility should be taken into consideration when explaining automated test results. Care should be taken to emphasize the strong reliability ("reproducibility") of results in computer interpretation and the general acceptance of automated reports by the profession. A quote from APA's *Guidelines for Computer-Based Tests and Interpretations* can be used to assure lay persons that computer-based testing is professionally appropriate and ethical: "A long history of research on statistical and clinical prediction has established that a well-designed statistical treatment of test results and ancillary information will yield more valid assessments than will an individual professional using the same information" (1986b, p. 9).

Another point to consider in using a computer-based interpretation report in forensic assessment is that two different computer interpretation services might actually produce somewhat different interpretations for the same protocol (i.e., the record of test responses). In theory, all computer-based MMPI interpretations for a specific protocol should be quite similar because they are based on the same correlate research literature. The underlying assumption on which computer interpretation is based is that the actuarially based (objectively validated) correlates are automatically applied to test indices. Computer systems that are based closely on research-validated indexes tend to have similar outputs. However, in practice, commercially available systems differ with respect to the information presented and the accuracy of the interpretations (Eyde, Kowal, & Fishburne, 1991).

The psychologist using an automated interpretation system in court should be familiar with the issues of computerized test interpretation generally and the validity research on the particular system used (see Eyde et al., 1991; Moreland, 1987).

TYPES OF FORENSIC ASSESSMENTS

In the following sections we examine a number of MMPI-based forensic assessments. When exploring the use of the MMPI, or any psychological evaluation procedure in forensic evaluations, it is important to keep in mind that a psychological evaluation, in this context, describes psychological characteristics, traits, states, symptoms, or adjustment and does not validate a legal proposition. Psychologists should not try to infer legal concepts from psychological test data (Grisso, 1986). For example, one cannot determine competency to stand trial or determine whether a particular defendant is not guilty by reason of insanity from psychological testing results alone. MMPI-based forensic assessment can shed light on the individual's psychological adjustment as he or she sees it and is willing to share self-observations with others.

Assessing Personal Injury Cases

One of the most frequent uses of MMPI-based forensic assessments is to evaluate the mental status of people involved in personal injury litigation who are alleging that they have been psychologically damaged. These claims of psychological injury may occur, for example, in lawsuits involving accidental injury, medical malpractice, sexual harassment, "hate crimes" (which may be the basis for later civil actions focusing on personal injury), or occupational stress.

The MMPI can be used as an aid in evaluating the presence of psychological distress or dysfunction (often relevant to legal claims for "pain and suffering") in litigants because the scales show the existence of symptoms in a reliable, valid manner in an objective framework. A higher degree of credence is usually placed on objectively interpreted procedures than on other types of information available to the psychologist (Butcher & Harlow, 1987).

In personal injury cases, the court or jury is often asked to decide whether or to what extent the litigant in the action has been psychologically injured or disabled and what amount of compensation should be awarded for the claim. Faced with such questions, expert witnesses testifying in the case may be asked to assess whether a plaintiff's complaints of psychological damage are due to one or more of the following: the alleged tort itself; one or more preexisting (i.e., before the alleged tort) conditions; harmful events or conditions that occurred after the alleged tort and for which the defendant is not alleged (by the plaintiff) to be responsible; stress; factitious disorder; malingering; paranoid delusion; or other factors. If the expert concludes that more than one factor is involved, he or she may be asked to make the much more difficult determination regarding the relative importance and possible interaction of each factor.

Forensic evaluations in personal injury cases may involve several elements: (a) the credibility of the litigant's self-report (see chapter 6); (b) the symptoms that the individual is reportedly experiencing; (c) the likely causes of actual symptoms; and (d) the intensity and extent of actual distress or dysfunction and likely (or possible) course of recovery.

Psychological evaluations in disability determinations have some inherent limitations. In a variety of cases, it may not be possible to determine whether a claimant's injuries are *actually* the result of organic posttraumatic changes or are based on preexisting personality factors (Marcus, 1983). No completely foolproof method of determining such distinctions is available at this time, although carefully conducted comprehensive psychological and neuropsychological assessments may be helpful in addressing the question. By selecting tests appropriate to the complaints, conducting careful interviews when possible, using the most valid and reliable test instruments, recording case notes and test reports, and reviewing relevant documents (such as previous records of assessment and treatment, school records, and records of previous civil or criminal legal cases), clinicians can be helpful in clarifying psychological factors in personal injury cases. If, for example, the individual responds to the MMPI in a cooperative manner and the validity scales do not show preclusive evidence of malingering or other distortions, the test profiles are likely to provide valuable information.

A number of MMPI measures can aid in determining whether an individual has attempted to present him- or herself in a slanted way. See chapter 6 for discussion of the use of the MMPI to assess malingering and other distortions.

Psychological testing can be of value in disability determinations in a number of ways. If the individual's approach to the test is valid, the test results can provide a useful evaluation of the client's symptomatic status. Psychological testing can also provide an indication of the severity of an individual's problems and the possible long-term course of the disorder.

In determining whether an individual who claims to have difficulties as a result of an injury, stressful experience, or exposure to toxic substances is manifesting symptoms consistent with such occurrences, several factors should be considered. As a baseline from which to judge personality test performances of disability claimants with cases pending, it is important to know how truly disabled people have responded on the relevant psychological measures. Research on personality characteristics of individuals who were actually disabled and were not awaiting a disability determination decision has been published (Butcher, 1987b). D. N. Wiener (1948a) and Warren and Weiss (1969) reported that groups of individuals who were actually disabled tended to produce MMPI profiles with scale scores in the nonpathological range, below a *T* of 70. Moreover, there were no characteristic MMPI profiles found for the various disability groups when disabled patients were classified according to type of disability.

Personality profiles of claimants pending disability determination, on the other hand, appear to be more exaggerated and generally more pathological (Pollack & Grainey, 1984; Sternbach, Wolf, Murphy, & Akeson, 1973). Expert witnesses must be familiar with the strengths and limitations of the research studies relevant to the assessments they are conducting. It is possible, for example, that the differences emerging from the studies cited above *may* be due to an element of acuteness in the disorder or a trend toward excessive symptom claiming to emphasize perceived disability, or they may indicate other factors.

Most MMPI research involving compensation cases reflects this increased level of psychological symptoms. In cases in which physical injury is claimed, the MMPI profile of compensation cases usually involves extreme scale elevations on *Hs*, *D*, and *Hy* (Repko & Cooper, 1983; Shaffer, Nussbaum, & Little, 1972). Snibbe, Peterson, and Sosner (1980) found that workers' compensation applicants had generally rather disturbed MMPI profiles (with high elevations on Scales *F*, *Sc*, *D*, *Hs*, *Hy*, and *Pd*), even though the 47 individuals in the research group had been drawn from four diagnostic groups according to type of claim (e.g., head injury, psychological stress and strain, low back pain, and miscellaneous).

In a study to determine possible motivational differences between disability applicants, Pollack and Grainey (1984) reported that claimants may respond to the test in an exaggerated manner in order to receive financial benefits. The idea that claimants present a more exaggerated picture of their adjustment than others was also supported by Parker, Doerfler, Tatten, and Hewett (1983), who found that individuals with prominent MMPI *Pt* scale scores in their profile code tended to report much more "intense" pain. Therefore, even when the test profiles are valid and interpretable, there may be some excessive responding in actually disabled clients.

Persons who are attempting to appear psychologically disturbed in psychological disability claims may exaggerate complaints. In a study assessing the possible psychological effects of exposure to Agent Orange during the Vietnam War, Korgeski and Leon (1983) contrasted veterans on the basis of whether there was objective evidence of exposure to the chemical during the war and whether the veteran believed that he had been exposed to the chemical. In the first comparison, there were no neurological or personality differences between the veterans with an objectively determined probability of being exposed and those who were clearly not exposed to Agent Orange. However, veterans who *believed* themselves to have been exposed to Agent Orange (whether there was evidence or not) reported more significant psychological disturbance than those who did not believe they had been exposed.

The claimant's overresponding often takes the form of exaggerating psychological symptoms, resulting in an elevated *F* scale score. S. Schneider (1979) found that the *F* scale of the MMPI identified the individuals who were presenting a great deal of psychopathology in connection with their disability determinations for a pension on grounds of having service-connected psychopathology. These findings are consistent with the research of Keller, Wigdor, and Lundell (1973), who studied individuals seeking compensation on the basis of psychologically disabling symptoms. The patients in this study were individuals who were seeking compensation on grounds that they were not employable but had no physical disability. These individuals were found to be identifiable with respect to MMPI-measured personality factors and life-style. Primarily, they produced elevated *F*-scale scores indicating an exaggeration of symptoms.

Research suggests that individuals seeking compensation for different problems may produce somewhat different MMPI profile patterns. Bowler, Rauch, Becker, Hawes, and Cone (1989), for example, reported that individuals manifesting somatoform disorder produced very different profiles than those for whom depression or anxiety was the prominent complaint.

S. Schneider (1979) reported that individuals applying for disability benefits as a result of psychopathology had elevated *Pa* and *Sc* scores reflecting an expression of severe and chronic disorder involving thought disturbance and personal deterioration. Similarly, in the study by Keller et al. (1973), these individuals presented significantly more psychopathology than controls on the MMPI, with scale elevations on *Hs*, *D*, *Hy*, *Pt*, and *Sc*. In addition, they were found to be low in self-esteem, dependent, depressed, and socially isolated.

Long-range consequences of disability are often of interest in personal injury cases. Psychologists may be asked to evaluate the extent of injury or damage to the individual and the possible length of time involved in the disability for purposes of establishing the amount of award in the suit. Personality assessment might be valuable in estimating how individuals will respond to rehabilitative efforts. Some research on the long-term consequences of physical and psychological disability in compensation claims has been reported with the MMPI and would be useful to consult if the course of disability and/or response to treatment is questioned.[7]

When considering the research that bears on MMPI-based assessments in personal injury cases (as in other types of forensic assessments), it is essential to evaluate the degree to which the participants in the research are truly comparable to the individual who is alleging personal injury; the degree to which the circumstances under which the research was conducted supports or limits its applicability to the individual's situation, and the appropriate weight to accord a particular research finding in light of the general array of relevant research findings (or *absence* of other applicable research findings). In all instances, the expert witness must carefully consider the strengths and weaknesses of both the MMPI and the research in terms of the particular assessment task. Qualifications or reservations about validity must be explicitly presented in the assessment report (see chapter 7).

[7] Cairns, Mooney, & Crane, 1984; Drasgow & Dreher, 1965; Dzioba & Doxey, 1984; Flynn & Salamone, 1977; Gilbert & Lester, 1970; Heaton, Chelune & Lehman, 1978; Kubiszyn, 1984; Kuperman & Golden, 1979; Levenson, Hirschfeld, & Hirschfeld, 1985; Newnan, Heaton, & Lehman, 1978; Roberts, 1984; Roberts & Reinhardt, 1980; Salomone, 1972; Wiltse & Rocchio, 1975.

Discussion of two special issues in psychological assessment of personal injury follows.

Assessment of posttraumatic stress disorder (PTSD) in injured workers. The Keane PTSD Scale in the MMPI-2 appears to measure negative response to stressful situations as did the Keane scale in the original MMPI (Litz et al., 1991). A recent study by Lyons and Keane (1992) provided further support for the MMPI-2 version of the Keane PTSD Scale.

Flamer (1992) conducted an investigation to determine if workers who were injured in industrial accidents showed more measurable psychopathology, particularly PTSD, than individuals who were reportedly experiencing chronic pain. Using workers' compensation claims, he grouped cases into three categories on the basis of the documented source of disability: workers with posttraumatic stress disorders (most of whom were also physically injured), chronic pain patients, and emotionally disturbed mental health patients. He examined their MMPI-2 clinical profiles and their scores on the Keane PTSD and Schlenger PTSD (Butcher et al., 1989; Jordan et al., 1991; Schlenger & Kukla, 1987; Schlenger et al., 1989) Scales. Their MMPI-2 profiles are shown in Figure 2-10.

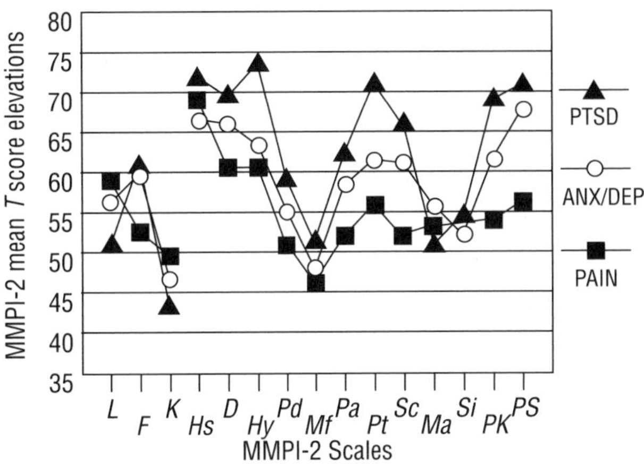

FIGURE 2-10. Mean MMPI-2 clinical profiles for PTSD, anxiety/depression, and chronic pain samples. (Source: Flamer & Birch, 1992. Adapted by permission.)

Consistent with the correlates for MMPI-2 scales, those workers with clearly defined posttraumatic symptoms showed more marked profile elevation on Scales 1, 2, 3, and 7 than did the other groups. In addition, the PTSD group showed more significant scale elevation on the PTSD scales than did the other groups. These findings are consistent with the observation that many individuals who are experiencing (either an immediate-onset or a delayed) reaction to a traumatic event show increased scale elevation on Scales 2 (Depression) and 7 (Psychasthenia).

In addition to evaluating these published MMPI-2 scales, Flamer (1992) has also conducted research on a PTSD scale for assessing posttraumatic symptomatology related to work injury. He developed a 35-item scale that significantly differentiated the posttraumatic injury cases from cases involving other claimants. This scale, provisionally titled the Work Place Trauma Scale for the MMPI-2, significantly differentiated the developmental group from other workers and showed sufficient specificity and sensitivity, detecting PTSD in 20 out of 24 cases.

Flamer (1992) cross-validated the scale with an additional 20 workers' compensation claimants and found that it differentiated well on cross-validation, detecting PTSD in 18 of 20 new cases. Although additional work needs to replicate these findings in other settings, this research supports the effectiveness of the MMPI-2 in identifying and differentiating individuals who are experiencing work-related stress.

Of course, PTSD also occurs among other populations and in other contexts (e.g., among military combatants, torture victims, and asylum seekers). The extensive research literature on the MMPI provides resources specifically relevant to these special populations and contexts.[8]

Assessment of behavioral and emotional consequences of head injury. The MMPI has apparently been the most widely used personality measure in neuropsychological test batteries because it provides a means of assessing behavioral and personality characteristics in an objective framework (K. B. Adams & Putnam, 1992). Psychologists assessing potential impact of organic damage on an individual's adaptive capacity find that the MMPI scales provide important

[8] For example, Eberly, Harkness, & Engdahl, 1991; Fairbank, Keane, & Malloy, 1983; Hyer, Leach, Boudewyns, & Davis, 1991; Kenderdine, Phillips, & Scurfield, 1992; Lyons & Keane, 1992; McCormick, Taber, & Kruedelbach, 1989; Nichols & Czirr, 1986; Penk et al., 1989; Pope & Garcia-Peltoniemi, 1991; Powell, Illovsky, O'Leary, & Gazda, 1988; Sutker, Bugg, & Allain, 1991; Wilson & Walker, 1990; see also chapter 6 of this volume.

differential information on emotional and behavioral symptoms that might accompany cognitive impairment.

Neuropsychological evaluation batteries have begun incorporating the MMPI-2 (K. B. Adams & Putnam, 1992; Gass, 1991, 1992). In a recent study, Beniak, Heck, and Erdahl (1992) administered both the MMPI and the MMPI-2 to a sample of people suffering from epilepsy and reported that the two versions of the MMPI produced comparable profiles. Those suffering from epilepsy tended to score high on the clinical Scales 2 and 8 on both forms. Scale 8 tends to be elevated in those who have epilepsy because of the neurological symptoms reflected in the subgroup of items on the scale (i.e., items pertaining to sensory and perceptual–motor problems). Thus, elevations on Scale 8 are often problematic because they do not allow for the important differential diagnosis between epilepsy and schizophrenia. However, Beniak et al. (1992) found that the new MMPI-2 content scale, BIZ, which is elevated for those suffering from schizophrenia, was *not* elevated for those suffering from epilepsy. This promising finding may provide important differential information for assessing those suffering from temporal lobe epilepsy.

Forensic Examinations Relevant to Asylum Seekers, Torture Victims, and Refugee Populations

Legal proceedings relevant to the rights, personal history, and current condition of asylum seekers, torture victims, and refugee populations may focus on the individual's credibility.

> *A critical aspect of asylum cases is the applicant's ability to convince the judge that he or she has a well-founded fear of persecution. In some cases, the applicant's own testimony may be the only evidence available. . . .*
>
> *Credibility is undercut by generalities, avoidance of eye contact, evasiveness and apparent uncooperativeness in answering questions. Some of these behaviors are culturally dependent, while others may be the consequences of the experiences that caused the applicant to seek asylum.*
>
> *Victims of torture or other severe trauma may be poor witnesses for themselves. Their shame and humiliation, anxiety, memory impairments and lack of trust often lead to confusing and apparently contradictory statements; an inability to recall times, dates and events; and a lack of emotional affect which may make their testimony unconvincing. . . . (Physicians for Human Rights, 1991, p. 12)*
>
> ◆ ◆ ◆
>
> *The very trauma or other form of persecution upon which the asylum claim is based may contribute to a numbed responsiveness, the appearance of which harms the applicant's credibility as a witness. The applicant, for example, may not cry when relating how his or her child was abducted by the police and never seen again. (Physicians for Human Rights, 1991, p. 20)*[9]

The MMPI validity scales can be exceptionally helpful in providing evidence of the individual's credibility.

The two more typical forensic uses of the MMPI validity scales can make it easy to overlook the usefulness of the MMPI with these populations. The first more typical forensic use of the MMPI validity scales is to help differentiate those who are *trying* to appear dysfunctional but are *feigning* (e.g., to escape responsibility for criminal acts or to obtain undeserved disability benefits) from those who not only *appear* but actually *are* dysfunctional. The second more typical use of the validity scales is to help differentiate those who are trying to *falsely* appear as if they lacked significant distress and dysfunction (e.g., to obtain a job or to be granted custody rights) from those who not only appear but also *actually* lack significant distress and dysfunction. These and other common uses of the validity scales are discussed in chapter 6.

Although these other more frequent forensic uses of the validity scales are important, it is also crucial to remember that some people may seem (e.g., during a

[9] See also Butcher, Egli, Shiota, & Ben-Porath, 1988; Herman, 1992; Pope & Garcia-Peltoniemi, 1991; Thomsen, Helwig-Larsen, & Rasmussen, 1984; Westermeyer, Williams, & Nguyen, 1992.

clinical or job interview, during a deportation hearing, or during a custody or criminal trial) as if they were feigning, exaggerating, or otherwise distorting the truth when in fact they are not. They may appear guilty when in fact they are innocent. They may appear unhurt when in fact they are deeply damaged. They may appear to be concocting the wildest, most improbable lies when in fact they are telling the truth.

In such situations, the validity scales can help establish or support the individual's credibility. As the passage quoted above (as well as the secondary references that were cited) emphasize, this use of the validity scales may be particularly helpful when conducting forensic examinations of asylum seekers, torture victims, and refugee populations.[10]

Psychological Assessment in Family Custody Cases

Psychologists and other mental health professionals are increasingly being called on to provide consultation on the personality and mental health adjustment of individuals who are involved in family custody dispute cases. Deed (1991) recently reviewed the pitfalls and challenges for psychologists conducting domestic court evaluations.

In providing expertise in forensic evaluations, psychologists are often asked to provide expert opinions about the emotional health of the parents and to assess possible adjustment problems and developmental issues for the child. Evaluations of parents and children tend to focus on family adjustment factors as well as potential problems in the family that might bear on the welfare of the minor. The use of psychological tests in family custody evaluations has been widely explored (e.g., Barnard & Jenson, 1984; Kelin & Bloom, 1986; Landberg, 1982; McDermott, Tseng, Char, & Fukunaga, 1978; and Woody, 1977).

Kelin and Bloom (1986) surveyed experienced professionals who conducted child custody examinations in forensic settings and reported that the MMPI was the most frequently administered psychological test in assessing parents. Over two thirds of respondents in the survey reported using the MMPI. The mean percentage of cases in which the MMPI was used was 87.8% for "testing of adults in child custody evaluations" (p. 341) and 48.3% for "testing of children and adolescents in child custody evaluations" (p. 341).

Personality assessments of parents who are enmeshed in family custody disputes are among the most difficult that psychologists face. Two major difficulties are often encountered: First, the quality of information that psychologists have available is often suspect; second, there is a general lack of appropriate measures for the setting.

With regard to the first problem, men and women in custody disputes tend to be very self-protective and assert their lack of problems, while at the same time tending to provide extremely negative and acrimonious information about their spouse. It is crucial that the professional conducting or reviewing the evaluation avoids reflexively accepting or rejecting these self-protective responses and claims about others; such aspects of the person's responses must be carefully explored and evaluated. Chapter 6 presents information on self-protective response sets that may be useful in such evaluations.

Second, available personality measures are often not developed with family custody considerations in mind and consequently need to be adapted for that purpose. Psychological test results in family court settings need to be interpreted from a somewhat different perspective than results in other settings.

Some studies suggest that particular MMPI patterns may be differentially associated with patients who do and who do not receive custody (Ollendick, 1984; Ollendick & Otto, 1983). Several other lines of empirical investigation bear on family custody evaluations, as described below.

MMPI profiles of parents of disturbed children. Several extensive reviews of research on parent personality in relation to child and adolescent psychopathology have been published (Hafner, Butcher, Hall, & Quast, 1969; Lachar & Sharp, 1979). Lahey, Russo, Walker, and Piacentini (1989), for example, found that mothers of children exhibiting conduct disorders had more deviant MMPI profiles when compared with mothers of children who suffered from

[10]Note: Readers interested in obtaining information about use of the MMPI-2 (in English language and translations relevant to various cultures) with torture victims, asylum seekers, and refugee populations may wish to contact Dr. Rosa Garcia-Peltoniemi of the Center for Victims of Torture, Minneapolis, MN.

other types of problems. Obviously, any inferences drawn from such research must take into account the difficulties of attempting to interpret statistical associations (e.g., caring for a child who suffers from a serious conduct disorder—as distinct from another disorder—may be so stressful for a parent that MMPI elevated scales may be a natural and understandable consequence).

Research on personality factors in marital distress. The MMPI has been used to help understand the personality characteristics of individuals who are experiencing marital distress. Some personality problems that are relevant to custody evaluations are reflected in MMPI responses.[11]

The recently developed Marital Distress Scale for the MMPI-2 (Hjemboe, Almagor, & Butcher, 1992) might prove of value in assessing couples participating in custody litigation. For example, some parties involved in family custody disputes may be remarried and are presently seeking custody of their children from a previous marriage now that they have become more maritally stable. Seeking a new custodial relationship with their children from their previous marriage, they may put the quality of their current marriage at issue before the family law court (if the state provides special courts that focus on family law).

Research on personality and adjustment factors in child physical and sexual abuse. A number of studies have attempted to identify responses that might characterize parents who abuse their children. The research suggests that some MMPI scale scores are statistically associated with higher risk for child abuse.[12] Other studies have focused on how abuse (e.g., incest) affects the personality and development of the victim/survivor. Psychological assessments of abuse victims/survivors need to consider the possibility of long-term consequences (Scott & Stone, 1986a, 1986b). When custody is at issue, the MMPI can be used to help assess the credibility of a parent's (or potential foster parent's) self-report, possible psychopathology, problems with alcohol or drugs, and characteristics that seem to be associated with safe, appropriate, and effective parenting.

Assessing Insanity and Competence to Stand Trial

Using the MMPI as an aid in determining whether an individual is psychologically able to stand trial is consistent with one of the main purposes of the original instrument. Starke Hathaway (1965) pointed out that "the MMPI was intended as an objective aid in the routine psychiatric case work-up of adult patients and as a method for determining the severity of the conditions" (p. 463). Consequently, much of the traditional MMPI research literature on clinical scale meanings and profile type correlates bears directly on the question as to the presence and extent of current, severe psychological problems.

Almost 20 years ago, Dahlstrom et al. (1975), in reviewing the literature on the use of the MMPI in the assessment of criminal behavior, observed that the instrument is frequently used in cases involving the question of whether defendants are competent to stand trial. In the same vein, Jay Ziskin (1981b) focused on the ways in which "assessment of psychopathology by means of the MMPI can be related to a number of legal issues" (p. 4). While emphasizing that *insanity* is a legal term that is not equivalent to a psychotic state, Ziskin noted that a psychotic state seemed to be an essential prerequisite for a professional opinion regarding issues of insanity.

> *If psychosis is present, then a description of the characteristics of the psychosis may support inferences concerning possession or lack of the requisite capacities for criminal responsibility. Conversely, in actual practice, failure to establish a psychosis will frequently negate lack of the requisite capacity. Also, in the criminal area, findings relative to prognosis or treatability may be relevant to disposition where a guilty verdict has been rendered. Availability of treatment and*

[11]See, for example, Arnold, 1970; Barrett, 1973; Barry, Anderson, & Thomas, 1967; Bloomquist & Harris, 1984; Cookerly, 1974; Hjemboe & Butcher, 1991; McAdoo & Connolly, 1975; Murstein & Glaudin, 1968; Ollendick, Otto, & Heider, 1983; Osborne, 1971; Snyder & Regts, 1990; Swan, 1957.

[12]Egeland et al., 1991; Land, 1968; Lund, 1975; Paulson, Afifi, Chaleff, Thomason, & Lui, 1975; Paulson, Afifi, Thomason, & Chaleff, 1974; Paulson, Schwemmer, & Bendel, 1976; Wright, 1970, 1976.

prospects for its success are factors the judge will take into consideration in the sentencing phase of the matter. (pp. 4–5)

A number of studies have attempted to assess the effectiveness of the MMPI in forensic insanity determinations or in determinations of possible differences between potentially insane individuals and those who have committed criminal offenses but are not legally insane.[13] It is important to keep in mind that when the MMPI is administered at some point *after* the crime, the results, if valid, reflect the individual's *current* (i.e., at the time of test administration) mental status, which may or may not be similar to the individual's mental status at the time that the crime was committed.

As with other forensic evaluations using the MMPI, evaluation of the defendant's test validity is especially important. Many individuals undergoing psychological evaluation in a correctional setting may attempt to dissemble in order to secure the most desirable verdict or sentence (Grossman & Wasyliw, 1988; Parwatikar, Holcomb, & Menninger, 1985; Rogers, Gillis, McMain, & Dickens, 1988; Wasyliw, Grossman, Haywood, & Cavanaugh, 1988). An example of a feigned effort to appear psychologically disturbed to avoid prosecution of a crime is presented in chapter 6.

Personality Adjustment of Criminal Offenders

In an effort to develop a comprehensive system for classifying convicted felons, Megargee and Bohn (1977; 1979) identified 10 types of criminal offenders by using their response to the MMPI. The 10 types are

1. **Able.** This profile type has moderate clinical scale elevations, usually on Scales 4 and 9. These individuals are considered to be charming, impulsive, and usually quite manipulative.
2. **Baker.** This profile cluster has moderate elevations with peak scores usually on Scales 2 and 4. These individuals tend to be considered inadequate, anxious, and constricted. Alcohol abuse is frequent.
3. **Charlie.** This profile tends to be indicative of extremely poor adjustment. Profile elevations are usually high, with several scale scores elevated above 70. The individuals are usually described as hostile, misanthropic, alienated, aggressive, and antisocial. A history of deviant behavior, criminal convictions, and substance abuse is common.
4. **Delta.** This profile configuration has a moderate to high elevation on Scale 4. These individuals are usually considered amoral, hedonistic, manipulative, and self-centered. They are viewed as impulsive stimulation seekers.
5. **Easy.** This profile type typically has low elevations, often below 70, with peak scores on Scales 4 and 3. These individuals tend to be bright and stable with good adjustment. Many show good personal relationships.
6. **Foxtrot.** Very high scale elevations (above 80) are characteristic. Scales 8, 9, and 4 tend to be elevated. These individuals are usually described as street-wise, tough, cynical, and antisocial. Long criminal histories and poor prison adjustment are common.
7. **George.** Moderate elevations are typical, particularly on Scales 1, 2, and 3. These individuals are usually described as hard working, submissive, and anxious. They are often able to make use of educational and other resources, if available.
8. **How.** Very high elevations are found with scores on at least three scales above 70. These individuals are described as unstable, agitated, and psychologically disturbed.
9. **Item.** This profile type contains low scale scores (usually below 70). This group is considered to be generally stable with minimal psychological problems.
10. **Jupiter.** This configuration has moderate to high elevations, typically on Scales 9, 7, and 8. Individuals in this category tend to be described as overcoming deprived backgrounds. They often do better than expected when released from prison.

[13]Blackburn, 1968; Boehnert, 1987; Craddick, 1962; Maxson & Neuringer, 1970; Roman & Gerbing, 1989; Schmalz, Fehr, & Dalby, 1989; Schretlen, Wilkins, Van Gorp, & Bobholz, 1992; Villanueva, Roman, & Tuley, 1988; Wilcock, 1964.

The Megargee and Bohn typology (1977; hereafter known as Megargee types) has been widely studied, and a number of demographic variables and prison behaviors have been associated with these profile types. In addition, the system's validity and reliability in the classification of felons has been widely explored. T. D. Kennedy (1986; see also Zager, 1988) provided a useful review of the research on the Megargee classification system, noting several studies that provided empirical tests of the system.[14]

A number of studies have supported the replicability of the 10 Megargee types across different inmate samples; the same types are found in fairly similar proportions across maximum and medium security facilities as well as minimum security programs and halfway houses.[15] However, the proportions of inmates in each classification vary somewhat according to the setting. Specific sample characteristics appear not to be associated with proportions of the different types across settings.

There is little empirical support for applying this classification scheme to female inmates (cf. Edinger, 1979) or to older inmates. Although the Megargee types can be found in many settings, correlates of the types have not been consistently found to generalize across settings. Some studies found *no* personal history, psychiatric, demographic, prison adjustment, or outcome variables to be differentially associated with any of the types. One type, C or Charlie, seems to be one that has most consistently been found to be predictive of psychiatric and behavioral maladjustment, including poor prison adjustment. Another type, H or How, also seems to be fairly consistently correlated with psychological and adjustment problems.

There is not enough information available at this time to address the question of which types are more stable. Some studies have questioned the stability of *any* of the Megargee types, finding a 60 to 90% change in type after only 4 months (Dahlstrom, Panton, et al., 1986; Johnson et al., 1983; Simmons et al., 1981). However, the issue of whether these changes reflect invalidating instability or actual personality changes in inmates remains open (Zager, 1983). For example, in one study of death row inmates who had their sentences commuted, the shifts away from pathological types Charlie and How into less pathological types Item, Easy, or George might be a valid reflection of changes in their mental state (Dahlstrom, Panton, et al., 1986).

In criminal cases, it may be exceptionally helpful to appraise people according to the Megargee felon classification typology in light of the research-based wealth of descriptive information (Wrobel, Calovini, & Martin, 1991). The resulting type can best be viewed, as with other aspects of MMPI profiles, as a source of potentially very useful hypotheses. These hypotheses can then be evaluated in the context of the full range of other information available.

The typology can be scored and processed manually, although it can be a somewhat onerous task. Many users of the classification system find computer-based processing faster and more cost effective. Research is in progress to translate the typology into MMPI-2 normative information (Megargee, Rivera, & Fly, 1991). Megargee (1992) found that a revised version of the Megargee rules for MMPI-2 classified 84% of the cases identically to the rules prepared for the original MMPI.

In light of the numerous published MMPI studies, there are, of course, sources presenting the relationship of MMPI profiles to other classification systems and to special types of criminal offenders.[16]

SUMMARY

The MMPI has become the most widely used measure of personality in applied psychology and is exten-

[14]Bohn, 1979; Booth & Howell, 1980; Dahlstrom, Panton, Bain, & Dahlstrom, 1986; Edinger, 1979; Edinger, Reuterfors, & Logue, 1982; Hanson, Moss, Hosford, & Johnson, 1983; Johnson, Simmons, & Gordon, 1983; Louscher, Hosford, & Moss, 1983; Megargee, 1984; Moss, Johnson, & Hosford, 1984; Motiuk, Bonta, & Andrews, 1986; Mrad, Kabacoff, & Duckro, 1983; Simmons, Johnson, Gouvier, & Muzyczka, 1981; Walters, 1986; Wrobel, Calovini, & Martin, 1991; Zager, 1983.

[15]Dahlstrom, Panton, et al., 1986; Edinger, 1979; Edinger et al., 1982; Johnson et al., 1983; Mrad et al., 1983; Walters, 1986.

[16]See, for example, Adams, 1976; Anderson & Holcomb, 1983; T. C. Carlson, 1990; Duthie & McIvor, 1990; Erickson, Luxenberg, Walbeck, & Seely, 1987; Forgac & Michaels, 1982; Grossman & Cavanaugh, 1989; Hall, Graham, & Shepherd, 1991; Hall, Maiuro, Vitaliano, & Proctor, 1986; Hall Shepherd, & Mudrak, 1992; Holcomb, Adams, & Ponder, 1985; Hunter, Childers, & Esmaili, 1990; Kalichman, 1990, 1991; Kalichman, Craig, Shealy, Taylor, Szymanowski, & McKee, 1989; Kalichman & Henderson, 1991; Kalichman, Shealy, & Craig, 1990; Kalichman, Szymanowski, McKee, Taylor, & Craig, 1989; Rader, 1977; Shealy, Kalichman, Henderson, Szymanowski, & McKee, 1991; Sutker, Allain, & Geyer, 1978.

sively used for many types of forensic evaluations. The MMPI and its two revised forms were described and compared in this chapter to provide an understanding of their similarities and differences. Information documenting the continuity of the traditional clinical scales was presented, indicating that the psychometric characteristics in the revised versions remain essentially the same as in the original version.

The advantages of using the MMPI and MMPI-2 in forensic evaluations were discussed and the strengths of the empirical assessment approach were highlighted. In addition, questions that are often addressed to experts offering MMPI-based testimony were examined and possible responses explored. Questions about possible cultural biases using the MMPI were considered, and several important resources providing multicultural factors were given in support of the test's utility with diverse cultural groups.

Computer-based interpretation of the MMPI was discussed because automated reports are frequently used in forensic testimony to eliminate the criticism of subjective interpretation. Both the advantages and the limitations of automated assessment in forensic settings were addressed.

Finally, uses of the MMPI in a variety of forensic settings were examined. Considerable research literature has accumulated in recent years that can be useful to psychologists involved in personal injury litigation cases. Numerous studies have found that psychological factors are often present in disability cases and that financial incentives may be correlated with prolongation and exacerbation of physical symptoms in such cases. MMPI research suggests that, at least in some instances, organically disabled patients who are not involved in litigation tend to produce more normal-range profiles than individuals involved in a claims process. More pathologically appearing profiles may reflect motivation to appear in considerable distress. Claimants who may be exaggerating psychological symptoms, for example, to appear psychologically disturbed for a Social Security disability determination claim, tend to produce MMPI profiles with extremely exaggerated features. However, these trends suggested by the research may not hold for all individuals in the types of cases studied and may not generalize to other types of similar cases. As emphasized repeatedly throughout this book, the MMPI is a useful, empirically based source of *hypotheses*.

The use of the MMPI in family custody evaluations was described. Increased use of the MMPI in psychological evaluations of parents and children in domestic or family law cases was noted. The MMPI is apparently the most frequently administered test in this setting. Considerable relevant research is available on the MMPI for assessing marital distress, parent pathology, and factors that may be (statistically) associated with child abuse.

Finally, the MMPI has a long and rich history in criminal courts and correctional settings. As an example, the offender typology developed by psychologist Edwin Megargee of Florida State University was discussed in detail. Other uses of the MMPI (e.g., in evaluating the psychological status of offenders in insanity determinations and in assessing offender mental health) were also reviewed.

CHAPTER 3

THE COURTS' RECOGNITION, USE, AND RESTRICTION OF MMPI-BASED TESTIMONY

The MMPI has appeared in a variety of contexts in the legal literature since its inception. Examined extensively by the federal and state courts (see appendixes E-1 and E-2), it has gained wide acceptance and usage in both civil and criminal litigation.

GENERAL EVIDENTIARY CONSIDERATIONS

The evidentiary admissibility of MMPI testing and its interpretation is controlled by the Federal Rules of Evidence (F.R.E.) in federal courts and by the specific evidentiary rules of the state in which a state court evaluating its admissibility sits. Many states have adopted the Federal Rules of Evidence in whole or in part, and evidentiary considerations tend to be similar from state to state.

The fundamental admissibility of MMPI results is governed by F.R.E. Rules 401, 402, and 404, or the state rules controlling relevancy and its limits. "Relevant evidence" is, according to F.R.E. Rule 401, "evidence having any tendency to make the existence of any fact that is of consequence to the determination of the action more probable or less probable than it would be without the evidence." The remainder of Article IV of the Federal Rules of Evidence limits the all-encompassing inquiry that F.R.E. Rule 401 seems to allow. Rule 403, for example, provides for the exclusion of relevant evidence on the grounds of prejudice, confusion, or waste of time. Rule 404 excludes evidence of a person's character, with listed exceptions. The considerations discussed in Rules 403 and 404 provide a basis on which MMPI results can be excluded from evidence.

Once the fundamental relevance questions are answered, the MMPI results are generally introduced into evidence as a basis of opinion testimony by expert witnesses. F.R.E. Rule 703 specifically authorizes use of information "reasonably relied upon by experts."

Within the parameter of the rules described above, expert witnesses are allowed to testify as to specialized knowledge that will assist the judge or jury to understand the evidence or to decide a fact in issue. The threshold question in determining admissibility of MMPI results in individual cases focuses on whether those results are sufficiently trustworthy to warrant their acceptance.

A federal court explored the origins and scientific bases of the test itself in copyright disputes regarding the MMPI. As background, the Federal Eighth Circuit Court of Appeals gave this description in its 1989 opinion in *Applied Innovations, Inc. v. Regents of the University of Minnesota*, 876 F.2d 626 (8th Cir. 1989):

> *Their basic hypothesis was that individuals who share a particular psychological symptom or personality trait or characteristic were likely to respond to certain groups of test statements in the same way and that each response to a particular test statement was indicative of a particular psychological symptom or personality trait or characteristic. 876 F.2D at 629.*
>
> ◆ ◆ ◆
>
> *The MMPI schedule was a comprehensive work and contained the 550 test statements, scale membership, scoring direction and*

> *T-score conversion data for the hypochondriasis, depression, hysteria, psychopathic deviate, sexual interest, question, truthfulness, and validity scales. 876 F.2d at 629.*

The process of identifying the personality traits in individuals and groups of persons, known as "building scales," was described in the trial court's factual findings and set forth in an earlier court's decision in *Regents of the University of Minnesota v. Applied Innovations, Inc.*, 685 F.Supp. 698 (D.C. Minn. 1987):

> *The authors then commenced on the long and tedious process of determining which of their 1,000 plus test items assisted in identification of particular personality traits, a process appropriately called building scales. Although there were some minor variations in the building of the individual scales, a crude, general description of the process is as follows. The authors selected individuals that had been diagnosed as manifesting the personality trait they were attempting to identify. Then Hathaway and McKinley would compare their responses to the test items to the responses of a group of Minnesota adults (typically friends and relatives of patients at the University of Minnesota Hospital) and a control group of University of Minnesota students. Based on this comparison, a particular test item was initially selected as a discriminating test item if the percentage frequency difference between the criterion group (individuals manifesting the clinical trait) and the group of Minnesota adults ("normals") was a statistically significant amount, which varied from one scale to another. 685 F.Supp. at 701.*

For years, the MMPI has been recognized by appellate courts across the country as a standard, reliable test when used correctly and appropriately. This longstanding recognition generally allows proponents of MMPI testing to avoid evidence restrictions placed on more experimental testing.

Scientific testing that is new or novel is generally severely restricted in courtroom use. Specific restrictions governing admission of experimental techniques were discussed in detail by two different courts. The cases included the 1923 case *Frye v. United States*, 293 F. 1013 (D.C. Cir. 1923), and the more recent case of *People v. Kelly*, 17 Cal.3d 24, 130 Cal.Rptr. 144, 549 P.2d 1240 (1976). California courts have dubbed the process through which courts weigh the merits and dangers of experimental techniques as the *Kelly/Frye test*, after the names of the two leading cases in the discussion. The California Supreme Court decided in 1989 that the MMPI is a standardized test that can no longer be considered novel or experimental. In deciding that no Kelly/Frye showing was required for expert opinion that relied on the MMPI, the court in *People v. Stoll*, 49 Cal.3d 1136, 265 Cal.Rptr. 111, 783 P.2d 698 (1989), declared that

> *No precise legal rules dictate the proper basis for an expert's journey into a patient's mind to make judgments about his behavior. In effect, however, California courts have deferred to a qualified expert's decision to rely on "standardized" psychological tests such as the MMPI to reach an opinion on mental state at the time acts were committed. . . . Such deference is no less appropriate here. Indeed, voir dire testimony indicated that qualified professionals routinely use raw material from the MMPI . . . as a basis for assessing personality, and drawing behavioral conclusions therefrom. 49 Cal.3d at 1154, 265 Cal.Rptr. at 122, 783 P.2d at 709.*
>
> ◆ ◆ ◆
>
> *The psychological testimony proffered here raises none of the concerns addressed by Kelly/Frye. The methods employed are* not *new to psychology or the law, and they carry no misleading aura of scientific infallibility. 49 Cal.3d at 1157, 265 Cal.Rptr. at 124, 783 P.2d at 711.*
>
> ◆ ◆ ◆
>
> *Moreover, as Dr. Mitchell testified, diagnostic use of written personality inventories such as the MMPI . . . has been established for decades. Modern courts have not resisted reference to these tests.* Id.
>
> ◆ ◆ ◆
>
> *Contrary to the dissent's claim, expert reliance on the MMPI . . . for this particular*

> *purpose* is not *a "revolutionary" development. 49 Cal.3d at 1158, 265 Cal.Rptr. at 125, 783 P.2d at 712.*
>
> ◆ ◆ ◆
>
> *It would be anomalous to view the MMPI and similar tests as a "new" technique at this late date.* Id.

Because the revised versions of the MMPI have maintained the traditional validity and clinical scales and because the psychometric properties are nearly identical between the MMPI and each of the revised versions, the revised versions would seem likely to pass any application of the Kelly/Frye test.

Even though courts accept the scientific reliability of MMPI testing, individual courts may acknowledge the fallibility of this testing. Courts deny evidentiary admission when the results may be misleading or inappropriate or when other testimony from experts suggests that the results should not be relied on as a source of the expert's opinion.

USE IN CRIMINAL CASES

Many appellate decisions that discuss the courtroom use of MMPI results involve criminal cases. In criminal cases, the use of the MMPI often focuses on whether test results indicate that the defendant's mental ability or functioning is sufficiently impaired to provide a defense to the crime charged.

Defenses of diminished capacity, impaired mental condition, and insanity are technical defenses that differ from state to state and are controlled by individual statutes. Use of the MMPI in criminal contexts may involve defensive use by the criminal defendant or rebuttal use by prosecution faced with a defense of impaired mental functioning.

The MMPI has been held to provide a reliable basis for a variety of expert opinions in criminal litigation. The *Stoll, supra*, court said that expert opinions that rely in part on the MMPI or on other standardized tests have been admitted "as circumstantial evidence that the defendant did not harbor the requisite criminal intent or mental state at the time he committed the charged act" or that the "defendant was not likely to commit certain acts in the future" 783 P.2d at 711.

Another area of criminal law in which the MMPI has been increasingly used and criticized in the past several years involves its use in establishing a "composite picture" or "profile" (not to be confused with an MMPI profile). The appellate court cases focus on whether testing may be used by a defendant to show that it is unlikely that he or she committed the crime charged because commission of the crime is inconsistent with the characterological "profile."

The appellate decisions reflect a dilemma with which criminal courts are increasingly faced: Psychological testimony may provide relevant testimony to assist the judge or jury in deciding whether the defendant had a culpable mental state, but psychological testimony should not be used to usurp the jury's role in deciding guilt or innocence. The decisions of courts across the country reflect both conflicting sides of this dilemma. Various decisions have both affirmed and rejected the use of MMPI profile evidence.

An Indiana appellate court in *Byrd v. State*, 579 N.E.2d 457 (Ind.App. 1 Dist. 1991), permitted the introduction of MMPI results to show that the criminal defendant's psychological "profile" was inconsistent with the mental requirement of "knowingly," an element of the crime of murder. The court said,

> *Byrd offered Dr. Davis's testimony only to show that Byrd's psychological profile and the MMPI test results were inconsistent with the knowing element of the crime of murder.* Record *at 1156, 1176–77; the results were not offered to show that Dr. Davis himself opined that Byrd did not knowingly kill Chafin. The MMPI results were admitted into evidence, so Dr. Davis's proffered testimony was based on facts in evidence; therefore, Dr. Davis's testimony met the proper foundational requirements for admissibility. 579 N.E.2d at 461.*

The most often reported use of "profile" testimony involves criminal allegations of sexual abuse, including pedophilia. In 1990, a California appellate court decided in the case of *People v. Ruiz*, 222 Cal.App.3d 1241, 272 Cal.Rptr. 368 (Cal.App. 1 Dist. 1990), that the MMPI profile type evidence that formed a basis for expert opinion would be admissible under the previous *Stoll, supra*, decision if the proper foundation for its use could be laid by the lawyers. The court held that

> *It follows that in the present situation, Ruiz was entitled to have Dr. Berg state his opinion that Ruiz was not a sexual deviant, or was not a pedophile, or was not likely to have committed the charged acts.*
>
> *Dr. Berg apparently had no intention of stating an opinion on any of these matters. Rather, he planned to testify that Ruiz did not have the psychological characteristics of a person suffering from pedophilia; i.e., that he did not match the profile of a pedophile. 222 Cal.App.3d at 1245, 272 Cal.Rptr. at 371.*
>
> ◆ ◆ ◆
>
> *Nonetheless, we see little reason to distinguish between the material underlying the expert's opinion in* Stoll *and the type of "profile" evidence underlying Dr. Berg's opinion in the present case.* Id.

Courts require that the MMPI's use be based on the purposes for which the test was designed and that expert testimony accompany its use. In 1986, a California appellate court in *People v. John W.*, 185 Cal.App.3d 801, 229 Cal.Rptr. 783 (Cal.App. 1 Dist. 1986), said that the test was not designed to inquire into certain topics. The expert witness had testified that the MMPI was "not particularly useful as applied to the topic of deviant sexuality" and thus could not have been, the reviewing court concluded, the basis of the expert witness's final opinion that the defendant was not a sexual deviant. The court said,

> *While Dr. Walker stated his belief that the MMPI was a reliable test, he conceded that it had never been "standardized in a sexual deviant population." Specifically, he stated that the publishers of the MMPI had not produced any profiles that one would expect from a person who is suffering from any sexual deviancy, so that the test is not particularly useful as applied to the topic of deviant sexuality. In that regard he admitted that "the main usefulness [of the MMPI] is whether they were honest or not on the test." 185 Cal.App.3d at 804–805, 229 Cal.Rptr. at 784.*

This decision incorporates inexact and misleading wording that psychological tests need to be *standardized* on various clinical groups. A more appropriate wording would involve the concept of having been *validated* for the specific group in question.

The courts also carefully acknowledged that MMPI results are fallible. The MMPI results and the expert opinion that accompanies these results are evidence to be weighed as any other scientific evidence presented to the trier of fact:

> *We also are persuaded that no reasonable juror would mistake an expert's reliance on standardized tests as a source of infallible "truth" on issues of personality, predisposition, or criminal guilt. Here, for example, Dr. Mitchell stated that the MMPI was essentially 70 percent accurate in diagnosing some patients, but "completely invalid" as to others. Although the witness expressed faith in his own methods, he recounted one instance in which an "admitted" child sex offender had tested "normal" on the MMPI. Thus, despite testimony regarding "validity scales," the test results—which were never actually described below—were not made to appear "fool proof."* People v. Stoll, *49 Cal.3d at 1159, 265 Cal.Rptr. at 125, 783 P.2d at 712.*

Underscoring the difficulty in evidentiary ruling regarding such issues as sexual deviance, *People v. John W.*, *supra*, was disapproved by the California Supreme Court in *People v. Stoll*, *supra*, as follows:

> *In* People v. John W. *(1986) 185 Cal.App.3d 801, 806–808, 229 Cal.Rptr. 783, the court suggested that repeal of the sexual psychopathy and MDSO schemes undercut* People v. Jones, supra, *42 Cal.2d 219, 266 P.2d 38, insofar as* Jones *authorizes admission of defense expert opinion on lack of deviance. However, the* John W. *court overlooked codification of the* Jones *character evidence rule in section 1102 [of the California Evidence Code]. To the extent* John W. *is inconsistent with our opinion on this point, it is disapproved. 49 Cal.3d at 1153, n. 18, 265 Cal.Rptr. at 121, 783 P.2d at 708.*

The California court in *Stoll*, *supra*, and other courts around the country continue to be unwilling to permit an expert witness to opine on the "truth or falsity" of the criminal charges. That decision remains the sole determination of the jury. A psychologist, called to testify as an expert on the existence of certain personality traits and likelihood of certain behavior, is generally not competent to testify as to the "truth" or "falsity" of criminal charges. Although opinion testimony is not made inadmissible solely because it embraces the ultimate issue to be decided by the trier of fact, an expert giving such an opinion must be otherwise qualified to do so. The *Stoll*, *supra*, court reasoned,

> *Here, of course, nothing in the voir dire testimony suggested that Dr. Mitchell was qualified to render a legal opinion as to whether all elements of the charged crimes could be proven beyond a reasonable doubt against Grafton and Palomo. However, since Dr. Mitchell immediately retracted his assessment of the charges, we need not explore this issue further. 49 Cal.3d at 1149, n. 13, 264 Cal.Rptr. at 118, 783 P.2d at 705.*

Other uses of psychological testing in criminal litigation settings include its offensive and defensive use in the sentencing phase of death penalty cases. In the states that use death as a sentence alternative to life imprisonment in designated cases (37 state and federal jurisdictions use death as a sentence for designated criminal activity), a sentencing inquisition into aggravating and mitigating circumstances follows conviction and precedes sentencing. The aggravation or mitigation evidence may include a variety of MMPI uses. Testing may show personality features that suggest reduced culpability. The treatment alternatives for a previously undiagnosed and untreated mental illness may argue against the likelihood of recidivism.

Because the stakes are so high, appellate courts allow the criminal defendant every opportunity to convince the judge or jury that life is a more appropriate sentence than death. When an Illinois trial court refused to adequately consider the defendant's mitigating psychological evidence, the Illinois Supreme Court in the case of *People v. Bodclair*, 129 Ill.2d 458, 136 Ill.Dec. 29, 544 N.E.2d 715 (1989), vacated the death sentence previously imposed and returned the case to the trial court for reevaluation and resentencing.

USE IN PERSONAL INJURY CASES

The MMPI has also been used extensively in a variety of civil litigation contexts. For example, MMPI test results have been used routinely in evaluating psychological injury in civil litigation cases. Plaintiffs, of course, tend to stress those MMPI results that are consistent with trauma; defendants tend to stress those MMPI results that are consistent with problematic personality traits that preceded the accident or incident in question. In *Abex Corporation v. Coleman*, 386 So.2d 1160 (Ala.Civ.App. 1980), the MMPI was one of three tests used to support the diagnosis of the plaintiff's psychological injuries. Similarly, the test formed part of a personal injury evaluation in *Valin v. Barnes*, 550 So.2d 352 (La.App. 3 Cir. 1989).

Lawsuits involving psychological damages have dramatically increased over the past few decades. With awards reaching as high as millions of dollars for damages that cannot physically be identified with the precision that an X ray provides in defining a fracture, psychological testing has gained increased importance in civil litigation. Except for physical injuries resulting from self-mutilation and suicide attempts associated with psychological trauma, the damages claimed in cases, such as the sexual exploitation case discussed in chapter 8, are almost always physically unobservable psychological reactions to the exploitation. Predictably, attorneys for the plaintiff attempt to make the damages "real" for the jury (personal injury attorney William A. Barton addressed this problem in his 1990 book, *Recovering for Psychological Injuries*), whereas attorneys for the defendant attempt to emphasize the difficulties in assessing injury inherent in relying on the self-report of the plaintiff.

Defensive use of the MMPI to show that a personal injury plaintiff is fabricating or distorting unobservable illnesses such as chronic pain or psychological impairment has become more frequent. Questions regarding use of the MMPI to identify possible malingering in litigation contexts has been the source of numerous psychological journal articles.

For example, Paul Lees-Haley, Lue T. English, and Walker J. Glenn wrote an article in 1991, "A Fake Bad Scale on the MMPI-2 For Personal Injury Claimants," describing use of the MMPI-2 in detecting malingerers in civil litigation contexts. For more detailed information regarding use of the MMPI in the assessment of malingering and other aspects of credibility, see chapter 6.

USE IN DOMESTIC RELATIONS CASES

The MMPI has been cited extensively in appellate cases involving custody evaluations and attempts to limit parental rights for the sake of the children's welfare. The general goal in custody evaluations is to establish custody and visitation arrangements that are in the best interests of the children involved. Courts are often faced with acrimonious dissolution proceedings in which allegations including neglect and abuse are leveled against one or both parents. MMPI-based assessment of parents can provide valuable information in identifying not only psychological and behavioral (e.g., substance abuse) problems that might argue against a grant of custody but also characteristics that may suggest mature parenting abilities (see chapter 2).

In *D.J. v. State Department of Human Resources*, 578 So.2d 1351 (Ala.Civ.App. 1991), the MMPI was accepted as evidence of a mother's mental state; the MMPI was accepted in a father's evaluation in *In Re Rodrigo S., San Francisco Department of Social Services v. Joan R.*, 225 Cal.App.3d 1179, 276 Cal.Rptr. 183 (Cal.App. 1 Dist. 1990); MMPI-based testing was appropriately used to evaluate the family in the custody dispute discussed in *Gootee v. Lightner*, 224 Cal.App.3d 587, 274 Cal.Rptr. 697 (Cal.App. 4 Dist. 1990); and in *Utz v. Keinzle*, 574 So.2d 1288 (La.App. 3 Cir. 1991), the MMPI was used in a custody dispute to evaluate two sets of parents.

MMPI testing has also been used to determine whether parental rights should be terminated (*State ex rel. LEAS in Interest of O'Neal*, 303 N.W.2d 414 [Iowa 1981]) and to decide when parental rights should be given to potential adoptive parents (*Commonwealth v. Jarboe*, 464 S.W.2d 287 [Ky. 1971]).

POSTTRAUMATIC STRESS DISORDER CONSIDERATIONS

The diagnosis of posttraumatic stress disorder, and the use of the MMPI to identify or detect the disorder, have played an increasing role in criminal and civil litigation since the conclusion of the war in Viet Nam. The presence of posttraumatic symptoms has been used as a defense in criminal prosecutions in cases in which veterans have had flashbacks to war experiences. In *State v. Felde*, 422 So.2d 370 (La. 1982), the test was used in the evaluation of a defendant diagnosed as suffering from a posttraumatic stress disorder. The test has also been used in civil litigations when psychological difficulties have followed, and may have been caused by, a traumatic event (see Lees-Haley, 1989; see also chapter 6 of this volume).

CONSTITUTIONAL CONSIDERATIONS

Mandatory MMPI testing as a prerequisite for entry into colleges or jobs has been challenged in recent years. These challenges have generally questioned whether mandatory testing violates any constitutionally protected rights, such as rights to privacy. The courts' answers conflict.

Psychological testing is increasingly used in connection with hiring decisions for high stress or high responsibility jobs. In 1991, a California appeals court in *Soroka v. Dayton Hudson Corp.*, 735 Cal.App.3d 654, 1 Cal.Rptr.2d 77 (Cal.App. 1 Dist. 1991),[1] enjoined Target stores from requiring that security officers pass a screening that included the MMPI. The court held that questions that address religious beliefs and sexual orientation likely invade individual privacy rights without showing a compelling reason for doing so (for discussions of objectionable items, please see relevant sections in chapter 2). The court said that the state constitutional guarantee of privacy protects both a job applicant and a job holder from being asked personal questions that are largely unrelated to the job in question.

Whereas the *Soroka* case focused on possible violation of (California) state constitutional rights, an earlier case, *McKenna v. Fargo*, 451 F. Supp. 1355

[1] On January 31, 1992, the California Supreme Court agreed to review the *Soroka* decision. The court had not yet issued its opinion when this book went to press.

(D.N.J. 1978), examined possible violations of the U.S. Constitution. Firefighters had sued the personnel manager and city of Jersey City, New Jersey, alleging that use of the MMPI in the selection process violated the First and Fourteenth Amendments of the U.S. Constitution. The court ruled against the plaintiffs. Judge Coolahan's decision stated,

> *Rarely does a case involve conflicting interests as important and as difficult to reconcile as those in this litigation. The psychological testing which Jersey City uses to screen applicants for its fire department has been challenged by plaintiffs as an invasion of the applicants' constitutional rights. In plaintiff's view, conditioning employment on psychological testing of questionable validity puts the applicants to a prohibited choice of sacrificing constitutional freedoms to secure prized employment or of looking for work elsewhere. Defendants contend that the condition is a reasonable and necessary one because the task of fighting fires is no ordinary job in difficulty or importance and because success depends critically on the psychological capabilities of firemen.*
>
> *There is good reason to scrutinize a government requirement which joins the words psychology and testing. Psychology is not yet the science that medicine is and tests are too frequently used like talismanic formulas. The Court has, therefore, carefully reviewed the extensive evidence generated by a long trial and has not arrived lightly at the conclusion that the defendant's psychological testing is constitutional. 451 F.Supp. at 1357.*

In Pennsylvania, a federal court also reached a conclusion that differed from *Soroka*. That court emphasized the reliability of the MMPI testing. Although one expert had testified in *Pennsylvania v. Flaherty*, 760 F.Supp. 472 (W.Dist.Pa. 1991), that "some studies have found the MMPI . . . 'inadequate' in predicting police and fire fighter performance" (760 F.Supp. at 486), the Pennsylvania court also found that "no one disputes that properly used psychological examinations help to screen out candidates whose temperament or personality may be incompatible with the critical demanding work of a police officer" 760 F.Supp. at 486. The expert who testified that the MMPI was "inadequate" conceded that the MMPI-2, a revision of the MMPI, was intended to reduce cultural and racial bias, although it was "too early to determine" its effectiveness, *Id.*

In an earlier case, *Valle-Axelberd and Associates, Inc. v. Metropolitan Dade County*, 440 So.2d 606 (Fla.3d DCA 1983), a Florida appellate court had upheld a county's choice of the second lowest bidder on contractual services, because the lowest bidder used the MMPI, which the community, witnesses said, perceived to be a "racially skewed" test.

In a similar inquiry, an Illinois court also emphasized the long-standing acceptance of the MMPI in deciding that the testing could be used as a college admission criterion. The use of the results of the MMPI and related psychological consultations was found not to be an arbitrary or capricious basis for denying admission of a student to a private college. In *Aronson v. North Park College*, 94 Ill.App.3d 211, 49 Ill.Dec. 756, 418 N.E.2d 776 (1981), the court said, "There is evidence that this test [MMPI] is a well-regarded psychological examination" and that all incoming students were required to take it.

SPECIAL LIMITATIONS

Raw data from the MMPI, without accompanying expert opinion and other data, such as personal interviews of the individual, may be inadmissible. MMPI data are often viewed as a "springboard" for the expert opinion. For example, in *Wesley v. State*, 575 So.2d 108 (Ala.Cr.App. 1989), the court held that testimony regarding MMPI results should be limited to the administering doctor. However, in another Alabama case, *Bailey v. Gold Kist, Inc.*, 482 So.2d 1224 (Ala.Civ.App. 1985), a doctor was allowed to use the results of the MMPI evaluated by another psychologist to testify as to the plaintiff's behavior patterns.

The *Byrd*, *supra*, court acknowledged the limitations of MMPI results and said that its use is "not as a primary source of information, but instead as a means of confirming or challenging clinical impressions previously gained through direct contact with the patient" 579 N.E.2d at 460.

Computer-generated MMPI profiles have raised special concerns for the courts. The computer analysis, rather than forming a part of the basis of an expert's opinion, may actually appear to give an opinion. That analysis was excluded from evidence in the Indiana case of *Sullivan v. Fairmont Homes, Inc.*, 543 N.E.2d 1130 (Ind.App. 1 Dist. 1989), when the expert's opinion was based on MMPI interpretations in which the testifying expert did not participate:

> *Dr. Bartleson does not consider himself to be an expert in the interpretation of the MMPI. The record does not show who programmed the computer, how the information provided by Sullivan was recorded and fed into the computer, or the scientific acceptability or reliability of the computerized result. 543 N.E.2d at 1133.*

Courts have also addressed the difficulty of using the original MMPI in the evaluation of adolescents. In his article, "Use of the MMPI With Adolescents in Forensic Settings," Robert Archer (1989) examined the problems inherent in using the MMPI to evaluate adolescents in litigation contexts because little cross-validation work has been done to determine how reliable the results are with adolescents. The MMPI-A (Butcher et al., 1992) should address most of the forensic questions addressed by Archer when its reliability becomes generally accepted by courts.

SUMMARY

This chapter reviewed some of the major appellate court decisions in which using a form of the MMPI was an issue. Although in the MMPI's early years, expert witnesses were called on to justify use of what was then a novel instrument (meaning what is termed in California the Kelly/Frye rule), this is no longer the case. The MMPI is the most widely used standardized test of personality and is likely the most widely cited personality assessment instrument in litigation. Such federal court decisions as *Regents of the University of Minnesota v. Applied Innovations, Inc.*, *supra*, and *Applied Innovations, Inc. v. Regents of the University of Minnesota*, *supra*, have affirmed the MMPI as a scientifically valid and accepted procedure for personality assessment.

Courts have both allowed and blocked MMPI testimony in criminal cases in which the MMPI was used to shed light on the defendant's mental status (e.g. *People v. Stoll*, *supra*; *Pennsylvania v. Flaherty*, *supra*). In such cases, the MMPI may be used to help determine whether the defendant is capable of standing trial, was capable of harboring the requisite understanding and intent for a particular crime, fits a "profile" of certain types of offenders, or is likely to respond well to certain types of remedial strategies (e.g., during sentencing).

Decisions about whether MMPI-based testimony is admissible in such cases tend to focus on two issues. First, is there adequate evidence that the MMPI is sufficiently reliable as a basis for the specific type of assessment at issue? The courts' general acceptance of the MMPI as an instrument for general personality assessment does not, in and of itself, grant or imply acceptance of the instrument for more specific assessments (e.g., reliably identifying perpetrators of child abuse through a specific MMPI profile). When the testimony relies on a computerized scoring and interpretation (*Sullivan v. Fairmont Homes, Inc.*, *supra*), the computer's methodology for scoring and interpretation must meet the tests of adequate reliability.

Second, does the MMPI-based testimony *help* the trier-of-fact (generally the jury; in some cases the judge) to understand the issues at hand and so to reach a decision, or does the testimony tend to *preempt* the trier-of-fact's job of deciding guilt or innocence? Courts have blocked MMPI-based testimony when it tends to decide the "ultimate issue" of the trial.

When used as a screening instrument for hiring, promotions, or college placement, the MMPI has passed legal scrutiny in some situations (e.g., *Pennsylvania v. Flaherty*, *supra*). However, items from the original MMPI have been identified by some courts as constituting an undue invasion of privacy or improper discrimination because of issues relating to religion, sexual orientation, and race (e.g., *Valle-Axelberd and Associates, Inc. v. Metropolitan Dade County*, *supra*; *Soroka v. Dayton Hudson Corp.*, *supra*). The revised versions of the MMPI (i.e., the MMPI-2 and MMPI-A) attempted to eliminate items that have been considered offensive or objectionable. Appendixes E-1 and E-2 provide annotated lists of recent federal and state appellate court cases in which use of the MMPI was at issue.

Chapter 4

THE EXPERT WITNESS PREPARES AND PRESENTS

THE INITIAL CONTACT WITH THE ATTORNEY

Psychologists and other mental health professionals who testify about the MMPI in court may wind up there in a variety of ways. Some may specialize in forensic assessments and encourage contacts from attorneys looking for expert witnesses. Some may focus on providing services to populations who frequently appear before the courts (e.g., battered women seeking restraining orders; parents who are divorcing and seeking custody of their children; chronic pain patients whose pain is due to work-related injury). Some psychologists with recognized expertise on the MMPI testify on technical aspects of MMPI administration, scoring, results, and interpretations. And some, never having been to court before, may be surprised to receive—without previous notice—a subpoena for the testing records of a patient they have not seen for several years.

Whatever the path to the court, the initial contact with the attorney is crucial. All too often, however, both attorney and potential expert witness may be rushed. A hurried phone conversation in which each individual finds no explicit disconfirmation of what he or she hopes or fantasizes about possible arrangements can provide a false, misleading, and dangerous substitute for a careful exploration of the potential for an effective working relationship.

No set of factors can cover all situations, but addressing each of the following issues in a systematic manner can help to prevent later mishaps and catastrophes.

The Task and the Client

What is it that the attorney wants? Many may reply that what they want is "consultation" or for the clinician to "look at the case." This is a good start, but what, more precisely, does the attorney have in mind?

Is the attorney seeking someone to conduct a psychological assessment of a party to an actual or potential legal case? Is the attorney looking for someone to review a third party's assessment and perhaps to testify regarding its adequacy and conclusions? Is the attorney simply looking for guidance in how to understand psychological aspects of a case but not looking for a potential witness? An attorney may be handling his or her first case in which psychological assessment is relevant and may be looking for extremely basic information about how to proceed.

Some attorneys may be able to spell out exactly what they are looking for (e.g., "I need someone to conduct a psychological evaluation of my client to determine whether she is mentally competent to execute a will"). Some may proceed in a step-by-step fashion in which the potential expert advances to the next step only if the previous step has been successfully completed. For example, an attorney may have taken on a new client who is alleging psychological injury as a result of job stress. The attorney may ultimately want one or more expert witnesses who will testify that, on the basis of a comprehensive psychological evaluation, the client has been severely psychologically disabled because of a variety of specific incidents that occurred at his or her job site.

The attorney may begin by asking the potential expert to listen to a brief description of the "facts" of the case (as presented by the attorney). The attorney may then ask a number of questions to probe the potential expert's attitude and tentative opinion. If, for example, a woman contacted as a potential expert says that she would not see the symptoms as described as constituting a severe psychological disability and that she would not view the job incidents as likely stressors, then the attorney may thank her for her time—which is all the thanks she may receive for a phone discussion that may have taken an hour or two, unless she has already established fee arrangements for this part of the process—and proceed to call another potential expert.

The next step is for the attorney to find a potential expert who, on hearing the attorney's recitation of the "facts," indicates that it is likely or at least possible that the job incidents caused a severe disability. The candidate (for potential expert) may then be asked to review the records.

If the potential expert continues to indicate an opinion that is favorable to the attorney's case, then the attorney may retain the clinician to take the next step: completing a psychological assessment of the client. In some instances, the attorney may ask for an oral summary of the potential expert's test findings and opinion. If these are unfavorable to the attorney's case, the process may end at that point. If the findings and opinion are supportive of the attorney's case, the potential expert may be hired for the next steps: preparing a written assessment report (see chapter 7) and offering testimony at a deposition and trial.

That the potential expert's responses at each step may cause the process to continue (i.e., the clinician will receive more business and hence more pay) or terminate (perhaps also decreasing the likelihood that this particular attorney will contact the potential expert for any future cases) can exert pressure that may affect the potential expert's responses, a topic to be discussed later in this book.

Those potential experts who have been frequently contacted by attorneys probably realize that there is at least one other reason an attorney may call. In a particular topic area (e.g., using the MMPI to screen applicants for police force or airline pilot positions; using the MMPI in the assessment of psychological harm suffered by rape victims/survivors) or geographic locale, there may be only a few (sometimes only one) widely known experts whose experience seems to qualify them almost uniquely for a particular case. In some instances, an attorney may have no intention of calling this individual as an expert. The attorney may, for example, believe (whether or not accurately) that the expert's testimony would be inherently damaging to his or her case. The attorney may, however, retain the expert (for as small a fee as possible) simply to ensure that the expert is not available to the opposing parties in the case. This strategy may not be disclosed by the attorney to the potential expert.

There are several variations by which an attorney may attempt to ensure that an expert does not play any role in a case (i.e., does not testify for the opposing attorney). The attorney may, for example, telephone the potential expert and, without offering to retain the expert, simply ask if he or she could spare perhaps 5 minutes to discuss an urgent matter. The attorney may imply (in varying degrees of nonspecificity) that the clinician is being considered as a potential expert.

Or the attorney may prevail on the clinician's (presumed) good nature, generosity, or collegiality, asking for some supposedly minor professional-to-professional consultation for which it would be churlish and greedy for the clinician to even think of charging. (After all, the whole conversation will take less than 5 minutes, and the attorney only wants to ask one very brief, very minor question.) The attorney may then give a two- or three-sentence summary of the case and ask a very simple question (e.g., "Would the MMPI be a good test to use in evaluating this plaintiff?" or "Is there a professional code of ethics that might be relevant?"). Having kept careful records of this professional consultation in which "crucial" information was shared with the clinician, the attorney is then in a position to move that the expert be excluded from being hired by or testifying for opposing counsel.

The clinician's own personal attorney may be of some help in such situations. The other attorney's conduct could be considered unethical in some jurisdictions. If a pattern of such conduct can be shown, other relief may be granted by the court, such as allowing the expert witness to be retained by the other side despite the nominal "consultation" by the previous attorney.

Yet another variation involves the attorney asking his or her client to call the clinician to ask for some information or advice (again involving a very brief disclosure of information about the case). Awareness of such strategies to "tie up" experts can enable potential experts to develop better procedures for handling consultations.

An initial contact from an attorney that is frequently disconcerting is to receive a subpoena for records relating to a former or current client. In some instances, a clinician, viewing what appears to be a valid, court-authorized (i.e., perhaps signed by a judge, although some are simply signed by an attorney) demand, may err by immediately turning over the requested records to the attorney. Such a response may constitute a serious error because, depending on the circumstances, the clinician may have been legally required to claim (therapist–patient) privilege on behalf of his or her client (see chapter 5). We recommend that a clinician receiving such a subpoena always consult with his or her own attorney before taking further action.

Finally, in clarifying the task, it is important to determine who the client is and where the responsibilities lie. Is the expert working for (e.g., is employed and paid by) the attorney? What problems may arise because the attorney's legal client becomes, in effect, the clinician's assessment client? Any potential conflicts need to be addressed during the initial contacts with the attorney. Clarification can become much more difficult in the criminal justice system, such as in cases in which the assessment is ordered by the court. Although there may be significant time pressures in such evaluations, clinicians must ensure that they clearly understand the tasks and that they do not act in such a way as to violate the accused's rights (e.g., R. D. Miller, 1990). In situations in which the clinician is called on to provide assessment (or treatment) services that are unwanted by the defendant or prisoner, Fersch (1980) believes that

> *it is easier to say that the psychologists' responsibility is to the judges or probation officers or whoever directs their work in the court. If these court personnel share a similar philosophy, then psychologists have at least two clients, the defendants (the traditional clients) and the court personnel, and psychologists' responsibilities to the two are bound to conflict at times. The ethical problems become more complex, however, when the various personnel within the court have differing philosophies, for this then multiplies the psychologists' clients. (p. 55)*

When the expert in a forensic setting has multiple and perhaps conflicting responsibilities to more than one individual, it is especially important to clarify whether the task is solely assessment or may include treatment or other interventions. Elwork (1992) presented a useful discussion of "psycholegal interventions that integrate traditional psychotherapeutic approaches with the contingencies of the legal context" (p. 181).

Readers interested in a more extensive discussion of issues related to conflicting responsibilities in the forensic arena are referred to *Who Is the Client?: The Ethics of Psychological Intervention in the Criminal Justice System* (Monahan, 1980). Other potential conflicts of interest are discussed in some of the following sections in this book.

Competence

The attorney may be looking to the clinician to help him or her understand the psychological issues relevant to the case. It is the clinician who bears the responsibility to clarify what the issues are and to ensure that he or she possesses adequate competence or expertise to address those issues. To a psychologist who has never had any training or experience in assessing children and who is about $500 short on office expenses this month, a call from an attorney looking for an expert to conduct a psychological evaluation of two children who may have experienced psychological trauma as the result of an auto accident can be *very* difficult to turn away.

The clinician has an ethical responsibility to be frank with the attorney regarding whether he or she has the proper background and credentials to serve as an expert in this particular case. In some instances, the clinician, even though thoroughly qualified to serve as an expert, may refer the attorney to someone whose particular history, skills, and characteristics seem better matched to a given case. For example, a psychologist may have conducted literally thousands of personality assessments using the MMPI and be thoroughly qualified to conduct an assessment of a young woman who is experiencing job stress because of alleged sexual harassment. However, the psychologist may want to suggest that the attorney consider hiring another assessment specialist who focuses on cases of sexual harassment in the workplace, has conducted research in that area, and has served as an expert witness in previous cases of this type.

The Golden Rule may be useful here. If the potential expert witness were to be charged with malpractice at some time in the future and were to contact an attorney, the clinician might be exceptionally dependent on the attorney to assess the legal issues relevant to the case and, even if the attorney were generally qualified to handle the case and "needed" the work, to refer the clinician to an attorney who might be better equipped (in terms of history, skills, and characteristics) to defend the clinician in this particular case. In the same way that the potential expert would expect the first attorney whom he or she contacted to make the best possible referral (if there were someone significantly better qualified to handle the case), attorneys have a right to expect that potential expert witnesses will level with them about who seems most likely to do the best job. Any significant lack of competence or expertise will likely provide a focus for vigorous and extended cross-examination.

For psychologists, policy documents of the APA emphasize the necessity of practicing only within the bounds of demonstrable competence and of accurately representing such competence (e.g., APA, 1981, 1992). State licensing laws and administrative regulations may also explicitly require that psychologists limit their practice to areas in which they are competent. For example, Article 8 ("Rules of Professional Conduct"), Section 1396 of California Title 16 states, "The psychologist shall not function outside his or her particular field or fields of competence as established by his or her education, training and experience."

Consider the following scenario: A psychologist with a doctorate in experimental psychology is asked to conduct a clinical examination of a litigant and to prepare a report. One step a psychologist might take in considering whether he or she possessed adequate general education and training in the clinical area would be to review the material in appendix C-2 on changing specialties. The individual must be certain that he or she possesses adequate education, training, and experience in the general area (e.g., clinical psychology) of relevant practice before assessing whether he or she has specific skills (e.g., administering and interpreting MMPIs or evaluating whether an individual is competent to stand trial) needed for the task.

Conflicts of Interest

The potential expert witness needs to inquire very specifically whether there are people, issues, or factors that would create an unacceptable actual or apparent conflict of interest. For example, a clinician may be asked by an attorney to provide an independent psychological assessment of a woman who is suing for custody of her children. The clinician, however, may once have been intimately involved with the woman and thus would be in no position to provide an objective assessment.

As another example, a psychologist may be asked to conduct an assessment of an individual who is filing a malpractice suit against a local hospital. The psychologist may have applied to the hospital repeatedly for a staff position and may have always been turned down. Were the psychologist to undertake such an assessment, his or her objectivity might be open to serious question. If the psychologist were to conclude that the plaintiff had been severely harmed because of wrongful acts by the hospital, it might seem to some that the psychologist's judgment would be influenced by anger and resentment at the hospital for failing to offer him or her a job. Alternatively, if the psychologist were to conclude that the plaintiff had suffered no harm whatsoever and that a careful history suggests no wrongdoing on the part of the hospital, it might appear to some that he or she were trying to curry favor with the hospital to increase the likelihood of later being hired.

In some instances, the potential expert witness must unilaterally decline (despite any urgings by the attorney) involvement in a case because of actual or apparent conflicts of interest. If there are relationships that involve confidentiality (e.g., the potential expert, as therapist, provided psychotherapy to the opposing attorney in this case), the potential expert may not be able to provide any specific information but may simply answer any of the attorney's requests for additional information with a statement such as, "I'm sorry, but participating in this case would constitute a potential or actual conflict of interest that I'm not at liberty to discuss."

In other instances, the potential expert bears a responsibility to disclose to the attorney factors that may be relevant to the case and that the attorney needs to be aware of in considering whether to retain the expert. In these instances, the potential expert has decided that the factors do not represent a legal, ethical, clinical, or professional barrier to participation in the case but that the attorney, apprised of these factors, may decide that another professional may be better suited to this case (e.g., that the attorney would be more comfortable working with another professional or that using this particular professional would needlessly complicate the case). For example, the potential expert may be best friends with the opposing attorney, may have coauthored a book with him or her, or may have filed one or more formal complaints against the opposing attorney with the state bar association.

Additional Aspects of Adequate Disclosure

The potential expert owes it to the attorney to provide an accurate picture of his or her strengths and weaknesses as an expert in the case at hand. Obviously, a conflict of interest or a lack of competence in the relevant issues are two of the primary aspects, but there are others. For example, is the potential expert currently under investigation by a hospital peer review committee, a professional ethics committee, or a state licensing agency? Has there been a complaint sustained under these auspices in the past? Does the expert have any record of significant violation of the law (something more than, say, a few parking tickets)? Has the expert ever been dismissed for cause from a paid or unpaid position?

Especially if the attorney is handling a "mental health" case for the first time, he or she may be unfamiliar with professional terminologies. For example, an attorney who addresses a potential expert witness as "Doctor" may need to be informed whether the witness actually does possess a degree at the doctoral level and whether the doctorate is an MD, a PhD, a PsyD, an EdD, a DSW, and so on, and what these various initials mean. This matter can become exceptionally troublesome if the potential expert has become accustomed to misstating his or her credentials or allowing others to make incorrect assumptions about his or her titles by not offering prompt correction and clarification. For example,

> *Many hospitals function as training institutions. Unfortunately, both the institution and the trainee may engage in extensive rationalization to attempt to justify fraudulently presenting therapists as having qualifications or credentials that they do not possess. Upper level graduate students may be introduced to patients and the public as "Dr. ___." Similarly, interns who are prohibited by the laws of their states and by formal ethical principles from presenting themselves as psychologists because they have not yet been licensed may be presented to patients and the public in a flagrantly deceptive manner. (Pope, 1990a, p. 1069)*

Three aspects of the credentialing process are essential for the potential expert to disclose to and discuss with the attorney: (a) degree level, (b) area of degree, and (c) licensing status. These aspects may become quite complex if the attorney is calling from another state that has different standards for licensing, qualifications for expert witnesses, and so on.

It is important for the expert to be familiar with the relevant professional association policies regarding these issues. For psychologists, the relevant documents include the *Ethical Principles of Psychologists and Code of Conduct* (APA, 1992; these principles and code are presented in appendix J), the *Casebook on Ethical Principles of Psychologists* (APA, 1987a), the *General Guidelines for Providers of Psychological Services* (APA, 1987b), the *Specialty Guidelines for the Delivery of Services* (APA, 1981), "Specialty Guidelines for Forensic Psychologists" (Committee on Ethical Guidelines for Forensic Psychologists, 1991; these Guidelines are presented as appendix C-1), the APA Policy on Training for Psychologists Wishing to Change Their Specialty (Abeles, 1982; Conger, 1976; this Policy on Training is presented as appendix C-2), and the lists of APA-accredited doctoral programs and APA-accredited predoctoral internship programs that generally appear in the December issue of *American Psychologist* (with supplementary lists sometimes appearing in the July issue). The section on education and training in chapter 8 provides examples of ways in which opposing attorneys can explore these issues during deposition and cross-examination.

Expert witnesses who conduct psychological assessments may feel betrayed if, at some late stage in the legal proceedings (perhaps while they are being cross-examined), they discover that the attorney that retained them has withheld some vital information from them. Similarly, attorneys may feel betrayed if potential experts withhold information that is relevant to the attorney's decision to retain the expert or to the attorney's approach to preparing and trying the case. As emphasized earlier, the Golden Rule exemplifies an important aspect of professional responsibility: The professional is obligated to disclose to the attorney relevant information just as the professional expects and wants the attorney to share all relevant information to which the professional is entitled.

No witness or attorney wants or deserves to be "blindsided" by information that should have been disclosed at an earlier point. Pope and Vetter (1991) provided one example in which a woman brought suit against a previous therapist for engaging in sexual intimacies with her. Her subsequent treating therapist was scheduled to testify on her behalf concerning the standard of care and the way in which the intimacies with the previous therapist had affected the woman. Only at a point immediately before he was to be deposed did the subsequent treating therapist disclose to the woman's attorney that he himself had been a perpetrator of therapist–patient sex.

Scheduling

Consider the following hypothetical scenario:

Attorney: Hello, Dr. Smith. I'm an attorney representing a plaintiff in a personal injury suit. My client was badly injured in an automobile accident. I believe it is clear that this trauma has affected her personality, her ability to work, her relationship with her family, and virtually all aspects of her life. What I'm looking for is someone who could take a look at her medical records, talk with her husband and her work supervisor, talk with her, and—I wouldn't presume to tell you how to do your job but—give her some general personality tests and also see if you can find any evidence of neuropsychological impairment. I need someone who can tell the jury just how much this accident has affected her and her life. You come highly recommended by [the attorney gives the name of someone you've never heard of] and I was wondering if you'd be interested in conducting this assessment and testifying for us as an expert witness.

Potential Expert: Well, I've done that kind of work before; it's a field I've specialized in. Part of my decision would depend on the time frame. Can you tell me what sort of schedule you have in mind?

Attorney: We're moving right along on this case. If you could review the records and complete the examination this evening and tomorrow morning—I can make my client available to you at your convenience any time this evening or before lunch tomorrow—I'd like to put you on the stand tomorrow afternoon.

This scenario may strike some readers as a gross exaggeration of some attorneys' tendency to wait until the last possible minute to prepare a case. It may strike other readers as a hauntingly familiar recreation of the general substance of some of the calls they have actually received. In any event, it is crucial that the potential expert find out and discuss the scheduling issues to ensure that there is adequate time to do the necessary work.

One scheduling issue involves the task: How extensive is the task proposed by the attorney? A comprehensive psychological and neuropsychological assessment, possibly including collateral family, employer, and co-worker interviews, may take much more time than an attorney might estimate. The psychological examination itself, if it involves taking a comprehensive history and administering a variety of tests, may take several sessions and, depending on the condition of the person being assessed and the stressfulness of the assessment procedures, the sessions may have to be spaced out over several days or weeks. The tests then need to be scored, interpreted, and considered in light of the other available information, such as records of previous assessment and treatment.

Another scheduling issue involves the availability of previous records and other documents. For some assessments, there may be numerous and diverse documents to review. There may be school, court, or employment records—some of them perhaps quite dated—that the expert will find necessary to understand the client's current condition and how distant or more recent events (such as surviving an airplane crash, being battered by a partner, or losing a child because of medical malpractice) may have affected that condition. If these records are not already in the attorney's or the client's possession, it may take a considerable amount of time and effort to track them down and obtain copies. Both potential expert and attorney need to discuss the types of documents or other information that the expert finds necessary to form a professional opinion and how long it may take to obtain them.

Yet another scheduling issue involves the potential expert's current work load and the sometimes unpredictable nature of forensic work. New cases can be relentlessly tempting despite a professional's vaguely nagging awareness that he or she is already overworked and overbooked. Participating in a single forensic case may mean canceling a day of patient appointments because of a deposition, only to find the scheduled deposition cancelled several times at the last possible moment for what may or may not appear to be a valid reason. Participation may also mean clearing a week of patient appointments so that one can travel to another city to testify, only to find the trial continued a number of times. Especially if one is seeing many patients on a regular basis, it may be difficult to meet the clinical needs of those patients while engaged in numerous court cases that demand that the expert be out of town frequently for long periods of time. Each professional's approach to treatment, clientele, personal resources, resilience, and ability to maintain a solid clinical practice despite sometimes unpredictable calls to testify are unique. Each professional must constantly and carefully monitor the status of current work load, potential for burnout or for being "stretched too thin," and ability to fulfill the various professional duties that he or she has undertaken.

Financial Arrangements

Professional health service providers may often be uncomfortable addressing fee issues, but it is important that the financial aspects of conducting a forensic assessment or otherwise participating in court proceedings be clarified during the initial contacts with the attorney. The professional should be frank and clear about the charges, including the methods and schedules of payment, about reimbursement for expenses, about payment for travel and lodging, and about all other aspects of the financial arrangements.

Depending on local laws and jurisdiction, there may be significant differences between being paid as an expert witness (i.e, one who has special knowledge and opinions that might help the trier of fact to understand the facts and issues) and as a percipient witness (also termed a lay or fact witness; i.e., one who was involved in some way, perhaps as an eyewitness or the subsequent treating therapist, and thus can help establish what the facts of the case are). Expert witnesses can usually command their customary fees, as long as they are reasonable. Percipient witness fees—which might be paid to an eyewitness to an automobile accident or to a shooting—may be set by law and are generally significantly lower than what experts tend to charge. Thus, an initial step in clarifying fee arrangements is to clarify whether one is being called to testify as an expert witness, a percipient witness, both, or in some other capacity.

In a typical case, the opposing counsel will often, depending on the jurisdiction, pay the witness's fee during the deposition conducted by the opposing counsel. If the professional is both an expert and a percipient witness, confusion can easily arise. For example, a professional may be the subsequent treating therapist of a plaintiff or defendant. The professional may be called on to testify both as a percipient witness (one who had direct knowledge of and about the plaintiff before, during, and after an automobile accident) and as an expert (someone qualified to form professional opinions about the psychological trauma and sequelae of injury sustained in automobile accidents). In some instances, again depending on jurisdiction, the deposition may be formally divided into, say, a morning session during which the professional provides (and is paid for) testimony as a percipient witness and an afternoon session during which the professional provides (and is paid for) testimony as an expert witness. Obviously, the deposing attorney may attempt to ask most or all of the questions during the morning session, when the professional's fees are at the lower percipient level. The professional may decline to answer such questions at that time by claiming, "I'm sorry, but answering that question would require an expert opinion."

As expert witnesses, professionals have a variety of ways in which they charge for their time and services. Probably the most common is the hourly charge. It should be clarified with the attorney if the hourly charge is the same for all work. Some professionals, for example, may charge more for appearances in court. Because forensic work can involve such diverse sets of tasks, it is important to note each type of work that may be involved—for example, phone consultations with the attorneys, interviews, psychological testing, scoring and interpreting tests, reviewing records, providing feedback about findings in oral or written form, traveling to and from depositions and courtroom testimony, time spent waiting to testify, time allotted for testing sessions or depositions that are cancelled with minimal notice, time spent in depositions or courtroom testimony—and the rates at which that work will be charged (e.g., same hourly fee for all work, differential hourly fees for different types of work, or a set fee for a specific task such as conducting an assessment or testifying at a deposition).

Particularly when an hourly fee is charged, the expert should provide guidance to the attorney concerning how long certain sorts of activities—such as administering, scoring, and interpreting an MMPI-2; conducting a comprehensive psychological and neuropsychological assessment; preparing a written forensic report—are likely to take (e.g., the probable minimum and maximum time as well as a "best estimate" on the basis of the circumstances as currently understood by the professional).

Some professionals find it easier to charge a set fee for each task. The professional arrives at such figures by estimating the average time each task tends to take. Obviously, if the tasks take a shorter time, the professional may "come out ahead"; but such occasional windfalls are balanced by cases that may take much more time than anyone would have anticipated. One benefit of the set fee for each task is that it clarifies completely for the attorney (and the attorney's client) exactly how much retaining this expert will cost.

By contrast, if an expert is charging by the hour, both the expert and the attorney may have virtually no idea how many hours will be needed to review the hundreds or thousands of pages of relevant documents that accumulate during legal proceedings (e.g., previous medical, psychological, educational, and legal records and depositions by other experts and by percipient witnesses). An expert may also, while preparing for a case, do extensive work in researching a special subsection of the research and professional literature. Even though the expert is an authentic expert, there may be an elaborate diversity of publications that need to be examined (or reexamined) as part of preparation. Attorneys (and their clients), particularly if they are not informed of this aspect of preparation in advance, may be taken off guard by such charges, which may seem excessive and unnecessary.

It is useful for expert and attorney to discuss the possible ways in which a fee arrangement might be challenged during deposition or in court. For example, an expert might charge a standard hourly fee (say, $200 per hour) for all time devoted to this case. If the trial is held in a different city, the expert may, under this arrangement, charge the standard fee for each hour he or she is out of town (using the rationale that travel is related to the case and that each hour out of town is an hour away from the professional's therapy practice or other income-producing work). The expert might get on a plane at night, fly to the city in which the trial is held, spend the night at a hotel near the courthouse, testify during the court's morning and afternoon session, then fly home exactly 24 hours after leaving. If the fee arrangement has explicitly set forth an hourly fee for this time, the expert has earned $4,800 for this trip. The opposing counsel may dwell, during cross-examination, on how some of the expert's income was earned, as follows:

Attorney: Let's see, you arrived in our fair city about 10 p.m. and checked into a hotel last night—is that your testimony?

Expert: Yes.

Attorney: And what time did you go to sleep?

Expert: Around 11 p.m.

Attorney: And what time did you get up this morning?

Expert: At 6 a.m.

Attorney: You slept from 11 p.m. last night until 6 a.m. this morning?

Expert: Yes.

Attorney: While you were asleep last night from 11 p.m. until midnight, you earned $200?

Expert: Well, actually I wouldn't put it quite that way. You have to understand that I calculate my fees so that. . . .

Attorney: Would you please answer the question with a "yes" or "no": Did you earn $200 while you were asleep last night from 11 p.m. to midnight?

Expert: [after looking to his or her attorney who remains unhelpfully silent] If you put it that way, yes.

Attorney: [looking at the jury who may be comparing and contrasting the way they earn wages to the way the expert earns wages] And you slept from midnight to 1 a.m.?

Expert: Yes.

Attorney: And during that hour of sleep you also earned $200?

Expert: Yes.

Attorney: So by 1 a.m.—just to make sure I have it right—you've earned [the attorney may have developed interesting ways of pronouncing, inflecting, and emphasizing the word *earned*] a total of $400 in regard to your participation as an expert witness in this case by sleeping two hours at the hotel. Is that correct?

Expert: Yes.

Attorney: Now from 1 a.m. to 2 a.m. you were also asleep, is that your testimony?

Perhaps the greatest blunder that a potential expert witness can make in creating fee arrangements is to allow a fee that is directly dependent on the outcome of the case. In some states, it is unethical for an attorney to pay such a fee to an expert witness.

On the face of it, such a fee arrangement would seem to create a clear conflict of interest: The expert might be viewed by the judge and jury as having a strong motive to shape testimony in such a way that maximizes the probabilities that the expert will be paid the highest possible amount.

Opposing attorneys can use such contingency fee arrangements to discredit a witness in a variety of ways. For example, the attorney may ask the expert to read from standard forensic psychology texts and ask him or her to comment on the prohibitions against contingency fees. David Shapiro, for example, served as president of the American Academy of Forensic Psychology and as chair of the ethics committee of the American Board of Professional Psychology. In his text *Forensic Psychological Assessment*, he emphasized, "The expert witness should never, under any circumstances, accept a referral on a contingent fee basis" (1991, p. 230). Another forensic specialist, Theodore Blau, who served as president of the APA, also stressed in his text *The Psychologist as Expert Witness* that "the psychologist should never accept a fee contingent upon the outcome of a case" (1984b, p. 336).

It is crucial to clarify that the expert is never to be paid to produce a particular opinion. Clever cross-examination, if the expert is not adequately prepared and does not speak clearly to this issue, can make it appear to the jury that the attorney has hired the witness to mouth particular testimony (and that, should the attorney have preferred and paid the requisite fee, could have just as well directed the expert to mouth the opposite). In all cases, the expert should be paid—and should make it clear that he or she is being paid—for performing a professional task or for his or her time and *not* for producing specific testimony. Pope and Bouhoutsos (1986) describe an instance in which an attorney was cross-examining an expert witness regarding the fee. The attorney asked the expert how much she was being paid to recite the opinion. The expert responded that the fee she charged was not for her opinion but for her time. "And just how much will you be paid for that?" sneered the attorney. The witness replied, "That depends on how long you keep me up here" (p. 140).

Each legitimate form of charging has its strengths and weaknesses. What is essential is that both expert and attorney clarify precisely the nature of possible charges by the expert, how the exact fee is to be determined, and the schedule for payment (see appendixes A and C-1). Some experts, for example, may wish to specify that all fees be paid in advance. Others may wish to specify that fees are to be paid within 30 days of the expert's submitting a written bill.

Once an agreement on the nature, method, schedule, and other factors relating to payment has been reached, a written agreement should be prepared to minimize possible misunderstandings or future disagreements stemming from divergent memories of the original financial arrangements (see appendix A).

Communication, Privilege, Secrets, and Surprises

Lines of communication among the various participants in a legal case can become tangled unless the expert and the attorney discuss aspects of mandatory, discretionary, and prohibited communications thoroughly during their initial contacts. Depending on the circumstances and the jurisdiction, a professional hired as a consultant to an attorney may be both able and required to keep confidential—from the court and from the opposing attorneys—all aspects of the consultant work. Such work may be privileged and thus be shielded—at least under normal circumstances—from all those who are not directly involved in preparing the attorney's case.

Again, depending on the circumstances and the jurisdiction, a professional hired as an expert witness may be obligated to disclose virtually all relevant information and opinions to the opposing attorney during deposition. In some situations, there may be exceptions; some communications between expert witnesses and attorneys may be privileged, and some of the professional's work for the attorney may be shielded as "work product."

If the professional is to administer, score, and interpret an MMPI as part of an assessment of the lawyer's client, to whom is the professional expected to provide the final report, the raw test data, and the MMPI form itself? How, for example, will the client receive feedback concerning the test? (see, e.g., Butcher, 1990; Finn & Tonsager, 1992; Fischer, 1985; Gass & Brown, 1992; Pope, 1992). Is the professional expected to meet with the client to review and discuss the results? Is it possible that the client will hear the results (and their implications) for the first time while the professional testifies as an expert witness in court? Is the professional obligated to provide the test report, raw test data, and the MMPI form to opposing counsel? Will the professional be able to request that such documents be delivered to a qualified psychologist who works for opposing counsel? If such a request is made, is there legal support for it in the jurisdiction? Discussion and clarification of such issues are crucial during initial contacts. (Some of these issues are addressed in appendixes C-1 and D.)

The potential for tangled communication may be heightened if the professional is not contacted by an attorney to discuss the possibility of conducting a psychological evaluation but rather is subpoenaed (as a percipient witness and custodian of documents) to provide information about a psychological evaluation that was conducted some time in the past. Because *any* evaluation may become the focus of a lawsuit or other demand for information, those who conduct evaluations must clarify the ethical and legal groundrules for providing or withholding information about an evaluation. Such clarification should become a routine part of any assessment practice and of any clinical practice more generally in which assessment is a component.

Pope and Vasquez (1991) presented a fictional vignette highlighting the sometimes bewildering aspects of unanticipated demands for information:

> *A seventeen-year-old boy comes to your office and asks for a comprehensive psychological evaluation. He has been experiencing some headaches, anxiety, and depression. A high school dropout, he has been married for a year and has a one-year-old baby, but has left his wife and child and returned to live with his parents. He works full time as an auto mechanic and has insurance that covers the testing procedures.*
>
> *You complete the testing. During the following year you receive requests for information about the testing from:*
>
> - *the boy's physician, an internist*
> - *the boy's parents, who are concerned about his depression*

- *the boy's employer, in connection with a workers' compensation claim filed by the boy*
- *the attorney for the insurance company that is contesting the worker's compensation claim*
- *the attorney for the boy's wife, who is suing for divorce and for custody of the baby*
- *the boy's attorney, who is considering suing you because he does not like the results of the tests*

> *Each of the requests asks for: the full formal report, the original test data, and copies of each of the tests you administered (for example, instructions and all items for the MMPI).*
>
> *To which of these people are you ethically or legally obligated to supply all information requested, partial information, a summary of the report, or no information at all? For which requests is having the boy's written informed consent for release of information relevant? (pp. 91–92)*

There may be circumstances of which the attorney is unaware that mandate communication of information obtained during the course of an assessment to third parties. For example, the attorney may be handling a wrongful discharge suit on behalf of a company's former employee. The attorney is a specialist in employment law but is generally unfamiliar with mental health law. The attorney hires a psychologist to conduct a comprehensive psychological evaluation of the woman who was fired and asks that information from her family also be gathered so that the psychologist can testify not only about the harm that the firing caused the former employee but also about the collateral stresses and disruptions the firing caused the woman's family.

As part of the evaluation, the psychologist schedules a meeting with the woman, her husband, and their 10-year-old daughter. He asks them as a group to discuss their history as a family, about what life was like while the mother was employed by the company, and what happened after she was fired. During this session, the daughter discloses a secret that she had never before shared with anyone: that she had been sexually molested by her uncle. The father becomes enraged and rushes from the room, shouting that he is going to kill the man who molested his daughter as soon as he can find him. At this point, the surprised psychologist may be faced with two responsibilities (again, depending on applicable law in that jurisdiction and the specific circumstances). The psychologist may be required to make an oral and subsequent written report to child protective services within a specified period of time regarding suspicions of child abuse. He or she may also be required to take reasonable steps to protect an identified third party (i.e., the uncle), whom the father has threatened to kill; taking these protective steps may involve disclosing information that would otherwise remain confidential. It is crucial that both expert and attorney discuss such issues, however unlikely they may appear to occur.

Other Needs and Expectations

Finally, it is important for both potential expert and attorney to discuss other services, materials, and so on, that each may need and expect from the other. For example, an expert may need a variety of previous records in order to form an adequate professional opinion. He or she may need records of previous assessments (particularly any previous administrations of the MMPI), school records, employment records, and medical records. If these are not already available, it may be much more efficient and effective for the attorney to secure them. A clinician in independent practice may make repeated phone calls and written requests (accompanied by a written release of information form signed by the client) to an employer, the client's previous therapist, a school system, or an attorney who handled previous cases for the client. None of these calls and requests may produce any significant results. A phone call from an attorney or a written request on stationery with a law firm's letterhead may attract much greater attention from the recipient. Putting the written request in the form of a subpoena may provide an even more salient cue for action by the recipient.

During the initial contacts, the expert can make clear why and how such previous records are a necessary part of the forensic assessment process and can reach agreement with the attorney about how the records are to be obtained. As with all basic aspects of the expert–attorney agreement, this understanding can be put in writing as a hedge against immediate misunderstanding or later faulty recollections.

As another example, the expert may also require time and services from the attorney in preparing for the deposition or for courtroom testimony. The expert may want to meet with the attorney several days before the deposition (and again immediately before the trial) to discuss findings, to cover questions to be asked during direct examination, and to anticipate the opposing attorney's possible approaches to cross-examination.

Some experts may find such sessions an essential aspect of adequate preparation. It helps to ensure that they are as knowledgeable as possible about the relevant facts and issues of the case and are as prepared as possible to state their professional opinions and the foundations for those opinions in the most clear and direct manner possible. If the attorney feels that such preparatory sessions are a waste of time and money, that they need only meet for a brief period immediately before the deposition or courtroom testimony, then this conflict in needs and expectations should be fully addressed and resolved (if possible) before the expert is hired. However, potential expert witnesses who are just beginning forensic work may be pleasantly surprised to find that many attorneys share the same concerns about fees, schedules, preparation, and so on, and will be happy to discuss them and prepare a written agreement (see appendix A).

CONDUCTING AN ASSESSMENT

Reviewing the Issues and the Literature

Having clarified the tasks that the attorney wants completed, the professional faces a significant responsibility in ensuring competence and currency in all relevant aspects. Assume, for example, that a professional has been retained to conduct a custody evaluation. The professional has vast experience in this area. In this particular case, however, while making an initial review of the case documents, the professional discovers that one of the parents has a chronic disease with which the professional has little familiarity. The rare disease tends to be associated with a somewhat shortened life span and may, in some instances, become debilitating. Part of the preparation for the assessment may involve extended consultation with medical specialists, a review of the professional literature to see if there is any discussion of a potential relation between the disease and the ability to provide adequate parenting, and a review of the assessment literature to determine the degree to which disease has been included or studied as a variable.

Virtually any case will have aspects for which the expert will need to "brush up" to ensure that recent research findings or related developments are taken into account. Sometimes these aspects may not be discovered until the midst of the assessment process. In some instances, the professional may need to tell an attorney that an assessment-in-progress should be supplemented (or in some instances, replaced) by an assessment conducted by a specialist. For example, a clinician who specializes in assessing women who have been raped may come to suspect, during the assessment process, that the woman is exhibiting signs of neuropsychological impairment. The impairment, if it exists, may be due to the rape (e.g., the rapist having beaten her about the head) or may be unrelated to the rape (perhaps involving a tumor, a blood clot, or a vessel rupture in the brain). However, if the clinician is not a specialist in neuropsychological assessment, he or she will need to note whatever signs indicate possible neuropsychological impairment and recommend that a qualified neuropsychologist or similar specialist conduct a comprehensive assessment (or at least review the data from the current assessment to see what further evaluation may be warranted).

Choosing the Tests to Fit the Tasks

Once the professional has refined the questions that the assessment is supposed to address and has reviewed the relevant issues and literature, selection of tests must meet at least one fundamental criterion: Is the test appropriate for the questions that the professional wants the assessment to address? The MMPI provides a general personality profile. It has been validated for a variety of uses. However, imagine that an attorney comes to a psychologist with the following proposition:

I handle only cases in which large companies have reason to believe that an employee has engaged in theft from the company's store. I represent the company. What I want you to do is to administer an MMPI to each employee that one of my client-companies suspects is stealing and let me know if they're guilty or not. I'll pay you $2,000 per employee, and I can guarantee that you'll be testing at least 10 employees a month. I don't need you to swear that you're absolutely certain that the person committed the theft or not. All I want is for you to write a test report giving your best professional opinion based solely on the MMPI as to whether you believe that the employee likely engaged in theft or not. All I want is some general indication so that we'll know whether to follow-up on the employee or not. Plus, we want something to put in the employee's personnel file to document that we had some reason to investigate fully and, where warranted, to fire them. You won't need to worry about getting sued: The companies will indemnify you, and I'll take out a $25 million professional liability policy on you. But I need an answer right now because I want to start the testing program this week. Will you take the job?

There are probably few psychologists who would not be painfully tempted by such an offer. The attorney is offering a minimum payment of $20,000 per month for administering and interpreting a few MMPIs. In addition, the psychologist would seem to be protected from losses that would be due to any malpractice suits.

The attorney seems to be asking simply for a little documentation—perhaps a paragraph per employee—that the companies could use in court were they to be sued for wrongful discharge or for some other cause related to the investigation and its outcome. Nevertheless, the psychologist must ask: Has the MMPI been adequately validated for this purpose? Have there been independent studies published in peer-reviewed journals that provide evidence that the MMPI can effectively distinguish between employees who have been stealing from their companies and employees who have not engaged in such theft?

As another example, there is no adequate evidence that MMPI scores, in and of themselves, provide comprehensive and adequate screening for neuropsychological damage. The MMPI, of course, may be used as *one* of the tests in a comprehensive psychological and neuropsychological assessment. Reitan and Wolfson (1985), for example, wrote that "the Minnesota Multiphasic Personality Inventory is also frequently administered with the HRNB [Halstead-Reitan Neuropsychological Test Battery], not as a neuropsychological procedure for evaluation of brain functions, but to provide information regarding any emotional distress or personality disturbance the patient may be experiencing" (p. 39). Similarly, Lezak (1983) noted that

the sheer variety of brain injuries and of problems attendant upon organicity probably helps explain the unsatisfactory results of MMPI scale and sign approaches. Moreover, the MMPI was not constructed for neuropsychological assessment and may be inherently inappropriate for this purpose. . . .

Thus, for brain damaged patients, acknowledgment of specific symptoms accounts for some of the elevation of specific scales. Premorbid tendencies and the patient's reactions to his disabilities also contribute to the MMPI profile. The combination of symptom description, the anxiety and distress occasioned by central nervous system defects, and the need for heroic adaptive measures probably account for the frequency with which brain damaged patients produce neurotic profiles. (pp. 611–613)

Psychologist Kirk Heilbrun (1992) of the Medical College of Virginia outlined several considerations for psychologists who are planning forensic assessments. He believes that adequate availability and documentation are two important criteria for test selection:

The test is commercially available and adequately documented in two sources. First, it is accompanied by a manual describing its development, psychometric properties, and

> *procedure for administration. Second, it is listed and reviewed in* Mental Measurements Yearbook *or some other readily available source. (p. 264)*

Tests should also meet the more general (i.e., for use in nonforensic as well as forensic settings) criteria regarding validity, reliability, administration, scoring, and interpretation as set forth in *Standards for Educational and Psychological Testing* (1985) and similar policy documents. Chapter 8 provides examples of detailed deposition and cross-examination questions to explore issues relating tests to assessment tasks in forensic settings.

Choosing the Tests to Fit the Individual

Although a test or assessment technique may have been demonstrated to possess adequate validity and reliability for the task at hand (e.g., selecting applicants best suited for police administration), the validation and reliability studies as well as collateral research need to be reviewed to ensure that demographic variables and other characteristics of the individual who is being assessed fit well with all of the empirical foundations for the inferences that will be drawn from the test results. Have the scoring and interpretation hypotheses for a specific test, for example, been validated for individuals who match the client's age, sex, race, and culture, if these are salient variables? To take extreme examples, one would not administer the English language MMPI to someone who did not read English, and one would not administer the MMPI to a 5-year-old child because the test was not designed for and has not been adequately validated for use with young children.

Thinking About Tests in Context

It is essential that the individual conducting an assessment be knowledgeable about the historical, cultural, and scientific context of the human factors that are to be assessed, of diagnostic categories, of the range of possible tests, and of assessment itself. No psychological tests, assessment conceptions, or methodologies were developed in a vacuum. All should be subjected to careful, informed, and continuing scrutiny.

At its worst, assessment can—whether intentionally or despite the best intentions—embody, strengthen, and serve the ends of racism, sexism, religious bigotry, and other destructive social forces. History, as well as the current scene, provides examples of research conducted in a prominent psychological laboratory of a major university using a test that *supposedly* demonstrated that men were intellectually superior to women and that Whites were intellectually superior to Blacks and American Indians; of the creation and application of specific diagnostic categories applied solely and oppressively to Blacks; and of methods of clinical assessment and intervention used as part of a systematic program of torture and political repression (Pope & Garcia-Peltoniemi, 1991; Pope & Johnson, 1987; Pope & Vasquez, 1991).

Perhaps the most sustained attention to concepts such as race as they may be misused in the construction, use, or interpretation of standardized psychological tests has focused on attempts to measure "intelligence." Contributing to the confusion has been the elusive nature of the concept that such tests supposedly measure intelligence. Many discussions of the concept seem to return to a long-standing self-referential or circular style of definition associated with psychologist Edwin G. Boring. For example, Professor Arthur Jensen used Boring's definition when defending the notion that intelligence tests are "really" a measure of intelligence. He was replying to critics who asserted that socioeconomic status, cultural advantages, and other factors may have been confounding variables causing tests to be "mis-aimed" (i.e., to measure factors other than general intelligence).

> *The notion is sometimes expressed that psychologists have mis-aimed with their intelligence tests. Although the tests may predict scholastic performance, it is said, they do not* really *measure intelligence—as if somehow the "real thing" has eluded measurement and perhaps always will. But this is a misconception. We can measure intelligence. As the late Professor Edwin G. Boring pointed out, intelligence, by definition, is what intelligence tests measure. (Jensen, 1972, pp. 75–76)*

Similarly, Professor Robert Herrnstein wrote,

> *Writing in the* New Republic *in 1923, Professor Edwin Boring of Harvard said, "Intelligence as a measurable capacity must at the start be defined as the capacity to do well in an intelligence test. Intelligence is what the tests test." Once we agree on a test, that is doubtless true, just as well-defined physical concepts like force and work can be identified with the instruments that measure them. (Herrnstein, 1973, p. 107)*

But is such an operational definition adequate as a foundation for understanding intelligence (or other concepts supposedly measured by psychological tests) and for developing, using, and interpreting intelligence tests? Professor Stephen Chorover examined this fundamental definition from another perspective.

> *To understand what Boring and Jensen are saying when they say that "intelligence is what IQ tests measure," consider the following example: Every automobile contains an instrument called a fuel gauge; its purpose is to measure the amount of fuel in the tank. Now, if one were to follow Boring's dictum, one might say, "Fuel as a measurable substance must* at the start *be defined as a substance capable of causing the fuel gauge to register." If that stipulation sounds satisfactory, and if no other definition is required concerning what fuel really is, let me suggest that the next time the fuel gauge on your car reads empty, you find a water hose and fill your tank from it. The car will thereafter take you about as far as Boring's dictum does, and it will do so with what he would have to call a full tank of fuel. (Chorover, 1979, p. 51)*

The expert witness must carefully consider such questions (e.g., of definition) in their historical, cultural, and scientific contexts when determining what factors or characteristics are to be assessed and what tests are to be used. As emphasized in chapter 1—especially in the extended quote by Faschingbauer (1979)—the original MMPI has been scrutinized in terms of its normative sample (which did not include Blacks, Hispanics, etc.). For example, psychologist Malcolm Gynther's (1972) review of the literature, "White Norms and Black MMPIs: A Prescription for Discrimination?" concluded that

> *blacks, whether normal or institutionalized, generally obtain higher scores than whites on Scales F, 8, and 9. Item and factor analyses reveal that these differences represent differences between blacks and whites in values, perceptions, and expectations rather than differences in level of adjustment (as a traditional interpretation of the findings would imply). . . . Studies . . . suggest that prospective black employees are disadvantaged when the MMPI is used for screening and that black psychiatric patients are less likely than whites to be diagnosed accurately by the MMPI. (p. 386)*

A study published 2 years after Gynther's (1972) review examined MMPIs "drawn from the files of patients referred for psychological testing in a public short-term treatment hospital serving an urban . . . racially mixed population" (Strauss, Gynther, & Wallhermfechtel, 1974, p. 55). "Profile analysis, Goldberg's composite, and a discriminant function were used to differentiate psychosis from behavior disorder on the basis of MMPI scores. These procedures . . . resulted in the misdiagnosis of blacks at a substantially higher rate than whites" (Strauss et al., 1974, p. 55).

In one of the most vivid demonstrations of possible difficulty applying White norms to Black individuals, psychologists Malcolm Gynther, Raymond Fowler, and Phillip Erdberg (1971) administered the original MMPI to 32 Black male and 56 Black female residents of a rural community. These individuals, who showed no evidence of significant psychopathology, who were recruited as "normally functioning" (p. 235) individuals, and who had no history of mental hospitalization or imprisonment, did *not* seem to be adequately assessed by the original MMPI.

> *Data were considered in terms of validity scores, profile scale scores, high point analysis, item analysis, Goldberg's neurotic–psychotic index, actuarial codebooks and computer summaries. All analyses indicated that our normal Ss would be considered as*

> *extremely deviant and, for the most part, psychotic. Classification errors of this magnitude suggest the need for a moratorium on interpreting profiles generated by Ss dissimilar in background and experience from normative groups. (Gynther et al., 1971, p. 237; see also Gynther, Altman, & Warbin, 1973)*

As Erdberg, a past president of the Society for Personality Assessment, clinical diplomate, and a member of the team that conducted this research, commented, "These [the people who participated in the study] were some of the most reasonable, least dysfunctional people you could ever want to meet. But if you judged them only by the MMPI scores, you would have [wrongly] thought that about 90% of them were flagrantly psychotic" (personal communication, May 14, 1992).

The following general resources provide additional research and points of view concerning the use of the MMPI for individuals of diverse racial and ethnic groups: Butcher and Pancheri (1976); Dahlstrom, Lachar, and Dahlstrom (1986); Greene (1987); and King, Carroll, and Fuller (1977). As noted earlier, the normative group for the MMPI-2, unlike that for the original MMPI, did not consist exclusively of Whites. For a discussion of the MMPI-2 normative group and research addressing the use of the MMPI-2 with various ethnic groups, see chapter 2.

Thinking about tests in context also means adequate consideration of what the test administrator and test interpreter may bring to the test situation. In some instances, the MMPI-based hypotheses are derived exclusively on an actuarial basis; much more often, especially in forensic settings, clinical judgment comes into play in deriving hypotheses from the basic test responses (see, e.g., Dawes, Faust, & Meehl, 1989; Meehl, 1954). In some cases, an individual conducting an assessment may be vulnerable to cultural stereotypes that result in biased and invalid initial hypotheses and final conclusions. For example, Jesse D. Geller (1988), on the faculty of the Department of Psychology at Yale University, reviewed research in which White clinicians were presented data about prospective patients. The research design systematically varied the IQ and race of each prospective patient while holding other factors constant.

> *The results . . . suggest that, when evaluating Blacks, White clinicians are in danger of relying on cultural stereotypes that do not apply to specific individuals, or that might not even be accurate characterizations of the group as a whole. Clearly the "facts" of the case did not dictate unequivocally the therapists' conclusions about the patient's strengths and weaknesses. Rather, they appear on various dimensions to have confused, unwittingly, the specific patient's abilities and problems with their probably unrecognized feelings and expectations about a whole class of patients. (p. 127)*

Only through careful, honest, and continuing attention to such potentially biasing "feelings and expectations" can an expert witness eliminate or at least minimize the likelihood that interpretations and conclusions will be distorted.

In summary, expert witnesses preparing to conduct an assessment have at least three major responsibilities related to historical, cultural, and scientific contexts. First, witnesses must be knowledgeable about and give careful consideration to the historical, cultural, and scientific context of the definition of the factors or characteristics to be assessed. All too often, such fundamentals may be overlooked or taken for granted. Chapter 8, which presents specific deposition and cross-examination questions, notes that even experienced expert witnesses may have difficulty defining such a fundamental term as *test*. Definitions have evolved out of specific historical, cultural, and scientific frameworks (see the chapters "Testing, Assessment, and Diagnosis" and "Cultural, Contextual, and Individual Differences" in Pope & Vasquez [1991], pp. 87–100 & 130–138). Adequate understanding of the concepts and definitions is based, in part, on an adequate knowledge of these frameworks.

Second, psychological tests and other assessment procedures also evolved out of specific historical, cultural, and scientific frameworks. Knowledge and consideration of these frameworks and how they contributed to strengths and weaknesses of various tests and procedures are essential. For example, if the normative group of a standardized psychological test excludes all people of color, what, if any, are the implications? A skilled cross-examiner may ask an expert witness how using a test in which all non-Whites were excluded from the norming differs from working for a mental health clinic that excludes all non-Whites from admission. The attorney may ask the witness how he or she justifies using a test in which "normal" seems, on a *de facto* basis (or on the operational basis of norming the test), to be equivalent to being White. Different experts may respond to such questions in different ways, but *no* expert should be caught off guard by such questions or encounter them for the first time on the witness stand. All witnesses have the responsibility to be aware of such issues, to be knowledgeable of the historical, cultural, and scientific context in which they have evolved, and to struggle earnestly and honestly with the complex dilemmas they present. Legitimate opinions, conclusions, and viewpoints may differ widely among experts on such questions, but the continuing struggle with them as psychologists undertake any assessment is basic to their integrity and one that everyone should share.

Third, no expert witness has grown up in a vacuum. Everyone has unique historical, cultural, and personal sets of experiences, influences, and viewpoints. These sets may influence the way one goes about planning, conducting, and interpreting a forensic assessment. It is not uncommon for clinical phenomena in a client to evoke a variety of reactions from a professional.[1] In some instances, for example, a psychologist who was sexually abused as a child or was raped or battered as an adult may be conducting an assessment to determine how deeply sexual or physical abuse may have harmed another individual; it is possible that the personal history of the psychologist may influence how he or she conducts the assessment (see Pope & Feldman-Summers [1992] for a discussion of this issue and data indicating that two thirds of female and one third of male clinical and counseling psychologists have experienced some form of sexual or physical abuse). To the degree that expert witnesses are "open and alert to these reactions, and can acknowledge . . . them nondefensively," it is possible that may even "constitute valuable sources of information" (Sonne & Pope, 1991, p. 176) that help the professional to ensure that the assessment is conducted sensitively, respectfully, and fairly. To be aware of one's limitations or potential biases—as well as one's strengths and potential to recognize and avoid, transcend, or at least take into account bias—is a continuing aspiration and significant responsibility.

To provide a full discussion of these issues is beyond the scope of this book. However, readers seeking additional examination of these issues may find the following references (in addition to those cited elsewhere in this book) useful: Baer (1981); Block and Dworkin (1976); L. S. Brown (1988, 1991); L. S. Brown and Root (1990); Cole and Bruner (1972); Denmark, Russo, Frieze, and Sechzer (1988); Gibbs and Huang (1989); Gossett (1975); Gould (1981); Guthrie (1976); Herek (1989); Herman (1992); E. E. Jones and Korchin (1982); J. M. Jones (1990a, 1990b); Lewis (1986); Malyon (1986a, 1986b); Mays and Comas-Diaz (1988); Mednick (1989); Pedersen, Draguns, Lonner, and Tribble (1989); Scarr (1988); Stanton (1960); Stricker et al. (1990); Tavris (1992); Unger (1979); and Walker (1989).

Informing the Client

The first section (Initial Contact With the Attorney) of this chapter emphasized the professional's responsibility to disclose to an attorney information that is relevant to the attorney's decision to hire the professional as a consultant, expert witness, or in some other role. Although the professional may assume that the attorney has fully informed the client about the nature and purpose of the assessment, that assumption is usually—at least in our experience—wrong. However, even if an attorney has briefed a client regarding the testing, the professional should review all significant and relevant aspects with the client so that the individual understands what will be happening, the implications of the assessment, how (and to whom) the results will be conveyed, and so on (see appendixes B and J).

It may be useful, after introductions have been made, to ask the client if he or she knows why the appointment has been scheduled. Some clients may

[1] Epstein & Feiner, 1979; Fromm & Pope, 1990; Heimann, 1950; Pope, Sonne, & Holroyd, 1993; Pope & Tabachnick, in press; Shafer, 1954; Singer, Sincoff, & Kolligian, 1989; Sonne & Pope, 1991.

have considerable information, but some may have "no idea why I was sent over here to see you." Some clients, in fact, may not understand that the professional *is* a professional (e.g., a psychologist), what that sort of professional does, and so on.

In virtually all cases, the professional has a responsibility to ensure that the client understands the process that is about to occur and freely consents to it. A written form may be useful in documenting such consent and in ensuring that all relevant items are covered (see appendix B). For example, does the client understand that you have been retained by the client's attorney (if that is the case) to conduct a psychological assessment? Does the client understand that you will be preparing a written report (if that is the case) and to whom you will be submitting the report (e.g., to the client's attorney)? Does the client understand that what you tell them may *not* be confidential (depending on the circumstances), but that you may be called as an expert witness to testify about the assessment and your findings and opinions? Does the client understand the arrangement and consent to it? Does the client have any questions, even if they concern topics that you have not covered?

Such issues become more complicated if the professional has not been retained by the client's attorney but by the opposing attorney. Moreover, there are instances in which a psychological assessment of an individual may have been ordered by the court and the individual may have diminished rights to informed consent.

Taking Adequate Notes

There is no standard way to take notes on an assessment, but professionals must ensure that they do not lose accurate and important information, especially because there may be a period of several years between the time that they conduct an investigation for a case and the time when the case actually comes to trial.

Opposing attorneys may take advantage, during a deposition and trial, of the ways in which the passage of time may obliterate or significantly distort the professional's memory of an assessment, the client, and the conditions of the assessment. For example, if a professional conducts 100 or 200 assessments each year and there is a gap of several years between the assessment and testimony, it is extremely difficult for the professional who lacks adequate notes to recall with any specificity the particular client.

In one case, an attorney was conducting a deposition several years after the psychologist's last session with the client. The attorney began one segment of the deposition by asking the psychologist to describe the individual whom he had assessed. The psychologist had complete records of the test data, the scoring, and the interpretation, but had not taken any notes regarding the appearance of the client. Unable to remember what the client looked like, the deponent was forced into a series of embarrassing admissions that he did not currently know whether the person whom he'd assessed was under 5′ tall, between 5 and 6′ tall, or over 6′ tall; that he did not know whether the individual was extremely thin, of moderate weight, or quite large; that he did not know whether the client did not need glasses or contact lenses, customarily wore glasses or contacts, wore them only for reading, or wore them while taking the psychological tests; and that he did not know what color eyes or hair the man had. Because the psychologist only had raw test data, scorings, and interpretations, he was unable to find records of what race or ethnic group the client belonged to. During the deposition, the opposing attorney spent some time exploring the fact that the deponent—who had presumably examined the client very carefully and was prepared to offer expert opinions on the individual—could not even say whether the client was Black, White, or of some other group.

However impressive an expert witness's testimony about the psychological status of a client might otherwise be during a trial, both judge and jury may be likely to discount testimony from an expert who, while being deposed, acknowledges that he or she had no idea of what the client looks like and can remember nothing of the client's height, weight, race, or other characteristics. Notes should not only help a professional to recall such fundamental personal characteristics but also ensure accurate recollection of such important factors as the following.

Vision. If the testing is at all dependent on the individual's ability to see (e.g., a test involving reading or a test involving copying geometric shapes), the professional needs to find out if the individual has any visual difficulties. For example, does the client normally wear glasses or contact lenses for reading or for the types of tasks involved in the testing? If so, is the client wearing those glasses or contacts now? (Unless asked, some clients may be reluctant to disclose that they forgot to bring their reading glasses; they may attempt to take the tests with a significant visual handicap.)

Is the light in the room adequate, or does it cause any problems? Does the light produce an annoying glare, or is it shining directly in the client's eyes? Some professionals may conduct assessment sessions in hospitals, clinics, prisons, schools, or office buildings in which the testing room is illuminated by florescent lights; such lights may cause headaches or visual problems for some individuals.

Hearing. If the assessment involves the individual's ability to hear (e.g., test instructions that are read aloud by the examiner or such tests as the Seashore Rhythm Test of the Halstead–Reitan Neuropsychological Test Battery), the professional needs to determine the degree to which the individual's ability to hear is attenuated to any significant degree. If a client customarily wears a hearing aid, is it in use and functioning properly throughout the examination? Are there any acoustical conditions in the room or external noises (e.g., loud noises in the hallway, construction work in an adjacent lot, or an air-conditioning unit producing an irritating rattle) that affect the individual's ability to hear clearly? As mentioned in chapter 2, the MMPI may be administered using American Sign Language to those who cannot hear (Brauer, 1992); this method of administration should be noted in the forensic report.

Mobility and access. Clients may have special physical needs that can, depending on the circumstances, be directly relevant to the adequacy and validity of the assessment process. For example, a client may use a wheelchair for mobility. However, the office building, hospital, or other locale of the assessment may not provide convenient access to the assessment room (e.g., the assessment room may be up three flights of stairs—with no working elevator—and have a very narrow entrance). The professional who is to conduct the assessment may be forced to consider alternative test cites (e.g., a cafeteria or lounge on the first floor) that may be extremely inappropriate for testing. Similarly, the assessment room's table on which the psychologist places the MMPI or lays out the materials of the WAIS-R, Bender-Gestalt Test, or Halstead–Reitan Neuropsychological Test Battery, may be constructed in such a way that its height and legs do not allow a person in a wheelchair to use it comfortably (or, in some cases, at all).

Such circumstances require the assessment specialist to confront two essential issues with care, candor, and integrity. First, can an adequate, valid, and fair testing be conducted under such conditions (with the additional requirement that the professional explicitly note consequent reservations, doubts, or qualifications about the validity of the process and results in the assessment report)? Second, what responsibilities do psychologists and other mental health professionals or expert witnesses functioning in such settings bear to ensure that changes are made so that the environment is accessible, convenient, and appropriate for all who seek (or are required to obtain) professional services?

Language, reading, and writing. To the extent that the assessment is dependent on oral or written language, is the individual fluent in the relevant language? For example, the professional may be conducting the assessment in English, but English may be a second, third, or subsequent language, perhaps recently acquired, for some test takers. To the extent that the individual does not adequately understand the instructions and the test itself, any results may be misleading.

An individual may be quite fluent in English but have difficulty reading or writing. Again, unless such factors are adequately assessed, test results may be quite misleading. An individual who, for example, can speak, read, and write several languages with great skill may be able to use English only conversationally, with little ability to read or write this language. A naive or incompetent professional might incorrectly conclude—having not inquired further about the discrepancy between the individual's ability to converse in English and the individual's relative inability to read and write in English—that the individual was dyslexic and dysgraphic.

Test administrators who use the MMPI-2 need to ensure (although the inventory provides internal checks) that clients currently have at least a fifth-grade reading level (Paolo et al., 1991; Butcher et al., 1989; see also chapters 2 and 8 of this volume).

Physical illness or disorders. As anyone who has tried to do even the most routine work while suffering from a bad case of the flu will instantly understand, illness or physical pain and disorders can affect an individual's ability to perform a task. Those conducting psychological assessments need to determine whether the individual is sick, in pain, or suffering from any physical disorder. The individual may not spontaneously volunteer such information. For example, the client may have been told by his or her attorney that the testing session is extremely important and that the client must by all means show up on time and complete the tests. The client may have woken up with an excruciating back spasm (perhaps precipitated by the stress of the legal proceedings and the fear and trembling evoked by the impending testing session), a sinus infection, or an attack of arthritis.

Even if there are scheduling problems (e.g., with an approaching trial) that would make it difficult to postpone the testing, the professional will need to determine whether tests administered under such conditions will have any real validity (e.g., can the client complete the test, and can the effects of the client's illness or physical distress be reliably factored into the interpretation of the results?) or whether it is mandatory that the testing be rescheduled.

The clinician also needs to determine whether neuropsychological impairment can be confidently (i.e., with good reason) ruled out. Neuropsychological impairment may not, as discussed previously, be readily identifiable from an MMPI profile but may, if undetected, lead to significantly misleading interpretations of the MMPI and other test results. Reitan and Wolfson (1985), for example, reviewed a number of case studies in which possible MMPI profile interpretations were *not* based on adequately validated research with neuropsychologically impaired individuals. In one case study, they noted a number of possible inferences that were based on a Conversion V profile, which results from the configuration of the Depression, Hypochondriasis, and Hysteria scores.

> *A Conversion V may have this significance in a psychiatric population, but there have been no studies of patients with neurological disorders that support the validity of this configuration in this group. There appear to be consistent indications that applying psychiatric criteria to neurological patients may have serious deficiencies. Researchers should investigate the possibly limited generality of the finding before recommending any clinical application and interpretation of a particular configuration of test data. . . .*
>
> *Although the items of the MMPI may be valid in terms of how they describe the feelings and complaints of this man, we must question their validity for interpretation within a psychiatric framework. For [the person evaluated], many of the items that contribute to the Hypochondriasis scale may represent valid problems which result from his brain disorder.* (pp. 285–286)

Drugs and medications. Has the person who is scheduled for assessment taken any legal or illegal drugs or other medications that might affect performance on the test? A variety of prescription as well as over-the-counter medications may cause drowsiness, irritability, difficulty concentrating, memory impairment, restlessness, hypervigilance, and other side effects that could produce misleading test results.

If the person regularly takes a medication (e.g., insulin, corticosteroids, anti-inflammatory agents, antianxiety agents, antidepressants, or Azidothymidine [AZT]), the professional needs to inquire if they have failed to take the customary dosage in the time period leading up to and including the testing session or sessions, whether they have changed dosages recently, whether they are experiencing any symptoms from the medication, and whether the medication continues to be adequately effective for its purpose.

Circumstances preceding the testing. Events leading up to the testing can profoundly affect testing results and foster misleading interpretations. As with many of the other factors mentioned in this section, the client may not spontaneously disclose such events. A battered woman may have been threatened and perhaps assaulted by her partner immediately before the testing session. The partner may have threatened her with harm should she participate in the session. A client may have experienced a recent death in the family that makes it hard to concentrate, may have gotten caught in a traffic jam that created excruciating anxiety about whether he or she would make it on time to the session, or may be worried about the last-minute arrangements he or she made for child care when the regular child care provider cancelled at the last minute. Careful, sensitive, and comprehensive inquiry can help ensure that the professional is aware of such factors.

Careful monitoring. In all instances, an assessment session must be carefully monitored. If the professional (or one of the professional's adequately trained and qualified assistants) is not present, there can be no assurance that the client filled out a self-report test such as the MMPI independently and under the standardized conditions required for validation (see the section on administration and scoring in chapter 8).

An unmonitored assessment can produce invalid, misleading, or otherwise extremely distorted results in many ways. One of the authors, for example,

> *observed a patient taking the MMPI in an outpatient waiting room while the psychologist worked in his office. Frequently when the patient marked down a response, the patient's spouse, who was reading along, commented, "Now that's not you! That's not what you believe. Change that answer!" The patient would re-read the item, reconsider, and then dutifully change the answer. (Butcher & Pope, 1990, p. 39)*

Professor Jack Graham described an interesting occurrence at a psychiatric ward (cited in Butcher & Pope, 1992). A group of patients sat attentively in a large circle. At intervals, some of the patients would raise their hands. Graham became intrigued and asked a member of the group to tell him what was going on. The person explained that one of the ward psychologists had given one of the patients an MMPI to fill out, asking him to return it to the psychologist's office later. The patient had asked the other residents for help. As the patient read aloud each MMPI item, the residents raised their hands to vote whether the item should be answered true or false.

The Committee on Professional Standards of the APA (1984) issued a formal ruling when a complaint was filed against a psychologist for failing to monitor administration of the MMPI (see chapter 8 for the text of their ruling). But there is another reason for avoiding unmonitored MMPI administration aside from the extraneous influences (e.g., "help" from friends or family or the test taker consulting an MMPI book) that can lead a person to fill out the form differently than if he or she were monitored in accordance with the findings of the Committee on Professional Standards. The presence of an individual monitoring the testing may be understood as one of the elements of standardization. As the Faschingbauer (1970) passage in chapter 8 (in the section on administration and scoring) vividly illustrates, for example, self-administering the test unmonitored in a private office can drastically skew the results. Unless results of an unmonitred test were interpreted in light of validation studies conducted in an unmonitored setting, the assumptions of standardization would be violated.

> *The assumption underlying standardized tests is that the test-taking situation and procedures are as similar as possible for everyone. When one departs from the procedures on which the norms are based, the standardized norms lose their direst applicability and the "standard" inferences drawn from those norms become questionable. (Pope & Vasquez, 1991, p. 93)*

Careful monitoring of an assessment using standardized tests such as the MMPI is a requirement of forensic evaluation.

While monitoring the test administration, the professional should note the duration of the testing session, any signs of test-taker fatigue, any breaks or interruptions, and any behaviors that might be relevant to interpreting the test.

Remaining Alert to Critical or Emergent Situations

As noted earlier, the professional needs to disclose to the attorney and client the conditions under which the professional may need to take prompt action that may breach customary confidentiality. While conducting the assessment and interpreting the results, the professional must remain alert to any signs that the client is an immediate danger to self or others (i.e., is suicidal or homicidal), is or is becoming gravely disabled, or may be in immediate danger (e.g., a client discloses during an assessment that her partner, who has battered her in the past, has threatened to kill her).

Depending on the clinical circumstances and relevant law, the professional may be obligated to take certain steps to protect the client or identifiable third parties. Similarly, if the client reports child abuse, the professional may be legally required to make an immediate oral report and subsequent written report to child protective services or other legal agencies. If the client is currently in therapy, that information should be obtained before or as part of the assessment—unless there is a compelling reason that this information should be withheld from the professional.

The degree to which the professional conducting the assessment, the client, the client's therapist, and the client's attorney work together to address critical or emergent situations will depend on the clinical needs of the patient, the unique circumstances of the case, the legal framework, and the exact nature of the crisis or danger. What is crucial is that the professional adequately address such contingencies during preparation for the assessment and remain alert to the possibility of such phenomena (even if the reason for the referral and the initial information seem to suggest that such possibilities are remote) while conducting and interpreting an assessment.

Ensuring Completeness and Considering Context

Before arriving at conclusions, it is important to review once again the choice of tests, the access to other sources of information (e.g., previous medical and assessment records and interviews with family members), and the scope and consistency of findings to help ensure that inferences are based on an adequate array of data and are placed in proper context. Any conclusions based on the MMPI alone *must* be viewed as hypotheses. These hypotheses can be evaluated in light of the support or contradiction provided by other sources of information about the individual. Psychologist Howard Garb (1988), for example, reviewed the available research studies "in which mental health professionals were given increasing amounts of information" (p. 442). He found a general increase in validity "when biographical, MMPI, or neuropsychological test data were added to demographic or psychometric information" (p. 442; see also Garb, 1984, 1992).

The previous sections of this chapter emphasized the importance of gathering such information as the conditions immediately preceding the testing (e.g., is the client extremely upset because he or she was caught in a traffic jam and was afraid of missing the assessment appointment). But expert witnesses conducting assessments have a responsibility to conduct an adequate review of records and to inquire specifically about incidents that may affect the interpretation of test results, even if the incidents occurred long ago.

Without a structured interview and adequate review of records, it is easy to arrive at compelling but thoroughly misinformed and misleading conclusions. Many clinicians, for example, may fail to inquire about a history of sexual abuse. In one research study, 50 charts of nonpsychotic female patients evaluated at a psychiatric emergency room (ER) were selected at random and reviewed. These charts were compared with 50 other charts of similar female patients; ER clinicians for the latter group of patients had been asked to include specific questions about possible child abuse in their structured interviews. The first group of charts recorded child abuse for only 6 of the 50 patients; the second group of charts recorded child abuse for 35 of the 50 patients (Briere & Zaidi, 1989).

Briere and Zaidi's (1989) research illustrates Harvard psychiatrist Judith Herman's (1992) observation that trauma victims or survivors will often be reluctant to volunteer their abuse history and have difficulty communicating it clearly.

> *The ordinary response to atrocities is to banish them from consciousness. Certain violations of the social compact are too terrible to utter aloud: this is the meaning of the word unspeakable.*
>
> *Attrocities, however, refuse to be buried. Equally as powerful as the desire to deny atrocities is the conviction that denial does not work. . . .*
>
> *This conflict between the will to deny horrible events and the will to proclaim them aloud is the central dialectic of psychological*

> *trauma. People who have survived atrocities often tell their stories in a highly emotional, contradictory, and fragmented manner which undermines their credibility and thereby serves the twin imperatives of truth-telling and secrecy. When the truth is finally recognized, survivors can begin their recovery. But far too often secrecy prevails, and the story of the traumatic event surfaces not as a verbal narrative but as a symptom. (1992, p. 1)*

Psychologist Lynne Rosewater's (1985, 1987) research found that MMPI profiles are likely to be misinterpreted—especially with a diagnosis of borderline personality disorder or schizophrenia—if abuse history is not taken into account during interpretations. Computerized interpretations may be especially prone to produce such discrepancies unless they have been specifically developed for this population. Herman, Perry, and van der Kolk (1989), in a study of people suffering from borderline personality disorder who had also suffered traumatic abuse, found that what is customarily termed borderline symptomatology could obscure the original trauma and make a diagnosis of PTSD difficult.

> *It appeared that memories of the abuse had become essentially ego syntonic. The subjects generally did not perceive a direct connection between their current symptoms and abusive experiences in childhood. This finding is compatible with observations from follow-up studies of trauma victims (30, 31) which indicate that fragments of the trauma may be transformed over time and relived in a variety of disguised forms, e.g., as somatic sensations, affect states, visual images, behavioral reenactments, or even dissociated personality fragments. (p. 494)*

A history of abuse is but one of many diverse factors that must be taken into account in arriving at an adequate understanding of test data and assessment results. Closed head injury, chronic medical conditions, and a history of previous involvement with the legal system are among other potentially critical factors in interpreting assessment findings. It is the expert witness's responsibility to ensure that all relevant previous records and other sources of information have been taken into account. If sources of information that may be crucial to the context and meaning of test data are missing or otherwise unavailable, that should be explicitly noted in a forensic report and testimony (see Case Illustration 2 in chapter 7).

Writing the Report

Putting the test findings and interpretations into an organized framework forces—or at least encourages—the professional to think through the various kinds of assessment data, to check emergent hypotheses against other sources of data, and to communicate clearly the implications of the data for understanding the individual and his or her behavior. A separate chapter (7) has been devoted to this task.

BEING DEPOSED AND TESTIFYING IN COURT

If the professional has clarified the tasks to be accomplished through formal psychological assessment and the ways in which the results are to be communicated, has chosen the assessment instruments or methods with care, has conducted the assessment scrupulously, and has considered the meaning of the results within their proper context, then much of the primary work of preparing to offer testimony in deposition and in court has been done. The professional's fundamental responsibility from this point on is to respond to proper questions in a way that tells the truth, the whole truth, and nothing but the truth. As an expert witness, the professional offers information and opinions that help the triers of fact (i.e., the jury or, in some instances, the judge) to understand phenomena and issues that are considered beyond common or lay knowledge.

And yet there are so many factors that can hamstring the professional's attempts to fulfill this responsibility. The sections that follow identify some of these major factors that tend to interfere with an expert witness's ability to present clearly, accurately, and helpfully the results of psychological assessments and conclusions and opinions that are based on those results.

Lack of Preparation

Lack of adequate preparation is a primary cause of disaster during depositions and in courtroom testimony. Louis Nizer's (1961) fundamental rule of preparation, quoted in chapter 1, applies to the expert witness as much as to the attorney. Forensic psychiatrist Robert Sadoff (1975) painted a vivid picture describing the consequences of inadequate preparation: "There is nothing more pitiful than to see a leading member of the community . . . brought to his knees under cross-examination because he is ill prepared. . . ." (p. 51). Brooten and Chapman (1987) estimate that "as a rule, at least four hours of preparation are required for any witness for every one hour to be spent in deposition or in court. In critical cases as much as six hours is advisable" (p. 176).

Allocating sufficient time to prepare is essential. Planning should allow enough time so that all necessary documents are available when the expert sits down to begin the review and preparation process. Ensuring that each of the points identified in this chapter have been fully addressed can help the witness avoid overlooking important matters.

A self-assessment can create justifiable confidence, identify areas of weakness, and serve as the final phase of adequate preparation. The expert can review all of the deposition and cross-examination questions discussed in chapter 8 as an important phase of this self-assessment. The expert can also review once again the factors that follow that often impair an expert's ability to testify clearly, accurately, and helpfully.

Lack of Familiarity With Forensic Settings and Procedures

Entering a new setting can be disorienting for any of us. Skills in one venue may not transfer easily to another. Readers are probably familiar with the clinical supervisor who can insightfully and incisively describe emerging clinical dynamics to a supervisee but becomes tongue-tied when standing in front of a packed lecture hall to deliver a clinical lecture. The psychometrician may be able to understand complex statistical relationships almost instantly and yet, even given adequate time, be unable to describe them clearly in the pages of a journal article. Those who were confidently assertive in their graduate school classes in clinical psychology, psychopathology, and treatment may have become timid and bewildered during their first days in a clinical internship in an inpatient setting; they did not know who was who, the procedures and routines, the jargon, and the lines of responsibility.

A similar phenomenon can happen to even the most skilled professional who sets foot in a deposition or courtroom for the first time. The very strangeness of the rules, procedures, language, and process can have an almost paralyzing effect. Because so many professionals will wind up in court—perhaps as a percipient witness for a client who was assessed or treated years ago—it is important to learn what the setting and process are like so as not to be caught off guard and make the various mistakes that are characteristic of someone who does not understand an environment with its own unique operating rules, culture, and dynamics. Watching *Perry Mason*, *Witness for the Prosecution*, and *L.A. Law* may not be adequate preparation for the experience.

Talking with colleagues who have testified in court is one good way to learn about the process, as is observing a trial. These methods, however, may be supplemented by reading accounts of trials and of trial procedures and strategies that may present a much more comprehensive, detailed, and coherent view of such aspects as attorney preparation, discussions among attorneys and the principals, legal briefs, jury deliberations, and other aspects that may not be apparent to those who observe a trial or who have the limited perspective of participation in one role (e.g., expert witness).

The following books may be useful to an expert witness or to anyone who is to take part in a court proceeding. Each has a slightly different perspective, but each presents important information about how trials and the legal proceedings leading up to them actually operate. Reading a variety of such accounts provides a more comprehensive understanding of the various perspectives and possibilities and of the patterns within the diverse permutations of legal actions.

Emily Couric's (1988) *The Trial Lawyers* might be a good book to begin with for someone who has little or no experience in the courtroom. The author has interviewed 10 prominent attorneys (including such well-known litigators as Linda Fairstein, Arthur Liman, Richard "Racehorse" Haynes, James Neal, and

Edward Bennett Williams). On the basis of her interviews, she describes how each handled one important case. The attorney describes the issues, the strategies, and the turning points. Brief excerpts of deposition and courtroom testimony are quoted to illustrate points. The 10 trials described in this book effectively convey the "shape" of a legal case, how it forms, the roles of the various parties, how evidence is identified and presented, and the adversarial process that is central to a trial.

A similar book is John Jenkin's (1988) *The Litigators*, an account of six trials that is based on interviews with high-profile attorneys. Alan Dershowitz's (1982) *The Best Defense*, the final example of this type of book, is similar to the others in that it provides accounts of 11 trials. Unlike the others, however, all of the trials involve the same attorney, and it is the attorney himself who is telling the stories.

The Trial Masters: A Handbook of Strategies and Techniques That Win Cases (Warshaw, 1984) is an extremely comprehensive book whose 51 chapters focus specifically on discrete aspects of a trial (e.g., conducting voir dire [see Glossary] and direct examination of a medical expert). In this edited book, a variety of attorneys, some of them quite well known (e.g., Louis Nizer, Vincent Bugliosi, Bruce Walkup, and Gerry Spence) provide a how-to-do-it (or at least a how-I-do-it) guide to understanding adversarial approaches.

Grutman and Thomas's (1990) *Lawyers and Thieves* is a much shorter book (224 pages) that serves as a good supplement to *The Trial Masters*. Whereas the longer volume focuses on approaches taken by attorneys in court, Roy Grutman's account of his own diverse experience tells more of the behind-the-scenes dealings by which attorneys try to gain advantage. As the title suggests, the book is more of an exposé.

The understanding of courtroom rules, dynamics, and culture is enhanced when the perspective—which in the preceding books is the attorney's perspective—is broadened. Prompted by her experience as a juror in a capital case that lasted 6 weeks, Robin Lakoff, professor of linguistics at the University of California, Berkeley, has provided an excellent analysis of life and language in court in her book *Talking Power: The Politics of Language* (1990). Those preparing to serve for the first time as an expert witness (the topic of some books listed later in this chapter) may find her discussion of the subject extremely helpful. For example, she begins an exploration of the special nature of testimony by noting,

> *The witness stand is not a place for comfortable conversation. Usually, the giver of information holds power, but a witness does not. A witness cannot control topics or their interpretation and has no say when the conversation begins and ends. . . . The lawyer–witness repartee may seem to an outside observer like especially snappy but otherwise normal conversation. But as in therapeutic discourse, its purpose and therefore its rules are different. To the observer, the discourse seems a dyad between lawyer and witness. But in terms of its function in a trial, both are in fact acting together as one participant, the speaker, with the jury as hearer. Without this understanding, much about the examination procedure would be unintelligible. (pp. 90–91)*

Whereas the works just listed provide relatively brief accounts of individual trials as well as trial strategies, dynamics, procedures, and perspectives, the late John D. MacDonald provided a much more detailed and comprehensive account of a single trial (in which one of the attorneys was F. Lee Bailey) in *No Deadly Drug* (1968). Briefer accounts can provide the basic patterns, but a longer book-length account (656 pages) can vividly portray, through careful attention to timing and detail, the ebb and flow of the extremely long and complex process that can occur between the time a case is filed and the trial is completed. MacDonald, author of the Travis McGee detective stories and numerous other novels, was an excellent writer. His descriptions of the extended direct and cross-examinations of the expert witnesses will be useful to virtually anyone preparing to serve in that role.

Another book focusing on a single case is *You Must Be Dreaming* (Noel & Watterson, 1992). A first-person account coauthored by one of the parties to the case and a professional journalist, this volume is especially informative in describing the deposition process, how the issues in a civil case can interact with issues that come before a licensing board and a professional ethics committee, and the movements toward settling a case. Other books concentrating on a single case are *Defendant* (Charles & Kennedy, 1985), *Betrayal* (Freeman & Roy, 1976), *Make No Law: The Sullivan Case and the First Amendment* (Lewis, 1991), and *The Sterilization of Carrie Buck* (J.D. Smith & Nelson, 1989), the latter two cases resulting in decisions by the U.S. Supreme Court. These books, by making the individuals about whom the witnesses are testifying so vividly real and immediate, serve as a crucial reminder of a witness's heavy responsibilities. Expert as well as lay testimony can profoundly and sometimes permanently affect the lives of those involved in judicial proceedings.

Expert witnesses may be particularly interested in understanding the ground rules, strategies, and dynamics of cross-examination. For a comprehensive description from a lawyer's perspective, perhaps the classic text is Francis Wellman's (1903/1936) *The Art of Cross-Examination*, especially his chapter on cross-examination of experts. This "how-to-do-it" text is extremely readable, quoting liberally from trial transcripts. One of the previously mentioned volumes, *The Trial Masters*, contains a number of chapters on cross-examination, including the ominously titled "Cross-Examination of the Adverse Medical Witness: Keep the Jury Laughing" (Peters, 1984; see also Kassin, Williams, & Saunders, 1990; Marcus, 1987; Younger, 1986a, 1986b).

The classic text for cross-examination of expert witnesses who testify regarding psychological assessment and related clinical matters was originally written by Jay Ziskin, *Coping With Psychiatric and Psychological Testimony* (1969). Ziskin, a psychologist and attorney, wrote a densely referenced guide for attorneys on how to attack (this is not too strong a word) forensic experts in the mental health field. A continuing theme of the text is

> *that movement toward a productive and valid law and behavioral science relationship can best be served by placing in the hands of lawyers, tools by which they can aid courts and juries to distinguish science from authoritarian pronouncement and validated knowledge from conjecture. (Ziskin, 1981a, p. 1)*

Now in its fourth edition and expanded from one volume to three, *Coping With Psychiatric and Psychological Testimony* (Ziskin & Faust, 1988; see also Faust & Ziskin, 1988) tends to be a source of considerable anxiety and perhaps panic for potential expert witnesses while bringing an anticipatory smile to many attorneys preparing for cross-examination. If the anxiety, panic, and other negative responses are not terminal or paralyzing, the expert witness can benefit immeasurably by confronting challenges posed in these volumes. The text encourages a rethinking of the foundations and sources of expertise, of the degree to which assertions (i.e., testimony) are supported by independently conducted research appearing in peer-reviewed scientific and professional journals, and of the likelihood that one's professional opinions may be biased, unsubstantiated, or vulnerable to attack. However stressful it may be to confront these vigorous challenges in the privacy of one's study, it is far less stressful than confronting them for the first time on the witness stand during cross-examination.

An ideal companion to the *Coping* text is Stanley Brodsky's (1991) *Testifying in Court: Guidelines and Maxims for the Expert Witness*. Brodsky, a psychologist who has testified as an expert witness in numerous trials, provides information, guidance, and support that can help restore the confidence of the expert witness who has been unable to cope with *Coping With Psychiatric and Psychological Testimony*. In a chapter titled "*Ziskin & Faust* Are Sitting on the Table," Brodsky observes that

> *those of us who testify have a reason to be grateful for the impetus to reconsider the* whats *and* hows *of our work. It can be quite constructive to say this in court. I find that an overview of the field, acknowledging the contributions of Faust and Ziskin and speaking to how we have attended to their issues, disarms attorneys and is part of nondefensive, positive testimony. (Brodsky, 1991, p. 203)*

This positive approach continues a theme he has elaborated previously in another work:

> *The testifying expert should know the research foundations and limitations of every clinical procedure employed, and should be prepared to defend its use. If the*

> *expert is strongly attacked, the attack will serve the useful purpose of reminding him or her of the need to be accountable. The cross-examination is a form of public examination and defense of what we know and how we know it. (Brodsky, 1989, p. 264)*

These guides to conducting and surviving cross-examination may be supplemented by detailed accounts of actual cases focusing on the cross-examination of expert witnesses providing testimony regarding assessment. Ron Rosenbaum's *Travels with Dr. Death* (1991; see also Tierney, 1982) provides a description of three trials in which a psychiatrist known as "Dr. Death" offers testimony and is cross-examined. Rosenbaum notes that the doctor's "lopsided record over the past twenty years favors his chances: going into these three trials he has testified against 124 murderers, and acting on his advice, juries have sentenced 115 of them to death" (pp. 206–207).

In order to impose the death penalty, the judge or jury must find that the defendant constitutes a continuing risk to society because he or she is likely to commit future acts of violence. The nature of Dr. Death's assessments in such trials may be troubling to many readers and illustrates vital issues regarding the scientific basis of expert testimony and the adequacy of cross-examination. Rosenbaum summarizes the doctor's customary style of testimony:

> *He'll take the stand, listen to a recitation of facts about the killing and the killer, and then—usually without examining the defendant, without ever setting eyes on him until the day of the trial—tell the jury that,* as a matter of medical science, *he can assure them the defendant will pose a continuing danger to society. (Rosenbaum, 1991, p. 210)*

A stark contrast to the success of the doctor described by Rosenbaum is the psychiatrist called to testify as an expert witness for the defense in the second trial (for spying) of Alger Hiss. The psychiatrist offered testimony, on the basis of his psychological evaluation, that the major prosecution witness, Whittaker Chambers, was afflicted with a personality disorder that included a propensity to lie. The psychiatrist had never met Mr. Chambers but had observed his testimony in court, reviewed the facts of his life, and studied his published writings. Thus, what the psychiatrist was setting forth as a solidly based psychological evaluation was derived *solely* from a study of Mr. Chambers's writings, a few facts about his life, and observation of him for awhile in one setting, the courtroom. The cross-examination of the defense psychiatrist has "frequently been described as the single most devastating cross-examination of an expert ever conducted" (Younger, 1986c, p. i). The verbatim transcript of this 3-day cross-examination was published as *Thomas Murphy's Cross-Examination of Dr. Carl A. Binger* (Younger, 1986c).

Trials of an Expert Witness (Klawans, 1991) presents a broad range of cases in which Harold Klawans testified as an expert witness. Unlike the previous two books, *Trials* provides first-person accounts of what it is like to be cross-examined.

Finally, experts and potential experts may find useful books that present the statutory and case law criteria for serving as an expert, rules of evidence, and similar information specific to testifying in a particular state (e.g., Kennedy, 1983; Kennedy & Martin, 1987; J. C. Martin, 1985; *West's California Codes: Evidence Code*, 1986), as well as more comprehensive guides to a specific state's laws as they are relevant to mental health professionals, such as APA's state-by-state series *Law and Mental Health Professionals* (e.g., M. O. Miller & Sales, 1986).

The Passage of Time

An expert may be retained by an attorney to conduct a psychological assessment, may conduct the assessment and write a report, and then may wait 3, 4, or 5 years until being deposed. Clinicians called as percipient or fact witnesses may have to cope with an even longer gap. They may have conducted a psychological evaluation of a therapy patient, the patient has completed therapy and terminated, and only 5, 10, or 15 years later does the therapist receive a subpoena. The subpoena may make a demand for the records and seek to compel the therapist to testify about the former client who is now suing for physical and emotional distress because of a slip and fall on an allegedly slippery floor in a department store.

When a professional prepares to offer testimony a considerable time after the assessment was conducted, there are at least three major aspects of the passage of time that need to be taken into account.

First, the professional needs to review carefully the test report and all documents (e.g., therapy notes and raw test data) related to it. Memory can be subtly faulty when attempts are made to recollect an assessment. The professional should be completely familiar with the report and related documents *before* arriving at the deposition. The professional's acumen, ability, judgment, and opinions may appear quite suspect if he or she must continually correct and clarify previous statements when the opposing attorney, who has likely studied the documents carefully, brings forth a succession of seemingly minor details that the professional has long since forgotten.

Second, the professional needs to ensure that his or her knowledge and expertise in the relevant areas are current. The state of the field may have changed significantly during the intervening years. Research published in peer-reviewed scientific and professional journals may have revised and refined norms, approaches, and the relevant database. Recent theory, research, and practice may have altered the context in which the original test findings are best understood.

Third, the professional needs to ensure proper acknowledgment that whatever inferences were drawn from the test data described the individual *at the time of the testing*. For example, however depressed a client may have been 5 years ago, the client may or may not be currently depressed. The professional must adequately acknowledge the possibility that the passage of time may have qualified or invalidated some (or all) of the test findings. In addition, the professional needs to avoid unwarranted assumptions that the individual's condition at the time of the testing necessarily reflected the individual's condition at an earlier time. For example, in criminal cases, the professional may be asked to examine a defendant a few days after the crime that the defendant is alleged to have committed. Such an assessment may have a variety of purposes (e.g., determining fitness to stand trial or the need for treatment before the trial). Insofar as such an evaluation may address the defendant's condition (e.g., state of mind) at the time that the crime occurred, inferences must be carefully based on the data. As Shapiro (1984) wrote,

> *The forensic clinician must never assume that the symptom picture which occurs at the time of the evaluation is the same as the symptom picture present at the time of the offense. There may be deterioration, or restitution, with the patient appearing more disturbed, or more intact, than at some time in the past. (p. 182)*

Carelessness

One of the most senseless ways an expert can participate in self-discrediting is through carelessness. MMPI forms and other test protocols need to be carefully checked to ensure that they have been scored correctly, that any columns of numbers (e.g., for MMPI clinical scales, for WAIS-R subscales, for Rorschach determinants, for Halstead–Reitan category test responses) accurately reflect the raw data, that the mathematical transformations of such numbers (e.g., adding them up for a scale or subscale value or using "correction" values) be performed without errors, that the proper norms or interpretive tables (e.g., for age on the WAIS-R) be applied, and so on. Such matters are exceptionally easy for opposing counsel (or their own experts) to check.

Even if an error—say, in adding up a clinical scale—seems to be relatively minor and virtually meaningless in the overall configuration of data, attorneys can be exceptionally effective in using the mistake as a vivid example of the fallibility, carelessness, or wrongness of an expert. Numerous questions may be put to the professional during deposition and trial to put the expert "on the spot," to focus attention on the expert's error, and to try to elicit even more damaging admissions from the distressed professional. Typical questions include the following:

- Knowing that this matter was so crucial for all parties involved in this unfortunate procedure and that you would be testifying under oath, you did not add that column of numbers carefully or even check to see if you'd made a mistake, did you?
- Did you use the same care in adding up this [incorrect] column of numbers that you did in carrying out your other so-called "assessment procedures"?
- Doctor, you have already reviewed the fees you charged for conducting the assessment. Did those

fees not include payment for you to make an effort to ensure the accuracy of the assessment?

- You have discussed the motivations of the defendant whom you evaluated, doctor. What motives did you have to write down the wrong sum on a formal report that you knew you'd be submitting to this court?
- Do you believe that in conducting this assessment you took adequate steps to ensure that the information you would be presenting to the court would be correct? [This sort of question is designed to make experts particularly uncomfortable. If they answer "yes" (i.e., that they believe that they took adequate steps to ensure that the information was correct), then they are shown to be clearly wrong because the steps they took were not adequate to detect the error. If they answer "no" (i.e., that they do not believe that they took adequate steps to detect errors), then they are probably in for a long and painful series of questions regarding why they declined to take adequate steps to ensure that the information was correct.]

Impartial and Adversarial Roles

In a trial, a judge is expected to be objective. He or she is to be impartial, not an adversary or proponent of either side (e.g., civil plaintiff and defendant or state prosecutor and criminal defendant). The role of the expert may be compared to that of the judge in this respect. The expert is offering testimony to help the jury and judge understand the issues at hand rather than to help one side or the other win the case. As forensic psychologist and clinical diplomate Herbert Weissman (1984) wrote,

> *The expert's obligation is to present material objectively and accurately, consistent with the bounds of knowledge in the given area, and to share fully with the trier of fact all that has been relied upon in the derivation of opinions, including the reasoning process upon which opinions are founded.* (p. 528)

And yet is this the type of expert that appears in court? Is this the type of expert that an attorney would actually hire to help win a case in an admittedly adversarial and often heatedly contentious process? Meier (1982; cited by Loftus, 1986) suggested otherwise: "I would go into a lawsuit with an objective, uncommitted, independent expert about as willingly as I would occupy a foxhole with a couple of non-combatant soldiers" (p. 1).

McCloskey, Egeth, and McKenna (1986) summarized the divisiveness of this issue as it was addressed in a conference on the psychologist as expert witness:

> *Most of the conference participants agreed that the most desirable role for the expert is that of impartial educator, and some held that this is the only ethically defensible position. It is clear that the law defines the role of the expert as that of an impartial educator called to assist the trier of fact. . . . Therefore, it was argued, the psychologist has the ethical responsibility to present a complete and unbiased picture of the psychological research relevant to the case at hand.*
>
> *Many conference participants disagreed, however, contending that the educator role is difficult if not impossible to maintain, both because of pressures toward advocacy from the attorneys who hire the expert, and because of a strong tendency to identify with the side for which one is working. Hence, they suggested, the psychologist should accept the realities of working within an adversary system, and seek to be a responsible advocate, presenting one side of an issue without distorting or misrepresenting the available psychological research.* (p. 5; see also Loftus, 1986; Hastie, 1986)

Despite the lack of clear unanimity in the field, what is crucial is that the expert witness be aware of the various intense, subtle pressures to distort facts and opinions. Some of the these pressures may be external. Trial attorneys, if successful, tend to be quite skilled at persuasion and influence. Far beyond the basic ability to avoid hiring an expert who will not provide a certain kind of testimony, the attorney may have an intuitive understanding of and instinctive ability to use the principles of social psychology, decision making, and so on, that many psychologists may envy. The pressures may also be internal. Some witnesses, for example, may have a desire to please the attorney or to try to be helpful.

There is nothing inherently wrong with such external and internal pressures. They are likely quite common to judicial proceedings. What is crucial is that the expert be aware of the pressures and ensure that they do not lead to a violation of the oath to tell the truth, the whole truth, and nothing but the truth. In their chapter "Therapist–Patient Sexual Intimacy on Trial: Mental Health Professional as Expert Witnesses," Pope and Bouhoutsos (1986) wrote,

> *The expert is not a hired gun, selling his or her "opinion" to the highest bidder. Nor can testimony be created or "shaped" in order to enrich a plaintiff, exonerate a defendant, or advance a purely personal point of view. The expert witness has a responsibility to fulfill the functions required by the court, and must resist all enticements—explicit or subtle, monetary, emotional, interpersonal, or ego-enhancing—to compromise this charge. (p. 137)*

Wagenaar (1988) compared the stance and role of the expert witness to that of a scientist presenting work in the context of peer-reviewed scientific journals.

> *Scientists, publishing the results of their experimental studies, will not be allowed to omit relevant parts of the literature. They would be corrected by colleagues during the process of peer evaluation. If a biased representation of the literature did slip through, it would be an error, not a result of a defendable strategy. Expert witnesses who cannot present a balanced account of the literature are not really experts. (p. 508)*

Finally, as emphasized in a previous section in this chapter on the clarification of tasks and clients, there are some situations that must be avoided altogether because they so clearly create a lack of objectivity and impartiality. The *American Bar Association Criminal Justice Mental Health Standards* (American Bar Association, 1989), for example, state clearly that "a professional who has been a defense or prosecution consultant in a given case ought not be called upon later to conduct an evaluation in that case. Under such circumstances, an objective evaluation would be impossible" (p. 12).

Words and Pictures

One of the worst occupational hazards of the professional is the tendency to think and speak in jargon. Even the simplest, most elegant ideas can be rendered ridiculous and incomprehensible if expressed in sufficiently baroque technical terms. No matter how sound the expert's opinions, he or she must—to be effective—be able to put them into words that can be clearly understood by the judge and jury. This may be difficult if the professional is used to speaking and writing jargon for an audience of other specialists who use the same jargon and understand what the words mean, or think that they understand what the words mean, or at least pretend to understand what the words mean. The witness may begin to explain the results of an MMPI-based assessment by saying something like the following:

> *The highest scales were 2 and 9. Both were at least two standard deviations above 50, but they were not statistically significantly different from each other so it is impossible to term this a 2-9 profile as opposed to a 9-2 profile—but the interpretations for the 2-9 and 9-2 would probably be isomorphic, since we have no empirical way to distinguish them. They have low profile definition. My professional opinion would be that this individual might be experiencing a unipolar or bipolar affective disorder, which may obscure or interact with or actually be the symptoms of neuropsychological impairment, so that the hypomanic symptomotology is due to somatopsychic origins such as cerebral vascular occlusions.*

The validity and meaningfulness of such a statement aside, would these words be easily comprehensible to a judge or jury who does not work with MMPI profiles and diagnostic categories on a day-to-day basis? Even some of the apparently simple terms may be quite misleading to a lay audience if the witness does not make clear which of several meanings a word is supposed to take. A "scale," for example, may be understood by many jurors as a mechanical device on which one places a letter, a human body, or a truck to determine the weight.

The expert needs to find a way to explain the basic nature of the MMPI as a foundation for testimony about a particular person's responses. Practicing such explanations not only with the attorney but also with friends who are *not* mental health professionals can be invaluable in helping an expert to describe how he or she arrived at an opinion in clear, everyday language.

Descriptions of the MMPI scales, research foundations, and specific profiles tend to become much more understandable, vivid, and memorable if they are accompanied by visual presentations. Displays can be examined by the judge and opposing attorney and marked for identification (as evidence or illustrative displays). In some states, such illustrative displays can be used by an expert witness in front of the jury if the expert testifies that the displays would aid his or her testimony. This limited use is permitted in some states even if the displays are not technically admissible *as* evidence because they are not actually admitted into evidence. They are used just to illustrate the testimony and are not taken into the jury room during deliberations.

Allowing judge and jury to see the array of validity, clinical, and content scales, the "average" responses of those in the normative groups as well as those in specific populations (e.g., patients with chronic pain, patients who have been hospitalized for schizophrenia, or successful applicants for managerial positions), and a specific individual's (e.g., a plaintiff or defendant) profile for comparison and contrast can provide a clarity and concreteness that may not be possible through use of words alone.

If the witness is able to present the information in a well-organized sequence, judge and jurors may be fascinated to learn exactly how a standardized psychological test works. In such instances, the expert witness is fulfilling the central responsibility of the testimony: helping the triers of fact to understand facts and issues that tend to lie outside the knowledge of the lay public.

The MMPI is ideal for such visual demonstrations. Available with this book are transparencies (for use with an overhead projector) showing some of the fundamental profiles of and information about the MMPI, MMPI-2, and MMPI-A (see appendix I). The profile that is at issue in the trial may be copied onto one of the blank transparencies. As an alternative, large graphic displays in the form of posters may be used for this purpose.

Listening

Good cross-examiners tend to be those who listen exceptionally well (e.g., Brodsky, 1991; Pope & Bouhoutsos, 1986). They attend to and exploit the lack of precision that all of us display when we try to express ourselves without reading from a script. They amplify and play with ambiguity, the ambiguity in the expert's responses and the ambiguity with which they may frame many of their questions. They listen to what we say, not what we intended to say. They hear what we said, not what we thought we said. As they pose a new question, they repeat what we said just a few minutes earlier, but the wording may be slightly different, the intonation and implication sending the meaning off in a different direction.

The person who testifies effectively and genuinely helps the judge and jury to understand the facts and issues tends to be someone who listens well during both direct and cross-examination. The attorney and the expert may have discussed at length exactly what the direct examination questions will be. The expert may have planned each response carefully. Yet attorneys may often wander from the intended path during the direct examination. In some instances, it may be because he or she is working from notes, and in rewording a question, the intended meaning shifts. In other instances, recent developments in the trial (e.g., testimony presented by the other side) may have made it necessary for the attorney to cover new ground with the expert, without having a chance to discuss these matters in adequate detail in advance. In still other instances, the judge may have sustained objections to certain questions or lines of questioning that had been planned in advance, forcing the attorney to improvise.

In all instances, the expert witness must listen carefully to each direct examination question. The recitation of prepared answers to questions that they no longer quite fit tends to confuse the jury and discredit the expert. Experts may gain exceptional credibility in spontaneous moments during which an attorney conducting direct examination reformulates a prepared question, unintentionally giving it a different meaning. The expert gives an answer that was not anticipated by the attorney, who registers, however subtly, surprise. In other instances, an attorney may try to lead an expert to provide "stronger" (in the sense of being favorable to the attorney's case) answers than the expert can justify. In such spontaneous moments, the expert may give the "wrong" answer (in the sense that it is not the answer that the attorney wanted or expected), and in subsequent examination the attorney and witness may appear to be arguing with one another, the attorney attempting to get the witness to acknowledge a point, the witness refusing to cooperate. To the degree that such moments are genuinely spontaneous, the jury may glimpse the independence and integrity of the witness in a way that is not obvious during the more rote portions of direct examination. Viewing the witness as a credible and significant source of information, the jury may find the professional more helpful in sorting out and understanding the facts and issues.

Similarly, the expert witness must listen with exceptional care to the questions during cross-examination (and to any questions that the judge may ask). If the question is not completely understood, the witness must ask for the question to be repeated or for adequate clarification. An alternative approach is for the witness to begin a response along the following lines: "If I understand correctly that you are asking [clarification or restatement of the question], then my answer is. . . ." Shapiro (1991) provides an example of a witness who listens carefully to a question and recognizes the many meanings that the word *validity* can have.

Attorney: Now then, Doctor, hasn't research shown that the MMPI is invalid?

Expert: I really cannot answer that question; would you be able to define what you mean by validity?

Attorney: Come now, you're a doctor, don't you know what validity is?

Expert: Certainly, Counselor, but there is predictive validity, construct validity, and face validity, to name only a few. You will have to define your terms more precisely before I can respond to the question.

Attorney: I withdraw the question. (p. 215)

Cognitive Processes Encouraging Error

However expert and professional the witness may be, he or she is still human. Errors are always possible. As noted above, carelessness is one factor that can make errors more likely. There are certain cognitive processes—typical ways that humans tend to think about or handle information—that may, if unacknowledged and neglected, tend to encourage errors.

Many of these cognitive processes are versions of a very human tendency to enter into what is known as a *cognitive set* and to view all additional information in terms of that set. A simple example of this tendency are the various series of childhood questions and answers in which the initial questions form a particular cognitive set and later lead to a wrong answer to a very easy question. For instance, one elementary school child may ask another the following:

> *How do you pronounce [spelling the letters]: M-a-c-D-o-n-a-l-d?*
> *How do you pronounce: M-a-c-H-e-n-r-y?*
> *How do you pronounce: M-a-c-D-o-u-g-l-e?*
> *How do you pronounce: M-a-c-H-i-n-e?*

The other child, having formed, through answering the first three questions, a cognitive set in which the letters seem to spell a Scottish name with the prefix pronounced as if it were "mack" will often use the same "mack" pronunciation for the final word, at which time the questioner laughs and points out that he or she has spelled the common word "machine."

Clients who take the MMPI may fall into such cognitive sets for responding. For example, some clients may tend to respond "no" to most questions, regardless of the content. For this reason, their profiles may not be valid, and the MMPI scoring keys have ways of identifying such responders (see chapters 2 and 6).

Those who conduct assessments must also be aware of their own tendencies to form cognitive sets that promote errors in making inferences about the individual who is being assessed. Chanowitz and Langer (1981), for example, found research evidence supporting the concept of *premature cognitive commitment*. Psychologist Ellen Langer (1989; see also Langer & Piper, 1987), professor at Harvard University, provided a concise description of the concept:

> *Another way that we become mindless is by forming a mindset when we first encounter something and then clinging to it when we reencounter that same thing. Because such mindsets form before we do much reflection, we call them* premature cognitive commitments. *(p. 22)*

Such premature cognitive commitment is evident in the childhood question and answer example cited earlier: The first encounter with the prefix "mac" forms a mindset that words beginning with m-a-c are various Scottish proper names. The tendency to use such a small chunk of information as if it meant the same thing in all contexts—forgetting other possible alternatives—can have profound implications for misdiagnosing individuals. Irving Weiner (1989), for example, noted the unfounded tendency of at least one professional to assume that a certain response to a certain Rorschach card inevitably indicates that the person is a victim of child sexual abuse (see the section on interpretation in chapter 8).

Describing similar examples, psychologist Robyn Dawes (1988b; see also Dickman & Sechrest, 1985) cited a university admissions committee's consideration of what seems to be an exceptionally well-qualified, highly sought applicant in engineering. One comment—in which a misspelling seems to be understood as a phenomenon that could only be a symptom of dyslexia—seemed to influence critically the view of this application.

> *Amy's high school loves her, and she wants to study engineering. Brown badly wants engineering students; unfortunately, Amy spells engineering wrong. "Dyslexia," says Jimmy Wren, a linguistics professor. After some debate, the committee puts her on the waiting list. (p. 152)*

The potential power of such cognitive sets to encourage error is magnified by the fact that in so many assessments, certain "facts" are known to the clinician that seem to offer a predetermined confirmation of a certain diagnosis or finding. As an extreme example, consider an expert witness reviewing records and providing testimony about a therapy client who committed suicide. Because the clinician already knows that the individual killed him- or herself, previous test and historical data may be interpreted retrospectively in light of this information, perhaps in a biased and unjustifiable manner (e.g., that the previous test results were clearly predictive of imminent suicide). Arkes, Saville, Wortmann, and Harkness (1981), for example, conducted research indicating that if professionals were given a symptom pattern, various alternative diagnoses, *and* the supposedly correct diagnosis, the professionals tended to overestimate significantly the probability that they would have chosen the correct diagnosis had they only known the symptom patterns and the diagnostic alternatives. This phenomenon is known as *hindsight bias*.

> *Those who know an event has occurred may claim that had they been asked to predict the event in advance, they would have been very likely to do so. In fact, people with hindsight knowledge do assign higher probability estimates to an event than those who must predict the event without the advantage of that knowledge. (Arkes et al., 1981, p. 252)*

A fascinating example of how a "known fact" can—through hindsight—influence interpretation of a broad array of other information is Freud's application of the principles of psychoanalysis to understanding the life of Leonardo da Vinci (Coles, 1973a, 1973b; see also Fischoff, 1982). The key to Freud's analysis was da Vinci's account of how, as an infant, he was touched on the lips by a vulture that swooped down out of the sky.

Freud's astonishing breadth of knowledge led him to recognize that, in Egyptian, the hieroglyph for "vulture" is the same as that for "mother." From this fundamental observation, Freud conducted an incisive and insightful psychoanalysis of da Vinci, about whose younger years there was virtually no other illuminating information. The analysis seemed to spring from and cohere through da Vinci's recollection of an event that seemed to represent themes concerning an intimate relationship with his mother.

It was only later discovered that the translation Freud had been using had contained an error. The Italian word for "kite" had been mistakenly translated into the German word for "vulture"; it was a kite, rather than a vulture, that had caressed da Vinci's lips as he lay in his cradle.

The potential power of cognitive sets to encourage error is magnified not only by hindsight bias but also by social influence and group process. A clinician who has conducted a psychological assessment and is attempting to make sense of the findings may be consciously or unconsciously influenced by the knowledge, which is based on a review of previous records of assessment and treatment, that at least three other clinicians have all agreed that the individual is suffering from a particular disorder (e.g., borderline personality disorder or posttraumatic stress disorder). The clinician may also be influenced by the fact that the individual and the individual's attorneys concur that a particular diagnosis or explanatory agent is relevant.

Solomon Asch (1956) was one of the first to conduct extensive research showing the sometimes uncanny ability of group pressure to influence individual decision making. More recently, Professor Irving Janis of Yale University (1972; see also Janis, 1982; Janis & Mann, 1977) explored the ways in which collaboration on certain types of decision making may tend to prematurely close off options and encourage a consensus that may not be warranted by the evidence.

Yet a third factor—in addition to hindsight bias and social influences—that can magnify the power of cognitive sets to encourage errors is *confirmation bias*. If a professional begins an assessment with a particular understanding of the client (perhaps including the likely diagnosis and etiology) or reaches such an understanding early on, the subsequent aspects of assessment may be severely biased. The choice of subsequent tests, interviews, and other sources, as well as the ways in which the resulting data are interpreted, may be shaped by a clinician's hypothesis to such a degree that it is virtually impossible or at least highly unlikely that the clinician will not find confirming data.

> *Confirmation bias is perhaps the best known and most widely accepted notion of inferential error to have come out of the literature on human reasoning. The claim . . . is that human beings have a fundamental tendency to seek information consistent with their current beliefs, theories or hypotheses and to avoid the collection of potentially falsifying evidence.* (Evans, 1989, p. 41)

Although potentially powerful, these cognitive processes that encourage error need not prevent an expert from reaching a valid opinion that is based on adequate evidence. What is crucial is that the expert remain constantly aware of and alert to these sources of bias and error and, when possible and appropriate, take steps to ensure that they are not interfering with fair and solidly based testimony.

Attempts to Be Funny

It is hard to be critical of humor. Gentle, self-deprecating humor can humanize an expert, showing that he or she—while taking the work *very* seriously—does not take him- or herself too seriously. Humor can make a point in a pleasant, vivid, and memorable way. It can relieve the tension that has built up during vigorous adversarial cross-examination.

But attempts at humor during testimony can just as often lead to disaster. One rule that expert witnesses may want to consider and possibly adopt is draconian: Never make a joke or a flip comment during a deposition. The temptation can be overwhelming. Opposing attorneys, sensing that an inexperienced witness may be naive, will do their best to create an informal atmosphere in which it appears that colleagues are just sitting around a table discussing various facts and opinions. What they hope that the witness does not recognize or eventually forgets is that all depositions are formal proceedings in which the witness is giving testimony under oath that will result in a written record. The witness may see an opportunity (often carefully and subtly created by the examining attorney) to make a joke, say something witty, use a clever and ironic turn of phrase, or speak sarcastically.

However funny, ironic, or clever such spontaneous utterances may be at the time, they will almost certainly lack all humor when the attorney reads them back to the witness in the courtroom in front of the jury. Almost everyone recognizes the principle that transporting humor from one setting to another is a difficult task; as so many after-dinner raconteurs have defensively explained after telling what had seemed to them so funny: "Well, you had to be there." The jury will *not* have been there. They will not have been present in what may have *seemed* the casual and relaxed atmosphere of the deposition. The attorney can be trusted to read the witness's words back with minimal context and with a very different inflection. No witness needs to go through the ordeal of sitting in court and explaining what must seem an unwarranted, bizarre, or mystifying comment by saying something such as, "Oh, I was just making a joke."

Expert witnesses need to take special care to avoid irony or sarcasm during depositions. In conversation, irony or sarcasm is generally made clear through vocal inflection and physical demeanor, neither of which will come through when the cross-examining attorney reads verbatim from a deposition transcript. As an exaggerated example, an exasperated deponent, having spent hours enduring savage questioning about the apparent lack of care in conducting a forensic assessment, may exclaim in bitter sarcasm, "I was obviously *trying* to be careless!" Those words can never be called back but are now part of the permanent record of the trial and may, if the deponent frequently testifies, be made available by the opposing attorney to attorneys in future cases in which the expert is to participate.

Even in the courtroom, where the witness can assess the mood of the jury and the jury in turn can see the demeanor and hear the inflection of the witness, humor can be extremely risky. However gentle and well meaning a joke made by a witness seems at the time, a skilled attorney tends to have a varied arsenal for turning the spontaneous comment to his or her advantage. In a criminal trial, for example, an expert may make what seems a perfectly appropriate and innocuous humorous comment, and virtually everyone in the courtroom may laugh. The attorney conducting cross-examination may pause until all laughter has died away, and then continues the pause. A *long* silence ensues. Finally, the attorney may ask the expert something along the lines of, "Do you think your assessment of the defendant is a fit subject for joking?"

Basically, the witness pondering this question has three options. First, he or she may answer "yes," an answer that will, when pursued by a skilled attorney, have some obvious disadvantages for the witness. Second, he or she may answer "no," inviting jurors and the attorney to reflect on his or her subsequent explanations about why, if the topic of the trial is not an occasion for joking, the expert used it as an occasion for joking. Third, the witness may attempt an elaborate and probably defensive explanation about how nothing was meant by the joke (which will probably be objected to by the attorney as nonresponsive to the question), about how humor has its place in even the most serious situations, and so on. Even if the witness offers a skilled theoretical exposition of justification, the attorney has succeeded in diverting attention from the expert's professional opinions. In other words, the attorney (with the help of the witness) has managed to change the subject.

Presenting clearly the results of a complex psychological and neuropsychological assessment is enough of a challenge for even the most skilled and seasoned expert witness without being forced to discuss unexpected and confusing side issues (e.g., the expert's joking about the case at hand) that are likely to make the task of helping the jury to understand difficult issues even more difficult. Trial attorney Louis Nizer provided a vivid case study of a professional comedian's attempts to be funny on the witness stand with disastrous results (see Nizer, 1961, chapter 3, pp. 233–286).

Aphasia–Agnosia

Aphasia and *agnosia* are two terms defined in the Glossary of this book and commonly used in reports of neuropsychological assessment. Aphasia indicates an inability to say something; agnosia indicates that one lacks knowledge in a certain area. As we apply this compound technical term to the expert witness, we are describing the condition in which the witness finds it all but impossible to say the words "I don't know" or to answer candidly that some subject matter is outside his or her realm of expertise.

Witnesses may be afflicted with this condition for all sorts of reasons. Some may not want to undermine their testimony by acknowledging that they are not experts in all areas relevant to the case. Some may not want to appear "dumb." Some may allow themselves to be seduced and manipulated by a skilled and prepared attorney who as part of deposition and cross-examination subtly leads the expert farther and farther from an area of genuine expertise and toward more and more grandiose claims of omniscience and infallibility.

Attorney Melvin Belli of San Francisco wrote of one of his *unsuccessful* cross-examinations. He was facing a modest and unassuming cardiologist who had provided solid testimony during direct examination. Again and again, Belli tried to draw him into areas in which he was not an expert. Each time, the expert refused to take the bait. According to Belli,

> *[the expert] refused to stray into any other field. When I asked him a question about gastroenterology, he replied, "I don't claim expertise in that area. I'm here as an expert on cardiology."*
>
> *"But you're an internist," I persisted. "Aren't all internists familiar with both cardiology and gastroenterology?"*
>
> *"Yes . . . but we don't claim to know all about them. . . ."*
>
> *"Well, . . . when you graduated from medical school . . ., didn't you think you knew all about medicine?"*
>
> *"Yes, I did . . . however, that was 30 years ago. Every medical student thinks he knows all about medicine when he graduates." (Belli & Carlova, 1986, p. 159)*

Belli described how the modest, thoughtful manner of the expert won over the jury. The expert's lack of a "know-it-all" attitude kept Belli from "scoring points" with the jury. Belli notes that he [Belli] lost this case.

The Wish to Star

The previously mentioned pitfalls are generally those of the ill-prepared expert or the professional who is new to the courtroom and is nervous and does not really know what to expect, making mistakes that are due to lack of knowledge, experience, and confidence. But there is a hazard that may be more often associated with those who are exceptionally knowledgeable, experienced, and confident: A very human tendency to want to be the center of attention *for the whole trial*, to be the star witness whose testimony overshadows and overwhelms the rest of the proceedings.

Anyone may be vulnerable to such feelings (or similar impulses), but the expert who lets these feelings influence his or her work, participation, opinions, and testimony almost certainly fails the crucial responsibility to be truthful and helpful to the triers of fact. Some may try to dictate trial strategy (e.g., what issues will be presented and what witnesses are to be called in what order) to the attorney who has retained him or her.

Such efforts—which subtly or not-so-subtly attempt to shape the proceedings in such a way that the expert is the powerful star and seeming raison d'etre of the proceedings—can be devastatingly counterproductive. For example, there is evidence that at least in some types of trials, it is far preferable to present and organize evidence or testimony in terms of a comprehensive "story" than in terms of witness-by-witness presentations (Pennington & Hastie, 1981, 1988, 1991, 1992; see the section Opening Statement and Presenting Witnesses in chapter 5 of this volume).

> *Ease of story construction mediates [jurors'] perceptions of evidence strength, judgments of confidence, and the impact of information about witness credibility. . . . When evidence is organized by stories, subjects make more decisions in the story direction compared with when the evidence is organized by witness. . . . A narrative* story sequence *is the most effective "order of proof" at trial. (Pennington & Hastie, 1992, pp. 202–203)*

The star witness's efforts to control trial strategy may prevent the emergence of such stories, the expert construing him- or herself as the central organizing force and focus for all evidence. Similarly, the star may offer testimony in such a way that the focus is on the expert rather than on what the expert has to say, how what the expert has to say can be helpful to the judge and jury in their tasks, and how what the expert has to say may fit into a coherent story or constellation.

Moreover, a relentless striving to star may make an expert witness much more vulnerable to effective cross-examination. The star may try to "win" all conflicts with the attorney conducting the cross-examination, may attempt to demonstrate cleverness and perhaps infallibility, and may strive to show that he or she is superior to opposing counsel. The counsel may subtly invite the expert to inflate expertise and claims, may try to outargue the expert, may try to one-up the witness in such a way that the witness finds it easy to "top" the attorney with a devastating rejoinder, and so on.

The witness may glory in the combat, registering every win with a smile and redoubling efforts to prevail with every minor misstep. What the judge and jury may accurately perceive, however, is someone who has lost sight of the task and responsibility of the expert, someone who has become hopelessly biased, someone who focuses on prevailing and starring rather than on honestly trying to answer both direct and cross-examination questions fully and honestly, and someone whose opinions and testimonies probably are not to be taken very seriously.

SUMMARY

Nothing invites disaster for the expert witness quite so reliably as lack of adequate preparation. The witness may need to spend many hours preparing for each hour he or she is deposed or testifies in court. A vigorous, informed, and skilled deposition or cross-examination conducted by the opposing attorney will expose seemingly minor shortcuts, oversights, and bits of unfinished business that may have overwhelming significance for the witness's credibility and effectiveness.

This chapter sought to organize the complex sequences of tasks, clients, issues, and responsibilities faced by the expert witness into a coherent set of practical steps that the witness can take to ensure proper preparation. There are three major sets of such steps.

The first set ensures that the initial contacts with the attorney who seeks the expert's services result (if the attorney decides to retain the expert and if the expert decides to work for the attorney) in a well-defined working agreement that clearly addresses such issues as identifying the tasks and clients, ensuring adequate competence or expertise, clarifying channels of communication, disclosing relevant information, specifying financial arrangements, identifying and avoiding potential conflicts of interest, and creating a reasonable schedule for conducting the work and, if necessary, testifying in court.

The second set of steps helps ensure that a forensic assessment is conducted in such a way that meets the highest ethical, legal, and professional standards. These steps involve reviewing the issues and literature relevant to the assessment, carefully choosing tests and assessment strategies that are appropriate for the assessment tasks and the individuals to be assessed, thinking about tests in their historical and cultural context, obtaining informed consent, creating adequate documentation, assessing factors (e.g., the individual's vision, hearing, and language abilities) that may affect the assessment process and inferences from test results, adequately monitoring all phases of testing, responding to critical or emergency situations, and writing a forensic report (which is addressed in chapter 7).

Once the expert witness has been employed by the attorney (or appointed by the court), the assessment has been conducted, and the forensic report completed, the expert witness now takes the third set of steps to prepare for deposition and courtroom testimony. These steps involve systematically addressing factors that tend to interfere with an expert's ability to present information clearly, accurately, and helpfully. Such factors include lack of adequate familiarity with forensic settings and procedures, the gap of time between completing the forensic assessment and testifying about the results of the assessment, carelessness, the tension between impartial and adversarial roles, the methods by which the expert attempts to communicate his or her findings and opinions, difficulties in listening carefully, cognitive processes that encourage errors of inference, a persistent inability of some experts to answer a question with the words "I don't know," and the wish to be a courtroom star.

Even the most experienced expert witnesses can benefit by using such systematic sequences of preparatory steps as a checklist. Conducting psychological and neuropsychological assessments and presenting the findings clearly in court is certainly no less complex an activity than flying a plane. Even the most experienced aviators use a checklist when making even the most routine flight. Because some of the steps in preparing to testify or to fly seem so easy, minor, and routine, the individuals taking those steps—being human and thus prone to human error—can forget a small but critical step unless using a checklist. As a final self-test to ensure that preparation has been adequate, the expert witness can review each of the deposition and cross-examination questions presented in chapter 8.

CHAPTER 5

THE ATTORNEY PREPARES AND PRESENTS

One of the most fundamental principles emphasized in this book for attorneys and expert witnesses alike is adequate preparation. Preparing to present and confront expert testimony using MMPI results requires the same diligence and work as any other aspect of the attorney's case. Fundamental to any use of the MMPI in trials is a commitment to the integrity of the case at issue. To achieve that commitment, the attorney must prepare in such a way that he or she not only understands the evidence and arguments to be put forth on behalf of the client but also anticipates the opposition's assumptions, approach, and documentation.

To illustrate the essential elements of preparation, this chapter discusses preparation from the point of view of a plaintiff's attorney in personal injury litigation involving psychological damages. Special problems inherent in the discovery in a criminal case are discussed later in this chapter.

The preparation described assumes that the case is scheduled to be tried by jury and that the issues include psychological damages. However, any litigation preparation—civil or criminal, prosecution or defense—requires the same fundamental understanding of and commitment to the strongest possible presentation of the case. This chapter specifically addresses preparation for hiring experts, pretrial motions, voir dire questions, opening statements, trial exhibits, and closing arguments. The first step in this preparation is pretrial research.

BACKGROUND RESEARCH

In this chapter, a personal injury case involving psychological damages illustrates the extensive research and discovery essential to almost any case involving the MMPI. After carefully obtaining the client's version of events and supportive documentation, the attorney needs to ensure that he or she is adequately familiar with the MMPI as a standardized psychological test (see chapter 2), with its legal history and context (see chapter 3), and with fundamental technical knowledge about evaluating, administering, scoring, and interpreting psychological tests (see chapters 4 and 8).

The attorney must be familiar with the MMPI items as well as the rationale behind the test, and its nature, reliability, and limitations. Taken alone and out of the context of the test (e.g., the MMPI scales), a response to a single MMPI item may be of questionable psychometric validity. The response to the item remains, however, a statement by the individual who took the MMPI. That statement may enhance or contradict other testimony. For example, the individual's responses to MMPI items about nightmares or suicide attempts may contradict the individual's deposition testimony about these experiences.

The lawyer reads the actual test items (see appendix F). Literally thousands of articles about the various forms of the MMPI have been published in respected, peer-reviewed scientific and professional journals. Although this book provides fundamental information about MMPI theory, research, and practice, the attorney (or an expert retained by the attorney) will need to conduct a literature search (perhaps beginning with some of the review articles cited in this book) to locate MMPI articles directly relevant to the case at issue. The successful attorney reviews—perhaps working with an expert consultant—this literature and its application to the case. To the extent that the attorney is unfamiliar with the test and the relevant literature published in peer-reviewed journals, he or she is inadequately prepared to try a case involving the MMPI.

RETAINING AN EXPERT

Retaining an expert may make the task of conducting background research, as outlined in the previous section, much easier. Moreover, expert testimony may significantly influence the outcome of a trial (see, e.g., Raitz, Greene, Goodman, & Loftus, 1990).

The initial sections of chapter 8 present areas of deposition and cross-examination questions for opposing experts, some of which focus on criteria for assessing competence. The attorney should evaluate the expert he or she is considering retaining in terms of the *same* criteria. The attorney needs to ensure that the professional has adequate education, training, credentials, and experience for the issues central to the case at hand (see also the section on competence in chapter 4). In addition, by reviewing chapter 4 ("The Expert Witness Prepares and Presents"), the attorney can supplement his or her understanding of the MMPI with a detailed understanding of the steps an expert witness must take in preparing for and conducting a forensic examination. This understanding will be invaluable to the attorney in communicating with and screening potential expert witnesses.

If the potential expert witness is a psychologist, the attorney can determine whether he or she obtained a doctorate from a graduate program accredited by the APA, whether an APA-accredited internship was completed, whether the individual is an APA fellow, and whether he or she is a diplomate of the American Board of Professional Psychology (again, see the section on competence in chapter 4; see also appendix C-2).

If the potential expert is a psychiatrist, the attorney should determine if all medical training institutions, including internships and residencies, were fully accredited, if the expert is certified by the American Board of Psychiatry and Neurology, and if he or she is certified as an expert witness by the American Board of Forensic Psychiatry. The initial sections of chapter 8 (on deposing and cross-examining expert witnesses) set forth other criteria for the attorney to review in choosing his or her own expert (e.g., occupational history, record of research, and authorship of articles relevant to the case that have been published in peer-reviewed scientific and professional journals).

Most experts have a curriculum vitae or other summary of qualifications that can be submitted to the (potentially) hiring attorney as an aid in answering these questions. Any expert who wants to make him- or herself available to a specific attorney should be willing to give candid and fully detailed answers to the full range of questions outlined in the initial sections of chapter 8.

The attorney may want to take some steps to verify independently some of this information. In cases in which the expert has been identified and endorsed by opposing counsel, transcripts may be subpoenaed from educational institutions; other documents can also be secured to verify the claims made by the expert. As noted in chapter 8, some "experts" have been known to exaggerate or simply invent qualifications. For example, one expert claimed to have been deemed by a prominent professional association to be one of the foremost authorities in a particular area. Careful research by the opposing attorney discovered that the professional association had made no such claim.

It is far preferable to discover the reliability of an expert's curriculum vitae and other claims *before* deciding whether to hire (or at least before the other attorney shows the unreliability of such claims during a sworn deposition or in court testimony in front of the jury). As emphasized in chapter 8, the fact that a professional has impressive credentials, is employed by a prestigious university or other institution, has a national or international reputation, or has testified frequently as an expert witness is no guarantee that claims about education, credentials, publications, and so on, are accurate.

Once credentials have been checked, the attorney needs to know if the expert can help the jury understand—on an emotional as well as an intellectual level—what happened to the client and how it relates to the issues before the court. Is the expert able to organize complex material and present it in everyday language? Can the expert help the jury to learn the connection between responses on an MMPI protocol and the client's experience? Some experts may have a thorough understanding of psychometric theory and practice but are unable to put it into language understandable to those who have not won a Nobel prize in mathematics. Some may be able to talk about tests clearly but are unable to help jurors get to know and understand the client's condition. The expert who gives a vivid, specific, and compelling description will be much more likely to help the jury to follow the client's story and to understand the client's experience.

If the attorney decides to retain an expert, the agreement should be adequately specific regarding such aspects as responsibilities, fees, scheduling, preparation of forensic reports (see chapter 7), and so on. The agreement should also be written to help guard against misunderstandings or faulty memory (see appendix A). There should be adequate discussion to prevent or at least minimize the chance that a conflict of interest (e.g., regarding the relationship of the expert to the opposing party or attorney in the case) is present or will emerge. Because the aspects of initial attorney–expert contacts and agreements are discussed in chapter 4, they are not repeated here.

The fact that an expert has been hired to evaluate MMPI results does not mean that the expert should be called to testify.[1] Fundamental questions to make this determination include the following:

1. Will the MMPI results help the judge or jury understand facts or theories at issue in the case?
2. Are the MMPI results consistent with the attorney's theory of the case?
3. If the MMPI results are inconsistent, is there a reason for the inconsistency?
4. Will the MMPI results confuse the judge or jury?

DOCUMENT PRODUCTION

Once the attorney has a fundamental understanding of (a) the client's version of events, (b) all supportive documentation that the client is able to supply, (c) the nature and function of the MMPI as it is relevant to the case, (d) the relevant diagnostic frameworks and categories, and (e) the expert's opinions and role (or roles) if one or more experts have been retained, *all* remaining available information concerning the case that is the subject of the litigation is obtained. This information is obtained through releases executed by the client, subpoenas, litigation procedures such as requests for production of documents, and depositions of the professionals involved.

All jurisdictions permit the parties to a civil litigation to inspect and copy any relevant designated documents that are not otherwise privileged. Some states require that the court order production of documents. Other states dictate that most routine document production occur without court intervention. Statutes or procedural rules of each jurisdiction control the timing of document production, inspection, and copying. Documents in control of persons other than the parties involved are generally not subject to the same rules concerning production of documents. In those cases, the records are obtained through a subpoena duces tecum, more commonly called a *subpoena to produce*.

In each case, the production request or subpoena lists both generally and specifically the documents requested. The term *document* is defined broadly to include any written material, correspondence, testing material, testing results (whether hand or computer scored), memoranda, audio tape recordings, video tape recordings, computer recordings (whether printed or otherwise stored), photographs, ledgers, and notes. Many of these documents are requested generally and then again specifically to ensure their production.

The documents requested of any expert who evaluates an MMPI include a comprehensive list of possible original documents to be copied. In the following hypothetical case, Ms. Mary Smith is suing Dr. A. Acme. Dr. Jones was retained by Dr. Acme's attorney to conduct a psychological evaluation of Ms. Smith using an MMPI. The subpoena duces tecum asked for all materials related to the administration, scoring, and evaluation of the MMPI, as well as to all consultations. The subpoena specifically enumerated materials as follows:

1. Dr. Jones's entire original file pertaining to the psychological examination (evaluation) of Mary

[1] As mentioned in the Preface, unless the context indicates otherwise, the term *MMPI* is frequently used—as in this passage—in a generic sense to refer to all three versions of the test (i.e., MMPI, MMPI-2, and MMPI-A).

Smith and any psychological testing, including but not limited to testing materials and results of the MMPI or any version of the MMPI.

2. All notes of conversations with any person, including Mary Smith or any person consulted in connection with this case or the examination (evaluation) of Mary Smith and any psychological testing, including but not limited to the MMPI or any version of the MMPI.
3. All scorings, computerized scorings, and hand scorings of any and all psychological tests or assessment instruments, including but not limited to the MMPI or any version of the MMPI.
4. All psychological testing documents for Mary Smith, including the original completed examinations (i.e., the actual answer form), score sheets, and notes written by Mary Smith or anyone else in connection with the testing.
5. All MMPI testing documents for Mary Smith, including the original completed examination, score sheets, and notes.
6. All documents that were reviewed in connection with your examination (evaluation) of Mary Smith or any aspect of the case of *Smith v. Acme*.
7. All reports and drafts of reports prepared in connection with your examination (evaluation) of Mary Smith or your evaluation in the case of *Smith v. Acme*.
8. A list of all documents, including computer-scored or computer-generated information, that you reviewed or wrote or that you discussed with any person in connection with your examination (evaluation) of Mary Smith or the evaluation of her MMPI testing, regardless of whether these documents are still in your possession.
9. The original file folders in which any information regarding Mary Smith is or has been stored.
10. All calendars that refer to appointments with Mary Smith or any person with whom you discussed the evaluation of Mary Smith or the case of *Smith v. Acme*.
11. All billing statements and payment records.
12. All correspondence with any person in any way relating to the case of *Smith v. Acme*.
13. All video tape recordings or audio tape recordings of or pertaining to Mary Smith.
14. The witness's curriculum vitae; a list of all articles, papers, chapters, books, or other documents he or she has written or published; a list of all articles, papers, chapters, books, or other documents, materials, or sources of information that he or she relied on in forming expert opinions regarding the matters at issue; transcripts from all institutions of higher learning attended by the expert; a list of all legal cases in which the expert has been endorsed in the last 5 years; a list of all attorneys and their addresses for each case in which the expert has been endorsed; and, in some cases, a copy of the expert's dissertation (thesis).
15. The originals of all correspondence, notes of conversations, and documents between and among the expert witness, attorneys (who retained the expert), representatives, and consultants of the attorneys in any way related to the case.

The original file (see Item 9 above), including the original file folder, is requested because short scribbled notes or notes on the reverse sides of documents can provide a wealth of information that might be missed when copies are requested. (See chapter 8 for deposition questions addressing the production, completeness, nature, and integrity of subpoenaed items.)

DEPOSITIONS

In civil litigation proceedings, depositions generally follow production of documents. A deposition is testimony taken under oath before any trial. A structured guide to important areas of deposition (which, if appropriate, may later become the basis of cross-examination in court) is presented in chapter 8. Although some attorneys may approach depositions and cross-examinations with the sole objective of, in Walter's (1982) words, "destroying the opponent's expert witness" (p. 10), a better strategy includes at least two (additional or alternative) tasks: (a) learning from the expert in such a way that the opposing attorney can better understand his or her own client and case and (b) assessing whether the opposing expert's testimony might be beneficial to one's own case. Walter (1982) presents examples of this latter approach.

PRETRIAL MOTIONS

To the extent practical, any questions about the admissibility of evidence are resolved before the jury is seated. If there is any question about the admissibility of test results because of novelty, that question should be addressed before the jury is seated by a motion in limine. (A motion in limine is made before the trial begins to limit certain types of evidence.) Interruptions, unless planned to alter the pace of the trial, are counterproductive.

Pretrial motions have another benefit, particularly in criminal cases. In the states that allow formal discovery, including depositions in criminal cases, the procedure outlined in this chapter can be used to obtain the expert's opinion and foundation for that opinion. However, many states do not routinely allow discovery depositions to be taken in criminal cases. Where depositions are not allowed, other court proceedings can provide much of the information. For example, a defense attorney may attack the validity and admissibility of the MMPI testing under F.R.E. Rule 702 and F.R.E. Rule 703.

The evidentiary hearing on the MMPI's validity allows an adequately prepared attorney to learn much of the information that could have been obtained through the civil discovery process. The subpoena duces tecum to the opposing expert witness should include all of the items identified in this chapter. The inquiry itself, however, is changed somewhat because the judge actually presides at the hearing, and the judge often severely restricts questioning. Therefore, the areas that seem most important (or least likely to be discovered through methods other than deposition) must be asked first. When the court restricts examination, the attorney, through offer of proof, explains on the record why the information is essential to adequately defend the client from the state's criminal allegations. A well-prepared, well-reasoned, and well-documented offer of proof may obtain extended inquiry.

The forensic use of any psychological testing requires that the attorney understand both the test administered and the results suggested by the test. A familiarity with the questions asked in the test as well as their general purpose in the evaluation process can help the attorney to understand, address, and exclude any incompatible testing results. For example, answering "true" to the following MMPI-2 questions might be construed to suggest problems with alcohol or drug use:

- I have had periods in which I carried on activities without knowing later what I had been doing. (true)
- I have had blank spells in which my activities were interrupted and I did not know what was going on around me. (true)

If the person tested had been suffering from psychosis or epilepsy, this interpretation might be wrong. The circumstances need to be considered by a competent clinician. This example highlights the difficulties in attempting to rely on a single response to an individual item and the crucial importance of obtaining and reviewing records of previous assessment and treatment. If a test interpretation is detrimental to the case, the attorney should ask the court before the trial to exclude the evidence because it is untrustworthy and likely to lead to confusion.

VOIR DIRE

First impressions are always important. Research has shown that first impressions with jurors are lasting and difficult to reverse (e.g., Kelven & Zeisel, 1966). In those jurisdictions that allow the attorneys to question the jury, the voir dire process gives attorneys the opportunity to create a strong first impression both for themselves and for their case. (Voir dire is the process of questioning potential jurors to determine which ones will be accepted as jurors for the trial and which ones will be excluded.)

The theme of an effective case presentation is developed early and followed through voir dire, opening statement, direct and cross-examination of witnesses, and closing arguments. A good theme is simple and is consistent with and supported by the evidence.

Voir dire has three general purposes: (a) to establish rapport between the attorney and the jurors; (b) to obtain information from the jurors in order to separate those jurors who are most likely to accept the theme from those who should be challenged; and (c) to educate the jurors about the case. The second and third purposes are particularly important when MMPI results or psychological testimony form an essential part of the case that the jury will hear.

In cases that involve substantial psychological testimony, the voir dire process is planned to identify the jurors who will accept the advocate's case. Many jurors distrust psychological testimony. Many distrust therapists and other clinicians, and they distrust the "mumbo-jumbo" testing on which some psychological testimony is based. The attorney needs to know who those jurors are. Closed-ended questions that are generally answered with "yes" or "no" are unlikely to generate answers that provide information. Open-ended questions that invite the jurors to openly share their feelings are more likely to obtain the information needed. Examples of closed-ended questions that will likely result in minimal information about the jurors include the following:

- This case may involve testimony from a psychologist about a test called the MMPI. Can you listen fairly to evidence from a psychologist?
- You will hear testimony about a test called the MMPI. Do you believe that psychological testing can help a psychologist to evaluate the emotional health of someone?
- Do you understand that the MMPI has been accepted in psychological communities for years?
- Do you understand that it is your responsibility to weigh the credibility of expert witnesses along with the credibility of any other witnesses in this case?

It is a rare juror who will respond to any of the above questions with anything except "yes." The answers reveal little or nothing about the jurors.

Examples of open-ended questions that are more likely to result in receiving valuable information from the jurors include the following:

- How do you feel about psychologists? Why?
- What do you think about testing that tries to evaluate a person's emotional condition?
- What do you think about psychological or emotional damages?
- What do you think about a person who would go to a psychiatrist or psychologist for help?

The attorney may not like the answers he or she receives from the juror, but it is better to learn those answers in voir dire than in an unfavorable verdict. Barton (1990) has provided additional examples of general open-ended questions intended to identify jurors who accept the idea of psychological damages.

OPENING STATEMENT AND CALLING WITNESSES

The opening statement is probably the most underestimated and poorly used phase in a jury trial. It is the first opportunity for the advocate to tell the client's story. It is difficult to overemphasize the importance of conveying a trial's complex evidence and information in the form of a coherent narrative. Cognitive psychologist Roger Schank (1990) summarized a wealth of research data (his own and others') into a basic principle:

> *People think in terms of stories. They understand the world in terms of stories that they have already understood. New events or problems are understood by reference to old previously understood stories and explained to others by the use of stories. We understand personal problems and relationships between people through stories that typify those situations. We also understand just about everything else this way as well. (p. 219; see also Schank, 1980; Schank & Abelson, 1977; Schank, Collins, & Hunter, 1986)*

In an article in the journal *Science*, Gordon Bower and Daniel Morrow of Stanford University (1990; see also Black & Bower, 1979; Bower & Clark, 1969; Morrow, Greenspan, & Bower, 1987) used much more technical language to describe the complex process by which people actively respond to stories:

> *We do not distinguish studies based on reading from those based on listening, since the input modality is irrelevant to the points at issue.*
>
> *Most researchers agree that understanding involves two major components. . . . First, readers translate the surface form of the text into underlying conceptual propositions. Second, they then use their world*

knowledge to identify referents (in some real or hypothetical world) of the text's concepts, linking expressions that refer to the same entity and drawing inferences to knit together the causal relations among the action sequences of the narrative. The reader thus constructs a mental representation of the situation and actions being described. This referential representation is sometimes called a mental model or situation model. Readers use their mental model to interpret and evaluate later statements in the text; they use incoming messages to update the elements of the model, including moving the characters from place to place and changing the state of the hypothetical story world. Readers tend to remember the mental model they constructed from the text, rather than the text itself. . . . The bare text is somewhat like a play script that the reader uses like a theater director to construct in imagination a full stage production. Throughout the story the narrator directs the reader's focus of attention to a changing array of topics, characters, and locations, thus making these elements temporarily more available for interpreting new information. (1990, p. 44)

Novelist Joan Didion (1979) put it this way: "We tell ourselves stories in order to live. . . . We interpret what we see, select the most workable of the multiple choices. We live . . . by the imposition of a narrative line upon disparate images" (p. 11).

For additional research and discussion regarding the nature and influence of narrative, see chapter 4 of this volume; see also Bakan, 1978; Chandler, Greenspan, and Barenboim, 1973; Emery and Csikszenmihalyi, 1981; Greenfield, 1983–1984; H. C. Martin, 1981–1982; Meringoff, 1980; Pearson and Pope, 1981–1982; Schafer, 1992; Schank, 1990; and Steinberg, 1982–1983.

The best litigators understand and use the power of narrative from the very beginning of a trial to its conclusion. A few outstanding attorneys—Gerry Spence in Wyoming, and Steve Rench and (Judge) Christopher Munch in Colorado—have spent decades crafting opening statements into storytelling. Chicago litigator Patricia Bobb (1992) believes that advocates can win their cases with opening statements. Recounting one of his trials, Gerry Spence described his typical opening: "I began my story like the old storyteller, setting the scene, creating the characters" (Spence & Polk, 1982, p. 298). In another trial, he actually used the words "once upon a time" in his opening statement: "'Ladies and gentlemen—my dear friends,' I began. 'Once upon a time . . .'" (Spence, 1983, p. 242). Nizer (1961, p. 37) describes making long opening statements without notes, taking the opportunity to make eye contact with each juror, and letting the honesty and sincerity of the statement invite the jurors' involvement. For examples of compelling opening statements and guides to creating them, see Habush (1984), Julien (1984), LaMarca (1984), Levin (1984), and J. D. MacDonald (1968).

The storytelling technique can be fatal to those who use it if the story rings false in any way, if it is not fully supported by the evidence, or if the truthfulness of the witness's testimony and the attorney's statements is not apparent. This approach heightens either the veracity or the falsity of the attorney's case. If attorneys do not have a valid story to tell—one that represents the truth as accurately and vividly as possible—it is better, as the old joke has it, to simply "bang on the table." Nizer (1961) wrote compellingly of this principle: If the story does not make sense in terms of the evidence, the testimony, common sense, and the jurors' own experience, the false story will bring down the case.

The storytelling technique requires the attorney to discard legal terminology and concepts and, instead, to tell a story with word pictures and imagery that allow the listener to identify with the client, to make sense of what will likely be complex information, and to want to hear the testimony. Nowhere is the storytelling technique more valuable than in the opening statement of a case involving psychological damages. The advocate has the opportunity either to reinforce skepticism about psychological damages and psychological testing or to use those tests to paint a vivid picture of harm. Specific descriptions that evoke images replace general wording. Humanizing the client through use of his or her name replaces all reference to "my client." Concentrating on the facts of the case replaces the traditional (and ineffective) opening statement disclaimers.

The first minutes of the opening statement are critical to inviting the members of jury into the case. Consider the first few minutes of two versions of the following opening statement:

> *STATEMENT 1: Ladies and gentlemen of the jury. It is a pleasure to have this opportunity to describe what I believe the evidence will show. This is a road map only. Nothing I say to you is evidence. The evidence in this case will come from that witness stand and from exhibits that the court accepts into evidence. The evidence in this case will include the testimony of a renowned psychologist. That psychologist examined my client and conducted several standard tests. He will testify that his conclusions, as confirmed by the psychological tests that he administered, show that my client was psychotic for over a year. The expert witness will tell you that my client's psychosis was caused because she went to a therapist for counseling and that therapist instead had sex with her. You will also hear evidence that, as a direct and proximate cause of the therapist's abuse of my client, she continues to suffer from a post-traumatic stress disorder. You will hear testimony from a board-certified psychiatrist that the conduct of Dr. Jones fell below the standard of care required of therapists in the community.*
>
> *STATEMENT 2: When Gail's 2-year-old son died in April of 1986, there were days she couldn't get out of bed. She cried for hours. Her little girl asked her mommy if she could help. Gail knew she had to do something to get better. She still had a daughter who needed her. She felt she couldn't do it alone. She turned for help to a person she thought she could trust. She turned to a counselor. This is about a betrayal of Gail's trust.*
>
> *The first counseling session was April 23, 1986. The doctor gave Gail a psychological test that showed her therapist that Gail was depressed and vulnerable. By May of 1986, the counselor was holding her hands. By June, he was kissing her, then he had sex with her. At each session, he held her, repeating, "God loves you, your boy is in heaven." By July, Gail began losing track of time. She found herself in her car, not knowing where she was or how she got there. August 4, 1986, was the first time Gail had seen her little boy since his funeral four months before. He was dressed in the same navy shorts and yellow shirt he had been wearing the day he died. She moved past the dining room table and reached to touch her son. Her hand passed through the air that moments before had, to her, been a 2-year-old boy. She later told her counselor how scared she was. He told her not to worry. He held her, fondled her, and repeated, "God loves you, your boy is in heaven." She began seeing and hearing other persons who were not really there. For 18 months, Gail never knew if the hand she reached out to touch was real.*
>
> *Doctors will explain, and independent testing confirms, that Gail was psychotic for more than a year and a half because her counselor, the person she thought she could trust, so confused her that she didn't know what was real and what wasn't.*

A strong opening statement cannot be made on the spur of the moment. It requires months of attention, thought, and structure. The opening statement should be drafted, revised, and delivered to any friend, associate, or secretary who will listen. They will tell you those areas that are unclear, repetitive, or boring.

Witnesses should be called and testimony elicited in such a way that adds support, clarity, detail, significance, and immediacy to the basic story that the attorney is trying to communicate to the jury. There is research supporting the notion that jurors may best organize the overwhelming information they encounter during a complex trial in terms of such narratives (see chapter 4). Pennington and Hastie (1992; see also Pennington and Hastie, 1981, 1988, 1991), for example, described their explanation-based story model as an "empirically supported image of the juror decision process that can serve as the basis for a unified, coherent discussion of the behavior of jurors in practical and scientific analyses" (1992, p. 203). Their research supports the view that the "story structure was a mediator of decisions and of the impact of credibility evidence" and that judgments made at the conclusion of a case "followed the prescriptions of the Story Model, not of Bayesian or linear updating models" (p. 189).

Nizer (1961) linked the story told by the witness to the jurors' perceptions of the witness's credibility: "We talk of the credibility of witnesses, but what we really mean is that the witness has told a story which meets the tests of plausibility and is therefore credible" (p. 11). (The Pennington and Hastie research addresses how jurors arrive at decisions about guilt or innocence in a criminal trial. Costanzo and Costanzo [1992] discuss jury decision making during the penalty phase of such trials when "the question is no longer 'What happened?' but 'What punishment does this defendant deserve?'" [p. 197]. V. L. Smith [1991] presented research concerning how jurors use a judge's instructions when the "judge's instructions are intended to educate untrained jurors in the legal concepts that apply to the case that they must decide" [p. 858; see also Elwork & Sales, 1985; Elwork, Sales, & Alfini, 1977, 1982; Luginbuhl, 1992]. For some of the fundamental concepts and research regarding how juries arrive at decisions, see the landmark works *The American Jury* [Kelven & Zeisel, 1966] and *Jury Verdicts* [Saks, 1977].)

Conley, O'Barr, and Lind (1978), discussed in detail the differences between testimony in *narrative style* and testimony in *fragmented style*. They noted, for example, that

> *if those hearing testimony believe that its style is determined by the lawyer, they may believe that use of a narrative style indicates the lawyer's faith in the witness' competence. Similarly, when the witness uses a fragmented style, presumable under the direction of the lawyer, the lawyer may be thought to consider the witness incompetent. (p. 1387)*

Similarly, Bank and Poythress (1982) wrote, "Both experienced mental health witnesses and recent experimental findings emphasize the superiority of the narrative style of testimony" (p. 188).

Providing opening statements and testimony in narrative style is one way of making the story more vivid. Other aspects of language may have similar effects. Bell and Loftus (1985; see also Erickson, Lind, Johnson & O'Barr, 1978; Lakoff, 1990), for example, noted,

> *Vivid detailed testimonies are more likely to be more persuasive than pallid testimonies for a variety of reasons. Relative to pallid information, vivid information presented at trials may garner more attention, recruit more additional information from memory, cause people to spend more time in thought, be more available in memory, be perceived as having a more credible source, and have a greater affective impact. (p. 663)*

TRIAL EXHIBITS

Demonstrative evidence has played an increasingly important role in litigation in the last decade. Jurors want to see the evidence. Trial exhibits lend vividness to direct testimony: The visual symbol illustrates and reinforces the spoken word. The best exhibits usually contain a minimal amount of information and are strongly illustrative. The MMPI lends itself to several types of exhibits.

One exhibit to consider is an enlargement of the MMPI basic scale profile (see appendix I). To the extent that the profile peaks help to explain a significant aspect of the case, the exhibit will assist a jury in remembering and understanding the MMPI evidence.

In the case that was the subject of the opening statements just described, if the offending doctor had administered an MMPI, enlargements of single questions taken directly from the MMPI, with the answers of the patient, might help to convince the jury that the doctor knew that his patient was vulnerable. (Note, however, that individual item responses may be psychometrically unreliable, as discussed elsewhere in this book; therefore, a knowledgeable expert may question this approach.) Examples include the following:

- I have nightmares every few nights. (true)
- My sleep is fitful and disturbed. (true)

- Much of the time my head seems to hurt all over. (true)
- I don't seem to care what happens to me. (true)

As previously discussed, lawyers and expert witnesses may have divergent views about singling out a response to an individual MMPI item. The expert may view the individual response in light of its lack of psychometric validity when taken out of context. The attorney, on the other hand, may view an individual's response to a specific MMPI item as a "statement" made by the individual, a statement that is relevant to the facts at issue before the court.

Another exhibit to consider, particularly in psychological damages cases, is an enlargement of the diagnostic criteria for those disorders suggested by the MMPI or diagnosed by experts. The diagnostic criteria for posttraumatic stress disorder, for example, include reexperiencing a trauma through recurrent and intrusive recollections of the event, recurrent dreams, and flashbacks, and psychological distress at exposure to events that symbolize or resemble the trauma. Each of the criteria that fit the case can be expanded by expert and lay witnesses from the general into a specific and compelling story through the details of the client's life.

Even the characteristics or symptoms of personality disorders can help form a compelling story in a case. For example, a formal chart or visual display of the diagnostic criteria for dependent personality disorder could be used to help a judge or jury understand that a therapist knew or should have known of the power that he or she possessed in the client's life.

Any exhibit that can help the jury to understand a complicated diagnosis should be considered. For example, the concept and diagnosis of multiple personality is often viewed with skepticism. In one trial, Colorado psychiatrist Marita J. Keeling used a hand-drawn exhibit to illustrate testimony about dissociation that helped the jury to understand the phenomenon in context of their own day-to-day lives. The jury heard the following (paraphrased) testimony:

> *There are a wide range of personalities in most of us. I am different when I am Dr. Keeling than when I am mommy to my children. Jane's personalities are sort of like my personalities, but her's became more distinct as a way to deal with trauma.*
>
> *Some of us seem to have one basic personality, no matter what the situation. Think of the businessman who wears a suit to the company Fourth of July picnic. Others of us seem to have quite a few different personalities or identities, and we move in and out of them fairly easily, depending on our mood and what the situation calls for. For example, when one of my children calls me at the office because there's been an injury, I'm mommy right away, no matter what else I've been working on.*
>
> *But some people, especially people who have suffered the kind of trauma that Jane has, may have quite a few different personalities but may not be able to move in and out of them so easily. Sometimes one personality takes over, and sometimes another. In extreme cases, like Jane's, some of the personalities are not even aware that there are other personalities.*
>
> *Some of Jane's personalities are sort of like the businessman I mentioned earlier who wears a three-piece wool suit to the Fourth of July picnic. Everyone else is dressed casually, but he seems somehow unaware of what a picnic is all about. He may only be aware that the temperature is in the high nineties and he's about to have a heatstroke. Some of Jane's personalities are sort of like that. When she is "her father's little girl"—which she often was in the presence of her former counselor—it was as if she were 5 years old. That personality is completely unaware that Jane is actually 35. She is as lost in the world of adults as the businessman in his heavy wool suit at the picnic. That "daddy's little girl" personality has become completely split off from the other personalities. It is as if her personalities were separated from each other.*

While she testified, Keeling referred to a large hand-drawn chart that had been marked as a trial exhibit. The chart consisted of four simple figures.

On the left was a circle. Keeling used the circle to illustrate the single identity of the businessman in the suit at the picnic.

Second from the left was a circle that had been divided by dotted lines into different "slices," much as a pie might be cut. These dotted lines showed the boundaries of different personalities or identities that most of us find ourselves experiencing. Earlier, Keeling had explained that a person might have many (i.e., far more than eight) such personalities. The dotted lines were meant, Keeling explained, to suggest that the personalities or identities tended to fit together well and—because the dividing lines were only dotted—the individual could move back and forth among the various identities according to the person's intentions and the circumstances.

Third from the left was the same divided circle; however, this time the sections were divided by solid rather than by dotted lines. This figure was used to illustrate how an individual's personalities or identities could become rigid: There could be difficulty moving from one to another, difficulty feeling that the various personalities or identities fit together into a familiar "self."

The fourth and final figure in the series showed the eight segments completely separated, as if someone had sliced a pie and then separated the pieces. Keeling used this figure to illustrate how dissociated and fragmented Jane's personalities had become. Her self was no longer basically unified; it was split into diverse personalities, some of which were completely unaware of the others.

Keeling's creative use of this exhibit seemed to be a turning point in the trial. The jurors, initially skeptical of the concept of multiple personalities, came not only to accept and appreciate the phenomenon but also to understand it in terms of their everyday lives. This form of narrative testimony (see chapter 4) illustrated with one or more exhibits can be extremely useful in communicating with a jury.

JURY INSTRUCTIONS

There are a number of possible jury instructions that address the unique problems associated with psychological damages cases.

A major defense in most civil claims involving psychological injury is that the person harmed was ill before the trauma occurred. This defense is often used in cases in which the litigation involves a defendant therapist who exploits a patient who has come to the therapist for help. Such a person usually seeks therapeutic help because he or she has a preexisting problem.

In Colorado, as in many states, an approved jury instruction discusses the exacerbation of preexisting conditions. C.J.I. (Colorado Jury Instruction) 6:8 requires that a jury attempt to separate the amount of damages caused by the negligence of the defendant from the preexisting damages. The instruction goes on to say,

> *If you are unable to separate the damages caused by the ailment or disability which existed before (the occurrence) and the damages caused by the (negligence) of the defendant, then the defendant is legally responsible for the entire amount of damages you find the plaintiff has incurred.*

The concept of a preexisting condition or disability is different from the notion of a vulnerability or frailty. In Colorado, as in most jurisdictions, the wrongdoer takes the plaintiff as he or she finds him. In *Fischer v. Moore*, 183 Colo. 392, 517 P.2d 458 (1973), the Colorado Supreme Court said that the tortfeasor "may not seek to reduce the amount of damages by spotlighting the physical frailties of the injured party" 517 P.2d at 459. A specific instruction highlighting the premise that the defendant takes the plaintiff as he or she finds the plaintiff sets a background for a closing argument that includes an appeal to fundamental fairness: Even the vulnerable deserve protection.

Every set of standard jury instructions contains language telling the jury that it should not consider bias, sympathy, or prejudice in its deliberations. Defense attorneys use the instruction to argue that the jury should not feel sorry for the plaintiff. A skilled and prepared plaintiff's attorney can respond in closing: "It is not sympathy that Gail wants. She is not asking for a verdict based on sympathy. She is not asking for a verdict based on charity. She is asking only that your verdict compensate her for what she has lost."

CLOSING ARGUMENTS

Good closing arguments tend to share common elements (see, e.g., Cartwright, 1984). The story or theme, developed throughout the case, is repeated in closing. The closing is organized, simple, and based on the truth. Like the opening statement, the closing argument tells a vivid and compelling story. Unlike the opening statement, the closing argument may involve appropriate emotion and obvious persuasion techniques.

The closing argument should not be a recitation of the testimony of witnesses or a depiction of time line. Most cases have a natural organization by major points. Argument by point is generally more effective than the stream-of-consciousness argument often used in closing arguments. A criminal defense closing argument, for example, may begin and conclude with the importance of the constitutional presumption of innocence. Other important points may include those facts that suggest that the wrong man is on trial because the wrong man was arrested or that the investigation that the police refused or failed to do could have uncovered facts that would have proved that the wrong man stands accused.

In a personal injury case, the points should include discussion of major issues such as liability, comparative negligence, economic damages, and noneconomic damages to the human spirit.

In any closing argument in which the application of MMPI results is discussed, the descriptions used by the attorney should avoid legal or technical words to the extent that this is practical. The MMPI results are used to help expand concepts that already make sense to the jury: A person's mental health is usually taken for granted; a person's mental health is one of the most important things he or she can possess.

To the extent that MMPI results are particularly compelling, those results might form the basis of a complete point to be argued in closing. For example, use of the MMPI might allow a graceful repetition in a liability argument as follows:

- Gail took this test because her doctor told her that it would help her get well.
- She did not know that her doctor would learn from this test that her sleep was fitful and tortured.
- She did not know that her doctor would learn from this test that she was afraid that she was losing her mind.
- She did not know that her doctor would learn from this test that she felt vulnerable and alone.
- She did not know, she could not have known, that the doctor she trusted would use the information that he got from this test to hurt her.

SUMMARY

A continuing theme throughout this book is the necessity for adequate preparation. Trial attorney Louis Nizer (1961) compared the work of the attorney preparing to go to trial to the work of the archaeologist who must find, exhume, and consider evidence and then attempt to assemble it in such a way that it reveals the truth. "This is the supreme test of preparation and, as any trial lawyer will admit, proper preparation is the be all and end all of trial success" (Nizer, 1961, p. 8).

This chapter provides a structured approach to the work done by the attorney in preparing and trying a case. The structure comprises a set of steps taken to ensure that all relevant information and evidence, no matter how obscure or well hidden, will emerge and that the truth that this information and evidence have to tell can be communicated in a clear and compelling story. The structured steps take the attorney through background research, retaining an expert, document production, depositions, pretrial motions, voir dire, opening statements and calling witnesses, trial exhibits, jury instructions, and closing arguments.

CHAPTER 6

ASSESSING MALINGERING AND OTHER ASPECTS OF CREDIBILITY

Evaluating the credibility of people involved in litigation is one of the most fundamental yet difficult forensic tasks. Is the defendant's bizarre demeanor and incoherent speech evidence of insanity or of great acting talent? Is the personal injury claimant really experiencing pain and suffering or simply using insufferable tactics to gain a lot of money painlessly? Is the parent seeking custody as good as he or she seems while testifying or simply good at deception? Deciding such questions is usually the responsibility of the "trier of fact" (usually the jury, sometimes the judge). Expert witnesses, whom the courts believe to supposedly possess special knowledge about issues, often testify about credibility to help the trier of fact address these questions.

Increasingly, psychological testing has become an important means for shedding light on credibility and related personality factors pertaining to the "truthfulness" of a person's claims before the court. The MMPI has seemingly become the most widely used instrument in such forensic assessments.

The MMPI is usually introduced in court without critical challenge (Adelman & Howard, 1984; see chapter 3 of this volume). The individual's response to psychological tests, conducted as part of the forensic evaluation, can provide information about the person's psychological functioning as it is relevant to the issues before the court.

Many psychological measures actually use the individual's own self-reported behavior and symptoms in the assessment, even though self-report in court testimony can be suspect in situations in which individuals are being asked to testify for or against themselves. The "truth and nothing but the truth" is often more of an ideal than a reality in courts when telling the absolute and complete truth might mean that the person loses everything sought.

Individuals who are being assessed in a forensic context sometimes make great efforts not to incriminate themselves or to provide information about themselves that would work against them. In many cases, individuals may simply answer MMPI test items dishonestly rather than undermine their own case.

The following sections focus on special issues in the use of the MMPI in assessing credibility.

RESPONDENT MOTIVATION TO CREATE PARTICULAR IMPRESSIONS

People being evaluated in a forensic assessment, whether in criminal, malpractice, personal injury, custody, or other types of cases, often tend to respond to personality test items in an effort to create a particular impression with the court. Individuals charged with capital crimes who are potentially facing long prison terms or the death penalty may attempt to convince the court that their crime was committed when they were in a psychotic state; those involved in personal injury litigation may attempt to present the view that their mental state has been adversely affected by the alleged injury; and those who are suing a corporation for damages because of a product failure that purportedly caused "mental anguish" may approach the testing with the idea of showing how disturbed their psychological adjustment is at this time as a result of using the product. In a different manner, a person who is seeking to obtain custody of a child in a domestic family dispute may present him- or herself as an extremely well-adjusted person, even if he or she is emotionally disturbed. Any psychological test procedure that does not take these natural response tendencies into account is likely to provide only limited, inaccurate, or misleading information.

One of the most valuable aspects of the MMPI in forensic evaluations is that it contains several measures that assess deviant response tendencies such as test defensiveness or tendencies to exaggerate symptoms.

The motivation of individuals who are being tested to present a distorted picture can take many forms. The individual's circumstances at the time of testing can often provide valuable clues to the possibility of a deceptive response approach. The type of assessment provides an important backdrop for MMPI interpretation. With a willing and capable test taker endorsing the items with a problem-focused attitude, the MMPI can provide a wealth of information about the client. Individuals being evaluated in forensic settings often are not as cooperative as those being assessed in clinical settings; therefore, symptomatic information provided by the instrument is often secondary to the perspective gained from careful evaluation of the validity indexes.

COACHING AND THE VALIDITY SCALES

Some individuals are carefully briefed as to the reason and rationale for the test, well beyond what the standard instructions for the test administration allow. *Extensive* briefing or coaching on the best approach to taking the test, whether advertent or not, occurs in some situations. Forensic psychologists conducting personality evaluations should keep in mind that the client may have been warned about the MMPI validity scales or actually told the best strategy to respond to the items by an attorney who says, "Don't answer any questions that might incriminate you" or "You should be aware of the fact that there are questions on the test that are designed to trap you if you aren't careful."

The extent to which such coaching has distorted test results can be difficult to determine. Under no circumstances should the expert intrude into privileged attorney–client communications. A careful appraisal of the validity scales will, in some cases, alert the expert witness that the client has produced an overly cautious or "managed" self-report. It might also be valuable for the professional who administers the MMPI to conduct an inquiry after testing is completed to assess the extent to which previous instructions may have influenced responses, as long as there is no inquiry into privileged communication with attorneys.

MMPI-BASED MEASURES OF RESPONSE INVALIDITY

The idea that people responding to the MMPI might not endorse the items in a truthful manner was carefully considered by Hathaway and McKinley, the original MMPI authors. Several control scales or validity measures were developed in the original instrument to assess profile validity. We review these measures, describe research that bears on their continued use in personality assessment today, and summarize the ways in which these scales operate on the MMPI-2. Next, we describe several new measures of protocol validity and illustrate their use. Several common types of invalidating approaches are illustrated. Later in the chapter, we also discuss pseudomeasures that purportedly provide useful information regarding response attitudes but that may provide more misinformation than useful interpretive guidelines.

THE CANNOT SAY (CS) SCORE

This MMPI index is the total number of items that were either unanswered or answered *both* "true" *and* "false" in the client's protocol.

In the original MMPI, *T* scores for the CS scale were actually provided on the profile sheet with an arbitrary mean score value of 30. However, this practice of providing *T* scores for the CS score was discontinued in MMPI-2 because the *T* scores were neither psychometrically sound nor clinically appropriate.

The shape of the distributions, in part because of the fact that people omit few and variable numbers of items, does not allow for the generation of meaningful *T* scores. The most appropriate use of the CS score involves simply the rough determination of whether the person endorsed enough items to provide useful information. Omissions greater than or equal to 30 items reflect an excessive number of omitted items and will likely attenuate the profile. Profiles with greater than this number of CS items should not be interpreted. In an empirical evaluation of item omissions, Clopton and Neuringer (1977) reported that excessive item omissions (i.e., greater than 30) can alter the MMPI scores by lowering scale elevations and altering the code type.

The rule of thumb cautioning against interpreting profiles with high CS counts, of course, assumes that the omitted items are scattered throughout the booklet and thus affect all of the clinical scales. (Interpretations for high CS scores are shown in Exhibit 6-1.)

One can be somewhat more precise in the interpretation of the CS score by evaluating where in the sequence of items in the booklet the omissions occur or whether a particular scale is actually affected by item omission. If all of the items a particular individual omits appear at the end of the booklet, one can actually score the traditional MMPI validity and clinical scales. That is, one is able to score the standard scales if the person has completed the first 370 items on the MMPI-2 or the first 350 items on the MMPI-A. Items that are deleted beyond these points influence only scales such as the MAC-R Scale or the MMPI-2 content scales that contain items that appear toward the end of the booklet.

Second, if the individual has actually responded to all items on a particular scale, even though the overall CS score numbers are high, then that particular scale might provide useful information. Knowing the actual response rate for the items composing each scale could add considerably to one's confidence in the interpretation of the scale. This information is available through some computer scoring programs. For example, the Minnesota Adolescent Report (MMPI-A) from National Computer Systems provides the percentage of items composing each scale that are actually endorsed by the individual (Butcher & Williams, 1992b). The practitioner can determine for each scale whether there has been a high percentage of items omitted.

In forensic settings, the CS score should be carefully evaluated because item omissions are a fairly common means for clients to distort the pattern pre-

EXHIBIT 6-1

Summary of Cannot Say Interpretative Rules for the MMPI-2 and MMPI-A in Forensic Evaluations

Omitting items on personality scales is a relatively common means for test takers in forensic settings to attempt to control the test.

Cannot Say scores (*Cs*) ≥ 30 indicate that the individual has produced an invalid protocol that should not be interpreted except under circumstances noted below. No other MMPI-2/MMPI-A scales should be interpreted.

If most of the omitted items occur toward the end of the booklet (after item 370 on MMPI-2 or 350 on MMPI-A), the validity and standard scales can be interpreted. However, the supplementary and content scales, which contain items toward the end of the booklet, should not be interpreted.

At the time of administration, if the individual has omitted items, the test should be returned with encouragement to try and complete all of the items.

Augmentation of profile scores by correcting for omitted items should be avoided.

Possible reasons for item omissions:

- Perceived irrelevance of items
- Lack of cooperation
- Defensiveness
- Indecisiveness
- Fatigue
- Low mood
- Carelessness
- Low reading comprehension

Adapted from Butcher & Williams (1992a) by permission.

sented. Even five or six omitted items, if they occur on a particular scale, can affect its reliability and validity.

Some authorities (e.g., Greene, 1991) have recommended augmenting profiles in which a number of items have been omitted. Two methods have been suggested for adjusting full-scale scores by estimating what the score would be if the individual had responded to all of the items. First, if the client was judged to have had time to complete the record but left out some items, then the items left unanswered that are scored on the scales are simply added to the total scale scores *as if* they had been endorsed in the deviant direction. Second, if the individual did not have time to complete the record, the full-scale score can be prorated by determining the proportion of endorsed items for those completed and applying this same proportion to the unanswered items on the scales.

Augmenting profiles in this manner in a forensic setting could be problematic because the individual has not actually answered those items. This procedure should be discouraged because it invites attack in cross-examination. For example, an attorney in cross-examination might ask the psychologist, "The client did not really endorse those items did he, Doctor?" Or, more likely, "You actually made up those MMPI scores, didn't you, Doctor?" Thus, although this creative approach may have uses in other contexts, it does not appear to be defensible in the forensic context.

THE LIE (*L*) SCALE

On the basis of work by Hartshorne and May (1928), Hathaway and McKinley developed a rational scale including statements proclaiming positive characteristics such as "At times I feel like swearing" (false) or "I get angry sometimes" (false) to assess the general characteristic that some individuals have to proclaim an unrealistic degree of personal virtue.

The *L* scale was devised, according to Dahlstrom et al. (1972), "to identify deliberate or intentional efforts to evade answering the test frankly and honestly" (p. 109). These items, asserting high moral value or an unusual quality of virtue, were scaled to provide an indication of whether the individual excessively asserts high virtue compared with people in general. Individuals who claim more than a few of these unrealistically positive characteristics are considered to be presenting a favorable view of themselves that is very unlikely to be accurate, even for individuals with model life-styles.

A general tendency to endorse the MMPI *L* items, often referred to as the Lie scale, suggests that the individual has likely responded to the other items in the inventory in such a manner as to deny any personal frailty or weakness and present the most favorable image. High-*L* scorers tend to deny even minor faults that most people would not object to endorsing in a self-report evaluation (see Exhibit 6-2 for a description of high-*L* characteristics).

Some studies have supported the value of the *L* scale as an indicator of the "good impression" profile. Burish and Houston (1976) found that the *L* scale correlated with denial. Joseph Matarazzo (1955), a former president of the APA who has conducted extensive research in the area of psychological assessment, found that the *L* scale was associated with lower levels of manifest anxiety.

Elevations on the *L* scale have also been reported among forensic patients who were paranoid and grandiose. Coyle and Heap (1965) concluded that some hospitalized patients were "pathologically convinced of their own perfection" (p. 729). Fjordbak (1985) found that high-*L* patients with normal profiles were often psychotic and showed paranoid features.

Interestingly, Vincent, Linsz, and Greene (1966) considered the usefulness of the *L* scale to be limited to unsophisticated clients. They reported that the *L* scale does not seem to detect the sophisticated individual who has been given instructions to falsify responses on the test. However, groups that tend to obtain higher scores on the *L* scale include college-educated applicants to airline flight jobs and parents being assessed in domestic court to determine who gets custody of the minor children, because these individuals tend to be asserting that they possess many virtues and no faults, even minor ones.

Graham, Watts, and Timbrook (1991), in a simulation study of faking using the MMPI-2, reported that the *L* scale appears to work the same in the revised version of the inventory as in the original MMPI. The *L* scale is identical *in item content* in the MMPI and MMPI-2. The main difference between the two forms

EXHIBIT 6-2

Summary of Interpretative Rules for the MMPI-2 *L* in Forensic Evaluations

T scores from 60–64, inclusive, indicate that the individual used a good impression response set to create the view that he or she is a virtuous person.

T scores from 65–69, inclusive, indicate possible profile invalidity due to an overly virtuous self-presentation.

T scores ≥ 70 suggest clear distortion of item responding in order to manipulate what others think of him or her.

Many individuals with high *L* scores produce low scores on the symptom scales. However, elevated *L* scale scores can be associated with other elevated MMPI-2 scale scores, particularly when the individual attempts to create a particular pattern of disability (e.g., physical problems).

The *TRIN* Scale (inconsistent true or false responding) can aid the interpreter in determining whether an elevated *L* score is due to a false or nay-saying response set.

Descriptors associated with elevations of *L*:

- Unwilling to admit even minor flaws
- Unrealistic proclamation of virtue
- Claims near-perfect adherence to high moral standards
- Naive self-views
- Outright effort to deceive others about motives or adjustment
- Personality adjustment problems

Adapted from Butcher & Williams (1992a) by permission.

is that originally Hathaway and McKinley rationally set or estimated the *T*-score distribution. In MMPI-2, the *T* scores were derived by a linear transformation that was based on the new normative samples.

L is a valuable scale for assessing impression management (see the discussion by Paulhus [1986]), which is often an important focus of forensic testimony. *L* scale elevations between 60 and 64 (unless otherwise indicated, "scores" in this chapter refer to *T* scores) suggest that the individual has been less than frank in the assessment and has probably underreported psychological symptoms and problems. Scores between 65 and 69 tend to reflect a strong inclination to accentuate the positive side of one's adjustment and to deny or suppress the possibility of personal frailty. With scores in this range, the clinical profile is less likely to provide a useful or accurate reflection of the individual's problem picture. Blatant distortion or conscious manipulation of the personality assessment process is associated with elevations above 70. This "fake good" pattern is unlikely to provide much valid personality or symptomatic information.

Recently, Baer, Wetter, and Berry (1992) conducted a meta-analysis of measures of underreporting psychopathology on the MMPI. They concluded that consistently effective cutting scores for many published indices have yet to be established. However, they recommended that

> *Until such research becomes available, clinicians using the MMPI-2 may be best advised to consider the L and K scales when making judgments about underreporting of psychopathology, as these scales showed reasonable mean effect sizes and have not been altered on the MMPI-2. (p. 523)*

THE INFREQUENCY (*F*) SCALE

One of the most useful measures in forensic assessment is the *F* scale, because many individuals in forensic evaluations tend to exaggerate symptoms in order to appear more psychologically disturbed than they actually are. The rationale for the development of the *F* scale was actually very straightforward. Paul Meehl and Starke Hathaway (cited in Dahlstrom & Dahlstrom, 1980) described it as follows:

> *The F variable was composed of 64 items that were selected primarily because they were answered with a relatively low frequency in either the true or false direction by the main normal group; the scored direction*

> *of response is the one which is rarely made by unselected normals. Additionally, the items were chosen to include a variety of content so that it was unlikely that any particular pattern would cause an individual to answer many of the items in the unusual direction. A few examples are these: "Everything tastes the same." (True) "I believe in law enforcement" (False) "I see things, animals, or people around me that others do not see" (True). The relative success of this selection of items, with deliberate intent of forcing the average number of items answered in an unusual direction downward, is illustrated in the fact that the mean score on the 64 items runs between two and four points for all normal groups. The distribution curve is, of course, very skewed positively; and the higher scores approach half the number of items. In distributions of ordinary persons the frequency of scores drops very rapidly at about seven and is at the 2 or 3 percent level by score twelve. Because of this quick cutting off of the curve the scores seven and twelve were arbitrarily assigned T scored values of 60 and 70 in the original F table. (Dahlstrom & Dahlstrom, 1980, p. 94)*

The *F* scale has been modified in the MMPI-2 and MMPI-A in several ways. First, in the MMPI-2, four items were dropped from the scale because of their objectionable content. Second, the *F* scale was empirically normed using linear *T* scores as opposed to the rationally derived setting of scale values, as was done in the original *F*-scale development. Third, an additional infrequency scale, *F(B)*, was developed to provide a measure of infrequency for the items that appear in the back of the booklet, because the original *F* scale contains only items that occur in the front half of the booklet.

The *F* scale for the MMPI-A was further revised to address more fully the tendency of adolescents to endorse items differently than adults (Butcher et al., 1992). Many of the items on the traditional *F* scale did not operate as infrequency items for younger people. Therefore, a new *F* scale for the MMPI-A, which was based on adolescent frequency tables, was developed for individuals between the age of 14 and 18. A separate set of 66 infrequency items, covering the full range of the items in the booklet, was obtained. The 66 *F* items are scattered throughout the 478-item booklet in the MMPI-A. To assess responding toward the end versus toward the front of the item pool, the *F* scale was divided into two equal parts, F_1 and F_2, each containing 33 items.

The *F* and the *F(B)* scales on the MMPI-2 and the *F*, F_1, and F_2 scales on the MMPI-A were developed without regard to content of the items by simply identifying the items that are infrequently endorsed in the general population. When individuals approach the items in an unselective way and attempt to present a picture of psychological disturbance, they usually obtain high scores on these scales. However, individuals with actual psychological problems tend to respond in a more selective and consistent manner to items. People who feign mental health problems on the MMPI, unless they have a background in psychology or the MMPI, will usually be unaware as to which items actually appear on the scales and what is the scored direction of particular items. Dissimulators, those who attempt to feign mental health problems, tend to overrespond to many extreme items.

The infrequency scales are very important forensic indicators because they provide an assessment of the extent to which the person has responded carefully and selectively to the content of the items. High *F* or *F(B)* scores ($T \geq 90$) threaten the validity and interpretability of the MMPI-2. Thus, the *F* scale has been referred to as a "fake bad" scale. Records with scores of 90 or above should be considered problematic for a straightforward interpretation of the clinical scales until possible reasons for the extreme responding can be determined.

We explore several possible hypotheses that might explain an elevated *F* or *F(B)* score. (See Exhibit 6-3 for the *F* scale and Exhibit 6-4 for the *F(B)* scale for a summary of possible meanings for *F*-scale elevations.) Each potentially invalid profile that is based on *F* or *F(B)* should be carefully evaluated to determine the possible source of invalidity. Potential sources of exaggerated responding include the following:

Careless Responding

Perhaps the individual got mixed up in responding to the items and marked responses in the wrong place

EXHIBIT 6-3

Summary of Interpretative Rules for the MMPI-2 *F* in Forensic Evaluations

The MMPI infrequency scales indicate unusual response to the item pool through claiming excessive, unlikely symptoms.

T scores below 50 may be associated with a response pattern that minimizes problems.

T scores from 60–79, inclusive, reflect a problem-oriented approach to the items.

T scores from 80–89, inclusive, indicate an exaggerated response set, which probably reflects an attempt to claim excessive problems. *VRIN T* scores ≤ 79 can be used to rule out inconsistent responding.

T scores from 90–109, inclusive, are possibly indicators of an invalid protocol. Some high *F* profiles are obtained in inpatient settings and reflect extreme psychopathology. *VRIN T* scores ≥ 79 can be used to rule out inconsistent profiles.

T scores ≥ 110 indicate an uninterpretable profile because of extreme item endorsements.

Interpretive hypothesis for elevated *F* scores:

- Confusion, reading problems
- Random responding (refer to *VRIN*)
- Severe psychopathology
- Possible symptom exaggeration
- Faking psychological problems
- Malingering

Adapted from Butcher & Williams (1992a) by permission.

EXHIBIT 6-4

Summary of Interpretative Rules for the MMPI-2 *F(B)* in Forensic Evaluations

The *F(B)* assesses exaggerated responding by examining infrequent responding to items in the back of the MMPI-2 booklet.

If *F* Scale is valid and *F(B)* ≥ 90, the standard scales are probably interpretable, but the scales containing items on the back of the booklet (e.g., content scales) should not be interpreted.

Interpretive hypotheses for elevated *F(B)* scores:

- Confusion, reading problems
- Random responding
- Severe psychopathology
- Possible symptom exaggeration
- Faking psychological problems
- Malingering

Adapted from Butcher & Williams (1992a) by permission.

on the answer sheet. Careful test administration can often eliminate this concern because proctoring of the exam could prevent such mix-ups in the instructions from occurring. (Some individuals, however, may still be "off" by one or two items when reading the booklet and marking responses on the answer sheet.)

An examination of the answer sheet can sometimes determine if the client became confused and mixed up on the test, for example, if an entire page of questions or a column of the answer sheet "bubbles" have been missed. Another way to evaluate the possibility of careless responding involves examining the consistency of the individual's response. One can determine, using validity indicators (such as the *VRIN* scale, discussed below), if the person has responded selectively to the content of the items or has responded in an inconsistent manner.

Random Responding

Random responding will produce highly deviant clinical profiles. However, the *F*-scale score will be so extremely elevated that the interpreter should not make personality inferences from the MMPI-2. There are two valuable indicators of randomness that should be carefully evaluated: *F* scores greater than 90 (usually random response sets will produce *F* scores greater than 120; see the profile in Figure 6-1). However, conservative test interpretation standards suggest that any *F* or *F(B)* scores of 80 or above for adults or of 70 or above for adolescents should be carefully evaluated for possible dissimulation.

The *VRIN* scale, to be discussed more fully below, produces a response consistency score that addresses

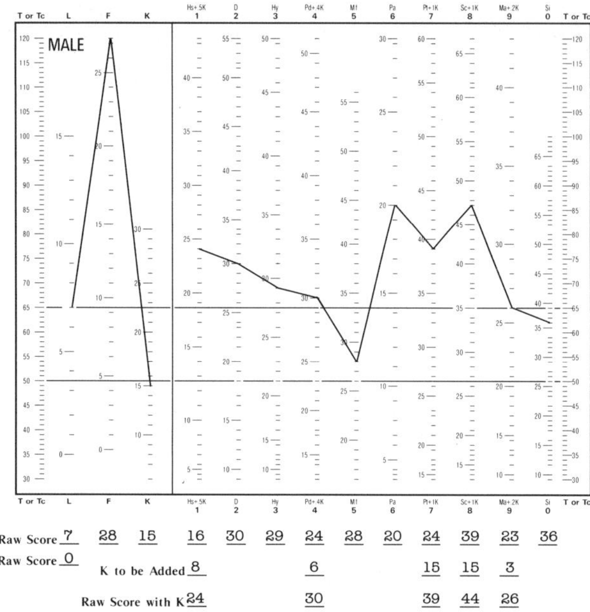

FIGURE 6-1. Random MMPI-2 basic profile.

the extent to which the individual has responded inconsistently to similar items. High *VRIN* scores are associated with random, careless, or noncontent-oriented responding. If the individual has a high score on *F* and a low to moderate score on *VRIN*, reasons other than a random response pattern should be evaluated to explain the high *F* score (e.g., actual or feigned psychopathology).

Rogers, Harris, and Thatcher (1983) found a better than 90% accuracy rate for MMPI random-response indicators (*F* and *T-R* [Test–Retest] Index; Greene, 1979) in discriminating randomly generated profiles from profiles obtained in a forensic evaluation program. More recently, Berry, Wetter et al. (1991) and Berry et al. (1992) found that the *F*, *F(B)*, and *VRIN* scales were effective at detecting random responding on the MMPI-2.

Stress or Distress

Extenuating, stressful circumstances in the individual's life can also influence infrequent item responding. Stressful life factors tend to be associated with elevated *F*-scale scores. Brozek and Schiele (1948; Schiele & Brozek, 1948) showed that increased *F*-scale elevation was associated with increased distress and an increase in neurotic symptomatology in individuals who were being systematically starved to 75% of their body weight in the Minnesota Experimental Semistarvation Studies during World War II.

Another obvious stressful circumstance that tends to produce extremely high *F* scores is admission to an inpatient psychiatric hospital or incarceration in a correctional facility. As a group, individuals in these settings tend to endorse a large number of extreme symptoms. Scheduling of the initial assessment or retesting at a later time, after the individual has had time to acclimate, usually results in more interpretable profiles. These findings reinforce the importance, when interpreting a profile, of being aware of the circumstances at the time of testing (see chapter 4).

Unusual Cultural Background

Another factor that could influence high *F* responding is membership in a particular cultural group or locale. Cheung, Song, and Butcher (1991) found that many of the items on the *F* scale did not work as infrequency items in the People's Republic of China. For example, the item "I believe there is a God" (false) was actually more frequently endorsed in the opposite direction in China than in the United States. A culturally specific *F* scale was subsequently developed using items that were infrequently endorsed in China. When assessing an individual, it is crucial to assure that the test protocol is scored using a culturally appropriate scoring key and set of norms (see chapter 4).

Severe Psychological Disturbance

High *F* scores can reflect extreme psychopathology (Gynther, Altman, & Warbin, 1973). In an empirical evaluation of murderers in pretrial psychological evaluations, Holcomb, Adams, Ponder, and Anderson (1984) reported that high *F*-scale scores were more often associated with psychopathology than with test invalidity.

Faking Mental Health Problems

High scores on the *F* scale can also reflect the tendency to exaggerate adjustment problems or feign mental illness. This extreme pattern of self-reported psychological disturbance has been found in situations in which the individual is attempting to portray disability perhaps to obtain compensation (Shaffer, 1981) or to escape punishment (Schretlin, 1988).

Extensive research on the MMPI *F* scale has shown it to be an effective measure of the tendency to exaggerate or fake mental health symptoms over a wide variety of settings and conditions.[1]

In many forensic evaluations, particularly those involving individuals who desire to appear psychologically disturbed, individuals respond less systematically and more on the basis of presenting extreme problems unselectively. Scores elevated above 80 suggest an extreme amount of symptom checking consistent with claiming an excessive amount of generally inconsistent symptoms or the experience of severe symptomotology that requires professional services.

THE SUBTLE DEFENSIVENESS (*K*) SCALE

The *K* scale was developed by Paul Meehl and Starke Hathaway (1946) for two purposes. The first was to detect the presence in some individuals of a tendency to present themselves in a socially favorable light, that is, to respond to items in a manner as to claim no personal weakness or psychological frailty. This tendency was observed to occur in some inpatients who had psychological problems but whose clinical profiles were normal. Moreover, the *L* scale did not appear to be effective in detecting their defensiveness.

The second reason for the development of the *K* scale involved the desire on the part of the scale developers to correct for test defensiveness in patients who had mental health problems but were defensive in their self-report descriptions. The scale developers assumed that the tendency some individuals have to present overly favorable self-views could be satisfactorily scaled and used to correct their clinical profiles to improve the discriminability as to whether the scores matched a criterion group. If patients were defensive (produced high *K* scores) then points could be added to their clinical scale scores.

The *K* factor was thus derived as an empirical correction for improving the discrimination between individuals who were defensive and did not accurately report mental health problems in clinical settings and those who were not defensive. Hathaway and Meehl originally determined the percentages of *K* scores that improved the identification of defensive patients using inpatient data. No efforts have been made to develop a *K* correction for other settings.

The *K* score appears to be a valuable indicator of the tendency to present a favorable self-report (see Exhibit 6-5 for a listing of the *K* scale correlates and interpretative guidelines). However, factors such as

EXHIBIT 6-5

Summary of Interpretative Rules for the MMPI-2 *K* Score in Forensic Evaluations

T scores ≥ 65 suggest possible defensive responding. Elevations in this range are common in forensic evaluations in which the individual is motivated to present a favorable image (e.g., family custody evaluations).

Scores on the *K* Scale are used to correct for defensive responding on several MMPI-2 scales (*Hs*, *Pd*, *Pt*, *Sc*, and *Ma*). Further research needs to clarify if *K* correction is appropriate for particular settings.

Individuals with less than high school education tend to produce, on average, lower *K* scores.

Absence of psychopathology cannot be assumed for profiles with an elevated *K* score and normal limits scale scores.

Interpretive hypotheses with elevated *K* scores:

- Defensiveness
- Possessing a great need to present oneself as very well adjusted
- A nay-saying response set (rule out with *TRIN*)

Adapted from Butcher & Williams (1992a) by permission.

[1] Anthony, 1971; Cofer, Chance, & Judson, 1949; Exner, McDowell, Pabst, Stackman, & Kirk, 1963; Fairbank, McCaffrey, & Keane, 1985; Gallucci, 1984; Gendreau, Irvine, & Knight, 1973; Grow, McVaugh, & Eno, 1980; Hawk & Cornell, 1989; Heaton, Smith, Lehman, & Vogt, 1978; Lundy, Geselowitz, & Shertzer, 1985; McCaffrey & Bellamy-Campbell, 1989; Pollack & Grainey, 1984; Rathus & Siegel, 1980; Rice, Arnold, & Tate, 1983; Rogers, Dolmetch, & Cavanaugh, 1983; Rogers, Harris, & Thatcher, 1983; Roman, Tuley, Villanueva, & Mitchell, 1990; Sweetland, 1948; Walters, White, & Greene, 1988; Schretlen & Arkowitz, 1990; Wasyliw et al., 1988; Wilcox & Dawson, 1977.

socioeconomic class and education have been shown to influence *K* scores (Butcher, 1990a; Dahlstrom et al., 1972). Interpretation of original MMPI *K*-corrected profiles required that adjustments be made for people with educations surpassing high school because the original *K* score was based on people with an eighth- or ninth-grade (depending on whether the arithmetic mean or median—see Glossary—is used) education. Because the average educational level in the United States today is higher than in the 1930s when the original norms were collected, the original *K* scores are elevated above 60 for most people. The MMPI-2 *K* score, which is based on a more representative sample, is more relevant for the majority of people today. However, individuals from lower educational backgrounds need to be given special interpretive considerations because, on average, *K* is slightly lower for those individuals with less than a high school education.

The *K* scale, as a correction factor, has not been without its critics. The MMPI Restandardization Committee considered dropping the *K* correction from the five corrected clinical scales; however, many validity studies have been based on *K*-corrected scores. Thus, for the sake of maintaining continuity on the clinical scales between the MMPI and MMPI-2, the *K* correction was maintained. However, several researchers have noted that the *K* scale, as a correction factor for test defensiveness, does not perform in a uniformly successful manner (Colby, 1989; Hunt, 1948; Schmidt, 1948; Wrobel & Lachar, 1982). Early studies by Hunt, Carp, Cass, Winder, and Kantor (1947) and Silver and Sines (1962) found that non-*K*-corrected scores worked as well as *K*-corrected scores in inpatient assessment.

There also has been the suggestion that the *K* correction might actually lower external test validity (Weed, Ben-Porath, & Butcher, 1990; Weed & Han, 1992). Consequently, a high *K* in a forensic assessment may prompt consideration that the *K*-corrected scores may, when compared with non-*K*-corrected scores, actually provide a *less* clear and *less* accurate understanding of the person who is being assessed. Profile sheets are available to enable clinicians to plot both *K*- and non-*K*-corrected profiles to compare the relative elevation of the particular scale without the influence of *K* (see sample case in appendix I). It should be emphasized, however, that in no case will a *K*-corrected score suggest an invalid descriptor.

THE DISSIMULATION (*F–K*) INDEX

In an effort to improve the detection of dissimulators on the MMPI, Gough (1947, 1950) developed an MMPI index using the relationship between the *F* and *K* scales, the *F–K* or Dissimulation Index, to assess the extent to which an individual has claimed nonexistent problems or has exaggerated complaints. Gough considered that extremely high *F* elevations along with low *K* scores indicated an invalid or dissimulated performance. This measure, the *F–K* Index, is determined by subtracting the raw score of the *K* scale from the raw score of the *F* scale. Gough originally recommended that an *F–K* score of 9 or above would serve as an indication that the profile was invalid because of exaggeration of symptoms. Others (e.g., Lachar, 1974) recommended that profiles with an *F–K* score of 12 or above be considered invalid because the original score suggested by Gough was considered so low that it resulted in the elimination of too many valid, interpretable profiles.

The *F–K* Index in which the *K* score is greater than the *F* score (resulting in a negative number) that is used to detect a "fake good" profile has not worked out well in practice and is not recommended for clinical use. Too many valid and interpretable protocols are rejected by this index when *K* is greater than *F*.

The *F–K* Index was recently supported by empirical studies in forensic assessment (Hawk & Cornell, 1989). In addition, a meta-analysis was conducted by Berry et al. (1991) to examine the effectiveness of MMPI-based measures in detecting faking. They found that the *F–K* Index significantly differentiated people who were malingering from people who were not malingering, although it was not as effective as the raw score or the *T* scores of the *F* scale taken alone (see Schretlen & Arkowitz, 1990; Wasyliw et al., 1989). Similarly, Graham et al. (1991) found that the *F–K* Index significantly detected faking on the MMPI-2 with a sample of undergraduate students who were instructed to try to appear psychologically disturbed on the test. However, the Index did not work as well as using the *F* scale alone. Although the *F–K* Index appears to be effective in detecting faking on the MMPI and MMPI-2 (Wetzler & Marlowe, 1990), it does not appear to add incremental validity beyond use of the *F* scale alone. There appears to be no advantage to using this index beyond that which is available from the *F* scale.

CONSISTENCY MEASURES

The validity of an individual's self-report is threatened by inconsistent or unreliable responding. A court could not accept an individual's testimony that he or she was simultaneously present at or absent from the scene of a crime. If an individual, in presenting pertinent self-descriptions as part of a psychological evaluation, endorses essentially identical items in an opposite way, then the accuracy of the response pattern is called into question.

Interest in devising a means of evaluating whether a client has consistently responded to MMPI items has resulted in fruitful research to detect this problematic response tendency. Originally, as a result of a scoring procedure, 16 items were repeated in the MMPI. Some investigators attempted to make use of this artifact to appraise response consistency (Buechley & Ball, 1952; Dahlstrom et al., 1972; Greene, 1991). These repeated item pairs, if answered differently by an individual, were considered to be a clear indication that the person was not approaching the MMPI items with a consistent, cooperative response orientation. The resulting *T–R* Index was somewhat limited by the relatively small number of items. If a person endorsed more than 4 items in an inconsistent manner, he or she was considered to be producing a low credibility record (Greene, 1991). However, because many groups produce two or three inconsistent responses, an important determination hinges on very small and probably insignificant numbers of items.

The 16 repeated items were viewed by the MMPI Restandardization Committee as problematic for several reasons and were not retained in the MMPI-2. The fact that there are no repeated items in MMPI-2 does *not* mean that response consistency cannot be evaluated. On the contrary, there are a number of items on the inventory that contain similar wording or possess content that reveal inconsistent responding. The Variable Response Inconsistency and True Response Inconsistency scales were developed from the revised item pool to assess response inconsistency in MMPI-2.

EXHIBIT 6-6

Summary of Interpretative Rules for the MMPI-2 and MMPI-A *VRIN* Scales in Forensic Evaluations

MMPI-2 *VRIN T* scores ≥ 80 or MMPI-A *VRIN* scores ≥ 75 indicate inconsistent random responding that invalidates the profile.

MMPI-2 *VRIN* scores from 70–79 or MMPI-A *VRIN* scores 70–74, inclusive, suggest a possibly invalid profile due to inconsistent responding.

Adapted from Butcher & Williams (1992a) by permission.

Variable Response Inconsistency (*VRIN*)

The *VRIN* scale is an empirically derived measure that is made up of pairs of items for which one or two of four possible configurations (true–false, false–true, true–true, false–false) would be considered semantically inconsistent. For example, answering "true" to "I do not tire quickly" and "false" to "I feel tired a good deal of the time," or vice versa, represents semantically inconsistent responses.

The *VRIN* score is based on the sum of inconsistent responses. As noted earlier, the *VRIN* scale may be used to help interpret a high *F* score. For example, a high *F* score in conjunction with a low to moderate *VRIN* score rules out the possibility that the former reflects random responding or confusion. (See Exhibit 6-6 for a summary of interpretive guidelines for *VRIN*.)

Figure 6-2 illustrates the interpretative value of the *VRIN* scale. This MMPI-2 profile was produced by a 36-year-old man who had recently been admitted to an inpatient psychiatric unit of a general hospital. Examination of the *F* scale suggests that the profile is uninterpretable because the *T* score is 118 and indicates the possibility that he has answered the items in

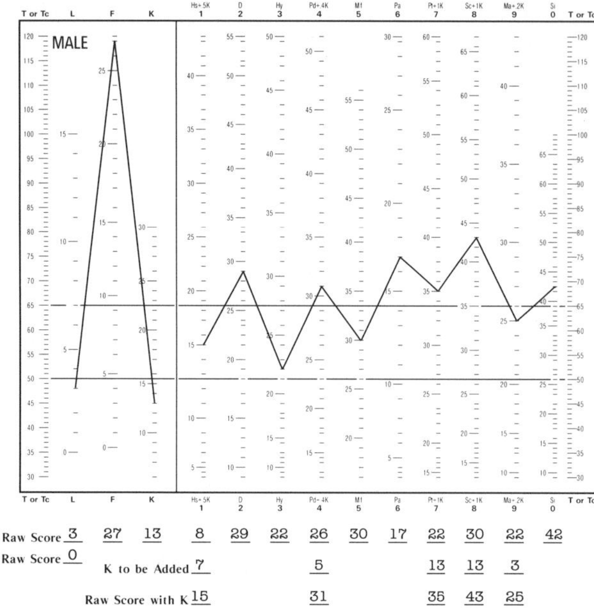

FIGURE 6-2. Basic MMPI-2 profile of a 36-year-old client with a high *F* score and a low *VRIN* scale score. (*VRIN* = 62; *TRIN* = 54.)

a random manner. However, the *VRIN*-scale score ($T = 62$) is in the valid range, signifying that he has not endorsed the items in a blatantly inconsistent manner. This rules out an interpretation that he has answered randomly. His clinical profile would be considered valid and interpretable.

However, the large number of symptoms he has endorsed, either as a result of a psychotic process or as an effort to draw attention to himself, requires further consideration. Although it has been possible to rule out random responding or carelessness as an explanation of his high *F*-scale elevation, one does not know why he has endorsed such broad-ranging, extreme symptoms. Further evaluation is needed to determine which of the possible alternative explanations is more likely.

True Response Inconsistency (*TRIN*)

The True Response Inconsistency scale or *TRIN* scale was designed to assess the tendency for some individuals to respond in an inconsistent manner by endorsing many items in the same direction (either true or false). The *TRIN* scale is made up of 20 pairs of items to which the same response is semantically inconsistent. For example, answering the items "Most of the time I feel blue" and "I am happy most of the time" both "true" or both "false" is inconsistent. Eleven of the 20 item pairs are scored inconsistent only if the client responds "true" to both items. Six of the item pairs are scored inconsistent only if the client responds "false" to both items. Three are scored inconsistent if the client responds "true" to both or "false" to both.

The scoring for *TRIN* is more complicated than the scoring of other MMPI-2 scales and should be carefully checked. First, the number of "true" and "false" inconsistent responses to the item pairs is determined. One point is added to the person's score for each of the 14 item pairs in which a "true" response is inconsistent. One point is subtracted for each of the 9 item pairs if a "false" response is obtained. Next, a constant of nine points is added to the scale in order to avoid negative raw score numbers. For example, if an individual endorsed four of the "true" item pairs and six of the "false" item pairs on *TRIN*, the score would be $4 - 6 + 9$, or 7. The test scorer should then convert the *TRIN* raw score to a *T* score.

The *T* scores for *TRIN* are constructed so that they will never be lower than 50. Any *T* score greater than 50 will be followed by either a "T," which denotes "true" response inconsistence ("yea saying"), or an "F," which denotes a "false" response inconsistency set ("nay saying"). Any *T* score greater than 80 is indicative of an extreme response set.

The *TRIN* score is particularly helpful in interpreting scores on Scales *L* and *K* because all but one of the items on these scales is keyed "false." Thus, an individual engaging in an inconsistent "false" response set may produce elevated scores on Scales *L* and *K* that have nothing to do with defensiveness or faking good. Conversely, an individual who answers the MMPI-2 items inconsistently "true" may produce very low scores on *L* and *K* that have nothing to do with being excessively open, self-critical, or overwhelmed by stress. Whenever extreme scores appear on Scales *L* and *K*, a careful examination of the score on *TRIN* is essential. (See Exhibit 6-7 for a summary of interpretive guidelines for *TRIN*.)

Figure 6-3 presents an example of an MMPI forensic evaluation that was invalidated by inconsistent responding (an "all false" pattern).

EXHIBIT 6-7

Summary of Interpretative Rules for the MMPI-2 and MMPI-A *TRIN* Scales in Forensic Evaluations

MMPI-2 *TRIN* T scores ≥ 80 or MMPI-A *TRIN* scores ≥ 75 indicate inconsistent responding because of yea- or nay-saying.

MMPI-2 *TRIN* scores from 70–79 or MMPI-A *TRIN* scores 70–74, inclusive, are suspect and suggest possible inconsistent responding.

A yea-saying response set is found in a *TRIN* score in the inconsistent true direction and indicated by a (T) following the score.

A nay-saying response set is found by a *TRIN* score in the inconsistent false direction and indicated by a (F) following the score.

Adapted from Butcher & Williams (1992a) by permission.

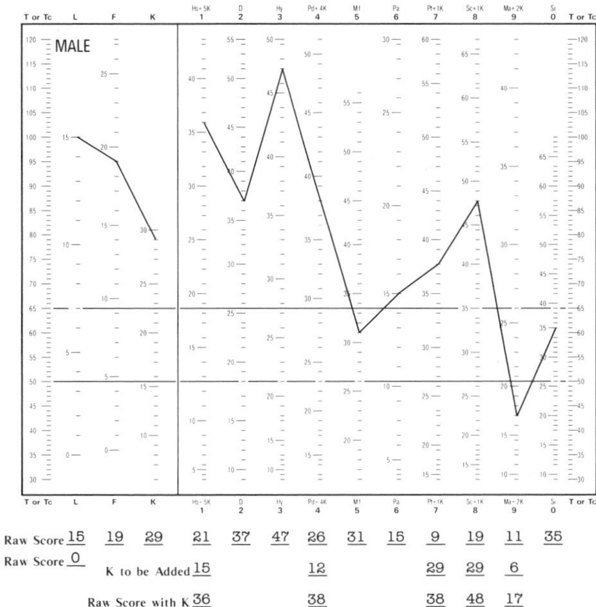

FIGURE 6-3. An all-false response pattern on the MMPI-2.

ASSESSING MALINGERING WITH THE MMPI AND MMPI-2

Malingering is defined as the intentional production of false or greatly exaggerated physical or psychological symptoms motivated by external incentives (American Psychiatric Association, 1987). It is often very difficult to demonstrate or detect malingering conclusively unless one actually observes that the behavior in question does not occur as reported. For example, some attorneys have been known to employ private detectives to watch an individual with an alleged physical injury to determine if he or she behaves in a manner contrary to the alleged injury.

Efforts to detect malingering through psychological test data have also been explored. Richard Rogers (1984) presented a useful model for detecting deception in forensic evaluations. He concluded that the MMPI offered "the widest array of psychometric research" (p. 101) in the area and pointed to cross-validated findings in identifying malingering through such means as exaggerated (or rare) responding, detection of defensiveness through excessive claims of virtue, and random or inconsistent responding. Rogers's model of malingering has received empirical support when applied in a forensic assessment setting (Heilbrun, Bennett, White, & Kelly, 1990).

MMPI AND MMPI-2 INDICATORS OF MALINGERING

We now discuss and illustrate further the three major indices of malingering suggested by Richard Rogers, and we describe a fourth approach that involves the evaluation of atypical patterns on MMPI and MMPI-2 results. The detection of faking on standardized psychological tests is an important consideration for the forensic psychologist not only for interpreting the particular test in question but also for better understanding the individual's general approach to the entire assessment process. Dalby (1988) wrote, "Given the evidence for generalized response set, the validity scores on these standardized measures may be useful in interpreting scores from concurrently administered instruments which do not contain validity indicators" (p. 54).

Rare Responding

Research on MMPI scales and malingering has consistently shown that the *F* scale and, to some extent, the *F–K* Index are valuable indicators of the tendency of some individuals to fake bad on the MMPI. Wasyliw et al. (1988) reported that MMPI indexes of malingering, particularly the *F* scale, were very effective in discriminating insanity defendants from individuals judged insane but not standing trial. Schretlen (1988) has recently reviewed the research evidence for the use of several psychological tests (MMPI, Rorschach, Bender-Gestalt, WAIS-R) in detection of malingering. He concluded that "it is probably indefensible to render expert testimony regarding the likelihood of malingering without psychological test data bearing on this question" (p. 473). His evaluation of the MMPI, thought to be the one most valuable means of detecting faking, was quite positive.

Berry, Baer, and Harris (1991) conducted a meta-analysis of 28 studies of faking bad or malingering on the MMPI. They found that most of the studies that have been conducted provided strong support for the MMPI's ability to detect malingering. They concluded, "The major finding of this review was that MMPI based scales for detecting faking are quite good at separating groups of subjects known or suspected of malingering from those completing the inventory honestly, with a mean overall effect size of 2.07" (p. 594).

Defensive Responding

In some settings, particularly in workers' compensation or personal injury litigation cases in which the individual is exaggerating or feigning physical injury or disability, the defensive profile pattern is a common harbinger of complaints without actual organic problems (Butcher & Harlow, 1987). Individuals in this setting often respond to the test items by claiming a high degree of virtue and denying (or minimizing) faults so that their claims of physical problems will seem more credible.

Inconsistent Responding

As Richard Rogers (1984) and others have noted, inconsistent responding on the MMPI items can reflect a general pattern of malingering on the test. Individuals who attempt to endorse extreme symptoms in an unselected fashion, endorse randomly, or respond according to an "all true" or "all false" response set tend to answer items on clinical scales in an inconsistent manner. Indices of inconsistency, such as *VRIN* and *TRIN* on MMPI-2, will help detect potential malingering or other invalidating response approaches.

Atypical MMPI and MMPI-2 Patterns

A fourth possible indicator of malingering on the MMPI-2 involves the presence of atypical response patterns. This approach is analogous to the reporting of incompatible physical symptoms such as "glove anesthesia" that cannot be explained by actual neural connections or other biological aspects. Those who malinger or dissimulate often give responses that are inconsistent with other clinical observations (J. M. MacDonald, 1976). This approach with the MMPI-2 involves the use of different sources of information within the test. That is, clients may present incompatible or inexplicable symptom patterns on the test that call into question the accuracy of the profile.

In this approach to detecting malingering, the interpreter matches behavior or symptoms from the client's responses to that of a modal or expected clinical pattern established by research on the particular sample involved or by the base rates for the relevant population. Research has established consistent or expected behavior patterns that can be evaluated through the various scales and indices. Hypotheses about an individual's expected behavior on the MMPI-2 can be matched with features of his or her actual behavior. Modal or expected MMPI-2 performances can be identified for a variety of clinical situations or phenomena. Clients who deviate from the expected performance, particularly with respect to the validity scale pattern, would be considered as possibly malingering. The following two examples illustrate instances in which the individual's MMPI-2 results are inconsistent with the expected MMPI-2 performance for the situation, suggesting that the client may have distorted the presentation of symptoms.

Example 1

In the first example, the MMPI-2 was used in a mental health treatment setting to determine treatment amenability and willingness to self-disclose (Butcher, 1990b). The expected validity pattern in this situation is that the individual presents honestly (low *L*) and openly (low *K*) and discusses mental health problems candidly (*F* between 60 and 89), as illustrated in Figure 6-4.

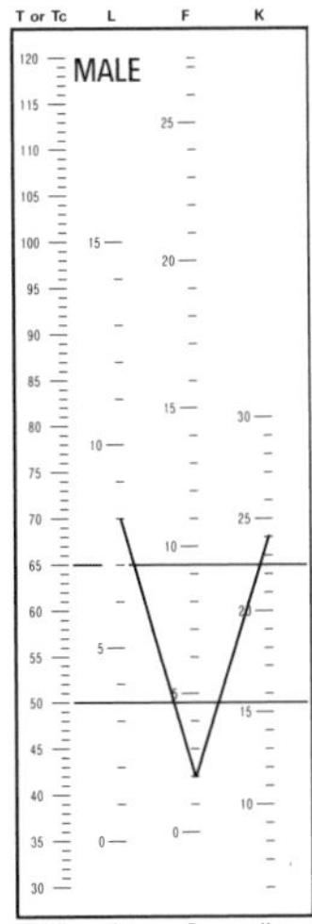

FIGURE 6-4. **An atypical validity pattern for a treatment-oriented patient.**

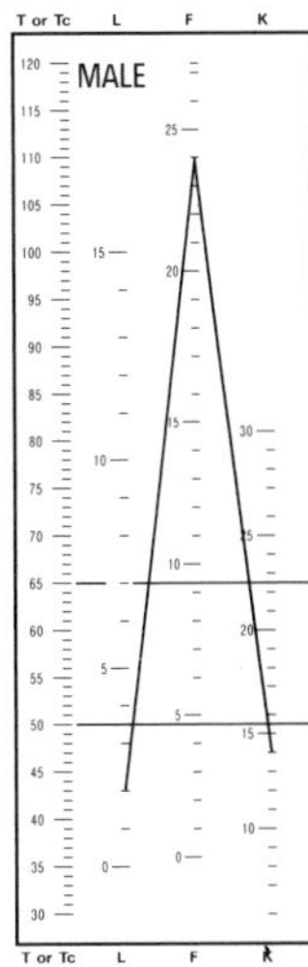

FIGURE 6-5. **An unlikely validity profile for an individual presenting a specific, accurate picture of his clinical symptoms.**

Example 2

In the second example, the MMPI-2 was administered in a medical clinic as part of an examination to determine if the individual was cooperating with the evaluation and presenting physical symptoms accurately. As the profile in Figure 6-5 shows, the individual has affirmed an excessive (relative to the expected) number of complaints.

COMMON FORENSIC VALIDITY PATTERNS

Several of the more common prototypical validity patterns found in forensic evaluations are now described and illustrated through case examples to show the relation among the various validity scales and their value in interpretation.

The Righteous Responder

Individuals with this validity pattern are projecting the most favorable social image possible, usually to create an impression that they are beyond reproach. The *L* score is quite prominent and may be accompanied by an elevation on the *K* scale. *F*-scale scores are typically low (i.e, less than average). Test takers profess to having very high moral values and assert that they have personal characteristics (e.g., high moral character) that they think will assure that their testimony will be credible. However, they seemingly claim too much virtue through asserting such unrealistically extreme qualities that even people who lead highly moral lives would not claim.

The case illustration in Figure 6-6 is an example of an individual (Mr. A) who subscribed to an extreme and exaggerated positive self-view so that his claims of other symptoms would be given a high degree of credence. In all likelihood, Mr. A engaged in conscious malingering of psychological and physical symptoms to convince the court of the legitimacy of his disability claims.

The situation is as follows. Mr. A, a 38-year-old litigant, claimed severe disability after *almost* being injured in a near-miss incident involving two airplanes. While taxiing a single engine airplane to depart on a charter flight, he was cleared to an active runway for takeoff by the air traffic controller. At the same time, a commercial jet airplane was cleared by a traffic control operator to land on the same runway. The jet airplane scraped the smaller plane, producing minor damages but no physical injury. Several months later, the litigant filed a workers' compensation claim for retraining in another field. Later (after the workers' compensation was used up), he filed a lawsuit against the government for damages (lost income) because he claimed that he was not able to follow up on his original aviation career plans (as an airline pilot) as a result of his alleged impaired mental state resulting from the incident. He reportedly became so tense, depressed,

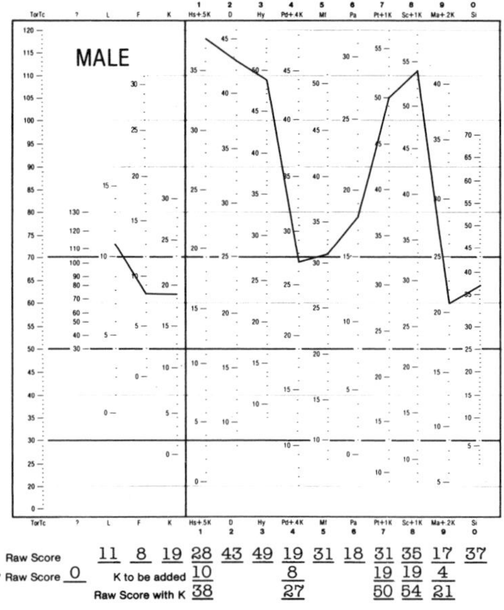

FIGURE 6-6. Basic MMPI profile of Mr. A.

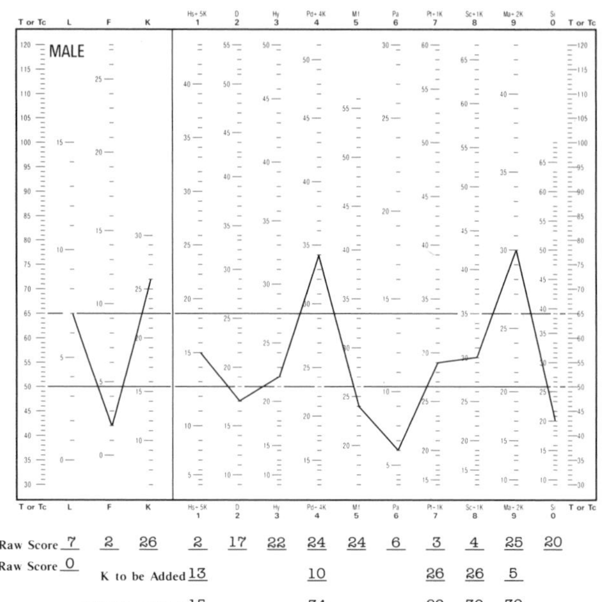

FIGURE 6-7. Basic MMPI-2 profile of Mr. B.

and stressed that he had to change his goals to a less lucrative career rather than to follow the original aviation career plans he was pursuing at the time of the incident.

His MMPI profile reflects an extreme tendency to present a highly virtuous picture of himself while at the same time asserting that he is suffering from extreme physical and mental fatigue and disability. Mr. A's apparent attempt to distort the MMPI personality appraisal, as reflected in the validity pattern, was consistent with other attempts on his part to "oversell" himself. For example, he had previously completed job application forms for airline positions that contained false information about his flying background and qualifications. His MMPI validity pattern was consistent with that of an individual who was falsely describing himself to create a particular impression.

The Defensive Self-Protector

As noted earlier, parents who are being assessed in a domestic court case to determine custody or establish visitation rights tend to present a very favorable self-portrait in their response to psychological testing. Figure 6-7 presents an MMPI-2 pattern typical of an individual who denies faults and asserts that he has no psychological problems or personal weaknesses (see Mr. B below). Even with his defensive profile, other aspects of his profile show a pattern of personality characteristics that probably reflect problem behavior.

The second hypothetical case study is as follows. Brenda (age 38) and Bob B (age 41), both White, have been divorced for about 3 years, and their relationship has continued to be troublesome. Reportedly, Mr. B has been very irregular with his alimony and child support payments to Ms. B, and Ms. B claims that he presently owes back alimony. On the other hand, Mr. B claims that his former wife has not lived up to the visitation program established by the court and has recently refused to let him see their daughter.

Mr. B was being evaluated in a domestic court assessment to determine if his parental visitation rights should be suspended. Investigation is currently under way to determine if he is guilty of sexually abusing his 9-year-old daughter, as alleged by his ex-wife. His daughter has not acknowledged that the abuse occurred, but his ex-wife insists that she has observed him fondling their daughter in the past and believes that the abuse continues. She also alleges that Mr. B has engaged extensively in other irresponsible behavior (financial, legal, and interpersonal) and that she does not wish to expose her child to his deviant behavior. Mr. B has a history of excessive drinking and problematic behavior, such as reckless driving and driving under the influence of alcohol. He told the psychologist that he agreed to the court-ordered MMPI-2 evaluation in an effort to "clear his name" and keep his visitation rights with his daughter.

Mr. B's MMPI-2 validity scale configuration shows a clear pattern of test defensiveness (see Appendix I for both *K*- and non-*K*-corrected profiles). He made an effort to place himself in the most favorable light, denying faults and projecting a very positive self-image. Although he attempted to present himself as a problem-free and well-adjusted individual, his MMPI-2 clinical pattern reflected a number of possible problems such as poor impulse control, antisocial behavior, and poor judgment. His problems are probably more extreme than the clinical scales suggest.

The court-appointed psychologist conducting the evaluation concluded that Mr. B's long history of problematic behavior along with his MMPI-2-based personality pattern supports the possibility that his negative behavior could produce a deleterious influence on the child. Closer supervision and more restricted family visitation were recommended pending review of visitation rights by the court.

A Case of Malingering in a Not Guilty by Reason of Insanity Plea

The following case involves an evaluation of a 22-year-old, unemployed Black woman (Ms. C) who pleaded that she was not guilty by reason of insanity after being arrested and charged with attempted aggravated murder following an incident in which she stabbed a taxi driver in the back. She was referred for psychological evaluation to determine her present condition and whether her present condition might bear on her allegation that she was insane at the time of the assault.

In the diagnostic interview, she appeared to be somewhat confused and seemed not to respond appropriately even to simple questions asked of her. She was administered the MMPI-2 as part of the forensic evaluation. Her MMPI-2 standard profile is shown in Figure 6-8, and her MMPI-2 supplemental profile is shown in Figure 6-9.

Ms. C's MMPI-2 validity pattern (see Figure 6-8) shows a clear symptom exaggeration and a very unlikely *F*-scale elevation, indicating that she claimed numerous, unrelated psychological problems and attitudes. According to her *F*-scale elevation, her clinical

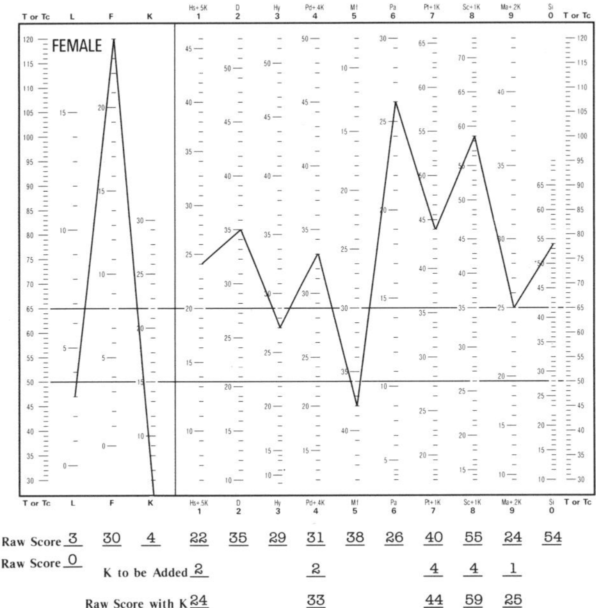

FIGURE 6-8. Basic MMPI-2 profile of Ms. C. (Source: Graham, 1992. Adapted by permission.)

profile is likely to be an exaggerated and uninterpretable pattern of symptoms.

As noted above, several possible explanations can be found for profiles with this level of elevation on the MMPI-2 *F* scale. It is important to rule out the possibility that this is a random profile. Ms. C has had limited education, and the examiner wondered if she could read well enough to complete a valid MMPI-2. Her low score on the *VRIN* scale ($T = 43$) indicates that she has endorsed similar items in a very consistent manner, thus eliminating the possibility that she had responded in a noncontent-oriented or random fashion (see Figure 6-9). If she simply had been confused, disoriented, or unable to read the items, she would have produced a higher *VRIN*-scale score. In addition, it is very unlikely that she was experiencing a psychotic process at the time of the testing. Individuals with extreme psychological disorders do not generally produce this extreme level of *F* elevation; instead, they tend to respond more selectively to symptoms, producing lower *F* scores.

Her extremely high *F*-score elevation is more likely the result of a false claim of psychological problems on her part. Ms. C's validity pattern more closely resembles those extremely exaggerated profiles found by Graham et al. (1991) in individuals who attempt to fake the MMPI-2 by claiming mental health problems

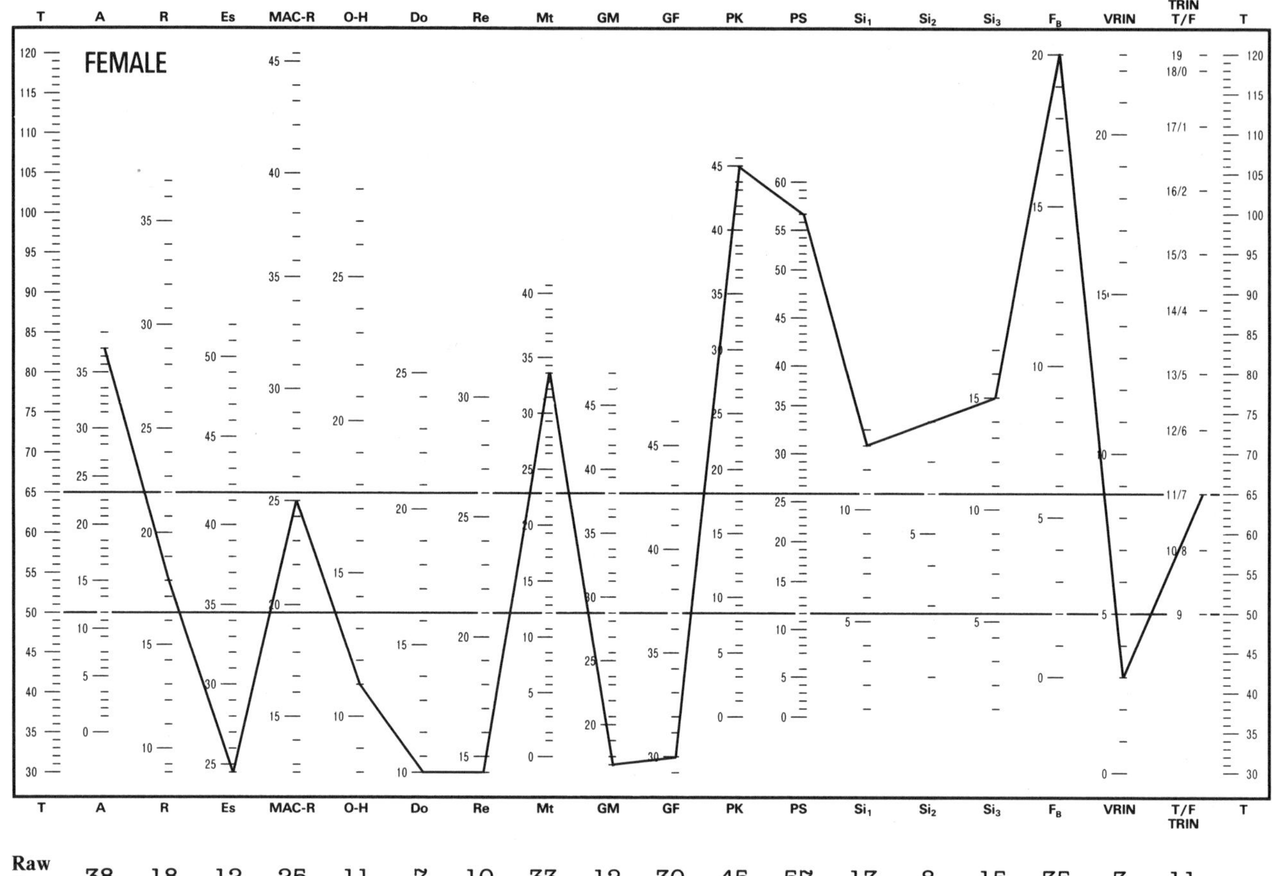

FIGURE 6-9. Supplementary MMPI-2 profile of Ms. C.

that they do not have. Other information obtained in the interview and background evaluation added substance to the conclusion that her MMPI-2 profile represented an effort to fake the test in order to appear psychiatrically disturbed.

PSEUDOMEASURES OF INVALIDITY

Subtle–Obvious Scales

Socrates often challenged his pupils with an interesting dilemma. If you were suddenly given omniscient powers through wearing a very special ring (Gyges Ring) that allowed you to know what others were thinking without their knowledge, would it be proper to use such information to your advantage? Psychologists working in forensic settings might not wish to debate the ethics of having this phenomenal power, although many would be delighted with the possible information such a device could provide. To know other people's secrets and motives without their being aware that they had disclosed them to us might even be considered by some to be an assessment psychologist's dream.

Interestingly, some psychologists have considered the MMPI "subtle" items to be just such a powerful technique—a way of assessing an individual without the test taker actually knowing that one has done so. We consider it important for psychologists to be aware of the flaws in this "technology," and we caution against relying on these indicators in forensic assessments.

Although the Wiener–Harmon subtle keys have been touted as a means of providing special information about clients, their track record as a credible source of information is actually poor. We now look at the question of item subtlety and the utility of the Wiener–Harmon subscales in more detail and examine recent research findings that bear on the question.

Theoretically, it is possible to develop items for a personality measure that have strong predictive validity but are not as obvious in content as other items on the scale (Jackson, 1971). A *subtle* item on a scale is defined as an item that predicts the criteria defining the scale but does not have an obvious content relationship to the construct in question. For example, some of the items on the *Pa* scale are not obviously related to criterion characteristics such as suspicion, mistrust, and paranoid thinking (e.g. "I am happy most of the time"). These items are thought to be subtle predictors and are believed by some to have special predictive properties.

Following the empirical scale construction doctrine underlying the MMPI (i.e., that all the items contained on an empirically derived scale are equally valid), Wiener and Harmon recognized that some items were less obviously related to content and were thought to be subtle predictors of the construct measured by the scale (Wiener, 1948). The subtle items were thought to have special properties in that they allowed the clinician to assess people without their being consciously aware that they were providing important personal information in the assessment.

Wiener and Harmon developed subtle and obvious subscales for several MMPI scales (*D*, *Hy*, *Pd*, *Pa*, and *Ma*). For a subtle item to work according to this premise, two item properties must be present: First, the content of the item should not be obviously related to the construct being measured; second, the item must predict the criterion as well as other items on the scale.

Unfortunately, the subtle subscales developed by Wiener and Harmon do not meet the second criterion. Two points should be considered. First, *the subtle items on the Wiener–Harmon subscales are likely to be chance items.* It is quite likely that the lack of content relevance in the subtle items results from the fact that they are imperfectly related to the criterion and were actually selected by chance as a result of incomplete validation procedures. (Starke Hathaway and McKinley used relatively small samples in their original scale development.) For example, in developing a scale to assess characteristic "x" using 550 items, chance alone would place 27 items on the scale. We assume that cross-validation would eliminate the chance items, leaving only those items that are valid indicators of the characteristic being assessed.

Second, *the research on the Wiener–Harmon subtle subscales shows that they are not valid predictors of the psychopathology they purportedly measure.* Hathaway (1965), who championed the empirical method of scale construction and generally held the view that subtle items on the scales had the special powers described above, actually expressed doubts about the efficacy of subtle items when compared with face-valid items:

> *It is apparent that the response-set issue began with worry about the fact that face valid questions seemed to invite distortion by faking good or bad. Subtle items appeared to be an obvious way to control this, but McCall (1958) concluded from a study of the D scale of the MMPI "The 60 items of the depression scale of the MMPI were shown to be differentially effective in distinguishing depressive from a matched group of nondepressive psychotics in proportion to their face validity, as determined a priori." Such a finding supports the possibility that face validity is a central source of item validity. Wiener (1948[b]) approached the problem by forming separate subscales using the subtle and the obvious items from empirical scales. It will be apparent below that the very reality of many personality variables is tied to face validity. There could not be a subtle scale that would have much value for such a variable. (p. 468)*

Several subsequent studies have shown that Hathaway's intuition was correct, at least with respect to the Wiener–Harmon subscales. The subtle subscales do not discriminate well enough in practice, and most studies show that they do not predict as clearly as the obvious items on the scale do.[2] In fact, Weed et al. (1990) found that the subtle items actually *lower* the validities of the full-scale score.

[2] Anthony, 1971; Berry, Baer, & Harris, 1991; Grossman, Haywood, Ostrov, Wasyliw, & Cavanaugh, 1990; Herkov, Archer, & Gordon, 1991; Nelson, 1987; Nelson & Cicchetti, 1991; Rogers, 1983; Schretlen, 1990; Timbrook, Graham, Keiller, & Watts, 1991; Wasyliw et al., 1988; Wrobel & Lachar, 1982.

Greene (1991) has recently reiterated the view that the subtle items give the interpreter a special way to evaluate invalid or unusual response attitudes. In his view, the difference in response to obvious as opposed to subtle items on a scale can be used as an indicator of test invalidity. However, there is inadequate empirical support for this view (Timbrook et al., 1991; Weed et al., 1990).

In most situations, personality and symptom scales work best for people who are willing to be assessed and are cooperative with the psychological evaluation. It is our own view that the Wiener–Harmon subtle subscales do not provide valid or useful information in any setting; however, they are especially problematic in forensic settings because they may tend to provide misleading information and detract from more valid and useful information that might be available in the test.

Complex Combinations of Validity Indexes

Greene (1991) has proposed a procedure designed to provide a measure of consistency of item endorsement by arithmetically combining the absolute values of the MMPI-2 validity scales, such as *F*, *F(B)*, and *VRIN* scores. For example, the raw scores of these scales would be summed and taken to represent a more accurate estimate of inconsistency than each measure taken separately. Caution should be exercised in simply combining these scales because each scale has somewhat different psychometric properties. For example, although *F* and *F(B)* were similarly derived scales, the number of items on each and the item response rates underlying the items differ. Ben-Porath and Tellegen (1992) have provided a similar caution about these arithmetically combined indices:

> *We similarly caution users of the MMPI-2 against premature and uncritical reliance on various indices and ratios derived from the validity scales such as those recommended by Greene (1991) in his recent book. These indices may have the appeal of computational objectivity and the appearance of scientific rigor. In reality, however, they are subjectively derived composites that may discard or inappropriately weigh information contained in the validity scales themselves. In our assessment, an adequate empirical basis remains to be established for indices such as those proposed by Greene. (p. 8)*

In conclusion, a simple summation of the raw scores of various MMPI-2 validity scales, without substantial empirical support, could mislead the interpreter into thinking it is a more powerful index than each scale considered separately. Adequate research support for combining the validity scales into summed indices has yet to be published.

SUMMARY

Few issues arise with such regularity during an expert witness's testimony as the credibility of the individual who was assessed. Is a defendant on trial for his or her life doing a good job of faking insanity but actually competent to stand trial? Is he or she apparently sane but actually managing to hide psychotic processes so that the lack of competence to stand trial only emerges through sophisticated psychological testing? Is the plaintiff in a personal injury suit malingering? Has the survivor of an airline crash, although suffering no serious physical injury, been psychologically traumatized? Are parents who are engaged in a bitter divorce and custody struggle telling the truth about the other's despicable behavior and about their own laudatory manners?

It is virtually impossible for expert witnesses and trial attorneys to avoid issues of assessing malingering and other aspects of credibility. In this chapter, we reviewed some of the issues, methods, and research related to credibility. The MMPI-2 and MMPI-A contain several measures that were designed to assess negative response approaches to the items. Several measures assess test defensiveness or the tendency to present a highly favorable image and to ignore or deny problems. The *L* and *K* scales were described as measures to assess tendencies to "look good" or present unrealistically favorable images on the test.

Other measures assess the opposite tendency—the desire to assert extreme problems or disability through responding to many items showing severe problems. The infrequency scales *F* and *F(B)* on the MMPI-2 and *F*, F_1, and F_2 on MMPI-A help the practitioner to determine if the client has exaggerated problems to create an aura of psychological frailty, personal injury, or inability to cope with present circumstances. Other useful measures assess the consistency or inconsistency with which the individual has approached the items. Two new scales, the *VRIN* scale and the *TRIN* scale, allow for the assessment of random responses or for nay-saying and yea-saying responses to the items.

The MMPI-2 and MMPI-A validity scales provide a very powerful tool for the forensic psychologist in appraising the response attitudes of clients. The validity scales can be effectively used in combination to provide hypotheses about the individual's approach to the test items and to the forensic evaluation. This chapter also provided a cautionary note about two validity approaches that may tend to obscure rather than clarify useful clues to the client's test-taking attitudes. The rationale for the Wiener–Harmon subtle subscales was discussed and flaws in these measures identified. The lack of adequate substantiating research for the subtle subscales was noted. The traditional MMPI-2 validity scales and the *VRIN* and *TRIN* scales appear to provide the forensic practitioner with substantial means for detecting deviant response attitudes on the MMPI-2 and MMPI-A.

Chapter 7

WRITING FORENSIC REPORTS

This chapter addresses the communication of MMPI-based test results through written forensic reports and provides illustrations of case reports.

The reasons for administration of the MMPI (and other tests) in forensic evaluations is an important consideration that will help determine the structure of the report. In many cases, MMPI-based evaluations become centrally involved in court cases although the evaluation might have been conducted for a purpose different from litigation, for example, in a medical evaluation or in a personnel screening situation. In other cases, attorneys or the court will request an evaluation to address the questions of psychological status, symptoms, diagnosis, and prognosis. In this chapter, we address reports that are specifically prepared for forensic testimony.

In forensic assessment, the psychologist is often asked to consult about a case before writing a report or testifying in court because the attorney needs to know what the expert will say as a basis for deciding whether to call the psychologist to testify (see The Initial Contact With the Attorney in chapter 4). Most forensic psychologists have probably had the experience of providing expert consultation on a case only to find that the attorney chose to ignore the test results and not call the expert to testify. Consider the following example:

A man in his mid-40s went to see a psychiatrist, reportedly for tension and sleeping difficulty. The psychiatrist, after administering (although probably not scoring or interpreting) an MMPI and interviewing the client for 15 minutes, provided medication to help him sleep. The man, a chronic alcoholic, went home and killed himself using the medication provided by the psychiatrist. The patient's wife filed a medical malpractice suit against the psychiatrist, charging that he failed to sufficiently evaluate her husband's problems and provided the means for his suicide. The psychiatrist's attorney contacted a psychologist to evaluate the patient's MMPI, administered on the day of his suicide, and to serve as a forensic witness on the case.

The results of a computer-generated scoring and interpretation of the patient's MMPI clearly supported the possibility that the psychiatrist did indeed fail to appropriately assess the client's high potential for suicide. The computer-based report on the patient actually warned about the possibility of suicide and the patient's possible abuse of prescription medications.

The attorney chose not to employ the psychologist as an expert witness in the case. It is unlikely that the plaintiff's side in the case was aware of the existence of the MMPI. Attorneys on both sides *must*, as outlined in chapters 5 and 8, conduct adequate discovery.

Psychologist Irving Weiner (1987) provided an informative discussion about the feelings that psychological consultants might have in such situations. He pointed out that

> *being in effect dismissed from the case before a written report has been prepared—can raise some disturbing questions concerning proper practice. . . . The answers to these questions touch upon some ethical and realistic considerations in the practice of law and psychology.* (p. 515)

However, Weiner further indicated that

> *the point is that it is entirely appropriate and consistent with prevailing practice for attorneys to question or reject the opinions of a consultant they have retained and to seek other consultants whose opinions will support more effectively the case they are trying to build. (p. 515)*

USE OF COMPUTER-BASED MMPI REPORTS IN FORENSIC CASES

As noted in chapter 2, computer-based psychological assessment can serve an important role in a forensic evaluation. Because of the potential advantages of computer-based interpretations, as discussed in chapter 2, many psychologists incorporate them in evaluations that are likely to be involved in litigation.

Computer reports are usually viewed as preliminary or provisional working papers, analogous to hypotheses that the practitioner might generate by researching the published literature to determine those that are likely relevant to the profile in question.

It is important for the automated-report user to be sufficiently familiar with the research literature to be able to cite the background sources if questioned in cross-examination. Forensic psychologist Theodore Blau (1984a), former president of the APA, pointed out that "when relying on computer-based test interpretation, the forensic psychologist should be familiar with the rationale and validity of the interpretations and be prepared to justify their utilization in the judicial matter at hand" (p. 184; see also appendix J of this book).

Should the computerized report be submitted as evidence in the case or modified to suit the client? A very important reason for the practitioner to be knowledgeable about the information incorporated in computer-based reports is that there may be hypotheses or descriptions in the report that may not apply to a particular case. In such instances, the practitioner may choose to use only those high-probability statements from the report that are deemed relevant to the case and ignore the others. This is appropriate because it is always the practitioner who has the final responsibility for deciding what elements of a psychological evaluation are appropriate for a particular client. However, if the opposing counsel conducts an adequate discovery, the computer-generated printout will be available as a basis for cross-examination. Therefore, as described below, the psychologist may wish to include in the written forensic report the reasoning process that led him or her to reject certain hypotheses set forth by the computer program.

There are situations in which a computerized report is introduced directly into evidence and becomes the center of direct and cross-examination. These usually are cases in which the computer-based report is used as a verification of or challenge against an interpretation made by a practitioner. Because any notes or test materials used to arrive at decisions can be subpoenaed, computer reports are more frequently finding their way into evidence in court cases.

The psychologist may, at times, be faced with discordant test findings or with a computer-based report that prints out a statement that is thought to be irrelevant in the present case.

As we discuss below, the practitioner may need to introduce in direct examination or defend in cross-examination the decision not to interpret seemingly discrepant findings or to include "off target" information that is printed out in a computerized report. Being well versed in what the MMPI measures will be important in such challenges. Forensic psychologist David Shapiro (1991), a former president of the American Academy of Forensic Psychology, advised that the expert witness try to anticipate what the controversial issues might be in the testimony and prepare carefully for them. He pointed out that

> *the expert needs to anticipate in advance what some of the challenges to the opinion will be, making a frank assessment of the weakest parts of the evaluation and opinion. One must attempt to deal with these in direct examination, rather than creating the impression that one is surprised by these questions when they arise on cross-examination. (pp. 206–207)*

PLANNING A FORENSIC REPORT

In this section, we consider a number of important general considerations for writing reports that might become the subject of forensic testimony. (For a

EXHIBIT 7-1

Features of Forensic Reports Based on the MMPI, MMPI-2, or MMPI-A

Comprehensive Includes all pertinent elements in the scale scores

Balanced Incorporates major aspects of the test performance, even hypotheses that might seem not to fit into the major conclusions of the case

Objective Incorporates established empirical correlates based on research

Instructional Includes unambiguous language so that lay persons can clearly understand the way the test is used

Assuring Includes an appraisal of the degree of confidence that the psychologist has in the reliability of the interpretations

Humility Provides interpretations and conclusions in an informative, direct, and unbiased tone

general discussion of report writing, see Tallent, 1993.) These points are also summarized in Exhibit 7-1.

The report should be *comprehensive* in scope; that is, it should include the major relevant interpretive elements in the MMPI results that bear on the question or questions involved in the case.

The report should be *balanced*, presenting clear and relevant features of the test scores. It is also important to note significant aspects of the profile that appear to produce disparate conclusions or that are discounted in the report. Noting discrepant findings, of course, runs the risk of pointing out possible weaknesses in the test-based information that the other side might capitalize on. However, one's task as an expert witness is not to win the case at all costs or to conceal aspects of evidence but rather to present as honestly and clearly as possible one's opinions and the bases for those opinions. As noted elsewhere, the Golden Rule seems a useful guide. If you were on the jury, would you not want to be aware of "discrepant" findings that are relevant to an expert witness's opinions and testimony? The process of pointing out and explaining disparate information can also be viewed as being consistent with an objective, scientific approach to test interpretation—a goal worth striving for in presenting test results in court. This process of pointing out disparate information can also be viewed as one's sworn duty when one takes an oath to tell the *whole* truth. It is important in test-based testimony not to select information in the test that supports a particular side at the expense of other pertinent features of the test. These contradictory elements, if important, may be brought out by the other side, making the forensic witness appear (perhaps accurately) biased or careless in preparation. An important goal in forensic testimony is to provide objective consultation to the court about the test results relevant to the case—not to win a case for the side that is paying one's fee.

Interpretations incorporated in the report should be based on the most *objective* information available from the scales and indices used. It is important for the psychologist to be knowledgeable about the resource information behind the interpretations included in the report. This specialized information often becomes the basis for cross-examination questions. Preparation for the cross-examination could include researching the relevant literature for references to document the interpretations in the report. It may be sufficient to cite standard textbook summaries of test-based information (Butcher & Williams, 1992a; Graham, 1990; Greene, 1991); however, if highly specific questions are being addressed, a more focused reference search may be required.

It is important that a forensic psychological report be written in clear, unambiguous language that serves to *instruct* nonpsychologists about the ways the test works. It is also important that the report be written in unambiguous language that is free of psychological jargon (see Ownby, 1987). In court settings, psychological reports are used by individuals who have no background in psychology and who are not likely to understand obscure psychological terms.

The report should contain information that allows the recipient to appraise the degree of confidence that the psychologist has in the reliability of the interpretations. The jury or the judge in the case needs to be *assured* of the credibility and relevance of the information provided. The "confidence" estimate provided by the psychological consultant as to the believability of the data allows recipients of the information to appropriately weigh this aspect of the testimony.

Finally, *humility* should be exercised in writing forensic reports that are based on psychological test results. Test-based psychological interpretations and conclusions are not absolutes but are probabilistic statements that are made to apply under certain conditions. The findings should be presented in an objective, informative, direct, and unbiased tone without the use of superlatives or slanted writing.

The makeup of the forensic report will depend in part on the questions about which the psychological consultant is being asked to testify. If the testimony is broad in scope, for example, centering around the question of suitability for parenting, then a very extensive diagnostic study, perhaps involving several interviews and many different tests, is needed. However, if the question being addressed is more limited (e.g., Did the test taker fake the MMPI? Does the score on the MAC-R Scale actually reflect alcoholism?), then a more focused report is appropriate.

A SAMPLE FORENSIC REPORT OUTLINE

The structure and content of a forensic report will vary depending on a variety of factors. The following outline is an example of just one way to organize a certain set of data and conclusions (see also the summary provided in Exhibit 7-2).

Test-taking Information and Analysis of Extratest Considerations

The extratest factors that bear on interpretation of the test results need to be carefully detailed. Any possible limiting condition should be described. For example, if the person's reading ability is marginal or if English is not the individual's native language, this should be noted. Any deviation from standard testing practice should also be noted. For example, if the individual had been administered the test items orally by a technician rather than being administered the booklet or standard audiocassette version of the instrument, these circumstances should be described. If the practitioner allowed the client to complete the test in an unsupervised setting, a clear problem for interpretation and an approach that cannot be justified in forensic practice, the report should clearly note the circumstances. This last situation is sufficient in most cases to have the test results declared hearsay and excluded from the proceedings. Chapter 4 discusses some of the reasons that failing to supervise the assessment process is poor practice that allows, if not invites, confounding factors inconsistent with the concept of a standardized test. (See also the discussion of the question, "Was the test administration directly monitored?" in the administration and scoring section of chapter 8; included in this discussion is the published

EXHIBIT 7-2

Suggested Outline for a Forensic MMPI/MMPI-2/MMPI-A Report

Extratest factors Includes descriptions of extraneous factors that could influence the evaluation

Appropriateness of the test Provides an indication of the relevance of the MMPI/MMPI-2/MMPI-A for the particular client

Test validity Includes a description of response or test-taking attitudes and an indication of whether the profiles are interpretable

Personality and symptomatic information Provides an integrated summary of relevant empirical scales and content indicators

Diagnostic considerations Summarizes test-based information relevant to descriptive diagnosis

Treatment or rehabilitation recommendations Offers hypotheses about treatment prognosis

Case considerations Summarizes information from the test that likely bears on specific aspects of the case

Report conclusions Concludes with a summary of the relevant aspects of the test interpretation for understanding the test taker's current forensic status

opinion of the APA's Committee on Professional Standards regarding adequate monitoring of test administration.)

Discussion of the Appropriateness of the Test for the Client

It is useful to include, near the beginning of the report, any appropriate statements regarding the relationship between the demographic data, personal history, and so on, of the client and the nature, norms, and interpretive research base of the test or tests. If it is not clear (on the basis of statements made elsewhere in the report, such as "Women of similar age, ethnicity, and circumstances who produce such profiles tend to be . . ."), questions of the appropriateness of the test for the individual should be explicitly discussed.

Discussion of Validity Considerations

A thorough interpretation and discussion of the individual's cooperativeness with the evaluation as reflected through the validity scales needs to be provided. As noted in chapter 6, this information often turns out to be the most important (and sometimes the only useful) information provided in forensic evaluations. The validity interpretation presents an overview of the credibility of the individual's self-report and gives the reader a clear understanding as to the degree of confidence one can have that the test profiles are valid and interpretable.

Description of Personality and Symptoms

In presenting the core personality and symptomatic description that is based on the traditional clinical scales of the MMPI, MMPI-2, and MMPI-A, it is important to incorporate two types of information: how well defined the scale score or profile configuration is and the extent of available research in the MMPI literature for similar cases.

As noted earlier, profile definition is an important consideration because it allows one to project with a higher degree of certainty whether the scores would likely be stable over time. Moreover, the more clearly defined profiles allow the interpreter to have more confidence in the matchup of the established empirical literature on high scale scores and code types.

The interpreter should be familiar with the research base in the MMPI literature for particular profile types or high scale elevations. If a particular interpretation is being made, for example, that high *Pd* individuals are typically viewed as impulsive and irresponsible, the psychologist should have an understanding and awareness of relevant resources to back up the statement.

Diagnostic Considerations

Although there have been several studies relating MMPI-based diagnostic patterns to the basic *Diagnostic and Statistical Manual of Mental Disorders* (3rd ed.; or 3rd ed., rev.; *DSM-III* or *DSM-III-R*; American Psychiatric Association, 1980 and 1987, respectively) categories (Ben-Porath et al., 1991; Manos, 1985; Savasir & Erol, 1990), it is usually not desirable to attempt *equating* MMPI diagnostic information to diagnoses that are based on the *DSM* in the report, because it opens the psychologist to the possibility of extensive cross-examination on issues irrelevant to the assessment.

The use of the MMPI approach to personality and clinical appraisal is an alternative approach to psychiatric diagnosis—one that provides a summary of symptoms and problems from the patient's self-reported perspective. MMPI-based diagnostic descriptions are more specific and are based on more empirical research than are *DSM*-based psychiatric categories.

Treatment or Rehabilitation Potential

In many cases, the potential for treatment or rehabilitation is pertinent to the report. In cases in which the individual is being charged with a major crime, the potential for rehabilitation might enter into sentencing or disposition. Similarly, in personal injury litigation, prognosis for rehabilitation might enter into damage awards.

Case Considerations

The report should provide a detailed discussion of case considerations, that is, inferences that are tailored to specific issues in the case. These, of course, will differ depending on the nature of the case. Cases involving personal injury will, for example, have a rather different focus than those involving determination of competency or insanity pleas. In this discussion, specific hypotheses or descriptions bearing on the court decision should be thoroughly described.

Report Conclusions

A summary of major points derived from the results of the testing should be presented along with conclusions that can be drawn from them. Recommendations for the court to consider should be succinctly presented.

SAMPLE FORENSIC REPORTS

This section presents two examples of MMPI-based forensic reports. In the first case ("Beatrice S."), a relatively brief report, based on the MMPI-2 and a 90-minute interview, was submitted to the court. Extensive demographic data, detailed history, and other information were available in other court documents and were not included in this report. In the second case ("Ms. Jones"), a more detailed report described the findings of a psychological and neuropsychological assessment that included administration of the MMPI.

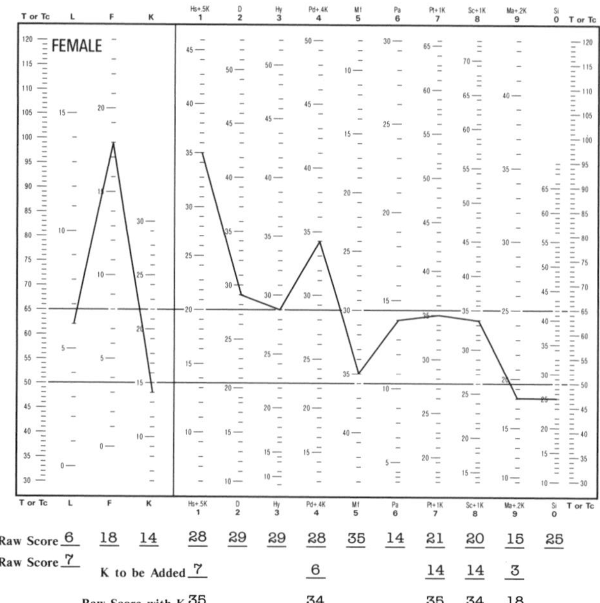

FIGURE 7-1. Basic MMPI-2 profile of Beatrice S.

Case 1: Beatrice S.

Background and context. Beatrice S., a 47-year-old hourly worker in the garment industry, was walking on the sidewalk in a commercial district of a large city on her way to work when she tripped on slippery pavement and fell in front of a drugstore. She helped herself up (there were no witnesses to the fall) and went inside to complain and ask for assistance. An assistant manager drove her to a hospital emergency room where she was treated and released after a relatively brief visit. Claiming that her back and neck injuries prevented her from working and caused continuous head and neck pain, sleeplessness, nausea, tension, and mental strain, she sought further treatment from her own physician and a doctor of chiropractic medicine. She was treated with several pain-relieving medications and chiropractic adjustments, but the pain allegedly persisted. She was finally hospitalized and placed in traction for about 10 days, but the pain reportedly became more intense after she was discharged. Following her discharge from the hospital, she filed a personal injury suit against the drugstore for negligence and sought damages for her intractable pain, loss of income, medical expenses, and mental suffering.

When she was evaluated by the physician assigned by the drugstore's insurance carrier to provide an evaluation (and consistent with the emergency room physician's initial report) her injuries were considered to be minimal and very unlikely to result in the extent of disability she claimed. Her medical evaluation included a psychological examination to evaluate the extent of psychological distress and mental impairment she claimed from the alleged injury (see MMPI-2 profiles in Figures 7-1 and 7-2).

Psychological report. *Behavioral observations.* Ms. S. was initially noncompliant with the psychological evaluation and refused to take the MMPI-2 at the request of the insurance carrier. After discussing the matter with her attorney, she rescheduled the appointment and complied with the evaluation. She was seen in a diagnostic interview for approximately an hour and a half and was administered the MMPI-2. She was generally hostile and brusque with the psychologist. During the interview, she presented herself as being in considerable pain, occasionally displaying pained mannerisms and facial expressions. She reportedly could not sit still to take the MMPI-2 in one sitting and got up several times and stretched. She complained at great length about her physical problems and how they had seemed to spread to other parts of her body after her traction treatment. During the interview, she was quite reluctant to explore areas of psychological conflict or past problems. She reluc-

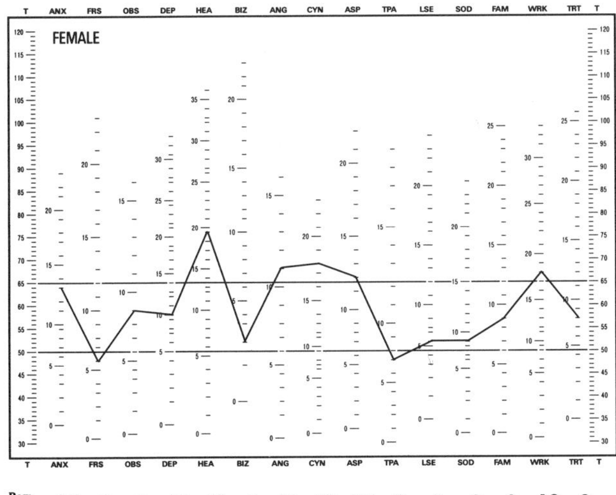

Raw Score 13 6 9 10 19 2 11 18 12 7 6 9 9 18 8

FIGURE 7-2. MMPI-2 content scale profile of Beatrice S.

tantly acknowledged that she has seen mental health counselors in the past, had been in marital therapy at one time, and had been in an inpatient alcohol abuse treatment program 1 year ago. She refused to acknowledge having mental health problems at this time and reiterated that her problems were purely physical.

Test-taking attitudes. Her lack of motivation to cooperate with the psychological evaluation was also reflected in her MMPI-2 performance. She did not complete the answer sheet as expected, omitting seven items. Moreover, she endorsed items in the extreme or rare direction regardless of content, as shown by her elevated score on the *VRIN* and *F* scales.

Validity considerations. Ms. S.'s validity scale scores indicate that she responded to the MMPI-2 items in an extremely exaggerated manner, claiming many more problems and symptoms than others do, even patients in mental health treatment programs. Her tendency to endorse many symptoms produced an exaggerated pattern of scores commonly found among individuals who malinger or distort health problems. Consistent with research on feigning extreme symptoms, there is a strong possibility that her symptom pattern is exaggerated in order for her to appear disabled.

Symptoms and behavior. Individuals with this MMPI-2 profile tend to present a pattern of chronic and extreme psychological maladjustment in which physical symptoms are the most prominent complaint. Apparently immature, moody, and rebellious, the client shows apparently serious problems with self-control in which aggressive behavior and interpersonal problems are possible. Although she may attempt to deny responsibility for her problems and to blame them on others, many individuals with this profile appear in treatment settings to escape responsibilities for problems that they have caused. Some may present minimal medical problems to gain attention or services. Because these physical complaints are less important in understanding her problem situation than are her personality problems, the possibility of personality maladjustment should be carefully evaluated.

She shows a low tolerance for frustration, and she may lose self-control easily. Her response content suggests that she has emotional control problems that could result in anger outbursts. Her immature behavior may be a part of a general tendency toward antisocial behavior. Beneath her vague and excessive medical complaints there appears to be an antisocial pattern of behavior that is probably of long-standing duration.

She appears to have problems in interpersonal situations. Her disregard for rules and her aggressive interpersonal style might create negative relationships with others.

Behavioral stability. Her MMPI-2 profile code is very well defined; that is, her code type is over 10 points higher than the next scale in the code. Her profile is likely to be similar on retest. In addition, this high profile definition suggests that the MMPI literature on the 1-4 personality type is likely to apply well in her case. The tendency to act out and show impulse control problems that is suggested by this MMPI-2 profile is probably of long-standing duration.

Diagnostic considerations. Ms. S. is likely to have prominent features of a personality disorder. Her excess somatic symptoms may be viewed as an effort to manipulate others. In addition, Ms. S. appears likely to have problems of an addictive nature. She has endorsed items in a manner similar to individuals who are experiencing alcohol or drug abuse problems. She has acknowledged that she has had a problem with alcohol abuse in the past. The extent to which alcohol abuse problems may have influenced other symptoms that she is reporting is not known.

Treatment or rehabilitation considerations. Her extreme somatic complaints may be secondary to long-standing personality problems. Possible secondary gain factors in her illness behavior should be carefully evaluated. Patients with this MMPI-2 profile are usually poor candidates for psychological intervention. They usually do not seek psychological treatment on their own. They tend to be only marginally cooperative in treatment programs. They are usually viewed as self-centered and immature and do not see much need for psychological therapy.

Her anger control problems are likely to adversely influence any rehabilitation efforts at this time. She is likely to terminate therapy early, possibly in anger. The manipulative behavior that patients with this pattern tend to show is likely to interfere with the development of trust in relationships, making the treatment relationship stormy.

She acknowledges having negative attitudes toward work and appears to view herself as unable to function productively in a work setting.

Case considerations. People with this pattern who are involved in personal injury claims tend to present with "excessive disability." Her extreme pattern of complaints is not internally consistent and appears to be an exaggerated effort to manipulate others to view her as disabled. Her pattern of symptom exaggeration is actually more extreme than one would expect from individuals who actually become physically disabled.

Case conclusions. In summary, Ms. S.'s scores on the MMPI-2 validity scales indicate that she responded to the MMPI-2 items in an extremely exaggerated manner, resembling individuals who are malingering rather than actual patients in distress. Her extreme pattern of physical complaints in the context of her MMPI-2 clinical profile reflects severe personality problems and suggests that her exaggerated symptom presentation is an effort to manipulate others to view her as disabled.

◆ ◆ ◆

The first case illustration presented an instance in which the MMPI-2 was the only standardized psychological test administered. In many instances, however, forensic evaluations will include a much broader range of assessment strategies. Some may include "intelligence" tests (e.g., WAIS-R) and projective tests (e.g., Rorschach or the Thematic Apperception Test [TAT]). Some may involve neuropsychological assessment (e.g., Burke, 1992; B. P. Jones & Butters, 1991; Lezak, 1983; Reitan & Wolfson, 1985). Some may involve behavioral and cognitive–behavioral methods of assessment.[1] In such instances, the expert witness must integrate a diverse set of data into a coherent forensic report.

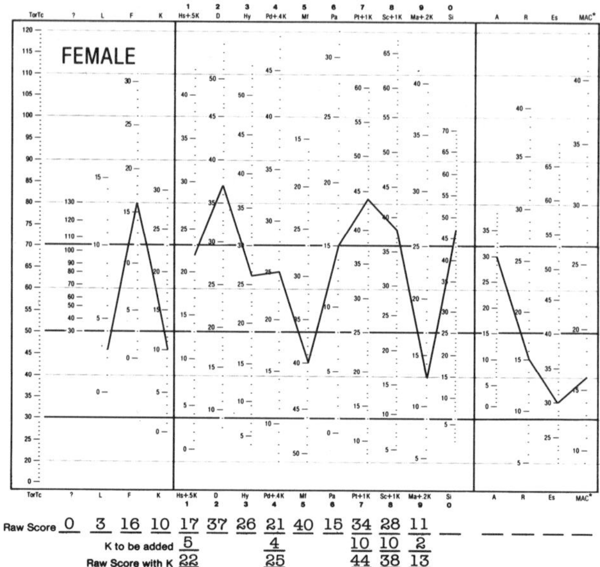

FIGURE 7-3. Computer-scored MMPI profile of Ms. Jones.

There is no "required" outline by which a clinician must organize such data. The organization must follow from the purpose and context of the assessment and from the assessment strategy and findings. The following case illustrates the integration of MMPI data (see Figure 7-3 and Exhibit 7-3) into a forensic report of psychological and neuropsychological assessment. It is, of course, but *one* of the possible ways in which these findings may be organized.

Case 2: Ms. Jones

Background and context. Ms. Jones had recently been placed under conservatorship and had been hospitalized (originally with her consent) as unable to

[1] For example, Bellack, Herson, & Kazdin, 1990; Haynes, 1991; Kazdin, 1978b; Kendall & Hollon, 1982; Levenson & Pope, 1992; Meichenbaum, 1977; Rachman, 1989; Singer, 1974.

EXHIBIT 7-3

Computer-Generated Interpretation for Ms. Jones—
The Minnesota Report: Adult Clinical System Interpretative Report

Validity considerations. This client has reported a number of extreme symptoms. She may be experiencing a great deal of stress which she feels the need to express. She may also be experiencing low self-esteem and may feel that she is having difficulty managing daily routines. While this MMPI profile is probably valid, it may reflect some exaggeration of symptoms due to her negative self-image. Individuals with this pattern are likely to be experiencing significant psychological problems.

Symptomatic pattern. A pattern of chronic psychological maladjustment characterizes individuals with this MMPI profile. The client is overwhelmed by anxiety, tension, and depression. She feels helpless and alone, inadequate and insecure, and believes that life is hopeless and that nothing is working out right. She attempts to control her worries through intellectualization and unproductive self-analyses, but she has difficulty concentrating and making decisions.

She is functioning at a very low level of efficiency. She tends to overreact to even minor stress, and may show rapid behavioral deterioration. She also tends to blame herself for her problems. Her life-style is chaotic and disorganized, and she likely has a history of poor work and achievement. She may be preoccupied with obscure religious ideas.

Interpersonal relations. Problematic personal relationships are also characteristic of such clients. She seems to lack basic social skills and is behaviorally withdrawn. She may relate to others ambivalently, never fully trusting or loving anyone. Many individuals with this profile have difficulty in intimate relationships.

Behavioral stability. This is likely to be a rather chronic behavioral pattern. Individuals with this profile may live a disorganized and pervasively unhappy existence. They may have episodes of more intense and disturbed behavior resulting from an elevated stress level.

Diagnostic considerations. Individuals with this profile show a severe psychological disorder and would probably be diagnosed as severely neurotic with anxiety disorder symptoms or mood disorder in a schizoid personality. The possibility of a more severe psychotic disorder, such as schizophrenic disorder, should also be considered, however.

Treatment considerations. Inpatients with this MMPI profile usually receive psychotropic medications for their extreme depression or intense anxiety. Many individuals with this profile seek and require psychological treatment for their problems along with any medication that is given. Because many of their problems tend to be chronic ones, an intensive therapeutic effort might be required in order to bring about any significant change. Patients with this profile typically have many psychological and situational concerns; thus it is often difficult to maintain a focus in treatment.

She probably needs a great deal of emotional support at this time. Her low self-esteem and feelings of inadequacy make it difficult for her to get energized toward therapeutic action. Her expectation for positive change in therapy may be low. Instilling a positive, treatment-expectant attitude is important for her if treatment is to be successful.

Individuals with this profile tend to be overideational and given to unproductive rumination. They tend not to do well in unstructured, insight-oriented therapy and may actually deteriorate in functioning if they are asked to be introspective. She might respond more to supportive treatment of a directive, goal-oriented type.

This MMPI interpretation can serve as a useful source of hypotheses about clients. This report is based on objectively derived scale indexes and scale interpretations that have been developed in diverse groups of patients. The personality descriptions, inferences, and recommendations contained herein need to be verified by other sources of clinical information, as individual clients may not fully match the prototype. The information in this report should most appropriately be used by a trained, qualified test interpreter. The information contained in this report should be considered confidential.

care for herself (based in part on suspected neuropsychological impairment), acutely suicidal, and psychotic. When she sought to leave the hospital and live independently (i.e., to have the conservatorship removed), both the conservator and the hospital staff refused. An attorney for a patients' rights organization, acting at Ms. Jones's request, brought legal challenge seeking her release from hospitalization and conservatorship.

During the legal proceedings taking place in 1988, the judge appointed a psychologist to conduct an independent psychological and neuropsychological assessment. The forensic report was to present a summary of Ms. Jones's background and to address issues related to neuropsychological impairment, suicidal risk, and psychosis, as relevant to continued involuntary hospitalization and conservatorship. Because the judge wanted an evaluation that would be independent in the sense of "untainted by prior assessments," she ordered that the psychologist form professional opinions that were based solely on interviews with and testing of Ms. Jones; consultations with other individuals (e.g., the conservator, hospital personnel, and family members) and review of records (hospital records and reports of previous assessments) were specifically excluded. These restrictions, as noted in other chapters (2, 4, and 8), may affect the interpretation of the test results and thus must be explicitly noted as a reservation about validity. The judge, commenting critically on some of the previous assessment reports of Ms. Jones (describing them, for exaple, as "long on conclusions but short on evidence"), specifically asked for a detailed report presenting a comprehensive test and interview data. She wanted to ensure that it contained sufficient evidence and detail to serve as one focus of deliberation (as well as opinion testimony and cross-examination) among the various court-appointed experts in this complex case.

Before accepting this appointment, the psychologist discussed with the judge the importance of taking into account all previous test data, hospital records, collateral interviews, and similar information before reaching any final conclusions about Ms. Jones. The psychologist also discussed with the judge the ways in which her restrictions would cause reservations about the validity of the report, and obtained the judge's assurance that, after this "untainted" report was submitted to the court, the psychologist would be able to review all prior information and records prior to testifying in court. The judge made part of the hearing record her recognition of the psychologist's stance (which was accepted without challenge by the attorneys) and her assurance that all expert witnesses would be provided an opportunity to review all relevant records, interviews, and other information before providing oral testimony at the subsequent proceedings.

Court-mandated report of psychological and neuropsychological assessment

Assessment of: Ms. _____ Jones

Assessment conducted by: ________________, PhD

Purpose of assessment: See attached judicial order

Date of assessment report: June 4, 1988

Date of assessment sessions: May 4, 9, 20, 22, 29, and 30, 1988

Assessment procedures

- Background Information Form (asking individual to provide written information about such issues as personal history, medical history, current condition, and treatment goals)
- Bender-Gestalt Test
- Clinical Interview and Observation
- Halstead-Reitan Neuropsychological Test Battery
- Minnesota Multiphasic Personality Inventory (MMPI), computer-scoring and interpretation provided by National Computer Systems (NCS; direct quotations about MMPI findings in the following forensic report were taken verbatim from the NCS interpretive report)
- Multidimensional Locus of Control Scale[2]
- Sentence Fragments
- Thematic Apperception Test (TAT)
- Wechsler Adult Intelligence Scale—Revised (WAIS-R)
- Wechsler Memory Scale
- Zung Self-Rating Depression Scale (SDS)

[2] Note: Readers unfamiliar with this scale may wish to consult Levenson, 1972, 1973a, 1973b, 1973c, 1974, 1975; Garcia & Levenson, 1975; Levenson & Mahler, 1975; Levenson & Miller, 1976; Logsdon, Bourgeois, & Levenson, 1978; Hyman, Robb, & Burrows, 1991.

Background information. The information in this section is based on Ms. Jones's account of her own history. Ms. Jones is a 30-year-old woman, widowed, the mother of four young children. She is currently hospitalized and living under conservatorship.

Born in Dallas, Texas, on January 3, 1958, Ms. Jones has a 40-year-old brother, who works as an architect, and a 38-year-old sister, who is unemployed. She reported that her mother, a homemaker currently aged 62, and her father, an accountant currently aged 58, were both emotionally disturbed and provided a chaotic, unpredictable, and sometimes terrifying environment during Ms. Jones's childhood years. They lived in a small two-bedroom apartment.

Her father, she said, suffered from a "a bad childhood." She said that her mother was diagnosed as "chronic schizophrenic," was "in mental hospitals on and off during the 1960s," and "was cured with lithium." [Note: She was certain, she said, that the medication was lithium, although this medication is more commonly associated with treatment of bipolar disorders than chronic schizophrenia.] She described both parents as heavy drinkers (as a result, she said, she consumes no alcohol).

According to Ms. Jones's account, her mother would run off from the father, taking the three children with her. They would travel and sleep in a station wagon, the mother screaming about what a terrible person her husband was. For example, Ms. Jones told of how her mother would march around the parking garages in which she parked the station wagon, carrying a sign describing the reprehensible acts of her husband. Ms. Jones remembered once returning to the station wagon to find that her mother had driven an ice pick into the dashboard. Ms. Jones was afraid that her mother would kill her, so she hid in a nearby store for the rest of the afternoon. She recounted being alone at night in the station wagon—her mother having walked off somewhere with the other children—and being very frightened.

Ms. Jones described feeling extremely insecure during the periods that her mother was away at the hospitals. One of her mother's most salient features, according to Ms. Jones, was the way she kept everything clean and neat. However, when her mother was away, "things got turned upside down." Ms. Jones began spending her time cleaning, "trying to make the apartment the way it was when she [the mother] was there." She remembered one occasion when the police were trying to contact Ms. Jones and her brothers at school. Ms. Jones managed to slip away and take the bus home "to an empty apartment, and started cleaning the whole place."

Although Ms. Jones's account raises questions (which cannot be definitively answered on the basis of the information available in this interview) of childhood emotional abuse, neglect, or both, she denied experiencing any childhood, teenage, or adult physical or sexual abuse, either actual or attempted (e.g., no incest, rape, battering, or harassment).

She described most of her school years as anxious and lonely. She was afraid of other people and intimidated by teachers. The ages of 12 and 13 were particularly bad, and she reported that she "felt like crying almost every day." At 14, her life changed: She met the man she would marry. Her life became much happier. She graduated high school and took some courses at the college level for 2 years. Her favorite courses were in art. She enjoyed playing the flute and sewing.

Her work experience lasted a year and a half. She was a salesclerk at a specialty store until right before her marriage (September, 1979). During recent years (before her hospitalization and conservatorship), she worked some mornings as a volunteer teacher's aid in the school her four children attend.

She described her husband as the most important person in her life. Now that he is dead (from an automobile accident 2 years ago), she said, her children are most important.

Early in the course of her marriage, she had an abortion. She had wanted to have the baby, but her husband was opposed, so she had the abortion in compliance with her husband's wishes. She was raised a Catholic, is currently a member of that faith, and is deeply religious. She now views her abortion with regret: "To me, it's murder now."

During the time period that she had the abortion, she began to manifest what she called a "germ phobia." Although her husband did his best to help her, the condition became worse. One year later, she reported, her husband hospitalized her, with her consent, in a locked unit. "I was having a nervous breakdown," she said. "I was banging my head against the wall until I was all bloody and I blacked out. I wanted to kill myself. I couldn't go out of the house. I went around opening door knobs with tissues; I couldn't touch anything. I would wash everything with ammonia—dishes, laundry. My hands and arms would break out." Although she had wanted to kill herself, her attempt was thwarted by her inability to locate her husband's gun. She reported that when they examined her head after the head-banging incidents, the doctors in the emergency room decided that she had brain damage.

She recounted that she stayed in the hospital for 4 days but found it easy to leave because of lax security. She returned to live with her husband.

She reported that in the intervening time period, she had seen perhaps "23 or 24" psychiatrists as well as a number of counselors and social workers. None, according to her, were very helpful. During this time, she reported, she has been overeating and has put on excess weight. She currently weighs (according to her report) 165 pounds and is 4′10″ tall.

According to her report, she has been physically healthy almost all of her life. To the best of her knowledge, there were no complications or abnormalities of any kind (e.g., no extended labor) involved in her birth, no physical impairments, no difficulties in menarche or other aspects of sexual development, and so on. She does not require glasses or hearing aids, according to her, and revealed no obvious visual or auditory impairments during the assessment sessions. Her only hospitalizations for physical conditions were once at age 12 for removal of her tonsils and four times to deliver her babies. (Her head banging did not, according to her, require hospitalization.) Aside from the head-banging incidents, she reported no serious accidents, illnesses, or assaults, no spells of dizziness, no loss of consciousness ("except every night when I go to sleep!"), and no prolonged or serious fevers. She reported that she had recently undergone a comprehensive medical examination after which the doctor told her that she was "perfectly healthy except for being overweight."

According to Ms. Jones, she is currently taking approximately 600 mg. of lithium per day as well as unspecified dosages of Stelazine.

Response to assessment. From the beginning, Ms. Jones made it clear that she becomes nervous and does not enjoy the types of tasks and situations involved in the assessment process. Tests that called for her to produce "answers" (e.g., the WAIS-R Vocabulary subtest) or perform specific tasks (e.g., the WAIS-R Block Design subtest)—especially if they were timed—seemed to remind her of the most stressful aspects of school. She experienced, and openly acknowledged, self-consciousness, self-doubt, and performance anxiety. The personality and projective tests, on the other hand, often seemed to draw her attention to personal concerns with which she was clearly uncomfortable or distressed.

Ms. Jones's difficulties with the assessment situation were increased when, shortly before the first session, her mother (according to Ms. Jones) strongly urged her not to follow through because the tests "will only show that you are crazy. They'll keep you locked up!"

Nevertheless, she worked hard and made intense, good-faith efforts to provide the most accurate responses of which she was capable. The MMPI scales (see Figure 7-3 and Exhibit 7-3) designed to detect random or deceptive responses suggested that "while this MMPI profile is probably valid, it may reflect some exaggeration of symptoms due to her negative self-image." Throughout, she was polite and cooperative. Taken in context, the responses appear to be valid bases for clinical inferences and professional judgments concerning her strengths, weaknesses, and characteristics.

Intellectual resources. The WAIS-R yielded the following summary scores:

Factor	IQ	Percentile
Verbal Scale	101	52nd
Performance Scale	89	24th
Full Scale	95	37th

These summary scores reflect intellectual ability best described as in the average range of intellectual functioning (about two thirds of all adults obtain IQs between 85 and 115). For Ms. Jones's age group, a difference between Verbal and Performance IQ of at least 9.23 is required for statistical difference at the 0.05 level of confidence. Thus, Ms. Jones's 12-point difference appears to be statistically significant, indicating substantially more ability in the Verbal than in the Performance areas.

The scaled scores for the WAIS-R subtests were as follows (listed in descending order from her strongest score on Digit Span to her weakest score on Picture Arrangement):

Subtest	Scaled score	Percentile for age
Digit Span	13	84
Similarities	12	75
Arithmetic	11	63
Information	10	50
Object Assembly	10	50
Block Design	9	50
Comprehension	9	37
Digit Symbol	9	37
Vocabulary	9	25
Picture Completion	8	25
Picture Arrangement	6	16

Digit Span primarily represents the functioning of short-term auditory memory, a resource dependent on the ability to attend to the numbers as they are read aloud by the examiner. Ms. Jones's strength in this area (she is among the top 16% of her age group) shows that she is able to mobilize her attention, at least for short periods of time. Her score on Arithmetic, at the 63rd percentile (her third highest score), reveals that she is able not only to attend (a relatively passive and automatic way of taking in information) but also to concentrate (a more active and effortful processing of information requiring the organization and manipulation of the information or data).

It is worth noting that her first and third highest scores are on subtests in which the data that she processes and uses to form her responses are numbers. It *may* be that numbers tend to be more emotionally neutral than words for her. Thus, she may find herself more able to attend, concentrate, and perform mental tasks with less distraction from personal, emotionally laden concerns characteristic of the obsessive ruminations (about germs, etc.) that she reports as plaguing her day-to-day life. This hypothesis that she is able to concentrate better on emotionally neutral numbers rather than on words that may evoke obsessive ruminations is consistent with the MMPI results about "difficulty concentrating and making decisions" discussed in a subsequent section of this report. (This possibility should be checked against school records, previous assessments, and other sources of information that were not, pursuant to the judicial order for this assessment, available during this assessment.)

Her score on Similarities reflects a high-average ability to think abstractly, more specifically to recognize and name an essential quality shared by pairs of objects. Again, it *may* be significant that her ability to engage in this type of thinking is due, in part, to the fact that the items themselves are presented abstractly, not in the context of interpersonal situations and sequences of events characteristic of some of the other subtests, such as Comprehension and Picture Arrangement.

Ms. Jones's scores on Information and Object Assembly are exactly at the average level. Block Design, although a little below average for the general population, is exactly average for people in her age group. Thus, she reveals no deficits in either her general store of factual information of the type often taught in primary and secondary schools or in her fundamental visual–motor (i.e., hand–eye) organization and coordination.

The Comprehension subtest requires an understanding of social situations and the ability to make social judgments. Ms. Jones's score, at the 37th percentile of her age group, suggests that although she can think abstractly (as she demonstrated on the Similarities subtest), she has relative difficulty applying this skill in the social realm, particularly when a social judgment is required.

Digit Symbol requires the test taker to copy a variety of simple patterns as quickly as possible during a limited period of time. Ms. Jones's score is close to average for the general population. Because other tests to be discussed later demonstrate her ability to draw much more complicated figures from memory, her lack of a strong performance on this subtest does not seem to represent inherent difficulty performing the discrete tasks involved. Two problems may be causing her some difficulty. First, this is the first part of the testing in which she was required to pick up a pencil and write down her response. In light of her anxiety concerning and dislike of the non-art courses in her schools, this subtest may have brought back unpleasant and distracting memories. Second, the slowed movements (technically termed *psychomotor retardation*) often associated with depression may have slowed her work.

Vocabulary is one measure of the breadth of concepts, ideas, and experience gained during one's lifetime. Ms. Jones's score at the 25th percentile for her age group may indicate that her learning in these areas, her ability to put that learning into words, or both, may be impaired by her personal emotional concerns.

Her lowest scores were on Picture Completion and Picture Arrangement, both of which present pictures of humans (although Picture Completion also has pictures of inanimate objects). Material presented in visual rather than verbal form may be much more emotionally evocative. Thus, Ms. Jones's emotional responses and interpersonal concerns may impair her ability to perform the tasks required by both of these subtests. Moreover, Picture Arrangement, on which she obtained her lowest score, requires the anticipation or understanding of complex sequences of human actions.

Her performance on the Wechsler Memory Scale was significantly above average, confirming her ability to attend, to concentrate, and to remember (using short-term memory), at least in the performance of clear and discrete tasks in a structured, supportive setting. She showed no substantial impairment in such areas as Information, Orientation, Mental Control, Digits Forward and Backward, Visual Reproduction, and Associate Learning. As with the WAIS-R, she did best with "emotionally neutral" information. For instance, the top level of the Digits subtests is 8 digits forward and 7 digits backward. She was able to perform at the top level on both subtests. In contrast, she made the most errors on the Logical Memory subtests, which involve listening to and repeating verbatim two stories of approximately a paragraph each. Both stories describe traumatic events that tend to elicit distressing emotional reactions that may have impaired her memory performance.

Neuropsychological factors

Lateral Dominance Examination:	exclusively right
Finger Tip Number Writing:	no errors
Tactile Finger Recognition:	no errors
Speech Sounds Perception:	1 error
Seashore Rhythm Test:	rank 3
Aphasia Screening Test:	no errors
Category Test:	23 errors
Trails A (1st admin.):	39.5 sec.
Trails B (1st admin.):	73.0 sec.
Trails A (2nd admin.):	34.5 sec.
Trails B (2nd admin.):	52.5 sec.
Strength of Grip:	R (right) = 26 kg.; L (left) = 23 kg.
Finger Oscillation:	R = 58; L = 52
Tactile Form Recognition:	R = 8″; L = 8″ (no errors)
Tactual Performance Test:	R = 8 min., 1 sec. L = 6 min., 51 sec. Both = 3 min., 42 sec. Total = 18 min., 34 sec. Memory = 9 Localization = 8
Halstead Impairment Index =	0.1

Taken as a whole, the test data, especially those related to the Bender-Gestalt Test and the Halstead–Reitan Neuropsychological Test Battery, do not suggest neuropsychological impairment. However, Ms. Jones's performance on two of the tests was in the range characteristic of those who have mild organic impairment. On the Trail Making Test, her time on Form B was 73 seconds, which is barely in the range (73–105) commonly associated with neuropsychological deficits. (Her performance on a second administration of this test was well within normal limits.) On the Tactual Performance Test, her total time was 18 minutes and 34 seconds; the range for mild impairment is 15.1–25.0 minutes (Reitan & Wolfson, 1985). It is worth noting that her performance on the memory and localization phases of this test were quite strong.

Ms. Jones's performance on the rest of the Halstead–Reitan tests was well within the normal range, with some of the test scores (e.g., Category Test and Speech Sounds Perception Test) at an above-average level. The Impairment Index of 0.1 is well within the range for those who are not organically impaired. On the Bender-Gestalt Test, there were no major distortions of the type indicative of central nervous system damage.

Cognitive–affective development, status, and styles. By her own report, Ms. Jones grew up in a chaotic home with parents who were suffering from alcoholism and severe emotional disorders. The world was and is a very frightening place for her. The MMPI profile is typical of those who tend to be "overwhelmed by anxiety, tension, and depression." It also suggests that she may be exceptionally sensitive to stress, even that which might be considered by most others to be relatively minor. Her association to the sentence fragment, "I get frightened . . . ," were the words, "by just about everything." In response to TAT Card 5, she tells a story about a woman who is alone and terrified, searching through the house for an intruder. When she completes the story, she adds, "I just took that from my own little world."

As a result of her difficult childhood, Ms. Jones seems to have developed two competing "pictures" or models of reality. One focuses on dangers and loss. In this threatening world, all is hopeless. The MMPI profile is characteristic of those who tend to feel "inadequate and insecure" and who tend to believe "that life is hopeless and that nothing is working out right."

Her other "world view" is almost a polar opposite. This is the idyllic world of an idealized family. All negative experiences are blotted out. People are perfectly loving. Thus, contrary to the ways in which she described him during the clinical interview, her father is described (in her first association to a sentence fragment using the word "father") as "the best dad anyone could have." Her responses on this and other projective tests describe both parents as making her feel loved, secure, and happy.

During her early life, she may have created the "good" world almost out of necessity, as a way to soothe herself and find something to affirm and hold onto in the midst of seemingly unendurable chaos and pain. There are, however, a number of costs involved. First, she limits herself by attempting to process the complexities of her experience in the world by using one or the other of two such rigid and simplified models, and she must deny or discount the information that does not fit. She is forced to deny aspects of her own experience. Second, the two models are so antithetical that she finds herself in confused swings between the two. It is virtually impossible for her to maintain both views at once. The resulting confusion will be discussed later.

As Ms. Jones described them, her parents were unable to help her with developmental tasks related to appropriate psychological separation from the parents. She has trouble leaving home, both literally and metaphorically. The MMPI profile suggests that she lacks "basic social skills and is behaviorally withdrawn." In response to TAT Card 2, she tells a story about a daughter who wants to go away to college but whose mother "just wants her to stay there on the farm."

Ms. Jones seems not to have developed a sense of herself as competent to go out into the world and handle things on her own. To the sentence fragment "Whenever they tell me to take care of things . . . ," her first response was, "I couldn't handle it." As noted above, the MMPI profile is one which is often associated with "negative self-image" and a belief that "life is hopeless." Her profile is also typical of those who "live a disorganized and pervasively unhappy existence." In one TAT story (7GF), the daughter asks herself, "What have I gotten myself into?" In another (6GF), a woman "looks like she's in trouble, like, 'What did I do now?'" And in still another (14), Ms. Jones says, "He looks very lonely. I think he's looking out at the world, wondering what he's doing here, wishing he wasn't here at all." Perhaps the quintessential story (13BG) conveying the inability to find one's own way in the world and meet its challenges is composed of only a few lines: "Hmmm, looks like somebody got lost. I think they were coming down the . . . is that a river? They were coming down the river on the boat and they pulled the boat up on the grass. I think they got lost in the hills. I don't think they find their way out. I think they died. That's it."

Believing herself to be inadequate to face life on her own, to be less capable than others, and to be in danger if she strays far from her childlike conception of "home," she feels herself as at the mercy of the "adults" around her and dependent on them for her survival. On the Multidiminsional Locus of Control Scale, Ms. Jones indicates that she sees the primary causal agent in her life as neither herself nor chance but rather powerful others. She marked that she "strongly" agreed with the statement, "I feel like what happens in my life is mostly determined by powerful people." She looks to others for care, safety, structure, and direction.

One implication of this orientation toward others is that she must avoid doing anything that might upset others and must actively attempt to please them. She refrains, for example, from directly expressing to others her anger at them. Another implication is that she must at all costs avoid being alone. To the sentence fragment, "When I get away from everybody else . . . ," her immediate response was, "I fall completely apart." Despite all the negative experiences involving her mother that Ms. Jones described during the clinical interview, she felt safer in her mother's presence and felt frightened, lonely, and desperate in her absence.

Tending to see herself as a child who must be guided and cared for (whether in the idyllic "good" world or in the treacherous "outside" world), Ms. Jones tends to feel little interest in activities for their own sake, to take little enjoyment in work or play that is primarily for herself, and to channel minimal energy independently into actions done on her own initiative. She seems to view herself almost as an extension of others and tends to live for them.

Ms. Jones has developed a rich and complex though often confused mental life that tends to make it hard for her to take constructive action, especially in times of stress or challenge. Her cognitive style seems to be the result of an extremely chaotic and painful childhood. In her adult life, it has enabled her, for the most part, to remain functional. However, it leaves her exceptionally vulnerable to stress. When the structure, support, and validation from others have been, for whatever reasons, inaccessible or inadequate, Ms. Jones has tended not to take action but rather to engage in mental activity. She begins elaborating, in her mind's eye and ear, both the threats of the "outside" world and the idyllic qualities of the world of "home." The MMPI profile suggests that she "attempts to control her worries through intellectualization and unproductive self-analysis, but she has difficulty concentrating and making decisions." In the initial, milder phase of stress, she does not attempt to express the tension and discharge the nervous energy through action. If the stress of her situation becomes more intense or if her coping resources become strained, this process of ideation becomes even more dominant in her life, and the content related to obsessive thoughts about germs becomes central. At such times, she clearly, according to her own report, manifests a thought disorder. During the clinical interview, she described periods in which she has believed that small people (about two inches tall) walk around in her house. During the interview she said that she realized that "something was wrong" with her mind during these periods; she understands (when she is not in these periods) that such small people do not really exist. There is no evidence from this assessment that she is *currently* psychotic or suffering from a thought disorder.

If her resources become even less adequate relative to the demands of her environment, she begins "acting out" through compulsive cleaning rituals and the measures she takes to avoid germs.

The obsessive and occasionally compulsive symptomatology concerning cleanliness and germs appears to reflect a number of Ms. Jones's concerns. First, it seems initially to have been a way of soothing herself in her mother's absence. She tried to make the apartment look as it did when her mother was home. In adopting this behavior, she was imitating—taking on the characteristics or identity of—her mother. Thus, she seems to have been attempting to deal with her feelings of loss or abandonment by taking on an important characteristic of the one who was absent. Second, the germs seem to represent threatening intrusions from the "outside" world. It is as if she were trying to make the world of "home" safe from those intrusions. Third, the germs may have symbolically become associated with her feelings about her abortion (a connection that she herself commented on). They may also have become associated with other losses (e.g., of her husband). Her obsessive-compulsive responses may represent attempts to deal with feelings of not only loss and abandonment but also of responsibility and guilt. In part, it may represent a mechanism of denial or an attempt to "undo" the damage.

It is important to note that this symptomatology is, by and large, what is technically termed "ego-dystonic." That is to say, Ms. Jones realizes that her obsessive-compulsive responses are unrealistic, even though she feels relatively helpless to prevent them. It is also important to note that medication (lithium and Stelazine) is apparently—at least by her report—helpful in lessening the harmful effects of these symptoms.

The test results indicate that Ms. Jones is currently severely depressed. Her SDS Index is 71 out of 100. Her MMPI profile is frequently produced by those with "severe psychological disorder," specifically "severely neurotic with anxiety disorder symptoms or mood disorder in a schizoid personality."

Ms. Jones also expresses an intense anger that, similar to her depression, is focused on and elicited by the death of her husband and her current state of involuntary hospitalization and conservatorship. On the Background Information Form, when asked what she would like to achieve in therapy, she wrote, "To be able to live with my husband's death, not to be in a constant state of depression and anger, and to be able to live a normal independent life without germ phobia." There is no evidence from this evaluation that Ms. Jones would express this anger in any way that would be physically harmful to others. Rather, she tends, as discussed earlier, to engage in extensive rumination. Much of her anger seems to be turned inward (i.e., back toward herself) in a way that intensifies her depression. The real danger is that she will harm herself.

In response to TAT Card 14, Ms. Jones describes a man who is in great emotional turmoil: "He's been hurt a lot in his life. Hmm. Well, maybe things will get better for him. Either that or he's gonna jump out the window."

Despite indicants of suicidal risk, there are a number of factors that suggest that independent functioning might be a reasonably safe, less restrictive alternative to hospitalization and conservatorship.

First, Ms. Jones has reported to me that she has promised God that she would never, no matter how bad things got, take her own life. Her report, taken in the full context of this assessment, seems credible.

Second, Ms. Jones's Catholic beliefs, with their reverence for life and clear prohibition against suicide, are very important to her.

Third, Ms. Jones's deepest and most enduring commitment seems to be to her children, who are being cared for in a foster home. To the sentence fragment, "Nothing is more important . . . ," she added the words, "than a good life for my children." She discussed, during the clinical interview, the responsibility she feels toward her four children despite the fact that they are (with her consent and approval) being raised in a foster home, the damage that would be caused to them were she to take her own life, and the fact that she would not, for their sake, take her own life.

There are additional factors that not only help her to manage her self-destructive impulses in a safe manner but also indicate potential for further growth and development.

Though often faint, Ms. Jones's hope for a happier life as a genuine possibility is expressed in the test data. In response to TAT Card 14, she describes a man so desperate that he may jump out the window. She reflects on the situation for a while and then continues her story, "I'm rooting for him. I think things will get better." Similarly, in response to TAT Card 8GF, Ms. Jones describes a woman "thinking about what went wrong in her life. And she's thinking that things haven't been fair, that she's gotten the rotten end of the deal. Hmmm. She's gonna try to figure out how she can make things better." To a sentence that began, "When life dealt her a blow, she . . . ," Ms. Jones added the words "she bounced right back." The fact that she was able to state specific goals for her therapy on the Background Information Form is basis for the inference that, at least to some degree, she believes that goals are possible to create and achieve.

Her statement of therapy goals and related discussions reveal that Ms. Jones has a fundamental grasp of the sources of her distress. The loss of her husband was an intensely traumatic event, and she acknowledges her need for support in the process of grieving and the attempt to continue with her life. The more extreme symptoms are ego-dystonic: She recognizes their unrealistic and self-defeating nature and wants to develop more fulfilling ways of functioning. This insight and motivation can serve her well in working toward change.

The fact that Ms. Jones has been plagued by what she calls her "germ phobia" for such a long time, the fact that hospitalization and conservatorship were deemed warranted, and the fact that, by her own report, she has initiated and then discontinued so many attempts at treatment are not hopeful signs. In addition, her MMPI profile suggests that her "low self-esteem and feelings of inadequacy make it difficult for her to get energized toward therapeutic action. Her expectation for change in therapy may be low." Nevertheless, the strengths listed above and the assessment data taken as a whole suggest that Ms. Jones may have both the motivation and the resources for change.

Hospitalization, conservatorship, and related implications. The assessment results, taken as a whole, support the following recommendations.

First, suicidal risk should be monitored with extreme care. However, the assessment results indicate that Ms. Jones is not currently suicidal and has made a firm commitment (on the basis of such factors as her oath to God, her belief in Catholicism, and her love of her children) never to take her own life. Thus, suicidal risk does not emerge—on the basis of the evidence available in this assessment—as a compelling reason to continue involuntary hospitalization at present. Continued monitoring and reassessment of her ability to handle her self-destructive impulses, however, seem warranted.

Second, Ms. Jones shows no evidence in this assessment of being currently psychotic or of currently exhibiting thought disorders. The results do not show evidence of "grave disability" that is due to mental, emotional, or behavioral disorder (e.g., disordered thought preventing an individual from appropriate use of food, clothing, shelter, and other aspects of self-care). Thus, the assessment results suggest that a current state of psychotic or disordered thinking is not a compelling reason to continue involuntary hospitalization or conservatorship.

Third, the assessment results, taken as a whole, do not indicate that Ms. Jones is suffering from neuropsychological impairment. Thus, neuropsychological impairment would not, according to this assessment, be a compelling reason to continue involuntary hospitalization or conservatorship.

Fourth, Ms. Jones states a credible desire to move to an outpatient basis in her therapy. There is no evidence from the assessment results that such a move is impossible or unwarranted. The MMPI profile suggests that she is more likely to benefit from a "supportive treatment of a directive, goal-oriented type." The option of providing a gradual move, through a half-way house or even day-treatment setting, should be considered.

Fifth, the psychotropic medications seem, according to her own report, helpful. These medications should likely be considered as an adjunct to, rather than a substitute for, supportive psychotherapy. Her MMPI profile is characteristic of those inpatients who "receive psychotropic medications for their extreme depression or intense anxiety. Many individuals with this profile seek and require psychological treatment for their problems along with any medication that is being given." Exploring the degree to which she will have continuing access to appropriate medications seems crucial.

Sixth, Ms. Jones appears to be correct in her belief that her husband's death is the precipitant and focus of her current depression and related distress. Therapy may be extremely useful in helping her through the grieving process. Some of her symptomatology may be understood as helping her to deny the reality of this traumatic event. A gentle, unhurried, and unthreatening approach to helping her to find ways to deal more directly with her feelings (especially depression and anger) and loss may be beneficial. The effectiveness (according to her report) of lithium suggests, though not conclusively, a bipolar component to her affective difficulties. If so, a strictly cognitive approach, such as cognitive therapy for depression, which research indicates is more appropriate for unipolar than bipolar depression, may not be effective. At some point, professionally led therapy groups or self-help groups composed of recently widowed people might be helpful. As previously noted, the MMPI profile suggests that supportive, directive, goal-oriented treatment may be most effective.

Special note. Exceptional care is warranted in considering the conclusions of this psychological and neuropsychological assessment. They should not be considered in isolation and do not—taken only by themselves—form an adequate basis for understanding Ms. Jones' current status.

Ms. Jones, according to her report, is currently taking lithium and Stelazine, which may be effective in ameliorating psychotic thought processes and suicidal risk; such medications are important to understanding these test results.

It is crucial to emphasize that the background information and all other data were obtained solely from Ms. Jones. In accordance with the judicial order for this assessment, no records of any kind (e.g., school and employment records, medical records, therapy records, and records of other psychological and neuropsychological assessments) were reviewed, nor was any information obtained from third parties (e.g., hospital personnel or family members). Thus, the chances that the findings and the inferences that are based on those findings were "prejudiced" by overreliance on previous diagnoses, records, and so on, have been minimized. However, it must be emphasized that lack of access to other sources of data (e.g., previous records or interviews with third parties) *severely* limits the opportunity to determine whether Ms. Jones's current state of psychological and neuropsychological functioning is consistent with or diverges from previous levels of development and functioning, to consider the test findings and other data in full and appropriate context, and to find corroboration for hypotheses or to explore discrepancies. Obtaining and examining such previous records of assessment, treatment, and so on, are essential to conducting an adequate and comprehensive assessment. It is my professional opinion that the findings and inferences presented in this report should *not* be relied on until they can be considered in the full context of previous records, collateral interviews, and so on.

◆ ◆ ◆

SUMMARY

Psychologists are often asked to prepare a written report addressing the relevant aspects of cases about which they are asked to testify. This chapter focused on the communication of MMPI-based test results in forensic reports. We detailed a number of important general considerations for psychologists to keep in mind when writing reports that might become the subject of forensic testimony. There is no *one* way to structure a report. The organization should be based on the purpose, the results, and the individual or agency to whom the report is addressed. In all reports, however, adequate information, qualifications, and reservations about the validity should be clear and explicit.

The chapter provided two examples of report organization. The first report outline was illustrated using a personal injury case in which the MMPI-2 was the only test administered. After the preliminary identifying information, the report presented (a) behavioral observations, (b) test-taking attitudes, (c) validity considerations, (d) symptoms and behavior, (e) behavioral stability, (f) diagnostic considerations, (g) treatment or rehabilitation considerations, (h) case considerations, and (i) case conclusions.

The second report outline was illustrated using a court-ordered psychological and neuropsychological assessment in which a variety of tests were administered. After preliminary identifying information, the report presented (a) purpose of the assessment; (b) date of the report; (c) dates of the assessment sessions; (d) assessment procedures; (e) background information; (f) response to assessment; (g) intellectual resources; (h) neuropsychological factors; (i) cognitive–affective development, status, and styles; (j) hospitalization, conservatorship, and related implications; and (k) a special note regarding validity.

Chapter 8

DEPOSITION AND CROSS-EXAMINATION OF THE EXPERT WITNESS: 80 BASIC QUESTIONS

No theme has been emphasized with more confidence than the necessity of thorough preparation for attorney and expert witness alike. Few aspects of legal proceedings require more extensive, detailed preparation for both attorney and expert witness than discovery through deposition and subsequent cross-examination. Louis Nizer (1961) compared the task of the attorney to the painstaking work of the archaeologist, searching for, exhuming, and sifting through records of the past as they emerge in expert testimony and other evidence.

> *How does he know where to search, and for what? This is the supreme test of preparation and . . . is the be all and end all of trial success. "The stupid man it will make bright, the bright, brilliant, and the brilliant, steady."* (p. 8)

This chapter was written as a guide for the attorney who is conducting that search. It was also written to help expert witnesses prepare for depositions and cross-examination.

Chapters 2 and 4 presented a number of possible cross-examination questions. In this chapter, we supplement those examples and provide a structured format that an attorney may use in exploring an expert witness's background, testimony, and the basis for that testimony. We present 80 basic questions (plus a few follow-up questions) created to help the attorney obtain information that is crucial to understanding assessment testimony. Obviously, expert witnesses preparing to testify about assessment must ensure that they understand both the nature of the questions and the answers relevant to a specific case.

Although attorneys conducting depositions or cross-examination may find it a useful strategy to jump occasionally from one topic to another (in order to determine how different aspects of the testimony fit together) and to return to a topic repeatedly (to assess the degree to which an expert's testimony on a specific topic is consistent during the long course of deposition and cross-examination), it is crucial that the attorney have a well-organized outline to ensure that all relevant questions are asked.

In the outline provided below, over 80 questions have been organized into a dozen basic categories, moving from initial information about the expert's background to the details of the expert's professional opinions. The twelve basic categories are

1. Compliance with the subpoena;
2. Education and training;
3. Illegal, unethical, or unprofessional behavior;
4. Occupational history;
5. Research and publication history;
6. Forensic history;
7. Knowledge of general issues of tests and psychometrics;
8. Knowledge of the MMPI;
9. Administration and scoring;
10. Interpretation;
11. The unexpected: testimony regarding specific claims and issues; and
12. Options and alternatives.

In this chapter, we make no distinction between questions to be put to the expert witness by opposing counsel during the deposition and during the trial.

Generally speaking, there is not one set of questions to be asked during discovery and a distinctly different set of questions for the trial. The questions tend to be used in an exploratory manner during depositions or to verify information implied by other sources (e.g., the expert's curriculum vitae or a written report of forensic assessment). This process helps the attorney to identify areas of inquiry and information that are likely to be useful during the trial and to gather specific factual information or claims that can be researched in preparation for the trial.

Perhaps the major difference between deposition and cross-examination during the trial (aside from the much larger scope of deposition inquiry giving way to the much more focused cross-examination issues that the deposition indicated would be useful) is that deposition questions are more frequently phrased in an open-ended manner (inviting the witness to expand responses as much as possible), whereas cross-examination questions during the trial are generally closed-ended, requiring a short, specific answer, often a "yes" or "no." However, even though the deposition questions may be phrased in an open-ended manner in an attempt to gather the maximum amount of information (and allow the expert to volunteer information), it is important for attorneys to ensure that they have obtained clear and specific answers to each question (if relevant) we describe.

The following questions, by no means exhaustive, exemplify ways that an attorney can explore and assess an expert's "expertise" and application of that expertise to the issues in dispute. Although each attorney has his or her own style, each case its own idiosyncrasies, and each expert a unique pattern of strengths and weaknesses, we recommend that the opposing attorney take advantage of the deposition to probe in *each* of the areas covered.

In some of the following sets of questions (e.g., Illegal, Unethical, or Unprofessional Behavior or Administration and Scoring), it is probably worth asking each question in the series, even if the curriculum vitae, reputation, and previous trial experience of the expert give no hint of the expert's vulnerability in these areas (see chapters 4 and 5). In other sections, a few questions of the type provided here will likely give the attorney a fairly accurate assessment of the expert's strengths and weaknesses in those areas. Obviously, what is learned during the deposition can become the basis for research an attorney conducts before the trial as well as for cross-examination at the trial.

The rules of evidence and other relevant strictures vary, of course, from jurisdiction to jurisdiction. The attorney will need not only to adapt the questions in this chapter to his or her own personal style, the issues relevant to the case at hand, and so on, but also to ensure that the content and wording are acceptable for the relevant jurisdiction. In some jurisdictions, for example, the attorney may be generally precluded from inquiring about a history of misdemeanors, and even questions about a history of felony convictions may be limited (e.g., to the number of convictions but not to the nature of the crimes).

We intend this chapter to be helpful to experts who enjoy or endure cross-examination as well as to novice and experienced attorneys. Practicing answers to the types of questions in this chapter can enhance the expert's expertise by allowing him or her to identify and strengthen weaknesses. Practice can also enable experts to become more comfortable and articulate in responding to a carefully prepared, vigorous, informed cross-examination.

Commentary on the content or implications follows most of the questions we present. In some instances, attorneys may want to alter questions relating to the content and psychometric properties of the MMPI as a hedge against the possibility that a pseudoexpert may have been well coached or simply memorized answers to the questions listed in this book. If other tests, in addition to the MMPI, have been used, the attorney may want to adapt the questions focusing on the MMPI (e.g., training in and understanding of the use of the instrument) so that they are applicable to each of the other tests. Thus, the attorney may ask all MMPI-specific questions, then adapt and ask them again for the WAIS-R, then again for the Rorschach, and so on, for each standardized test or method of assessment.

COMPLIANCE WITH SUBPOENA DUCES TECUM

Have you complied fully with each and every element of the subpoena to produce? Are there any items that you did not make available?

As discussed in chapter 5, the attorney has generally subpoenaed all documents relevant to the case. The attorney has prepared areas of specific deposition questions on the basis of a previous review of these documents. It is worth asking the deponent to indicate under oath whether each element specified in the subpoena was produced. In some instances, such general questions as these may not seem sufficient; the attorney may want to take the items mentioned in the subpoena one by one and ask if the deponent supplied all relevant documents. If some or all of the documents were not supplied in a timely manner, the attorney may wish to consider suspending the deposition until the documents are delivered and deposition questions can be planned on the basis of a careful review. Alternatively, the attorney may wish to conduct part of the deposition immediately but reserve the right to complete the deposition once the missing documents have been made available.

Were any of these documents altered in any way? Were any of them recopied, erased, written over, enhanced, edited, or added to in any way since the time each was originally created? Are the photocopies made available true and exact replicas of the original documents without any revision?

Chart notes, original test forms, and other documents may have been copied over, rewritten, or otherwise altered. Obtaining the deponent's testimony under oath concerning the authenticity of the documents is important. In one case, for example, an expert, when questioned in detail about the completeness of assessment documents, acknowledged having submitted the MMPI answer sheet to a company that provided computer scoring and interpretation services. The expert had copied by hand the profile from the computer printout onto another form. Had the attorney not inquired specifically about these matters, he would not have known that the test had been scored and interpreted by computer. The expert's previous testimony about the meaning of the results had not been completely consistent with customary interpretations. Asked about the missing computer printout, the expert testified that the computer-generated profile and interpretation had somehow been misplaced. The expert's attempt to substitute a hand-copied replica of the computer-generated profile and to omit (until asked under oath) any mention of the original computer profile leads to the next set of questions: missing documents.

Have any documents falling within the scope of the subpoena or otherwise relevant to the case been lost, stolen, misplaced, destroyed, or thrown away? Are any documents you made, collected, handled, or received that are within the scope of this subpoena or otherwise relevant to the case absent from the documents made available to me?

Depositions are part of the discovery process, and discovering that certain documents are missing or have otherwise become "unavailable" is crucial. This issue extends beyond expert witnesses and applies to a variety of percipient or fact witnesses as well.

If there is any doubt that all relevant documents are still extant and have been supplied in complete and unaltered form, the attorney should learn in detail from the deponent his or her (or the institute's, company's, or business's for which he or she works) customary procedures for handling documents as well as the procedures for handling documents relevant to this case. Any discrepancies between the customary procedures and the procedures in this case should be carefully explored.

The deponent's testimony can later be verified by deposing other witnesses (clerical workers who prepared, filed, or otherwise handled or were familiar with the documents in question or the customary ways in which documents were handled; administrators who developed and monitored policies and procedures for document handling; and other professionals who may have reviewed the documents) and consulting relevant sets of documents *about* the documents in question. For example, customary or mandatory procedures for handling documents may be set forth in a policies and procedures manual, in written job descriptions for the expert (if he or she works within an organization), in governmental rules and regulations, in sets of standards maintained by accrediting agencies (e.g., the Joint Commission on Accreditation of Healthcare Organizations [JCAHO], located in Chicago, Illinois, sets forth specific requirements for a variety of documents to be maintained by hospitals, clinics, and other organizations that are JCAHO-accredited), and other sources.

Documents prepared by an expert witness specifically in connection with the forensic proceedings (e.g., "personal" notes and the other items that were specified for the initial subpoena in chapter 5) as well as a wide range of preexisting or collateral documents can play an influential (and sometimes determinative) role in trial preparation and in the trial itself. In a chapter in *Product Liability of Manufacturers 1988: Prevention and Defense*, Richard D. Williams (1988) reviewed issues faced by corporations about preserving or disposing of corporate records. He pointed out that documents that are retained by a corporation may be quite damaging. Understanding how an individual (e.g., expert witness) or organization created policies for keeping or eliminating documents, what those policies are (or were at the relevant time), the rationale for the policies, and the ways in which the policies were implemented and monitored can be essential to adequate preparation for trial.

EDUCATION AND TRAINING

Please list the degrees you've earned, identifying the type of degree, the awarding institution, and the year the degree was granted. Please also list the internships you've completed, including the type, institution, and year.

In most instances, the expert will have provided a curriculum vitae that lists this information. If so, the attorney can ask if the vitae is current, comprehensive, and completely accurate. If any of the information is lacking from the document itself, it should be elicited. See chapter 5 for items (such as transcripts, dissertations, etc.) relevant to this and many of the following questions that should be requested in the initial subpoena.

[For witnesses presenting themselves as psychologists] Do you meet all criteria of the American Psychological Association's educational requirements for the practice of psychology?

In some states, those who have no graduate or undergraduate degrees or other recognized formal training may term themselves *therapists*, *counselors*, *behavioral specialists*, or similar titles and conduct what they term *psychological services*. They may then come to refer to themselves (or to accept others referring to them) as *psychologists*. In some cases, the individual may have a BA, BS, MA, MS, MPhil, or other psychology degree but lack a doctorate in psychology (although they may possess a doctoral degree in some unrelated field).

The *General Guidelines for Providers of Psychological Services* (Board of Professional Affairs, [APA] Committee on Professional Standards, 1987), adopted by the APA Council of Representatives as a matter of formal policy for the Association, is applicable to all members of the Association who provide services.

> *These General Guidelines apply to psychological service functions offered by psychologists, regardless of their specialty, of the setting, or of the form of remuneration given to them. Professional psychology has a uniform set of guidelines just as it has a common code of ethics. . . . These General Guidelines apply equally to individual practitioners and to those who work in a group practice, an institutional agency, or another organizational setting. (p. 712)*

The *General Guidelines* provide the following definition for the term *providers of psychological services*:

> *This term subsumes two categories of providers of psychological services. The two categories are as follows:*
>
> *A. Professional psychologists. Psychologists have a doctoral degree in psychology from an organized, sequential program in a regionally accredited university or professional school. . . . Specific definitions of professional psychologists by each of the recognized specialties are provided in the* Specialty Guidelines for the Delivery of Services. . . .
>
> *B. Other persons who provide psychological services. Qualifications and supervision for these persons are commensurate with their responsibilities and are further delineated in these policies . . . and in the Spe-*

> cialty Guidelines for the Delivery of Services. *(p. 713)*

Similarly, as the *Model Act for State Licensure of Psychologists* (APA, 1987b) states,

> *The Act recognizes the doctorate as the minimum educational requirement for entry into the professional practice as a psychologist.*
>
> *Applicants for licensure shall possess a doctoral degree in psychology from an institution of higher education. The degree shall be obtained from a recognized program of graduate study in psychology as defined by the rules and regulations of the board. (p. 698)*

Both the *General Guidelines* and the *Model Act* reflect an APA policy decision made at its January 1977 meeting after considering the report of the Ad Hoc Task Force on Master's-Level Issues and subsequent recommendations made by a meeting of the Executive Committees of the Board of Professional Affairs, the Education and Training Board, and representatives of the Board of Scientific Affairs (see Conger, 1977). The first segment of this policy decision appears below.

> *RESOLUTION ON THE MASTER'S-LEVEL ISSUE*
>
> *I. The title "Professional Psychologist" has been used so widely and by persons with such a wide variety of training and experience that it does not provide the information the public deserves.*
>
> *As a consequence, the APA takes the position and makes it a part of its policy that the use of the title "Professional Psychologist," and its variations such as "Clinical Psychologist," "Counseling Psychologist," "School Psychologist," and "Industrial Psychologist" are reserved for those who have completed a Doctoral Training Program in Psychology in a university, college, or professional school of psychology that is APA or regionally accredited. In order to meet this standard, a transition period will be acknowledged for the use of the title "School Psychologist," so that ways may be sought to increase opportunities for doctoral training and to improve the level of the educational codes pertaining to the title.*
>
> *The APA further takes the position and makes part of its policy that only those who have completed a Doctoral Training Program in Professional Psychology in a university, college, or professional school of psychology that is APA or regionally accredited are qualified independently to provide unsupervised direct delivery of professional services including preventive, assessment, and therapeutic services. The exclusions mentioned above pertaining to school psychologists do not apply to the independent, unsupervised, direct delivery of professional services discussed in this paragraph. (Conger, 1977, p. 426)*

The *Ethical Principles of Psychologists and Code of Conduct* (APA, 1992) emphasize the importance of accurately representing one's credentials:

> *Psychologists do not make public statements that are false, deceptive, misleading, or fraudulent, either because of what they state, convey, or suggest or because of what they omit, concerning their research, practice, or other work activities. . . .*
>
> *Psychologists claim as credentials for their psychological work, only degrees that (1) were earned from a regionally accredited educational institution or (2) were the basis for psychology licensure by the state in which they practice. ([303(a)], p. 1604)*

The *Casebook on Ethical Principles of Psychologists* (APA, 1987a), which was written to "furnish precedents for the Association, for future APA Ethics Committees, and for state and local ethics committees of psychologists . . . [and] document the efforts of the Association to police its own house" (p. vii), describes a relevant case:

> *An attorney, representing an insurance company that was contesting the payment of claims for an extensive psychological examination and therapy, charged that Psycholo-*

gist A had falsely represented herself as a clinical psychologist trained in personality assessment. The attorney alleged that the psychologist, although licensed to practice in the state on the basis of having a master's degree in experimental psychology, had obtained clinical training and her Ph.D. from a nonaccredited university. Furthermore, her academic records indicated no evidence of coursework, training, or supervised experience in personality assessment. In addition, the attorney reported that their claims reviewer had observed that the mental health treatment reports the company received from Psychologist A were virtually identical to each other.

Ms. A responded to the Ethics Committee that she was an Associate of APA and that her application for that status clearly stated that her degree was a master's in psychology from a terminal program in a regionally accredited university. She had obtained further training through a nonaccredited Ph.D. clinical psychology program, which she realized APA did not recognize. (The program consisted primarily of reading projects with 6 weeks a year in residence.) She had, however, subsequently performed "postdoctoral" work through an internship at a local psychiatric hospital. She thought that so long as "Ph.D." did not appear on her stationery, she had not violated APA policy; however, Ms. A acknowledged that she did use the title "clinical psychologist" on her stationery to denote the area of her practice. **Adjudication:** *The Ethics Committee considered two issues. First, Ms. A was licensed and therefore legally able to practice in her state. Secondly, although she did not claim to have a Ph.D. in either the APA* Membership Directory *or on her stationery, she nonetheless presented herself to the public as a clinical psychologist. The Ethics Committee found Ms. A in violation of General Principle 2 and Principle 2.a. because her degree was from a nonaccredited university and from a psychology training program that did not meet minimal requirements for clinical training, a situation clearly at variance with the APA* Specialty Guidelines *criteria for the use of the title "clinical psychologist. . . ."*

Ms. A's behavior was in serious violation of professional standards. . . . The Committee . . . recommended to the Board of Directors that she be dropped from membership in the Association. The Board approved this recommendation. (pp. 24–25)

It is useful for the attorney to have copies of the relevant ethics codes, casebooks, guidelines for providers of services as well as any specialty guidelines, and the laws and regulations governing licensure or certification in the state or states in which the deponent lives and works as well as (if different) the state in which the legal proceedings are occurring. The attorney can discover the extent to which the deponent meets—or fails to meet—the criteria in each domain. This information may be directly relevant to the deponent's qualifications and limitations to serve as an expert in the issues at hand and in the judicial jurisdiction. (See section on competence in chapter 4; see also APA Policy on Training for Psychologists Wishing to Change Their Specialty [Conger, 1976], which is reprinted in appendix C-2.)

Which of these degrees or internships is relevant to your expertise and the testimony you will be providing?

Some experts have earned degrees (or, in more rare instances, have completed internships) in unrelated areas (see appendix C-2). The degrees may nonetheless sound impressive to a judge or jury and may provide an unfounded aura of expertise for the issues at hand. Some experts will readily acknowledge that a degree in, say, nuclear physics or classical languages is irrelevant and does not add to their expertise in a particular case. Such a candid acknowledgment can be made part of the record and, if necessary, used at the trial (e.g., if the attorney who hired the expert dwells glowingly on this degree while attempting to qualify the witness as an expert).

Other experts, however, never wanting to concede *anything* to an opposing counsel, will, perhaps without thinking the response through clearly, give a vague affirmation of the potential relevance of a clearly irrelevant degree, imagining that all of his or her life experience adds to expertise and enhances judgment. Any such claims should be explored in detail during the deposition. In some instances, an expert will at some point back down and admit that the irrelevant degree is in fact irrelevant to any expertise involved in the case at hand. This honest acknowledgment of irrelevance can be contrasted, perhaps during the trial itself, with the expert's earlier claim of relevance. In other instances, an expert will never concede that an irrelevant degree (or training program, work experience, etc.) is in fact irrelevant. The more careful and detailed the questioning, the more strained and sometimes outlandish the rationales become. Such self-serving (i.e., in terms of the expert's attempts to falsely inflate the sources of his or her expertise) statements can often be useful at later points when quoted back to the expert. By attempting to stretch their expertise beyond its realistic limits, experts can discredit themselves in devastating ways, create mistrust for the content of their opinions, and offer a more effective form of rebuttal for their own testimony than could any other expert.

Which of your training programs and internships were fully accredited the full time you were in attendance?

Some schools may have impressive names (perhaps similar to the names of solid, reputable, and even "famous" institutions) but may have had (during the time the expert was enrolled) significant deficits, as noted by accrediting agencies. For psychologists serving as experts, it is worth asking specifically whether the graduate training program and the internship were approved by the APA and if not, why not. Lists of graduate training programs and internships that have been reviewed and approved can be obtained directly from APA's Office of Accreditation and are usually published on an annual basis in the December issue (with supplements sometimes appearing in the July issue) of the Association's journal of record, *American Psychologist* (see, e.g., "APA-Accredited Predoctoral Internships for Doctoral Training in Psychology: 1990," 1990; "APA-Accredited Programs in Professional Psychology: 1990," 1990; "Supplement to Listing of APA-Accredited Doctoral and Predoctoral Internship Training Programs in Psychology," 1991; appendix C-2; see also section on competence in chapter 4 of this volume). The criteria for accreditation appear in the *Accreditation Handbook* (APA, 1986a).

If the deponent affirms that the graduate program and internship were fully accredited, ask if they were fully accredited during the full time period that the individual participated.

If the deponent testifies that the university or professional school granting the doctorate or the internship was *not* fully accredited during the full time period that he or she participated, ask the deponent to describe the program's deficiencies that prevented accreditation. Ask also if the deponent has received subsequent training qualifying for a doctorate that did meet the standards set forth by the APA. If not, inquire as to the reasons that the deponent has either not sought or not been admitted to such a course of training.

Please give the full names, titles, and, if known, current addresses and telephone numbers of the directors of each graduate training program and internship at the time the expert was enrolled.

If it is assumed that not all people who offer themselves as experts always tell the complete truth about all matters relevant to their testimony, then it is worth checking the veracity of their deposition testimony. Asking for the name of the director of each graduate training program and internship serves at least three major purposes.

First, it gives the deposing attorney a way to check the veracity and completeness of the expert's testimony about his or her own training. A call to the director of a graduate program may lead to the discovery that, for example, contrary to the expert's testimony, the expert only attended a graduate program for 2 years and did not receive a doctoral degree; that the expert's training and graduate degree were actually in social psychology rather than clinical psychology, and thus the expert in fact had no training in psychological assessment generally or the MMPI in particular; or that the expert failed courses or was formally censured. In some instances, an expert may have never had any connection whatsoever with a program from which he or she claimed to have a degree.

Second, the expert is put on notice that the attorney plans to ask detailed questions and to verify the expert's responses. A less-than-honest deponent may be disconcerted by the likelihood that the attorney will discover—through careful questioning and verification of claims—perjured testimony offered in previous cases and false testimony already given under oath in the current case (in previous affidavits and in testimony already given in this deposition). In light of this likelihood, the deponent may also respond to subsequent questions during the deposition and later at the trial in a different way than if he or she were confident that inflated or entirely bogus claims about training and other aspects of expertise would not be seriously scrutinized.

Third, even if the expert's testimony is completely accurate and contains no serious omissions or distortions to which graduate training and internship directors might be called to testify, the directors who trained the deponent may themselves be potentially impressive rebuttal witnesses (e.g., a judge or jury may tend to give more weight to a more senior professional who directed a training program than to that professional's student). Those who trained the expert may also be excellent sources of information about other potential expert witnesses who might offer rebuttal testimony.

Did you ever leave a doctoral degree-granting program without obtaining a doctoral degree or were you ever asked to leave a degree-granting program? Did you ever fail to complete successfully a clinical practicum, field placement, internship, or similar program, or were you ever asked to leave a practicum, field placement, internship, or similar program?

Unsuccessful experiences with training programs may not be listed on curriculum vitaes but may be directly relevant to judgment and expertise. If, as the previous question and discussion note, the expert anticipates that the attorney will be checking the veracity of the testimony, he or she may tend to be more forthcoming about programs that were not completed.

If the expert acknowledges such experiences, the attorney should elicit detailed information and explanation. In some instances, the program that the expert was unable to complete successfully—and may have been asked to leave—may be directly relevant to his or her claimed expertise. The expert may, for example, have been asked to leave a program because of perceived incompetence in the area of assessment. Student evaluations, correspondence, and other material in the student's file at the school—which may still be kept in administrative offices and which may ultimately be accessible to the attorney (e.g., not protected by specific privilege)—may contain statements or information bearing specifically on the aptitude, stability, judgment, professionalism, ethics, or biases of the expert.

Please name each course, workshop, and so on, in psychological testing and assessment in which you actually enrolled, the institution at which it was offered, the year in which you took the course, the full name of the professor or other individual who taught the course, how many cumulative hours the course involved, whether you successfully completed the course and, if so, what your grade was.

A careful inquiry into specific courses in assessment enables an attorney to evaluate the expert's actual training in testing, diagnosis, and other aspects of psychological assessment. Formal training in testing is one of the prerequisites for basic competence and advanced expertise. Experts may hold impressive degrees, job titles, publication records, and similar indicants of expertise. They may have been admitted to testify as experts in numerous previous cases. They may view themselves as having a sort of generalized expertise: Whatever topic they turn their attention to is a topic for which they consider themselves experts.

And yet no expert is an expert in all areas. A world famous therapist may have had no training whatsoever in psychological testing and other aspects of assessment. A renowned expert in anorexia nervosa, phobic fears of heights, or borderline personality disorder may have had no training in the administration, scoring, and interpretation of tests that might be useful in identifying the presence, absence, severity, or complications of such conditions. Only by careful inquiry into such factors as an expert's training and experience are the limits as well as the foundations of expertise revealed.

Taking a look at the expert's grades in assessment courses may be quite revealing. Some experts, of course, may claim to have received only As in such courses; if a transcript obtained later by opposing counsel shows otherwise, the expert may have difficulty explaining why he or she inflated the grade while testifying under oath during the deposition. Experts who have failed or obtained low grades in assessment courses may also be legitimately challenged regarding the basis of their expertise.

If the attorney has subpoenaed the transcripts, as described in chapter 5, determining the accuracy of the deponent's responses will be an easier task and can be completed much more quickly.

How many hours in each of the previously listed courses, workshops, and so on, were devoted specifically to the MMPI?

Once the extent of training in psychological testing and assessment has been established, it is important to determine the degree to which this training addressed the MMPI. It is likely that general courses in testing and assessment devoted a minority of their total hours to the MMPI in order to cover an adequate range of basic assessment instruments (e.g., Wechsler Adult Intelligence Scale, Rorschach, Bender-Gestalt). If an expert has named only one assessment course that met for a total of 30 hours, the hours that such a course focused on the MMPI may be quite limited. The expert's description of the course content can be compared with a description provided by the instructor who taught the course or with a course catalog.

If the expert has taken coursework in the MMPI *only* very recently, it is reasonable to inquire if genuine expertise can be acquired in so short a time (i.e., without a substantial number of years of experience in using the instrument). If the expert has taken coursework in the MMPI *only* in the distant past, it is reasonable to inquire whether, as described elsewhere in this volume (see chapter 4, "The Expert Witness Prepares and Presents"), the expert's training and knowledge base are current and up-to-date.

Have you received training in the MMPI-2 or MMPI-A? What recent books on the revised MMPI have you reviewed? What recent research articles on the revised MMPI have you reviewed? Which of these books and articles do you consider most relevant to your expert opinions in this case?

These questions will help the attorney discover the degree to which the expert witness is adequately aware of the revised instruments, knowledgeable about them, and trained in their use.

ILLEGAL, UNETHICAL, OR UNPROFESSIONAL BEHAVIOR

Has anyone ever filed a complaint against you with a licensing board in this or any other state, province, or jurisdiction?

This section of questions may seem pointless with experts possessing certain kinds of qualifications and reputations. The individual may in fact have served on a licensing board. Nevertheless, it is our strong recommendation that *each* question in this section be asked of a potential expert. There have been cases in which members of licensing boards, ethics committees, and so on, have themselves been found to have violated formal standards. These findings of violation may not be widely known. Only by asking—and in some cases, by making an independent investigation—can an attorney find out whether an expert may have a record of engaging in questionable or even reprehensible acts that would be relevant to the credibility of his or her testimony.

It is probably best to avoid using the following form for the questions in this set: "Has any licensing board found you to have violated the licensing law?" No matter how carefully worded, such questions tend to allow the experts ways to conceal violations by semantic juggling. Experts may have reached some sort of stipulated settlement or similar carefully worded agreement with a licensing board that enables them to answer "no" to counsel's question through some technicality in wording (e.g., it was not a violation of a licensing "law" but rather a licensing "regulation"; it was not the licensing "board" that found a violation but rather an administrative "tribunal"; it was technically not a "violation" but rather a "failure to comply"). Nevertheless, if the attorney learns of the settlement or other pertinent information, it may be a key component in shedding a more accurate light on the expert's "expertise." Consequently, the best way to learn of the myriad ways in which a licensing board may have resolved a complaint against an expert is to ask if any complaints have been *filed*. If the expert answers "yes," then the nature and disposition of the complaint can be fully explored.

It is crucial to emphasize that even the most scrupulous expert may have been subjected to one or more invalid and entirely groundless complaints. In such cases, the honest expert answers a deposition question about whether a licensing complaint has been filed with a candid "yes." The importance of opposing counsel finding out all details regarding the disposition of such groundless complaints is obvious. Were opposing counsel to make such a groundless complaint a focus of cross-examination (i.e., assuming that the judge or jury will view the mere existence of a complaint as a discrediting fact), the attorney who originally called the expert could present in detail the licensing board's exculpatory findings, thus simultaneously "rehabilitating" an expert whose history has been cast in a false light *and* implicitly casting valid aspersions on the cross-examining attorney for presenting information in an incomplete, unfair, and misleading manner.

In cases in which there has been a complaint, it may be well worth the attorney's time to obtain all available documentation regarding the matter. Documents relating to formal complaints filed with licensing boards are often a matter of public record and may be obtained from the relevant board or governmental agency.

In some instances, documentation may reveal that an expert's characterization of the nature or disposition of the complaint does not match what actually happened. In other instances, the cross-examining attorney may learn additional information that may be extremely useful (e.g., that the expert did not comply with the licensing board's terms of probation).

Has anyone ever filed a complaint against you with any ethics committee, professional standards review committee, peer review board, or any other organization, association, institution, committee, or board—whether governmental, private, or other?

Aside from state licensing boards, a variety of review agencies receive and evaluate complaints against mental health professionals. These include local, state, or national ethics committees for the various mental health professional associations (e.g., the American Psychological Association and American Psychiatric Association), county or state patients' rights offices, hospital peer review boards, credentialing organizations (e.g., the American Board of Professional Psychology), community mental health center professional standards committees, and the quality assurance departments of clinics.

Have you ever been convicted of or pleaded nolo contendere to a crime or been a defendant or plaintiff in a malpractice or other civil suit?

Obviously, the fact that an expert witness has been convicted of or pleaded guilty or nolo contendere to or otherwise resolved criminal charges in such a way that might indicate guilt may be relevant to that witness's credibility and capacity to serve as an expert. Similarly, one or more findings that the witness committed malpractice or similar torts may bear directly on the case at hand.

Beyond the issues raised concerning criminal, unethical, or unprofessional behavior as determined by courts of law (or by licensing agencies, ethics committees, and the other boards or associations noted in the previous questions), however, is the issue of potential bias. If, for example, someone has participated in the legal system as a plaintiff and, regardless of the outcome of the case they initiated, always testifies for plaintiffs in similar suits, the question of potential bias is a legitimate one to raise and explore.

OCCUPATIONAL HISTORY

Please list all professional positions you have held since graduate school.

Like educational background, occupational history is often provided in the form of a resumé or curriculum vitae. The attorney should always ask the expert if the information is comprehensive, correct, and current. It may be worth asking a follow-up question along the following lines: "Then there is no job or position that you omitted for any reason?" This follow-up question helps to prevent an expert from concealing a position and later claiming that it was omitted simply because "it didn't seem worth mentioning" or "it was not relevant to the case at hand." Any positions that the expert omits from the curriculum vitae and mentions at the deposition only when the attorney asks about omitted material deserve careful scrutiny. It may be that the expert was fired for cause or was otherwise found to have committed acts that might cast doubt on credibility or expertise.

The dates of each position should be examined to ensure that there are no gaps. When gaps appear, or when the expert has moved from one level to a seemingly lower level (e.g., from full-time tenured professor at a major university to full-time, untenured position at an unaccredited university within the same city), the attorney conducting the deposition should inquire fully. There may, of course, be a perfectly reasonable explanation, but the attorney needs to understand the explanation rather than simply assume that the expert's employment history is actually as glowing as it appears on the curriculum vitae.

Which of these positions involved your administering, scoring, or interpreting the MMPI?

This question will enable the attorney to begin understanding the extent of the expert's work experience with the MMPI. Some positions, such as clinical director or supervisor of interns, may be purely administrative and denote a time during which the expert had no day-to-day experience with the MMPI, although the position title might misleadingly imply otherwise to a judge or jury. As with the follow-up questions under the section Education and Training, questions in this area can begin to focus with increasing precision on the extent of experience with the MMPI that each position provided. To develop additional sources of information, the attorney may also want to ask the following in relationship to some of the settings: "In that position, who was your immediate supervisor?" and "Do you know if that individual is still at the setting or how I can contact him or her?"

RESEARCH AND PUBLICATION HISTORY

Have you conducted any research or published any books, chapters, articles, or other documents that involved the MMPI?

This area of questioning serves at least two major purposes. First, it helps to define more clearly exactly what claim the deponent has to expertise regarding the MMPI. Careful questioning can help the attorney learn how the expert views the nature of and evidence for his or her expertise as they are reflected in a history of research and publication. Rationales for not submitting research to peer-reviewed journals and reputable publishers should be explored so that the attorney can understand and evaluate fully the expert's approach to these issues. Few experts will fail to present rationales for their approach. Only by learning these rationales during the deposition will the attorney be able to assess their persuasiveness, validity, and relevance.

As with some of the previous information in this chapter, research and publication are usually presented in the form of a curriculum vitae. If so, the attorney should, as with the previous areas of inquiry, ask if the curriculum vitae is complete, accurate, and up-to-date and then ask a follow-up question such as, "So there is no research study or any document you've presented publicly in the form of a book, chapter, article, monograph, or any other form concerning the MMPI that you have omitted from the curriculum vitae for any reason?"

When the expert has written articles and other documents, it is important for the attorney to learn the publisher, date of publication, and any other information necessary to locate the publication. Unless the attorney is familiar with journals in the field of psychological assessment, it is useful to inquire if any of the journals submitted the expert's work to peer review before publication. As noted in a later section of this chapter, the process of peer review is important to the scientific process of ensuring the merit, accuracy, and integrity of new findings. There are some journals that do not provide peer review (i.e., do not send manuscripts on an anonymous basis to outside experts in the field who evaluate their scientific and professional worth and worthiness for publication) and some that will, in exchange for payments by the author, publish manuscripts.

The attorney may also want to inquire if any of the journals are published by or in association with any scientific, academic, or professional organization. For example, *Psychological Assessment*, *American Psychologist*, and *Professional Psychology: Research and Practice* are among the journals published by the APA; *American Journal of Psychiatry* and *Hospital and Community Psychiatry* are among the journals published by the American Psychiatric Association; *Psychological Science* and *Current Directions in Psychological Science* are journals published by the American Psychological Society.

An issue separate from publishing articles in reputable, peer-reviewed journals is that of publishing books. Judges and juries are often impressed by authorship of a technical book on a subject that is a focus of a trial. It is important for an attorney to discover, during the deposition, whether one or more books for which the deponent claims authorship were published by reputable publishers. In some instances, what are often called "vanity presses" will publish virtually any volume for an author, as long as the author pays the expenses. In other instances, an author may be claiming authorship of one or more books for whom the publisher was actually the author or the author's institute or corporation.

An example of this latter situation occurred in the trial of the policemen charged with using excess force to subdue Mr. Rodney King. The case received extensive publicity because when Mr. King was arrested in 1991, an amateur photographer captured part of the event on a home videocamera, and the resulting videotape was shown repeatedly on television news programs. After the taping began, the film showed at least 56 baton swings by various policemen (Serrano, 1992).

One former policeman called by the defense and appearing as an expert witness in police techniques claimed that there were only about 20 instances in which Mr. King was actually hit, although the film showed at least 56 apparent hits. The judge "ordered the comments stricken from the court record" (Serrano, 1992, p. B3). The reason that the individual's testimony was disallowed may have been due in part to cross-examination focusing on the books he had written as the basis or evidence of his expertise. "Under cross-examination, [the expert witness] acknowledged that he published the two books he wrote about police techniques" (Serrano, 1992, p. B3).

If a clinician has no record of research or other work published in peer-reviewed scientific and professional journals or by reputable, independent publishing companies, the attorney may want to inquire more specifically if there is any evidence that the individual is recognized by his or her peers as a genuine expert with the instrument. Careful questioning can help the attorney learn how the expert views the nature of and evidence for his or her expertise as they are reflected in a history of research and publication. Rationales for not submitting research to peer-reviewed journals and reputable publishers should be explored so that the attorney can understand and evaluate fully the expert's approach to these issues. Few, if any, experts will fail to present rationales for their approach. Only by learning these rationales during the deposition can the attorney assess their persuasiveness, validity, and relevance.

The second major purpose for obtaining a complete list of all publications relevant to the MMPI is to explore what the expert has publicly asserted in the past regarding the nature, uses, and implications of the MMPI. In other words, is the expert's testimony in the current case consistent with what the expert has previously written?

FORENSIC HISTORY

Have you previously testified as an expert witness regarding the MMPI in any civil, criminal, or administrative procedure, or any other proceeding or setting?

As with the previous area of questioning, this line of inquiry will help the attorney to understand the deponent's basis for asserting expertise regarding the MMPI (i.e., the extent to which other courts have admitted testimony from the clinician as an expert) and to obtain transcripts of previous deposition or court testimony to determine the degree to which it is consistent with the expert's testimony in the current case.

Have you previously testified as an expert witness in any cases not mentioned above?

This area of inquiry will help the attorney to understand the extent to which the expert has forensic experience. Follow-up questions may explore the degree to which the pattern of previous testimony may suggest bias.

KNOWLEDGE OF GENERAL ISSUES OF TESTS AND PSYCHOMETRICS

What is a psychological test?

It is surprising that those who administer, score, and interpret standardized psychological tests may never have thought carefully about what a test is. Initial inquiry at this fundamental level may help an attorney to begin assessing the degree to which an individual has genuine expertise and understands the nature of testing as opposed to following a "cookbook" method of test use or "improvising" opinions. The individual's response may also help the attorney to assess the degree to which the individual can communicate clearly and concretely to a judge or jury. Some individuals may be quite knowledgeable in the area of psychometrics and inferences from test data but may be incapable of putting their knowledge into words that can be understood by those without special training (see chapter 4).

One possible answer to this initial question was proposed by Cronbach in the original edition of his classic text (1960; see also Cronbach, 1990): "A test is a systematic procedure for comparing the behavior of two or more persons" (p. 21). Note that the "behavior" may be oral (e.g., an individual telling what he or she sees when looking at a Rorschach card) or written (e.g., marking down "true" or "false" responses on the MMPI).

One of the most important aspects of the definition suggested by Cronbach is that the procedure for comparing behavior is *systematic*. For many tests, the system used to measure and compare behavior is *standardized*. The MMPI, like the Rorschach, the WAIS-R, and the Halstead-Reitan Neuropsychological Test Battery, is a standardized test. A standardized test presents a standardized set of questions or other stimuli (such as inkblots) under generally standardized conditions; responses from the individual are collected in a standardized format and scored and interpreted according to certain standardized norms or criteria. The basic idea is that all individuals who take the test take the same test under the same conditions. Obviously, not all aspects are exactly equivalent. One individual may take the test during the day in a large room; another may take the test at night in a small room. The assumption is, however, that in all essential respects (i.e., those that might significantly affect test performance), all individuals are taking the "same" test.

Because characteristics of the individual taking the test or the testing circumstances may significantly influence test results and interpretations, experts must be aware of the research literature that addresses these factors. For some tests, it may tend to make a difference whether the examiner and the examinee are similar or different in terms of gender, race, or age. For most popular tests, systematic investigations have indicated which factors need to be taken into account in the scoring or interpretation of the tests so that extraneous or confounding factors do not distort the results.

Later sections of this chapter focus in more detail on such aspects as administration (e.g., whether the expert followed the standard procedures for administering the test or whether special individual characteristics or testing circumstances were adequately taken into account and discussed in the forensic report); the basic issue in this section is assessing the deponent's understanding and ability to communicate the fundamental nature of a standardized test.

Are you able to distinguish retrospective accuracy from predictive accuracy? [Alternative or follow-up questions could involve distinguishing sensitivity from specificity, or Type I error from Type II error, as noted in the Glossary of this book.]

This is a simple yes-or-no question. If the expert indicates understanding of these concepts, the attorney may want to ask a few follow-up questions to ensure that the answer is accurate.

If the expert replies "no," then the attorney may consider a subsequent question such as, "So would it be fair to say that you did not take these two concepts into account in your assessment?" If the witness has indicated inability to distinguish between the two concepts, he or she is in a particularly poor position to assert subsequently that the concepts were taken into account in the assessment.

If the witness does indicate that although he or she is unable to distinguish the two forms of accuracy, he or she nevertheless took them into account in the assessment, the attorney may ask the witness to explain the meaning of these two seemingly contradictory statements and how the two forms of accuracy were taken into account in the assessment.

On the other hand, if the witness testifies that it would be a fair statement that retrospective and predictive accuracy were not taken into account in the assessment, then the attorney may ask additional questions to clarify that the witness has no information to provide regarding the two forms of accuracy, cannot discuss any of his or her professional opinions in terms of these forms of accuracy, did not weigh (when selecting the test or tests to be administered) the types of available tests or evaluate the test results in light of these forms of accuracy, and so on.

The two concepts are simple but are crucial to understanding testing that is based on standardized instruments such as the MMPI (see, e.g., Gambrill, 1990). Assume that a hypothetical industrial firm announces that they have developed a way to use the MMPI to identify employees who have shoplifted. According to their claims (which one should greet with skepticism), the MMPI, as they score and interpret it, is now a test of shoplifting. *Predictive accuracy* begins with the test score. This hypothetical new MMPI score (or profile) will be either positive (suggesting that the employee who took the test is a shoplifter) or negative (suggesting that the individual is not a nonshoplifter). The predictive accuracy of this new test is the probability, given a positive score, that the employee actually *is* a shoplifter, and the probability, if the employee has a negative score, that the individual *is not* a shoplifter. Thus, the predictive accuracy, as the name implies, refers to the degree (expressed as a probability) that a test is accurate in classifying individuals or in predicting whether or not they have a specific condition, characteristic, and so on.

Retrospective accuracy, on the other hand, begins not with the test but with the specific condition or characteristic that the test is purported to measure. In the example above, the retrospective accuracy of this hypothetical MMPI shoplifting test denotes the degree (expressed as a probability) that an employee who is a shoplifter will be correctly identified (i.e., caught) by the test.

Confusing the "directionality" of the inference (e.g., the likelihood that those who score positive on a hypothetical predictor variable will fall into a specific group versus the likelihood that those in a specific group will score positive on the predictor variable) is, in a more general sense, a cause of numerous errors in assessment and in testimony on assessment, assessment instruments, and assessment techniques. Cross-examination must carefully explore the degree to which testimony may be based on such misunderstandings.

Psychologist Robyn Dawes (1988a) provided a vivid example. Assume that the predictor is cigarette smoking (i.e., whether an individual smokes cigarettes) and that what is predicted is the development of lung cancer. Dawes observes that there is around a 99% chance (according to the actuarial tables) that an individual who has lung cancer is a chronic smoker. This impressive statistic *seems* to indicate or imply that whether one is a chronic smoker might be an extremely effective predictor of whether he or she will develop lung cancer. But the chances that a chronic smoker will develop lung cancer are (again, according to the actuarial tables) only around 10%.

Using these same statistics in another context, an expert witness might indicate reasonable certainty that, on the basis of a defendant's showing a particular MMPI profile, the defendant is a rapist. The witness's foundation for such an assertion might be that a research study of 100 rapists indicated that virtually all of them showed that particular MMPI profile (similar to the statistics indicating that virtually all people with lung cancer have been smokers). The problem is in trying to make the prediction in the other direction: What percentage of all individuals (i.e., a comprehensive and representative sample that includes a full spectrum of nonrapists as well as rapists) showing that particular MMPI profile are *not* rapists? Without this latter information (based on solid, independently conducted research published in peer-reviewed scientific or professional journals), there is no way to determine whether the particular MMPI profile is effective in identifying rapists. To borrow again from the statistics on lung cancer, it may indeed be true that a 99 or 100% of a sample of rapists showed the particular profile, but it may also be true that only about 10% of the individuals who show that profile are rapists. Thus, the evidence that the witness is presenting would actually suggest that there is a 90% chance that the defendant was *not* a rapist.

The confusion of predictive and retrospective accuracy may be related to the logical fallacy known as *affirming the consequent*. In this fallacy, the fact that *x* implies *y* is erroneously used as a basis for inferring that *y* implies *x*. Logically, the fact that all versions of the MMPI are standardized psychological tests does *not* imply that all standardized psychological tests are versions of the MMPI.

When selecting a standardized psychological assessment instrument, what aspects of validity do you consider?

Expertise in MMPI administration, scoring, and interpretation requires at least a basic knowledge of validity issues (see, e.g., *Standards for Educational and Psychological Testing*, 1985). Although follow-up questions—keyed to the content and detail of the initial response—are necessary, beginning inquiry in the area of validity by asking an open-ended question during the deposition can enable an attorney to obtain a general idea of how knowledgeable the deponent is in this area.

The attorney can assess the degree to which the deponent's initial response addresses the various kinds of validity. Although there are a variety of ways in which validity can be viewed and assessed, Cronbach (1960) set forth four basic types.

Predictive validity indicates the degree to which test results are accurate in forecasting some future outcome. For example, the MMPI may be administered to all individuals who seek services from a community mental health center. The results may be used to predict which patients will be able to participate in and benefit from group therapy. Research to validate the MMPI's predictive validity for this purpose would explore possible systematic relationships between MMPI profiles and patient responses to group therapy. The responses to group therapy might be measured in any number of ways, including the group therapist's evaluation of the patient's participation and progress, the patient's own self-report or self-assessment, and careful evaluation by independent clinicians.

Concurrent validity indicates the degree to which test results provide a basis for accurately assessing some other current performance or condition. For example, a clinician or researcher might develop the hypothesis that certain MMPI profiles are pathognomonic signs of certain clinical diagnostic groups. (A pathognomonic sign is one whose presence always and invariably indicates the presence of a clinical diagnosis.) To validate (or invalidate) this hypothesis, MMPI profiles might be compared with the diagnoses as currently determined in a clinic by more detailed, comprehensive, and time-consuming methods of assessment (e.g., extended clinical interviews conducted by independent clinicians in conjunction with a history of the individuals and a comprehensive battery of other psychological and neuropsychological tests). If the MMPI demonstrates adequate concurrent validity in terms of this hypothesis, the MMPI could be substituted—at least in certain situations—for the more elaborate and time-consuming methods of assessing diagnosis.

Content validity indicates the degree to which a test, as a subset of a wider category of performance, adequately or accurately represents the wider category of which it is a subset. For example, the bar examination and the psychology licensing examination supposedly measure some of the basic knowledge, skills, or abilities necessary to practice as an attorney or a psychologist. The degree to which such examinations accurately reflect or represent this larger domain is the content validity.

Construct validity indicates the degree to which a test accurately indicates the presence of a presumed characteristic that is described (or hypothesized) by some theoretical or conceptual framework. For example, a researcher might develop a theory that there are four basic interpersonal styles that attorneys use in developing rapport with juries. According to this theory, each attorney uses the one basic style that is most consistent with his or her core personality. The researcher then hypothesizes that these styles can be identified according to an attorney's MMPI profile (i.e., the researcher theorizes that one set of MMPI profiles indicates a Type One core personality and a Type One interpersonal style for developing rapport with a jury, another set of MMPI profiles indicates a Type Two core personality and a Type Two interpersonal style, etc.). Assessing the validity of such possible indicants of a theoretical construct is a complex task that involves attention to other external sources of information thought to be relevant to the construct, intercorrelations of test items, and examination of individual differences in responding to the test items (see *Standards for Educational and Psychological Testing*, 1985).

Conceptualizations about test validity continue to emerge and constructs continue to evolve. Those interested in reviewing the evolving understanding of test validity are encouraged to read Geisinger's (1992) fascinating account.

When selecting psychological assessment instruments, what aspects of reliability do you consider?

A basic knowledge of reliability issues is also—as with validity issues—fundamental to expertise in MMPI administration, scoring, and interpretation (see, e.g., *Standards for Educational and Psychological Testing*, 1985). Again, an open-ended question may be the best approach to this area of inquiry during the deposition.

Reliability refers to the degree to which a test produces results that are free of measuring errors. If there were no measuring errors at all, then it is reasonable to assume that test results would be consistent.

Reliability is another way of describing how consistent the results of a test are. Consider the following hypothetical situation. For the purposes of the example, assume that there are two completely identical people. If they are completely identical and if a test (such as the MMPI) were completely reliable (i.e., free from any measuring errors), then both people should produce the same responses to the test. However, now assume that one of these two identical people takes the test at nine a.m. when she is rested and alert. The other person takes the same test at two a.m. when she has just been awakened from a sound sleep and is tired and groggy. Differences in test results between these two otherwise identical people might be due purely to the times at which the test was administered. If the test were supposedly a measure of personality (such as the MMPI) and if the personalities of these hypothetically identical people were the same, then different test results do not actually represent a difference in personality but rather a difference or error in measurement (i.e., the time or conditions under which the test was administered).

Statistical techniques have been developed that indicate the degree to which a test is reliable. Such statistical analyses are often reported in the form of *reliability coefficients*. The coefficient will be a number that falls in the range of zero (for no reliability) to one (indicating perfect reliability).

The coefficient may indicate the reliability between subsequent administrations of the same test (e.g., administering the MMPI-2 to a group of individuals and then administering the same MMPI-2 to the same group 1 week or 1 month later). Reports of this type of reliability will often refer to the *test–retest* reliability (or the coefficient of stability). They may indicate, using a coefficient of equivalence, the reliability between different forms of the same test. For example, a large group of individuals might be randomly divided in half. One half would be given the original MMPI, and the other half would be given the MMPI-2; 1 week later, the half that took the original MMPI would take the MMPI-2 and vice versa. Reliability between subsequent administrations (perhaps under different conditions) of the same test is often termed *stability*; reliability between different forms of the same test is often termed *equivalence* (Cronbach, 1960).

In some instances, test items will be divided independently into two halves as a way to estimate the reliability of the test. This method estimates the *split-half* reliability. The resulting coefficient, often measured using a statistical method known as the

Spearman-Brown formula, is often termed the coefficient of *internal consistency*.

What types of scales were involved in the various tests and methods of assessment that you considered in selecting the instruments and diagnostic frameworks that you used in the case at hand?

Different forms of measurement use different scales. The scales can refer to scores on a test or to the categories into which test responses fall. There are four basic types of scales.

The first type of scale is termed *nominal*. As the Latin root (nomen, meaning "name") from which we derive a number of similar English words (e.g., nominate, denomination, and nomenclature) implies, nominal scales simply provide names to two or more different categories, types, kinds, or classes. A two-category nominal scale might be invented to describe the various individuals in a courtroom: participants and observers. The same population might be described using a more detailed nominal scale with categories such as jurors, prosecution team, defense team, and so on. Note that the categories are listed in no particular order. Assigning an individual to a particular group on a nominal scale indicates only that the individual is in a group that is different from the others.

If placement of an individual (or object, verbal response, etc.) into a particular group indicates that an individual (or object, etc.) is in a different group from all others, then there can be no overlap among groups. That is to say, the groups must be *mutually exclusive*: Placement in one group indicates that the person, object, response, and so on, does not belong in any of the other groups. Thus, the four categories of mammals, living things, humans, and whales do *not* constitute a nominal scale in the sense used here because the categories are not mutually exclusive (i.e., a particular individual may be placed in more than one of the categories). Individuals who take the MMPI are asked to use a nominal scale in responding to each of the items; the scale has two values: "true" and "false."

The second type of scale does place its categories in a particular order and is termed an *ordinal* scale. For example, an attorney might evaluate all the cases he or she has ever tried and sort them into three categories: "easy," "moderate," and "difficult." The scale indicates that cases in the middle group were harder for the attorney to try than cases in the easy group, but there is no information about how much harder. The scale only places the items (in this instance, legal cases) in three ordered categories, each category having more (or less) of a particular attribute (such as difficulty) than the others.

The third type of scale is a particular kind of ordinal scale in which the interval between each group is the same. An example of an *interval* scale is any listing of the days of the week: Wednesday, Thursday, Friday, Saturday, Sunday, and so on. When events are classified according to this interval scale, it is clear that the temporal distance between Wednesday and Thursday is the same as that between Saturday and Sunday or any other two consecutive days. An important characteristic of an interval scale (that sets it apart from the fourth type of scale described below) is that there is no absolute or meaningful zero point. Some people may begin their week on Mondays, others on Saturdays, still others on Sundays; from time to time a "3-day weekend" leads into a week that "begins" on Tuesday. The Fahrenheit scale for measuring temperature is an example of an interval scale: the zero on the scale is arbitrary.

The fourth type of scale is a scale of equal intervals in which the zero point is absolute, and it is termed a *ratio* scale. An example of a ratio scale is one's weight. The zero point is not arbitrary. As the name of the scale implies, the ratios may be meaningfully compared. For example, a person who weighs 100 pounds is twice as heavy as a person who weighs 50 pounds, and a person who weighs 200 pounds is twice as heavy as a person who weighs 100 pounds. Such ratios do *not* hold for the other three types of scales. For example, because the zero point on the Fahrenheit scale is arbitrary, one cannot accurately state that 40° is twice as hot as 20° or that 200° is twice as hot as 100°.

The deponent's explanation of these different types of scales and their meaning for different assessment instruments that were considered (e.g., the MMPI, the WAIS-R, the Rorschach, a sentence-completion test) will indicate the degree to which he or she understands this aspect of psychological assessment and can communicate it effectively to a judge or jury.

What is a T *score, and what are its psychometric properties?*

Understanding the nature of the *T* score is essential to understanding the MMPI (see chapter 2). Both the original MMPI and the revised versions (MMPI-2 and MMPI-A) are based on *T* scales, although there are significant differences between the original and later versions that will serve as the focus of subsequent questions.

The raw scores (e.g., of the content scales) of the MMPI are translated—through statistical methods—into a *T*-score distribution. A *T scale* is a distribution of scores in which the mean is 50 and the standard deviation is 10. It is important to ensure that the expert understands the nature of this distribution, of a mean, and of a standard deviation.

The mean is one of three major ways of describing the *central tendency* of a distribution of scores (i.e., the "center" around which all the other scores seem to cluster). The arithmetic *mean* can be defined statistically as the sum of all scores divided by the number of scores. In other words, the mean is the arithmetic average of the scores. The *median*, which is the second measure of central tendency, is that number that is in the "middle" of the distribution: half of the scores fall below the median, and the other half of the scores fall above the median. The third measure of central tendency is the *mode*, which indicates the score that appears most often. If there were seven IQ scores—98, 100, 102, 102, 103, 103, and 103—then the mode would be 103 because it appears most often (i.e., three times out of seven).

The *standard deviation* is one way of describing the "scatter" of a distribution of scores—the degree to which the scores vary from the central tendency. The statistical formula for the standard deviation is somewhat complicated. Each score is subtracted from the mean to produce a deviation from the mean. Each of these deviations is squared. (A number is squared when the number is multiplied by itself. The square of 2—that is to say, 2 times 2—is 4; the square of 3—that is, 3 times 3—is 9; the square of 4 is 16.) These squared deviations are then added together into a total sum of squares. The total sum of squares is then divided by the number of scores.[1]

This total sum of squares divided by the number of scores (or the number of scores minus one) is the *variance* (i.e., the degree to which the scores vary from or vary around the mean). The *standard deviation* is the square root of the variance. The larger the standard deviation, the farther the scores tend to fall from the mean.

If the *T* scale describes a normal distribution, the distribution is said to fall into a bell-shaped curve. In the normal distribution, 68% of the scores fall within one standard deviation of the mean; 95% fall within two standard deviations of the mean; and 99% fall within three standard deviations of the mean. These percentages apply only to a normal or normalized *T* scale and not necessarily to a linear *T* scale or a uniform *T* scale (for information about the *T* scale and its various forms, see chapter 2 and the Glossary).

Most of the original MMPI validity and clinical scales were derived according to the formula for linear *T* scores (Dahlstrom et al., 1972) except *L* and *F*, for which the mean values were arbitrarily set. Each of these scales was separately derived, and each has a slightly different skew. Thus, the distributions are not *uniform* nor are they normal. This is to say, a particular *T* score does not fall at the same percentile rank across all scales (Colligan et al., 1983).

The original MMPI's lack of uniformity among the clinical scales has been somewhat problematic (e.g., when comparing scores on different scales). In MMPI-2 and MMPI-A, however, this lack of uniformity was resolved by developing linear *T* scores that did possess uniformity across given percentile values. This scale norming, referred to as uniform *T* scores, is described in the MMPI-2 manual (Butcher et al.,

[1] This is the formula for determining the variance or standard deviation in *descriptive* statistics. In *inferential* statistics, the sum of squares is divided not by the number of scores but rather by the number of scores minus one. In descriptive statistics, one is simply trying to describe the scores or numbers that are available (e.g., the IQ scores of the children in one sixth-grade classroom). In inferential statistics, one is trying to use the scores or numbers that are available—called the *sample*—as a basis for drawing inferences about a wider group of scores or numbers—called the *population* (e.g., attempting to use the IQ scores of the sample of children in one sixth-grade classroom to infer or estimate the IQ scores for the population of all sixth-grade students in the school system).

1989) and is discussed extensively by psychologists Auke Tellegen and Yossef Ben-Porath (1992b).

KNOWLEDGE OF THE MMPI

Please describe the normative group for the original MMPI.

The basic group of individuals who served to define the original MMPI's psychometric standards of "normal" were 724 people, most of whom had accompanied patients to university hospitals in Minneapolis in the late 1930s (see chapter 2). That is to say, relatives, friends, and acquaintances who came to the hospital with patients (or to visit patients)—and a much smaller group of airline workers and Civilian Conservation Corps workers—were recruited to serve as "normals" for the purpose of scale construction (which provided in turn the "norms" for the test). People were excluded from the normative sample if they themselves were currently receiving medical care from a physician or hospital. As a result of such factors as time (the late 1930s) and circumstance (the demographics of the population in the area from which the normative sample was recruited), all of the normative sample were White (Dahlstrom et al., 1975). Thus, the "norms" of the original MMPI were defined by a sample that did not include individuals from Black, Asian American, Hispanic, American Indian, and certain other ethnic groups.

Some experts may find it difficult to explain the rationale for using a test that seems to equate, however unintentionally, the concept of "normal" or "normative" with being White. The more general demographic characteristics of the sample that provided the norms for the original MMPI may have clinical implications that the cross-examining attorney can explore. For example, Faschingbauer (1979) wrote

> *The original Minnesota group seems to be an inappropriate reference group for the 1980s. The median individual in that group has an eighth-grade education, was married, lived in a small town or on a farm, and was employed as a lower level clerk or skilled tradesman. None was under 16 or over 65 years of age, and all were white. As a clinician I find it difficult to justify comparing anyone to such a dated group. When the person is 14 years old, Chicano, and lives in Houston's poor fifth ward, use of original norms seems sinful. (p. 385)*

Please describe the normative group for the MMPI-2.

The basic group of individuals who served to provide normative standards for the MMPI-2 was composed of 2,600 people (1,462 women and 1,138 men) drawn at random from seven regions of the United States (California, Minnesota, North Carolina, Ohio, Pennsylvania, Virginia, and Washington state). The normative sample—which, unlike the normative sample for the original MMPI, includes individuals who are Black, Asian American, Hispanic, American Indian, and so on—is more generally reflective of the U.S. population in terms of age, gender, and minority representation (see chapter 2).

Is it true that the normative group for the MMPI-2 scored about half of one standard deviation above the mean on the clinical scales of the original MMPI? Doesn't this mean that the group was not really normal? Doesn't this mean that the means are "off" somehow?

Expert witnesses who use the MMPI-2 (or original MMPI) but are not adequately familiar with it may be unable to answer this question. It is true that the normative sample for the revised MMPI scored about one half of a standard deviation above the mean (both mean and standard deviation are explained in a previous section of this chapter) on the original MMPI. This would seem, in the absence of additional information, to suggest that there is something wrong with the sample *or* that pathology has increased among the supposedly "normal" population during the decades since the original norms were established.

However, those who are knowledgeable about the tests will be able to explain that the difference seems largely the result of differences in instructional sets and unanswered items. When the original norms were compiled, those who took the test were allowed to leave blank any items that they were unsure about or that they believed were inapplicable (Hathaway & McKinley, 1940). Consequently, more than 30 items were typically unanswered on each form. The contemporary instructions for the MMPI and MMPI-2, however, encourage test takers to try to answer all items. As a result, only about two items are left unanswered on each form. Thus, more deviant items are, on average, endorsed on each form, and the normative sample for the MMPI-2 scored about a half of one standard deviation higher on the clinical scales of the original MMPI. As described previously (see chapter 2), when other groups of "normals" are scored on MMPI-2 norms, they tend to score around $T = 50$ (Butcher, Graham, et al., 1989).

On the original MMPI, at what level is a clinical score generally considered significant?

This question and the one that follows (i.e., clinical significance level for the MMPI-2) will be unnecessary if the deponent's previous responses have shown at least basic familiarity with the MMPI. The level of clinical significance is one of the first and most fundamental facts that people learn about the MMPI. The level is clearly marked on the profile sheet, so that even if the deponent played no role in administering or scoring the test, he or she can easily see the significance level. This question and the one that follows will be most useful if the deponent has shown little or no evidence of any education, experience, or knowledge regarding the MMPI. They will help reveal whether the deponent has even the most rudimentary understanding of the instrument. On the original MMPI, a score on a clinical scale is generally considered significant when it reaches or exceeds 70.

On the MMPI-2, at what level is a clinical score generally considered significant?

The significance level for the MMPI-2 scales differs from that of the original MMPI (see chapter 2). On the MMPI-2, a score on a clinical scale is generally considered significant when it reaches or exceeds 65.

What scales on the MMPI or MMPI-2 indicate the degree to which a specific test protocol is valid? Please describe each scale.

This question is still relatively simple—the deponent may read the scales directly on the profile sheet—but does require an understanding of what each scale means (see chapter 6).

Four major validity scales are common to both the original MMPI and the MMPI-2.

The *Cannot Say* score—generally indicated by a question mark—is simply the number of items for which the test taker did not provide a clear answer. In some instances, the test taker may have left the item blank. In other instances, the test taker may have filled in both the "true" and the "false" response blank for a given item. As noted previously, most test takers leave blank two or fewer items.

Any time a test taker fails to provide answers for more than, say, 5 or 10 items, there is the possibility that clinical and other scale scores may be distorted. Profiles that are based on tests in which at least 20 items have no clear answer should be interpreted with exceptional caution; profiles that are based on tests in which at least 30 items have no clear answer are invalid.

A significant elevation on the *Lie (L) scale* suggests that the test taker may have distorted answers in order to present him- or herself in a more favorable light. An individual who is trying to put up a "good front" may deny or minimize problems.

A significant elevation on the *Frequency or Infrequency (F) scale* suggests that the test taker may have distorted answers in order to invent or exaggerate problems.

A significant elevation on the *Subtle Defensiveness (K) scale* suggests that the test taker may have distorted answers in a more subtle way than that measured by the *L* scale. In effect, the individual has responded defensively—in a more sophisticated way than those with elevated *L* scales—in order to present a more favorable image. The *K* scale is not only a measure of validity but also a basis for correcting for defensiveness. The deponent may describe the way in which the *K* score led to a statistical adjustment of the clinical scales known as a K *correction*. It is important that both social class and education be taken into account when considering the *K* scale.

In addition to these scales that appear on both the original and the revised MMPI, three validity scales appear only on the MMPI-2.

The F(B) *scale* is similar to the *F* scale. However, the *F* scale is based on items that appear within the first 370 items of the original MMPI. Thus, the *F* scale measures possible exaggeration of symptoms only in the early and middle parts of the test. The *F(B)* scale is composed of 40 items that appear in the second half of the MMPI-2. A significant elevation on the *F(B)* scale suggests possible exaggeration of symptoms.

The *True Response Inconsistency* (TRIN) *scale* measures inconsistency in responding to items. The *TRIN* scale is composed of pairs of items for which responding "true" to both items or "false" to both items constitutes a contradiction. For example, consider two items in a hypothetical test: (a) I always enjoy trying cases in which the MMPI-2 is the focus, and (b) I never enjoy trying cases in which the MMPI-2 is the focus. To answer "true" to both items would be contradictory, a likely indicant of indiscriminant acquiescence (or yea-saying). (In contrast to those who are indiscriminately acquiescent in their responses and who score high on *TRIN*, random responders tend to score around 50 on *TRIN*.)

The *Variable Response Inconsistency* (VRIN) *scale* is a measure of random responding. It is comprised of pairs of items for which some pattern of true–true, true–false, false–false, or false–true constitutes a contradiction.

These validity scales are discussed in more detail in chapter 6.

Are the clinical scales on the original MMPI and MMPI-2 based on normalized T *distributions? If not, what is the nature of the scale?*

Neither the MMPI nor the MMPI-2 clinical scales are normalized *T* distributions.

The original MMPI used a *linear* transformation of raw clinical scores. That this linear transformation was not a normalization (and did not result in normalized *T* scores) has been the cause of much confusion among those who are not adequately familiar with the test. As Colligan et al., (1983) wrote,

> *It is widely believed that the standard scores plotted on the profile sheet [for the original MMPI] are normalized T scores. This assumption would mean that a score, on any scale, falling at T 70 would be at approximately the 98th percentile for the normative group. This is not the case. The so-called T scores on the MMPI are not T scores by the usual definition of being derived from probabilities related to the normal curve. Rather, they are simply a linear transformation to a mean of 50 and a standard deviation of 10, a procedure that preserves the remarkably skewed distribution of some of the underlying raw scores. Thus, scale elevations of similar degree in terms of T scores unfortunately, do not have equivalent meanings in terms of deviations from the mean (that is, percentile rank). (pp. xiv–xv)*

There is an additional aspect regarding *T* scores and the original MMPI that an attorney may wish to explore during discovery. In some instances, he or she may wish to ask the opposing expert detailed questions about the scoring and interpretation of scores in this regard; in other instances, the attorney may wish to provide the raw test data, scoring notations, and MMPI report to another expert for review regarding these issues. The additional aspect concerns the *T*-score format on the MMPI profile sheet and the tables of norms provided in standard reference works on the MMPI. As Roger Greene (1980) wrote,

> *The purified sample of Minnesota normals is the most frequently used normative group [for the original MMPI] since it forms the basis for the norms on the standard profile sheet. Hathaway and Briggs (1957) formulated the purified Minnesota normative sample by removing from the original Minnesota group any case with incomplete test protocols or background records. This "purified" sample was then used to derive the T-score equivalents for each raw score on each scale for both K-corrected and non-K-corrected profiles. . . . Non-K-corrected profiles, however, cannot be plotted directly on the profile sheet. . . . The reader should note that T-scores derived from the norms provided in the* Handbook *and most other MMPI reference works will not correspond exactly with the T-scores on the standard profile sheet, for the* Handbook *and other references provide norms based on the* original *(nonpurified) Minnesota normative group*

> *but the standard profile sheet is based on the* purified *sample. This discrepancy can be the source of considerable confusion. (pp. 21–22)*

The clinical scales of the MMPI-2 also do *not* use normalized *T* scores. They do, however, differ from the simple linear transformations of the *T* scores on the original MMPI. The scores for the clinical scales (except for Scales 5 and 0) were converted into *uniform T* scores. As a result, the scales not only have a mean of 50 and a standard deviation of 10 but also represent the same level of deviation (i.e., percentile value) from the norm at each level of elevation (e.g., 65, 70, and 80; see appendix H).

What reading level is required for the MMPI-2?

A fifth- or sixth-grade reading level is required (Paolo et al., 1991; see also Butcher, 1990a).

ADMINISTRATION AND SCORING

Did you administer the MMPI [MMPI-2 or MMPI-A]?

In some cases, the deponent may be testifying about one or more MMPI protocols that he or she personally administered (or that were administered under his or her supervision). In other cases, one or more of the protocols may have come from other sources (e.g., previous MMPIs—some perhaps years or decades old—that were part of the test taker's previous clinical records; MMPIs administered by an independent clinician appointed by the court; or MMPIs administered by the test-taker's current therapist). It is important to clarify who was responsible for administration.

Whether the deponent or some third party was responsible for administering the test, it is also important to clarify whether the responsible party actually administered the test (e.g., gave the instructions, personally monitored the person during the entire time that he or she took the test, and then collected the completed form) or whether the responsible party delegated some or all of the administrative tasks to a supervisee, clerical worker, employee, or colleague. Because, as previously discussed, the validity of a standardized test such as the MMPI is dependent on a standardized method of administration, the way in which the test is administered and monitored becomes crucial. Faschingbauer (1979) made this point vividly by referring to his own experience:

> *We know, for example, that the MMPI can provide false information when the usual mental health testing environment is altered. Hence, we were taught as students to be concerned about the settings in which tests are administered. Some of us had this point personally accentuated when we sneaked off to take the MMPI in our offices only to be startled by the unusually high elevations this private setting produced. To be reliable and valid any test should be administered in a setting close to that employed in normative studies. (p. 384)*

If the person responsible for the administration delegated the task of administration to a third party, it is important to discover adequately detailed information about this third party. For example, who trained the person who actually administered the test? How much experience does the person have in administering MMPIs? How is that person supervised? How has that person's work (particularly in regard to MMPI administration) been evaluated? Does that person have any formal clinical training? What information (about the MMPI administration in the current case) did that person convey to the person who was responsible for test administration? Was that information in oral or written form? Does it appear in the formal report? Did the person who actually administered the MMPI keep any written records of this particular administration? Did the test taker ask the person who administered the test any questions? If so, how did the person who actually administered the MMPI respond? Did the test taker make any comments while taking the test? If so, what were they? Did the test taker take any breaks while taking the MMPI? If so, for how long?

What instructions were given to the test taker?

The questions in this set are relevant regardless of whether the deponent, someone under the deponent's supervision, or some unrelated third party actually administered the test. The purpose of this set of questions is to discover the conditions under which the test was administered (and, for example, whether they adequately met the criteria for a standardized test), the deponent's extent of knowledge (which may be severely limited if the deponent did not personally administer the test) about those conditions, and the deponent's understanding of the implications of those conditions. Did, for example, the person who administered the test include instructions regarding attempting to answer all items (an issue that, as previously noted, can affect validity)? If so, how were the instructions worded?

How was the test taker's reading level assessed?

If there is any question at all about the test taker's reading level (because of such factors as education, neuropsychological impairment affecting language processing, or reliance on English as a second or third language), it is useful to discover the degree to which the reading level was assessed. The MMPI does have some internal checks, but if there is any reasonable question about the test taker's reading level, the deponent may be asked to explain the degree to which the internal checks have shown validity, the basis for deciding whether some other form of assessing reading level should have been included as part of a careful assessment process, and the full array of information on which his or her professional opinion about the reading level is based. (If the person taking the test does not have an adequate reading ability in English, the attorney may also want to inquire about any forms—such as those for informed consent for testing—that the deponent had the person "read" and sign.)

Was the test administration directly monitored?

If no one was with the test taker during the entire period that the test was taken, it is impossible to determine the degree to which the test taker may have relied on other sources for filling out the test. The test taker may, for example, have consulted written materials. Chapter 4 provides examples of settings in which third parties sometimes "helped" the test taker fill out the test by indicating which response blanks should be filled in. To administer the MMPI without adequate monitoring violates the published opinion of the APA's Committee on Professional Standards who held that whenever a psychologist

> *does not have direct, first-hand information as to the condition under which the test is taken, he or she is forced (in the above instance, unnecessarily) to assume that the test responses were not distorted by the general situation in which the test was taken (e.g., whether the client consulted others about test responses). Indeed, the psychologist could have no assurance that this test was in fact completed by the client. In the instance where the test might be introduced as data in a court proceeding, it would be summarily dismissed as hearsay evidence. (Committee on Professional Standards, 1984, p. 664)*

Was any phase of the assessment audiotaped, videotaped, or otherwise recorded?

If so, the taped record should have been produced in response to the subpoena duces tecum. The attorney may consider asking the deponent how audio- or videotaping might have affected the assessment (see the following question). For example, if a person is sensitive to being observed (e.g., becomes self-conscious or inhibited) or if he or she has paranoid traits, might not the sensitivity or the traits be exacerbated by the taping of an assessment session? The deponent might also be asked if he or she is aware of any published research or discussion regarding how recording an assessment session may affect the assessment process and results.

What conditions of test administration did you consider as potentially affecting the validity of this test?

As previously noted, a variety of factors can affect the validity or interpretation of a test, and psychologists are ethically required to explicitly note their reservations regarding validity in any test report (see chapters 4, 6, and 7). The attorney may want to explore this issue in detail. What sort of lighting was available in the room? Were there any extraneous noises or interruptions? Was the client taking any medication or suffering from any illness while taking the test? Does the client require glasses or contact lenses for reading? If so, was the client wearing the glasses or contact lenses while taking the test?

Has anyone but you had access to the original completed response form?

This question addresses the integrity of the original test data and the security of the test form itself. If other people beside the test administrator handled the form or had access to it, the attorney may want to explore in detail the specific circumstances. Has the original completed test form been kept in a locked or otherwise secured locale?

Has the original completed response form been altered in any way by anyone? Did anyone except the test taker make marks on, erase, or change the original form in any way?

These questions also address the integrity of the original test data. The person who administered the test and is preparing to submit it for machine scoring may, for example, have worried that the test taker's pencil marks will not be sufficiently dark to register on the machine. He or she may decide to make the original marks darker to ensure proper scoring by the machine. If the administrator or anyone else has attempted to enhance the test in this way, a careful exploration of the process can be useful. How can the administrator be certain that the correct response slot for each item was enhanced?

There may be other instances in which the test taker left a large number of items blank. The administrator may have scanned the test form quickly, noticed the missing responses, and asked the test taker how he or she would answer these items.

Whatever the circumstances, the attorney should have a clear picture of exactly how the test was administered, the degree to which the requirements of standardization (in regard to administration) were met, and the possibility that the original, authentic responses may have changed in some manner.

Were any test data discarded, destroyed, recopied, or lost? Are all of the documents involved in the administration and taking of the test present in their original form?

As a hypothetical example, a patient may be given an MMPI-2 immediately on admission to a hospital. However, because the patient appears to be psychotic, only half of the items are filled in. The patient is given some medication and, a few hours later, another MMPI-2 is administered. This time the patient fills in all the items but seems to have filled them in randomly (i.e., the *VRIN* scale is significantly elevated). Finally, the next day, the MMPI-2 is again administered. This time the patient seems sufficiently motivated, alert, and oriented to produce a valid profile. The psychologist who conducts psychological testing on the unit files the valid profile in the patient's chart, discarding the two previous protocols as incomplete, invalid, and useless. Only by asking directly about all documents relating to the administration and taking of psychological tests will an attorney likely discover the previous administrations of the test, information that may be key to understanding information relevant to the trial.

As another hypothetical example, a patient at a mental health clinic may sue the clinic and a number of staff members for malpractice. One of the staff members may fear that certain chart notes and test data may support the patient's case. At some point the staff member may surreptitiously go through the patient's file and "weed out" all documents that might significantly support the patient's charges. Again, only by asking specific questions of all those involved (while they are under oath) is an attorney most likely to discover that the test data that have been provided to him or her as part of the discovery process are somehow incomplete, changed, or supplemented with bogus data created "after the fact."

Who scored this test?

In some instances, the test may have been hand scored. It is worth finding out whether the deponent or some third party did the actual calculations that converted the raw data (i.e., the marks that the test taker made in the "true" and "false" slots) into scale scores and an MMPI profile. In other instances, the test may have been scored by machine. Some clinicians may have personal computers (or computers in their hospital, clinic, university, or other setting) that have programs that scan and score an MMPI. Still other clinicians may send the raw data to an individual or institution (such as National

Computer Systems) that provides scoring and interpretation services.

Did the scoring differ in any way whatsoever from the scoring method set forth in the MMPI manual?

As emphasized previously, the strength and validity of a standardized test is dependent on the standardization. To the degree that the standardized methods for scoring are altered (without additional validation and standardization), the test is no longer standardized. The reliability, validity, and interpretations that are associated with the standardized test do not automatically transfer to methods of scoring that deviate from those specified in the manual and the research literature.

What steps have you taken to ensure that the scoring of this test is accurate and free from error?

No matter how a test is scored, there may be errors. If the test was hand scored, the person doing the scoring may have misread some of the responses (e.g., scored a "true" as a "false" on a specific item), may have made mathematical errors in adding up the raw scores on each scale, may have made errors in translating the raw scores into scale scores, or may have made errors in plotting the profile on the form. If the individual who administered the test used a personal computer to score the test, he or she may have used an unauthorized scoring program with a "bug" in the software that reads and scores the responses. If the test was sent to a distant location for scoring, what assurance does the deponent have that the test was not incorrectly labeled in some way, that it was not somehow mixed up with one of the other test forms that was received by the facility, or that the report that was returned did not contain scoring or other errors?

By asking detailed questions in this area, the attorney can discover the degree to which the deponent has taken appropriate and careful steps to verify that the scoring (and other) information is accurate. Has, for example, the deponent personally checked the scoring and the profile against the raw data? If not, why not? The failure to take such fundamental steps *may* (or may not) indicate a lack of care in reaching professional opinions. (Chapter 4 presents possible cross-examination questions for expert witnesses who present test data that contains scoring or computational errors.) In any event, such information will help the attorney to discover the extent to which MMPI scores that are introduced into evidence (or that form a basis of an expert's opinion) are likely to be accurate and reliable.

Were there any changes made in the test format, mode of administration, instructions, language, or content?

This question is intended to be comprehensive in scope, picking up several themes that have been addressed in more limited form in previous questions. Again, the purpose is to discover the degree to which a standardized test was actually administered and scored in a standardized manner. The deponent needs to acknowledge, explain, and adequately justify any deviations from the standard instructions, content, administration, and so on.

> *When a test user makes a substantial change in test format, mode of administration, instructions, language, or content, the user should revalidate the use of the test for the changed conditions or have a rationale supporting the claim that additional validation is not necessary or possible.* (APA, 1985, p. 41).

INTERPRETATION

By what method were these interpretative statements derived from the MMPI scores and profiles?

The deponent may have hand scored the MMPI and looked up the relevant profiles in a set of actuarial tables or code book. The deponent may have used a computer-based scoring and interpretation service that provides a printout of the scores, profile, and interpretation. It is important for the attorney to discover the method or basis by which the scores and profile are "translated" into interpretative statements about the test taker. At this point, we are only addressing the general issues of personality assessment (e.g., "the person who took the test appears to be clinically depressed because of certain scale elevations"); more specific inferences and interpretation are addressed later in this chapter.

The fact that a computer was used to score and interpret the test and that the test report appears in the form of a computer printout may lend an aura of authority, omniscience, and infallibility that is unwarranted (O'Dell, 1972). The *Ethical Principles of Psychologists and Code of Conduct* (APA, 1992) emphasize that "psychologists who offer assessment or scoring procedures to other professionals accurately describe the purpose, norms, validity, reliability, and applications of the procedures and any special applications and any special qualifications applicable to their use" ([208(a)], pp. 1603–1604).

Psychologists who rely on computer services as a component of forensic evaluations are responsible for choosing services that have shown demonstrable validity. "Psychologists select scoring and interpretation services (including automated services) on the basis of evidence of validity of the program and procedures as well as on other appropriate considerations" ([208b], p. 1604).

The *Guidelines for Computer-Based Tests and Interpretations* (APA, 1986b) state that "the original scores used in developing interpretive statements should be given to test users. The matrix of original responses should be provided or should be available to test users on request" (p. 21). The *Guidelines* also state that "the manual or, in some cases, interpretive report, should describe how the interpretive statements are derived from the original scores" (p. 21).

Readers seeking a more extended discussion of the standards and rationale for linking interpretive statements clearly to raw data or standardized scores are referred to the *Ethical Principles of Psychologists* (APA, 1992), *Guidelines for Computer-Based Tests and Interpretations* (APA, 1986b), and *Standards for Educational and Psychological Testing* (1985).

Do you have any reservations or qualifications regarding the validity of the interpretations that you are presenting?

Few deponents are likely to assert that interpretations that are based on the MMPI are infallible. The attorney can obtain a clear and comprehensive explanation of the sources of possible error and the degree to which and basis on which the deponent believes the interpretations may be somewhat inaccurate, incomplete, misleading, or downright wrong.

What other documents or sources of information would you consider important or relevant to interpreting this MMPI profile?

This question invites the deponent to go on record—under oath—regarding the sources of information that could affect the interpretation of the MMPI. It is important to emphasize that statements about a specific MMPI test taker that are based on books, computer printouts, and so on, whether derived from actuarial tables (e.g., "92% of the individuals who were inpatients in psychiatric hospitals and who exhibited this profile on the MMPI showed the following personality characteristics . . .") or other sources *must* be considered hypotheses. The degree to which these hypotheses are supported by, are consistent with, are modified by, or are seemingly contradicted by other sources of information is crucial to an informed understanding of the nature and strength of an MMPI-based interpretation.

Depending on the situation, other sources of information that might be relevant to evaluating the hypotheses derived from a specific MMPI profile could include previous or subsequent administrations of the MMPI, findings from other psychological or neuropsychological tests, assessments from clinical interviews or behavioral observation, medical records, school records, the personal history of the individual (e.g., significant life events and developmental influences), interviews with relatives or friends, employment records, previous or current court records or related legal documents, and current circumstances (e.g., those that might raise the possibility of malingering).

If there are sources of information that seem relevant to the attorney but are not mentioned by the deponent, the attorney may want to ask about each source to discover the deponent's rationale for viewing it as relevant or irrelevant to interpreting the profile.

Have you carefully reviewed all of these documents or sources of information (i.e., those named by the

deponent in responding to the previous question) that you consider important or relevant to interpreting this MMPI profile?

Unless the deponent gives a comprehensive "yes" in responding to this question, the attorney may wish to mention each of the sources of information to discover whether the deponent carefully reviewed it, the rationales for instances in which documents from other sources of information were not reviewed, and the possible impact that failure to consider specific sources of information may have on the interpretation of the MMPI.

[For a written assessment report or other document submitted by the expert witness] ***At any point in your written report, did you present the work, conclusions, or words of others without honestly acknowledging that these came from other sources?***

Those who hand score an MMPI may look up published descriptions of the relevant profiles and copy these descriptions verbatim without indicating the source. Those who submit MMPI forms to a computerized scoring and interpretation service may copy the service's report verbatim, as part of the clinician's own report without acknowledging that these words came from a different source. While preparing forensic reports that are based on the MMPI, other standardized psychological tests, or other sources, the expert may copy passages word-for-word from published articles or clinical textbooks on psychopathology without providing the proper reference.

Imwinkelried (1982, pp. 289–290) cited Schwartz's account of the trial in which Sirhan Sirhan was charged with killing Robert Kennedy. The prosecutor noticed that a defense psychiatrist had apparently copied passages from a variety of published works into his report with no acknowledgment of the source material. The prosecutor asked the expert witness to read the relevant passages from his report and then presented the original sources for the passages. The prosecutor then subjected the witness to a series of cross-examination questions about whether he had been taught in college to indicate clearly (e.g., through quotation marks, footnotes, or explicit statements) any instances in his own writing when the words he was using were not his own, the customary ways in which he had acknowledged using the ideas and words of others in his previous writings, whether in writing his papers for various courses he had indicated when he had copied from the works of others, and so on. Imwinkelried emphasized that such unreferenced verbatim copying may approach plagiarism, that the prosecutor in the Sirhan trial had condemned the defense psychiatrist for this unacknowledged usage in his closing argument, and that the defense attorney "virtually apologized" (p. 290) for this expert witness's testimony.

It is important for expert witnesses to make appropriate acknowledgment of source material. For example, a computerized interpretation of an MMPI is generally considered a "professional-to-professional" consultation. If the expert has used a computerized interpretation service, that fact should be noted in the forensic report (see, e.g., the second example of a forensic assessment report in chapter 7). Similarly, if the expert quotes verbatim from the report (or from other sources), those verbatim quotations should be placed within quotation marks (see the second example in chapter 7).

THE UNEXPECTED: TESTIMONY REGARDING SPECIFIC CLAIMS AND ISSUES

No matter how thoroughly an attorney has prepared his or her side of the case and no matter how favorable the opinions formed by the expert witnesses whom he or she has designated, the attorney is likely, at least occasionally, to encounter one or more surprises from opposing experts. The surprise can occur either before the trial or, if discovery has been inadequate, during the trial itself.

The claims and issues raised by opposing experts may be so unexpected, sweeping, and compelling that the attorney's conception of the case is threatened. The attorney encounters theories, terms, "facts," and opinions that are entirely unfamiliar (at least to the attorney and the attorney's experts) and perhaps seemingly irrefutable. The opinions formed by the attorney's own experts now seem inadequate, trivial, or, in extreme instances, completely irrelevant.

As examples of such unexpected developments, consider the three following fictional scenarios.

Scenario 1: *A prison guard slams a club against the back of Mr. A's head. The guard claims that Mr. A made a threatening move toward him and that he [the guard] used a mild-to-moderate blow to subdue the prisoner. Mr. A claims that he had done nothing wrong (although he was moving rapidly—not in a threatening manner—at the time he was struck) and that the guard had often harassed him on the basis of Mr. A's race and sexual orientation. Mr. A wants to bring suit against the prison but faces the hurdle of proving (as would be required by the idiosyncrasies of state law) that the damage he sustained from the blow was "severe."*

Prison records indicate little or no damage. The prison physician, an internist, performed a neurological examination to assess possible damage to the occipital region (i.e., the part of the brain at the back of the head) and could find no severe problems. The prison psychologist administered an MMPI, allowing the prisoner to take the form back to his cell to complete, as the sole screening device for neuropsychological impairment resulting from the blow and found no evidence of such impairment.

An attorney who often handles cases on behalf of abused prisoners reviews the prison records and finds no adequate basis for a law suit. However, the prisoner's family had arranged for a "specialist" in neuropsychology to examine the prisoner. The neuropsychologist administered the MMPI in conjunction with a comprehensive battery of tests. The neuropsychologist asserts that Mr. A was severely harmed. She comes up with such a bizarre explanation that the attorney is tempted to dismiss it outright as prima facie *quackery. The neuropsychologist claims that the blow to the back of the head caused little damage to the back of the brain that would, because of complex factors, be overtly obvious but considerable damage to the front of the brain that caused severe problems through a phenomenon she terms* contrecoup brain damage.

How can the attorney determine the legitimacy of this theory and its applicability to the prisoner's condition?

◆ ◆ ◆

Scenario 2: *Ms. B filed suit against her employer of 20 years, alleging wrongful termination. She seeks to recover damages as a result of the psychological stress she endured when she was unable to find other work, was unable to make payments on (and subsequently was evicted from) her house, and became so traumatized that she became unable to care for herself.*

Her attorney took her case pro bono *and retained, at her own expense, an expert witness. The expert witness conducted a series of clinical interviews and administered the MMPI twice over a 2-month period. The expert witness was prepared to testify that Ms. B's current condition seemed to be due chiefly to the trauma of being fired unexpectedly (and for no good reason, according to what employment records were available through discovery).*

The company who had fired Ms. B, however, was prepared to present four expert witnesses, one of whom had conducted an extensive psychological assessment. The assessment had been videotaped and made available to the three other experts for review. All four experts were prepared to testify that the MMPI was not a valid instrument for evaluating Ms. B's "special condition." The experts relied on their clinical judgment and also on a test they termed "Multiplicity Indices of Conjoint and Covert Development (MICCD)." The MICCD, which two of the experts had created and used for 30 years, was described as illuminating subintentional aspects of personality that the MMPI and other commonly used tests were too insensitive to evaluate. The MICCD showed clearly that Ms. B had suffered from a life-long subintentional personality defect or vulnerability known as "eschatological morbidity with pronounced teleological complications." Any problems she now had were due to this life-long condition that had only now become apparent (and would have become apparent regardless of her employment or financial status).

Ms. B's attorney and her expert had heard of neither the MICCD nor the diagnosis put forth by the four defense experts. Through discovery, they were able to find four books on the subject, all of which were self-published by the defense experts. No research on the test or diagnosis had been published in peer-reviewed journals, although the authors, some of whom were professionally prominent, had mentioned both the test and diagnosis in "theoretical" articles (explaining the constructs and rationale) and "practice" articles in professional journals (explaining how to conduct an assessment using the MICCD and how to treat eschatological morbidity by regressing the patient into a variety of past lives, an approach termed multiple regression therapy*).*

Is there any hope that Ms. B's attorney with her one expert can counter the impressive unanimity of the four prominent defense experts? What steps can be taken to discover the nature and foundation of this new testimony?

◆ ◆ ◆

Scenario 3*: Mr. C browses through a large supermarket for several hours. He walks the aisles, tastes the free samples offered by food companies promoting new products, takes a butcher knife from the kitchenware section, and attempts to rob a cashier at a checkout counter at knife point. When the cashier moves too slowly in handing over the money, Mr. C stabs her to death, runs from the store, but is soon apprehended. The entire incident was captured on videotape by the supermarket's videomonitor.*

The prosecutor believes that she has a reasonably easy homicide case because of the numerous eyewitnesses as well as the videotape. The defense attorney has raised defenses involving mental impairment. To counter this defense, the prosecutor has retained an expert witness who has conducted an extensive forensic assessment using the MMPI-2 and other standardized tests. The expert is prepared to testify that Mr. C suffers no disorders that would be relevant to the case. The prosecutor soon learns, however, that prominent defense experts will testify that Mr. C was temporarily insane (or at least suffered from diminished capacity) at the time of the alleged killing. They will assert that the high sugar (and food additive) content of the free samples consumed by Mr. C caused an intense metabolic and psychotropic reaction, as a result of which Mr. C became temporarily deranged and unable to understand or control his actions. Not only will he plead not guilty to the criminal charges, his attorneys are filing a multimillion dollar civil claim against the supermarket (and the food companies who urged Mr. C to sample their products) for causing this tragedy.

How do the prosecutor and the defense attorneys representing the supermarket and food companies contend with these claims?

There is no magical way that the attorney can simply "know" whether such claims are exceptionally well founded, entirely bogus, or somewhere in between. Theories that have the ring of authority, common sense, and inevitability may be ludicrously fallacious. Concepts that seem bizarre, counterintuitive, and just downright silly may, in fact, be valid.

Without careful, informed, and thorough inquiry, the attorney will only be guessing at the validity of an unexpected, sweeping claim by an opposing expert and will be in no position to contend adequately with the testimony. The extended section that follows was developed to help attorneys (and expert witnesses) to confront, explore, analyze, and understand such specific claims and issues when they arise during the course of legal proceedings.

Although many of the sets of questions listed earlier are relatively straightforward and uncomplicated (e.g., whether an expert witness has received a doctorate from an APA-approved graduate program or whether the witness has ever been disciplined for an ethics violation), informed, systematic, and useful examination of the interwoven, often obscure strands of assumptions, theories, terms, facts, inferences, and opinions forming the basis of unexpected expert testimony tends to be much more complex and fraught with potential difficulties.

Examining such claims is comparable in some ways with dismantling a complex mechanical device, viewing each component from various perspectives, seeing what it is made of and why, and then reassembling the mechanism to see how the parts work together, what makes the machine "go," and to what purposes the machine can be put. Nothing so forcefully illustrates Louis Nizer's axiom, quoted repeatedly in this book, about the absolute necessity of careful and thorough case preparation.

Whenever a deponent provides a professional opinion or makes any claim or assertion about the MMPI, about other assessment instruments and techniques, about generally accepted practice or theory, about research results, about the published scientific and professional literature, or about *any important fact or issue* (even if it only concerns the context of the issue at hand or what might be considered a peripheral, collateral, or tangential issue), the deposition process *must* help the attorney discover the evidence supporting the claim and the degree to which such evidence is valid, reliable, consistent, authentic, and specifically applicable to the issue at hand.

Psychology bases claims regarding the effectiveness of an intervention or the accuracy of assessments or predictions on impartial, systematic investigation. Professor Irving Weiner, editor of the *Journal of Personality Assessment*, has emphasized the importance of refraining from making claims for validity that are not supported by empirical evidence.

> *A psychologist commenting on the assessment of alleged sexual abuse was heard to identify a "certain sign": If a girl sees Card IV on the Rorschach as a tree upside down, then she has been a victim of sexual abuse. Whatever tortuous rationale might be advanced on behalf of such an influence, there is not a shred of empirical evidence to support it. Indeed, there is precious little evidence to support any isomorphic relationship between specific Rorschach responses and specific behavioral events. Psychologists who nevertheless use Rorschach responses in this way are behaving unethically, by virtue of being incompetent. (Weiner, 1989, pp. 829–830)*

Weiner's conclusion reflects the longstanding tradition in psychology that for methods of assessment "validity has always been an ethical imperative" (Messick, 1980, p. 1020). Similarly, Professor Jerome L. Singer (1980), director of clinical and community psychology training at Yale University, has discussed how the need to base clinical interventions on methods whose validity or effectiveness is established through research constitutes "a central ethic of the profession" (p. 372). In a statement of formal policy, the APA's Council of Representatives has repeatedly emphasized that psychological interventions should be "based on the available scientific evidence of efficacy" (Fox, 1989, p. 1024).

Psychology's (and other scientific disciplines') emphasis on validity as an "ethical imperative" and careful attention to "scientific evidence" is consistent with the federal appellate decision in *Kenosha Liquor Company v. Heublein*, 895 F.2d 418 (7th Cir. 1990). The court's basic finding was that the opinions of a well-qualified expert were generally admissible but that they were "worthless without data and reasons" 895 F.2d at 420, as explained below.

At issue in the case was whether one of Heublein's brands of liquor, specifically Jose Cuervo tequila, was essential to the business health of the Kenosha Liquor distributing company. Kenosha carried a variety of brands, but only one (Jose Cuervo) was produced by Heublein. Heublein contended that Jose Cuervo was not crucial to Kenosha because it accounted for less than 10% of their sales.

"Kenosha Liquor defended the motion by relying on Steve L. Barsby, an economist who maintained that Jose Cuervo is one of Kenosha Liquor's 'magnet brands' essential to its business" 895 F.2d at 419. The expert referred to the fact that almost 90% of the tequila that Kenosha sold was Jose Cuervo and that the attractiveness of this brand enabled Kenosha sales representatives to make contacts with buyers and thus to have an opportunity to sell other brands carried by the distributor.

What the court emphasized in its decision is that however well-credentialed, the expert presented opinions that were not adequately supported by research and other facts.

> *Even if Barsby said that losing Jose Cuervo would cost Kenosha Liquor 10%, 20%, 50%, even 99.44% of its business, this would be unimportant. For he presented no foundation for his conclusion. Barsby did not report the results of a statistical study of the effect of losing certain brands of liquor. From 1967–72 Barsby (who holds a Ph.D. in economics from the University of Oregon) was an assistant professor at the University of Arizona; since 1972 he has been in private industry and consulting. So he must have professional skills, but he did not use them. The only* fact *he presented is that Jose Cuervo accounts for 90% of Kenosha Liquor's tequila sales. This does not imply anything about Kenosha Liquor's status as a "dealer" unless connected to a probable consequence of termination. The expert offered no summary of similar terminations of other dealers, no data about consequences of product cut-offs outside the liquor business. 895 F.2d at 420.*

Judge Easterbrook, writing the unanimous decision, summarized the court's finding that expert opinion, even when offered by a skilled and well-qualified expert, has no value and should be accorded no weight unless adequately founded on data and reasons:

> *Opinions are admissible under Fed. R. Evid. 702, but admissibility does not imply utility. See* Mid-State Fertilizer Co. v. Exchange National Bank, *877 F.2d 1333, 1338-40 (7th Cir. 1989);* Richardson v. Richardson-Merrell, Inc., *857 F.2d 823, 829-32 (D.C.Cir. 1988). Expert opinions are worthless without data and reasons. Kenosha Liquor has a worthless opinion, and Heublein is entitled to judgment. 895 F.2d at 420.*

Such issues of validity can easily be obscured when a witness (a) lists either numerous examples (the sheer number of statements about an issue masking the degree to which there is underlying validity) or one or two exceptionally vivid case studies, (b) uses reasoning that embodies the cognitive processes encouraging error (such as mistaking retrospective accuracy for predictive accuracy) described in chapter 4, or (c) inappropriately uses research from other contexts that may have limited or no relevance to the issues before the court.

The expert may refer to "published opinions and statements by an authority," but is the author of these opinions and statements an authentic and recognized authority? Does he or she have a sufficient body of work on the relevant topic that has met the criteria of peer-reviewed publication in scientific and professional journals and that has subsequently been recognized as authoritative (e.g., frequently cited in other articles published in recognized, peer-reviewed scientific and professional journals)? Have the authority's opinions and statements been effectively refuted by other writers? Have these "published opinions and statements" been taken out of context so that they are misleading and perhaps less than completely relevant to the issue at hand? Are the published opinions and statements dated and perhaps no longer representative of (and perhaps antithetical to) the views that the author now holds?

The *Kenosha Liquor Company v. Heublein* decision discussed above emphasized that "expert opinions are worthless without data and reasons" 895 F.2d at 420. Obviously the "authoritative opinions and statements" that are cited secondhand by a testifying expert should meet the same criteria of "data and reasons" that apply to the expert's own work and opinions. The difficulties faced by the attorney conducting the deposition or cross-examination often become much more complex as the relevant issues proliferate and intertwine.

In the approach suggested here, the attorney in essence becomes a scientist, seeking all relevant data and evaluating them carefully according to specific scientific principles. The attorney obtains as much information as possible from the expert witnesses during deposition.

Then, much as one scientist may attempt to replicate a research study previously conducted by another scientist (to see if he or she obtains the same results), the attorney obtains all materials (raw test data, scoring keys, and published research reports mentioned by the expert) and examines the data to see the degree to which the expert's testimony presented them fully, accurately, and in context. The attorney will also (see chapter 5) conduct an independent search of the literature to see if there are relevant publications that were not mentioned by the expert.

If the attorney approaches the deposition of an opposing expert *only* to intimidate, "rattle," cast aspersions, and wring out statements damaging to the witness's credibility and the opposing party's case, then the attorney is likely to lose a vital opportunity to understand the issues and evidence more fully and to be in a better position to try the case.

To help attorneys untangle and examine overwhelmingly complex and intertwined issues comprehensively, we recommend using a systematic set of 16 fundamental questions about each relevant issue. The list of areas of inquiry that follow can be used both as a "road map" to the extensive discussion and analysis that follows and also as an outline for deposition or cross-examination questioning:

1. the adequacy with which the expert portrays the studies, information, or publications;
2. relevance;
3. internal consistency;
4. research foundation;
5. definition and consistent application of evaluative criteria;
6. number of investigations;
7. sample size;
8. criteria for "success";
9. duration of study;
10. questionable applications;
11. level of effectiveness;
12. reliability and validity;
13. independent verification;
14. ethically questionable research practices;
15. publication in peer-reviewed academic, scientific, or professional journals; and
16. accounting for the base rate.

Checking off each set of questions for each issue during the deposition process can help to ensure that no relevant information is overlooked and that the attorney has obtained the information necessary to understand the expert witness's testimony.

To illustrate the process by which this systematic approach can be applied during deposition to extremely detailed, complex, and intertwined issues, the following section presents the set of 16 fundamental questions as they might be put to an expert witness in a hypothetical case. Because the material in this book, as well as sets of MMPI-related questions in previous sections of this chapter, will enable attorneys to assess the validity of MMPI-based claims and because unexpected testimony of the type exemplified in the three scenarios at the beginning of this section threatens (for the unprepared attorney) to trivialize, throw into question, or render seemingly irrelevant testimony that is based on the MMPI and other well-accepted, empirically validated, commonly used standardized psychological tests, we have chosen a case in which the MMPI appears only occasionally and peripherally. The focus should be on the general principles of systematic exploration and analysis of unexpected claims and theories rather than on the intricacies of the MMPI that are addressed elsewhere in this volume.

The hypothetical case involves an administrative hearing of a male therapist who has been sexually intimate with his clients. The therapist does not dispute that the intimacies occurred but asks the administrative law judge to impose minimal sanctions and to allow him to return to practice (i.e., to allow him to maintain a psychology license) as a rehabilitated professional.

The hypothetical expert witness for the defense, during direct examination, has provided testimony regarding two issues. First, the witness has attempted to establish that there is no scientific evidence that therapist–client sexual intimacies generally tend to cause harm and that in fact there is persuasive evidence that such intimacies may be no more likely to cause harm than sexual activity in other contexts (e.g., marital relations) and may even be beneficial. Therefore, the witness concludes, the therapist has likely caused no harm and does not deserve discipline.

Second, the expert in this hypothetical case testifies that the defendant has been reliably identified as a certain type of impaired professional on the basis of an MMPI profile, was subsequently assigned to an appropriate rehabilitation program for that type of perpetrator, and has been, according to a current MMPI assessment, completely rehabilitated and no longer constitutes any risk of reoffending should he be permitted by the administrative law judge and the licensing board to resume practice.

The following questions can help the attorney conducting the deposition or cross-examination to understand the foundation, accuracy, validity, comprehensiveness (e.g., has essential information been omitted), context, and relevance of the expert's claims about these issues. However, the questions can be adapted to fit a variety of specific claims regarding similar issues in other types of cases (e.g., criminal or personal injury).

Questions Regarding Relative Harmfulness

1. Does the study, information, or publication actually support the claims represented by the expert?

The expert witness in the hypothetical case may have attempted to introduce studies such as those presented in *The Love Treatment*, written by psychiatrist Martin Shepard (1971). This book of case studies is used by Shepard to suggest that under the right conditions, sex in a professional context may be harmless and might even be helpful. Yet a careful reading of the cases themselves can provide evidence that would tend to refute those claims. As Fritz C. Redlich (1977), professor of psychiatry and dean of the Yale University Medical School commented,

> *Shepard recommends "mature" sexual relationships with patients, but every case in the book (verbatim accounts of patients' sexual relationships with other therapists) testifies to the breakdown of trust and regard and to the hostility and disappointment that follow the sexual involvement. The book also illustrates the psychopathological motivations of therapists who become thus involved. Such behavior satisfies the needs of the therapist, which are incompatible with good therapy, and not the legitimate needs of patients.* (p. 150)

This segment illustrates one of the most important aspects of trial preparation: obtaining and carefully reviewing the materials cited by all experts. Unless the attorney reads the books, articles, papers, and so on, cited by opposing experts, he or she is in a poor position to assess the degree to which an expert's testimony may represent the truth, the *whole* truth, and *nothing but* the truth about the scientific and professional literature as well as about more popular books, vanity press books, self-published volumes, privately distributed monographs, unpublished studies, and so on.

Experts may not be maliciously motivated or attempting to "pull a fast one." They may simply be insufficiently familiar with the material that is the subject of their testimony. They may not have read it carefully (or only read summaries of it in secondary sources). They may be misremembering parts of the material or forgetting other parts. As Redlich (1977) pointed out, a study or publication purporting (even according to the author) to support one position may actually undermine that position, suggest other positions, or reveal a complexity to the issue that has not been recognized or adequately highlighted by the author or expert witness.

Whenever MMPI-2 or other standardized test data are presented as supporting a position, the data themselves should be checked for accuracy, research design (if relevant), context, and other factors that may not have been fully identified or assessed by the study's authors or expert witness. Subsequent questions will exemplify various approaches to obtaining information useful in exploring accuracy, research design, context, and so on.

2. Is the study, information, or publication actually relevant to the claims represented by the expert?

The expert in this hypothetical case may have introduced an article "Therapist as Sex Partner Better Than 'Surrogate'" (1976), reported by the International Medical News Service. This article reports a presentation by psychologist Martin H. Williams describing a program of intensive "body work" for helping certain patients. This approach, in which "the emphasis is on arousal" (p. 11), involves encouragement of patients to discuss their reactions and to express or ventilate their thoughts. The article quotes Williams as saying that this approach in which therapists have sex with patients "makes more sense" than the Masters and Johnson type of work using "surrogates."

Although the title of this article and the fact that it discusses sex between therapists and patients as useful for some types of patients and problems might misleadingly seem—on a superficial level and without further examination or information—to support the expert witness's claim in this hypothetical case that therapist–patient sex is not generally harmful and may even be helpful, closer reading and examination indicate otherwise. For example, this approach (at least as described in the article) is appropriate only for patients who have certain types of sexual difficulties and are seeking help for those sexual difficulties. Moreover, the individual conducting the arousing "body work" is becoming sexually involved with the patient within a specific framework and has obtained adequately specialized training for that purpose. Thus, even if Williams's account as reported in the article were to be accepted at face value, it would *only* be applicable to therapists who have been specially trained to engage safely and therapeutically in sexually arousing activities with patients and to instances in which the patients were specifically seeking sex therapy. It has no more relevance, similarity, or applicability to what is generally conceptualized as therapist–patient sexual intimacies in most licensing hearings, civil suits, and the clinical literature than the early work of William Masters and Virginia Johnson using sex surrogates.

Terminology, then, is a crucial factor in assessing the degree to which cited material may or may not be relevant. A given term or phrase (e.g., "therapist," "therapy," or "sex partner") may have a variety of significantly different meanings according to the theoretical orientation, situation, topic, context, or person who uses the term. An article or book may use the same terms as those that are at issue before the court and yet have entirely different meanings than the terms used in the legal proceedings. Until the meanings can be adequately assessed, no reflexive assumption should be made that even a commonly used term always carries the same definition in all usage.

Even at this point (i.e., when lack of relevance has been shown to be due to significant differences between the issues addressed by an article as cited and described by an expert witness and the behaviors at issue before the court), the opposing attorney's analysis of the article and its actual meaning have barely begun. *No inferences should ever be drawn* from or about such articles (or books, etc.), their wording, or the way in which they are presented (e.g., by the hypothetical expert in this case) until the attorney (and all others—including readers of this book—encountering such material) has read the article and knows what it actually says.

Selective presentations are just that—selective—and may, however unintentionally, form the basis of erroneous or misleading inferences. Obviously, a number of other factors, in addition to use of similar or identical terminology, discussed in this book may be essential in understanding such material and should be examined before inferences are drawn, attributions made, or conclusions reached about the material. Such factors include the datedness of the material (as mentioned previously, an author who has expressed a particular conclusion or opinion may later, perhaps in light of new data, reach different—perhaps contrary—conclusions or opinions), research foundation, the sample size, number of independent studies, publication in peer-reviewed scientific and professional journals, and so on.

The use of similar terminology can obscure important and sometimes essential differences between the studies, information, or publications presented by an expert witness and the matters that are at issue before the court. Research and assessment data from the MMPI and other standardized psychological tests can likewise distract the attention of the attorney, judge, and jury from the fact that these data—however impressive they may be in vividness, sheer mass, or elaborate patterns—may have little or no relevance to the issues at hand. Again, careful examination of the documents on which the expert witness is relying can provide the basis for an appropriate cross-examination.

3. Do the data—viewed from all reasonable perspectives—add up?

The hypothetical expert witness might present a study that is based on a psychiatrist's evaluation of his or her own work that appears to lend support to the notion that therapist–client sex is not generally harmful and may, under proper circumstances (i.e., by certain therapists for certain patients with certain problems), be therapeutic. McCartney (1966) claimed to have had success, during the 40-year period in which he studied this intervention, in three fourths of the 1,500 psychoanalyses in which he had engaged in sex with patients.

In reviewing the numbers presented by McCartney, Pope and Bouhoutsos (1986, pp. 57–59) calculated the number of hours per week that the psychiatrist devoted to these psychoanalytic patients on whom he had been trying out his sexualized intervention on a trial basis. The calculations reveal that he would have been spending 600 hours *per week* on these particular patients. This somewhat taxing schedule may be viewed from yet another perspective: McCartney (1966, p. 236) emphasized that these psychoanalytic clients accounted for only about a fourth (26%) of his client load.

This example highlights at least four major principles of questioning expert witnesses and reviewing their data.

First, as mentioned previously, the attorney must obtain the original source materials cited by or relied on by the expert. Only then can information that may not be disclosed in the testimony (e.g., the number of patients, percentage of time spent with them, etc., in McCartney's study) become evident.

Second, McCartney conducted and reported research investigating the efficacy of an intervention that he had developed and put into practice. The lack of independent verification of the validity of an intervention indicates that essential evidence concerning the effects is missing. For a clinician (or a group of clinicians, a research team, an agency, an institution, etc.) to be the sole judge of whether their theories are valid, their interventions sound and safe, and their work productive and reliable is comparable to allowing an attorney in a trial to be sole judge of whether he or she won the case.

A subsequent question in this chapter highlights the crucial significance of determining whether evidence was independently obtained, especially in light of the considerable research evidence in the areas of cognitive psychology, decision making, and so on, demonstrating the ways that judgments and even perceptions about one's own hypotheses and work can be biased. Moreover, there may be extrinsic motivation that calls into question the objectivity of research. Thus, for example, research sponsored by a drug company may show that its own drugs are far superior to all others, or research sponsored by the tobacco industry may show that smoking cigarettes is harmless; the degree to which the beliefs, interests, and procedures of the sponsorship may in some way have influenced—however subtly or unintentionally—the research should be fully explored.

Third, because McCartney's presentation reviewed findings about an experimental procedure involving human subjects or participants (i.e., his patients), the issue of providing proper safeguards and informed consent for those exposed to the risks of an unvalidated intervention needs to be fully explored. A question later in this series highlights the importance of verifying that all evidence that the expert witness cites or relies on was gathered in accordance with legal, ethical, professional, and all other appropriate standards for trial or investigatory procedures that might expose third parties to risk of harm.

Fourth, numerical data should be reviewed thoroughly to ensure that statistical assumptions and implications are sound. The McCartney data illustrate the necessity of examining carefully the internal consistency and related patterns or implications of the data (i.e., the number of hours he must have devoted each week to his patients). The case of *People v. Collins*, 68 Cal. 2d 319, 66 Cal. Rptr. 497, 438 P.2d 33 (1968) illustrates an instance in which the assumptions were unsound. The prosecutor devised a hypothetical example that was based on the testimony of an eyewitness to a crime. The eyewitness had described a number of the alleged robbers' characteristics (e.g., their race, the way they wore their hair, and the color of their car). The characteristics matched those of the defendants. The prosecutor's hypothetical example asked that an expert witness assume that each of the characteristics had a particular probability (e.g., the probability that a person has a mustache). The prosecutor then asked the witness to calculate the probability that all these characteristics would occur simultaneously (which, during closing argument, he would assert indicated the probability that the two defendants—who had all of the characteristics described by the eyewitness and included in the hypothetical example—were the actual perpetrators).

The expert witness in mathematics testified that the probability of all these characteristics occurring together could be calculated by multiplying the probabilities together. As Mendenhall, Wackerly, and Scheaffer (1990) described in "The Multiplicative Law of Probability" for independent events, the probability of the independent events all occurring is the product of their independent probabilities (p. 51; see also Howell, 1992; Paulos, 1988; Ross, 1988; and Scheaffer, 1990, for a more extended discussion of probabilities). When all the probabilities were multiplied, the resulting probability (1 out of 12 million) was so small that the two defendants seemed, on the basis of this testimony, to be, beyond all reasonable doubt, the two individuals described by the eyewitness.

The California Supreme Court overturned the conviction on the basis of a variety of errors in this mathematical analysis. A central error was that the various characteristics were *not* independent and thus could not be validly multiplied together to obtain the probability of all characteristics occurring together. As Justice Sullivan wrote for the majority,

> *While we discern no inherent incompatibility between the disciplines of law and mathematics and intend no general disapproval or disparagement of the latter as an auxiliary in the fact-finding processes of the former, we cannot uphold the technique employed in the instant case. . . . Mathematics, a veritable sorcerer in our computerized society, while assisting the trier of fact in the search for truth, must not cast a spell over him. 68 Cal. 2d 319, 66 Cal. Rptr. 497, 438 P.2d 33 (1968) at 497.*

The assumption of independence is common to many statistical tests (e.g., those in validity and reliability studies of standardized psychological tests; statistical analyses of research concerning the efficacy of medical, psychological, or behavioral interventions) presented as the basis of expert testimony.

> *Statistical tests . . . nearly always assume random and independent selection of the data. Although this process is relatively easy to understand, often its importance is overlooked. If the assumptions of random and independent selection are not met, then the results of subsequent statistical manipulations will have little if any meaning. (Young & Veldman, 1981, p. 43)*

Attorneys and expert witnesses may find it particularly useful to study Thompson and Schumann's (1987) review of what they term the *prosecutor's fallacy,* in which it is falsely assumed that "one can determine the probability of a defendant's guilt by subtracting the incident rate of a 'matching' characteristic from [the number] one" (p. 170) and the *defense attorney's fallacy,* in which it is falsely assumed that "associative evidence is irrelevant, regardless of the rarity of the 'matching' characteristic" (p. 171).

4. Do the claims made by the expert witness rest on research or comparable data?

The hypothetical expert witness may cite a work such as psychologist Zoltan Gross's (1977) "Erotic Contact as a Source of Emotional Learning in Psychotherapy" as empirical support for the notion that therapist–patient sexual involvement need not have negative outcome but may in some cases be positive for patients. For example, Gross explained that

> *while it is true that verbal clues may trigger significant emotional reactions, physical contact, and its special case erotic contact, is a much more reliable triggering action. It is, also, a very powerful source of learning in psychotherapy for both same and opposite sexed people. A touch, like a picture, may convey more information than a thousand words. Touching a person produces an awareness of affect which when focused upon (let me refer you to Gendlin on this point) can illuminate self process with a vividness unmatched by verbal description. . . .*
>
> *In order for meaningful physical communication to occur, however, therapists must remain centered upon the task of learning. (pp. 7–8)*

By obtaining a copy of this paper, however, the attorney is in a position to establish that the paper itself presents no quantifiable data in support of its arguments. The author has advanced a thesis about his view of the value of erotic contact for patients but makes no pretense about supporting his views with research data. The attorney can point out that the expert attempting to present this paper as research evidence is providing testimony that is not accurate.

Examination of the extent to which testimony rests on a research base of empirical data should not be unnecessarily limited to the central issue. Experts may cite or base their testimony on other studies, information, or publications that provide auxiliary data, a context for understanding the central issue, a standard to which data about the central issue may be compared or contrasted, or an argument through example.

That such studies, information, or publications may seem peripheral, contextual, or collateral does not diminish their potential importance in helping the judge and jury to understand the issues at hand. They deserve careful scrutiny. For example, psychologist Martin Williams (1992) maintained that those for whom therapist–patient sexual intimacies may have been a "positive experience" (p. 414) might be less motivated to participate in studies and that damage to women who become sexually involved with a therapist might simply be attributable to a sexually intimate relationship per se rather than to sex in the context of therapy. Williams (1992, p. 415) cited Andrea Dworkin's (1987) book *Intercourse* as an example of the view that "heterosexual relationships are structured to cause harm to women." Dworkin wrote that

> *intercourse itself is immune to reform. In it, female is bottom, stigmatized. Intercourse remains a means or the means of making a woman inferior. . . . In the experience of intercourse, she loses the capacity for integrity because her body . . . is entered and occupied. What is taken from her in that act is not recoverable. (p. 137)*

Dworkin suggests that a "central paradigm for intercourse" is "incestuous rape" (p. 194). If sexual intercourse between a male therapist and a female patient is to be evaluated against a presumptive context in which more general male–female intercourse is comparable to incestuous rape, then it may be difficult to discern any unusual harm caused by the occurrence of intercourse in the context of therapy. Dworkin's thesis has another possible implication in light of M. H. Williams's (1992) suggestion that a patient for whom sex with a therapist had been a "positive experience" might be reluctant to become involved in any of the studies to date. The notion that more general male–female intercourse is comparable to incestuous rape might form the basis for the hypothetical expert witness's inference that the specific therapeutic context might be a buffer—at least in some instances—against the devastating harm that occurs regularly, in Dworkin's (1987) view, in other forms of intercourse (i.e., intercourse that is not between a therapist and a patient).

The hypothetical expert witness's testimony in this regard highlights two important areas of inquiry for the attorney. First, M. H. Williams's (1992) article cited by the expert offered no critique of the evidence supporting Dworkin's (1987) theory. It is important that the attorney inquire carefully of the expert what sources of empirical research or other evidence are available that would confirm the validity of this theory. Moreover, it is important to obtain these sources for careful, independent examination.

Second, the attorney should ask the expert if he or she is aware of any empirical research or other evidence that might contradict the notion that therapist–patient sexual intimacy might be no more harmful (and might even be a more positive experience) than intercourse that occurs in other contexts. For example, studies have collected data so that "the effects of sexual involvement with a therapist could be compared to consensual sexual involvement with a spouse, long- and short-term extramarital liaisons, and sexual involvements traditionally considered traumatic (e.g., rape, incest)" (Pope, 1990c, p. 478).

Thus, the attorney must learn not only what research published in peer-reviewed scientific and professional journals is available to support or discredit an expert's opinion but also the degree to which the expert is aware of this research and took it into account in arriving at his or her opinion.

5. What are the expert's criteria for adequate or acceptable research evidence? Are these criteria consistently applied?

The hypothetical expert witness may claim that, for a variety of reasons, none of the research conducted to date is reliable for establishing that therapist–patient sexual intimacies cause harm. Gross (1977; see also Shepard, 1971) maintained that the moral climate prevented an objective exploration of the issues. M. H. Williams (1992) maintained that in attempts to show an association between therapist–patient sexual intimacy and harm, "the causality may not be possible to define empirically" (p. 416). Riskin (1979; see Pope & Bouhoutsos [1986] for a discussion of Riskin's research proposal) argued that finding out whether therapist–patient sexual intimacy is generally harmful or helpful must await experimental research in which an independent variable is sexual involvement with a therapist; that is, he recommended conducting research in which patients were randomly assigned to "sex" and "no sex" treatment groups as the only way to reliably infer whether such intimacies are positive or negative.

When an expert witness asserts that the available body of studies, information, or publications fail to constitute an adequate basis for a specific inference (e.g., that therapist–patient sex presents a risk for harm), there are three specific areas of inquiry that the attorney should cover.

First, what are the expert's criteria for an "adequate basis"? That is, the expert is maintaining that the available studies, information, and publications do not form an adequate basis for the inference at issue. What, in the witness's expert opinion, are the criteria for an adequate basis for this inference? What are the necessary and sufficient conditions for making the inference? What are the decision-making rules that the expert uses in evaluating the available evidence and in determining whether a given body of evidence constitutes an adequate basis for the inference? Hypothetically, is there any body of evidence *possible* that would adequately support the inference, or do the expert's criteria exclude not only the studies, information, and publications that have appeared to date but also all *possible* methods of gathering data and sources of information?

Allowing the judge and jury to understand whether the expert believes that he or she could ever, under any conditions, draw the inference or reach the conclusion at issue may be crucial to a thorough understanding of the testimony. Are these criteria generally accepted in the relevant field of study? Do they represent a universal consensus, or are they at least generally accepted by authorities in the field? What publications can the expert cite that support the view that these criteria are generally accepted? Can the expert provide adequate evidence that these criteria are held by a majority in the field or are otherwise generally accepted? To what degree have the criteria set forth by the expert been challenged by others in the field? Have any challenges or presentations of alternate sets of criteria (i.e., different from those defined by the expert witness) been taken seriously in the field; do they represent one or more respectable minority viewpoints?

For example, the expert may have testified that a diagnosis of borderline syndrome was an unjustified inference because no psychological testing was conducted. In support of this specific criterion, the witness cites a passage from psychiatrist Otto Kernberg's (1975) authoritative text, *Borderline Conditions and Pathological Narcissism*: "Its [borderline personality organization's] detection through the use of projective tests makes sophisticated psychological testing an indispensable instrument for the diagnosis of borderline personality organization" (p. 25). The attorney should ask if there are any authoritative texts or other creditable sources that maintain that sophisticated psychological testing is *not* an indispensable criterion for arriving at this diagnosis.

Second, what evidence did the witness review in arriving at the opinion that the available evidence does not meet the criteria? It is possible that the witness was unaware of certain studies or information that did meet the witness's own criteria, overlooked them in the evaluation, or forgot to cite them during earlier testimony? For example, in the area of harm and therapist–patient sex, diverse research methodologies have been used to investigate

> *the effects of abuse on patients who did not return to a subsequent therapy as well as those who did, have compared patients who were subjected to abuse by a prior therapist with matched groups of patients who were not victimized, and have explored the sequelae as evaluated variously by the patients*

> *themselves, by subsequent therapists, and by independent clinicians through methods including observation, clinical interviews, and standardized psychological testing.* (Pope, 1990b, p. 232)

An independent search of the literature by the attorney may locate studies, information, and publications that were not considered by the expert.

Third, has the expert witness used these criteria for inference consistently in all phases of testimony in the current case, in testimony rendered in other cases, in his or her own previous articles, chapters, books, papers, teachings, and public or professional lectures and statements? For example, if the hypothetical expert witness states that the available studies, information, and publications do not meet well-defined criteria for inference, does the witness's other testimony—for example, that a specific type of therapist is a better sex partner than a surrogate (for which the hypothetical expert cites "Therapist as Sex Partner Better than 'Surrogate'" [1976]), that erotic contact can help a patient learn (for which the hypothetical expert cites Gross [1977]), or that intercourse in general is comparable to incestuous rape (for which the expert cites Dworkin [1987])—meet these same specific criteria for validity (i.e., are there studies, information, or publications that provide evidence that *is adequate* for the hypothetical expert's claims in a way that the evidence—if any—that therapist–patient sex presents a risk for harm *is inadequate*)?

These three aspects of an expert witness's criteria for the adequacy of research or other forms of evidence for drawing inferences have been a focus of litigation related to the harmfulness of cigarette smoking. Witnesses for the tobacco industry, for example, have testified that

> *evidence supporting the hypothesis that smoking harms or at least endangers humans does not meet certain scientific criteria (e.g., Patterson, 1987): (a) the animal studies—in which isolated variables are randomly assigned in a controlled environment (e.g., precise control of exactly how much smoke is inhaled over specified temporal intervals, of all facets of diet that might interact with smoking effects, of all environmental variables, of relevant genetic predispositions)—cannot be assumed to have direct implications for another species (i.e., humans), and (b) none of the human studies involve random assignment to smoking and nonsmoking groups or adequate isolation of variables; for example, all smokers are self-selected (thus introducing a bias of indeterminable magnitude), and those smokers who do volunteer for studies may differ in significant ways from those smokers who decline to participate.* (Pope, 1990b, p. 231)

As one defense expert, a professor who came to be known as the toxicologist "who discovered that tobacco does not cause cancer" (Jenkins, 1989, p. 176), testified, "On the basis of my own research over many years, and based on all the papers I have read and the people I have talked to, I have come to the conclusion that it's not been proven that cigarette smoke causes cancer" (Jenkins, 1989, p. 176).

Consistency in the application of the criteria for inferring that a substance places an individual at risk for developing cancer (and could thus be a contributing causative agent) is a significant issue in these trials. A plaintiff's attorney outlined what he perceived to be a potential if not actual inconsistency in the application of these criteria:

> *The tobacco companies have an interesting outlook on what causes cancer. . . . Their standards of cancer causation are rather loose, for everything but tobacco! So, they will go into questions about the exposures of your client to anything other than tobacco: Did the decedent ever eat brussels sprouts? Did he ever eat charcoaled meats? But when it comes to tobacco, then nothing's been proven!* (Jenkins, 1989, p. 176)

For an account of litigation focusing on the criteria for inference and consistency in their application, the reader is referred to the chapter, "The Cigarette Wars" (pp. 121–241), in John Jenkin's (1989) informative book, *The Litigators*.

Questions Regarding Rehabilitation

As previously mentioned in this section regarding specific inferences, the second portion of the expert witness's testimony in this hypothetical case maintains that the defendant has been reliably identified as a certain type of impaired professional on the basis of an MMPI profile, was subsequently assigned to an appropriate rehabilitation program for that type of perpetrator, and has been, according to a current MMPI assessment, completely rehabilitated and no longer constitutes any risk of reoffending should he be permitted by the administrative law judge and the licensing board to resume practice. Important areas of inquiry for deposition and trial are discussed below.

6. How many systematic investigations were completed?

That is to say, how many research studies have been undertaken and completed to validate the effectiveness of the rehabilitation program and the MMPI's effectiveness in measuring the results of the rehabilitation program? Of those, how many demonstrated effectiveness? How many failed to demonstrate effectiveness? How many showed indeterminate results?

Harvard Professor E. Bright Wilson wrote that "there have been many ludicrous cases of conclusions drawn from an insufficient number of experiments" (1952, p. 46), after earlier noting that "the proper number of replications for a given case depends on the magnitude of the differences worth looking for, the uniformity . . ., and the precision of the technique of observation" (1952, p. 46).

7. For those systematic investigations that produced evidence that the rehabilitation approach was effective, what was the size of the sample?

A study that, according to a deponent, "proves" a certain hypothesis may seem much less impressive once it is discovered that it included only one (or two, or three) individuals in the sample. Once the size of the sample has been determined, the nature or characteristics of those in the sample (e.g., How were they chosen? Are they truly representative?) can, if relevant, be explored.

Professor E. B. Wilson, quoted in the previous section, described how withholding of precise statistics can be used to give a false or misleading aura of scientific confidence and evidence. He described "an investigation in which chickens were subjected to a certain treatment. It was then reported that 33.3 per cent of the chickens recovered, 33.3% died, and no conclusion could be drawn from the other 33.3 per cent because that one ran away" (1952, p. 46).

8. How was "success" measured?

What measures or criteria were used to determine whether offenders were fully rehabilitated? What is the reliability of each measure? (This is a particularly important issue because, as previously discussed, validity cannot exceed reliability.) What kind of validity do the measures demonstrate?

This more detailed line of questioning (for which we are using the topic of therapist–patient sex as an example) underscores the ways in which the authoritative "aura" of a test and the substantial body of work that may support its validity and reliability may—however unintentionally—be inappropriately focused on a specific topic, task, or issue. The MMPI, for example, is a widely used standardized personality measure. Experts appearing for both sides in a judicial adversarial proceeding may testify truthfully that the MMPI is a widely used and generally accepted test that has shown substantial validity and reliability.

The wealth of supporting research and the common acceptance and use of the MMPI, however, may or may not be relevant to a very specific use. For example, the UCLA (University of California, Los Angeles) Post Therapy Support Program attempted to use the MMPI to help determine which patients (who had been sexually abused by a previous therapist) would benefit from the program's group therapy services (Pope & Bouhoutsos, 1986). However, traditional MMPI patterns associated with suitability and lack of suitability for group therapy appeared to have virtually no predictive validity for this special subset of patients (i.e., people who had been sexually intimate with a previous therapist and were seeking subsequent therapy in this setting). For example, some of the most severely abused patients whose MMPI profiles suggested would not be able to participate meaningfully in, let alone benefit from, outpatient group therapy were among those patients who responded most positively to this treatment modality and who found it an important part of their recovery process.

The MMPI's wide acceptance and demonstrated (through research published in peer-reviewed scientific and professional journals) validity in so many areas should never substitute for scrutiny of its appropriateness and effectiveness in regard to a very specific population, setting, or task.

In the example of the hypothetical licensing hearing used to illustrate the issues in this section, it would be important to ask the witness if the MMPI (or other instruments and methods of assessment) has shown evidence of reliability and validity in identifying therapist-offenders who may have been "rehabilitated"? In these studies, how was rehabilitation defined? Just as a specific medical procedure (such as an appendectomy) may be of enormous use for a given task (i.e., treating appendicitis) but not be useful for a variety of other tasks (e.g., treating glaucoma, dandruff, broken bones, and diabetes), a test such as the MMPI may be exceptionally effective in performing some tasks but not others. The point of the questions in this line of discovery is to identify exactly how validity and reliability have—or have not—been established.

If judgments about the perpetrator's likelihood of becoming sexually involved with a patient sometime in the future are not validated using reliable measures, the research literature suggests that those judgments may be quite misleading. For example, Schnelle (1974) studied interventions designed to ensure that frequently truant children would begin attending school regularly. Parents found that the intervention was effective and reported that their children's attendance had improved significantly. A check of school records, however, revealed that there had been no change in attendance. In a similar manner, those involved in rehabilitation efforts may become quite convinced that such programs are effective even if there is no change in the therapist's likelihood of engaging in sex with a patient.

9. Was the time period covered by the research appropriate to the hypothesis?

If the research is to serve as a solid basis for stating with reasonable certainty that the rehabilitated offenders will not reoffend again over the course of their career, then obviously the research must describe an adequate follow-up of more than just a few years. J. McCord (1978; see also McCord & McCord, 1959a, 1959b) described a careful study of an intervention that is similar in some ways to the much briefer study by Schnelle (1974) reported in the previous section. McCord described a program designed by physician Richard Clark Cabot. Five hundred boys, seemingly at risk for juvenile delinquency or subsequent antisocial activities, were randomly assigned to a preventive treatment program or to a control group of "matched mates" (p. 284). The preventive treatment program lasted about 5 years and included such resources as family visits, academic tutoring, medical and/or psychiatric services, summer camp, Boy Scouts, YMCA (Young Men's Christian Association), and a variety of community programs.

As with the Schnelle (1974) study of school attendance, the Cabot intervention seemed exceptionally valuable to those who participated. The subjective judgments supported the effectiveness of the intervention.

However, a sufficient follow-up during a 30-year period after the intervention allowed an adequate evaluation of the evidence. As with the Schnelle (1974) study, the objective measures told a different story from the favorable subjective endorsements by those who provided services involved in the intervention and those who received the services. The objective measures of the 30-year follow-up showed that

> 1. *Men who had been in the treatment program were more likely to commit (at least) a second crime.*
> 2. *Men who had been in the treatment program were more likely to evidence signs of alcoholism.*
> 3. *Men from the treatment group more commonly manifested signs of serious mental illness.*
> 4. *Among men who had died, those from the treatment group died younger.*
> 5. *Men from the treatment group were more likely to report having had at least one stress-related disease. . . .*
> 6. *Men from the treatment group tended to have occupations with lower prestige.*
> 7. *Men from the treatment group tended more often to report their work as not satisfying. (J. McCord, 1978, p. 288)*

Published research must not only use valid and reliable measures of success, as outlined in section 8 above, but also cover a time period appropriate to the hypothesis being tested.

10. Did the perpetrator's previous knowledge of or experience with the MMPI (or other instruments used to assess rehabilitation) invalidate, qualify, or in any way raise questions about the findings?

Therapists who have engaged in sex with clients may have received extensive training in such standardized psychological tests as the MMPI. The therapist may be thoroughly familiar with the instrument, may have privately taken the test numerous times, and may have administered, scored, and interpreted the test literally hundreds or thousands of times. Familiarity and expertise with a test may invalidate an assessment of an individual who takes that test. This principle is perhaps most obvious with a standardized test such as the WAIS-R. Anyone who has studied the test or administered it once or twice likely knows all the answers to the test (e.g., understands the "best" answers to such subtests as Similarities and Comprehension and has previous knowledge of the forms used in Object Assembly).

Similarly, anyone who has studied the MMPI professionally may be in a position to present a desired profile without running afoul of the items customarily used to assess validity or distortions. If, for example, expert witnesses testify that they understand the test, know how each of the items is scored on the various scales, can determine how the responses will determine the individual profile, then what reason do they have for believing that another clinician—in this instance the therapist who engaged in sex with clients—does not possess the same information and understanding and thus could subvert the purpose of the test in a way that untrained individuals would not have sufficient training, information, and experience to carry out?

11. What level of success did the rehabilitation program demonstrate?

The hypothetical expert witness may testify that one or more formal studies using the MMPI has demonstrated that a specific intervention is effective. But this vague statement needs clarification. For each study, were all participants rehabilitated successfully? If not, what percentage were rehabilitated? There can be a great difference between sets of studies that supposedly demonstrate effective rehabilitation. In one successful (as characterized by the hypothetical expert witness) set, perhaps a few (say, 30 of 150) of the participants were rehabilitated. To this expert, the rehabilitative intervention was a success because it worked with some of the participants. In another successful set of studies, perhaps a majority of the participants were rehabilitated. To the hypothetical expert witness describing the success of these studies, they were successful because most of the individuals in the studies were rehabilitated. And in a third set of studies, all of the participants in each study were rehabilitated. It is only when the attorney inquires about the details of studies—about, for example, the success-level criterion by which each study was judged a success or failure—that the information necessary for the judge or jury to make an informed evaluation of the testimony is elicited.

12. If the rehabilitation program depended on an accurate classification of offenders (i.e., offenders are divided into different types, with each type associated with a specific rehabilitation plan and "prognosis"), what are the reliability and validity of the classification system, as formally and impartially assessed?

Attempting to classify offenders (e.g., on the basis of nature and duration of offense, developmental stages, environmental or life-event factors, demographics, archetypes, professional history or training, or presence or absence of various forms of psychopathology) may constitute an integral component of a hypothetical approach to rehabilitation. If the hypothetical expert witness is offering assurances that offenders are fully rehabilitated on the basis of a specific classification system, the attorney can inquire about the evidence regarding the validity and reliability of the classification system. Is there clear and compelling evidence that such assessments—even when they are based on such a widely accepted instrument as the MMPI—are effective and accurate?

Attempts to classify using methods of classification for which empirical support for validity and reliability are missing can—as in Weiner's (1989) previously cited example of using the Rorschach to identify child abuse—be quite misleading. Chapman and Chapman (1962, 1969)[2] were among the earliest investigators to demonstrate the ways in which illusory correlations and other factors can provide impressive but invalid support for classification systems.

The importance of specifying clearly the type of classification system (see, e.g., Meehl & Golden, 1982), the criteria for classification, and the reliability of classification is illustrated in the following classification of patients who filed malpractice complaints against psychologists. The chair of the APA Insurance Trust studied an impressive array of data: 10 years of insurance carrier information regarding malpractice complaints. The carrier data for the APA were reported as showing

> *that the greatest number of actions are brought by women who lead lives of very quiet desperation, who form close attachments to their therapists, who feel rejected or spurned when they discover that relations are maintained on a formal and professional level, and who then react with allegations of sexual improprieties. (Brownfain, 1971, p. 651; see Pope, 1990b, for discussion of these data)*

In this system of classifying complaints, the largest category is described as consisting of false allegations of sexually "improper" behavior filed by desperate–attached–spurned women. Before allowing introduction of this classification system and this finding into courtroom testimony, it would seem important for an attorney to discover the criteria for placing plaintiffs in or out of this category. It would also seem important to discover the reliability of the classification system. For example, would a fair cross-section of psychologists with expertise in this area be in substantial agreement as they independently classified 10 years of cases according to this system? Would the reliability statistic be sufficiently high to make the system trustworthy (rather than a reflection of the assumptions, expectations, and agenda of whoever is doing the classifying in a specific instance)?

As emphasized in previous sections of this chapter, it is crucial that the aura of authority and the evidence for validity and reliability of the MMPI for a given set of tasks *not* be inappropriately transferred to other methods of assessment that are used in conjunction with the MMPI or to sets of tasks for which the MMPI's validity and reliability has not been sufficiently established.

13. Was the investigation conducted by a disinterested party?

We all share a very human trait: When we develop or endorse a particular intervention or method of classification, we are not disinterested observers of its efficacy, its intended results, or its unintentional side effects. Psychologist Robert Rosenthal (1988), professor of psychology at Harvard University, was one of the pioneers calling attention to the potentially profound effects of expectations and bias in research, assessment, and arriving at decisions.[3]

Careful inquiry should explore who funded the research and the nature of the organization that conducted the research. Such information may raise questions about possible bias. For example, if *all* the research regarding whether an item or intervention (e.g., cigarettes or a drug to increase alertness and mental acuity) causes harm or beneficial effects has been sponsored by the organization that developed the item or intervention or who markets or profits from its distribution or use, then more detailed questions addressing issues of bias are warranted.

Similarly, the independence and objectivity of the expert witness who reviews the research and offers

[2] See also Acorn, Hamilton, & Sherman, 1988; Brown & Smith, 1989; Dawes, 1989; Dickman & Sechrest, 1985; Dowling & Graham, 1976; Lueger & Petzel, 1979; Meehan & Janik, 1990; Schaller & Maass, 1989; Smither, Collins, & Buda, 1989; Spears, Van der Pligt, & Eisler, 1986; Tversky & Kahneman, 1973; and Winkel, 1990.

[3] See also Barber, 1976; Bell, Raiffa, & Tversky, 1988; Dawes, 1988a; Gambrill, 1990; Kahneman, Slovic, & Tversky, 1982; Langer & Abelson, 1974; Yates, 1990.

testimony should be carefully examined. For example, if the hypothetical expert witness is testifying that a particular act is not grossly negligent and did not cause harm or undue risk to a patient, it may be useful to know if the expert has engaged in the practice or if he or she is employed by a facility in which the practice has occurred (e.g., a health care facility that has been subjected to a number of law suits or other complaints regarding the practice).

If the expert receives a large amount of income from or does regular work for an organization or company, then potential bias in the witness's testimony that may bear on the organization's or company's fortunes should not be overlooked. Attorney Bruce Walkup (1984; see also Imwinkelried, 1982; Jenkins, 1989; Wellman, 1903/1936) provides a case study of an actual trial showing how careful preparation and detailed questioning can reveal such bias in his chapter, "Impeaching the Expert."

14. *Was the research conducted in a way that meets the highest ethical, legal, clinical, and similar applicable standards?*

When the expert witness cites studies, information, or publications to support his or her opinions, attorneys should always inquire if it is the expert's testimony that the evidence was obtained in a way that meets all formal ethical, legal, clinical, and similar applicable standards.

The Nuremberg trials forced into public awareness the atrocities committed by the otherwise seemingly respectable Nazi doctors and other professionals; many of these atrocities were committed in the name of scientific research, trial interventions, or experimental psychotherapeutic or rehabilitation approaches.[4] The resulting Nuremberg Code's (1991; see also Amas, 1991) first and fundamental principle is that the "voluntary consent" (to participate or to refuse to participate) of any individual placed at risk by research is "absolutely essential."

Despite the clarity and importance of this code, physicians, mental health professionals, and others have occasionally violated it, with sometimes disastrous, even fatal results.[5]

In regard to the hypothetical expert witness's testimony about rehabilitation interventions, it is important to note the evidence that people who enter treatment with therapists who have become sexually involved with patients are at increased risk for therapist–patient sexual intimacies. "The best single predictor of exploitation in therapy is a therapist who has exploited another patient in the past" (Bates & Brodsky, 1989, p. 141). A pamphlet distributed to all licensed therapists in California notes that "80% of the sexually exploiting therapists have exploited more than one client" (California Department of Consumer Affairs, 1990, p. 14). The APA Insurance Trust (1990) concluded that the "recidivism rate for sexual misconduct is substantial" (p. 3). The executive directors of the California licensing boards for psychology, social work, and marriage and family counseling reviewed the experience of those boards and concluded that, for therapists who have become sexually involved with a patient, "prospects for rehabilitation are minimal and it is doubtful that they should be given the opportunity to ever practice psychotherapy again" (Callanan & O'Connor, 1988, p. 11).

In the absence of adequate validation (e.g., independently conducted research, published in peer-reviewed scientific and professional journals and adequately replicated; see, for example, Pope, 1990b, 1990c; Pope & Vetter, 1992), rehabilitation interventions are by nature and definition implemented on a trial or experimental basis. To the extent that the hypothetical expert witness cites evidence for the efficacy of a rehabilitation intervention (or assessment of "rehabilitated" status for the therapist), was such evidence collected in a way that ensured that future patients of the therapist (who would, according to the data presented by psychologists Carolyn Bates and Annette Brodsky [1989] and others, be placed at increased risk for sexual intimacies by that therapist) were accorded full, voluntary, informed consent as mandated by the Nuremberg Code and other standards for those placed at risk for harm by experimental or trial interventions?

[4] See, for example, Annas & Grodin, 1992; Cocks, 1985; Gallagher, 1990; Lifton, 1986; Muller-Hill, 1988; and Proctor, 1988.

[5] See, for example, Annas & Grodin, 1991; Beecher, 1963, 1966; J. H. Jones, 1981; Levine, 1988; Pope & Garcia-Peltoniemi, 1991; Pope & Vasquez, 1991; and Rothman, 1991.

In asking any expert if all of the studies, information, and publications that form the basis for his or her expert opinion or are otherwise cited meet the highest ethical, legal, clinical, and similar standards, the expert may ask what specific standards the attorney is referring to. The attorney's questioning after such an inquiry by the expert may proceed in two phases. First, the attorney may ask what, if any, standards the expert is aware of and what, if any, he or she used to evaluate the studies, information, and publications.

Second, the attorney may cite specific standards and ask the expert if the studies or interventions violate these standards in any way or if, in the expert's professional opinion, they fully comply with the spirit and letter of the standards. Examples of such standards are provided by the APA (1982, 1992) and Levine (1988).

The expert can be asked how he or she formed the opinion (e.g., what documents were obtained and reviewed) that the research met the standards reflected in the Nuremberg Code and other codes. The expert's care and attention to this issue may be reflective of adequate or inadequate care and attention to other aspects of his or her work and opinion. Did, for example, the expert obtain and review the informed consent forms by which those future patients of therapists who were returned to practice after trial or experimental rehabilitation interventions gave their fully informed and voluntary consent to be put at risk as part of the experimental trials (see Pope & Vetter, 1991; Sonne & Pope, 1991)? The attorney can subpoena or otherwise obtain the informed consent forms (as well as procedures by which the informed consent process was implemented and monitored) used by those who are attempting to develop, use, or study any experimental or trial (i.e., yet to be adequately validated by independently conducted and sufficiently replicated research published in peer-reviewed journals) rehabilitation intervention that places future patients at risk for harm if these interventions are cited by or relied on by the hypothetical expert witness.

15. Was an adequately detailed report of the research published in a peer-reviewed academic, scientific, or professional journal?

Submitting not only "results" but also methodology, size and nature of sample, statistical procedures, and conclusions to scientific journals that use anonymous peer review is one of the primary, though not infallible, ways by which professions ensure the legitimacy, integrity, and reliability of findings.

> *The scientific journal is the repository of the accumulated knowledge of a field. . . . In fact, scientists "will get to really know a field only if [they] become sufficiently involved to contribute to it" (Orne, 1981, p. 4). . . . The preparation of a manuscript for journal publication is an integral part of the individual research effort. (APA, 1983, p. 17)*

Newspaper interviews, television appearances, books, chapters, convention presentations, workshops, and personal appearances have their valuable place in the dissemination of psychological information. But when research findings and other conclusions that are purportedly based on rigorous systematic investigation avoid the detailed scrutiny of respected journals, it raises important questions and can have widespread, enduring consequences. Sommers and Sommers (1983), for example, examined a "loophole through which data can find their way into textbooks without ever going through the journal review process" (p. 983). In their study, they noted

> *the ease with which tentative information may become virtual fact. Textbooks are a major source of information for our students, and ultimately for the public. They represent psychological science to a wide audience. Textbooks authors bear the responsibility for seeing that the information that they quote is not only correct, but accurate. (pp. 983–984)*

This responsibility is no less for expert witnesses—and for the attorneys who cross-examine them—than it is for textbook authors. Sommers and Sommers found several useful "warning flags. The most prominent was the lack of publication in refereed sources" (p. 984).

Martin Gardner, whose contributions Harvard Professor Stephen Jay Gould described as "a priceless national resource" (1987, p. 241), elaborated the theme stated by Summers and Summers:

> *The modern pseudo-scientist . . . stands . . . outside the closely integrated channels through which new ideas are introduced and evaluated. . . . He does not send his findings to the recognized journals. . . . He . . . published books only when he or his followers can . . . have them privately printed. (Gardner, 1963, p. 38)*

Harold Klawans (1991) recounted his testimony as an expert witness in a case focusing on articles by a Dr. Karr that supported the use of colchicine for degenerative disk disease. (In the case at hand, administration of colchicine had apparently caused the death of a patient suffering from degenerative disk disease.) Klawans had reviewed these articles yet testified that he knew of no articles in the medical literature that supported the use of colchicine for degenerative disc disease. He seemed, at best, to be impeaching himself by offering apparently contradictory testimony. His testimony prevailed, however, when he explained the significance of peer-reviewed scientific and professional journals. In the following excerpt from the trial testimony, in which Klawans responds to the attorney's questions, Klawans is the first speaker.

> *"Karr's articles exist. So do Batman comic books and* Hustler. *None of them represents competent medical authority. . . ."*
>
> *"Karr's articles are part of the medical literature."*
>
> *"They are not. . . ."*
>
> *"Why not?"*
>
> *"The medical literature is a body of printed material which has a recognized degree of authority. In journals, what constitutes that authority is fairly easy to define. The articles, once submitted to a journal, must be scrutinized and judged by appropriate authorities before being accepted for publication—a process called refereeing . . . [Karr's articles] were published in a non-refereed, throw-away journal sent out by a drug company."*
>
> *"So you arbitrarily decide what is and isn't a medical journal."*
>
> *"Not me. . . . The Library of Congress. They put together the index of all authoritative journals. It is called the* Index Medicus." *(pp. 122–123)*

A comparable index of authoritative journals in the area of psychology is the APA's annual publication, *Psychological Abstracts*, which currently summarizes data from articles in over 1,400 journals in the social and behavioral sciences.

Any expert witness might claim to be able to use the MMPI to reliably identify abused children, to predict whether a rapist is likely to offend in the future, to differentiate those alcoholics who will drink again from those alcoholics who will never again drink alcohol, or to determine whether a criminal defendant had in fact stolen a car. The expert witness may have previously held news conferences, conducted workshops, written books, or appeared on talk shows to publicize his or her effectiveness in using the MMPI to conduct such assessments. It is of great significance, however, whether the expert has previously submitted evidence for these claims to scientific journals and whether the claims have been independently verified by other investigators. Bates and Brodsky (1989) outline a particularly troubling instance in which research data concerning therapists who engage in sex with their patients (conceptualizing them as "impaired professionals") was presented at an annual meeting of the APA and received newspaper coverage. The research has apparently never appeared in a scientific journal. According to Bates and Brodsky, the APA audience and newspaper readers were probably unaware that the psychologist who conducted the survey had been engaging in therapist–patient sexual intimacies and, several years after the APA convention presentation, pleaded guilty to a sex-abuse charge.

Publication in authoritative peer-reviewed scientific and professional journals is a fundamental criterion for distinguishing generally accepted theories, methodologies, assessment techniques, interventions, and findings from what Peter Huber (1991) terms "junk science":

> *There is . . . a straightforward test for judges to determine which methods, procedures, and theories have not been "generally accepted" by other scientists: the absence of*

peer-reviewed publication. Writing is the medium of science. . . . Only a much firmer emphasis on the written word can bridge the wide gulf between oral testimony in court and the only medium accepted by scientists themselves for communicating important findings and theories. A witness whose views have survived peer review in a professional journal will already have been forced into a candid disclosure of cautions and qualifications; good journals won't publish without them. If the published claim is of any importance, publication will also mobilize other scientists to repeat, verify, contradict, or confirm. By requiring professional publication as a basis for expert opinion, judges will help line up the larger community of scientists to shadow the necessarily smaller community of expert witnesses. (Huber, 1991, p. 202)

16. How has the apparently low rate of reporting been taken into account in the validation study?

Assuming that rehabilitation methods are actually tested for their effectiveness, then some attempt must be made to see if offenders actually reoffend in the years after the rehabilitation attempt. This raises two issues that can be explored during the deposition. First, are the patients who are involved in this validation research accorded adequate informed consent, a topic covered in the discussion of a previous area of questioning.

Second, how can the investigator determine whether the supposedly rehabilitated offender is reoffending? Therapists have been able to engage in sex with their patients in virtually all imaginable circumstances, even when under mandated supervision for a previous offense. Bates and Brodsky (1989), for example, reported an instance in which a malpractice suit was filed against both the therapist–perpetrator and his licensing board-approved supervisor who was conducting the rehabilitation and monitoring. If therapists can engage in sexual intimacies with their patients without detection, investigators may have to rely on patients' reports to learn of offenses. Yet the evidence suggests that an extremely small percentage of victims file complaints with a licensing board (Pope, 1990b; Pope & Vasquez, 1991; Pope & Vetter, 1991).

For example, a 5-year validation study might examine a seemingly promising but completely worthless rehabilitation method as applied to 10 offenders. Assume that each of the offenders, having completed a comprehensive but ineffective rehabilitation program, will offend again with another patient within the next 5 years of the study. If each of the 10 new victims has only a 5% chance of reporting the offense, then the binomial probabilities indicate that there is a 59.9% likelihood that *none* of them will report. Thus, an impressively presented but completely worthless rehabilitation program has more than a 50% likelihood of demonstrating complete effectiveness, even if *all* of the offenders reoffend with another patient. If the investigator does not acknowledge and take into account the base rate of reporting, he or she might report that the rehabilitation program was 100% successful (i.e., no evidence of any new offenses) when in fact there was 100% recidivism (see Pope, 1990b).

Of course it is possible that not all offenders will reoffend during the 5-year period of the formal validation study. If we assume that several will delay reoffending until after the 5-year period (perhaps assuming that once the study is completed there will be less chance that their offenses will be detected), the probability that the worthless program will be reported as 100% effective increases significantly. Moreover, if the reporting rate is actually much less than 5%, as some evidence suggests, then it becomes very difficult *not* to find that a completely worthless rehabilitation program is 100% effective if one does not take the base rate of reporting into account in analyzing and reporting the data.

What is crucial is that the attorney inquire about such factors so that the evidence supporting the efficacy of an intervention or method of classification can be clearly understood. Failure to take into account base rates is a common error in assessments (see the chapter "Assessment, Testing, and Diagnosis" in Pope & Vasquez, 1991, pp. 87–100). Both high and low base rates can be a source of faulty and misleading inferences.

The work of O'Dell (1972), cited in the discussion of the first question in this chapter's section on interpretation, explored ways in which high base-rate assessment statements, presented in computer-generated format, may create a false aura of accuracy and authority. Tallent (1958) similarly explored the tendency of high base-rate statements about an individual's personality or clinical condition, when couched in what he called "prosecuting-attorney" format using ominous clinical jargon, to *seem* valid and compelling regardless of any other factors. An example of such a jargon-based statement is, "The amount of libidinal energy used in maintaining defenses reduces his ability to function at times" (Tallent, 1958, p. 243). These high base-rate statements tend to be extremely nonspecific, generally lack usefulness, and do tend to provide the evidence supporting the validity of an assessment or intervention that they appear (unexamined in light of the base rate) to provide. As Gynther and Gynther (1976) wrote, "We can be accurate nearly all of the time, if we say a psychiatric patient is 'anxious.' We need to discover meaningful ways in which one person differs from another" (p. 261).

Low base rates, as discussed previously in regard to the assessment of rehabilitation programs, can also cause numerous interpretive errors. Another example was provided by Livermore, Malmquist, and Meehl (1968). In their example, one assumes that an amazingly accurate test is developed that can identify those who will kill and those who will not kill at a 95% effectiveness rate (i.e., it will be wrong only 5% of the time). However, the base rate of killers in the community is 1 out of every 1,000 (i.e., only 1 person per 1,000 will actually kill someone). The test is tried out on 100,000 people in the community. Because 1 out of every 1,000 in the community will kill, then the group of 100,000 people contains 100 people who will kill. The test is correct in making predictions about 95% of these 100 people who *will* kill: 95 of them it classifies as future killers (which is a correct assessment) and the remaining 5 it classifies as people who will not kill (which is a wrong assessment).

However, the test must also be applied to the 99,900 people who will *not* kill, and it will be wrong in classifying 5% of them. The only way in which it can wrongly classify people who will not kill is to predict (wrongly) that they *will* kill. Thus, it wrongly predicts that 4,995 (5% of 99,900) of the 99,900 nonkillers will kill. Therefore, even this amazingly accurate (95%) test will make a total of 5,090 (95 plus 4,995) predictions that people will kill, but only 95 of these predicted killers are actual killers. The low base rate has confounded the test's ability to be a useful instrument for differentiating those who will kill from those who will not kill.

OPTIONS AND ALTERNATIVES

Having discovered and inquired in systematic detail about expert witness's opinions and their foundation, the attorney needs now to discover the scope of the expert's examinations and considerations.

In arriving at your diagnosis (or other conclusion), what alternatives did you consider?

If, for example, the expert witness asserts that a comprehensive psychological and neuropsychological assessment indicates that the individual is suffering from bipolar affective disorder (i.e., manic–depressive mood syndrome), what other possible diagnostic categories (or explanations for the individual's behavior) did the expert consider or "rule out"? In some cases, the attorney may want to list possible alternatives and ask the expert to explain why he or she did not arrive at each alternative diagnosis.

Is there any other source of information that you did not take into account (e.g., because it was not available or because the expert chose not to administer a particular test) that might be relevant or that might change your opinion?

If the expert acknowledges that there might be some source of information that would be relevant to forming an accurate diagnosis (or other conclusion), the attorney can then ask (a) how such a source of information might alter the expert's opinion, (b) whether the expert is less certain of his or her opinion in the absence of this information, and (c) why the information was not obtained. In most cases, the attorney will find it useful to inquire about the steps that the expert took (or failed to take) to discover whether there were previous records of assessment, previous records of treatment, school records, legal records, and so on, and to ask in each case of a step not taken *why* the expert did not take the step to obtain relevant information. In some instances, the attorney may discover that the opposing attorney who retained the expert had possession of (or access to) such records or information but did not make them available to the expert; if so, this situation and its implications should be carefully explored.

SUMMARY

One of the most difficult tasks facing the attorney in a case involving the MMPI is deposing and cross-examining the expert witness. The attorney him- or herself must become (or make an attempt to become) as knowledgeable as the expert witness about the MMPI as an instrument, about its use in the case at hand, and about the complex and detailed framework of psychological theory, research, and practice within which the MMPI results and other evidence in the case will be understood.

This chapter provides a structured guide to deposing the expert to obtain information that will be useful in understanding the case and in subsequent cross-examination. This structured guide includes sets of specific questions in such areas as the expert witness's compliance with the subpoena duces tecum, education and training, questionable behavior, occupational history, previous research and publication, history of previous participation in legal cases, general knowledge of tests and psychometrics, specific knowledge of the MMPI, administration and scoring of the MMPI and other tests in the case at hand, interpretive issues, complex and specific claims and issues, and options and alternatives.

Nizer's (1961) analogy of trial preparation to the work of the archaeologist suggests that each piece of information that is obtained during deposition must be carefully turned over, weighed, and considered. The advice given to expert witnesses being deposed also applies to attorneys conducting depositions or cross-examinations: Does the attorney genuinely and completely understand the witness's response? Does it make sense? Does it fit the question that the attorney asked? Does it fit with the emerging picture that is forming from the accumulating evidence and testimony? Does the witness's response itself raise additional questions or suggest other lines of inquiry?

One of the most important aspects of trial preparation involves independent investigation and verification of the witness's responses. For example, an expert witness may, during a deposition, make claims about his or her own credentials, about research published in peer-reviewed scientific and professional journals, and about scoring procedures for the MMPI-2 and other standardized tests. All such assertions should be checked out by the attorney. No deposition should be concluded until all relevant questions from the structured sets of inquiry presented in this chapter are fully answered. However, even after the deposition has been completed, trial preparation should not be concluded until the witness's responses have been investigated for accuracy, consistency, and validity.

Chapter 9

SOME FINAL THOUGHTS

The appendixes following this final chapter include a variety of specialized information and materials (e.g., sample expert witness–attorney agreement, sample form for informed consent for forensic assessment, specialty guidelines for forensic psychologists, APA policy for psychologists wishing to change their specialty, annotated list of state and federal case law relevant to the MMPI, lists of items in the MMPI, MMPI-2, and MMPI-A, and comparative information on the MMPI, MMPI-2, and MMPI-A) that we hope will be useful to expert witnesses and attorneys both in preparation for and during trials. This final chapter concludes the text of this book with a few final considerations.

FUNDAMENTAL RULES

This book attempts to provide a context and focus for examining the use of the MMPI, MMPI-2, and MMPI-A in forensic settings. In exploring this central focus and broader context, we drew together a great diversity of information, issues, and questions. This compilation of research, dilemmas, and possibilities can be overwhelming to expert witness and attorney alike. Those who are new to this area—psychologists who have never set foot in court and attorneys who have never heard of the MMPI—must confront complex, unfamiliar information and procedures. Those who are experienced in this area—expert witnesses who are seasoned and attorneys who may know more than some psychologists about the MMPI—are aware of the infinite number of ways in which issues at the trial, sets of test scores, personalities of the participants, unanticipated evidence, and sequences of testimony and cross-examination can create unique (and sometimes unpleasant) surprises, dilemmas, and confrontations in the courtroom. Consequently, the material in this book can seem overwhelming. At least it has to us as we have tried to consider what was most important to include and how best to organize it.

Throughout the book, we have suggested possible guidelines or approaches that may be helpful to the reader in coping with information and complexity that can lead to feelings of being overwhelmed. For example, we have presented a sequence of questions that both attorneys and expert witnesses can use in planning for cross-examination.

In this final chapter, we want to return to four fundamental rules that we believe are the most useful in coping with the sometimes overwhelming array of facts, tasks, and standards involved in the use of the MMPI, MMPI-2, and MMPI-A in court.

One fundamental principle applies equally to expert witnesses and attorneys: Prepare. As emphasized throughout the book, thorough preparation is crucial. The expert witness or attorney who walks into court unprepared invites disaster. Adequate preparation requires time, effort, and self-discipline. Before accepting any case, expert witnesses and attorneys must ensure that they have adequate time to prepare as well as personal (e.g., motivation, energy, and eagerness) and professional (e.g., access to relevant information and consultation) resources to prepare adequately. Reviewing the suggested steps for preparation in this book as well as the possible cross-examination questions can help expert witnesses and attorneys to monitor and assess the degree to which they accomplish the task of preparation.

A second fundamental principle, particularly relevant for expert witnesses who provide MMPI-based testimony is this: Let the objective test results speak for themselves. As discussed in previous chapters, the MMPI (particularly the revised versions) can provide a great range and depth of invaluable information in forensic cases if the results can be communicated clearly to the jury. If the expert witness has a good working knowledge of the meaning of the scales, the database of the test, and the relevant research, he or she can present the findings with such clarity that the jury can "see" (particularly if appropriate exhibits are used; see, for example, chapter 5 and appendix I) what the test reveals about the individual and means for the questions at issue before the court.

A major pitfall is the tendency to misleadingly portray hunches and guesses that lack empirical support as if they were conclusively demonstrated. Expert witnesses must be clear—with themselves and with the court—concerning what testimony is based solidly on well-accepted, adequately validated, and sufficiently standardized assessment instruments. Perhaps another way of stating this principle (with a slightly different focus) is this: Stick with the data. Of course, professionals may be called on to give opinions with greater and lesser degrees of certainty. However, the jury has a right to know when the expert is engaging in speculation, using psychological constructs that have not been empirically validated or relying on a nonstandardized (and yet to be validated) method of administering (e.g., using a short form of the MMPI that has not been adequately validated), scoring, or interpreting a standardized test. Many of the questions presented in chapter 8 will help clarify these issues for attorneys who are confronting such testimony and for expert witnesses who are preparing to testify.

In some cases, the only relevant information from an MMPI is that the protocol is invalid. This fact alone may help everyone involved to better understand the situation (i.e., that the test results suggest that the individual was not accurately responding to the items) and may provide a perspective not readily available from other tests or testimony. In such cases, the expert witness must refrain from any temptation to depart from the principle of sticking with the data. Although expert opinions may derive from a variety of sources, expert opinion that purports to be based on the MMPI should not involve interpretation of clinical or content scales when the validity scales show that the profile is clearly invalid.

A third fundamental principle is especially useful for expert witnesses: Tell the truth. Regardless of whether one is making initial contact with an attorney, talking with an individual who is being assessed, writing a forensic report, or testifying, telling the truth is essential. In this book, we have tried to explore some of the factors that can make this task difficult. The adversarial nature of our courtroom process, the potential role conflicts and conflicts of interest, and tendencies not to disclose that one is ignorant of certain facts exemplify some of these factors. During cross-examination, the expert witness is likely, at least occasionally, to be baffled and caught off guard by lines of inquiry, to be unwilling to acknowledge that he or she neglected to complete certain preparatory tasks (e.g., reviewing previous records or keeping up with the current professional literature in relevant areas), to be uncertain how to respond to difficult questions, and to "go blank."

Regardless of the circumstances, once one adequately understands the question and realizes that the cross-examining attorney is entitled to an answer, the basic rule is always: Tell the truth. No matter how easy it is to forget this fundamental principle, fortunately we are always reminded of it when we take the oath right before we testify.

The fourth fundamental principle is especially useful for attorneys: Trust the jury. No case is perfect. An attorney's handling of a case, before and during the trial, always has weaknesses as well as strengths. No attorney's work has ever been completely free of blunders. And trials almost always contain the unexpected. In the midst of even the most difficult circumstances, trusting the jury is imperative. While preparing and trying a case, the attorney must present the evidence as clearly as possible in a way that conveys in a direct and immediate sense the story of what happened and how it is relevant to the claims at issue. The process of voir dire and jury selection attempts to produce the best, most open, and most unbiased jury possible. To respect and trust those jurors to make a fair decision on the basis of the evidence and arguments can be the central and organizing principle for attorneys in even the most difficult trials.

THE EXPERT WITNESS VERSUS THE ATTORNEY

Addressed to two separate readerships, this volume may seem at times to express contradictory views. For example, one section may suggest "avoid focusing on, emphasizing, or relying on responses to an individual item," whereas another section may suggest "inquire about responses to and meanings of individual items." These apparent contradictions result from addressing a volume to two groups of professionals whose roles are sometimes in conflict and from the adversarial nature of the American judicial system.

It is our belief that the psychometric properties of individual items make it unwise to attempt actuarial interpretations on the basis of responses to an individual item. It is unlikely that the witness will be able to produce or refer to adequately validated actuarial databases for such individual item responses that have been published in peer-reviewed scientific or professional journals. Although at times an expert witness might consider using an individual item response to *illustrate* a general trend that has been identified by a more general actuarial method and supported by other sources of data, such use may—depending on context, qualification, and clarification—seem to imply that the individual item response itself warrants interpretation and is supported by actuarial tables or interpretive rules. If this implication is subjected to vigorous and informed cross-examination, the witness is likely to be in for a rough time.

While expert witnesses consequently should avoid highlighting responses to individual items, attorneys conducting discovery and subsequently, if appropriate, cross-examination would do well to obtain and explore the expert's knowledge of, understanding of, use of, and professional opinions about the meaning of responses to individual items and the degree to which such responses are a valid source of inference about the person who was assessed. The attorney's inquiries will help him or her to understand the degree to which the expert uses this standardized test appropriately.

This adversarial process of careful, detailed discovery and vigorous cross-examination is one that has great potential for ensuring that expert witnesses are genuine experts. Expert witnesses must be prepared to explain clearly how a test works *and* how it does not work (i.e., unjustified or inappropriate uses), even when responding to tough, adversarial questions. Anticipation of such questioning may enable experts to be better prepared for their testimony and to learn more about the tests that they are using. Covert rehearsal (e.g., Kazdin, 1978a) of responses to the type of questions in chapters 2, 4, and 8 as well as trying out answers informally in front of friends and colleagues (while allowing them to comment on the responses and ask questions) can help experts to identify problem areas in their knowledge of tests and their ability to communicate that knowledge in clear, everyday language.

This process of discovery and cross-examination also has great potential for enabling the trier of fact to understand appropropriate and inappropriate uses of standardized psychological tests. Only when jurors (or the judge in nonjury trials) adequately understand how a test works are they in the best position to decide how much weight to give to test results or to expert opinions that are based on test results. Observing the expert witness responding to vigorous, informed, and carefully planned cross-examination can also help the jurors to evaluate the expert's knowledge, credibility, and integrity.

THE EXPERT WITNESS AND THE ATTORNEY

Although the very nature of trials creates at least a *seeming* (but not necessarily actual) adversarial relationship between the expert witness and the attorney who conducts discovery and cross-examination, a collaborative relationship can be fostered between the expert and the attorney who employed him or her. Each has a responsibility to help educate and prepare the other. The expert witness can help educate the attorney regarding the use of psychological tests. The attorney can help educate the expert in trial procedures and the specifics of a particular case. Each also has a responsibility to educate the other regarding the ethics of their respective domains and to help ensure that all matters related to the endeavor are handled in a completely ethical manner.

There are dangers in the collaborative relationship. The adversarial nature of trials can exert pressures—both subtle and powerful—leading the expert to be "for" the attorney who employs him or her and "against" the attorney who conducts discovery and cross-examination. The very understandable impulse to want to help the employing attorney may, in fact, be a more profound threat to the expert's objectivity and responsibility to tell the truth than the potentially adversarial relationship with the other attorney. These issues are examined in chapter 4. It is crucial that both expert and employing attorney be aware of and monitor such factors to ensure that they do not subvert their own integrity or the integrity of their work.

FEAR AND TREMBLING IN THE COURTROOM

Expert witnesses and attorneys are not computers that contain information and are programmed to present it clearly and accurately in court. Expert witnesses and attorneys—despite some reports, stereotypes, and well-known jokes that can be simultaneously demeaning and funny to the contrary—are human. So it is not surprising that we may feel anxious or even panic-stricken at the prospect of walking into the adversarial atmosphere of the courtroom. All three of the authors of this book have, at least on occasion (if not almost constantly for one of the authors) felt nervous before and during court appearances. It is important to acknowledge that this is a normal and understandable human reaction to what can be an extremely challenging experience.

Part of the rationale for this book is to help people prepare for court experiences. Adequate preparation can help reduce uncomfortable (and sometimes debilitating) anxiety. Of course, for some people, a little anxiety before any demanding task such as a court appearance may be adaptive and useful. It may help motivate them to prepare adequately and to be more alert. But excessive anxiety is more likely to impair preparation and presentation as well as make life miserable for the individual. It tends to make some people "lock up," "freeze," and "go blank" in court; it makes others talk in a forced or stilted manner, and it makes still others babble almost uncontrollably. In almost all instances, it makes it difficult for an individual to concentrate, listen carefully, and speak clearly.

Paradoxically, reading this book may stir up anxiety in many readers. Attorneys may find it difficult to believe that they can ever learn enough about psychological tests and the principles of psychometrics, research, theory, and practice to conduct an adequately informed discovery and cross-examination, whereas expert witnesses may wonder if they can survive a vigorous cross-examination by someone who is knowledgeable about kurtosis, contrast errors, Lambda, reliability coefficients, dyscalculia, peer-reviewed journals, beta errors, and the social discomfort content scale. Part of the framework and content of this book evolved from the workshops conducted by the authors on forensic assessment and related psychological, legal, and professional issues. During parts of such workshops, the nervousness of some participants becomes both visible and audible.

It is crucial to recognize that such anxiety, when confronting detailed information in an important area of professional practice, is completely normal and understandable. Appearing in court—as an expert witness or an attorney—is demanding, challenging work that requires substantial knowledge, expertise, and preparation. Confronting the areas in which one may be less than adequately knowledgeable, expert, and prepared is likely to evoke some anxiety. Responding appropriately to the anxiety involves a reasonably simple task, although one that may require considerable time and effort: becoming familiar with the material.

Anxiety about acknowledging and exploring areas of complex information with which we are unfamiliar (and *all* expert witnesses and attorneys, no matter how knowledgeable, how experienced, or how widely known, published, or respected, encounter such areas) but which are relevant to our work can also elicit less adaptive responses such as denial, resentment (at the exacting demands of the work), anger (on the part of attorneys at expert witnesses who come up with all this information and on the part of expert witnesses at attorneys who focus on this information in discovery and cross-examination), paralyzing fear, and rationalization (e.g., pretending that one already knows this information or that it will never be relevant or important in forensic settings).

Alertness to the possibility of these less adaptive impulses can help prevent them from controlling our behavior. If the less adaptive responses continue to be tempting, the following consideration may be helpful. No matter how uncomfortable it is to read about the complex, detailed information relevant to forensic assessments, it tends to be much less uncomfortable for the expert witness to become adequately familiar with the material during trial preparation than to encounter the material for the first time during cross-examination; similarly, it is generally less agonizing for an attorney to work through this material adequately during preparation than to encounter it for the first time from an expert witness called by opposing counsel.

SCOPE AND LIMITATIONS OF THIS BOOK

We have tried in this book to present some basic information and considerations that would be useful to professionals who use or encounter the MMPI in court. Although focusing primarily on the MMPI, this book also offered information, theory, research, hypothetical cases, discussions, dilemmas, and suggestions that are not directly relevant to the MMPI. For example, such issues as expert witness–attorney fee arrangements, informed consent for assessments, role conflicts experienced by witnesses, unexpected testimony and its complications, and attorneys' opening statements are discussed.

Through addressing such contextual or additional issues, we hoped to create a book that would provide some flexibility and that could serve as one of the basic handbooks or sourcebooks an expert witness could use in preparing for trial. In the process, difficult choices had to be made about what material to include while still keeping the book at a size unlikely to cause pulled muscles or chronic back problems for those who might carry it to court with them. Despite this selectivity, on an individual basis, virtually every reader will find at least some portion of the book to be extraneous to their concerns. For example, those expert witnesses and attorneys whose forensic practice is limited exclusively to criminal cases will likely find the material on personal injury litigation of little direct value. Similarly, the sample forms in the appendixes may not be useful to those who have already developed forms more specific to their own practice or for whom state laws or other factors would require major changes. However, we hope that even the case examples and other material that may not be directly relevant to a reader may still be potentially useful, if only by analogy.

We have tried to present material about the MMPI so that much of it will illustrate more general principles of test construction, use, interpretation, testimony, and cross-examination. Although the book does mention a few other standardized psychological tests (see, for example, chapters 7 and 8 and the Glossary), it presents no substantial discussion of any tests except the MMPI. We hope, however, that the approach we have taken in this book will be valuable to colleagues who develop similar volumes for other useful tests such as the WAIS-R, the Rorschach, and the Halstead-Reitan Neuropsychological Test Battery.

BROADER ETHICAL RESPONSIBILITIES

In closing, perhaps the most useful perspective is to step back and take a look at the forensic context in which MMPI-based testimony and cross-examination occur. Throughout this book we have discussed ethical responsibilities of both expert witnesses and attorneys as they deal with each other, with the principle participants in the case (e.g., the individual who is being assessed), with their colleagues, and with the judge and jury in a particular trial. We have also tried to highlight some of the major ethical pitfalls and dilemmas (e.g., conflicting roles and responsibilities) that are likely to arise.

To the extent that ethical dilemmas or violations are made more likely or are intensified by the larger systems, individual expert witnesses, attorneys, and other readers must consider the degree to which they bear an ethical responsibility to attempt to address those issues. Are there laws, rules of evidence, or courtroom procedures, for example, that seem unjust or likely to promote error, confusion, or misconduct, or that fail to specify clearly the responsibilities and standards to which expert witnesses and attorneys should be and can be held accountable? Do graduate training programs in law, psychology, and other relevant disciplines provide adequate training in forensic practice, ethical issues, and professional standards? Do professional associations adequately fulfill their responsibilities to provide clear standards, adequate involvement of the membership in the formation of those standards, satisfactory procedures for assuring adequate accountability to those standards, and sufficient education and open discussion of those standards? Are there unnecessary, unjustifiable, or unexamined conflicts among ethical, legal, professional, and related standards or responsibilities (see, e.g., Pope & Bajt, 1988; Pope & Vasquez, 1991)?

Experience with and examination of these larger systems in which we function makes it difficult to assert that they are without problems or that the problems have been adequately discussed and addressed. The work of expert witnesses and attorneys and the larger systems in which they function exerts a profound effect on the lives of so many people, not only those who appear as plaintiffs or defendants in civil, criminal, and administrative cases but also those who represent the more general society. To the extent that the system of justice does not operate as well as it should, or at least as well as it can or might, we are negligent as a society, as responsible members of that society, and as professionals who work within the legal system. To ignore problems with this system helps ensure that such problems continue and likely grow worse.

None of us practices in a vacuum. Each of us is affected by and shares responsibility for the broader context. Continuing appreciation of the context—or rather, contexts—in which we attempt to fulfill our professional responsibilities as expert witnesses and attorneys is crucial to our professional ability and integrity. Acknowledging and responding to problems in the system are no less important.

As professionals, expert witnesses and attorneys have been entrusted by society to help make our system of justice work. If we have anything to profess, it begins with this: We must take our work—and all its inescapable responsibilities—seriously.

Appendix A

Sample Agreement Between Expert Witness and Attorney

As discussed in chapter 4, expert witnesses may use any of a variety of approaches in reaching agreement with an attorney regarding fees. The example presented in this appendix sets forth one such approach. What is important is that the written agreement provide a clear understanding between both individuals concerning the manner in which the fees are to be calculated and paid. One aspect of the sample agreement that follows is that all fees are to be paid in advance. This helps to prevent situations in which the expert witness has conducted an assessment, written a report, billed the attorney, but not received full payment when due.

This sample agreement, of course, should be adapted to meet the needs of the individual expert witness, the specific circumstances of the assessment, and any applicable legislation, case law, and other standards or regulations in the relevant jurisdiction.

Before using any such agreement, the expert witness should always and in all circumstances review the form with his or her own professional liability attorney (i.e., not the attorney who is hiring the individual as an expert witness) to ensure that it fully meets the applicable ethical, legal, and professional standards as well as the needs and approaches of the expert witness.

CONSULTANT AGREEMENT
[NAME OF EXPERT WITNESS]

Initial Case Review and Consultation

There is an initial, nonrefundable case-opening, review, and consultation fee of [an amount equal to 10 times the professional's hourly rate] to be paid in advance of opening work on the case.

If work in the [city or town in which expert witness practices] area (i.e., the area within 20 miles of [location of expert witness's office]) during this phase (i.e., before I am retained or disclosed as an expert witness) exceeds 10 hours, an advance of [an amount equal to 10 times the clinician's hourly rate] is due immediately; each additional hour (beyond the initial 10) will be billed at the rate of [professional's hourly rate] per hour. Each time the advance is depleted, a subsequent advance of [an amount equal to 10 times the clinician's hourly rate] is due immediately, against which each additional hour will be billed at the rate of [hourly rate] per hour. Unlike the initial case-opening, review, and consultation fee of [an amount equal to 10 times the clinician's hourly rate], which is nonrefundable, the unused portion of any of these subsequent [an amount equal to 10 times the clinician's hourly rate] advances (during this period prior to naming or endorsing me as an expert witness) will be returned should my services no longer be needed.

Disclosure as an Expert Witness

If, based on the initial review and consultation, you decide to disclose me as an expert witness in the case, an additional nonrefundable payment of [an amount equal to 10 times the clinician's hourly rate] must be received by me in advance of my being named as an expert witness.

If work in the [city or town] area (i.e., the area within 20 miles of [office]) during this phase exceeds 10 hours, an advance of [an amount equal to 10 times the clinician's hourly rate] is due immediately; each additional hour (beyond the initial 10) will be billed at the rate of [hourly rate] per hour. Each time the advance is depleted, a subsequent advance (for work to be done within [city or town]) of [an amount equal to 10 times the clinician's hourly rate] is due immediately, against which each additional hour will be billed at the rate of [hourly rate] per hour. Unlike the [an amount equal to 10 times the clinician's hourly rate] fee for case opening and the [an amount equal to 10 times the clinician's hourly rate] fee for endorsement as expert witness—both of which are nonrefundable—the unused portion of any of these subsequent [an amount equal to 10 times the clinician's hourly rate] advances (during this period prior to naming or endorsing me as an expert witness) will be returned should my services no longer be needed.

It is understood that the opposing attorney(s) will pay my hourly fee for the deposition itself at the time that I am deposed. [As noted in chapter 4, the party or parties responsible for paying an expert witness for time spent in deposition varies from jurisdiction to jurisdiction.]

Work Conducted Outside the [City or Town] Area

For any travel out of [city or town], the charge is [eight times the hourly rate] per 24-hour period (or fraction thereof), plus expenses (transportation as discussed, food, lodging, and delivery of documents via such carriers as Federal Express), to be received by me at least 1 week prior to the scheduled departure from the [city or town] area.

If I do not receive any of the payments called for hereunder exactly when due, I shall stop all work and vacate all appointments, in which event you agree to assume sole responsibility for any and all damages or expenses that may result to you or your client(s).

In the event of any litigation arising under the terms of this agreement, the prevailing party shall recover their reasonable attorneys' fees.

If you agree to these terms, please sign below and return a signed copy to me along with the case-opening fee.

______________________________ ____________________

Signature Date

Appendix B

Sample Informed Consent Form for Conducting Forensic Assessments

As with agreements between expert witnesses and attorneys (see chapter 4 and appendix A), there are many approaches to issues of informed consent when conducting forensic assessment. This appendix presents one possible example of a written informed consent form for assessments involving the MMPI-2. Obviously, such forms must be tailored to the specific nature, purpose, and circumstances of the assessment; the approach of the expert witness; the needs of the individual being assessed; and to all applicable legislation, case law, standards, and regulations.

Expert witnesses may find it useful to have one or more versions of these forms on a computer file. A comprehensive form, tailored to the individual's approach and practice, may contain numerous statements; the expert witness may then edit a copy of the file, before printing it out, to ensure that it is most relevant to the individual assessment at hand.

Again, as with written agreements between expert witnesses and attorneys, *before* using any such agreement, the expert witness should always review the form with his or her own professional liability attorney (i.e., not the attorney who is hiring the individual as an expert witness) to ensure that it fully meets the applicable ethical, legal, and professional standards (e.g., regarding informed consent) as well as the needs and approaches of the expert witness.

Where appropriate, and where time permits, the expert witness may fax or mail copies of the form to both the attorney who has arranged the assessment and to the individual who is to be assessed. This will provide each of them an opportunity to study the form and to consult with each other and perhaps with third parties before the initial assessment session. At the initial assessment session, the expert witness can review the form with the individual to ensure that he or she adequately understands and consents to the assessment process.

Providing the consent form to both the attorney and the individual to be assessed in advance of the first session can help prevent situations in which an attorney may have simply told the client some version of the following:

1. "I want you to talk with Dr. ________ this Wednesday morning at 10:00 a.m."
2. "Please call the Generic Institute and make an appointment. Just tell them who you are and that I referred you, and they'll know what to do."
3. "This afternoon, the paralegal will drive you to another set of offices where they'll give you some tests."
4. "Please have my secretary arrange for you to meet with the Generic Group sometime next week."

In the absence of adequate advance explanation, clients may arrive at the expert witness's office having literally no idea why their attorney has asked them to make the trip.

It is important for the expert witness to take time to review the form on a point-by-point basis to ensure that the client adequately understands the process that is about to take place. The expert witness can use the form as part of the process of informed consent but must not assume that the mere presence of the form completes the process.

> *Providing information in written form can be vital in ensuring that clients have the information they need. But the form cannot be a substitute for an adequate process of informed consent. At a minimum, the clinician must discuss the information with the client and arrive at a professional judgment that the client has adequate understanding of the relevant information.*
>
> *Clinicians using consent forms must ensure that their clients have the requisite reading skills. Illiteracy is a major problem in the United States; clinicians cannot simply assume that all of their clients can read. Moreover, some clients may not be well versed in English, perhaps having only rudimentary skills in spoken English as a second or third language. (Pope & Vasquez, 1991, p. 85)*[1]

INFORMED CONSENT FOR FORENSIC ASSESSMENT

Your attorney has asked that I conduct a psychological assessment in connection with your court case. This form was written to give you information about the assessment process. The assessment will contain two parts. In the first part, I will give you a form (called the MMPI-2) containing a number of statements. You will be asked to indicate whether or not you believe that each of these statements applies to you. (We will discuss the instructions in detail when I give you the form.)

In the second part of the assessment, I will interview you. During the interview, I will ask you questions about yourself and ask you to talk about yourself. There may, of course, be areas that you are reluctant to talk about. If so, please be sure to tell me that the questions are making you uncomfortable or that you have reasons for not providing the information. We can then talk about your concerns.

It is important that you be as honest as possible when answering the questions on the MMPI-2 form and during the interview. Information that is incomplete, wrong, or misleading may be far more damaging than if I am able to find out about it now and put it in context in my report and/or testimony. It is important for us to discuss any concerns you have in this area.

Although I will try to be thorough when I interview you, I may not ask about some areas or information that you believe is important. If so, please tell me so that we can discuss it.

I am a [psychologist, psychiatrist, or other professional title] licensed by the state of [name of state]. If you have reason to believe that I am behaving unethically or unprofessionally during the course of this assessment, I urge you to let me know at once so that we can discuss it. If you believe that I have not adequately addressed your complaints in this area, there are several agencies whom you may consult, and, if you believe it appropriate, you may file a formal complaint against me. One agency is the state governmental board that licenses me to practice: [name, address, and phone number of the licensing board]. Other agencies are the ethics committees of my state professional association, [name, address, and phone number], and national professional association, [name, address, and phone number]. However, you have assurance that I will conduct this assessment in an ethical and professional manner and will be open to discussing any complaints you have in this area.

Please check each item below to indicate that you have read it carefully and understand it.

- ❑ I understand that Dr. _______ has been hired by my attorney, [fill in attorney's name], to conduct a psychological assessment using the MMPI-2 and a clinical interview.
- ❑ I understand that Dr. _______ intends to administer a test called the Minnesota Multiphasic Personality Inventory–Revised (MMPI-2), which takes about 1 or 2 hours for me to fill out.
- ❑ I understand that the MMPI-2 is a set of questions developed to help learn about and understand the personality of the person who answers the questions.

[1] For a more extended discussion, see Pope & Vasquez's chapter "Informed Consent and Informed Refusal," 1991, pp. 74–86.

- ❑ I understand that it is important for me to be honest and accurate when answering questions on the MMPI-2 form and during the interview.
- ❑ I understand that Dr. _______ will score, interpret, and write a formal report about me based on the results of the MMPI-2.
- ❑ I authorize Dr. _______ to send a copy of this formal report to my attorney and to discuss the report with him or her.
- ❑ I understand that Dr. _______ will not provide me with this written report but that I may, if I choose, schedule an additional appointment with Dr. _______ to discuss the results of this assessment.
- ❑ I authorize Dr. _______ to testify about me and this assessment in depositions and trial(s) related to my legal case.
- ❑ I understand that if I disclose certain types of special information to Dr. _______, he/she may be required or permitted to communicate this information to other people. As previously discussed with Dr. _______, examples of such special information include reports of child or elder abuse and threats to kill or violently attack a specific person.

If you have read, understood, and checked off each of the prior sections, please read carefully the following statement and, if you are in agreement, please sign the statement.

Do *not* sign if you have any further questions or if there are any aspects that you don't understand or agree to; contact your attorney for guidance concerning how to proceed so that you fully understand the process and can decide whether you wish to continue.

Consent Agreement: I have read, agreed to, and checked off each of the previous sections. I have asked questions about any parts that I did not understand fully. I have also asked questions about any parts that I was concerned about. By signing below, I indicate that I understand and agree to the nature and purpose of this testing, how it will be reported, and to each of the points listed above.

_______________________________________ _______________________

Signature Date

____

Name (please print)

APPENDIX C-1

Specialty Guidelines for Forensic Psychologists

Committee on Ethical Guidelines for Forensic Psychologists

The "Specialty Guidelines for Forensic Psychologists,"[1] while informed by the *Ethical Principles of Psychologists and Code of Conduct* (APA, 1992) and meant to be consistent with them, are designed to provide more specific guidance to forensic psychologists in monitoring their professional conduct when acting in assistance to courts, parties to legal proceedings, correctional and forensic mental health facilities, and legislative agencies. The primary goal of the *Guidelines* is to improve the quality of forensic psychological services offered to individual clients and the legal system and thereby to enhance forensic psychology as a discipline and profession. The *Specialty Guidelines for Forensic Psychologists* represent a joint statement of the American Psychology-Law Society and Division 41 of the American Psychological Association and are endorsed by the American Academy of Forensic Psychology. The *Guidelines* do not represent an official statement of the American Psychological Association.

The *Guidelines* provide an aspirational model of desirable professional practice by psychologists within any subdiscipline of psychology (e.g., clinical, developmental, social, or experimental), when they are engaged regularly as experts and represent themselves as such, in an activity primarily intended to provide professional psychological expertise to the judicial system. This would include, for example, clinical forensic examiners; psychologists employed by correctional or forensic mental health systems; researchers who offer direct testimony about the relevance of scientific data to a psycholegal issue; trial behavior consultants; psychologists engaged in preparation of amicus briefs; or psychologists, appearing as forensic experts, who consult with, or testify before, judicial, legislative, or administrative agencies acting in an adjudicative capacity. Individuals who provide only occasional service to the legal system and who do so without representing themselves as forensic experts may find these *Guidelines* helpful, particularly in consultation with colleagues who are forensic experts.

While the *Guidelines* are concerned with a model of desirable professional practice, to the extent that they may be construed as being applicable to the advertisement of services or the solicitation of clients, they are intended to prevent false or deceptive advertisement or solicitations and should be construed in a manner consistent with that intent.

I. PURPOSE AND SCOPE

A. Purpose

1. While the professional standards for the ethical practice of psychology, as a general discipline, are addressed in the American Psychological Association's *Ethical Principles of Psychologists*, these ethical principles do not relate, in sufficient detail, to current aspirations of desirable professional conduct for forensic psychologists. By design, none of the *Guidelines* contradicts any of the *Ethical Principles of Psychologists*; rather, they amplify those *Principles* in the context of the practice of forensic psychology, as herein defined.

[1] From Committee on Ethical Guidelines for Forensic Psychologists, 1991.

2. The *Guidelines* have been designed to be national in scope and are intended to conform with state and Federal law. In situations where the forensic psychologist believes that the requirements of law are in conflict with the *Guidelines*, attempts to resolve the conflict should be made in accordance with the procedures set forth in these *Guidelines* [IV(G)] and in the *Ethical Principles of Psychologists*.

B. Scope

1. The *Guidelines* specify the nature of the desirable professional practice by forensic psychologists, within any subdiscipline of psychology (e.g., clinical, developmental, social, experimental), when engaged regularly as forensic psychologists.

a. "Psychologist" means any individual whose professional activities are defined by the American Psychological Association or by regulation of the title by state registration or licensure, as the practice of psychology.

b. "Forensic psychology" means all forms of professional psychological conduct when acting, with definable foreknowledge, as a psychological expert on explicitly psycholegal issues, in direct assistance to courts, parties to legal proceedings, correctional and forensic mental health facilities, and administrative, judicial, and legislative agencies acting in an adjudicative capacity.

c. "Forensic psychologist" means psychologists who regularly engage in the practice of forensic psychology as defined in I(B)(1)(b).

2. The *Guidelines* do not apply to a psychologist who is asked to provide professional psychological services when the psychologist was not informed at the time of delivery of the services that they were to be used as forensic psychological services as defined above. The *Guidelines* may be helpful, however, in preparing the psychologist for the experience of communicating psychological data in a forensic context.

3. Psychologists who are not forensic psychologists as defined in I(B)(1)(c), but occasionally provide limited forensic psychological services, may find the *Guidelines* useful in the preparation and presentation of their professional services.

C. Related Standards

1. Forensic psychologists also conduct their professional activities in accord with the *Ethical Principles of Psychologists* and the various other statements of the American Psychological Association that may apply to particular subdisciplines or areas of practice that are relevant to their professional activities.

2. The standards of practice and ethical guidelines of other relevant "expert professional organizations" contain useful guidance and should be consulted even though the present *Guidelines* take precedence for forensic psychologists.

II. RESPONSIBILITY

A. Forensic psychologists have an obligation to provide services in a manner consistent with the highest standards of their profession. They are responsible for their own conduct and the conduct of those individuals under their direct supervision.

B. Forensic psychologists make a reasonable effort to ensure that their services and the products of their services are used in a forthright and responsible manner.

III. COMPETENCE

A. Forensic psychologists provide services only in areas of psychology in which they have specialized knowledge, skill, experience, and education.

B. Forensic psychologists have an obligation to present to the court, regarding the specific matters to which they will testify, the boundaries of their competence, the factual bases (knowledge, skill, experience, training, and education) for their qualification as an expert on the specific matters at issue.

C. Forensic psychologists are responsible for a fundamental and reasonable level of knowledge and understanding of the legal and professional standards that govern their participation as experts in legal proceedings.

D. Forensic psychologists have an obligation to understand the civil rights of parties in legal proceedings in which they participate, and manage their professional conduct in a manner that does not diminish or threaten those rights.

E. Forensic psychologists recognize that their own personal values, moral beliefs, or personal and professional relationships with parties to a legal proceeding may interfere with their ability to practice competently. Under such circumstances, forensic psychologists are obligated to decline participation or to limit their assistance in a manner consistent with professional obligations.

IV. RELATIONSHIPS

A. During initial consultation with the legal representative of the party seeking services, forensic psychologists have an obligation to inform the party of factors that might reasonably affect the decision to contract with the forensic psychologist. These factors include, but are not limited to

1. the fee structure for anticipated professional services;

2. prior and current personal or professional activities, obligations, and relationships that might produce a conflict of interests;

3. their areas of competence and the limits of their competence; and

4. the known scientific bases and limitations of the methods and procedures that they employ and their qualifications to employ such methods and procedures.

B. Forensic psychologists do not provide professional services to parties to a legal proceeding on the basis of "contingent fees," when those services involve the offering of expert testimony to a court or administrative body, or when they call upon the psychologist to make affirmations or representations intended to be relied upon by third parties.

C. Forensic psychologists who derive a substantial portion of their income from fee-for-service arrangements should offer some portion of their professional services on a *pro bono* or reduced fee basis where the public interest or the welfare of clients may be inhibited by insufficient financial resources.

D. Forensic psychologists recognize potential conflicts of interest in dual relationships with parties to a legal proceeding, and they seek to minimize their effects.

1. Forensic psychologists avoid providing professional services to parties in a legal proceeding with whom they have personal or professional relationships that are inconsistent with the anticipated relationship.

2. When it is necessary to provide both evaluation and treatment services to a party in a legal proceeding (as may be the case in small forensic hospital settings or small communities), the forensic psychologist takes reasonable steps to minimize the potential negative effects of these circumstances on the rights of the party, confidentiality, and the process of treatment and evaluation.

E. Forensic psychologists have an obligation to ensure that prospective clients are informed of their legal rights with respect to the anticipated forensic service, of the purposes of any evaluation, of the nature of the procedures to be employed, of the intended uses of any product of their services, and of the party who has employed the forensic psychologist.

1. Unless court ordered, forensic psychologists obtain the informed consent of the client or party, or their legal representative, before proceeding with such evaluations and procedures. If the client appears unwilling to proceed after receiving a thorough notification of the purposes, methods, and intended uses of the forensic evaluation, the evaluation should be postponed and the psychologist should take steps to place the client in contact with his/her attorney for the purpose of legal advice on the issues of participation.

2. In situations where the client or party may not have the capacity to provide informed consent to services or the evaluation is pursuant to court order, the forensic psychologist provides reason-

able notice to the client's legal representative of the nature of the anticipated forensic service before proceeding. If the client's legal representative objects to the evaluation, the forensic psychologist notifies the court issuing the order and responds as directed.

3. After a psychologist has advised the subject of a clinical forensic evaluation of the intended use of the evaluation and its work product, the psychologist may not use the evaluation work product for other purposes without explicit waiver to do so by the client or the client's legal representative.

F. When forensic psychologists engage in research or scholarly activities that are compensated financially by a client or party to a legal proceeding, or when the psychologist provides those services on a *pro bono* basis, the psychologist clarifies any anticipated further use of such research or scholarly product, and obtains whatever consent or agreement is required by law or professional standards.

G. When conflicts arise between the forensic psychologist's professional standards and the requirements of legal standards, a particular court, or a directive by an officer of the court or legal authorities, the forensic psychologist has an obligation to make those legal authorities aware of the source of the conflict and to take reasonable steps to resolve it. Such steps may include, but are not limited to, obtaining the consultation of fellow forensic professionals, obtaining the advice of independent counsel, and conferring directly with the legal representatives involved.

V. CONFIDENTIALITY AND PRIVILEGE

A. Forensic psychologists have an obligation to be aware of the legal standards that may affect or limit the confidentiality or privilege that may attach to their services or their products, and they conduct their professional activities in a manner that respects those known rights and privileges.

1. Forensic psychologists establish and maintain a system of record keeping and professional communication that safeguards a client's privilege.

2. Forensic psychologists maintain active control over records and information. They only release information pursuant to statutory requirements, court order, or the consent of the client.

B. Forensic psychologists inform their clients of the limitations to the confidentiality of their services and their products (See also Guideline IV E) by providing them with an understandable statement of their rights, privileges, and the limitations of confidentiality.

C. In situations where the right of the client or party to confidentiality is limited, the forensic psychologist makes every effort to maintain confidentiality with regard to any information that does not bear directly upon the legal purpose of the evaluation.

D. Forensic psychologists provide clients or their authorized legal representatives with access to the information in their records and a meaningful explanation of that information, consistent with existing Federal and state statutes, the *Ethical Principles of Psychologists*, the *Standards for Educational and Psychological Testing*, and institutional rules and regulations.

VI. METHODS AND PROCEDURES

A. Because of their special status as persons qualified as experts to the court, forensic psychologists have an obligation to maintain current knowledge of scientific, professional and legal developments within their area of claimed competence. They are obligated also to use that knowledge, consistent with accepted clinical and scientific standards, in selecting data collection methods and procedures for an evaluation, treatment, consultation or scholarly/empirical investigations.

B. Forensic psychologists have an obligation to document and be prepared to make available, subject to court order or the rules of evidence, all data that form the basis for their evidence or services. The standard to be applied to such documentation will be subject to reasonable judicial scrutiny; this standard is higher than the normative standard for general clinical practice. When forensic psychologists conduct an examination or engage in the treatment of a party to a legal proceeding, with foreknowledge that their professional services will be used in an adjudicative forum, they incur a special responsibility to provide the best documentation possible under the circumstances.

1. Documentation of the data upon which one's evidence is based is subject to the normal rules of discovery, disclosure, confidentiality, and privilege that operate in the jurisdiction in which the data were obtained. Forensic psychologists have an obligation to be aware of those rules and to regulate their conduct in accordance with them.

2. The duties and obligations of forensic psychologists with respect to documentation of data that form the basis for their evidence apply from the moment they know or have a reasonable basis for knowing that their data and evidence derived from it are likely to enter into legally relevant decisions.

C. In providing forensic psychological services, forensic psychologists take special care to avoid undue influence upon their methods, procedures, and products, such as might emanate from the party to a legal proceeding by financial compensation or other gains. As an expert conducting an evaluation, treatment, consultation, or scholarly/empirical investigation, the forensic psychologist maintains professional integrity by examining the issue at hand from all reasonable perspectives, actively seeking information that will differentially test plausible rival hypotheses.

D. Forensic psychologists do not provide professional forensic services to a defendant or to any party in, or in contemplation of, a legal proceeding prior to that individual's representation by counsel, except for persons judicially determined, where appropriate, to be handling their representation *pro se*. When the forensic services are pursuant to court order and the client is not represented by counsel, the forensic psychologist makes reasonable efforts to inform the court prior to providing the services.

1. A forensic psychologist may provide emergency mental health services to a pretrial defendant prior to court order or the appointment of counsel where there are reasonable grounds to believe that such emergency services are needed for the protection and improvement of the defendant's mental health and where failure to provide such mental health services would constitute a substantial risk of imminent harm to the defendant or to others. In providing such services the forensic psychologist nevertheless seeks to inform the defendant's counsel in a manner consistent with the requirements of the emergency situation.

2. Forensic psychologists who provide such emergency mental health services should attempt to avoid providing further professional forensic services to that defendant unless that relationship is reasonably unavoidable [see IV(D)(2)].

E. When forensic psychologists seek data from third parties, prior records, or other sources, they do so only with the prior approval of the relevant legal party or as a consequence of an order of a court to conduct the forensic evaluation.

F. Forensic psychologists are aware that hearsay exceptions and other rules governing expert testimony place a special ethical burden upon them. When hearsay or otherwise inadmissible evidence forms the basis of their opinion, evidence, or professional product, they seek to minimize sole reliance upon such evidence. Where circumstances reasonably permit, forensic psychologists seek to obtain independent and personal verification of data relied upon as part of their professional services to the court or to a party to a legal proceeding.

1. While many forms of data used by forensic psychologists are hearsay, forensic psychologists attempt to corroborate critical data that form the basis for their professional product. When using hearsay data that have not been corroborated, but are nevertheless utilized, forensic psychologists have an affirmative responsibility to acknowledge the uncorroborated status of those data and the reasons for relying upon such data.

2. With respect to evidence of any type, forensic psychologists avoid offering information from their investigations or evaluations that does not bear directly upon the legal purpose of their professional services and that is not critical as support for their product, evidence, or testimony, except where such disclosure is required by law.

3. When a forensic psychologist relies upon data or information gathered by others, the origins of those data are clarified in any professional product. In addition, the forensic psychologist bears a special responsibility to ensure that such data, if relied upon, were gathered in a manner standard for the profession.

G. Unless otherwise stipulated by the parties, forensic psychologists are aware that no statements made by a defendant, in the court of any (forensic) examination, no testimony by the expert based upon such statements, nor any other fruits of the statements can be admitted into evidence against the defendant in any criminal proceeding, except on an issue respecting mental condition on which the defendant has introduced testimony. Forensic psychologists have an affirmative duty to ensure that their written products and oral testimony conform to this Federal Rule of Procedure (12.2[c]), or its state equivalent.

1. Because forensic psychologists are often not in a position to know what evidence, documentation, or element of written product may be or may lend to a "fruit of the statement," they exercise extreme caution in preparing reports or offering testimony prior to the defendant's assertion of a mental state claim or the defendant's introduction of testimony regarding a mental condition. Consistent with the reporting requirements of state or federal law, forensic psychologists avoid including statements from the defendant relating to the time period of the alleged offense.

2. Once a defendant has proceeded to the trial state, and all pretrial mental health issues such as competency have been resolved, forensic psychologists may include in their reports or testimony any statements made by the defendant that are directly relevant to supporting their expert evidence, providing that the defendant has "introduced" mental state evidence or testimony within the meaning of Federal Rule of Procedure 12.2(c), or its state equivalent.

H. Forensic psychologists avoid giving written or oral evidence about the psychological characteristics of particular individuals when they have not had an opportunity to conduct an examination of the individual adequate to the scope of the statements, opinions, or conclusions to be issued. Forensic psychologists make every reasonable effort to conduct such examinations. When it is not possible or feasible to do so, they make clear the impact of such limitations on the reliability and validity of their professional products, evidence, or testimony.

VII. PUBLIC AND PROFESSIONAL COMMUNICATIONS

A. Forensic psychologists make reasonable efforts to ensure that the products of their services, as well as their own public statements and professional testimony, are communicated in ways that will promote understanding and avoid deception, given the particular characteristics, roles, and abilities of various recipients of the communications.

1. Forensic psychologists take reasonable steps to correct misuse or misrepresentation of their professional products, evidence, and testimony.

2. Forensic psychologists provide information about professional work to clients in a manner consistent with professional and legal standards for the disclosure of test results, interpretations of data, and the factual bases for conclusions. A full explanation of the results of tests and the bases for conclusions should be given in language that the client can understand.

a. When disclosing information about a client to third parties who are not qualified to interpret tests results and data, the forensic psychologist complies with Principle 16 of the *Standards for Educational and Psychological Testing*. When required to disclose results to a nonpsychologist, every attempt is made to ensure that test security is maintained and access to information is restricted to individuals with a legitimate and professional interest in the data. Other qualified mental health professionals who make a request for information pursuant to a lawful order are, by definition, "individuals with a legitimate and professional interest."

b. In providing records and raw data, the forensic psychologist takes reasonable steps to ensure that the receiving party is informed that raw scores must be interpreted by a qualified professional in order to provide reliable and valid information.

B. Forensic psychologists realize that their public role as "expert to the court" or as "expert representing the profession" confers upon them a special responsibility for fairness and accuracy in their public statements. When evaluating or commenting upon the professional work product or qualifications of another expert or party to a legal proceeding, forensic psychologists represent their professional disagreements with reference to a fair and accurate evaluation of the data, theories, standards, and opinions of other expert or party.

C. Ordinarily, forensic psychologists avoid making detailed public (out-of-court) statements about particular legal proceedings in which they have been involved. When there is a strong justification to do so, such public statements are designed to assure accurate representation of their role or their evidence, not to advocate the positions of parties in the legal proceeding. Forensic psychologists address particular legal proceedings in publications or communications only to the extent that the information relied upon is part of a public record or consent for that use has been properly obtained from the party holding any privilege.

D. When testifying, forensic psychologists have an obligation to all parties to a legal proceeding to present their findings, conclusions, evidence, or other professional products in a fair manner. This principle does not preclude forceful representation of the data and reasoning upon which a conclusion or professional product is based. It does, however, preclude an attempt, whether active or passive, to engage in partisan distortion or misrepresentation. Forensic psychologists do not, by either commission or omission, participate in a misrepresentation of their evidence, nor do they participate in partisan attempts to avoid, deny, or subvert the presentation of evidence contrary to their own position.

E. Forensic psychologists, by virtue of their competence and rules of discovery, actively disclose all sources of information obtained in the court of their professional services; they actively disclose which information from which source was used in formulating a particular written product or oral testimony.

F. Forensic psychologists are aware that their essential role as expert to the court is to assist the trier of fact to understand the evidence or to determine a fact in issue. In offering expert evidence, they are aware that their own professional observations, inferences, and conclusions must be distinguished from legal facts, opinions, and conclusions. Forensic psychologists are prepared to explain the relationship between their expert testimony and the legal issues and facts of an instant case.

Appendix C-2

APA Policy on Training for Psychologists Wishing to Change Their Specialty

Possession of a doctoral degree from an accredited institution does not, in and of itself, constitute adequate educational preparation to practice in all areas of psychology. A doctorate in experimental psychology, for example, does not provide adequate preparation for clinical practice. In assessing their own competence as it is relevant to an area of forensic practice, psychologists may find it helpful to consider the two policy statements of the American Psychological Association (APA) that follow.

The first policy statement was adopted by the APA's Council of Representatives at the January 23–25, 1976, meeting (Conger, 1976; reprinted by permission):

> *Council adopts the following as official policy of the APA:*
>
> 1. We strongly urge psychology departments currently engaged in doctoral training to offer training for individuals, already holding the doctoral degree in psychology, who wish to change their specialty. Such programs should be individualized, since background and career objectives vary greatly. It is desirable that financial assistance be made available to students in such programs.
> 2. Programs engaging in such training should declare so publicly and include a statement to that effect as a formal part of their program description and/or application for accreditation.
> 3. Psychologists seeking to change their specialty should take training in a program of the highest quality, and, where appropriate, exemplified by the doctoral training programs and internships accredited by the APA.
> 4. With respect to subject matter and professional skills, psychologists taking such training must meet all requirements of doctoral training in the new psychological specialty, being given due credit for relevant course work or requirements they have previously satisfied.
> 5. It must be stressed, however, that merely taking an internship or acquiring experience in a practicum setting is not, for example, considered adequate preparation for becoming a clinical, counseling, or school psychologist when prior training had not been in the relevant area.
> 6. Upon fulfillment of all formal requirements of such training program, the students should be awarded a certificate indicating the successful completion of preparation in the particular specialty, thus according them due recognition for their additional education and experience.
> 7. This policy statement shall be incorporated in the guidelines of the Committee on Accreditation so that appropriate sanctions can be brought to bear on university and internship training programs which violate paragraphs

> 4 and/or 5 of the above. (Conger, 1976, p. 424)

In reaffirming and amending its previous policy, the Council of Representatives approved the following statement of policy at its January 22–24, 1982 meeting (Abeles, 1982, p. 656; reprinted by permission):

> *The American Psychological Association holds that respecialization education and training for psychologists possessing the doctoral degree should be conducted by those academic units in regionally accredited universities and professional schools currently offering doctoral training in the relevant specialty, and in conjunction with regularly organized internship agencies where appropriate. Respecialization for purposes of offering services in clinical, counseling, or school psychology should be linked to relevant APA approved programs.*

Statement of Principles Relating to the Responsibilities of Attorneys and Psychologists in Their Interprofessional Relations

An Interdisciplinary Agreement Between the New Mexico Bar Association and the New Mexico Psychological Association

[*Note from the authors of this book:* In order to avoid the confusion of tasks, roles, and procedures, the Board of Bar Commissioners of the New Mexico Bar Association and the New Mexico Psychological Association created and formally approved the document that follows (Spring & Foote, 1986). The document was adopted on August 30, 1986; the copyright is held by the State Bar of New Mexico. Attorneys and psychologists in other states may want to consider adopting a similar statement.]

These principles should govern the interprofessional relations of psychologists and attorneys.

I. THE PATIENT-CLIENT

The welfare of the patient-client is the paramount and joint goal of these principles.

II. THE PSYCHOLOGISTS AND THE LAW

1. Psychologists shall refrain from giving legal advice.

2. Psychologists shall refrain from interfering with established lawyer–client relationships.

III. ATTORNEYS AND PSYCHOLOGICAL CARE

1. Attorneys shall refrain from giving psychodiagnostic opinions.

2. Attorneys shall refrain from interfering with established psychologist–patient relationships.

IV. AN ATTORNEY'S RESPONSIBILITIES

An attorney's responsibility is always first to his client. However, in his relationships with psychologists, an attorney has the following responsibilities:

1. Testimony: An attorney should keep the psychologist informed as to the status of the litigation and in particular inform him sufficiently in advance of:

   a. deposition and trial settings;

   b. vacated deposition and trial settings; and

   c. pre-trial settlements.

2. Fees: The services of a psychologist in a legal matter involve the consumption of the psychologist's time and the utilization of his facilities and his expertise. As a result, the attorney shall make proper arrangements with all involved psychologists beforehand for payment for the psychologist's services either directly by his client or by the attorney himself through advancement of costs. An attorney is not expected to advance costs for psychologist services involving treatment.

   An attorney who requests information from a psychologist solely to advance his knowledge of psychology is responsible personally for prompt payment of those services.

3. Background: An attorney should attempt to familiarize himself with the psychological litera-

The Statement of Principles included in appendix D is used by permission of the New Mexico Bar Association and New Mexico Psychological Association.

ture in order that he may have some initial understanding of the problem and so that he might be able to specify the information requested from the psychologist and understand the psychologist's explanation and report.

4. Confidentiality: An attorney must know the applicable law relating to confidentiality in the psychologist–patient relationship, such as the psychotherapist–patient privilege, Rule 504, New Mexico Rules of Evidence and the disclosure of information provision of the New Mexico Mental Health and Developmental Disabilities Code, N.M.Stat.Ann. Section 43-1-19 (1978). The attorney shall refrain from asking a psychologist to disclose confidential information other than as provided by law.

5. Client Preparation: An attorney should inform his client as to the nature and purposes of any psychological evaluation and should identify the potential uses of information to be gathered during the evaluation.

V. A PSYCHOLOGIST'S RESPONSIBILITIES

A psychologist's primary responsibility is always the well-being of his patient. The psychologist must maintain the confidentiality of patient communications as provided by New Mexico law. The psychologist acting as psychotherapist must claim the psychotherapist–patient privilege on behalf of his patient, recognizing that this privilege may be waived or excepted under New Mexico law. In any event, the psychologist must obtain a valid authorization from his patient or the patient's guardian before confidential information may be disclosed. A psychologist involved in the legal process has the following responsibilities:

1. Records: Given a valid authorization, the psychologist should promptly transfer information from his records to the requesting attorney. Psychologists have no proprietary interest in test or interview responses, whether written, taped, or otherwise recorded.

2. Reports: Given a valid authorization, reports covering a summation of psychological facts and opinions and their significance shall be furnished upon request by the treating psychologist or the psychologist specifically engaged to do such work. The attorney should specify the items he wishes covered in that report.

3. Psychological Testing Materials: Secured instruments, such as Rorschach or TAT cards, testing manuals, or other copyrighted materials, should be forwarded only to certified psychologists retained by the requesting attorney.

4. Psychological Evaluations: Before evaluating a person, the psychologist must inform the person of the nature and purposes of the psychological evaluation and must identify the potential uses of the information to be gathered during the evaluation.

5. Conferences: Given a valid authorization, attorneys may confer with psychologists either to:

a. gain psychological information on a topic of the attorney's interest, or

b. discuss psychological aspects of the case of a particular client with the treating psychologist or with one engaged to render such opinions. This may include a discussion of testimony that may be elicited at trial.

6. Testimony: Psychologist may be requested to testify either in court or by deposition. Cooperation between both attorneys and psychologists should allow for setting of court or deposition testimony for mutual convenience; while a subpoena may be necessary, it is not a substitute for direct communication between the attorney and psychologist for purpose of setting a time for testimony.

A psychologist should familiarize himself with the basic requirements of court procedure.

A psychologist should limit his testimony to his opinion and its basis. He should leave the representation of his patient and advancement of the patient's interest to the patient's attorney.

7. Fees: Psychologists may use the expenditure of their time, office facilities, and funds as a basis for arriving at a reasonable fee for services rendered pursuant to these principles. If an attorney fails to give timely notification of a change in the scheduled time for the psychologist's services, which makes the psychologist unavailable for other remunerative work, the psychologist may charge

for the time set aside. A reasonable fee for the psychologist's time spent in preparation for testimony by deposition or in the courtroom is the same rate charged for usual psychological services. A reasonable fee for deposition or courtroom testimony is no more than double the usual rate for psychological services.

VI. GRIEVANCE PROCEDURE

Any grievance regarding the Principles set forth above shall be referred to a grievance panel for hearing. The New Mexico Bar Association and the New Mexico Psychological Association will each provide six committee members and one co-chairman to serve on grievance panels which will be composed of two lawyers, two psychologists, and one co-chairman. The co-chairman for a grievance panel will choose two panel members from each profession.

Grievance panels are intended to resolve disputes arising out of the Principles set forth above; they are not intended as a substitute for the bodies governing the ethical conduct of the respective professions. Breaches of the ethical code of either profession or violations of law are to be referred to the appropriate body for consideration.

Appendix E-1

Federal Cases Involving the MMPI

This appendix lists federal appellate decisions that mention the MMPI. Each citation is accompanied by a brief statement showing the relation of the MMPI to the case. This brief statement is not intended to provide a complete description of the case or of issues unrelated to the MMPI. All significant issues raised in any case should be examined through review of the full case opinions and subsequent appellate opinions that affirm or reject the legal precedent set out in the original case.

Western District of Arkansas
Gray v. University of Arkansas, 658 F.Supp. 709 (W.D.Ark. 1987). MMPI evaluation of coach used in sex discrimination case.

Eastern District of Arkansas
Fairchild v. Lockhart, 744 F.Supp. 1429 (E.D.Ark. 1989). MMPI used in evaluation of petitioner.

Northern District of California
Hernandez v. Heckler, 621 F.Supp. 439 (D.C.Cal. 1985). MMPI tests used in evaluation of plaintiff.

District of Colorado
Reighley v. International Playtex, Inc., 604 F.Supp. 1078 (D.Colo. 1985). Reference article pertaining to MMPI listed in footnote 4.

Southern District of Florida
Stockett v. Tolin, 791 F.Supp. 1536 (S.D.Fla. 1992). In this sexual harassment case, the MMPI was part of an evaluation which found that the victim suffered severe emotional distress as the result of the harassment.

Gant v. Sullivan, 773 F.Supp. 376 (S.D.Fla. 1991). MMPI could not be administered because of individual's extreme inability to read or write.

Northern District of Georgia
Fields v. Harris, 498 F.Supp. 478 (N.D.Georgia 1980). MMPI used in evaluation of claimant.

Southern District of Illinois
Wilson v. Lane, 697 F.Supp. 1500 (S.D.Ill. 1988). MMPI used in evaluation of plaintiff as alcoholic.

Northern District of Illinois, Eastern Division
Winters v. Iowa State University, 768 F.Supp. 231 (N.D.Ill. 1991). MMPI used in negative recommendation to Chicago Police Department in regard to plaintiff.

Northern District of Indiana
Shidler v. Bowen, 651 F.Supp. 1291 (N.D.Ind. 1987). MMPI used in evaluation of claimant.

Mitchell v. Heckler, 590 F.Supp. 131 (N.D.Ill. 1984). MMPI ignored by administrative law judge in disability benefits dispute; MMPI had been used in diagnosis of plaintiff.

Lee v. Heckler, 568 F.Supp. 456 (N.D.Ind. 1983). MMPI used in evaluation of plaintiff.

Stokes v. U.S., 538 F.Supp. 298 (N.D.Ind. 1982). MMPI used in evaluation of appellant in competency case.

Northern District of Iowa
Stone v. Harris, 492 F.Supp. 278 (N.D.Iowa 1980). MMPI administered to plaintiff in disability benefits hearing.

District of Kansas
Elbrader v. Belvins, 757 F.Supp. 1174 (D.Kan. 1991). MMPI used in evaluation.

Ringer v. Sullivan, 772 F.Supp. 548 (D.Kan. 1991). Plaintiff completed MMPI in disability case.

Caldwell v. Sullivan, 736 F.Supp. 1076 (D.Kan. 1990). MMPI one of several tests used in evaluation of plaintiff.

Ash v. Sullivan, 748 F.Supp. 804 (D.Kan. 1990). MMPI one of tests used in evaluation of plaintiff.

Durflinger v. Artiles, 563 F.Supp. 322 (D.Kan. 1981). MMPI used in evaluation of alleged perpetrator in wrongful death action.

Western District of Kentucky
Canterino v. Wilson, 546 F.Supp. 174 (W.D.Ky. 1982). Results of 30 MMPI tests used by defendants to show lack of psychological injury to plaintiffs.

District of Maine
Taylor v. Heckler, 605 F.Supp. 407 (D.Me. 1984). Two MMPI tests used in evaluation of plaintiff and in testimony for plaintiff.

District of Maryland
U.S. v. Rigatuso, 719 F.Supp. 409 (D.Md. 1989). MMPI test results produced invalid profile and evidence of malingering.

Union Trust Co. of Maryland v. Charter Medical Corp., 663 F.Supp. 175 (D.Md. 1986). Extension of sublicense to use MMPI condition of acquisition in dispute.

Western District of Michigan
Simonds v. Blue Cross-Blue Shield of Michigan, 629 F.Supp. 369 (W.D.Mich. 1986). MMPI used in evaluation of plaintiff rendered invalid.

District of Minnesota
Regents of the University of Minnesota v. Applied Innovations, Inc., 685 F.Supp. 698 (D.Minn. 1987). MMPI the subject of copyright dispute.

Doe v. Hennepin County, 623 F.Supp. 982 (D.C.Minn. 1985). Family's psychologist claimed that court-approved psychologist improperly administered and interpreted MMPI tests.

Southern District of Mississippi
Kirksey v. City of Jackson, Miss., 461 F.Supp. 1282 (S.D.Miss. 1978). Use of MMPI in police candidate testing mentioned in civil rights action.

Northern District of Mississippi
Hill v. Thigpen, 667 F.Supp. 314 (N.D.Miss. 1987). MMPI used in evaluation of defendant. Controversy in that defense was not given adequate time to use results.

Eastern District of Missouri
Russell v. Sullivan, 758 F.Supp. 490 (E.D.Mo. 1991). MMPI used in evaluation of plaintiff.

Western District of Missouri
May v. U.S., 572 F.Supp. 725 (W.D.Mo. 1983). MMPI mentioned. Used in evaluation of plaintiff.

Mikel v. Abrams, 541 F.Supp. 591 (W.D.Mo. 1982). MMPI mentioned in case.

Harbour v. Bowen, 659 F.Supp. 732 (W.D.Mo. 1987). MMPI used in evaluation of plaintiff.

Smith v. Armontrout, 632 F.Supp. 503 (W.D.Mo. 1986). MMPI mentioned as one of tests directed to be given to Smith. See also 604 F.Supp. 840 (W.D.Mo. 1984).

District of Montana
Marmon v. Califano, 459 F.Supp. 369 (D.Mont. 1978). Administrative law judge's treatment of doctor's statements about MMPI results was reversed. Case remanded.

District of New Jersey
LaCorte v. Bowen, 678 F.Supp. 80 (D.N.J. 1988). MMPI one of tests given plaintiff at therapeutic center.

McKenna v. Fargo, 451 F.Supp. 1355 (D.N.J. 1978). Discussion of psychological testing challenged on constitutional grounds.

District of New Mexico
U.S. v. Dennison, 652 F.Supp. 211 (D.N.M. 1986). MMPI one of tests used in evaluation of defendant.

Southern District of New York
Guardsmark, Inc. v. Pinkerton's, Inc., 739 F.Supp. 173 (S.D.N.Y. 1990). Advertising use of MMPI in evaluating security personnel sparked suit of false advertising and unfair competition.

Eastern District of North Carolina
Edwards v. Bowen, 672 F.Supp. 230 (E.D.N.C. 1987). MMPI one of tests used in evaluation of plaintiff.

Southern District of Ohio
Isaac v. Sullivan, 782 F.Supp. 1215 (S.D.Ohio 1992). MMPI scores suggested somatic concerns that a doctor interpreted as indicating a personality disorder.

Tourlakis v. Morris, 738 F.Supp. 1128 (S.D.Ohio 1990). Defendant Tourlakis proffered testimony of doctor who was prepared to testify that MMPI scores showed a battered woman profile.

Northern District of Ohio
Lingo v. Secretary of Health and Human Services, 658 F.Supp. 345 (N.D.Ohio 1986). MMPI used in evaluation of plaintiff.

Northern District of Ohio, Eastern Division
Palmer v. Sullivan, 770 F.Supp. 380 (N.D.Ohio 1991). MMPI used in evaluation of claimant. No evidence of malingering.

Western District of Oklahoma
U.S. v. Barnes, 551 F.Supp. 22 (W.D.Okla. 1982). MMPI one of tests used to evaluate defendant.

Eastern District of Pennsylvania
U.S. v. Kosma, 749 F.Supp. 1392 (E.D.Pa. 1990). Defendant unable to complete MMPI because of concentration problems.

Western District of Pennsylvania
Commonwealth of Pennsylvania v. Flaherty, 760 F.Supp. 472 (W.D.Pa. 1991). MMPI-2 used in selection of police officers; effectiveness questioned.

U.S. v. Slayman, 590 F.Supp. 962 (W.D.Pa. 1984). Two separate MMPI tests used to evaluate defendant.

District of Puerto Rico
Diaz v. Secretary of Health and Human Services, 791 F.Supp. 905 (D.P.R. 1992). The administrative law judge erred when he denied an application for disability benefits. Psychiatric evaluations which included psychological testing showed evidence of many problems including depression, sleep problems, and motor retardation, which the judge ignored in his decision.

District of South Carolina
Kay v. Secretary of Health and Human Services, 683 F.Supp. 136 (D.S.C. 1988). MMPI one of several tests used in evaluation of plaintiff.

District of South Dakota
Holmberg v. Bowen, 687 F.Supp. 1370 (D.S.D. 1988). MMPI used in evaluation of plaintiff.

Western District of Tennessee
Sterling v. Velsicol Chemical Corp., 647 F.Supp. 303 (W.D.Tenn. 1988). MMPI used to evaluate one man in extensive personal injury case involving chemical waste burial site.

Middle District of Tennessee
Grubbs v. Bradley, 552 F.Supp. 1052 (M.D. Tenn. 1982). MMPI one of tests listed as part of inmate classification process.

Eastern District of Texas
Vanderbilt v. Lynaugh, 683 F.Supp. 1118 (E.D.Tex. 1988). MMPI one of tests listed as administered to petitioner.

Southern District of Texas
Ruiz v. Estelle, 503 F.Supp. 1265 (S.D.Tex. 1980). MMPI was the sole test given to evaluate or diagnose personality abnormalities of the inmates in the Texas Department of Corrections. Since the test cannot be understood by people with less than sixth-grade reading ability, the court concluded that it was useless for evaluating inmates who read at lower levels. The court also discussed the difficulty posed by lack of qualified personnel to supervise and evaluate diagnostic testing.

Western District Virginia
Brown v. Bowen, 682 F.Supp. 858 (W.D.Va. 1988). MMPI used in evaluation of plaintiff. Court reversed where administrative law judge discredited evidence of psychologist who administered MMPI.

Eastern District of Washington
Carr v. Sullivan, 772 F.Supp. 522 (E.D. Wash. 1991). MMPI used in evaluation of claimant.

Western District of Wisconsin
Corbecky v. Heckler, 588 F.Supp. 882 (W.D.Wis. 1984). MMPI used in evaluation of plaintiff.

District of Wyoming
Poindexter v. Bowen, 685 F.Supp. 1545 (D.Wyo. 1988). MMPI one of tests used in evaluation of claimant ordered by administrative law judge.

District of Columbia
Poulin v. Bowen, 817 F.2d 865 (D.C.Cir. 1987). French version of MMPI used in early evaluation of plaintiff and mentioned in footnote 79 of case.

U.S. v. Byers, 740 F.2d 1104 (D.C.Cir. 1984). MMPI one of several tests used in examination of defendant. Mentioned in footnote 20 of the dissent.

U.S. v. Alexander, 471 F.2d 923 (D.C. Cir. 1973). MMPI one of tests used to evaluate defendant. Short discussion of testimony.

Second Circuit
Daley v. Koch, 892 F.2d 212 (2nd Cir. 1989). MMPI one of tests used in psychological evaluation of police officer candidate.

Berry v. Schweiker, 675 F.2d 464 (2nd Cir. 1982). MMPI used as part of examination of appellant.

Third Circuit
Zettlemoyer v. Fulcomer, 923 F.2d 284 (3rd Cir. 1991). MMPI one of tests used to evaluate defendant.

Fourth Circuit
Murphy v. Bowen, 810 F.2d 433 (4th Cir. 1987). In an action challenging denial of Social Security disability benefits, the results of two psychological examinations conflicted. The MMPI was administered orally in the first examination because the individual could not read. In the second psychological assessment, the evaluator "administered a Rorschach test rather than the MMPI" 810 F.2d at 435. The second evaluator maintained that the MMPI was only 65% effective when given orally. This assertion was not challenged in the case.

Gross v. Heckler, 785 F.2d 1163 (4th Cir. 1986). MMPI mentioned in case and used in evaluation of claimant.

U.S. v. Burgess, 691 F.2d 1146 (4th Cir. 1982). MMPI one of tests used to evaluate defendant mentioned in footnote 18.

Jacobs v. U.S., 350 F.2d 571 (4th Cir. 1965). MMPI used in evaluation of defendant upon entering correctional facility. Doctor opined that Jacobs was feigning illness.

Fifth Circuit
U.S. v. Doe, 871 F.2d 1248 (5th Cir. 1989). Defendant claimed MMPI tests results were of questionable validity. Court upheld use of results.

Harrell v. Bowen, 862 F.2d 471 (5th Cir. 1988). MMPI mentioned in case.

Lowenfield v. Butler, 843 F.2d 183 (5th Cir. 1988). MMPI used in evaluation of defendant who was denied a stay of execution.

Dawsey v. Olin Corp., 782 F.2d 1254 (5th Cir. 1986). MMPI used in evaluation of plaintiff. Clinical interview did not bear out results of MMPI.

Rumbaugh v. Procunier, 753 F.2d 395 (5th Cir. 1985). Validity of MMPI test results questioned because of extremity of defendant's score. Mentioned in dissent.

Gray v. Lucas, 677 F.2d 1086 (5th Cir. 1982). MMPI results used to support theory of mental disturbance in defendant. Mentioned in case.

U.S. v. Harper, 450 F.2d 1032 (5th Cir. 1971). MMPI used in evaluation of defendant.

Sixth Circuit
Young v. Secretary of Health and Human Services, 925 F.2d 146 (6th Cir. 1990). MMPI one of tests used in evaluation of claimant.

Davis v. Secretary of Health and Human Services, 915 F.2d 186 (6th Cir. 1990). MMPI used in evaluation of claimant.

Atterberry v. Secretary of Health and Human Services, 871 F.2d 567 (6th Cir. 1989). MMPI used by consulting (not treating) physician to evaluate claimant.

Allen v. Redman, 858 F.2d 1194 (6th Cir. 1988). MMPI used as part of evaluation of defendant.

Mullen v. Bowen, 800 F.2d 535 (6th Cir. 1986). MMPI used in evaluation of claimant.

Williamson v. Secretary of Health and Human Services, 796 F.2d 146 (6th Cir. 1986). MMPI used in evaluation of claimant who doctor believed was taking test with "bad faith effort."

Seventh Circuit
Daniels v. Pipefitters Association Local Union No. 597, 945 F.2d 906 (7th Cir. 1991). Plaintiff had to take MMPI because union would not send pro forma letter of recommendation. Racial discrimination case.

Anderson v. Sullivan, 925 F.2d 220 (7th Cir. 1991). MMPI used in evaluation of plaintiff.

U.S. ex rel. Securities and Exchange Commission v. Billingsley, 766 F.2d 1015 (7th Cir. 1985). MMPI used in evaluation of defendant.

U.S. v. Bohle, 445 F.2d 54 (7th Cir. 1971). MMPI used in evaluation of defendant. Discussion as to admissibility of MMPI results given over telephone.

Eighth Circuit
Pratt v. Sullivan, 956 F.2d 830 (8th Cir. 1992). Plaintiff took MMPI three different times. The results showed progressive intensification of symptoms over time.

Lubinski v. Sullivan, 952 F.2d 214 (8th Cir. 1991). MMPI used in evaluation of claimant.

Kenley v. Armontrout, 937 F.2d 1298 (8th Cir. 1991). MMPI used in evaluation of defendant.

Coffin v. Sullivan, 895 F.2d 1206 (8th Cir. 1990). MMPI used in evaluation of claimant.

Wheeler v. Sullivan, 888 F.2d 1233 (8th Cir. 1989). MMPI profile rendered invalid because Wheeler "endorsed most test items in a pathological direction, . . ." 888 F.2d at 1235.

U.S. v. Barta, 888 F.2d 1220 (8th Cir. 1989). MMPI used in evaluation of defendant.

Buck v. Bowen, 885 F.2d 451 (8th Cir. 1989). MMPI one of many tests used to evaluate claimant.

Bryant v. Bowen, 882 F.2d 1331 (8th Cir. 1989). MMPI used in one evaluation of claimant.

Freels v. United States Railroad Retirement Board, 879 F.2d 335 (8th Cir. 1989). MMPI used in evaluation of claimant.

Applied Innovations, Inc. v. Regents of the University of Minnesota, 876 F.2d 626 (8th Cir. 1989). University sued for copyright infringement against company for exclusive ownership of MMPI. Extensive discussion, history, and description of MMPI.

Bland v. Bowen, 861 F.2d 533 (8th Cir. 1988). MMPI used in evaluation of claimant.

Rush v. Secretary of Health and Human Services, 738 F.2d 909 (8th Cir. 1984). MMPI used in evaluation of claimant.

McDonald v. Schweiker, 698 F.2d 361 (8th Cir. 1983). MMPI used in evaluation of claimant.

Houghton v. McDonnell Douglas Corp., 627 F.2d 858 (8th Cir. 1980). MMPI mentioned as one of tests used by Mayo Clinic for pilots. Mentioned in footnote 8.

Doe v. Department of Transportation, Federal Aviation Administration, 412 F.2d 674 (8th Cir. 1969). MMPI used in evaluation of applicant.

Marion v. Gardner, 359 F.2d 175 (8th Cir. 1966). MMPI used in evaluation of ward of Marion in petition for Social Security benefits.

Ninth Circuit
Mathis v. Pacific Gas and Electric Co., 891 F.2d 1429 (9th Cir. 1989). Two plaintiffs denied access to nuclear plant because they "failed" MMPI.

Fife v. Heckler, 767 F.2d 1427 (9th Cir. 1985). MMPI used in evaluation of claimant.

Gallant v. Heckler, 753 F.2d 1450 (9th Cir. 1984). MMPI mentioned in dissent as to mental state of claimant.

U.S. v. Harris, 534 F.2d 1371 (9th Cir. 1976). MMPI used in evaluation of key prosecution witness.

Tenth Circuit
Casias v. Secretary of Health and Human Services, 933 F.2d 799 (10th Cir. 1991). MMPI mentioned in case and used in evaluation of claimant.

Hays v. Murphy, 663 F.2d 1004 (10th Cir. 1981). MMPI mentioned in footnote 14 as standard psychological test.

Eleventh Circuit
Card v. Singletary, 963 F.2d 1440 (11th Cir. 1992). A defendant's capital murder conviction had been affirmed by the Florida Supreme Court and he sought to be

released through a federal habeas corpus writ. The court held that neither the MMPI results suggesting psychotic disturbance nor other evaluation data were sufficient to set aside the conviction.

U.S. v. Manley, 893 F.2d 1221 (11th Cir. 1990). MMPI used in one evaluation of defendant.

Smith v. Zant, 855 F.2d 712 (11th Cir. 1988). MMPI used to evaluate defendant in case that was vacated on grant of rehearing en banc, May 2, 1989.

Messer v. Kemp, 831 F.2d 946 (11th Cir. 1987). MMPI one of several tests used to evaluate defendant. Mentioned in footnote 10.

Moon v. Bowen, 794 F.2d 1499 (11th Cir. 1986). MMPI used to evaluate claimant.

MacGregor v. Bowen, 786 F.2d 1050 (11th Cir. 1986). MMPI used in evaluation of claimant.

Popp v. Heckler, 779 F.2d 1497 (11th Cir. 1986). MMPI scores rendered invalid because claimant attempted to appear in a very unfavorable light.

U.S. v. Lindstrom, 698 F.2d 1154 (11th Cir. 1983). MMPI used in evaluation of witness in case.

State Cases Involving the MMPI

This appendix lists state appellate decisions that mention the MMPI. Each citation is accompanied by a brief statement showing the relation of the MMPI to the case. This brief statement is not intended to provide a complete description of the case or of issues unrelated to the MMPI. All significant issues raised in any case should be examined through review of the full case opinions and subsequent appellate opinions that affirm or reject the legal precedent set out in the original case.

Alabama

C.M.B. v. State, 594 So.2d 695 (Ala.Crim.App. 1991). MMPI results in "lower normal range" considered in effective waiver of rights by 15-year-old defendant.

Prince v. State, 584 So.2d 889 (Ala.Crim.App. 1991). MMPI results used in testimony of a psychologist as to mental capability of defendant.

D.J. v. State Department of Human Resources, 578 So.2d 1351 (Ala.Civ.App. 1991). MMPI used as evidence of mother's mental state.

Carter v. Reid, 540 So.2d 57 (Ala. 1989). MMPI used to evaluate plaintiff. Validity not an issue.

Ex Parte Brown, 540 So.2d 740 (Ala. 1989). MMPI one of three tests used to evaluate defendant's ability to stand trial as an adult.

McGahee v. State, 554 So.2d 454 (Ala.Crim.App. 1989). Results of MMPI alleged to be defective. Motion made to employ expert to testify about results.

Brannon and the B.F. Goodrich Company v. Sharp, 554 So.2d 951 (Ala. 1989). MMPI used to evaluate plaintiff. Test validity not an issue.

Wesley v. State, 575 So.2d 108 (Ala.Crim.App. 1989). Testimony as to MMPI results deemed as limited to administering doctor.

Ford v. State, 515 So.2d 34 (Ala.Crim.App. 1986). Doctor felt that results of MMPI test could have been affected by defendant's "malingering" or "faking bad."

Musgrove v. State, 519 So.2d 565 (Ala.Crim.App. 1986). MMPI used in testimony of doctor to disprove claims of defendant's insanity.

McCrory v. State, 505 So.2d 1272 (Ala.Crim.App. 1986). MMPI taken by victim and defendant outside the scope of this case.

Bailey v. Gold Kist, Inc., 482 So.2d 1224 (Ala.Civ.App. 1985). Doctor allowed to use results of MMPI, evaluated by another psychologist, to testify as to plaintiff's behavior patterns.

Bailey v. State, 421 So.2d 1364 (Ala.Crim.App. 1982). Witness was not allowed to testify as to results of MMPI test because he was not qualified as an expert.

Smith v. State, 411 So.2d 839 (Ala.Crim.App. 1981). Psychologist found no major disorder at time of testing, but believed defendant was suffering from psychosis during commission of crime.

Abex Corporation v. Coleman, 386 So.2d 1160 (Ala.Civ.App. 1980). MMPI test one of three used to support diagnosis of plaintiff's psychological injuries.

Kyzer v. State, 399 So.2d 317 (Ala.Crim.App. 1979). Evidence of MMPI presented by defense in mitigation phase of death penalty action.

Luster v. State, 221 So.2d 695 (Ala.Ct.App. 1969). Undisputed expert testimony including MMPI data suggesting psychotic pathology insufficient evidence of insanity to disturb jury's finding.

Alaska

Adamson v. University of Alaska, 819 P.2d 886 (Alaska 1991). MMPI mentioned as element of thorough evaluation of plaintiff.

Wade v. Anchorage School District, 741 P.2d 634 (Alaska 1987). MMPI used to diagnose patient. Validity not questioned.

Martin v. State, 664 P.2d 612 (Alaska Ct.App. 1983). Defense of diminished capacity largely centered on results of MMPI test.

Alto v. State, 565 P.2d 492 (Alaska 1977). MMPI results consistent with psychosis part of support for reversing determination of sanity.

Arizona

State v. Winters, 160 Ariz. 143, 771 P.2d 468 (1989). Court of Appeals held that MMPI results had no merit in case and that its use was not probative under these circumstances.

State v. McMurtry III, 151 Ariz. 105, 726 P.2d 202 (1986). MMPI test results allowed as evidence of defendant's habitual criminalism and defendant's sanity.

Makinson v. Industrial Commission of Arizona, 134 Ariz. 246, 655 P.2d 366 (1982). Psychiatrist based diagnosis of plaintiff on MMPI and two personal visits.

Arkansas

Willmon v. Allen Canning Co., 828 S.W.2d 868 (Ark.Ct.App. 1992). The appellate court reversed the decision of the Worker's Compensation Commission that had denied benefits to an employee. The MMPI results that showed an "abnormal profile" helped to convince the court that physical trauma was prolonged by a psychological conflict and was compensable.

Freemen v. City of DeWitt, 301 Ark. 581, 787 S.W.2d 658 (1990). MMPI used by psychiatrist in recommendations for police officer candidates. Validity not in question.

Wade v. Mr. C. Cavenaugh's and Cigna Ins. Co., 298 Ark. 363, 768 S.W.2d 521 (1989). MMPI mentioned in case.

Wade v. Mr. C. Cavenaugh's and Cigna Ins. Co., 756 S.W.2d 923 (Ark.Ct.App. 1988). MMPI suggested a "normal profile."

Garibaldi v. Deitz, 25 Ark. 136, 752 S.W.2d 771 (1988). MMPI noted in dissenting opinion as one of tests used to evaluate plaintiff.

Boyd v. General Industries and Aetna Life & Casualty, 22 Ark.App. 103, 733 S.W.2d 750 (1987). MMPI recognized as "objective" test. Results were not "negative" in the normal sense.

Allen v. State, 488 S.W.2d 712 (Ark. 1973). MMPI one of several tests administered in criminal forensic setting.

California

People v. Kelly, 1 Cal. 4th 495, 3 Cal.Rptr.2d 677, 822 P.2d 385 (1992). In an appeal from a judgment of death, the court discussed evidence from the three phases (guilt, sanity, and penalty) of the criminal prosecution. In the sanity phase, defense presented an expert psychologist who administered the MMPI and opined that the defendant had a "psychotic-like disturbance."

Soroka v. Dayton Hudson Corp., 753 Cal.App.3d 654, 1 Cal.Rptr.2d 77 (Cal.App. 1 Dist. 1991). Use of MMPI in employment setting was unconstitutional.

In Re Rodrigo S., San Francisco Department of Social Services v. Joan R., 225 Cal.App.3d 1179, 276 Cal.Rptr. 183 (Cal.App. 1 Dist. 1990). MMPI evaluation of father used in testimony.

Gootee v. Lightner, 224 Cal.App.3d 587, 274 Cal.Rptr. 697 (Cal.App. 4 Dist. 1990). MMPI used to evaluate family in custody dispute.

People v. Kelly, 51 Cal.3d 931, 800 P.2d 516 (1990). MMPI used in evaluation of defendant.

People v. Ruiz, 220 Cal.App.3d 537, 269 Cal.Rptr. 465 (1990). MMPI and other accepted test results deemed admissible to show that an individual was not likely to commit crime. MMPI not subject to Kelly/Frye test.

People v. Ruiz, 222 Cal.App.3d 1241, 272 Cal.Rptr. 368 (Cal.App. 1 Dist. 1990). Ruling that psychologist may give opinion based partly on MMPI results as to character of defendant, but not allowed to testify that defendant did not possess certain characteristics shared by pedophiles, unless material used was reliable basis for such opinion.

People v. Stoll, 49 Cal.3d 1136, 265 Cal.Rptr. 111, 783 P.2d 698 (1989). Court recognized validity of MMPI used in testimony as evidence of defendant's good character. Extensive discussion.

People v. Jackson, 193 Cal.App.3d 875, 238 Cal.Rptr. 633 (1987). MMPI one of several tests mentioned in case that were scheduled to be given to defendant. Trial court did not err in allowing time for these tests.

People v. John W., 185 Cal.App.3d 801, 229 Cal.Rptr. 783 (Cal.App. 1 Dist. 1986). General discussion of test as it relates to determining sexual deviance. MMPI not standardized in regard to a sexually deviant population.

People v. Coleman, 38 Cal.3d 69, 211 Cal.Rptr. 102, 695 P.2d 189 (1985). Use of MMPI in forming an opinion as to defendant's past mental state questioned.

People v. Moore, 166 Cal.App.3d 540, 211 Cal.Rptr. 856 (Cal.App. 2 Dist. 1985). Defendant attempted to have "fixed" MMPI to show his insanity.

In the Matter of Cheryl H., Dennis H. v. Los Angeles County Department of Social Services, 153 Cal.App.3d 1098, 200 Cal.Rptr. 789 (Cal.App. 2 Dist. 1984). MMPI used in evaluation of family.

Ballard v. State Bar of California, 35 Cal.3d 274, 197 Cal.Rptr. 556, 673 P.2d 226 (1983). MMPI results previously read into evidence were sufficient after State Bar misplaced original results.

Insurance Company of North American v. Workers' Compensation Appeals Board of the State of California, 122 Cal.App.3d 905, 176 Cal.Rptr. 365 (1981). MMPI used to diagnose employee. Results discussed.

People v. Nicholas, 112 Cal.App.3d 249, 169 Cal.Rptr. 497 (Cal.App. 1 Dist. 1980). Gross exaggeration on tests rendered results invalid. Doctors considered it medically improper to draw any conclusions from those results.

Gay v. Workers' Compensation Appeals Board, 96 Cal.App.3d 555, 158 Cal.Rptr. 137 (1979). MMPI used in evaluation of claimant.

People v. Phillips, 90 Cal.App.3d 356, 153 Cal.Rptr. 359 (1979). MMPI one of tests used in evaluation of defendant/appellant.

People v. Arbuckle, 150 Cal.Rptr. 778, 587 P.2d (1978). MMPI one of several tests administered to defendant. Mentioned in footnote 1.

People v. Cox, 82 Cal.App.3d 211, 147 Cal.Rptr. 73 (1978). MMPI used by psychiatric social worker to evaluate defendant.

People v. Humphrey, 45 Cal.App.3d 32, 119 Cal.Rptr. 74 (1975). MMPI administered orally in evaluation of defendant.

People v. Coogler, 71 Cal.2d 153, 454 P.2d 686 (1969). MMPI used in evaluation of defendant by clinical psychologist.

Colorado

B.B. v. People, 785 P.2d 132 (Colo. 1990). MMPI one of tests used to evaluate B.B.

People v. Roark, 643 P.2d 756 (Colo. 1982). MMPI not used as a basis for assessing defendant's mental condition. Defendant was "faking bad" and rendered results unreliable.

District of Columbia

McEvily v. District of Columbia Department of Employment Services, 500 A.2d 1022 (D.C. 1985). MMPI used to evaluate McEvily.

Delaware

State v. Shields, 593 A.2d 986 (Del. 1990). MMPI one of many tests used to evaluate defendant.

Florida

DuBois v. DuBois, 586 So.2d 423 (Fla.App. 4 Dist. 1991). MMPI used to evaluate appellant. Results used in testimony.

Flanagan v. State, 586 So.2d 1085 (Fla.App. 1 Dist. 1991). MMPI mentioned in case re: controversy over whether tests results can reliably exclude a person from "profile" of a sexual deviant.

Grey v. Eastern Airlines, Inc., 480 So.2d 1341 (Fla.App. 1 Dist. 1985). MMPI one of tests used to evaluate appellant.

Valle-Axelberd and Associates, Inc. v. Metropolitan Dade County, 440 So.2d 606 (Fla.App. 3 Dist. 1983). Firm lost contract to firm that does not use MMPI. (MMPI became suspect when witnesses testified that it was perceived by the community to be racially skewed.) Appellate court upheld action.

Georgia

Stripling v. State, 261 Ga. 1, 401 S.E.2d 500 (1991). MMPI used to evaluate defendant.

Christenson v. State, 261 Ga. 80, 402 S.E.2d 41 (1991). MMPI used to evaluate defendant.

Jacobs v. Pilgrim, 186 Ga.App. 260, 367 S.E.2d 49 (1988). MMPI used to diagnose plaintiff. Used to show causal relationship with accident.

Patillo v. State, 258 Ga. 255, 368 S.E.2d 493 (1988). Court denied continuance to research MMPI results.

In re D.H., 178 Ga.App. 119, 342 S.E.2d 367 (1986). Evaluations of parents included MMPI. Discussion of results.

Ford v. State, 255 Ga. 81, 335 S.E.2d 567 (1985). Results of short form MMPI invalidated by Ford's "faking sick."

Idaho

O'Loughlin v. Circle A. Construction, 112 Idaho 1048, 739 P.2d 347 (1987). MMPI used to evaluate appellant. Mentioned briefly.

Illinois

Iwanski v. Steamwood Police Pension Board, 596 N.E.2d 691 (Ill.App. 1 Dist. 1992). Psychological testing that included MMPI results marked by depression, anxiety, and dysfunction supported a finding of nondisability.

People v. Scott, 148 Ill.2d 479, 594 N.E.2d 217 (Ill. 1992). The court affirmed the death sentence in a murder case. The MMPI testing showed no evidence of any thought disorder that would affect the defendant's ability to work with his attorney.

Johnson v. May, 223 Ill. App. 3d477, 165 Ill.Dec. 828, 585 N.E.2d 224 (Ill.App. 5 Dist. 1992). A psychological examination, including MMPI testing, resulted in a diagnosis of severe posttraumatic stress disorder. The jury's award of nothing for disability was in error, and the evaluation warranted a new trial on damages.

Amoco Oil Company v. Industrial Commission, 218 Ill.App.3d 737, 161 Ill.Dec. 397, 578 N.E.2d 1043 (1991). MMPI used to evaluate claimant.

People v. Camden, 219 Ill.App.3d 124, 161 Ill.Dec. 565, 578 N.E.2d 1211 (1991). MMPI used to evaluate defendant.

People v. Beehn, 205 Ill.App.3d 533, 151 Ill.Dec. 101, 563 N.E.2d 1207 (1990). MMPI used in evaluation of defendant.

In re L.M., 205 Ill.App.3d 497, 150 Ill.Dec. 872, 563 N.E.2d 999 (1990). MMPI mentioned in case, but not used to evaluate parents.

Illinois Mutual Ins. Co. v. Industrial Commission, 201 Ill.App.3d 1018, 147 Ill.Dec. 679, 559 N.E.2d 1019 (1990). MMPI used to evaluate claimants.

McDaniel v. Industrial Commission, 197 Ill.App.3d 981, 145 Ill.Dec. 442, 557 N.E.2d 212 (1990). MMPI used to evaluate claimant.

May v. Industrial Commission, 195 Ill.App.3d 468, 141 Ill.Dec. 890, 552 N.E.2d 258 (1990). MMPI used to evaluate claimant.

People v. Boclair, 129 Ill.2d 458, 136 Ill.Dec. 29, 544 N.E.2d 715 (1989). MMPI test results used in doctor's testimony as to his evaluation of defendant.

People v. Britz, 123 Ill.2d 446, 124 Ill.Dec. 15, 528 N.E.2d 703 (1988). MMPI used to evaluate defendant. Results were in a range that indicated exaggeration; therefore deemed invalid.

People v. Thompson, 166 Ill.App.3d 909, 117 Ill.Dec. 795, 520 N.E.2d 1146 (1988). MMPI test given to defendant in navy. Results read into testimony and accepted.

People v. Eckhardt, 156 Ill.App.3d 1077, 109 Ill.Dec. 349, 509 N.E.2d 1361 (1987). MMPI used to show that defendant was not malingering.

People v. Littlejohn, 144 Ill.App.3d 813, 98 Ill.Dec. 555, 494 N.E.2d 677 (1986). State entered MMPI results into evidence against defendant.

Roulette v. Department of Central Management Services, 141 Ill.App.3d 394, 95 Ill.Dec. 587, 490 N.E.2d 60 (1986). When rejected police officer candidate requested all documents, his MMPI profile was not included. He brought action to retrieve it.

People v. Gacy, 103 Ill.2d 1, 82 Ill.Dec. 391, 468 N.E.2d 1171 (1984). Defendant attempted to make himself look in worse condition than he actually was with MMPI test.

Aronson v. North Park College, 94 Ill.App.3d 211, 49 Ill.Dec. 756, 418 N.E.2d 776 (1981). Student required to take MMPI. Results and her refusal of counseling led to her dismissal. She brought suit against school for violation of her rights.

People v. Cooper, 64 Ill.App.3d 880, 381 N.E.2d 1178 (1978). MMPI results confirmed insecurity and hostility and supported the conclusion that the defendant was "sexually dangerous."

Indiana

Byrd v. State, 593 N.E.2d 1183 (Ind. 1992). Results of the MMPI were held inadmissible to prove that defendant's character was inconsistent with committing intentional murder.

Byrd v. State, 579 N.E.2d 457 (Ind.App. 1 Dist. 1991). Issue as to whether doctor should be allowed to proffer expert opinion about MMPI results already entered into evidence.

Ellis v. State, 567 N.E.2d 1142 (Ind. 1991). MMPI mentioned in case.

Ulrich v. State, 550 N.E.2d 114 (Ind.App. 3 Dist. 1990). Doctor not allowed to answer whether he believed that allegations of sexual activity by defendant were consistent with the profile and results obtained from the MMPI.

Isom v. Isom, 538 N.E.2d 261 (Ind.App. 3 Dist. 1989). MMPI results used in testimony to decide child custody dispute.

In the Matter of John L. Hudgins, 540 N.E.2d 1200 (Ind. 1989). MMPI used to evaluate attorney in disciplinary proceeding.

Sullivan v. Fairmont Homes, Inc., 543 N.E.2d 1130 (Ind.App. 1 Dist. 1989). MMPI interpretation was computer generated and doctor testifying was not an MMPI expert. Appellate court ruled that that evidence was hearsay and not allowed.

Van Cleave v. State, 517 N.E.2d 356 (Ind. 1987). Psychologist used results of MMPI as basis for opinion that defendant was excellent candidate for vocational rehabilitation.

City of Greenwood v. Dowler, 492 N.E.2d 1081 (Ind.App. 1 Dist. 1986). MMPI test results used in evaluation of police officer candidate.

Iowa

State v. Randle, 484 N.W.2d 220 (Iowa Ct.App. 1992). A sexual abuse victim waived her physician-patient privilege when she authorized release of documents to the Department of Criminal Investigations, and, therefore, the victim's MMPI results were admissible to show that she experienced little stress 5 days after the alleged offense.

State ex rel. LEAS in Interest of O'Neal, 303 N.W.2d 414 (Iowa 1981). MMPI one of tests used to evaluate parents in parental rights termination.

Gosek v. Garmer and Stiles Co., 158 N.W.2d 731 (Iowa 1968). MMPI used in discussion of worker's disability.

Kansas

West v. Martin, 11 Kan.App.2d 55, 713 P.2d 957 (1986). MMPI subject of admissibility of evidence argument.

Rund v. Cessna Aircraft Co., 213 Kan. 812, 512 P.2d 518 (1974). MMPI one of tests used in evaluation of claimant.

State of Kansas v. Kilpatrick, 201 Kan.6, 439 P.2d 99 (1968). MMPI one of several tests used in evaluation of defendant.

Kentucky

Commonwealth v. Jarboe, 464 S.W.2d 287 (Ky. 1971). MMPI given to potential adoptive parents.

Louisiana

Cheramie v. J. Wayne Plaisance, Inc., 595 So.2d 619 (La. 1992). Plaintiff evaluated by psychologist with MMPI.

Ward v. Commercial Union Ins. Co., 591 So.2d 1286 (La.App. 3 Cir. 1991). MMPI used in evaluation of plaintiff.

Castille v. Great Atlantic & Pacific Tea Co., 591 So.2d 1299 (La.App. 3 Cir. 1991). MMPI used to evaluate plaintiff.

Bankston v. Alexandria Neurosurgical Clinic, 583 So.2d 1148 (La.App. 3 Cir. 1991). Bankston alleged that doctors destroyed her MMPI test, along with other tests, "with conspiracy to deny plaintiff due course of justice." Appellees asked court to sanction her.

Miley v. Landry, 582 So.2d 833 (La. 1991). MMPI used in evaluation of Miley.

State v. Widenhouse, 582 So.2d 1374 (La.App. 2 Cir. 1991). MMPI used to evaluate defendant.

Utz v. Kienzle, 574 So.2d 1288 (La.App. 3 Cir. 1991). MMPI used, along with interviews, in custody battle to evaluate the two sets of parents.

Whatley v. Regional Transit Authority, 563 So.2d 1194 (La.App. 4 cir. 1990). MMPI used in evaluation of plaintiff.

Broussard v. Grey Wolf Drilling Company, 562 So.2d 1006 (La.App. 3 Cir. 1990). MMPI part of evaluation of plaintiff.

Valin v. Barnes, 550 So.2d 352 (La.App. 3 Cir. 1989). MMPI used to evaluate party in personal injury.

Cronier v. Cronier, 540 So.2d 1160 (La.App. 1 Cir. 1989). MMPI part of evaluation of husband in custody dispute.

Miles v. Dolese Concrete Co., 518 So.2d 999 (La. 1988). MMPI used in evaluation of workers' compensation plaintiff. Some discussion of MMPI.

Miles v. Dolese Concrete Co., 507 So.2d 2 (La.App. 1 Cir. 1987). MMPI used in evaluation of workers' compensation plaintiff.

State v. Bowman, 491 So.2d 1380 (La.App. 3 Cir. 1986). MMPI used to evaluate defendant. Portions read into testimony pertaining to plea of insanity.

Laborde v. Velsicol Chemical Corp., 474 So.2d 1320 (La.App. 3 Cir. 1985). MMPI used in one of many evaluations of plaintiff.

Lewis v. East Feliciana Parish School Board, 452 So.2d 1275 (La.App. 1 Cir. 1984). MMPI one of several tests used in evaluation of plaintiff.

Droddy v. Cliff's Drilling, Inc., 471 So.2d 223 (La. 1985). MMPI given to plaintiff three different times to determine whether he was being truthful.

Bunch v. Bunch, 469 So.2d 1191 (La.App. 3 Cir. 1985). MMPI used to evaluate wife in custody dispute.

State v. Felde, 422 So.2d 370 (La. 1982). MMPI used in evaluation of defendant, who was characterized as having posttraumatic stress disorder.

State v. Freeman, 409 So.2d 581 (La. 1982). MMPI used by state to establish defendant's ability to aid and participate in her own defense.

Walton v. William Wolf Baking Co., Inc., 406 So.2d 168 (La. 1981). MMPI used to evaluate plaintiff on three occasions.

Smith v. Angelle, 339 So.2d 922 (La.App. 3 Cir. 1976). MMPI one of tests used in evaluation of claimant.

Maine

State v. Bridges, 413 A.2d 937 (Me. 1980). MMPI not used to evaluate defendant because the doctors believed it would prove inconclusive. Brief discussion.

State of Maine v. Howard, 405 A.2d 206 (Me. 1979). Defendant attempted to introduce a report that contained MMPI results, but defendant did not lay proper foundation.

State v. Buzynski, 330 A.2d 422 (Me. 1974). Defendant unsuccessfully attempted to have a doctor's testimony concerning MMPI results stricken.

Maryland

Scott v. Prince George's County Department of Social Services, 76 Md.App. 357, 545 A.2d 81 (Md.App. 1988). MMPI used in evaluation of appellant in parental rights dispute.

Bremer v. State, 18 Md.App. 291, 307 A.2d 503 (1973). MMPI one of several tests used in one evaluation of defendant/appellant.

Massachusetts

Commonwealth v. Goulet, 402 Mass. 299, 522 N.E.2d 417 (Mass. 1988). MMPI administered to defendant, whom doctor opined was "faking bad."

Commonwealth v. Meech, 403 N.E.2d 1174 (Mass. 1980). MMPI used to evaluate defendant on behalf of the defense.

Michigan

Adkerson v. MK-Ferguson Co., 191 Mich.App. 129, 477 N.W.2d 465 (Mich.App. 1991). Employee who was terminated because of his MMPI scores brought action for damages. Personal representative of former employee appealed.

In the Matter of Farley, 469 N.W.2d 295 (Mich. 1991). Mother in parental rights dispute given MMPI twice to help indicate progress through therapy.

People v. Bowman, 141 Mich.App. 390, 367 N.W.2d 867 (Mich.App. 1985). MMPI used in evaluation of defendant.

People v. Arroyo, 138 Mich.App. 246, 360 N.W.2d 185 (Mich.App. 1984). Expert witness for defendant testified defendant was legally insane based on an interview and MMPI results.

Minnesota

Loveland v. Kremer, 464 N.W.2d 306 (Minn.App. 1990). MMPI mentioned in case.

Matter of Reinstatement of Williams, 433 N.W.2d 104 (Minn. 1988). MMPI used in evaluation of lawyer and used in petition for reinstatement.

J.E.P. v. J.C.P., 432 N.W.2d 483 (Minn.App. 1988). MMPI used to evaluate both a husband and a wife in protective order hearing.

In re Miera, 426 N.W.2d 850 (Minn. 1988). MMPI used to evaluate judge and his employee in dispute of sexual harassment by judge.

State v. Jurgens, 424 N.W.2d 546 (Minn.App. 1988). MMPI given to defendant three times over number of years. All three were brought into sanity issue.

In re Bolen, 416 N.W.2d 449 (Minn. 1987). Lawyer used MMPI to reinforce mitigating circumstances in suspension of probation hearing.

Matter of Welfare of J.A.R., 408 N.W.2d 692 (Minn.App. 1987). MMPI used in evaluation of juvenile while incarcerated.

Bjerke v. Wilcox, 401 N.W.2d 97 (Minn.App. 1987). MMPI used to evaluate father, mother, father's fiancee, and mother's new husband in custody dispute.

Petersen v. Kidd, 400 N.W.2d 413 (Minn.App. 1987). MMPI used as part of evaluation of plaintiff.

Rosen v. Rosen, 398 N.W.2d 38 (Minn.App. 1986). Disputed MMPI results for both parents used in custody dispute.

Novotny v. Novotny, 394 N.W.2d 256 (Minn.App. 1986). MMPI used to evaluate both parents in custody dispute.

Hreha v. Hreha, 392 N.W.2d 914 (Minn.App. 1986). Petitioner filed for change of custody. MMPI used in evaluation of respondent.

Jorschumb v. Jorschumb, 390 N.W.2d 806 (Minn.App. 1986). MMPI used to evaluate both parents in custody dispute. Appellant claimed that his being denied access to psychological tests of appellee rendered testing psychologist's testimony inadmissible.

Matter of Welfare of P.L.C. and D.L.C., 384 N.W.2d 222 (Minn.App. 1986). MMPI used in evaluation of father in guardianship dispute against grandfather.

Hoffa v. Hoffa, 382 N.W.2d 522 (Minn.App. 1986). MMPI used in evaluation of both parents in custody dispute.

Riewe v. Arnesen, 381 N.W.2d 448 (Minn.App. 1986). Disclosure of use of MMPI test results to defense counsel on afternoon before trial ruled not for purpose of taking advantage of defense.

Matter of Welfare of D.D.K., 376 N.W.2d 717 (Minn.App. 1985). MMPI used as part of evaluation of both parents in hearing to terminate all parental rights.

Matter of Welfare of R.B. and B.B., 369 N.W.2d 353 (Minn.App. 1985). Father required, as part of visitation order, to submit to MMPI test in neglect due to sexual abuse proceeding.

Application for Discipline of McCallum, 366 N.W.2d 100 (Minn. 1985). Lawyer required to take MMPI and psychiatric examination as condition of petitioning for reinstatement.

State v. Cermak, 365 N.W.2d 238 (Minn. 1985). MMPI used in evaluation of codefendant.

Newmaster v. Mahmood, 361 N.W.2d 130 (Minn.App. 1985). Plaintiff was evaluated with MMPI in order to help determine the "economic impact" of her injuries.

Matter of Welfare of A.K.K., 356 N.W.2d 337 (Minn.App. 1984). MMPI used in evaluation of mother in termination of parental rights hearing.

State v. Bouwman, 354 N.W.2d 1 (Minn. 1984). MMPI had been used in evaluation and treatment of defendant before the commission of the crime.

Enebak v. Noot, 353 N.W.2d 544 (Minn. 1984). MMPI used as part of evaluation of plaintiff in review of committal to a mental facility.

Wills v. Red Lake Municipal Liquor Store, 350 N.W.2d 452 (Minn.App. 1984). MMPI mentioned as example in case cited within this case.

Halper v. Halper, 348 N.W.2d 360 (Minn.App. 1984). MMPI used in evaluation of both parents in custody dispute.

McClish v. Pan-O-Gold Baking Co., 336 N.W.2d 538 (Minn. 1983). Rehabilitation psychologist testified that McClish was unemployable in this competitive labor market. His opinion was based partly on MMPI scores.

Cornfeldt v. Tongen, 262 N.W.2d 684 (Minn. 1977). MMPI mentioned in medical malpractice case.

Hagen v. Swenson, 306 Minn. 257, 236 N.W.2d 161 (1975). Qualifications of expert testifying as to MMPI results challenged and upheld.

Haynes v. Anderson, 304 Minn. 185, 232 N.W.2d 196 (1975). Plaintiff appealed an order requiring her to submit to a MMPI test. Discussion of MMPI.

Saholt v. Northwest Airlines, Inc., 290 Minn. 393, 188 N.W.2d 772 (1971). MMPI used in evaluation of worker's compensation claimant.

Mississippi

King v. State, 503 So.2d 271 (Miss. 1987). MMPI mentioned in opinion of judge specially concurring to decision of case.

Bethany v. Stubbs, 393 So.2d 1351 (Miss. 1981). MMPI used to evaluate mental patient petitioning for habeas corpus.

Missouri

In Interest of S.A.J. and S.L.J., 818 S.W.2d 690 (Mo.App. 1991). Appellant was evaluated with MMPI at one time during series of parental rights hearings.

Bussell v. Leat, 781 S.W.2d 97 (Mo.App. 1989). MMPI used by defendant to have plaintiff's mental condition evaluated. Discussion of administering doctor's qualifications.

State v. Taylor, 745 S.W.2d 173 (Mo.App. 1987). MMPI mentioned in case. Defendant, on appeal, claimed trial court erred in overruling his objection to the state's cross-examination of administering psychologist.

State v. Kennedy, 726 S.W.2d 884 (Mo.App. 1987). MMPI mentioned in case.

State v. Quillar, 683 S.W.2d 656 (Mo.App. 1986). MMPI used to evaluate appellant on three separate occasions.

Juvenile Office of Cape Girardeau County v. M.E.J., 666 S.W.2d 957 (Mo.App. 1984.) MMPI used in evaluation of appellant in parental rights termination.

In Interest of C.L.M., 625 S.W.2d 613 (Mo. 1981). MMPI one of tests used to evaluate mother in parental rights hearing.

Montana

State v. Brodniak, 221 Mont. 212, 718 P.2d 322 (Mont. 1986). MMPI used as part of evaluation of victim.

Nebraska

Van Winkle v. Electric Hose & Rubber Co., 214 Neb. 8, 332 N.W.2d 209 (Neb. 1983). MMPI used to evaluate plaintiff two separate times.

Davis v. Western Electric, 210 Neb. 771, 317 N.W.2d 68 (Neb. 1982). Plaintiff refused to take MMPI.

New Jersey

New Jersey State Parole Board v. Cestari, 224 N.J.Super. 534, 540 A.2d 1334 (N.J.Super.A.D. 1988). MMPI used in evaluation of defendant.

New Mexico

Matter of Ayala, 112 N.M. 109, 812 P.2d 358 (N.M. 1991). MMPI mentioned in case. Psychologist testified that Ayala "faked" test answers.

New York

People v. Berrios, 150 Misc.2d 229, 568 N.Y.S.2d 512 (Sup. 1991). MMPI one of four standardized tests used in evaluation of defendant.

H. Jon Geis, P.C. v. Landau, 117 Misc.2d 396, 458 N.Y.S.2d 1000 (N.Y. Civ.Ct. 1983). MMPI mentioned in case under "Brown and Dunbar, 'MMPI Difference Between Fee-Paying and Non-fee-paying Psychotherapy Clients,' *Journal of Clinical Psychology*, October 1978, Vol. 54, No. 4."

Buehler v. New York Telephone Co., 89 A.D.2d 664, 453 N.Y.S.2d 105 (App.Div. 3 Dept. 1982). Case brought because claimant refused to take MMPI because her disability was orthopedic.

North Carolina

Matter of Kennedy, 103 N.C.App. 632, 406 S.E.2d 307 (N.C. App. 1991). MMPI used to evaluate entire family in juvenile neglect case.

State v. Huff, 325 N.C. 1, 381 S.E.2d 635 (N.C. 1989). Results of MMPI given to defendant were discounted by psychologist because validity scale indicated that answers were not accurate measures of his condition.

In re Parker, 90 N.C.App. 423, 368 S.E.2d 879 (N.C.App. 1988). MMPI mentioned in case.

State v. Mancuso, 321 N.C. 464, 364 S.E.2d 359 (N.C. 1988). MMPI one of tests used to evaluate defendant.

State v. Hoyle, 49 N.C.App. 98, 270 S.E.2d 582 (N.C.App. 1980). MMPI test results ruled hearsay and highly prejudicial. Administering psychologist not present to be cross-examined. Other reasons discussed.

North Dakota

Kopp v. North Dakota Workers' Compensation Bureau, 462 N.W.2d 132 (N.D. 1990). MMPI used in evaluation of plaintiff.

Oberlander v. Oberlander, 460 N.W.2d 400 (N.D. 1990). MMPI results used extensively in evaluation of both parents in custody dispute.

In Interest of C.K.H., 458 N.W.2d 303 (N.D. 1990). The case discussed the termination of parental rights to five children. The mother had been married twice. The court's order terminated parental rights of the mother and both her husband, who had fathered four of the children, and her ex-husband, who had fathered one. The MMPI was used to support a finding that the second husband was "self-centered, selfish and egocentric" 458 N.W. 2d at 307.

State v. Skjonsby, 417 N.W.2d 818 (N.D. 1987). MMPI test results refuted. Three MMPIs were administered.

Sexton v. J.E.H., 355 N.W.2d 828 (N.D. 1984). MMPI used to evaluate mother in parental rights termination.

Gramling v. North Dakota Workers' Compensation Bureau, 303 N.W.2d 323 (N.D. 1981). Plaintiff asserts violation of due process with respect to MMPI test results. Discussion of issue in case.

Ohio

Cleveland Civil Service Commission v. Ohio Civil Rights Commission, 57 Ohio St.3d 62, 565 N.E.2d 579 (1991). MMPI used in evaluation of police department applicant. MacAndrew Alcoholism Scale mentioned.

State v. Ambrosia, 587 N.E.2d 892 (Ohio App. 6 Dist. 1990). Results of MMPI not allowed as character evidence in rape case.

Pinger v. Behavioral Science Center, Inc., 52 Ohio App.3d 17, 556 N.E.2d 209 (1988). Plaintiff sued company retained by his employer to conduct psychological testing. MMPI one of tests adminstered.

In re Barnes, 31 Ohio App.3d 201, 510 N.E.2d 392 (1986). MMPI mentioned in case.

Oklahoma

In the Matter of L.S., 805 P.2d 120 (Okl.App. 1990). MMPI not given by doctor because patient couldn't read. Another doctor administered it orally.

State ex rel. Oklahoma Bar Association v. Colston, 777 P.2d 920 (Okl. 1989). MMPI one of several tests used to evaluate attorney in disciplinary proceeding.

Haworth v. Central National Bank of Oklahoma City, 769 P.2d 740 (Okl. 1989). MMPI mentioned in case.

Reynolds v. State, 717 P.2d 608 (Okl.Crim. 1986). Testimony of M. Thomas, who administered MMPI, not allowed in case.

Faulkenberry v. Kansas City Southern Railway Co., 661 P.2d 510 (Okl. 1983). Two separate MMPI tests' results used in case.

Jones v. State, 648 P.2d 1251 (Okl.Crim. 1982). MMPI used as one of methods of evaluating defendant.

Oregon
State ex rel. Juvenile Department v. DeVore, 108 Or.App. 426, 816 P.2d 647 (1991). MMPI used to evaluate mother in parental rights termination.

State v. Huntley, 302 Or. 418, 730 P.2d 1234 (1986). MMPI used to evaluate defendant.

Short v. State Accident Insurance Fund Corporation, 79 Or.App. 423, 719 P.2d 894 (1986). MMPI used more than one time to evaluate claimant.

Gasper v. Adult and Family Services Division, 77 Or.App. 209, 712 P.2d 167 (1986). MMPI one of tests used to evaluate claimant.

Berwick v. Adult and Family Services Division, 74 Or.App. 460, 703 P.2d 994 (1985). MMPI used in evaluation of petitioner.

Ferguson v. Industrial Indemnity Co., 70 Or.App. 46, 687 P.2d 1130 (1984). MMPI used to evaluate claimant.

State ex rel. Juvenile Department v. Grannis, 67 Or.App. 565, 680 P.2d 660 (1984). Results of MMPI used in testimony against mother in parental rights termination.

Matter of Swartzfager, 290 Or. 799, 626 P.2d 882 (1981). MMPI test given to mother rendered invalid because she had preconceived notions.

Pennsylvania
Marsico v. Workmen's Compensation Appeal Board (Dept. of Revenue), 588 A.2d 984 (Pa.Commw.Ct. 1991). Two MMPI tests used in evaluation of the claimant.

Moore v. Unemployment Compensation Board of Review, 578 A.2d 606 (Pa.Commw.Ct. 1990). MMPI mentioned in case.

In re Adoption of Stunkard, 551 A.2d 253 (Pa.Super. 1988). MMPI used to evaluate father in parental rights termination case.

Wool v. Workmen's Compensation Appeal Board, 450 A.2d 1081 (Pa.Commw.Ct. 1982). MMPI used to evaluate claimant.

South Carolina
Howle v. PYA/Monarch, Inc., 288 S.C. 586, 344 S.E.2d 157 (S.C.App. 1986). MMPI used in evaluation of plaintiff.

South Dakota
State v. Titus, 426 N.W.2d 578 (S.D. 1988). MMPI used in diagnosis of defendant.

People in Interest of M.J.B., 364 N.W.2d 921 (S.D. 1985). MMPI used to evaluate parents in therapy to correct domestic situation. Parental rights termination case.

Tennessee
State v. Payne, 791 S.W.2d 10 (Tenn. 1990). MMPI used in evaluation of defendant.

Wade v. Aetna Casualty and Surety Co., 735 S.W.2d 215 (Tenn. 1987). MMPI mentioned in case.

State v. Dicks, 615 S.W.2d 126 (Tenn. 1981). MMPI one of several tests used in evaluation of appellant. Testimony of psychologist who administered tests not allowed in trial in guilt and innocence phase.

Texas
Johnson v. King, 821 S.W.2d 425 (Tex.App.-Fort Worth 1991). MMPI used in evaluation of plaintiff.

Davis v. Davis, 794 S.W.2d 930 (Tex.App.-Dallas 1990). MMPI used to evaluate father in custody dispute.

City of Dallas v. Cox, 793 S.W.2d 701 (Tex.App.-Dallas 1990). Extensive discussion of officer's grid sheet, which contained MMPI information. Discussion of MMPI testing procedure.

Ochs v. Martinez, 789 S.W.2d 949 (Tex.App.-San Antonio 1990). MMPI mentioned in footnote to case.

Moss v. State, 704 S.W.2d 939 (Tex.App. 3 Dist. 1986). MMPI results showed defendant to be normal. Defendant was taking antipsychotic drugs at the time, which may be responsible for a showing of normal.

Matter of Franklin, 699 S.W.2d 689 (Tex.App. 6 Dist. 1985). MMPI one of tests used in evaluation of Franklin.

Williams v. State, 649 S.W.2d 693 (Tex.App. 7 Dist. 1983). Psychologist explained MMPI, used results on a chart, and gave his opinion of appellant based on those results.

Utah

State v. Bryan, 709 P.2d 257 (Utah 1985). MMPI mentioned in footnote as one of two tests administered to defendant by a psychologist.

Virginia

M.E.D. v. J.P.M., 3 Va.App. 391, 350 S.E.2d 215 (1986). MMPI one of several tests used in evaluation of father.

Washington

State v. Rice, 110 Wash.2d 577, 757 P.2d 889 (1988). MMPI used in evaluation of defendant. Also used in argument that defendant had time to fabricate evidence of mental disease while incarcerated.

State v. Harris, 106 Wash.2d 784, 725 P.2d 975 (1986). MMPI used in evaluation of defendant but was unscored. Court denied motion for new trial based on new evidence including the scored MMPI.

DeHaven v. Gant, 42 Wash.App. 666, 713 P.2d 149 (1986). Admissibility of MMPI results argued.

State v. Walker, 40 Wash.App. 658, 700 P.2d 1168 (1985). MMPI used in evaluation of defendant.

State v. Despenza, 38 Wash.App. 645, 689 P.2d 87 (1984). MMPI used in evaluation of victim. Testimony as to those results refused.

In re Mosley, 34 Wash.App. 179, 660 P.2d 315 (1983). MMPI used in evaluation of mother in parental rights termination appeal.

Bertsch v. Brewer, 96 Wash.2d 973, 640 P.2d 711 (1982). In this case, admission of MMPI tests results, without the laying of a proper foundation, was prejudicial and necessitated a new trial.

West Virginia

Weece v. Cottle, 352 S.E.2d 131 (W.Va. 1986). MMPI used in evaluation of mother in custody dispute.

State v. Duell, 332 S.E.2d 246 (W.Va. 1985). MMPI test results rendered invalid because they were scored with the wrong gender scale.

Wyoming

Zabel v. State, 765 P.2d 357 (Wyo. 1988). The same expert whose testimony was allowed in *Brown v. State*, 736 P.2d 1110 (Wyo. 1987) (discussed in following case) testified in this case. The case was reversed because the expert expanded her testimony beyond discussing the validity scoring as she had in *Brown v. State*, *supra*, and into improper evaluation of and comment on credibility.

Brown v. State, 736 P.2d 1110 (Wyo. 1987). An expert testified that the MMPI validity scales suggested that the alleged sexual assault victim tested had approached the test from a truthful fashion, neither exaggerating nor covering up. The testimony was held not to be an inappropriate comment on the witness's truthfulness.

APPENDIX F

Listing of MMPI, MMPI-2, and MMPI-A Items

THE ORIGINAL MMPI

M: Rewritten items in MMPI-2 (62)
D: Deleted items in MMPI-2 (90)
R: Repeated items deleted in MMPI-2 (16)
[ ]: MMPI-2 rewritten items

1 I like mechanics magazines.
2 I have a good appetite.
3 I wake up fresh and rested most mornings.
4 I think I would like the work of a librarian.
5 I am easily awakened by noise.
6 I like to read newspaper articles on crime.
7 My hands and feet are usually warm enough.
8 My daily life is full of things that keep me interested.
9 I am about as able to work as I ever was.
10 There seems to be a lump in my throat much of the time.
M **11** A person should try to understand his dreams and be guided by or take warning from them. [People should try to understand their dreams and be guided by or take warning from them.]
12 I enjoy detective or mystery stories.
13 I work under a great deal of tension.
D **14** I have diarrhea once a month or more.
15 Once in a while I think of things too bad to talk about.
16 I am sure I get a raw deal from life.
M **17** My father was a good man. [My father is a good man, or (if your father is dead) my father was a good man.]
18 I am very seldom troubled by constipation.
M **19** When I take a new job, I like to be tipped off on who should be gotten next to. [When I take a new job, I like to find out who it is important to be nice to.]
20 My sex life is satisfactory.
21 At times I have very much wanted to leave home.
22 At times I have fits of laughing and crying that I cannot control.
23 I am troubled by attacks of nausea and vomiting.
24 No one seems to understand me.
25 I would like to be a singer.
26 I feel that it is certainly best to keep my mouth shut when I'm in trouble.
27 Evil spirits possess me at times.
M **28** When someone does do me a wrong I feel I should pay him back if I can, just for the principle of the thing. [When people do me a wrong, I feel I should pay them back if I can, just for the principle of the thing.]
M **29** I am bothered by acid stomach several times a week. [I am bothered by an upset stomach several times a week.]
30 At times I feel like swearing.

31 I have nightmares every few nights.

32 I find it hard to keep my mind on a task or job.

33 I have had very peculiar and strange experiences.

34 I have a cough most of the time.

35 If people had not had it in for me I would have been much more successful.

36 I seldom worry about my health.

37 I have never been in trouble because of my sex behavior.

M 38 During one period when I was a youngster I engaged in petty thievery. [Sometimes when I was young I stole things.]

39 At times I feel like smashing things.

40 Most any time I would rather sit and daydream than do anything else.

41 I have had periods of days, weeks, or months when I couldn't take care of things because I couldn't "get going."

42 My family does not like the work I have chosen (or the work I intend to choose for my life work).

43 My sleep is fitful and disturbed.

44 Much of the time my head seems to hurt all over.

45 I do not always tell the truth.

46 My judgement is better than it ever was.

M 47 Once a week or oftener I feel suddenly hot all over, without apparent cause. [Once a week or oftener I suddenly feel hot all over, for no real reason.]

M 48 When I am with people, I am bothered by hearing very queer things. [When I am with people, I am bothered by hearing very strange things.]

49 It would be better if almost all laws were thrown away.

50 My soul sometimes leaves my body.

51 I am in just as good physical health as most of my friends.

52 I prefer to pass by school friends, or people I know but have not seen for a long time, unless they speak to me first.

D 53 A minister can cure disease by praying and putting his hand on your head.

54 I am liked by most people who know me.

M 55 I am almost never bothered by pains over the heart or in my chest. [I am almost never bothered by pains over my heart or in my chest.]

M 56 As a youngster I was suspended from school one or more times for cutting up. [I was suspended from school one or more times for bad behavior.]

M 57 I am a good mixer. [I am a very sociable person.]

D 58 Everything is turning out just like the prophets of the Bible said it would.

59 I have often had to take orders from someone who did not know as much as I did.

60 I do not read every editorial in the newspaper every day.

61 I have not lived the right kind of life.

62 Parts of my body often have feelings like burning, tingling, crawling, or like "going to sleep."

D 63 I have had no difficulty in starting or holding my bowel movement.

64 I sometimes keep on at a thing until others lose their patience with me.

M 65 I loved my father. [I love my father, or (if your father is dead) I loved my father.]

66 I see things or animals or people around me that others do not see.

67 I wish I could be as happy as others seem to be.

M 68 I hardly ever feel pain in the back of the neck. [I hardly ever feel pain in the back of my neck.]

D 69 I am very strongly attracted by members of my own sex.

D 70 I used to like drop-the-handkerchief.

71 I think a great many people exaggerate their misfortunes in order to gain the sympathy and help of others.

72 I am troubled by discomfort in the pit of my stomach every few days or oftener.

73 I am an important person.

74 I have often wished I were a girl. (Or if you are a girl) I have never been sorry that I am a girl.

75 I get angry sometimes.

76 Most of the time I feel blue.

77 I enjoy reading love stories.

78 I like poetry.

79 My feelings are not easily hurt.

80 I sometimes tease animals.

81 I think I would like the kind of work a forest ranger does.

82 I am easily downed in an argument.

M 83 Any man who is able and willing to work hard has a good chance of succeeding. [Anyone who is able and willing to work hard has a good chance of succeeding.]

84 These days I find it hard not to give up hope of amounting to something.

85 Sometimes I am strongly attracted by the personal articles of others, such as shoes, gloves, etc., so that I want to handle or steal them though I have no use for them. [Sometimes I am so strongly attracted by the personal articles of others, such as shoes, gloves, etc., that I want to handle or steal them, though I have no use for them.]

86 I am certainly lacking in self-confidence.

87 I would like to be a florist.

88 I usually feel that life is worth while.

89 It takes a lot of argument to convince most people of the truth.

90 Once in a while I put off until tomorrow what I ought to do today.

91 I do not mind being made fun of.

92 I would like to be a nurse.

93 I think most people would lie to get ahead.

M 94 I do many things which I regret afterwards (I regret things more or more often than others seem to). [I do many things which I regret afterwards (I regret things more than others seem to).]

D 95 I go to church almost every week.

96 I have very few quarrels with members of my family.

97 At times I have a strong urge to do something harmful or shocking.

D 98 I believe in the second coming of Christ.

99 I like to go to parties and other affairs where there is lots of loud fun.

100 I have met problems so full of possibilities that I have been unable to make up my mind about them.

101 I believe women ought to have as much sexual freedom as men.

102 My hardest battles are with myself.

103 I have little or no trouble with my muscles twitching or jumping.

104 I don't seem to care what happens to me.

M 105 Sometimes when I am not feeling well I am cross. [Sometimes when I am not feeling well I am irritable.]

106 Much of the time I feel as if I have done something wrong or evil.

107 I am happy most of the time.

108 There seems to be a fullness in my head or nose most of the time.

109 Some people are so bossy that I feel like doing the opposite of what they request, even though I know they are right.

110 Someone has it in for me.

111 I have never done anything dangerous for the thrill of it.

112 I frequently find it necessary to stand up for what I think is right.

113 I believe in law enforcement.

M 114 Often I feel as if there were a tight band about my head. [Often I feel as if there is a tight band around my head.]

115 I believe in a life hereafter.

M 116 I enjoy a race or game better when I bet on it. [I enjoy a race or game more when I bet on it.]

M 117 Most people are honest chiefly through fear of being caught. [Most people are honest chiefly because they are afraid of being caught.]

M 118 In school I was sometimes sent to the principal for cutting up. [In school I was sometimes sent to the principal for bad behavior.]

M 119 My speech is the same as always (not faster or slower, or slurring; no hoarseness). [My speech is the same as always (not faster or slower, no slurring or hoarseness).]

120 My table manners are not quite as good at home as when I am out in company.

121 I believe I am being plotted against.

122 I seem to be about as capable and smart as most others around me.

123 I believe I am being followed.

124 Most people will use somewhat unfair means to gain profit or an advantage rather than to lose it.

125 I have a great deal of stomach trouble.

126 I like dramatics.

127 I know who is responsible for most of my troubles.

M 128 The sight of blood neither frightens me nor makes me sick. [The sight of blood doesn't frighten me or make me sick.]

M 129 Often I can't understand why I have been so cross and grouchy. [Often I can't understand why I have been so irritable and grouchy.]

130 I have never vomited blood or coughed up blood.

131 I do not worry about catching diseases.

132 I like collecting flowers or growing house plants.

133 I have never indulged in any unusual sex practices.

134 At times my thoughts have raced ahead faster than I could speak them.

135 If I could get into a movie without paying and be sure I was not seen I would probably do it.

M 136 I commonly wonder what hidden reason another person may have for doing something nice for me. [I often wonder what hidden reason another person may have for doing something nice for me.]

137 I believe that my home life is as pleasant as that of most people I know.

138 Criticism or scolding hurts me terribly.

139 Sometimes I feel as if I must injure either myself or someone else.

140 I like to cook.

M 141 My conduct is largely controlled by the customs of those about me. [My conduct is largely controlled by the behavior of those around me.]

142 I certainly feel useless at times.

M 143 When I was a child, I belonged to a crowd or gang that tried to stick together through thick and thin. [When I was a child, I belonged to a group of friends that tried to be loyal through all kinds of trouble.]

144 I would like to be a soldier.

145 At times I feel like picking a fist fight with someone.

M 146 I have the wanderlust and am never happy unless I am roaming or traveling about. [I am never happy unless I am roaming or traveling around.]

147 I have often lost out on things because I couldn't make up my mind soon enough.

148 It makes me impatient to have people ask my advice or otherwise interrupt me when I am working on something important.

149 I used to keep a diary.

150 I would rather win than lose in a game.

151 Someone has been trying to poison me.

152 Most nights I go to sleep without thoughts or ideas bothering me.

153 During the past few years I have been well most of the time.

154 I have never had a fit or convulsion.

155 I am neither gaining nor losing weight.

156 I have had periods in which I carried on activities without knowing later what I had been doing.

157 I feel that I have often been punished without cause.

158 I cry easily.

159 I cannot understand what I read as well as I used to.

160 I have never felt better in my life than I do now.

161 The top of my head sometimes feels tender.

M 162 I resent having anyone take me in so cleverly that I have had to admit that it was one on me. [I resent having anyone trick me so cleverly that I have to admit I was fooled.]

163 I do not tire quickly.

164 I like to study and read about things that I am working at.

165 I like to know some important people because it makes me feel important.

166 I am afraid when I look down from a high place.

167 It wouldn't make me nervous if any members of my family got into trouble with the law.

168 There is something wrong with my mind.

169 I am not afraid to handle money.

170 What others think of me does not bother me.

171 It makes me uncomfortable to put on a stunt at a party even when others are doing the same sort of things.

172 I frequently have to fight against showing that I am bashful.

173 I liked school.

174 I have never had a fainting spell.

175 I seldom or never have dizzy spells.

176 I do not have a great fear of snakes.

M 177 My mother was a good woman. [My mother is a good woman, or (if your mother is dead) my mother was a good woman.]

178 My memory seems to be all right.

M **179** I am worried about sex matters. [I am worried about sex.]

180 I find it hard to make talk when I meet new people.

181 When I get bored I like to stir up some excitement.

182 I am afraid of losing my mind.

183 I am against giving money to beggars.

M **184** I commonly hear voices without knowing where they come from. [I often hear voices without knowing where they come from.]

185 My hearing is apparently as good as that of most people.

186 I frequently notice my hand shakes when I try to do something.

187 My hands have not become clumsy or awkward.

188 I can read a long while without tiring my eyes.

189 I feel weak all over much of the time.

190 I have very few headaches.

191 Sometimes, when embarrassed, I break out in a sweat which annoys me greatly.

192 I have had no difficulty in keeping my balance in walking.

193 I do not have spells of hay fever or asthma.

194 I have had attacks in which I could not control my movements or speech but in which I knew what was going on around me.

195 I do not like everyone I know.

196 I like to visit places where I have never been before.

197 Someone has been trying to rob me.

198 I daydream very little.

199 Children should be taught all the main facts of sex.

200 There are persons who are trying to steal my thoughts and ideas.

201 I wish I were not so shy.

202 I believe I am a condemned person.

203 If I were a reporter I would very much like to report news of the theater.

204 I would like to be a journalist.

205 At times it has been impossible for me to keep from stealing or shoplifting something.

D **206** I am very religious (more than most people).

207 I enjoy many different kinds of play and recreation.

208 I like to flirt.

209 I believe my sins are unpardonable.

210 Everything tastes the same.

211 I can sleep during the day but not at night.

212 My people treat me more like a child than a grown-up.

213 In walking I am very careful to step over sidewalk cracks.

214 I have never had any breaking out on my skin that has worried me.

215 I have used alcohol excessively.

216 There is very little love and companionship in my family as compared to other homes.

217 I frequently find myself worrying about something.

218 It does not bother me particularly to see animals suffer.

219 I think I would like the work of a building contractor.

M **220** I loved my mother. [I love my mother, or (if your mother is dead) I loved my mother.]

221 I like science.

222 It is not hard for me to ask help from my friends even though I cannot return the favor.

223 I very much like hunting.

M **224** My parents have often objected to the kind of people I went around with. [My parents often objected to the kind of people I went around with.]

225 I gossip a little at times.

226 Some of my family have habits that bother and annoy me very much.

227 I have been told that I walk during sleep.

228 At times I feel that I can make up my mind with unusually great ease.

M **229** I should like to belong to several clubs or lodges. [I would like to belong to several clubs.]

230 I hardly ever notice my heart pounding and I am seldom short of breath.

231 I like to talk about sex.

232 I have been inspired to a program of life based on duty which I have since carefully followed.

233 I have at times stood in the way of people who were trying to do something, not because it amounted to much but because of the principle of the thing.

234 I get mad easily and then get over it soon.

235 I have been quite independent and free from family rule.

236 I brood a great deal.

237 My relatives are nearly all in sympathy with me.

238 I have periods of such great restlessness that I cannot sit long in a chair.

239 I have been disappointed in love.

240 I never worry about my looks.

241 I dream frequently about things that are best kept to myself.

242 I believe I am no more nervous than most others.

243 I have few or no pains.

244 My way of doing things is apt to be misunderstood by others.

245 My parents and family find more fault with me than they should.

246 My neck spots with red often.

247 I have reason for feeling jealous of one or more members of my family.

248 Sometimes without any reason or even when things are going wrong I feel excitedly happy, "on top of the world."

D **249** I believe there is a Devil and a Hell in afterlife.

M **250** I don't blame anyone for trying to grab everything he can get in this world. [I don't blame people for trying to grab everything they can get in this world.]

251 I have had blank spells in which my activities were interrupted and I did not know what was going on around me.

252 No one cares much what happens to you.

253 I can be friendly with people who do things which I consider wrong.

254 I like to be with a crowd who play jokes on one another.

M **255** Sometimes at elections I vote for men about whom I know very little. [Sometimes in elections I vote for people about whom I know very little.]

M **256** The only interesting part of newspapers is the "funnies." [The only interesting part of newspapers is the comic strips.]

257 I usually expect to succeed in things I do.

D **258** I believe there is a God.

259 I have difficulty in starting to do things.

260 I was a slow learner in school.

261 If I were an artist I would like to draw flowers.

262 It does not bother me that I am not better looking.

263 I sweat very easily even on cool days.

264 I am entirely self-confident.

265 It is safer to trust nobody.

266 Once a week or oftener I become very excited.

267 When in a group of people I have trouble thinking of the right things to talk about.

268 Something exciting will almost always pull me out of it when I am feeling low.

269 I can easily make other people afraid of me, and sometimes do for the fun of it.

270 When I leave home I do not worry about whether the door is locked and the windows closed.

M **271** I do not blame a person for taking advantage of someone who lays himself open to it. [I do not blame a person for taking advantage of people who leave themselves open to it.]

272 At times I am all full of energy.

M **273** I have numbness in one or more regions of my skin. [I have numbness in one or more places on my skin.]

274 My eyesight is as good as it has been for years.

275 Someone has control over my mind.

276 I enjoy children.

M **277** At times I have been so entertained by the cleverness of a crook that I have hoped they would get by with it. [At times I have been so entertained by the cleverness of some criminals that I have hoped they would get away with it.]

278 I have often felt that strangers were looking at me critically.

279 I drink an unusually large amount of water every day.

280 Most people make friends because friends are likely to be useful to them.

281 I do not often notice my ears ringing or buzzing.

282 Once in a while I feel hate toward members of my family whom I usually love.

283 If I were a reporter I would very much like to report sporting news.

284 I am sure I am being talked about.

285 Once in a while I laugh at a dirty joke.

286 I am never happier than when alone.

287 I have very few fears compared to my friends.

R **288** I am troubled by attacks of nausea and vomiting.

289 I am always disgusted with the law when a criminal is freed through the arguments of a smart lawyer.

R **290** I work under a great deal of tension.

291 At one or more times in my life I felt that someone was making me do things by hypnotizing me.

292 I am likely not to speak to people until they speak to me.

293 Someone has been trying to influence my mind.

294 I have never been in trouble with the law.

D **295** I liked "Alice in Wonderland" by Lewis Carroll.

296 I have periods in which I feel unusually cheerful without any special reason.

297 I wish I were not bothered by thoughts about sex.

298 If several people find themselves in trouble, the best thing for them to do is to agree upon a story and stick to it.

299 I think that I feel more intensely than most people do.

300 There never was a time in my life when I liked to play with dolls.

301 Life is a strain for me much of the time.

R **302** I have never been in trouble because of my sex behavior.

303 I am so touchy on some subjects that I can't talk about them.

M **304** In school I found it very hard to talk before the class. [In school I found it very hard to talk in front of the class.]

305 Even when I am with people I feel lonely much of the time.

306 I get all the sympathy I should.

307 I refuse to play some games because I am not good at them.

R **308** At times I have very much wanted to leave home.

309 I seem to make friends about as quickly as others do.

R **310** My sex life is satisfactory.

R **311** During one period when I was a youngster I engaged in petty thievery.

M **312** I dislike having people about me. [I dislike having people around me.]

M **313** The man who provides temptation by leaving valuable property unprotected is about as much to blame for its theft as the one who steals it. [The person who provides temptation by leaving valuable property unprotected is about as much to blame for its theft as the one who steals it.]

R **314** Once in a while I think of things too bad to talk about.

R **315** I am sure I get a raw deal from life.

316 I think nearly anyone would tell a lie to keep out of trouble.

317 I am more sensitive than most other people.

R **318** My daily life is full of things that keep me interested.

319 Most people inwardly dislike putting themselves out to help other people.

M **320** Many of my dreams are about sex matters. [Many of my dreams are about sex.]

321 I am easily embarrassed.

322 I worry over money and business.

R **323** I have had very peculiar and strange experiences.

324 I have never been in love with anyone.

325 The things that some of my family have done have frightened me.

R **326** At times I have fits of laughing and crying that I cannot control.

327 My mother or father often made me obey even when I thought that it was unreasonable.

R **328** I find it hard to keep my mind on a task or job.

329 I almost never dream.

330 I have never been paralyzed or had any unusual weakness of any of my muscles.

R **331** If people had not had it in for me I would have been much more successful.

332 Sometimes my voice leaves me or changes even though I have no cold.

R **333** No one seems to understand me.

334 Peculiar odors come to me at times.

335 I cannot keep my mind on one thing.

336 I easily become impatient with people.

337 I feel anxiety about something or someone almost all the time.

338 I have certainly had more than my share of things to worry about.

339 Most of the time I wish I were dead.

340 Sometimes I become so excited that I find it hard to get to sleep.

341 At times I hear so well it bothers me.

342 I forget right away what people say to me.

M **343** I usually have to stop and think before I act even in trifling matters. [I usually have to stop and think before I act even in small matters.]

344 Often I cross the street in order not to meet someone I see.

M **345** I often feel as if things were not real. [I often feel as if things are not real.]

346 I have a habit of counting things that are not important such as bulbs on electric signs, and so forth.

347 I have no enemies who really wish to harm me.

348 I tend to be on my guard with people who are somewhat more friendly than I had expected.

349 I have strange and peculiar thoughts.

350 I hear strange things when I am alone.

351 I get anxious and upset when I have to make a short trip away from home.

352 I have been afraid of things or people that I knew could not hurt me.

353 I have no dread of going into a room by myself where other people have already gathered and are talking.

354 I am afraid of using a knife or anything very sharp or pointed.

355 Sometimes I enjoy hurting persons I love.

356 I have more trouble concentrating than others seem to have.

357 I have several times given up doing a thing because I thought too little of my ability.

358 Bad words, often terrible words, come into my mind and I cannot get rid of them.

359 Sometimes some unimportant thought will run through my mind and bother me for days.

360 Almost every day something happens to frighten me.

361 I am inclined to take things hard.

R **362** I am more sensitive than most other people.

363 At times I have enjoyed being hurt by someone I loved.

364 People say insulting and vulgar things about me.

365 I feel uneasy indoors.

R **366** Even when I am with people I feel lonely much of the time.

367 I am not afraid of fire.

368 I have sometimes stayed away from another person because I feared doing or saying something that I might regret afterwards.

D **369** Religion gives me no worry.

D **370** I hate to have to rush when working.

371 I am not unusually self-conscious.

D **372** I tend to be interested in several different hobbies rather than to stick to one of them for a long time.

D **373** I feel sure that there is only one true religion.

374 At periods my mind seems to work more slowly than usual.

D **375** When I am feeling very happy and active, someone who is blue or low will spoil it all.

D **376** Policemen are usually honest.

377 At parties I am more likely to sit by myself or with just one other person than to join in with the crowd.

D **378** I do not like to see women smoke.

379 I very seldom have spells of the blues.

D **380** When someone says silly or ignorant things about something I know about, I try to set him straight.

381 I am often said to be hotheaded.

382 I wish I could get over worrying about things I have said that may have injured other people's feelings.

383 People often disappoint me.

384 I feel unable to tell anyone all about myself.

385 Lightning is one of my fears.

386 I like to keep people guessing what I'm going to do next.

D **387** The only miracles I know of are simply tricks that people play on one another.

388 I am afraid to be alone in the dark.

389 My plans have frequently seemed so full of difficulties that I have had to give them up.

M 390 I have often felt badly over being misunderstood when trying to keep someone from making a mistake. [I have often felt bad about being misunderstood when trying to keep someone from making a mistake.]

391 I love to go to dances.

392 A windstorm terrifies me.

D 393 Horses that don't pull should be beaten or kicked.

394 I frequently ask people for advice.

395 The future is too uncertain for a person to make serious plans.

396 Often, even though everything is going fine for me, I feel that I don't care about anything.

397 I have sometimes felt that difficulties were piling up so high that I could not overcome them.

398 I often think, "I wish I were a child again."

399 I am not easily angered.

400 If given the chance I could do some things that would be of great benefit to the world.

401 I have no fear of water.

402 I often must sleep over a matter before I decide what to do.

D 403 It is great to be living in these times when so much is going on.

404 People have often misunderstood my intentions when I was trying to put them right and be helpful.

405 I have no trouble swallowing.

406 I have often met people who were supposed to be experts who were no better than I.

407 I am usually calm and not easily upset.

D 408 I am apt to hide my feelings in some things, to the point that people may hurt me without their knowing about it.

D 409 At times I have worn myself out by undertaking too much.

M 410 I would certainly enjoy beating a crook at his own game. [I would certainly enjoy beating criminals at their own game.]

411 It makes me feel like a failure when I hear of the success of someone I know well.

D 412 I do not dread seeing a doctor about a sickness or injury.

413 I deserve severe punishment for my sins.

414 I am apt to take disappointments so keenly that I can't put them out of my mind.

415 If given the chance I would make a good leader of people.

416 It bothers me to have someone watch me at work even though I know I can do it well.

M 417 I am often so annoyed when someone tries to get ahead of me in a line of people that I speak to him about it. [I am often so annoyed when someone tries to get ahead of me in a line of people that I speak to that person about it.]

418 At times I think I am no good at all.

M 419 I played hooky from school quite often as a youngster. [When I was young I often did not go to school even when I should have gone.]

D 420 I have had some very unusual religious experiences.

M 421 One or more members of my family is very nervous. [One or more members of my family are very nervous.]

D 422 I have felt embarrassed over the type of work that one or more members of my family have done.

D 423 I like or have liked fishing very much.

D 424 I feel hungry almost all the time.

D 425 I dream frequently.

426 I have at times had to be rough with people who were rude or annoying.

427 I am embarrassed by dirty stories.

D 428 I like to read newspaper editorials.

D 429 I like to attend lectures on serious subjects.

D 430 I am attracted by members of the opposite sex.

431 I worry quite a bit over possible misfortunes.

432 I have strong political opinions.

D 433 I used to have imaginary companions.

434 I would like to be an auto racer.

D 435 Usually I would prefer to work with women.

436 People generally demand more respect for their own rights than they are willing to allow for others.

437 It is all right to get around the law if you don't actually break it.

438 There are certain people whom I dislike so much that I am inwardly pleased when they are catching it for something they have done.

439 It makes me nervous to have to wait.

440 I try to remember good stories to pass them on to other people.

D **441** I like tall women.

D **442** I have had periods in which I lost sleep over worry.

443 I am apt to pass up something I want to do because others feel that I am not going about it in the right way.

D **444** I do not try to correct people who express an ignorant belief.

M **445** I was fond of excitement when I was young (or in childhood). [I was fond of excitement when I was young.]

446 I enjoy gambling for small stakes.

447 I am often inclined to go out of my way to win a point with someone who has opposed me.

M **448** I am bothered by people outside, on the street-cars, in stores, etc., watching me. [I am bothered by people outside, on the streets, in stores, etc., watching me.]

449 I enjoy social gatherings just to be with people.

450 I enjoy the excitement of a crowd.

451 My worries seem to disappear when I get into a crowd of lively friends.

D **452** I like to poke fun at people.

D **453** When I was a child I didn't care to be a member of a crowd or gang.

D **454** I could be happy living all alone in a cabin in the woods or mountains.

455 I am quite often not in on the gossip and talk of the group I belong to.

D **456** A person shouldn't be punished for breaking a law that he thinks is unreasonable.

D **457** I believe that a person should never taste an alcoholic drink.

458 The man who had most to do with me when I was a child (such as my father, step-father, etc.) was very strict with me.

D **459** I have one or more bad habits which are so strong it is no use fighting against them.

D **460** I have used alcohol moderately (or not at all).

461 I find it hard to set aside a task that I have undertaken, even for a short time.

D **462** I have had no difficulty starting or holding my urine.

M **463** I used to like hopscotch. [I used to like to play hopscotch and jump rope.]

464 I have never seen a vision.

465 I have several times had a change of heart about my life work.

M **466** Except by a doctor's orders I never take drugs or sleeping powders. [Except by doctor's orders I never take drugs or sleeping pills.]

D **467** I often memorize numbers that are not important (such as automobile licenses, etc.).

M **468** I am often sorry because I am so cross and grouchy. [I am often sorry because I am so irritable and grouchy.]

469 I have often found people jealous of my good ideas, just because they had not thought of them first.

D **470** Sexual things disgust me.

M **471** In school my marks in deportment were quite regularly bad. [In school my marks in classroom behavior were quite regularly bad.]

472 I am fascinated by fire.

473 Whenever possible I avoid being in a crowd.

D **474** I have to urinate no more often than others.

475 When I am cornered I tell that portion of the truth which is not likely to hurt me.

D **476** I am a special agent of God.

M **477** If I were in trouble with several friends who were equally to blame, I would rather take the whole blame than to give them away. [If I was in trouble with several friends who were as guilty as I was, I would rather take the whole blame than give them away.]

D **478** I have never been made especially nervous over trouble that any members of my family have gotten into.

479 I do not mind meeting strangers.

480 I am often afraid of the dark.

481 I can remember "playing sick" to get out of something.

482 While in trains, busses, etc., I often talk to strangers.

D **483** Christ performed miracles such as changing water into wine.

D **484** I have one or more faults which are so big that it seems better to accept them and try to control them rather than to try to get rid of them.

485 When a man is with a woman he is usually thinking about things related to her sex.

D **486** I have never noticed any blood in my urine.

487 I feel like giving up quickly when things go wrong.

D 488 I pray several times every week.

D 489 I feel sympathetic towards people who tend to hang on to their griefs and troubles.

D 490 I read in the Bible several times a week.

D 491 I have no patience with people who believe there is only one true religion.

492 I dread the thought of an earthquake.

D 493 I prefer work which requires close attention, to work which allows me to be careless.

494 I am afraid of finding myself in a closet or small closed place.

M 495 I usually "lay my cards on the table" with people I am trying to correct or improve. [I am usually very direct with people I am trying to correct or improve.]

D 496 I have never seen things doubled (that is, an object never looks like two objects to me without my being able to make it look like one object).

D 497 I enjoy stories of adventure.

D 498 It is always a good thing to be frank.

499 I must admit that I have at times been worried beyond reason over something that really did not matter.

500 I readily become one hundred per cent sold on a good idea.

501 I usually work things out for myself rather than get someone to show me how.

502 I like to let people know where I stand on things.

D 503 It is unusual for me to express strong approval or disapproval of the actions of others.

M 504 I do not try to cover up my poor opinion or pity of a person so that he won't know how I feel. [I do not try to cover up my poor opinion or pity of people so that they won't know how I feel.]

505 I have had periods when I felt so full of pep that sleep did not seem necessary for days at a time.

506 I am a high-strung person.

507 I have frequently worked under people who seem to have things arranged so that they get credit for good work but are able to pass off mistakes onto those under them.

D 508 I believe my sense of smell is as good as other people's.

509 I sometimes find it hard to stick up for my rights because I am so reserved.

510 Dirt frightens or disgusts me.

511 I have a daydream life about which I do not tell other people.

D 512 I dislike to take a bath.

D 513 I think Lincoln was greater than Washington.

D 514 I like mannish women.

D 515 In my home we have always had the ordinary necessities (such as enough food, clothing, etc.).

516 Some of my family have quick tempers.

517 I cannot do anything well.

M 518 I have often felt guilty because I have pretended to feel more sorry about something than I really was. [I often feel guilty because I pretend to feel more sorry about something than I really do.]

D 519 There is something wrong with my sex organs.

520 I strongly defend my own opinions as a rule.

521 In a group of people I would not be embarrassed to be called upon to start a discussion or give an opinion about something I know well.

522 I have no fear of spiders.

D 523 I practically never blush.

D 524 I am not afraid of picking up a disease or germs from door knobs.

525 I am made nervous by certain animals.

526 The future seems hopeless to me.

527 The members of my family and my close relatives get along quite well.

D 528 I blush no more often than others.

529 I would like to wear expensive clothes.

D 530 I am often afraid that I am going to blush.

M 531 People can pretty easily change me even though I thought that my mind was already made up on a subject. [People can pretty easily change my mind even when I have made a decision about something.]

532 I can stand as much pain as others can.

D 533 I am not bothered by a great deal of belching of gas from my stomach.

534 Several times I have been the last to give up trying to do a thing.

D 535 My mouth feels dry almost all the time.

536 It makes me angry to have people hurry me.

D 537 I would like to hunt lions in Africa.

D 538 I think I would like the work of a dressmaker.

539 I am not afraid of mice.

D 540 My face has never been paralyzed.
D 541 My skin seems to be unusually sensitive to touch.
D 542 I have never had any black, tarry-looking bowel movements.
543 Several times a week I feel as if something dreadful is about to happen.
544 I feel tired a good deal of the time.
D 545 Sometimes I have the same dream over and over.
D 546 I like to read about history.
547 I like parties and socials.
D 548 I never attend a sexy show if I can avoid it.
549 I shrink from facing a crisis or difficulty.
550 I like repairing a door latch.
551 Sometimes I am sure that other people can tell what I am thinking.
552 I like to read about science.
553 I am afraid of being alone in a wide-open place.
D 554 If I were an artist I would like to draw children.
555 I sometimes feel that I am about to go to pieces.
D 556 I am very careful about my manner of dress.
D 557 I would like to be a private secretary.
558 A large number of people are guilty of bad sexual conduct.
559 I have often been frightened in the middle of the night.
560 I am greatly bothered by forgetting where I put things.
D 561 I very much like horseback riding.
562 The one to whom I was most attached and whom I most admired as a child was a woman (mother, sister, aunt, or other woman.)
563 I like adventure stories better than romantic stories.
564 I am apt to pass up something I want to do when others feel that it isn't worth doing.
D 565 I feel like jumping off when I am on a high place.
D 566 I like movie love scenes.

MMPI-2 NEW ITEMS (107)

371 I have often wished I were a member of the opposite sex.
373 I have done some bad things in the past that I never tell anybody about.
374 Most people will use somewhat unfair means to get ahead in life.
375 It makes me nervous when people ask me personal questions.
376 I do not feel I can plan my own future.
377 I am not happy with myself the way I am.
378 I get angry when my friends or family give me advice on how to live my life.
379 I got many beatings when I was a child.
380 It bothers me when people say nice things about me.
381 I don't like hearing other people give their opinions about life.
382 I often have serious disagreements with people who are close to me.
383 When things get really bad, I know I can count on my family for help.
384 I liked playing "house" when I was a child.
387 I can express my true feelings only when I drink.
475 Often I get confused and forget what I want to say.
476 I am very awkward and clumsy.
477 I really like playing rough sports (such as football or soccer).
478 I hate my whole family.
479 Some people think it's hard to get to know me.
480 I spend most of my spare time by myself.
481 When people do something that makes me angry, I let them know how I feel about it.
482 I usually have a hard time deciding what to do.
483 People do not find me attractive.
484 People are not very kind to me.
485 I often feel that I'm not as good as other people.
486 I am very stubborn.
487 I have enjoyed using marijuana.
488 Mental illness is a sign of weakness.
489 I have a drug or alcohol problem.
490 Ghosts or spirits can influence people for good or bad.
491 I feel helpless when I have to make some important decisions.
492 I always try to be pleasant even when others are upset or critical.
493 When I have a problem it helps to talk it over with someone.

494 My main goals in life are within my reach.
495 I believe that people should keep personal problems to themselves.
496 I am not feeling much pressure or stress these days.
497 It bothers me greatly to think of making changes in my life.
498 My greatest problems are caused by the behavior of someone close to me.
499 I hate going to doctors even when I'm sick.
500 Although I am not happy with my life, there is nothing I can do about it now.
501 Talking over problems and worries with someone is often more helpful than taking drugs or medicine.
502 I have some habits that are really harmful.
503 When problems need to be solved, I usually let other people take charge.
504 I recognize several faults in myself that I will not be able to change.
505 I am so sick of what I have to do every day that I just want to get out of it all.
506 I have recently considered killing myself.
507 I often become very irritable when people interrupt my work.
508 I often feel I can read other people's minds.
509 Having to make important decisions makes me nervous.
510 Others tell me I eat too fast.
511 Once a week or more I get high or drunk.
512 I have had a tragic loss in my life that I know I'll never get over.
513 Sometimes I get so angry and upset I don't know what comes over me.
514 When people ask me to do something I have a hard time saying no.
515 I am never happier than when I am by myself.
516 My life is empty and meaningless.
517 I find it difficult to hold down a job.
518 I have made lots of bad mistakes in my life.
519 I get angry with myself for giving in to other people so much.
520 Lately I have thought a lot about killing myself.
521 I like making decisions and assigning jobs to others.
522 Even without my family I know there will always be someone there to take care of me.
523 At movies, restaurants, or sporting events, I hate to have to stand in line.
524 No one knows it but I have tried to kill myself.
525 Everything is going on too fast around me.
526 I know I am a burden to others.
527 After a bad day, I usually need a few drinks to relax.
528 Much of the trouble I'm having is due to bad luck.
529 At times I can't seem to stop talking.
530 Sometimes I cut or injure myself on purpose without knowing why.
531 I work very long hours even though my job doesn't require this.
532 I usually feel better after a good cry.
533 I forget where I leave things.
534 If I could live my life over again, I would not change much.
535 I get very irritable when people I depend on don't get their work done on time.
536 If I get upset I'm sure to get a headache.
537 I like to drive a hard bargain.
538 Most men are unfaithful to their wives now and then.
539 Lately I have lost my desire to work out my problems.
540 I have gotten angry and broken furniture or dishes when I was drinking.
541 I work best when I have a definite deadline.
542 I have become so angry with someone that I have felt as if I would explode.
543 Terrible thoughts about my family come to me at times.
544 People tell me I have a problem with alcohol, but I disagree.
545 I always have too little time to get things done.
546 My thoughts these days turn more and more to death and the life hereafter.
547 I often keep and save things that I will probably never use.
548 I've been so angry at times that I've hurt someone in a physical fight.
549 In everything I do lately I feel that I am being tested.
550 I have very little to do with my relatives now.
551 I sometimes seem to hear my thoughts being spoken out loud.

552 When I am sad, visiting with friends can always pull me out of it.
553 Much of what is happening to me now seems to have happened to me before.
554 When my life gets difficult, it makes me want to just give up.
555 I can't go into a dark room alone even in my own home.
556 I worry a great deal over money.
557 The man should be the head of the family.
558 The only place where I feel relaxed is in my own home.
559 The people I work with are not sympathetic with my problems.
560 I am satisfied with the amount of money I make.
561 I usually have enough energy to do my work.
562 It is hard for me to accept compliments.
563 In most marriages one or both partners are unhappy.
564 I almost never lose self-control.
565 It takes a great deal of effort for me to remember what people tell me these days.
566 When I am sad or blue, it is my work that suffers.
567 Most married couples don't show much affection for each other.

MMPI-A ITEMS

1: Items appearing on the original MMPI
2: Items appearing on the MMPI-2
N: New items appearing only on the MMPI-A
R1: Items appearing on the original MMPI, not on the MMPI-2, but rewritten from the original MMPI
R2: Rewritten items from the MMPI-2
R*: Rewritten items from MMPI-2, but the same as original MMPI items

1 2 **1** I like mechanics magazines.
1 2 **2** I have a good appetite.
1 2 **3** I wake up fresh and rested most mornings.
1 2 **4** I seldom worry about my health.
1 2 **5** I am easily awakened by noise.
1 2 **6** My father is a good man, or (if your father is dead) my father was a good man.
1 2 **7** I like to read newspaper articles on crime.
1 2 **8** My hands and feet are usually warm enough.
1 2 **9** My daily life is full of things that keep me interested.
1 2 **10** I am about as able to work as I ever was.
1 2 **11** There seems to be a lump in my throat much of the time.
N **12** My teachers have it in for me.
1 2 **13** I enjoy detective or mystery stories.
1 2 **14** I work under a great deal of tension.
1 2 **15** Once in a while I think of things too bad to talk about.
1 2 **16** I am sure I get a raw deal from life.
1 2 **17** I am troubled by attacks of nausea and vomiting.
1 2 **18** I am very seldom troubled by constipation.
1 2 **19** At times I have very much wanted to leave home.
1 2 **20** No one seems to understand me.
1 2 **21** At times I have fits of laughing and crying that I cannot control.
1 2 **22** Evil spirits possess me at times.
1 2 **23** I feel that it is certainly best to keep my mouth shut when I'm in trouble.
1 2 **24** When people do me a wrong, I feel I should pay them back if I can, just for the principle of the thing.
1 2 **25** I am bothered by an upset stomach several times a week.
1 2 **26** At times I feel like swearing.
1 2 **27** I shrink from facing a crisis or difficulty.
1 2 **28** I find it hard to keep my mind on a task or job.
1 2 **29** I have had very peculiar and strange experiences.
N **30** Sometimes I use laxatives so I won't gain weight.
1 2 **31** I have never been in trouble because of my sex behavior.
1 2 R2 **32** I have sometimes stolen things.
N **33** I'm afraid to go to school.
1 2 **34** At times I feel like smashing things.
1 2 **35** I have had periods of days, weeks, or months when I couldn't take care of things because I couldn't "get going."
1 2 **36** My sleep is fitful and disturbed.
1 2 **37** Much of the time my head seems to hurt all over.

1 2 38 I do not always tell the truth.
1 2 R2 39 If people had not had it in for me, I would be much more successful.
1 2 40 My judgment is better than it ever was.
1 2 41 Once a week or oftener I suddenly feel hot all over, for no real reason.
1 2 42 I am in just as good physical health as most of my friends.
1 2 R2 43 I prefer to pass by people I know but have not seen for a long time, unless they speak to me first.
1 2 44 I am almost never bothered by pains over my heart or in my chest.
1 2 45 Most anytime I would rather sit and daydream than do anything else.
1 2 46 I am a very sociable person.
1 2 47 I have often had to take orders from someone who did not know as much as I did.
1 2 48 I do not read every editorial in the newspaper every day.
1 2 49 I have not lived the right kind of life.
1 2 R2 50 Parts of my body often feel like they are burning, tingling, or "going to sleep."
1 2 R2 51 My family doesn't like the kind of work I plan to do.
1 2 52 I sometimes keep on at a thing until others lose their patience with me.
1 2 53 I wish I could be as happy as others seem to be.
1 2 54 I hardly ever feel pain in the back of my neck.
1 2 55 I think a great many people exaggerate their misfortunes in order to gain the sympathy and help of others.
1 2 56 I am troubled by discomfort in the pit of my stomach every few days or oftener.
N 57 My parents do not like my friends.
1 2 58 I am an important person.
1 2 59 I have often wished I were a girl. (Or if you are a girl) I have never been sorry that I am a girl.
1 2 60 My feelings are not easily hurt.
1 2 61 I enjoy reading love stories.
1 2 62 Most of the time I feel blue.
1 2 63 It would be better if almost all laws were thrown away.
1 2 64 I like poetry.
1 2 65 I sometimes tease animals.
1 2 66 I think I would like the kind of work a forest ranger does.
1 2 67 I am easily downed in an argument.
1 2 68 These days I find it hard not to give up hope of amounting to something.
N 69 I think school is a waste of time.
1 2 70 I am certainly lacking in self-confidence.
1 2 71 I usually feel that life is worthwhile.
1 2 72 It takes a lot of argument to convince most people of the truth.
1 2 73 Once in a while I put off until tomorrow what I ought to do today.
1 2 74 I am liked by most people who know me.
1 2 75 I do not mind being made fun of.
1 2 76 I would like to be a nurse.
1 2 77 I think most people would lie to get ahead.
1 2 R* 78 I do many things which I regret afterwards (I regret things more or more often than others seem to).
1 2 79 I have very few quarrels with members of my family.
1 2 80 I have been suspended from school one or more times for bad behavior.
1 2 81 At times I have a strong urge to do something harmful or shocking.
1 2 82 I like to go to parties and other affairs where there is lots of loud fun.
1 2 83 I have met problems so full of possibilities that I have been unable to make up my mind about them.
1 2 84 I believe women ought to have as much sexual freedom as men.
1 2 85 My hardest battles are with myself.
1 2 86 I love my father, or (if your father is dead) I loved my father.
1 2 87 I have little or no trouble with my muscles twitching or jumping.
1 2 88 I don't seem to care what happens to me.
1 2 89 Sometimes when I am not feeling well I am irritable.
1 2 90 Much of the time I feel as if I have done something wrong or evil.
1 2 91 I am happy most of the time.

1 2 **92** I see things or animals or people around me that others do not see.

1 2 **93** There seems to be a fullness in my head or nose most of the time.

1 2 **94** Some people are so bossy that I feel like doing the opposite of what they request, even though I know they are right.

1 2 **95** Someone has it in for me.

1 2 **96** I have never done anything dangerous for the thrill of it.

1 2 **97** Often I feel as if there is a tight band around my head.

1 2 **98** I get angry sometimes.

1 2 **99** I enjoy a race or game more when I bet on it.

1 2 **100** Most people are honest chiefly because they are afraid of being caught.

1 2 R2 **101** In school I have sometimes been sent to the principal for bad behavior.

1 2 **102** My speech is the same as always (not faster or slower, no slurring or hoarseness).

1 2 **103** My table manners are not quite as good at home as when I am out in company.

1 2 **104** Anyone who is able and willing to work hard has a good chance of succeeding.

1 2 **105** I seem to be about as capable and smart as most others around me.

1 2 **106** I have a great deal of stomach trouble.

1 2 R2 **107** Most people will use somewhat unfair means to get what they want.

N **108** Sometimes I make myself throw up after eating so I won't gain weight.

1 2 **109** I know who is responsible for most of my troubles.

1 2 **110** The sight of blood doesn't frighten me or make me sick.

1 2 **111** Often I can't understand why I have been so irritable and grouchy.

1 2 **112** I do not worry about catching diseases.

1 2 **113** I have never vomited blood or coughed up blood.

1 2 **114** I like collecting flowers or growing house plants.

1 2 **115** I frequently find it necessary to stand up for what I think is right.

1 2 **116** At times my thoughts have raced ahead faster than I could speak them.

1 2 **117** If I could get into a movie without paying and be sure I was not seen, I would probably do it.

1 2 **118** I often wonder what hidden reason another person may have for doing something nice for me.

1 2 **119** I believe that my home life is as pleasant as that of most people I know.

1 2 **120** I believe in law enforcement.

1 2 **121** Criticism or scolding hurts me terribly.

1 2 **122** I like to cook.

1 2 R2 **123** My conduct is mostly controlled by the behavior of those around me.

1 2 **124** I certainly feel useless at times.

1 2 R2 **125** I belong to a group of friends who try to stick together through all kinds of trouble.

1 2 **126** I believe in a life hereafter.

1 2 **127** I would like to be a soldier.

1 2 **128** At times I feel like picking a fist fight with someone.

1 2 **129** I have often lost out on things because I couldn't make up my mind soon enough.

1 2 **130** It makes me impatient to have people ask my advice or otherwise interrupt me when I am working on something important.

1 2 R2 **131** I keep a diary.

1 2 **132** I believe I am being plotted against.

1 2 **133** I would rather win than lose in a game.

1 2 **134** Most nights I go to sleep without thoughts or ideas bothering me.

1 2 **135** During the past few years I have been well most of the time.

1 2 **136** I believe I am being followed.

1 2 **137** I feel that I have often been punished without cause.

1 2 **138** I have never had a fit or convulsion.

1 2 **139** I cry easily.

1 2 **140** I am neither gaining nor losing weight.

1 2 **141** I cannot understand what I read as well as I used to.

1 2 142 I have never felt better in my life than I do now.
1 2 143 The top of my head sometimes feels tender.
2 R2 144 I have a problem with alcohol or drugs.
1 2 145 I resent having anyone trick me so cleverly that I have to admit I was fooled.
1 2 146 I do not tire quickly.
1 2 147 I like to know some important people because it makes me feel important.
1 2 148 I am afraid when I look down from a high place.
1 2 149 It wouldn't make me nervous if any members of my family got into trouble with the law.
1 2 150 What others think of me does not bother me.
1 2 151 It makes me uncomfortable to put on a stunt at a party even when others are doing the same sort of things.
1 2 152 I have never had a fainting spell.
1 2 R2 153 I like school.
1 2 154 I frequently have to fight against showing that I am bashful.
1 2 155 Someone has been trying to poison me.
1 2 156 I do not have a great fear of snakes.
1 2 157 I seldom or never have dizzy spells.
1 2 158 My memory seems to be all right.
1 2 159 I am worried about sex.
1 2 160 I find it hard to make talk when I meet new people.
1 2 161 I have had periods in which I carried on activities without knowing later what I had been doing.
1 2 162 When I get bored I like to stir up some excitement.
1 2 163 I am afraid of losing my mind.
1 2 164 I am against giving money to beggars.
1 2 165 I frequently notice my hand shakes when I try to do something.
1 2 166 I can read a long while without tiring my eyes.
1 2 167 I feel weak all over much of the time.
1 2 168 I have very few headaches.
1 2 169 My hands have not become clumsy or awkward.
1 2 170 I like to study and read about things that I am working at.
1 2 171 Sometimes, when embarrassed, I break out in a sweat which annoys me greatly.
1 2 172 I have had no difficulty in keeping my balance in walking.
1 2 173 There is something wrong with my mind.
1 2 174 I do not have spells of hay fever or asthma.
1 2 175 I have had attacks in which I could not control my movements or speech but in which I knew what was going on around me.
1 2 176 I do not like everyone I know.
N 177 I sometimes think about killing myself.
1 2 178 I wish I were not so shy.
1 2 179 I enjoy many different kinds of play and recreation.
1 2 180 I like to flirt.
1 2 R2 181 My family treats me like a child.
1 2 182 My mother is a good woman, or (if your mother is dead) my mother was a good woman.
1 2 183 In walking I am very careful to step over sidewalk cracks.
1 2 184 There is very little love and companionship in my family as compared to other homes.
1 2 185 I frequently find myself worrying about something.
1 2 186 I think I would like the work of a building contractor.
N 187 I have a physical problem that keeps me from enjoying activities after school.
1 2 188 I like science.
1 2 189 It is not hard for me to ask help from my friends even though I cannot return the favor.
1 2 190 I very much like hunting.
1 2 R2 191 My parents often object to the kind of people I go around with.
1 2 192 I gossip a little at times.
1 2 193 My hearing is apparently as good as that of most people.

1 2 **194** Some of my family have habits that bother and annoy me very much.
1 2 **195** At times I feel that I can make up my mind with unusually great ease.
1 2 **196** I hardly ever notice my heart pounding and I am seldom short of breath.
1 2 **197** I like to talk about sex.
1 2 **198** I like to visit places where I have never been before.
1 2 **199** I have been inspired to a program of life based on duty which I have since carefully followed.
1 2 **200** I have at times stood in the way of people who were trying to do something, not because it amounted to much but because of the principle of the thing.
1 2 **201** I get mad easily and then get over it soon.
1 2 **202** I have been quite independent and free from family rule.
1 2 **203** I brood a great deal.
1 2 **204** My relatives are nearly all in sympathy with me.
1 2 **205** I have periods of such great restlessness that I cannot sit long in a chair.
1 2 **206** I have been disappointed in love.
1 2 **207** I never worry about my looks.
1 2 **208** I dream frequently about things that are best kept to myself.
1 2 **209** I believe I am no more nervous than most others.
1 2 **210** I have few or no pains.
1 2 **211** My way of doing things is apt to be misunderstood by others.
1 2 **212** Sometimes without any reason or even when things are going wrong I feel excitedly happy, "on top of the world."
1 2 **213** I don't blame people for trying to grab everything they can get in this world.
1 2 **214** I have had blank spells in which my activities were interrupted and I did not know what was going on around me.
N **215** My parents do not really love me.
1 2 **216** I can be friendly with people who do things which I consider wrong.
1 2 **217** I like to be with a crowd who play jokes on one another.
1 2 **218** I have difficulty in starting to do things.
1 2 **219** I believe I am a condemned person.
1 2 R2 **220** I am a slow learner in school.
1 2 **221** It does not bother me that I am not better looking.
1 2 **222** I sweat very easily even on cool days.
1 2 **223** I am entirely self-confident.
1 2 **224** At times it has been impossible for me to keep from stealing or shoplifting something.
1 2 **225** It is safer to trust nobody.
1 2 **226** Once a week or oftener I become very excited.
1 2 **227** When in a group of people I have trouble thinking of the right things to talk about.
1 2 **228** Something exciting will almost always pull me out of it when I am feeling low.
1 2 **229** When I leave home I do not worry about whether the door is locked and the windows closed.
1 2 **230** I believe my sins are unpardonable.
1 2 **231** I have numbness in one or more places on my skin.
1 2 **232** I do not blame a person for taking advantage of people who leave themselves open to it.
1 2 **233** My eyesight is as good as it has been for years.
1 2 **234** At times I have been so entertained by the cleverness of some criminals that I have hoped they would get away with it.
1 2 **235** I have often felt that strangers were looking at me critically.
1 2 **236** Everything tastes the same.
1 2 **237** I drink an unusually large amount of water every day.
1 2 **238** Most people make friends because friends are likely to be useful to them.
1 2 **239** I do not often notice my ears ringing or buzzing.
1 2 **240** Once in a while I feel hate toward members of my family whom I usually love.
1 2 **241** If I were a reporter I would very much like to report sporting news.

1 2 242 No one cares much what happens to you.
1 2 243 Once in a while I laugh at a dirty joke.
1 2 244 I have very few fears compared to my friends.
1 2 245 In a group of people I would not be embarrassed to be called upon to start a discussion or give an opinion about something I know well.
1 2 246 I am always disgusted with the law when a criminal is freed through the arguments of a smart lawyer.
1 2 247 I have used alcohol excessively.
1 2 248 I am likely not to speak to people until they speak to me.
1 2 249 I have never been in trouble with the law.
1 2 250 My soul sometimes leaves my body.
1 2 251 I wish I were not bothered by thoughts about sex.
1 2 252 If several people find themselves in trouble, the best thing for them to do is to agree upon a story and stick to it.
1 2 253 I think that I feel more intensely than most people do.
1 2 254 There never was a time in my life when I liked to play with dolls.
1 2 255 Life is a strain for me much of the time.
1 2 256 I am so touchy on some subjects that I can't talk about them.
1 2 R2 257 In school I find it very hard to talk in front of the class.
1 2 258 I love my mother, or (if your mother is dead) I loved my mother.
1 2 259 Even when I am with people I feel lonely much of the time.
1 2 260 I get all the sympathy I should.
1 2 261 I refuse to play some games because I am not good at them.
1 2 262 I seem to make friends about as quickly as others do.
1 2 R2 263 A person who leaves valuable property unprotected is about as much to blame when it is stolen as the one who steals it.
1 2 264 I dislike having people around me.
1 2 265 I think nearly anyone would tell a lie to keep out of trouble.
1 2 266 I am more sensitive than most other people.
1 2 267 Most people inwardly dislike putting themselves out to help other people.
1 2 268 Many of my dreams are about sex.
1 2 269 My parents and family find more fault with me than they should.
1 2 270 I am easily embarrassed.
1 2 R2 271 I worry about money.
1 2 272 I have never been in love with anyone.
1 2 273 I am afraid of using a knife or anything very sharp or pointed.
1 2 274 I almost never dream.
1 2 275 I have never been paralyzed or had any unusual weakness of any of my muscles.
1 2 276 Sometimes my voice leaves me or changes even though I have no cold.
1 2 R2 277 My mother or father often makes me obey even when I think it is unreasonable.
1 2 278 Peculiar odors come to me at times.
1 2 279 I cannot keep my mind on one thing.
1 2 280 I am apt to pass up something I want to do when others feel that it isn't worth doing.
1 2 281 I feel anxiety about something or someone almost all the time.
1 2 282 I easily become impatient with people.
1 2 283 Most of the time I wish I were dead.
1 2 284 Sometimes I become so excited that I find it hard to get to sleep.
1 2 285 I have certainly had more than my share of things to worry about.
1 2 286 I am sure I am being talked about.
1 2 287 At times I hear so well it bothers me.
1 2 288 I forget right away what people say to me.
1 2 289 At times I am all full of energy.
1 2 290 Often I cross the street in order not to meet someone I see.
1 2 291 I often feel as if things are not real.
1 2 292 I like parties and socials.
1 2 293 I have a habit of counting things that are not important such as bulbs on electric signs, and so forth.

1 2 **294** I have no enemies who really wish to harm me.

1 2 **295** I tend to be on my guard with people who are somewhat more friendly than I had expected.

1 2 **296** I have strange and peculiar thoughts.

1 2 **297** I get anxious and upset when I have to make a short trip away from home.

1 2 **298** I have periods in which I feel unusually cheerful without any special reason.

1 2 **299** I hear strange things when I am alone.

1 2 **300** I have been afraid of things or people that I knew could not hurt me.

1 2 **301** I have no dread of going into a room by myself where other people have already gathered and are talking.

1 2 **302** The things that some of my family have done have frightened me.

1 2 **303** Sometimes I enjoy hurting persons I love.

1 2 **304** Whenever possible I avoid being in a crowd.

1 2 **305** I have more trouble concentrating than others seem to have.

1 2 **306** I have several times given up doing a thing because I thought too little of my ability.

1 2 **307** Bad words, often terrible words, come into my mind and I cannot get rid of them.

1 2 **308** Sometimes some unimportant thought will run through my mind and bother me for days.

1 2 **309** Almost every day something happens to frighten me.

1 2 **310** I usually have to stop and think before I act even in small matters.

1 2 **311** I am inclined to take things hard.

1 2 **312** While in trains, busses, etc., I often talk to strangers.

1 2 **313** People should try to understand their dreams and be guided by or take warning from them.

1 2 **314** People say insulting and vulgar things about me.

1 2 **315** Someone has control over my mind.

1 2 **316** At parties I am more likely to sit by myself or with just one other person than to join in with the crowd.

1 2 **317** People often disappoint me.

1 2 **318** I have sometimes felt that difficulties were piling up so high that I could not overcome them.

1 2 **319** I love to go to dances.

1 2 **320** At periods my mind seems to work more slowly than usual.

1 2 **321** At times I have enjoyed being hurt by someone I loved.

1 2 **322** I enjoy children.

1 2 **323** I enjoy gambling for small stakes.

1 2 **324** If given the chance I could do some things that would be of great benefit to the world.

1 2 **325** I have often met people who were supposed to be experts who were no better than I.

1 2 **326** It makes me feel like a failure when I hear of the success of someone I know well.

1 2 **327** I often think, "I wish I were a child again."

1 2 **328** I am never happier than when alone.

1 2 **329** If given the chance I would make a good leader of people.

1 2 **330** People generally demand more respect for their own rights than they are willing to allow for others.

1 2 **331** I enjoy social gatherings just to be with people.

1 2 **332** At one or more times in my life I felt that someone was making me do things by hypnotizing me.

1 2 **333** I find it hard to set aside a task that I have undertaken, even for a short time.

1 2 **334** I have often found people jealous of my good ideas, just because they had not thought of them first.

1 2 **335** I enjoy the excitement of a crowd.

1 2 **336** I do not mind meeting strangers.

1 2 **337** Someone has been trying to influence my mind.

1 2 **338** I can remember "playing sick" to get out of something.

1 2 **339** My worries seem to disappear when I get into a crowd of lively friends.

1 2 **340** I feel like giving up quickly when things go wrong.

1 2 **341** I like to let people know where I stand on things.

2 **342** I can express my true feelings only when I drink.

1 2 **343** I have had periods when I felt so full of pep that sleep did not seem necessary for days at a time.

N **344** I cannot wait for the day when I can leave home for good.

N **345** My friends are often in trouble.

1 2 **346** I have no fear of water.

2 **347** I am not happy with myself the way I am.

1 2 **348** I would like to wear expensive clothes.

1 2 **349** I am afraid of being alone in a wide-open place.

1 2 **350** I feel uneasy indoors.

1 2 **351** The only interesting part of newspapers is the comic strips.

1 2 **352** I have reason for feeling jealous of one or more members of my family.

1 2 **353** I have nightmares every few nights.

1 2 **354** I can easily make other people afraid of me, and sometimes do for the fun of it.

1 2 **355** I am not easily angered.

2 **356** I have done some bad things in the past that I never tell anybody about.

2 **357** It makes me nervous when people ask me personal questions.

2 **358** I do not feel I can plan my own future.

2 **359** I get angry when my friends or family give me advice on how to live my life.

1 2 **360** I very seldom have spells of the blues.

1 2 **361** It is all right to get around the law if you don't actually break it.

2 **362** I don't like hearing other people give their opinions about life.

2 **363** I often have serious disagreements with people who are close to me.

N **364** I am often upset by things that happen in school.

2 **365** When things get really bad, I know I can count on my family for help.

2 R2 **366** I have gotten many beatings.

1 2 **367** I am often said to be hotheaded.

1 2 **368** I wish I could get over worrying about things I have said that may have injured other people's feelings.

1 2 **369** I feel unable to tell anyone all about myself.

1 2 **370** My plans have frequently seemed so full of difficulties that I have had to give them up.

1 2 **371** The future is too uncertain for a person to make serious plans.

1 2 **372** Often, even though everything is going fine for me, I feel that I don't care about anything.

1 2 **373** People have often misunderstood my intentions when I was trying to put them right and be helpful.

1 2 **374** I have no trouble swallowing.

1 2 **375** I am usually calm and not easily upset.

1 2 **376** If I was in trouble with several friends who were as guilty as I was, I would rather take the whole blame than give them away.

1 2 **377** I am apt to take disappointments so keenly that I can't put them out of my mind.

1 2 **378** I am often so annoyed when someone tries to get ahead of me in a line of people that I speak to that person about it.

1 2 **379** At times I think I am no good at all.

1 2 R2 **380** Often I have not gone to school even when I should have.

1 2 **381** One or more members of my family are very nervous.

1 2 **382** I have at times had to be rough with people who were rude or annoying.

1 2 **383** I worry quite a bit over possible misfortunes.

2 **384** It bothers me when people say nice things about me.

1 2 **385** I am apt to pass up something I want to do because others feel that I am not going about it in the right way.

1 2 R2 **386** I like excitement.
1 2 **387** I have never seen a vision.
1 2 **388** I am often sorry because I am so irritable and grouchy.
1 2 R2 **389** In school my grades in classroom behavior (conduct) are quite regularly bad.
1 2 **390** I am fascinated by fire.
1 2 **391** When I am cornered I tell that portion of the truth which is not likely to hurt me.
1 2 **392** I deserve severe punishment for my sins.
1 2 **393** I readily become one hundred percent sold on a good idea.
1 2 R2 **394** I must admit that I have at times been overly worried about something that really didn't matter.
1 2 R2 **395** I have often worked for people who take credit for good work but who pass off mistakes on those who work for them.
1 2 **396** Some of my family have quick tempers.
1 **397** I prefer work which requires close attention to work which allows me to be careless.
1 2 **398** The members of my family and my close relatives get along quite well.
1 2 **399** The future seems hopeless to me.
1 2 **400** People can pretty easily change my mind even when I have made a decision about something.
1 2 **401** It makes me angry to have people hurry me.
1 2 **402** Several times a week I feel as if something dreadful is about to happen.
1 2 **403** I like to read about science.
1 2 **404** I sometimes feel that I am about to go to pieces.
2 **405** I hate my whole family.
1 2 **406** A large number of people are guilty of bad sexual conduct.
1 2 R2 **407** The person to whom I have been most attached and whom I have most admired is a woman (mother, sister, aunt, or other woman).
2 **408** Some people think it's hard to get to know me.
1 **409** I like to read newspaper editorials.
2 **410** I spend most of my spare time by myself.
1 **411** I like to attend lectures on serious subjects.
1 **412** I have had periods in which I lost sleep over worry.
1 **413** I could be happy living all alone in a cabin in the woods or mountains.
1 R1 **414** I have one or more bad habits that are so strong it is no use fighting against them.
1 2 **415** I cannot do anything well.
2 **416** I am very stubborn.
2 **417** Ghosts or spirits can influence people for good or bad.
N **418** I am not responsible for the bad things that are happening to me.
2 **419** My main goals in life are within my reach.
2 **420** Mental illness is a sign of weakness.
2 **421** I feel helpless when I have to make some important decisions.
N **422** All my troubles would vanish if only my health were better.
2 **423** I believe that people should keep personal problems to themselves.
2 R2 **424** I am not feeling much stress these days.
N **425** I think my teachers at school are stupid.
2 **426** Although I am not happy with my life, there is nothing I can do about it now.
N **427** I hate to admit feeling sick.
1 2 **428** There are persons who are trying to steal my thoughts and ideas.
2 **429** I have some habits that are really harmful.
2 **430** When problems need to be solved, I usually let other people take charge.
2 **431** Talking over problems and worries with someone is often more helpful than taking drugs or medicines.
2 **432** I recognize several faults in myself that I will not be able to change.
1 2 **433** When I am with people, I am bothered by hearing very strange things.
2 **434** I hate going to doctors even when I'm sick.

N 435 I would rather drive around with my friends than go to school activities or athletic events.

N 436 I want to go to college.

2 437 When I have a problem it helps to talk it over with someone.

N 438 My parents do not understand me very well.

1 2 439 I often hear voices without knowing where they come from.

N 440 I have spent nights away from home when my parents did not know where I was.

2 441 People do not find me attractive.

N 442 People should always follow their beliefs even if it means bending the rules to do it.

N 443 I have missed a lot of school in my life because of sickness.

2 444 It bothers me greatly to think of making changes in my life.

N 445 I often get into trouble for breaking or destroying things.

2 446 People are not very kind to me.

1 2 447 I usually expect to succeed in things I do.

N 448 Most people think they can depend on me.

N 449 I find it hard to break bad habits.

N 450 I get along with most people.

N 451 We don't have trouble talking to each other in my family.

N 452 The only good thing about school is my friends.

N 453 Others say I throw temper tantrums to get my way.

N 454 Others in my family seem to get more attention than I do.

N 455 I am often told that I do not show enough respect for people.

N 456 I like to shock people by swearing.

N 457 I do the things I am supposed to do around home.

N 458 I sometimes get into fights when drinking.

N 459 My school grades are average or better.

N 460 I have never run away from home.

N 461 I often have to yell to get my point across.

N 462 I often have to lie in order to get by.

N 463 I have no close friends.

N 464 Others tell me that I am lazy.

N 465 I don't like having to get "rough" with people.

N 466 At school I am very often bored and sleepy.

2 R2 467 I enjoy using marijuana.

2 R2 468 I often get confused and forget what I want to say.

N 469 Sometimes I do the opposite of what others want just to show them.

1 2 470 I have a cough most of the time.

N 471 I avoid others to keep from being teased or tormented.

N 472 I have many secrets that I keep to myself.

N 473 I don't seem to have as much fun as others my age.

N 474 People often tell me I have a problem with drinking too much.

N 475 I am usually very quiet around other people.

N 476 I have a close friend whom I can share secrets with.

N 477 My friends often talk me into doing things I know are wrong.

N 478 I have done some bad things I didn't want to do because my friends thought I should.

Appendix G

Description of MMPI, MMPI-2, and MMPI-A Scales

SECTION 1: MMPI AND MMPI-2 SCALES

Validity Scales

Cannot Say Score (?). This score is not a psychometric scale but rather the number of items the individual omitted; it is used as an index of cooperativeness. If the test taker has deleted more than 30 items, the response record is probably insufficient for interpretation. This is particularly the case if the item deletions occur in the first 370 items. If the item deletions are at the end of the booklet (beyond Item 370), the validity and clinical scales can be interpreted, but the supplemental and MMPI-2 content scales should not be interpreted.

Lie Scale (*L*). In the MMPI-2, as in the original MMPI, the *L* scale is a measure of the individual's willingness to self-disclose personal information and to endorse negative self-views. Individuals who score high on this scale ($T > 60$) are presenting an overly favorable picture of themselves. If the *L* score is greater than 65, the individual is claiming virtue not found among people in general.

Subtle Defensiveness Scale (*K*). The *K* scale was developed as a measure of test defensiveness and as a correction for the tendency of some people to deny problems. Five MMPI scales are corrected by adding a portion of *K* to the total score: *Hs*, *Pd*, *Pt*, *Sc*, and *Ma*. The *K* scale appeared to operate for MMPI-2 normative test takers much as it did for the original MMPI subjects. Consequently, the *K* weights originally derived by Meehl were maintained in the MMPI-2. Slight changes in the norms for *K* in the MMPI-2 make the scale somewhat less elevated for higher socioeconomic status (SES) individuals than in the past. The slightly higher *K* score for the MMPI-2 normative sample does not raise the *T* scores for corrected scales (Butcher, 1990a). Low SES clients appear slightly lower on the *K* scale than do individuals from the normative sample. Some adjustment in the interpretation of profiles from test takers from very low socioeconomic or educational levels may be needed.

In the MMPI-2, practitioners can evaluate both *K*-corrected and non-*K*-corrected profiles if they desire, because non-*K*-corrected profiles are now available.

Infrequency Scales: *F* and *F(B)*. The *F* scale was developed for the original MMPI as a measure of symptom exaggeration or the tendency to claim an excessive number of psychological problems. (See more extensive discussion in chapter 6.) Originally, the *F* scale contained 64 items. The *F* scale in the MMPI-2 contains 60 items. If the *F* score is approximately 30 raw score points, it is suggestive of a random response set.

An additional invalidity measure, the *F(B)* scale or Back Side *F* scale, was developed for the revised version of the MMPI to detect possible deviant responding to items located toward the end of the item pool. Some test takers may modify their approach to the items part way

The material included in appendix G, section 1, was adapted by permission from Butcher, 1992a; Butcher, Graham, Williams, & Ben-Porath, 1990, copyright 1990 by the Regents of the University of Minnesota; and Butcher & Williams, 1992a, copyright 1992 by the Regents of the University of Minnesota.

through the test and answer in a random or unselective manner. Because the items on the *F* scale occur earlier in the test, before Item 370, the *F* scale might not detect deviant response patterns occurring later in the booklet.

The 40-item *F(B)* scale was developed following the same method used for the original *F* scale, by including items that had low endorsement percentages in the normal population.

Consistency Scales: *VRIN* and *TRIN*. Two new validity scales have been introduced in the MMPI-2 and MMPI-A to assist the practitioner in evaluating the validity of the profile. These scales are based on the analysis of the individual's response to the items in a consistent or inconsistent manner.

The first scale, *TRIN* or True Response Inconsistency, is made up of pairs of items in which a combination of two "true" or two "false" responses is semantically inconsistent. For example, "I am happy most of the time" and "Most of the time I feel blue" cannot be answered in the same direction if the test taker is responding consistently to the content. The *TRIN* scale can aid in the interpretation of scores on the *L* and *K* scales, because the former is made up of items that are keyed "false" and the latter is made up of items all but one of which is keyed "false." Thus, an individual who inconsistently responds "false" to MMPI-2 items will have elevated scores on Scales *L* and *K* that do not reflect intentional misrepresentation or defensiveness. An individual whose *TRIN* score indicates inconsistent "true" responding will have deflated scores on Scales *L* and *K* that do not reflect a particularly honest response pattern or lack of ego resources.

The *VRIN* scale may be used to help interpret a high score on *F*. *VRIN* is made up of pairs of (true–false; false–true; true–true; false–false) patterns. For example, answering "true" to "I am greatly bothered by forgetting where I put things" and "false" to "I forget where I leave things" is inconsistent. The scale is scored by summing the number of inconsistent responses. A high *F* score in conjunction with a low to moderate *VRIN* score rules out the possibility that the *F* score reflects random responding.

Clinical Scales

As explained in chapter 2, the clinical scales are virtually identical in MMPI and MMPI-2 in terms of item composition and psychometric properties. Their distributions and recommended cutoff points differ slightly because the *T*-score distributions are based on different samples and use a slightly different *T*-score generation procedure. Empirical correlates for the clinical scales are essentially the same in all three versions. It is important to emphasize again that not all correlates will fit all test takers who score in a particular range.

Scale 1: Hypochondriasis (*Hs*). *High Scorers.* Excessive bodily concern; somatic symptoms that tend to be vague and undefined; epigastric complaints; fatigue, pain, and weakness; lacks manifest anxiety; selfish, self-centered, and narcissistic; pessimistic, defeatist, and cynical outlook on life; dissatisfied and unhappy; makes others miserable; whines and complains; demanding and critical of others; expresses hostility indirectly; rarely acts out; dull, unenthusiastic, and unambitious; ineffective in oral expression; has longstanding health concerns; functions at a reduced level of efficiency without major incapacity; not very responsive to therapy and tends to terminate therapy when therapist is seen as not giving enough attention and support; seeks medical solutions to problems.

Scale 2: Depression (*D*). *High Scorers.* Depressed, unhappy, and dysphoric; pessimistic; self-deprecating; guilty; sluggish; somatic complaints; weakness, fatigue, and loss of energy; agitated, tense, high strung, and irritable; prone to worry; lacks self-confidence; feels useless and unable to function; feels like a failure at school or on the job; introverted, shy, retiring, timid, and seclusive; aloof; maintains psychological distance; avoids interpersonal involvement; cautious and conventional; has difficulty making decisions; nonaggressive; overcontrolled; denies impulses; makes concessions to avoid conflict; motivated for therapy.

Scale 3: Hysteria (*Hs*). *High Scorers.* Reacts to stress and avoids responsibility through development of physical symptoms; has headaches, chest pains, weakness, tachycardia, and anxiety attacks; symptoms appear and disappear suddenly; lacks insight about causes of symptoms; lacks insight about own motives and feelings; lacks anxiety, tension, and depression; rarely reports delusions, hallucinations, or suspiciousness; psychologically immature, childish, and infantile; self-centered, narcissistic, and egocentric; expects attention and affection from others; uses indirect and devious means to get attention and affection; does not express hostility and resentment openly; socially involved; friendly, talkative, and enthusiastic; superficial and immature in interpersonal relationships; shows interest in others for selfish reasons; occasionally acts out in sexual or aggressive manner with little apparent insight; initially enthusiastic about treatment; responds well to direct advice or suggestion; slow to gain insight into causes of own behavior; resistant to psychological interpretations.

Scale 4: Psychopathic Deviate (*Pd*). *High Scorers.* Antisocial behavior; rebellious toward authority figures; stormy family relationships; blames parents for problems; history of underachievement in school; poor work history; marital problems; impulsive; strives for immediate gratification of impulses; does not plan well; acts without considering consequences of actions; impatient; limited frustration tolerance; poor judgment; takes risks; does not profit from experience; immature, childish, narcissistic, self-centered, and selfish; ostentatious and exhibitionistic; insensitive; interested in others in terms of *how* they can be used; likeable and usually creates a good first impression; forms shallow and superficial relationships and is unable to form warm attachments; extraverted and outgoing; talkative, active, energetic, and spontaneous; intelligent; asserts self-confidence; has a wide range of interests; lacks definite goals; hostile, aggressive; sarcastic, and cynical; resentful and rebellious; acts out; antagonistic; aggressive outbursts, assaultive behavior; little guilt over negative behavior; may feign guilt and remorse when in trouble; is free from disabling anxiety, depression, and psychotic symptoms; likely to have personality disorder diagnosis (antisocial or passive–aggressive); prone to worry; is dissatisfied; shows absence of deep emotional response; feels bored and empty; poor prognosis for change in therapy; blames others for problems; intellectualizes; may agree to treatment to avoid jail or some other unpleasant experience but is likely to terminate before change is effected.

Scale 5: Masculinity–Femininity (*Mf*). *Men: Very High Scorers ($T > 80$).* Shows conflicts about sexual identity; insecure in masculine role; effeminate; aesthetic and artistic interests; intelligent and capable; values cognitive pursuits; ambitious, competitive, and persevering; clever, clear thinking, organized, and logical; shows good judgment and common sense; curious; creative, imaginative, and individualistic in approach to problems; sociable; sensitive to others; tolerant; capable of expressing warm feelings toward others; passive, dependent, and submissive; peace loving; makes concessions to avoid confrontations; good self-control; rarely acts out.

Men: High Scorers ($T = 70–79$). May be viewed as sensitive; insightful; tolerant; effeminate; showing broad cultural interests; submissive and passive. (In clinical settings, the patient might show sex role confusion or heterosexual adjustment problems.)

Men: Low Scorers ($T < 35$). "Macho" self-image, presents self as extremely masculine; overemphasizes strength and physical prowess; aggressive, thrill seeking, adventurous, and reckless; coarse, crude, and vulgar; harbors doubts about own masculinity; has limited intellectual ability; narrow range of interests; inflexible and unoriginal approach to problems; prefers action to thought; is practical and nontheoretical; easygoing, leisurely, and relaxed; cheerful, jolly, and humorous; contented; willing to settle down; unaware of social stimulus value; lacks insight into own motives; unsophisticated.

Women: High Scorers ($T > 70$). Rejects traditional feminine roles and activities; traditional masculine interests in work, sports, and hobbies; active, vigorous, and assertive; competitive, aggressive, and dominating; coarse, rough, and tough; outgoing, uninhibited, and self-confident; easygoing, relaxed, and balanced; logical and calculated; unemotional and unfriendly.

Women: Low Scorers ($T < 35$). Describes self in terms of stereotypical female role; doubts about own femininity; passive, submissive, and yielding; defers to males in decision making; self-pity; complaining and fault finding; constricted; sensitive; modest; idealistic.

Scale 6: Paranoia (*Pa*). *Extremely High Scorers ($T > 75$).* Blatantly psychotic behavior; disturbed thinking; delusions of persecution and/or grandeur; ideas of reference; feels mistreated and picked on; angry and resentful; harbors grudges; uses projection as defense; most frequently diagnosed as schizophrenia or paranoid state.

Moderate Scorers ($T = 65–74$ for men; $T = 71–74$ for women). Paranoid predisposition; sensitive; overly responsive to reactions of others; feels he or she is getting a raw deal from life; rationalizes and blames others; suspicious and guarded; hostile, resentful, and argumentative; moralistic and rigid; overemphasizes rationality; poor prognosis for therapy; does not like to talk about emotional problems; difficulty in establishing rapport with therapist.

Extremely Low Scorers ($T < 35$). Should be interpreted with caution. In a clinical setting, low Scale 6 scores, in the context of a defensive response set, may suggest frankly psychotic disorder; delusions, suspiciousness, ideas of reference; symptoms less obvious than for high scorers; evasive, defensive, and guarded; shy, secretive, and withdrawn.

Scale 7: Psychasthenia (*Pt*). *High Scorers.* Anxious, tense, and agitated; high discomfort; worried and apprehensive; high strung and jumpy; difficulties in concentrating; introspective and ruminative; obsessive and compulsive; feels insecure and inferior; lacks self-confidence; self-doubting, self-critical, self-conscious, and self-derogatory; rigid and moralistic; maintains high standards for self and others; overly perfectionistic and conscientious; guilty and depressed; neat, orderly, organized, and meticulous; persistent; reliable; lacks ingenuity and originality in problem solving; dull and formal; vacillates; is indecisive; distorts importance of problems and overreacts; shy; does not interact well socially; hard to get to know; worries about popularity and acceptance; sensitive; physical complaints; shows some insight into problems; intellectualizes and rationalizes; resistant to interpretations in therapy; expresses hostility toward therapist; remains in therapy longer than most patients; makes slow but steady progress in therapy.

Scale 8: Schizophrenia (*Sc*). *Very High Scorers ($T = 80–90$).* Blatantly psychotic behavior; confused, disorganized, and disoriented; unusual thoughts or attitudes; delusions; hallucinations; poor judgment.

High Scorers ($T = 65–79$). Schizoid life-style; does not feel a part of social environment; feels isolated, alienated, and misunderstood; feels unaccepted by peers; withdrawn, seclusive, secretive, and inaccessible; avoids dealing with people and new situations; shy, aloof, and uninvolved; experiences generalized anxiety; resentful, hostile, and aggressive; unable to express feelings; reacts to stress by withdrawing into fantasy and daydreaming; difficulty separating reality and fantasy; self-doubts; feels inferior, incompetent, and dissatisfied; sexual preoccupation and sex role confusion; nonconforming, unusual, unconventional, and eccentric; vague, long-standing physical complaints; stubborn, moody, and opinionated; immature and impulsive; high-strung; imaginative; abstract and vague goals; lacks basic information for problem solving; poor prognosis for therapy; reluctant to relate in meaningful way to therapist; stays in therapy longer than most patients; may eventually come to trust therapist.

Scale 9: Hypomania (*Ma*). *High Scorers ($T > 75$).* Overactivity; accelerated speech; may have hallucinations or delusions of grandeur; energetic and talkative; prefers action to thought; wide range of interests; does not use energy wisely; does not see projects through to completion; creative, enterprising, and ingenious; little interest in routine or detail; easily bored and restless; low frustration tolerance; difficulty inhibiting expression of impulses; episodes of irritability, hostility, and aggressive outbursts; unrealistic and unqualified optimism; grandiose aspirations; exaggerates self-worth and self-importance; unable to see own limitations; outgoing, sociable, and gregarious; likes to be around other people; creates good first impression; friendly, pleasant, and enthusiastic; poised and self-confident; superficial relationships; manipulative, deceptive, and unreliable; feelings of dissatisfaction; agitated; may have periodic episodes of depression; difficulties at school or work; resistant to interpretations in therapy; attends therapy irregularly; may terminate therapy prematurely; repeats problems in stereotyped manner; not likely to become dependent on therapists; becomes hostile and aggressive toward therapist.

Moderate Scorers ($T > 65$, ≤ 74). Overactivity; exaggerated sense of self-worth; energetic and talkative; prefers action to thought; wide range of interest; does not use energy wisely; does not see projects through to completion; enterprising and ingenious; lacks interest in routine matters; becomes bored and restless easily; low frustration tolerance; impulsive; has episodes of irritability, hostility, and aggressive outbursts; unrealistic and overly optimistic at times; shows some grandiose aspirations; unable to see own limitations; outgoing, sociable, and gregarious; likes to be around other people; creates good first impression; friendly, pleasant, and enthusiastic; poised and self confident; superficial relationships; manipulative, deceptive, and unreliable; feelings of dissatisfaction; agitated; views therapy as unnecessary; resistant to interpretations in therapy; attends therapy irregularly; may terminate therapy prematurely; repeats problems in stereotyped manner; not likely to become dependent on therapist; becomes hostile and aggressive toward therapist.

Low Scorers ($T < 35$). Low energy level; low activity level; lethargic, listless, apathetic, and phlegmatic; difficult to motivate; reports chronic fatigue and physical exhaustion; depressed, anxious, and tense; reliable, responsible, and dependable; approaches problems in conventional, practical, and reasonable way; lacks self-confidence; sincere, quiet, modest, withdrawn, and seclusive; unpopular; overcontrolled; unlikely to express feelings openly.

Scale 0: Social Introversion (*Si*). *High Scorers (T > 65).* Socially introverted; is more comfortable alone or with a few close friends; reserved, shy, and retiring; uncomfortable around members of opposite sex; hard to get to know; sensitive to what others think; troubled by lack of involvement with other people; over-controlled; not likely to display feelings openly; submissive and compliant; overly accepting of authority; serious; slow personal tempo; reliable and dependable; cautious, conventional, and unoriginal in approach to problems; rigid and inflexible in attitudes and opinions; difficulty making even minor decisions; enjoys work; gains pleasure from productive personal achievement; tends to worry; is irritable and anxious; moody; experiences guilt feelings; has episodes of depression or low mood.

Low Scorers (T < 45). Sociable and extroverted; outgoing, gregarious, friendly, and talkative; strong need to be around other people; mixes well; intelligent, expressive, and verbally fluent; active, energetic, and vigorous; interested in status, power, and recognition; seeks out competitive situations; has problem with impulse control; acts without considering the consequences of actions; immature and self-indulgent; superficial and insincere relationships; manipulative and opportunistic; arouses resentment and hostility in others.

MMPI-2 Supplemental Scales

Addiction Acknowledgement Scale (AAS). This scale assesses the extent to which the individual has endorsed content relevant to alcohol or drug use and abuse.

Addiction Proneness Scale (APS). This scale assesses the tendency for the individual to have life-style characteristics associated with the development of alcohol and drug abuse problems. High scorers endorse items reflecting hedonistic, irresponsible, and impulsive behavior.

MacAndrew Scale-Revised (MAC-R). High scorers have been found to be prone to developing problems of addiction such as alcohol or drug abuse, pathological gambling, or other addictive problems.

Anxiety (A). Individuals scoring high on this scale are viewed as anxious, tense, obsessional, and generally maladjusted.

Repression (R). Individuals scoring high on this scale tend to be overcontrolled. They deny problems and tend to gloss over personal frailties. They are seen as constricted and inhibited.

Ego Strength (Es). This scale assesses the ability of the individual to tolerate stress and to benefit from treatment.

Dominance (Do). This scale measures the extent to which the individual is dominant in social and interpersonal contexts.

Responsibility (Re). This scale addresses the extent to which the individual holds attitudes of social responsibility.

Overcontrolled Hostility (O–H). This scale assesses the personality style of overcontrolled hostility or the possibility that the individual represses conflict to the extent that explosive behavior could occur.

Keane Posttraumatic Stress Disorder (PTSD). This scale assesses the symptoms of the syndrome of post-traumatic stress disorder.

Marital Distress Scale (MDS). This scale assesses marital relationship problems.

MMPI-2 Content Scales

Anxiety (ANX). High scorers on ANX report general symptoms of anxiety including tension, somatic problems (i.e., heart pounding and shortness of breath), sleep difficulties, worries, and poor concentration. They fear losing their minds, find life a strain, and have difficulties making decisions. They appear to be readily aware of these symptoms and problems, and they are willing to admit them.

Fears (FRS). A high score on FRS indicates an individual with many specific fears. These specific fears can include blood; high places; money; animals such as snakes, mice, or spiders; leaving home; fire; storms and natural disasters; water; the dark; being indoors; and dirt.

Obsessiveness (OBS). High scorers on OBS have tremendous difficulties making decisions and are likely to ruminate excessively about issues and problems, causing others to become impatient. Having to make changes distresses them, and they may report some compulsive behaviors, such as counting or saving unimportant things. They are excessive worriers who frequently become overwhelmed by their own thoughts.

Depression (DEP). High scores on this scale characterize individuals with significant depressive thoughts. They report feeling blue, uncertain about their future, and uninterested in their lives. They are likely to brood, be unhappy, cry easily, and feel hopeless and empty. They may report thoughts of suicide or wishes that they were dead. They may believe that they are condemned or have committed unpardonable sins. Other people may not be viewed as a source of support.

Health Concerns (HEA). Individuals with high scores on HEA report many physical symptoms across several body systems. Included are gastrointestinal symptoms (e.g., constipation, nausea and vomiting, or stomach trouble), neurological problems (e.g., convulsions, dizzy and fainting spells, or paralysis), sensory problems (e.g., poor hearing or eyesight), cardiovascular symptoms (e.g., heart or chest pains), skin problems, pain (e.g., headaches or neck pains), respiratory troubles (e.g., coughs, hay fever, or asthma). These individuals worry about their health and feel sicker than the average person.

Bizarre Mentation (BIZ). Psychotic thought processes characterize individuals high on BIZ. They may report auditory, visual, or olfactory hallucinations and may recognize that their thoughts are strange and peculiar. Paranoid ideation (e.g., the belief that they are being plotted against or that someone is trying to poison them) may be reported as well. These individuals may feel that they have a special mission or powers.

Anger (ANG). High scores on ANG suggest anger control problems. These individuals report being irritable, grouchy, impatient, hotheaded, annoyed, and stubborn. They sometimes feel like swearing or smashing things. They may lose self-control and report having been physically abusive toward people and objects.

Cynicism (CYN). Misanthropic beliefs characterize high scorers on CYN. They expect hidden, negative motives behind the acts of others, for example, believing that most people are honest simply because of fear of being caught. Other people are to be distrusted because people use each other and are only friendly for selfish reasons. They likely hold negative attitudes about those close to them, including fellow workers, family, and friends.

Antisocial Practices (ASP). In addition to holding similar misanthropic attitudes as high scorers on CYN, high scorers on ASP report problem behaviors during their school years and other antisocial practices, such as being in trouble with the law, stealing, or shoplifting. They report sometimes enjoying the antics of criminals and believe that it is all right to get around the law, as long as it is not broken.

Type A (TPA). High scorers on TPA are hard-driving, fast-moving, and work-oriented individuals who frequently become impatient, irritable, and annoyed. They do not like to wait or to be interrupted. There is never enough time in a day for them to complete their tasks. They are direct and may be overbearing in their relationships with others.

Low Self-Esteem (LSE). High scores on LSE characterize individuals with low opinions of themselves. They do not believe that they are liked by others or that they are important. They hold many negative attitudes about themselves, including beliefs that they are unattractive, awkward and clumsy, useless, and a burden to others. They certainly lack self-confidence and find it hard to accept compliments from others. They may be overwhelmed by all the faults they see in themselves.

Social Discomfort (SOD). High scorers on SOD are very uneasy around others, preferring to be by themselves. When in social situations, they are likely to sit alone rather than joining in the group. They see themselves as shy and dislike parties and other group events.

Family Problems (FAM). Considerable family discord is reported by high scorers on FAM. Their families are described as lacking in love, quarrelsome, and unpleasant. They even may report hating members of their families. Their childhood may be portrayed as abusive, and their marriages may be seen as unhappy and lacking in affection.

Work Interference (WRK). A high score on WRK is indicative of behaviors or attitudes likely to contribute to poor work performance. Some of the problems relate to low self-confidence, concentration difficulties, obsessiveness, tension and pressure, and decision-making problems. Others suggest lack of family support for career choice, personal questioning of career choice, and negative attitudes towards co-workers.

Negative Treatment Indicators (TRT). High scores on TRT characterize individuals with negative attitudes towards doctors and mental health treatment. High scorers do not believe that anyone can understand or help them. They have issues or problems that they are not comfortable discussing with anyone. They may not want to change anything in their lives, nor do they feel that change is possible. They prefer giving up rather than facing a crisis or difficulty.

SECTION 2: MMPI-A SCALES

Validity Scales

Cannot Say (*?*). This score equals the total number of unanswered items. A defensive protocol is suggested if the raw score is greater than 30.

Lie (*L*). As in the MMPI-2, this scale is a measure of a rather unsophisticated, overly "virtuous" test-taking attitude. Elevated scores ($T > 65$) suggest that the individual is presenting him- or herself in an overly positive light and attempting to create an unrealistically favorable view of his or her adjustment.

Infrequency (*F*). Adolescent response to personality items has traditionally been shown to be somewhat exaggerated or extreme. Adolescents tend to score high on the original MMPI *F* scale. One reason for this is that many of the original MMPI *F* items were inappropriate as infrequency indicators for adolescents—they were endorsed differently than in adult samples. Consequently, for MMPI-A, new infrequency items were obtained by examining endorsement frequencies of the normative sample. Items that were endorsed by fewer than 20% of the sample were identified as *F* items. The *F* scale in the MMPI-A contains 66 items. Consequently, the number of *F* items suggestive of a random response set is 33. The items on this scale are answered in the nonkeyed direction by most people. High scores ($T > 80$) suggest some extreme responding that may be due to reading difficulties, confusion, inconsistent responding, exaggeration, or possibly serious psychopathology.

F_1 and F_2. These subscales were developed by dividing the 66-item *F* scale into two equal halves. Extreme elevations on F_2, in the absence of extreme elevations on F_1, suggest that the first half of the MMPI-A (i.e., the basic scales) can be interpreted but that scales in the second half of the booklet (i.e., content scales and supplementary scales) are invalid.

Defensiveness (*K*). As in the original MMPI, this scale measures an individual's willingness to disclose personal information and to discuss his or her problems. High scores ($T > 65$) reflect possible reluctance to disclose personal information, provided *TRIN* is not elevated above 74. The *K* score is not used to correct for defensiveness in adolescent profiles as it is for adults.

True Response Inconsistency (*TRIN*). The *TRIN* scale is made up of pairs of items to which a combination of "true" or "false" responses is semantically inconsistent. Extreme scores ($T \geq 75$) on either end of the range reflect a tendency to answer inconsistently false (i.e., nea saying, at the low end of the range) or to answer inconsistently true (i.e., yea saying, at the upper end of the distribution). Raw scores are converted to linear *T* scores that are based on the adolescent normative sample.

Variable Response Inconsistency (*VRIN*). The *VRIN* scale is made up of pairs of items for which one or two of four possible configurations (true–false, false–true, true–true, and false–false) represents semantically inconsistent responses. The scale is scored by summing the number of inconsistent responses. Extreme *VRIN* scores ($T \geq 75$) indicate the presence of an invalid response style.

Basic Scales

Scale 1: Hypochondriasis (*Hs*). High scorers present numerous vague physical problems and may be unhappy, self-centered, whiny, complaining, and attention demanding. They are dissatisfied with life and cynical toward others.

Scale 2: Depression (*D*). High scores reflect depressed mood, low self-esteem, and feelings of inadequacy. Elevations may reflect great discomfort and need for change or symptomatic relief. High

The material included in appendix G, section 2, was adapted by permission from Butcher & Williams, 1992b and C. L. Williams et al., 1992.

scorers are pessimistic, unhappy, indecisive, withdrawn, and feel useless.

Scale 3: Hysteria (*Hy*). High scorers may rely on defenses such as denial and repression to deal with stress. They tend to be dependent and naive. They show little insight into problems. High levels of stress may be accompanied by physical symptoms.

Scale 4: Psychopathic Deviate (*Pd*). Elevations measure acting-out behaviors and rebelliousness; disrupted family relations; lying; impulsiveness; and school or legal difficulties. Alcohol or drug problems may be present.

Scale 5: Masculinity–Femininity (*Mf*). High-scoring boys are described as having an unusual pattern of feminine interests. Because the direction of scoring is reversed, high-scoring girls are seen as having stereotypically masculine or more "macho" interests.

Scale 6: Paranoia (*Pa*). Elevations on this scale are often associated with being suspicious, aloof, shrewd, guarded, worrying, and overly sensitive. High scorers may be hostile and argumentative. Problems in school are common.

Scale 7: Psychasthenia (*Pt*). High scorers may be tense, anxious, preoccupied, obsessional, and rigid. They tend to have low self-confidence.

Scale 8: Schizophrenia (*Sc*). High scorers may have an unconventional or schizoid life-style. They can be withdrawn, shy, and moody, and feel inadequate, tense, and confused. They may have unusual or strange thoughts, poor judgment, and erratic moods. School problems and low personal achievement are probable.

Scale 9: Mania (*Ma*). High scorers may be impulsive and overly energetic. Acting-out behavior and school problems occur among high scoring adolescents.

Scale 0: Social Introversion–Extraversion (*Si*). High scorers are introverted, shy, withdrawn, socially reserved, submissive, overcontrolled, lethargic, conventional, tense, inflexible, and guilt prone. Low scorers are extraverted, outgoing, gregarious, expressive, and talkative.

Supplementary Scales

Anxiety (A). High scores suggest anxious, tense, obsessional, and generally maladjusted individuals.

Repression (R). High scorers tend to be overcontrolled. They deny problems and gloss over personal frailties.

MacAndrew Scale–Revised (MAC–R). High scorers are prone to developing problems with addiction and tend to be risk takers and exhibitionistic.

Alcohol and Drug Problem Acknowledgement (ACK). High scores indicate the individual has endorsed content relevant to alcohol or drug use and related problems.

Alcohol and Drug Problem Proneness (PRO). High scores suggest the tendency to develop alcohol or drug use problems, including association with a negative peer group.

Immaturity (IMM). The IMM scale developed in accordance with Loevinger's distinction between the preconformist and conformist stages of maturation.

Content Scales

Anxiety (a-anx). Adolescents who score high on a-anx report many symptoms of anxiety, including tension, frequent worrying, and difficulties sleeping (e.g., nightmares, disturbed sleep, and difficulty falling asleep). They report difficulties concentrating, confusion, and an inability to stay on task. They appear aware of their problems and how they differ from others.

Obsessiveness (a-obs). Adolescent high scorers on a-obs report worrying beyond reason, often over trivial matters. They may have ruminative thoughts about "bad words" or may count unimportant items. They have times when they are unable to sleep because of their worries. They report great difficulty making decisions and frequently dread having to make changes in their lives. They report that others sometimes lose patience with them.

Depression (a-dep). Adolescents who score high on a-dep report many symptoms of depression. Frequent crying spells and fatigue are problems. They are dissatisfied with their lives, and they feel that others are happier. They have many self-deprecative thoughts, including beliefs that they have not lived the right kind of life, feelings of uselessness, and beliefs that they are condemned and their sins unpardonable. Their future seems hopeless and their lives seem uninteresting and not worthwhile. Suicidal ideation is possible. They report loneliness even when with other people. Their future seems too uncertain for them to make serious plans, and they have periods when they are unable to "get going." A sense of hopelessness is characteristic.

Health (a-hea). Adolescents with high scores on a-hea report numerous physical problems that interfere with their enjoyment of after-school activities and that contribute to significant school absence. They may report that their physical health is worse than that of their friends. Their physical complaints cross several body systems. Included are gastrointestinal problems (e.g., constipation, nausea and vomiting, or stomach trouble), neurological problems (e.g., numbness, convulsions, fainting and dizzy spells, or paralysis), sensory problems (e.g., hearing difficulty or poor eyesight), cardiovascular symptoms (e.g., heart or chest pain), skin problems, pain (e.g., headaches or neck pain), and respiratory problems.

Alienation (a-aln). High scorers on a-aln, one of the adolescent-specific content scales, report considerable emotional distance from others. They believe that they are getting a raw deal from life and that no one cares about or understands them. They do not believe that they are liked by others nor do they get along with others. They feel that they have no one, including parents or close friends, who understands them. They feel that others are out to get them and are unkind to them. They have difficulty self-disclosing and report feeling awkward when having to talk in groups of people. They do not appreciate hearing others give their opinions.

Bizarre Mentation (a-biz). Adolescents scoring high on a-biz report very strange thoughts and experiences, including possible auditory, visual, and olfactory hallucinations. They characterize their experiences as strange and unusual, and they believe that there is something wrong with their minds. Paranoid ideation (e.g., the belief that they are being plotted against or that someone is trying to poison them) may also be reported. They may believe that others are trying to steal their thoughts and ideas or control their minds, perhaps through hypnosis. They may believe that evil spirits or ghosts possess or influence them.

Anger (a-ang). Adolescents with high scores on a-ang report considerable anger control problems. They often feel like swearing, smashing things, or starting a fistfight, and they frequently get into trouble for breaking or destroying things. They report having considerable problems with irritability and impatience with others. They have been told that they throw temper tantrums to get their own way. They indicate that they are hot headed and often have to yell in order to make a point. Occasionally they get into fights, especially when drinking.

Cynicism (a-cyn). Misanthropic attitudes are held by adolescents scoring high on a-cyn. They believe that others are out to get them and will use unfair means to gain an advantage. They look for hidden motives whenever someone does something nice for them. They believe that it is safer to trust nobody because people make friends in order to use them.

Conduct Problems (a-con). Adolescents scoring high on a-con report a number of different behavioral problems, including stealing, shoplifting, lying, breaking or destroying things, being disrespectful, swearing, and being oppositional. Members of their peer group are often in trouble and frequently talk them into doing things they know they should not do. At times they try to make other people afraid of them, just for the fun of it.

Low Self-Esteem (a-lse). Adolescents with high a-lse scores have very negative opinions of themselves including being unattractive, lacking self confidence, feeling useless, having little ability, having several faults, and not being able to do anything well. They are likely to yield to others' pressure, changing their minds or giving up in arguments. They tend to let other people take charge when problems have to be solved and do not feel that they are capable of planning their own future.

Low Aspirations (a-las). High scorers on a-las, an adolescent-specific content scale, are disinterested in being successful. They do not like to study and to read about things, dislike science, dislike lectures on serious topics, and prefer work that allows them to be careless. They do not expect to be successful. They report difficulty starting things, and they quickly give up when things go wrong. They let other people solve problems, and they avoid facing difficulties. Others also tell them that they are lazy.

Social Discomfort (a-sod). Adolescents with high scores on a-sod find it very difficult to be around others. They report being shy, and they much prefer to be alone. They dislike having people around them and frequently avoid others. They do not like parties, crowds, dances, or other social gatherings. They have difficulty making friends and do not like to meet strangers.

Family Problems (a-fam). Adolescents with high a-fam scores report considerable problems with their parents and other family members. Family discord, jealousy, fault finding, anger, beatings, serious disagreements, lack of love and understanding, and limited communication characterize these families. These adolescents do not believe they can count on their families in times of trouble.

School Problems (a-sch). Numerous difficulties in school characterize adolescents scoring high on a-sch, another of the adolescent-specific content scales. Poor grades, suspension, truancy, negative attitudes towards teachers, and dislike of school are characteristic of high scorers. The only pleasant aspect of school for such youth is their friends. They do not participate in school activities or sports. They believe that school is a waste of time. Some of these individuals may report being afraid to go to school. Others indicate that they are told that they are lazy, and they are frequently bored and sleepy at school.

Negative Treatment Indicators (a-trt). High scorers on a-trt indicate negative attitudes towards doctors and mental health professionals. They do not believe that others are capable of understanding them nor that others care what happens to them. They are unwilling to take charge and face their problems or difficulties. They report several faults and bad habits that they feel are insurmountable. They do not feel they can plan their own future. They will not assume responsibility for negative things in their lives. They also report great unwillingness to discuss their problems with others and indicate that there are some issues that they would never be able to share with anyone. They report being nervous when others ask them personal questions, and they have many secrets they feel are best kept to themselves.

Appendix H

Psychometric Properties of the MMPI, MMPI-2, and MMPI-A Compared

Original MMPI	MMPI-2	MMPI-A
Contains 566 items.	Contains 567 items.	Contains 478 items.
Contains 16 repeated items.	Contains no repeated items.	Contains no repeated items.
Contains a number of objectionable content areas: sexual preference, religion, and bowel and bladder functioning. Some items contain outmoded language.	Objectionable and outmoded items have been deleted. About 14% of items were reworded in more modern language.	Objectionable items have been eliminated, and items were reworded from the adolescent's perspective.
Contains numerous nonworking, nonscored items.	Eliminated nonworking items. Substituted new items dealing with suicide, drug and alcohol abuse, Type A behavior, interpersonal relations, and treatment compliance.	Nonworking items have been eliminated, and specific adolescent items have been included.
Contains 4 validity scales: ?, *L*, *F*, and *K*.	Contains 7 validity scales: ?, *L*, *F*, *K*, *F(B)*, *VRIN*, and *TRIN*.	Contains 8 validity scales: ?, *L*, *F*, F_1, F_2, *K*, *VRIN*, and *TRIN*.
Contains the 10 standard scales: *Hs*, *D*, *Hy*, *Pd*, *Mf*, *Pa*, *Pt*, *Sc*, *Ma*, and *Si*.	Contains the 10 nearly identical standard scales in the original MMPI: *Hs*, *D*, *Hy*, *Pd*, *Mf*, *Pa*, *Pt*, *Sc*, *Ma*, and *Si*. The difference is that a few items with objectionable content were eliminated from *F*, *Hs*, *D*, *Mf*, and *Si*.	Contains the traditional standard scales as in the MMPI-2. The number of items on the *Mf* and *Si* scales was reduced slightly to shorten the inventory.
K correction added to *Hs*, *Pd*, *Pt*, *Sc*, and *Ma*.	*K* correction added to *Hs*, *Pd*, *Pt*, *Sc*, and *Ma*.	*K* correction is not used in the MMPI-A.
Age range of normative sample: 16–65 years.	Age range of normative sample: 18–84 years.	Age range of normative sample: 14–18 years.

The material included in appendix H is used by permission from Butcher, 1992b.

Original MMPI	MMPI-2	MMPI-A
Assesses alcohol and drug problems; contains the 49-item MAC Scale.	Assesses alcohol and drug problems; contains the 49-item MAC-R Scale. Four objectionable items have been deleted; however, four new items, which empirically separated alcoholic patients from other psychiatric patients, were substituted.	Assesses alcohol and drug problems; contains MAC-R Scale to assess addiction potential.
	Two new substance abuse indicators have been developed: APS (Addiction Potential Scale) and AAS (Addiction Acknowledgment Scale).	Two new substance abuse indicators have been developed. PRO (Alcohol and Drug Problem Proneness Scale) and ACK (Alcohol and Drug Problem Acknowledgment Scale).
When the 13 validity and standard scale scores are factor analyzed, typically, four factors emerge: A, R, *Mf*, and *Si*.	When the MMPI-2 validity and standard scores are factor analyzed the same four factors emerge in similar magnitude: A, R, *Mf*, and *Si*.	When MMPI-A validity and standard scales are factor analyzed the same 4 factors emerge and are similar: A, R, *Mf*, and *Si*.
The Harris-Lingoes subscales are available for providing content-based hypotheses for clinical scale interpretation.	The Harris-Lingoes subscales are available in the MMPI-2.	The Harris-Lingoes subscales are available in the MMPI-A.
The Serkownek subscales for *Si* are available for developing content-based hypotheses.	New subscales for *Si* are available for generating content-based hypotheses.	The *Si* subscales from the MMPI-2 are contained in MMPI-A.
The Koss-Butcher empirically based "critical items" are available for the MMPI.	The Koss-Butcher "critical items" are virtually intact in the MMPI-2. Moreover, two item sets (depressed–suicide and alcohol–crises) have been expanded by about four items each on the basis of new empirical item analyses.	No empirically derived "critical item" lists have been developed for the MMPI-A.
The Wiggins content scales provide a psychometrically sound measurement of the content of an individual's responses.	A new set of 15 content scales has been developed to assess the major content dimensions in the MMPI-2. These rationally and statistically constructed scales provide highly reliable and valid indicants of the major content themes in the MMPI-2.	A new set of 15 adolescent problem-oriented content scales has been developed according to a rational and statistical strategy.

Original MMPI	MMPI-2	MMPI-A
The original MMPI norms were based on 724 visitors to the university hospitals and some special groups such as CCC Workers.	The MMPI-2 normative sample was randomly solicited from several states: California, Minnesota, North Carolina, Ohio, Pennsylvania, Virginia, and Washington. A total of 1,138 men and 1,462 women were included.	The MMPI-A normative sample was obtained from private and public schools in California, Minnesota, New York, North Carolina, Ohio, Pennsylvania, Virginia, and Washington state. A total of 805 boys and 815 girls were included.
Mean educational level of original sample was 8th grade, similar to the 1940 census data.	Mean educational level was 13 years, similar to the 1980 census data.	Educational level of normative sample was 8th, 9th, 10th, 11th, and 12th grade.
Item omissions were allowed and actually encouraged in the original MMPI data collection, producing high Cannot Say scores. This resulted in a lower mean profile for the normative group compared with more contemporary samples when omitted items are discouraged.	Response to all items in the MMPI-2 was encouraged. Mean profiles are less affected by item omission.	Item omissions were discouraged in the MMPI-A normative data collection.
The original *T* scores for the MMPI were linear *T* scores. No effort was made to have equivalent *T* scores across scales.	The MMPI-2 *T* scores for the 8 clinical scales and the 15 content scales are uniform *T* scores that are based on a single composite scale score distribution. A given level of *T* is *equivalent* in terms of percentile rank across the clinical scales.	The MMPI-A *T* scores for the 8 clinical scales and the 15 content scales are uniform and comparable with MMPI-2 *T* scores.
Percentile ranks across scales vary for a given *T*-score elevation.	The percentile rank for a given *T* score is uniform across the original 8 clinical scales and 15 content scales. ***T* score** / **Percentile** 50 / 55 55 / 73 60 / 85 65 / 92 70 / 96 75 / 98 80 / 99	The percentile rank for a given *T* score is uniform across the 8 original clinical scales and 15 content scales. ***T* score** / **Percentile** 50 / 55 55 / 73 60 / 85 65 / 92 70 / 96 75 / 98 80 / 99
No test–retest data were collected from the original normative sample.	One-week test–retest data are available for a subsample of the MMPI-2 normative sample ($n = 82$ men and 111 women):	One-week test–retest data are given for boys and girls in the normative sample ($n = 45$ boys and 109 girls):

Scale	MMPI-2 Men	MMPI-2 Women	MMPI-A Boys and Girls
L	.77	.81	.61
F	.78	.69	.55
K	.84	.81	.75
1	.85	.85	.79
2	.75	.77	.78
3	.72	.76	.70
4	.81	.79	.80
5	.82	.73	.82
6	.67	.58	.65
7	.89	.88	.83
8	.87	.80	.83
9	.83	.68	.70
0	.92	.91	.84

Original MMPI	MMPI-2	MMPI-A
Only age and gender were obtained from individuals from the original normative sample.	Extensive biographical and life-event information was obtained from the MMPI-2 normative sample.	Extensive biographical and life-event information was obtained from the MMPI-A normative sample.
The original normative sample was essentially rural, White men and women in Minnesota.	The MMPI-2 normative sample is more diverse in terms of socioeconomic level, ethnic group membership, and residence.	The MMPI-A normative sample is diverse in terms of ethnicity and residence.

	MMPI-2 Men	MMPI-A Boys
White	82.0%	76.5%
Black	11.1%	12.4%
American Indian	3.3%	2.6%
Hispanic	3.1%	2.2%
Asian	0.5%	2.9%

	MMPI-2 Women	MMPI-A Girls
White	81.0%	75.9%
Black	12.9%	12.3%
American Indian	2.7%	3.2%
Hispanic	2.6%	2.0%
Asian	0.9%	2.8%

Original MMPI	MMPI-2	MMPI-A
Manual scoring keys are available for the MMPI.	Manual scoring keys are available for the MMPI-2.	Manual scoring keys are available for the MMPI-A.
Tape-recorded and computer-administered format versions are available for the MMPI.	Tape-recorded and computer-administered format versions are available for the MMPI-2.	Tape-recorded and computer-administered format versions are available for the MMPI-A.
An MMPI scoring and interpretation system for the MMPI is available from National Computer Systems (NCS).	A computer scoring and interpretation program (Minnesota Report) for the MMPI-2 is available from NCS.	A computer interpretation program (Minnesota Report) for the MMPI-A is available from NCS.

Appendix I

Fifty-seven Illustrations for Presenting the MMPI in Court and Classroom

EXHIBIT I-1

Suggested Points for Presenting the MMPI-2 in Court

Describe the MMPI in terms of being an objective, paper and pencil personality scale that has been widely researched and validated.

Describe how widely used the MMPI is in clinical assessment, and cite references to support its broad use.

Provide a rationale for the original development of the MMPI as an objective means of classifying psychological problems.

Explain the empirical scale construction approach.

Describe and illustrate how the MMPI was validated, and explain the correlate base for the clinical scales.

Illustrate how the MMPI is used in personality description and clinical assessment.

If pertinent to the case, describe the MMPI revision (and MMPI-2/MMPI-A).

Describe and illustrate how the clinical scales of the revised versions (MMPI-2/MMPI-A) are composed of the same items and possess the same psychometric properties as the original version of the scales. Traditional scale reliabilities and validities have been assured in the revised version.

How can the credibility and validity of a particular MMPI profile be determined?

What does the MMPI/MMPI-2/MMPI-A measure for the particular client?

The above suggestions are provided for explaining the MMPI/MMPI-2/MMPI-A in court. The information provided in chapters 2 and 6 and in appendix G provide the necessary background for the suggested points.

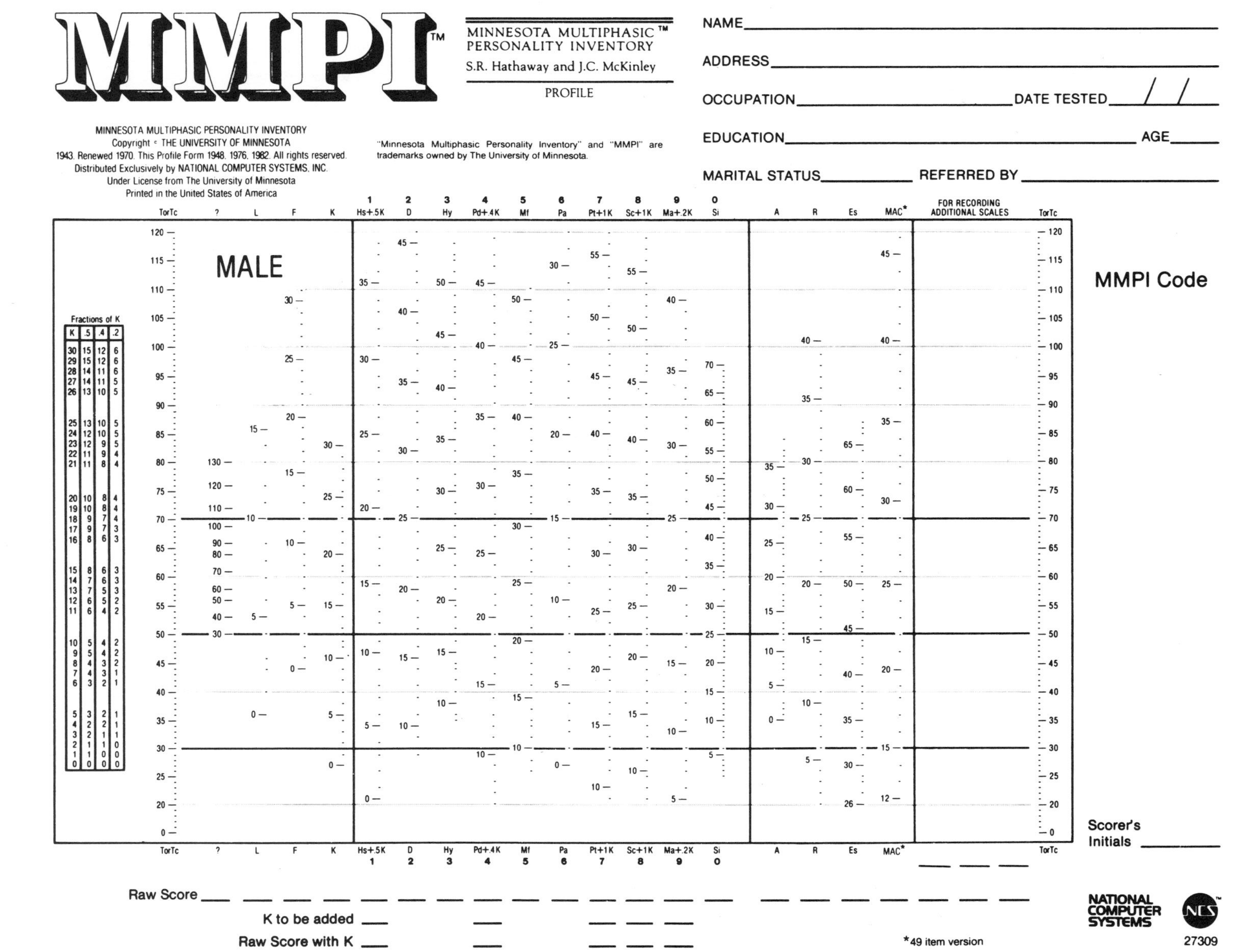

FIGURE I-1. MMPI profile for men. Reprinted with permission of the publisher from *Minnesota Multiphasic Personality Inventory*. Copyright © by the Regents of the University of Minnesota 1942, 1943 (renewed 1970), 1982. This form 1948, 1970, 1982.

MMPI™

MINNESOTA MULTIPHASIC™ PERSONALITY INVENTORY
S.R. Hathaway and J.C. McKinley
PROFILE

NAME ______
ADDRESS ______
OCCUPATION ______ DATE TESTED __/__/__
EDUCATION ______ AGE ______
MARITAL STATUS ______ REFERRED BY ______

FEMALE

Fractions of K

K	.5	.4	.2
30	15	12	6
29	15	12	6
28	14	11	6
27	14	11	5
26	13	10	5
25	13	10	5
24	12	10	5
23	12	9	5
22	11	9	4
21	11	8	4
20	10	8	4
19	10	8	4
18	9	7	4
17	9	7	3
16	8	6	3
15	8	6	3
14	7	6	3
13	7	5	3
12	6	5	2
11	6	4	2
10	5	4	2
9	5	4	2
8	4	3	2
7	4	3	1
6	3	2	1
5	3	2	1
4	2	2	1
3	2	1	1
2	1	1	0
1	1	0	0
0	0	0	0

TorTc ? L F K Hs+.5K (1) D (2) Hy (3) Pd+.4K (4) Mf (5) Pa (6) Pt+1K (7) Sc+1K (8) Ma+.2K (9) Si (0) A R Es MAC* FOR RECORDING ADDITIONAL SCALES TorTc

MMPI Code

Raw Score ______
K to be added ______
Raw Score with K ______

Scorer's Initials ______

*49 item version

NATIONAL COMPUTER SYSTEMS NCS 27309

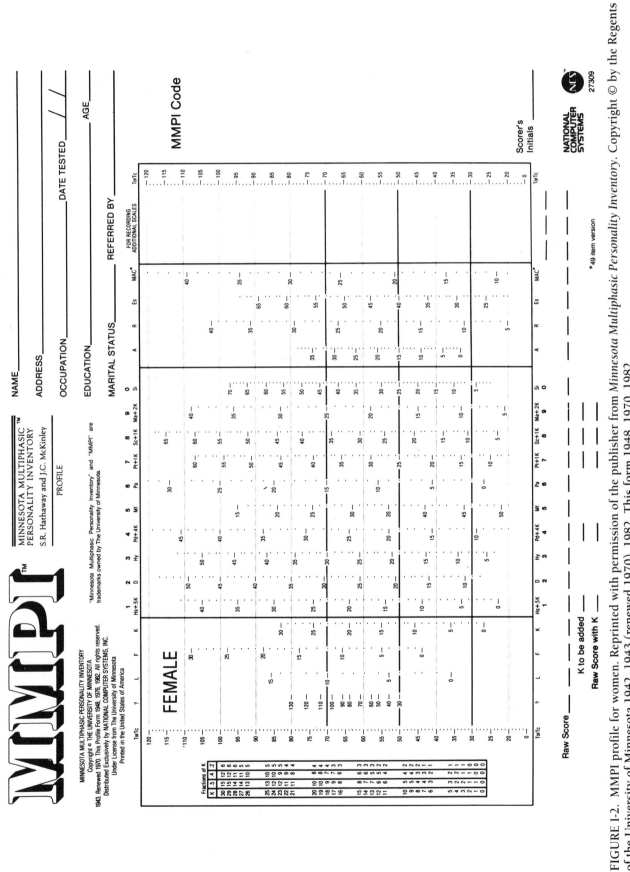

FIGURE I-2. MMPI profile for women. Reprinted with permission of the publisher from *Minnesota Multiphasic Personality Inventory*. Copyright © by the Regents of the University of Minnesota 1942, 1943 (renewed 1970), 1982. This form 1948, 1970, 1982.

MMPI-2™ S.R. Hathaway and J.C. McKinley

Minnesota Multiphasic Personality Inventory-2™

Profile for Basic Scales

Name__________

Address__________

Occupation__________ Date Tested __/__/__

Education_____ Age_____ Marital Status_____

Referred By__________

MMPI-2 Code__________

Scorer's Initials__________

Fractions of K

K	.5	.4	.2
30	15	12	6
29	15	12	6
28	14	11	6
27	14	11	5
26	13	10	5
25	13	10	5
24	12	10	5
23	12	9	5
22	11	9	4
21	11	8	4
20	10	8	4
19	10	8	4
18	9	7	4
17	9	7	3
16	8	6	3
15	8	6	3
14	7	6	3
13	7	5	3
12	6	5	2
11	6	4	2
10	5	4	2
9	5	4	2
8	4	3	2
7	4	3	1
6	3	2	1
5	3	2	1
4	2	2	1
3	2	1	1
2	1	1	0
1	1	0	0
0	0	0	0

MALE

T or Tc | L | F | K | Hs+.5K 1 | D 2 | Hy 3 | Pd+.4K 4 | Mf 5 | Pa 6 | Pt+1K 7 | Sc+1K 8 | Ma+.2K 9 | Si 0 | T or Tc

Raw Score___

? Raw Score___

K to be Added___

Raw Score with K___

NATIONAL COMPUTER SYSTEMS

24001

FIGURE I-3. MMPI-2 basic profile for men. Reprinted with permission of the publisher from *Minnesota Multiphasic Personality Inventory-2*. Copyright © by the Regents of the University of Minnesota 1942, 1943 (renewed 1970), 1989. This form 1948, 1970, 1982, 1989.

MMPI-2™ S.R. Hathaway and J.C. McKinley
Minnesota Multiphasic Personality Inventory-2™

Profile for Basic Scales

Name ________

Address ________

Occupation ________ Date Tested __/__/__

Education ______ Age ____ Marital Status ______

Referred By ________

MMPI-2 Code ________

Scorer's Initials ________

Fractions of K

K	.5	.4	.2
30	15	12	6
29	15	12	6
28	14	11	6
27	14	11	5
26	13	10	5
25	13	10	5
24	12	10	5
23	12	9	5
22	11	9	4
21	11	8	4
20	10	8	4
19	10	8	4
18	9	7	4
17	9	7	3
16	8	6	3
15	8	6	3
14	7	6	3
13	7	5	3
12	6	5	2
11	6	4	2
10	5	4	2
9	5	4	2
8	4	3	2
7	4	3	1
6	3	2	1
5	3	2	1
4	2	2	1
3	2	1	1
2	1	1	0
1	1	0	0
0	0	0	0

FEMALE

T or Tc | L | F | K | Hs+.5K 1 | D 2 | Hy 3 | Pd+.4K 4 | Mf 5 | Pa 6 | Pt+1K 7 | Sc+1K 8 | Ma+.2K 9 | Si 0 | T or Tc

Raw Score ___

? Raw Score ___

K to be Added ___

Raw Score with K ___

NATIONAL COMPUTER SYSTEMS

24001

FIGURE I-4. MMPI-2 basic profile for women. Reprinted with permission of the publisher from *Minnesota Multiphasic Personality Inventory-2*. Copyright © by the Regents of the University of Minnesota 1942, 1943 (renewed 1970), 1989. This form 1948, 1970, 1982, 1989.

MMPI-2™ S.R. Hathaway and J.C. McKinley
Minnesota Multiphasic Personality Inventory-2™

Profile for Content Scales
Butcher, Graham, Williams and Ben-Porath (1989)

Name ______

Address ______

Occupation ______ **Date Tested** __/__/__

Education ______ **Age** ______ **Marital Status** ______

Referred By ______

Scorer's Initials ______

MALE

T ANX FRS OBS DEP HEA BIZ ANG CYN ASP TPA LSE SOD FAM WRK TRT T

Raw Score — — — — — — — — — — — — — — —

NATIONAL COMPUTER SYSTEMS NCS™

24002

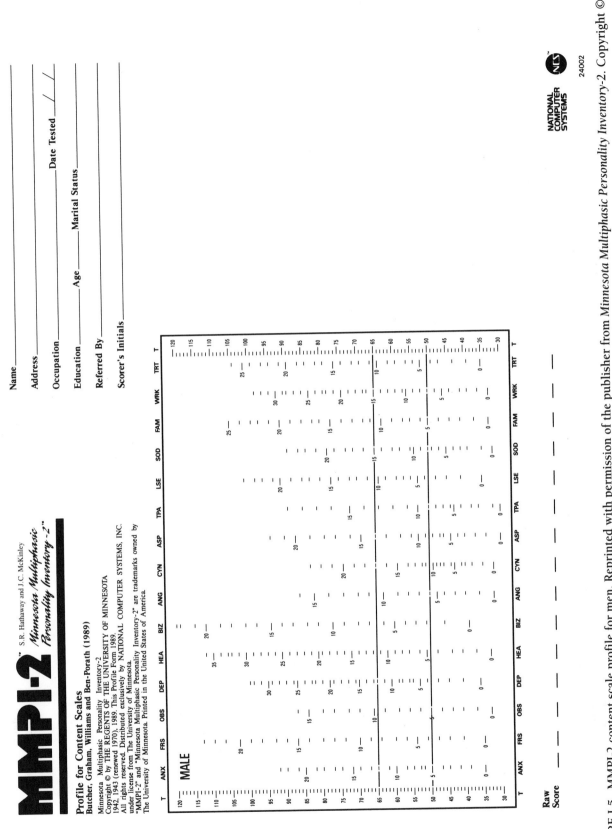

FIGURE I-5. MMPI-2 content scale profile for men. Reprinted with permission of the publisher from *Minnesota Multiphasic Personality Inventory-2*. Copyright © by the Regents of the University of Minnesota 1942, 1943 (renewed 1970), 1989. This form 1948, 1970, 1982, 1989.

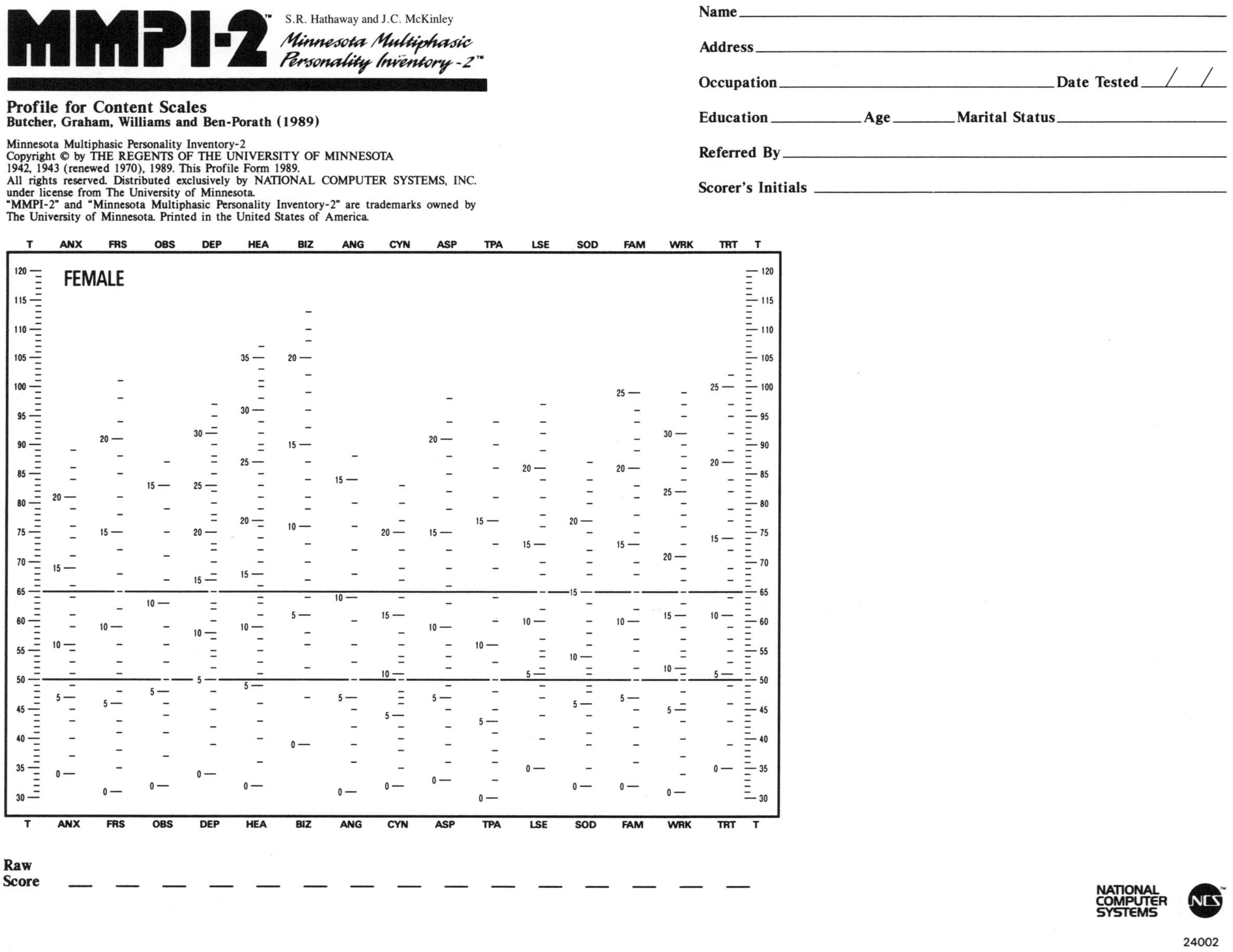

MMPI-2™ S.R. Hathaway and J.C. McKinley
Minnesota Multiphasic Personality Inventory-2™

Profile for Content Scales
Butcher, Graham, Williams and Ben-Porath (1989)

Name ____________
Address ____________
Occupation ____________ Date Tested __/__/__
Education ______ Age ______ Marital Status ______
Referred By ____________
Scorer's Initials ____________

T ANX FRS OBS DEP HEA BIZ ANG CYN ASP TPA LSE SOD FAM WRK TRT T

FEMALE

Raw Score ___ ___ ___ ___ ___ ___ ___ ___ ___ ___ ___ ___ ___ ___ ___

NATIONAL COMPUTER SYSTEMS
24002

FIGURE I-6. MMPI-2 content scale profile for women. Reprinted with permission of the publisher from *Minnesota Multiphasic Personality Inventory-2*. Copyright © by the Regents of the University of Minnesota 1942, 1943 (renewed 1970), 1989. This form 1948, 1970, 1982, 1989.

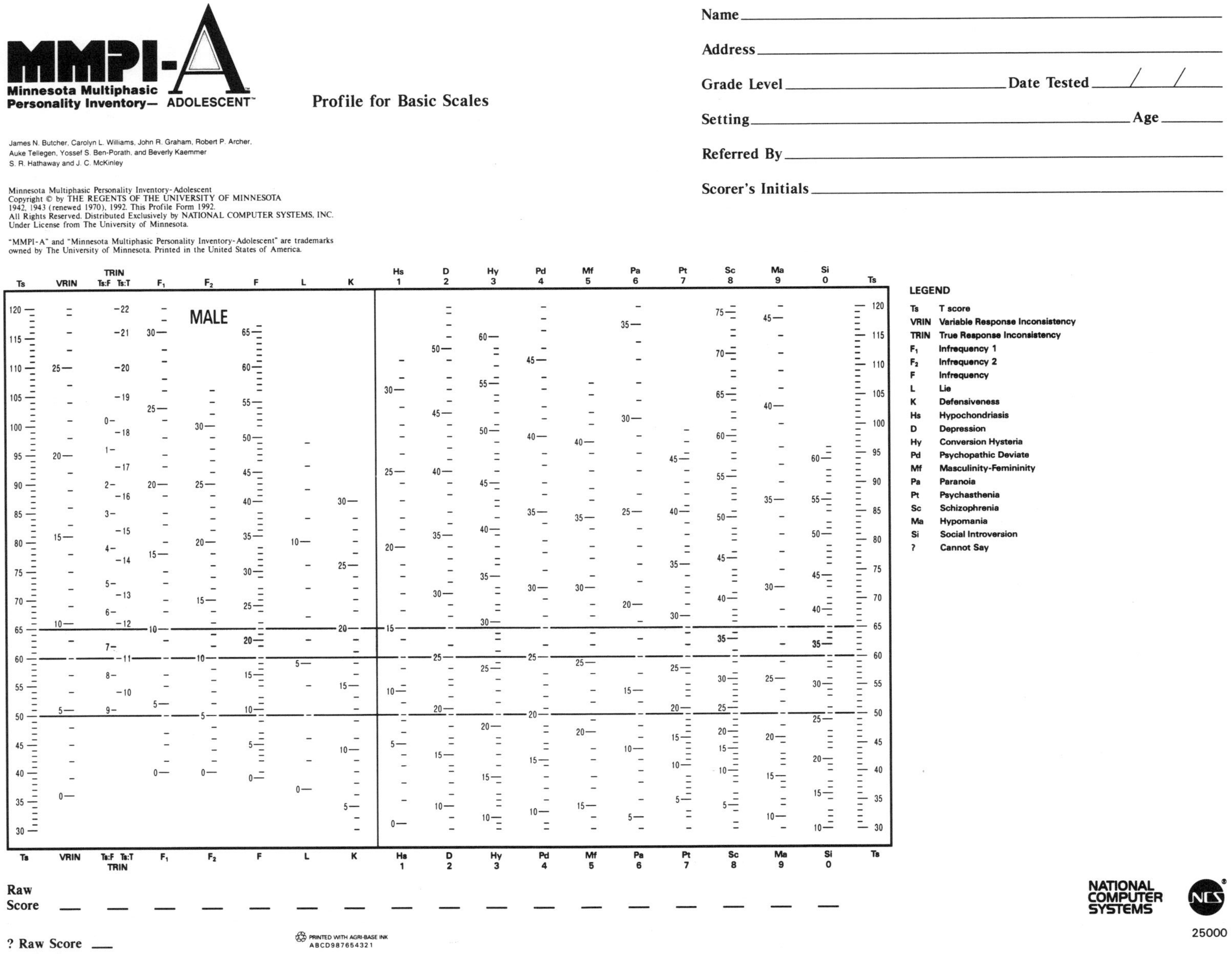

MMPI-A
Minnesota Multiphasic Personality Inventory— ADOLESCENT™

Profile for Basic Scales

James N. Butcher, Carolyn L. Williams, John R. Graham, Robert P. Archer, Auke Tellegen, Yossef S. Ben-Porath, and Beverly Kaemmer
S. R. Hathaway and J. C. McKinley

Name ______
Address ______
Grade Level ______ Date Tested __/__/__
Setting ______ Age ______
Referred By ______
Scorer's Initials ______

MALE

Ts | VRIN | TRIN (Ts:F Ts:T) | F₁ | F₂ | F | L | K | Hs 1 | D 2 | Hy 3 | Pd 4 | Mf 5 | Pa 6 | Pt 7 | Sc 8 | Ma 9 | Si 0 | Ts

Raw Score ___ ___ ___ ___ ___ ___ ___ ___ ___ ___ ___ ___ ___ ___ ___ ___ ___ ___

? Raw Score ___

LEGEND

- Ts T score
- VRIN Variable Response Inconsistency
- TRIN True Response Inconsistency
- F_1 Infrequency 1
- F_2 Infrequency 2
- F Infrequency
- L Lie
- K Defensiveness
- Hs Hypochondriasis
- D Depression
- Hy Conversion Hysteria
- Pd Psychopathic Deviate
- Mf Masculinity-Femininity
- Pa Paranoia
- Pt Psychasthenia
- Sc Schizophrenia
- Ma Hypomania
- Si Social Introversion
- ? Cannot Say

PRINTED WITH AGRI-BASE INK
ABCD987654321

NATIONAL COMPUTER SYSTEMS NCS® 25000

FIGURE I-7. MMPI-A basic scale profile for males. Reprinted with permission of the publisher from *Minnesota Multiphasic Personality Inventory-A*. Copyright © by the Regents of the University of Minnesota 1942, 1943 (renewed 1970), 1989, 1992. This form 1948, 1970, 1982, 1989, 1992.

MMPI-A
Minnesota Multiphasic Personality Inventory— ADOLESCENT™

Profile for Basic Scales

James N. Butcher, Carolyn L. Williams, John R. Graham, Robert P. Archer, Auke Tellegen, Yossef S. Ben-Porath, and Beverly Kaemmer
S. R. Hathaway and J. C. McKinley

Name ____________________

Address ____________________

Grade Level ____________ Date Tested ___/___/___

Setting ____________ Age ______

Referred By ____________________

Scorer's Initials ____________________

FEMALE

Ts | VRIN | TRIN (Ts:F Ts:T) | F_1 | F_2 | F | L | K | Hs 1 | D 2 | Hy 3 | Pd 4 | Mf 5 | Pa 6 | Pt 7 | Sc 8 | Ma 9 | Si 0 | Ts

Raw Score ___ ___ ___ ___ ___ ___ ___ ___ ___ ___ ___ ___ ___ ___ ___ ___ ___ ___

? Raw Score ___

LEGEND

- Ts T score
- VRIN Variable Response Inconsistency
- TRIN True Response Inconsistency
- F_1 Infrequency 1
- F_2 Infrequency 2
- F Infrequency
- L Lie
- K Defensiveness
- Hs Hypochondriasis
- D Depression
- Hy Conversion Hysteria
- Pd Psychopathic Deviate
- Mf Masculinity-Femininity
- Pa Paranoia
- Pt Psychasthenia
- Sc Schizophrenia
- Ma Hypomania
- Si Social Introversion
- ? Cannot Say

PRINTED WITH AGRI-BASE INK
ABCD987654321

NATIONAL COMPUTER SYSTEMS
25000

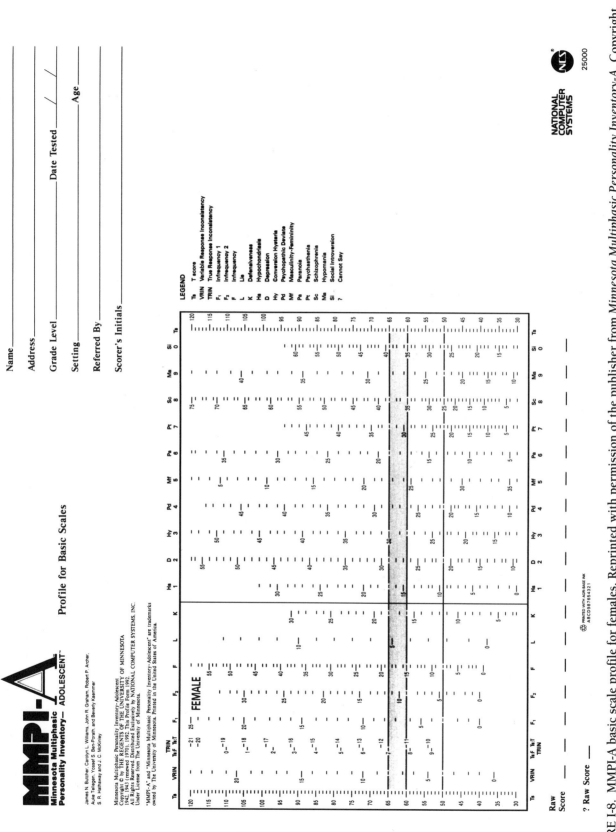

FIGURE I-8. MMPI-A basic scale profile for females. Reprinted with permission of the publisher from *Minnesota Multiphasic Personality Inventory-A*. Copyright © by the Regents of the University of Minnesota 1942, 1943 (renewed 1970), 1989, 1992. This form 1948, 1970, 1982, 1989, 1992.

MMPI-A
Minnesota Multiphasic Personality Inventory— ADOLESCENT™

Profile for Content and Supplementary Scales

James N. Butcher, Carolyn L. Williams, John R. Graham, Robert P. Archer, Auke Tellegen, Yossef S. Ben-Porath, and Beverly Kaemmer

Name ____________
Address ____________
Grade Level ____________ Date Tested __/__/__
Setting ____________ Age ______
Referred By ____________
Scorer's Initials ____________

Content

MALE

Ts | A-anx | A-obs | A-dep | A-hea | A-aln | A-biz | A-ang | A-cyn | A-con | A-lse | A-las | A-sod | A-fam | A-sch | A-trt | Ts

Raw Score __ __ __ __ __ __ __ __ __ __ __ __ __ __ __

Supplementary

Ts | MAC-R | ACK | PRO | IMM | A | R | Ts

Raw Score __ __ __ __ __ __

LEGEND

Ts	T score
A-anx	Adol. Anxiety
A-obs	Adol. Obsessiveness
A-dep	Adol. Depression
A-hea	Adol. Health Concerns
A-aln	Adol. Alienation
A-biz	Adol. Bizarre Mentation
A-ang	Adol. Anger
A-cyn	Adol. Cynicism
A-con	Adol. Conduct Problems
A-lse	Adol. Low Self-Esteem
A-las	Adol. Low Aspirations
A-sod	Adol. Social Discomfort
A-fam	Adol. Family Problems
A-sch	Adol. School Problems
A-trt	Adol. Negative Treatment Ind.
MAC-R	MacAndrew Alcoholism-Revised
ACK	Alcohol/Drug Problem Acknow.
PRO	Alcohol/Drug Problem Proneness
IMM	Immaturity
A	Anxiety
R	Repression

PRINTED WITH AGRI-BASE INK
ABCD987654321

NATIONAL COMPUTER SYSTEMS
25006

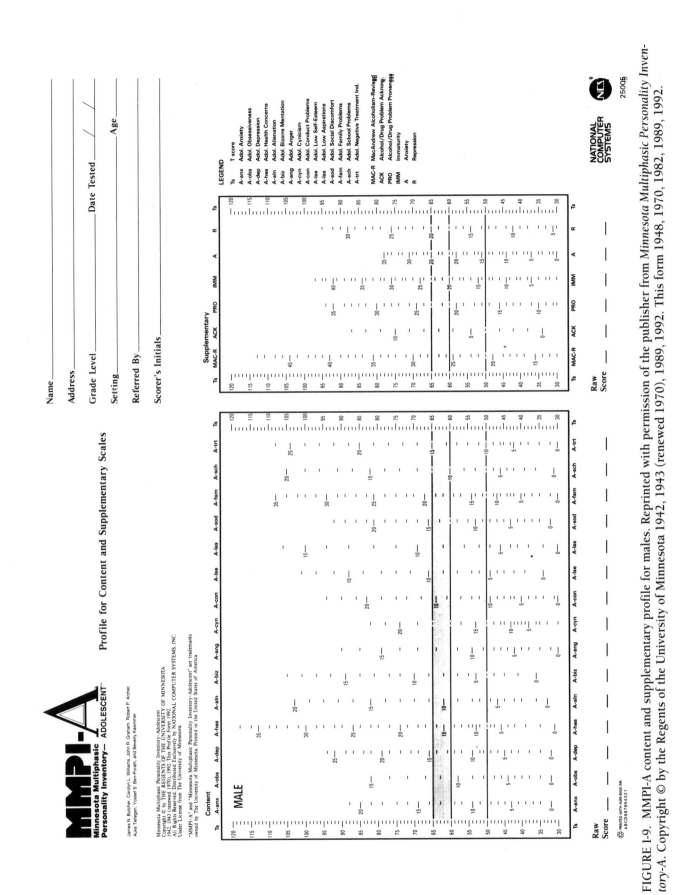

FIGURE I-9. MMPI-A content and supplementary profile for males. Reprinted with permission of the publisher from *Minnesota Multiphasic Personality Inventory-A*. Copyright © by the Regents of the University of Minnesota 1942, 1943 (renewed 1970), 1989, 1992. This form 1948, 1970, 1982, 1989, 1992.

MMPI-A
Minnesota Multiphasic Personality Inventory— ADOLESCENT™

Profile for Content and Supplementary Scales

James N. Butcher, Carolyn L. Williams, John R. Graham, Robert P. Archer, Auke Tellegen, Yossef S. Ben-Porath, and Beverly Kaemmer

Name ____________________

Address ____________________

Grade Level ____________ Date Tested ___/___/___

Setting ____________ Age ______

Referred By ____________________

Scorer's Initials ____________________

Content

FEMALE

Ts A-anx A-obs A-dep A-hea A-aln A-biz A-ang A-cyn A-con A-lse A-las A-sod A-fam A-sch A-trt Ts

Raw Score ___ ___ ___ ___ ___ ___ ___ ___ ___ ___ ___ ___ ___ ___ ___

Supplementary

Ts MAC-R ACK PRO IMM A R Ts

Raw Score ___ ___ ___ ___ ___ ___

LEGEND

Ts	T score
A-anx	Adol. Anxiety
A-obs	Adol. Obsessiveness
A-dep	Adol. Depression
A-hea	Adol. Health Concerns
A-aln	Adol. Alienation
A-biz	Adol. Bizarre Mentation
A-ang	Adol. Anger
A-cyn	Adol. Cynicism
A-con	Adol. Conduct Problems
A-lse	Adol. Low Self-Esteem
A-las	Adol. Low Aspirations
A-sod	Adol. Social Discomfort
A-fam	Adol. Family Problems
A-sch	Adol. School Problems
A-trt	Adol. Negative Treatment Ind.
MAC-R	MacAndrew Alcoholism-Revised
ACK	Alcohol/Drug Problem Acknow.
PRO	Alcohol/Drug Problem Proneness
IMM	Immaturity
A	Anxiety
R	Repression

PRINTED WITH AGRI-BASE INK
ABCD987654321

NATIONAL COMPUTER SYSTEMS NCS®

25005

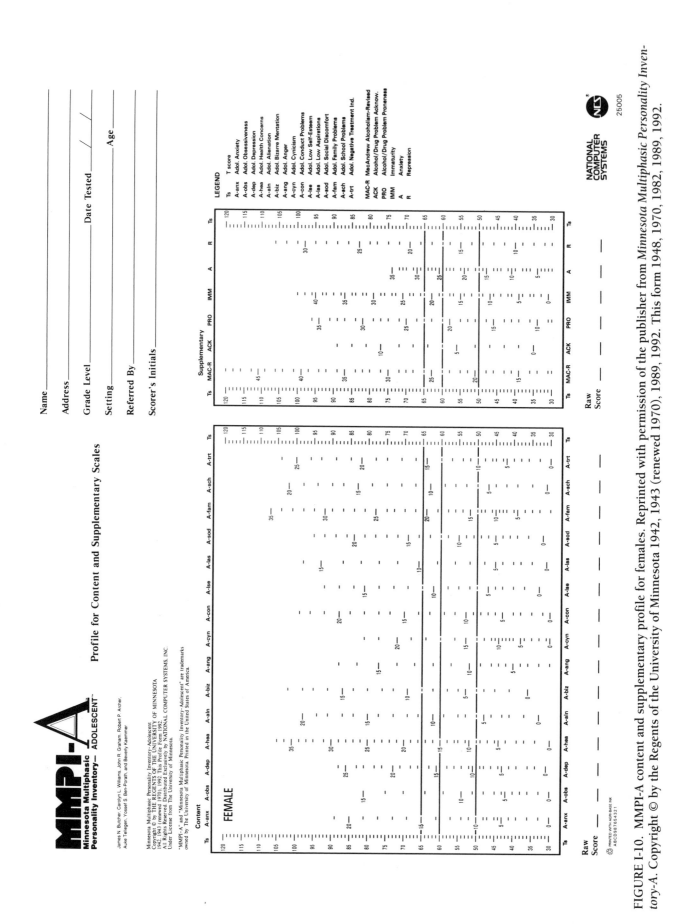

FIGURE I-10. MMPI-A content and supplementary profile for females. Reprinted with permission of the publisher from *Minnesota Multiphasic Personality Inventory-A*. Copyright © by the Regents of the University of Minnesota 1942, 1943 (renewed 1970), 1989, 1992. This form 1948, 1970, 1982, 1989, 1992.

MMPI-2™ S.R. Hathaway and J.C. McKinley
Minnesota Multiphasic Personality Inventory-2™

Profile for K- and Non-K-Corrected Basic Scales

Name ______
Address ______
Occupation ______ Date Tested __/__/__
Education ______ Age ______ Marital Status ______
Referred By ______
MMPI-2 Code ______
Scorer's Initials ______

MALE (K-Corrected)

T or Tc | L | F | K | Hs+.5K 1 | D 2 | Hy 3 | Pd+.4K 4 | Mf 5 | Pa 6 | Pt+1K 7 | Sc+1K 8 | Ma+.2K 9 | Si 0 | T or Tc

Fractions of K

K	.5	.4	.2
30	15	12	6
29	15	12	6
28	14	11	6
27	14	11	5
26	13	10	5
25	13	10	5
24	12	10	5
23	12	9	5
22	11	9	4
21	11	8	4
20	10	8	4
19	10	8	4
18	9	7	4
17	9	7	3
16	8	6	3
15	8	6	3
14	7	6	3
13	7	5	3
12	6	5	2
11	6	4	2
10	5	4	2
9	5	4	2
8	4	3	2
7	4	3	1
6	3	2	1
5	3	2	1
4	2	2	1
3	2	1	1
2	1	1	0
1	1	0	0
0	0	0	0

Raw Score ___
? Raw Score ___
K to be Added ___
Raw Score with K ___

MALE (Non-K-Corrected)

T | L | F | K | Hs 1 | D 2 | Hy 3 | Pd 4 | Mf 5 | Pa 6 | Pt 7 | Sc 8 | Ma 9 | Si 0 | T

Raw Score ___
? Raw Score ___

NATIONAL COMPUTER SYSTEMS
24006

FIGURE I-11. MMPI-2 K- and non–K-corrected basic scale profile for men. Reprinted with permission of the publisher from *Minnesota Multiphasic Personality Inventory-2*. Copyright © by the Regents of the University of Minnesota 1942, 1943 (renewed 1970), 1989. This form 1948, 1970, 1982, 1989.

MMPI-2™ S.R. Hathaway and J.C. McKinley
Minnesota Multiphasic Personality Inventory-2™

Profile for K- and Non-K-Corrected Basic Scales

Minnesota Multiphasic Personality Inventory-2

Name ______
Address ______
Occupation ______ Date Tested __/__/__
Education ______ Age ______ Marital Status ______
Referred By ______
MMPI-2 Code ______
Scorer's Initials ______

Fractions of K

K	.5	.4	.2
30	15	12	6
29	15	12	6
28	14	11	6
27	14	11	5
26	13	10	5
25	13	10	5
24	12	10	5
23	12	9	5
22	11	9	4
21	11	8	4
20	10	8	4
19	10	8	4
18	9	7	4
17	9	7	3
16	8	6	3
15	8	6	3
14	7	6	3
13	7	5	3
12	6	5	2
11	6	4	2
10	5	4	2
9	5	4	2
8	4	3	2
7	4	3	1
6	3	2	1
5	3	2	1
4	2	2	1
3	2	1	1
2	1	1	0
1	1	0	0
0	0	0	0

FEMALE (K-Corrected)

T or Tc | L | F | K | Hs+.5K 1 | D 2 | Hy 3 | Pd+.4K 4 | Mf 5 | Pa 6 | Pt+1K 7 | Sc+1K 8 | Ma+.2K 9 | Si 0 | T or Tc

Raw Score ___
? Raw Score ___
K to be Added ___
Raw Score with K ___

FEMALE (Non-K-Corrected)

T | L | F | K | Hs 1 | D 2 | Hy 3 | Pd 4 | Mf 5 | Pa 6 | Pt 7 | Sc 8 | Ma 9 | Si 0 | T

Raw Score ___
? Raw Score ___

NATIONAL COMPUTER SYSTEMS

24006

FIGURE I-12. MMPI-2 K- and non–K-corrected basic scale profile for women. Reprinted with permission of the publisher from *Minnesota Multiphasic Personality Inventory-2*. Copyright © by the Regents of the University of Minnesota 1942, 1943 (renewed 1970), 1989. This form 1948, 1970, 1982, 1989.

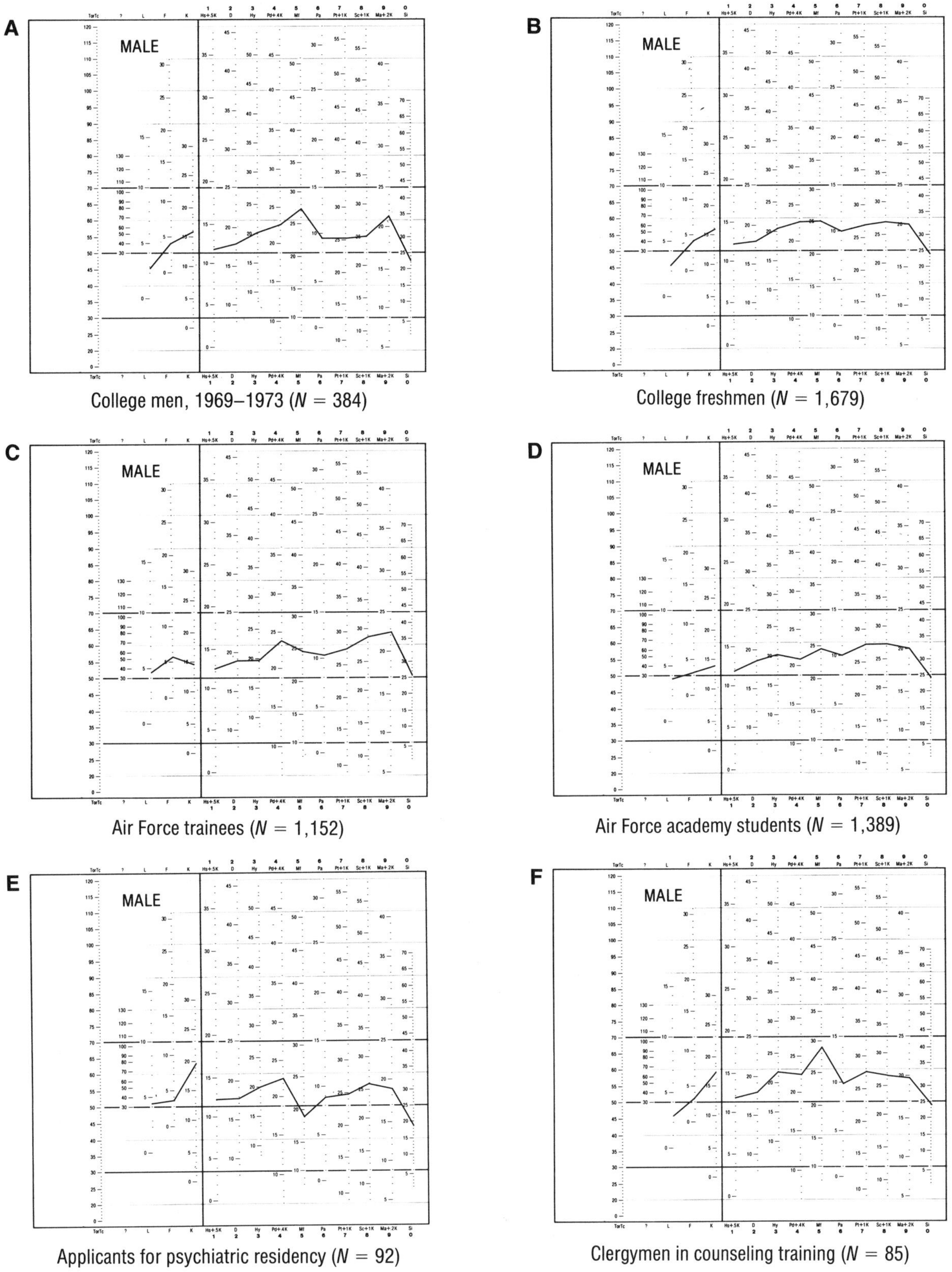

FIGURE I-13. Group mean profiles for several samples of "normal" men, illustrating the inaccuracy of the original MMPI in characterizing normal individuals. (Sources: *A*, Schneider & Cherry, 1976; *B*, Loper, Robertson, & Swanson, 1968; *C*, Bloom, 1977; *D*, Lachar, 1974; *E*, Garetz & Anderson, 1973; *F*, Jansen & Bonk, 1973. Adapted by permission.)

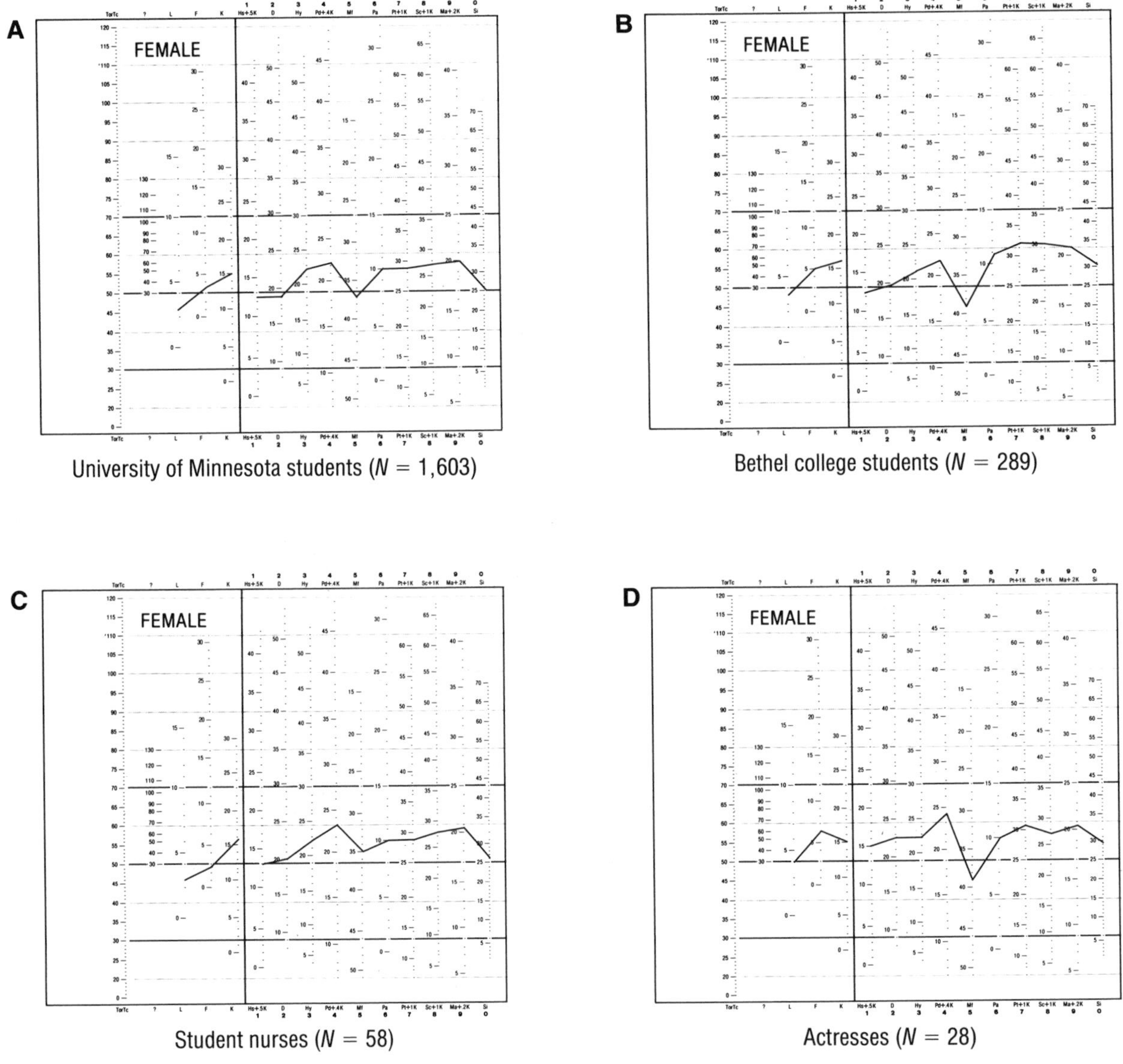

FIGURE I-14. Group mean profiles for several samples of "normal" women, illustrating the inaccuracy of the original MMPI in characterizing normal individuals. (Sources: *A*, Loper, Robinson, & Swanson, 1968; *B*, Butcher & Pancheri, 1976; *C*, Wolf, Freinck, & Shaffer, 1964; *D*, Taft, 1961. Reprinted by permission.)

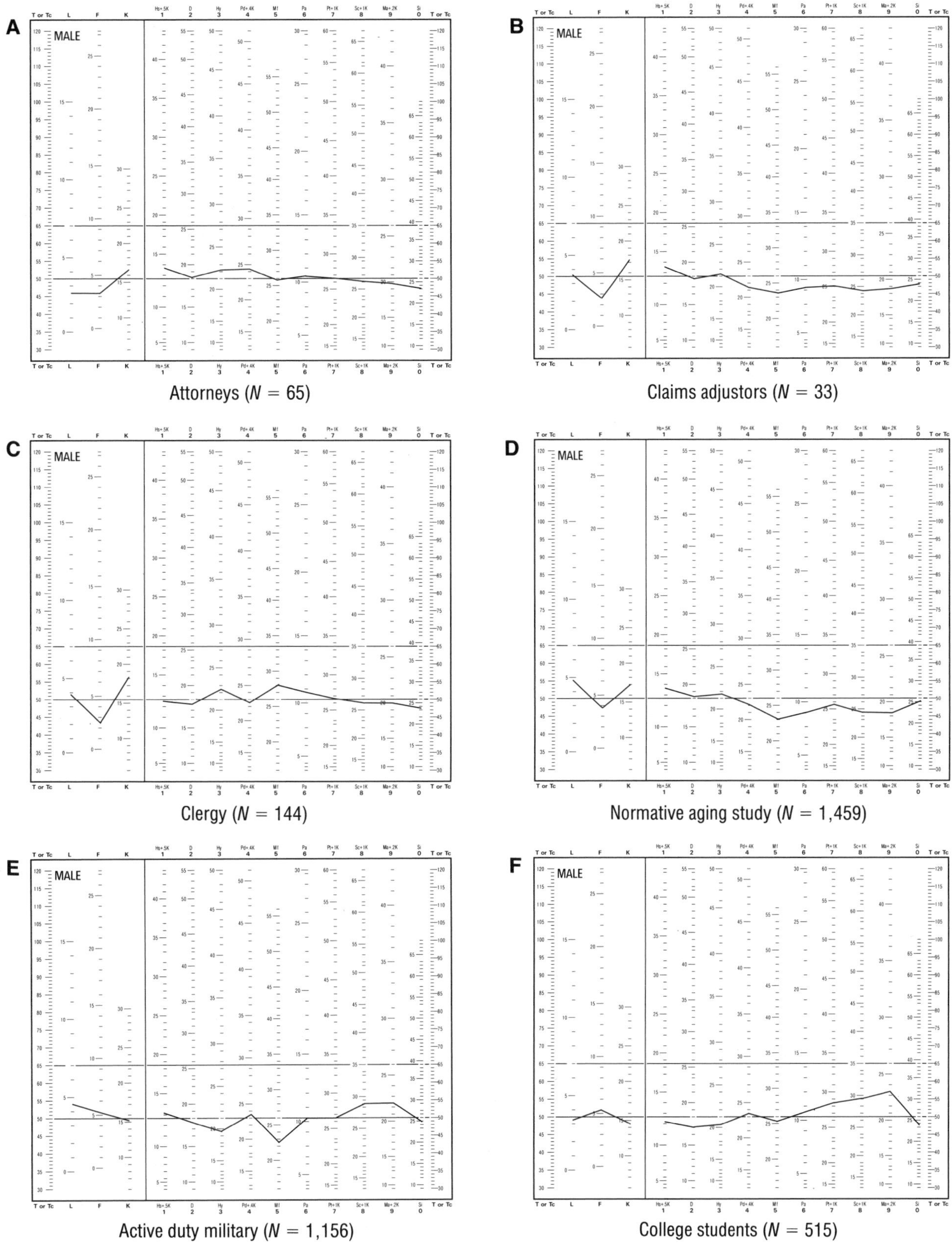

FIGURE I-15. Group mean MMPI-2 profiles of several groups of "normal" men, illustrating how contemporary "normal" samples are characterized by the new norms. (Sources: *A*, *B*, *C*, Putnam, Adams, & Butcher, 1992; *D*, Butcher et al., 1991; *E*, Butcher, Jeffrey, et al., 1990; *F*, Butcher, Graham, et al., 1990. Reprinted by permission.)

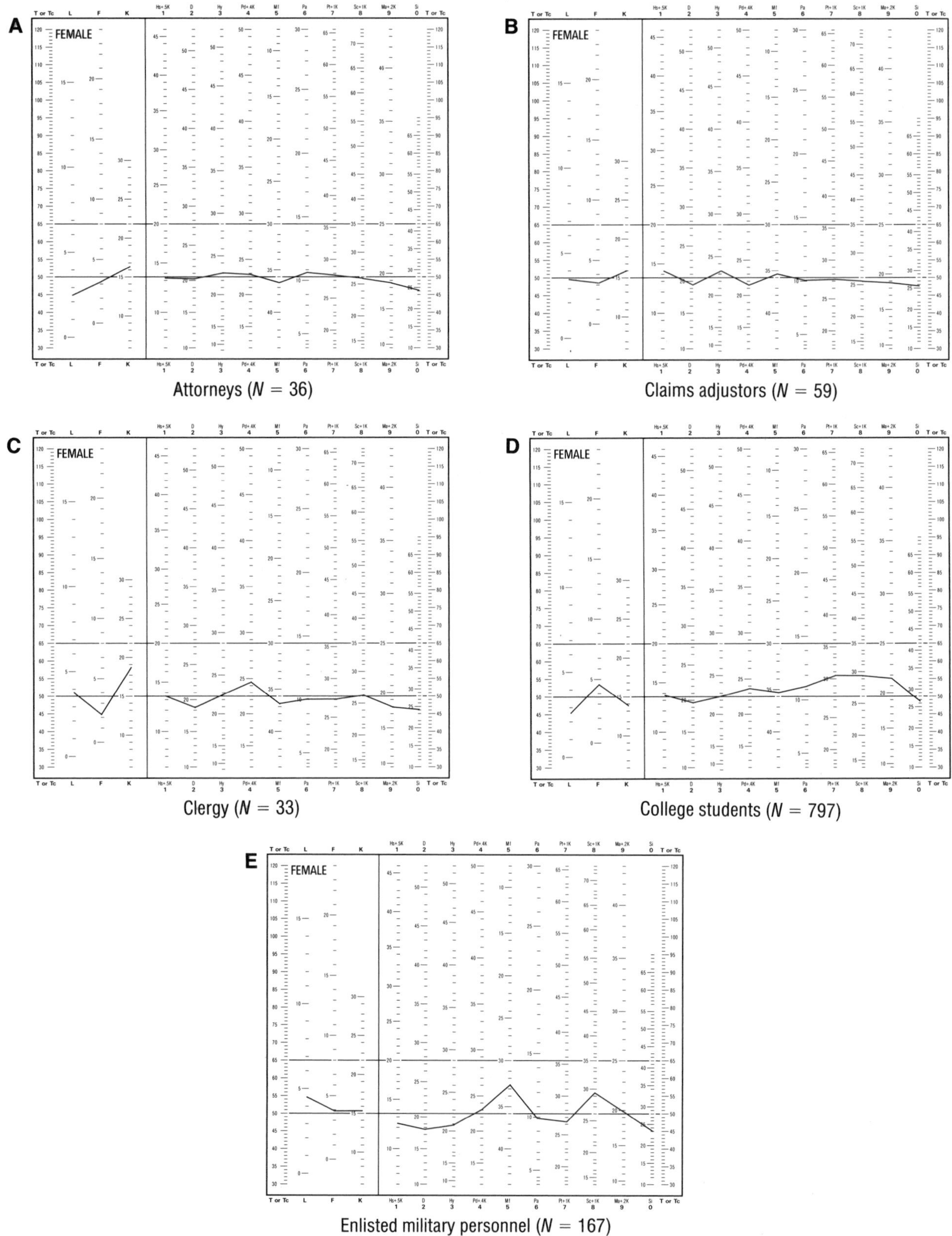

FIGURE I-16. Group mean MMPI-2 profiles of several groups of "normal" women, illustrating how contemporary "normal" samples are characterized by the new norms. (Sources: *A*, *B*, *C*, Putnam, Adams, & Butcher, 1992; *D*, Butcher, Graham, et al., 1990; *E*, Egeland, Erickson, Butcher, & Ben-Porath, 1991. Reprinted by permission.)

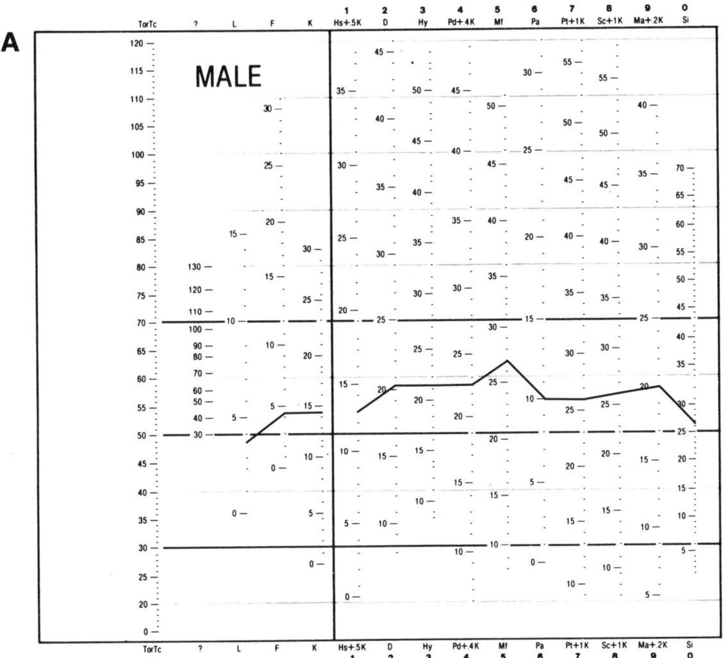

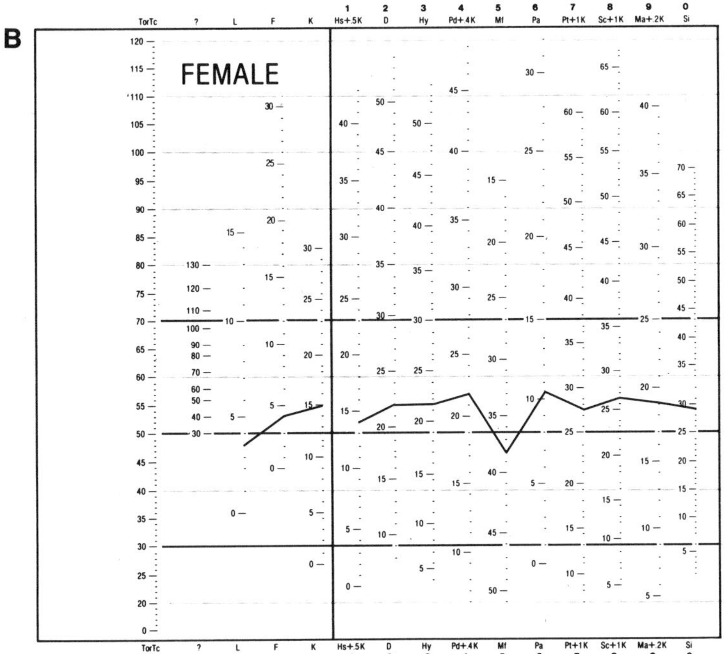

FIGURE I-17. Group mean profiles of the MMPI-2 restandardization samples (*A*: men; *B*: women), plotted on the original MMPI norms to illustrate the inaccuracy of the original inventory to characterize "normal" individuals. (Source: Butcher, Dahlstrom, Graham, Tellegen, & Kaemmer, 1989. Reprinted by permission.)

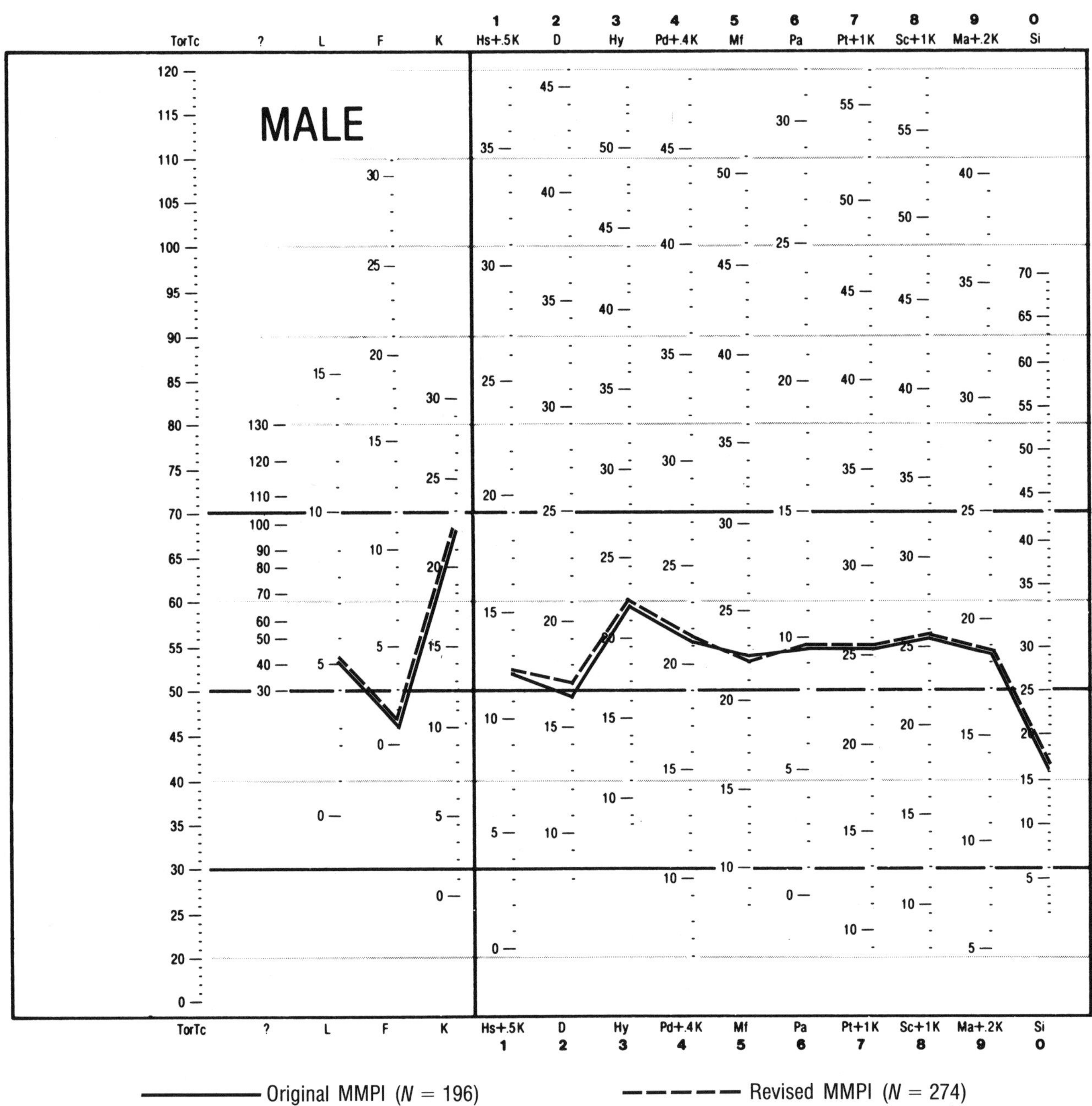

FIGURE I-18. Basic profiles of two groups of airline pilot applicants who had been administered either the original MMPI or the revised MMPI, with both profiles plotted on the original MMPI norms. (Source: Butcher, 1992c. Reprinted by permission.)

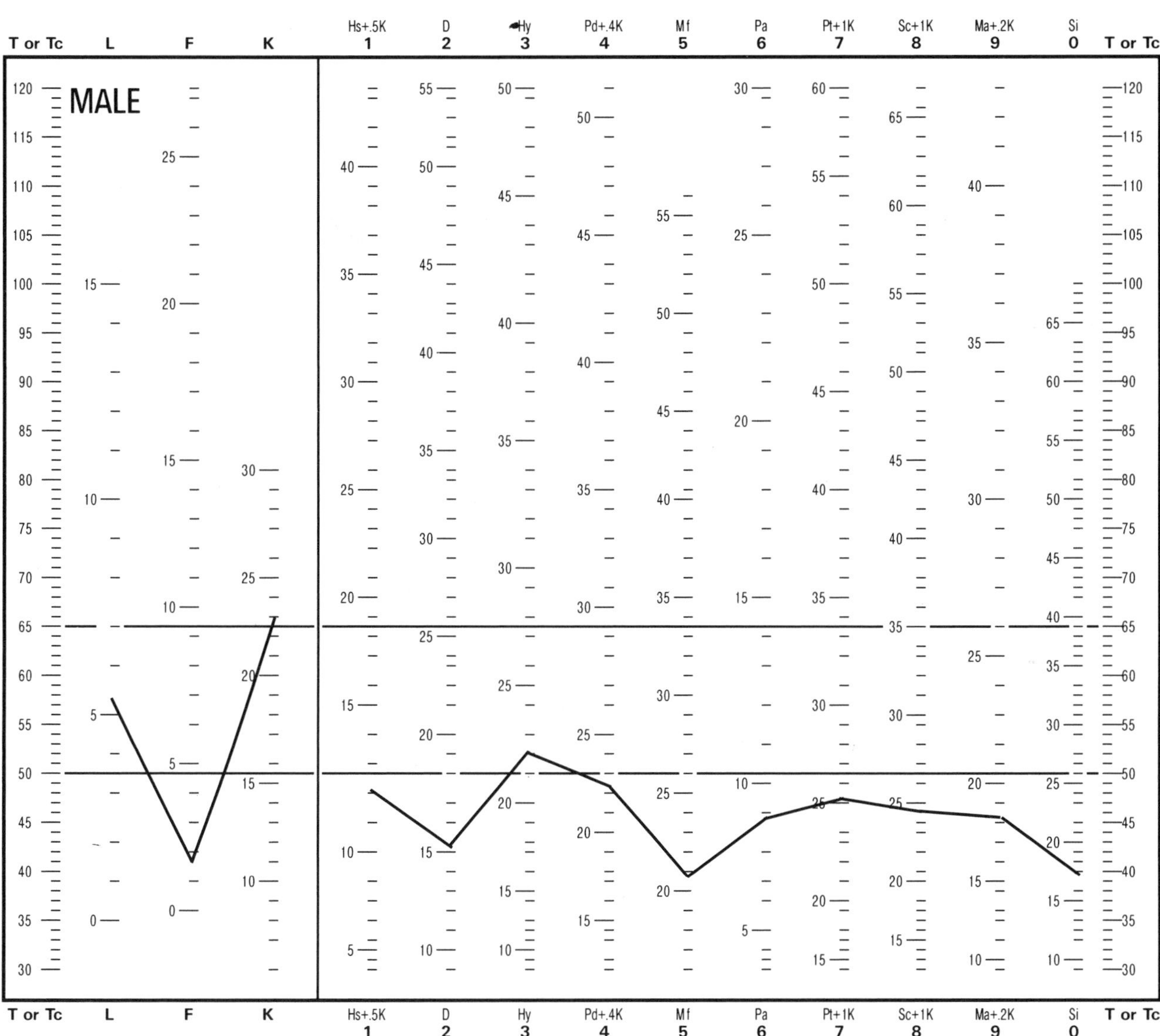

FIGURE I-19. MMPI-2 basic profile of airline pilot applicants ($N = 437$), illustrating how well-adjusted individuals who present themselves in a positive light score on the MMPI-2 norms. (Source: Butcher, 1992c. Used by permission.)

TABLE I-1

Geographic Distribution of Individuals in the MMPI-2 Restandardization Sample

	Males		Females	
Location	**Frequency**	**%**	**Frequency**	**%**
California	112	9.8	132	9.0
Minnesota	266	23.4	296	20.3
North Carolina	181	15.9	307	21.0
Ohio	196	17.2	254	17.4
Pennsylvania	123	10.8	182	12.5
Virginia	109	9.6	144	9.9
Washington	106	9.3	111	7.6
Military[a]	18	1.6	6	0.4
Indian Reservation[b]	27	2.4	30	2.1
TOTAL	1,138	100.0	1,462	100.2

Note: From Dahlstrom & Tellegen (1992). Reprinted by permission.
[a]Active duty personnel tested on several U.S. military bases.
[b]American Indian adults residing on a federal reservation in the state of Washington.

TABLE I-2

Ethnic Group Distribution of Individuals in the MMPI-2 Restandardization Sample

	Males				Females			
	Restandardization				Restandardization			
Ethnic Group	Frequency	%	Adjusted %	Census	Frequency	%	Adjusted %	Census
Asian	6	0.5	0.5	1.5	13	0.9	0.9	1.5
Black	126	11.1	11.1	10.1	188	12.9	12.9	10.9
Hispanic	35	3.1	[a]	[a]	38	2.6	[a]	[a]
American Indian	38	3.3	3.3	0.5	39	2.7	2.7	0.5
White	933	82.0	83.7	85.2	1,184	81.0	82.4	84.7
Other	0	0	1.3	2.7	0	0	1.1	2.3
TOTAL	1,138	100.0	99.9	100.0	1,462	100.1	100.0	99.9

Note: From Dahlstrom & Tellegen (1992). Reprinted by permission.
[a]Adjusted to conform to U.S. Census categories (Hispanic individuals were classified as: 56% "White," 44% "Other").

TABLE I-3

Age Distribution of Individuals in the MMPI-2 Restandardization Sample

	Males			Females		
Age Range	**Frequency**	**%**	**Census**	**Frequency**	**%**	**Census**
18–19	19	1.7	5.7	29	2.0	5.1
20–29	269	23.6	26.4	373	25.5	24.1
30–39	331	29.1	20.1	438	30.0	18.7
40–49	177	15.6	14.4	224	15.3	13.7
50–59	144	12.7	14.3	178	12.2	14.3
60–69	134	11.8	11.0	143	9.8	12.0
70–79	55	4.8	6.0	65	4.5	9.0
80–84	9	0.8	2.2	12	0.8	4.0
TOTAL	1,138	100.0	100.1	1,462	100.1	100.9

Note: Values have been corrected since the population data were reported in the 1989 MMPI-2 Manual. From Dahlstrom & Tellegen (1992). Reprinted by permission.

TABLE I-4

Distribution of Occupations for the Individuals in the MMPI-2 Restandardization Sample

	Males			Females		
Occupation Group	**Frequency**	**%**	**Census**	**Frequency**	**%**	**Census**
Professional	479	42.1	15.5	581	39.7	15.7
Managerial	168	14.8	16.8	109	7.5	5.5
Skilled	164	14.4	37.8	51	3.5	13.1
Clerical	37	3.3	12.4	328	22.4	42.0
Laborer	132	11.6	17.3	73	5.0	23.8
None of the above	154	13.5	0.0	309	21.1	0.0
(Missing data)	4	0.4	0.0	11	0.8	0.0
TOTAL	1,138	100.1	99.8	1,462	100.0	100.1

Note: From Dahlstrom & Tellegen (1992). Reprinted by permission.

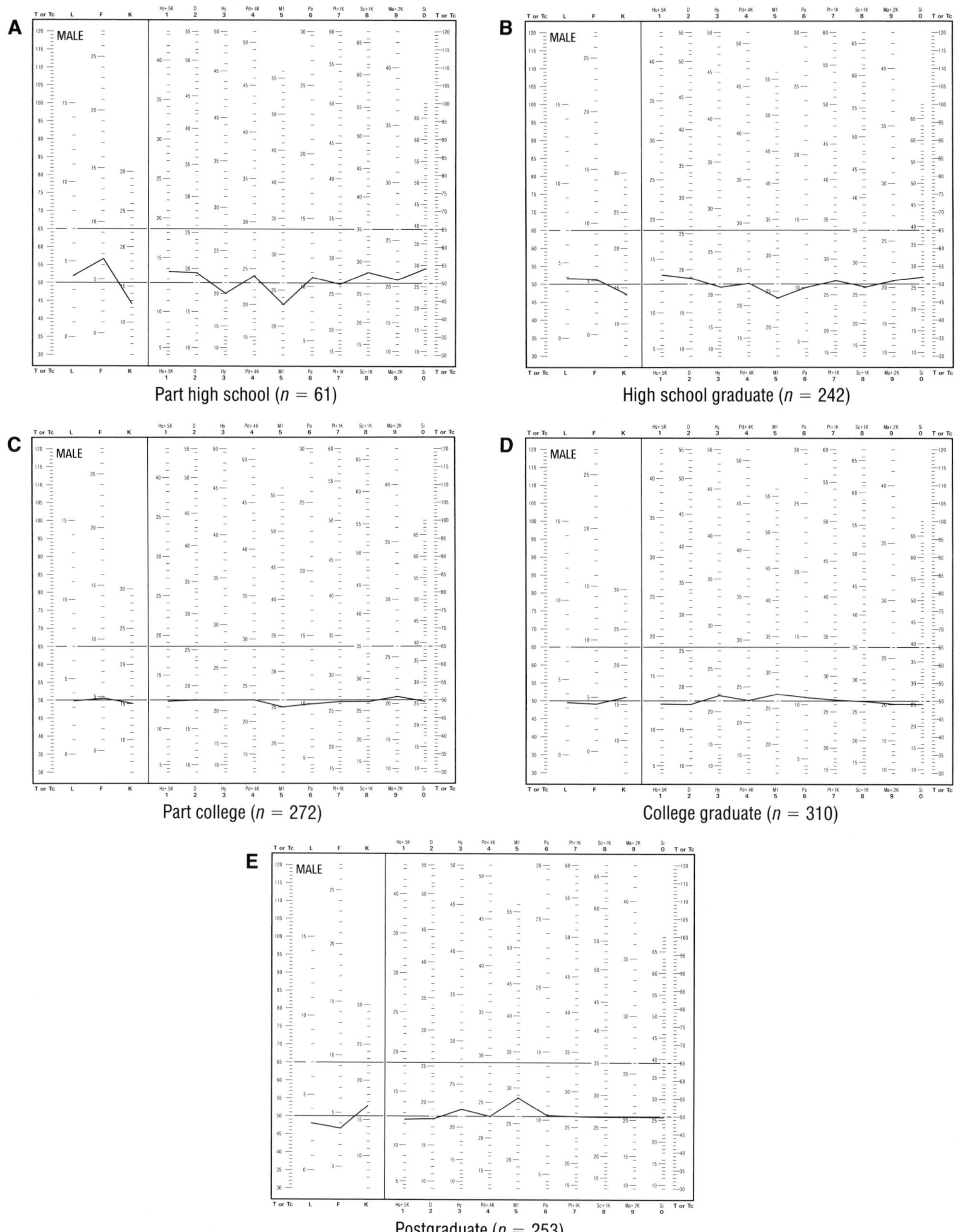

FIGURE I-20. Group mean profiles of men in the MMPI-2 restandardization sample according to levels of education. (Source: Butcher, 1990c. Adapted by permission.)

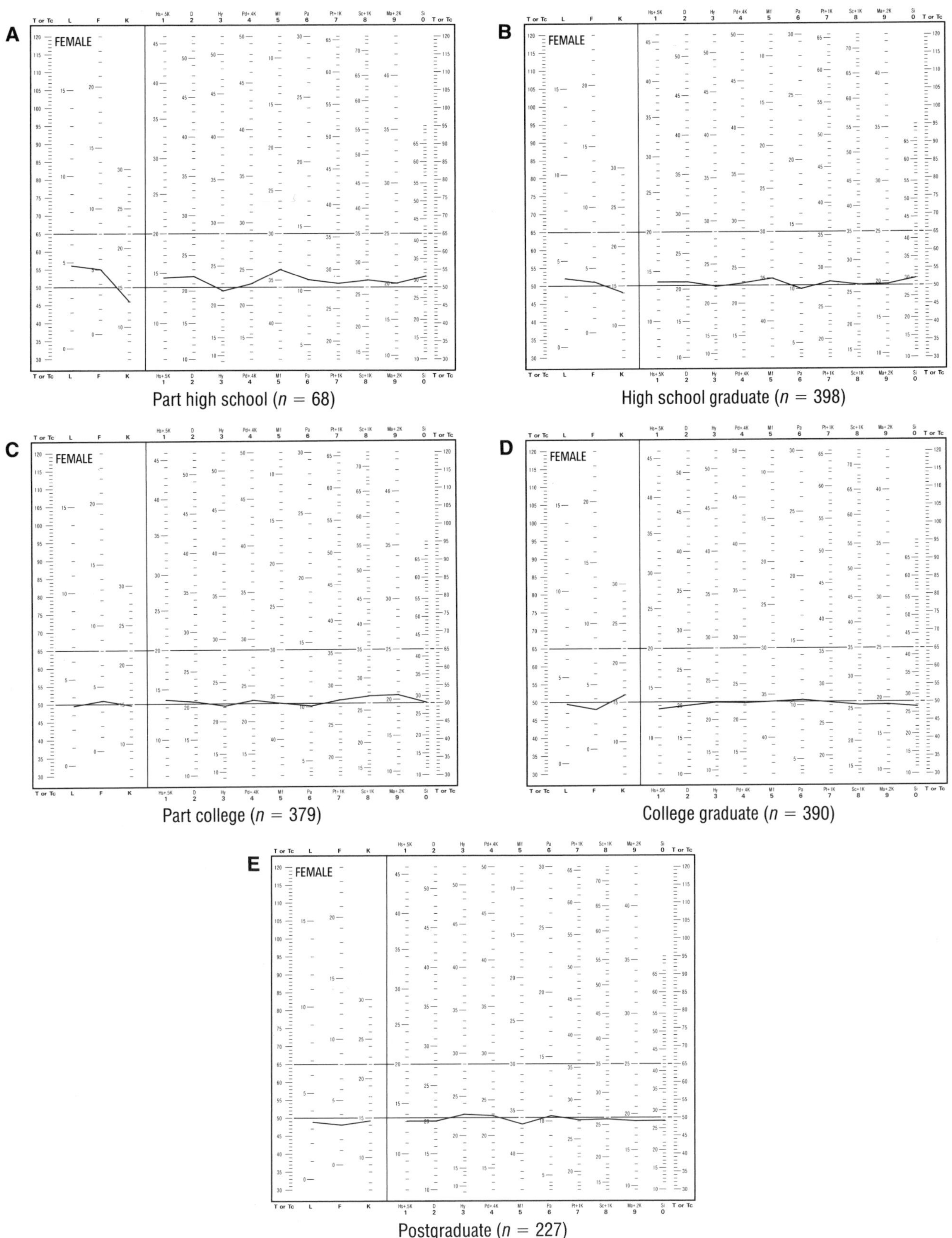

FIGURE I-21. Group mean profiles of women in the MMPI-2 restandardization sample according to levels of education. (Source: Butcher, 1990c. Adapted by permission.)

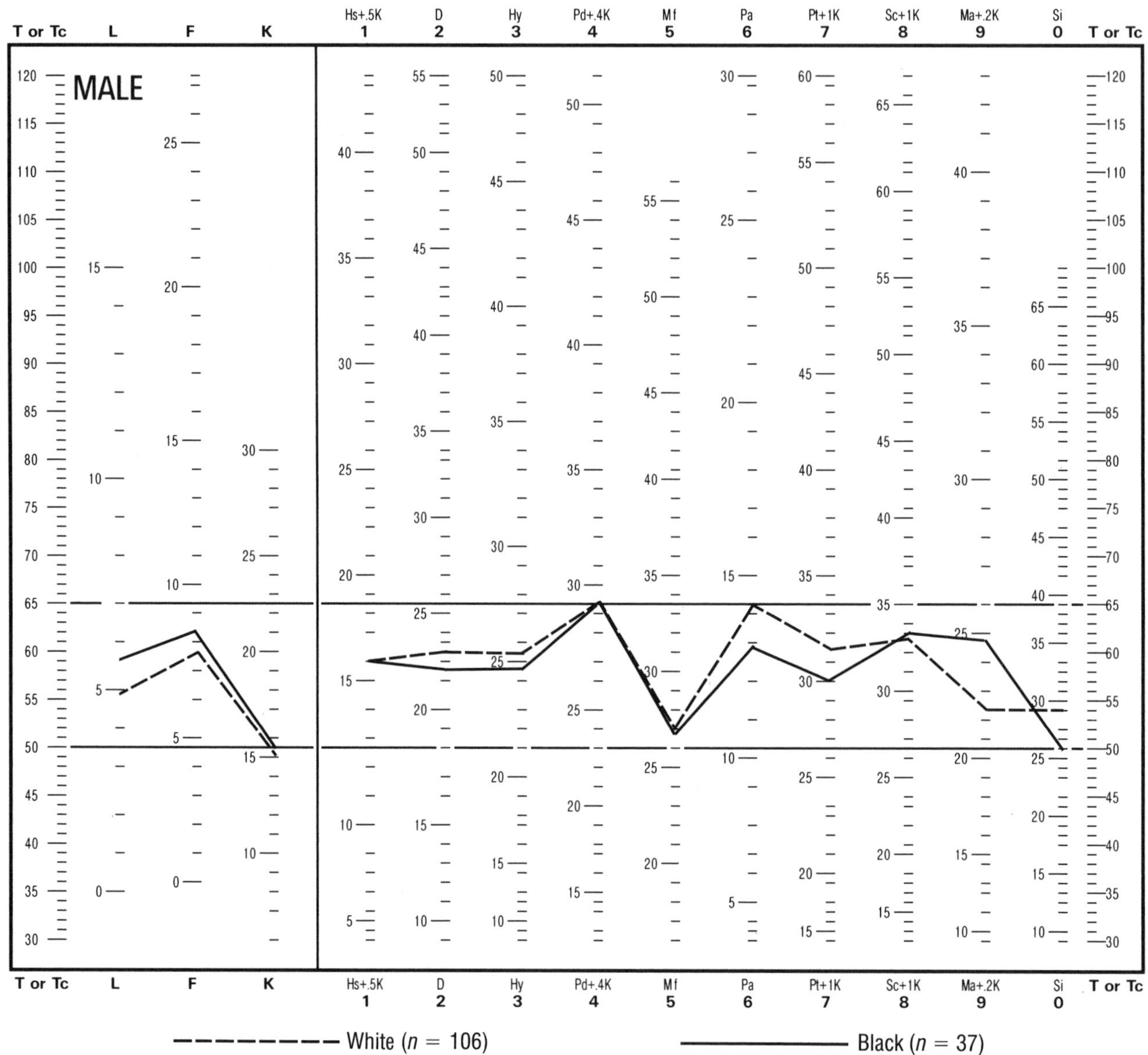

FIGURE I-22. Group mean MMPI-2 clinical scale profile of White and Black men who had been court-ordered to take the MMPI-2. (Source: Shondrick, Ben-Porath, & Stafford, 1992. Used by permission.)

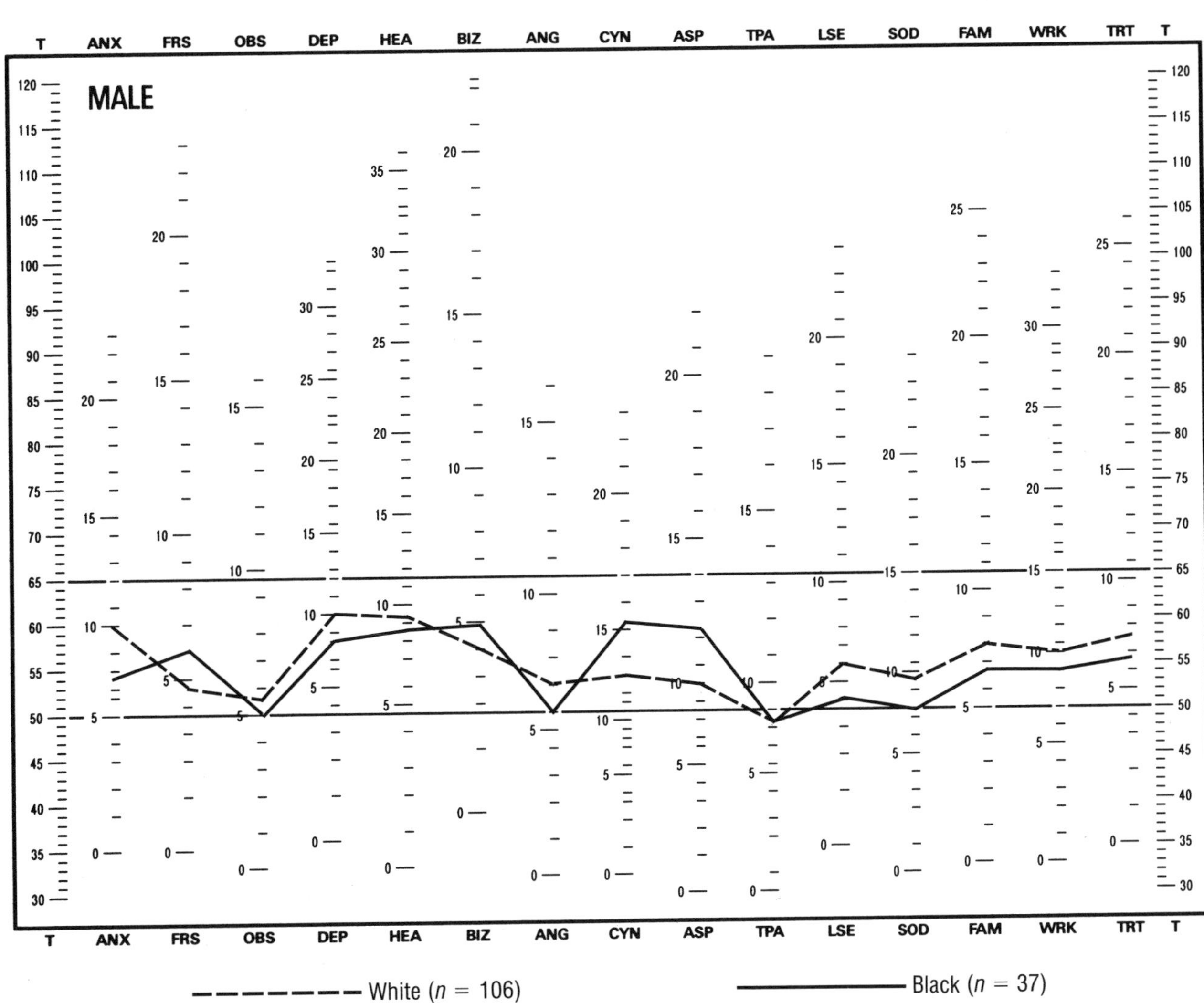

FIGURE I-23. Group mean MMPI-2 content scale profile of White and Black men who had been court-ordered to take the MMPI-2. (Source: Shondrick, Ben-Porath, & Stafford, 1992. Used by permission.)

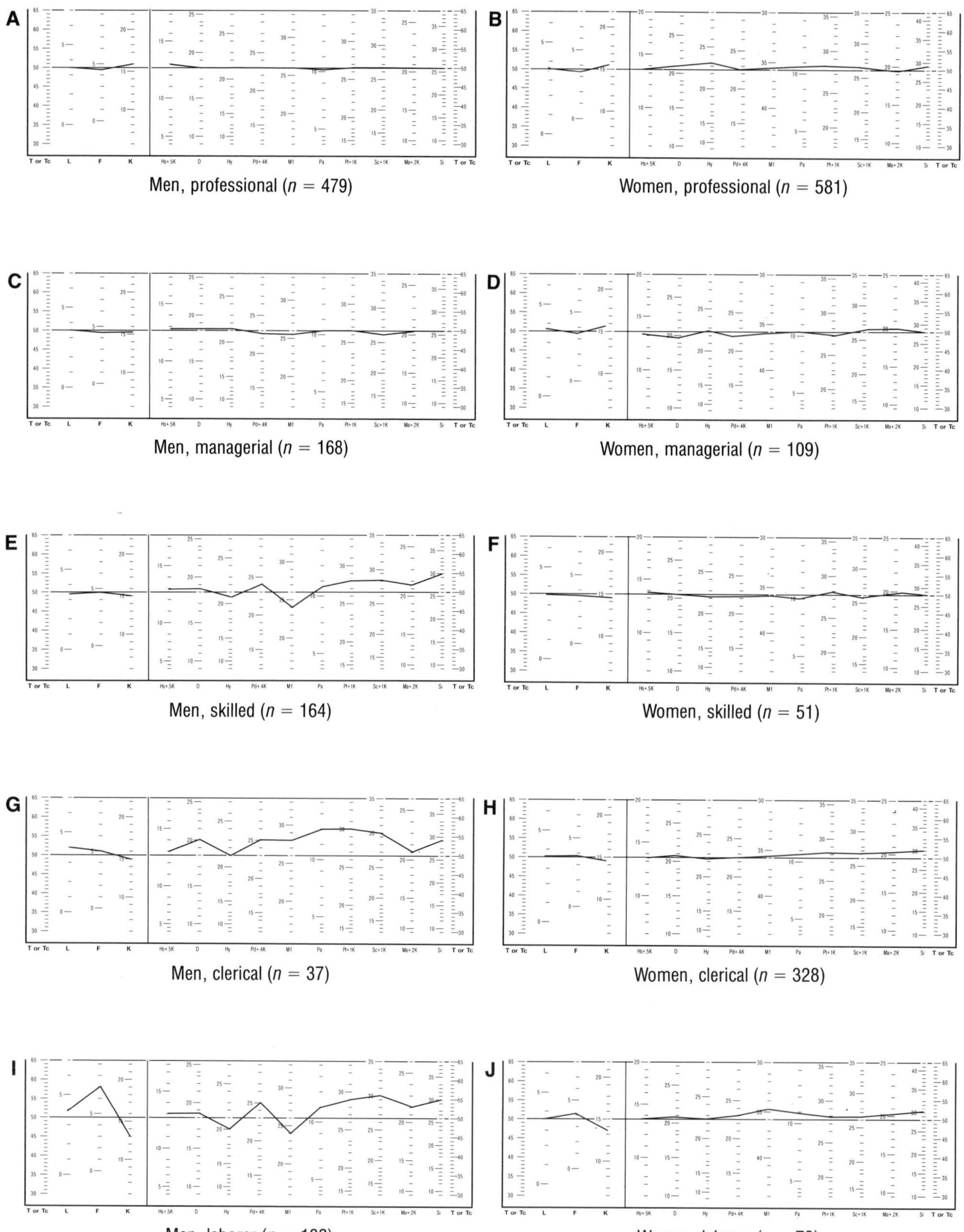

FIGURE I-24. Mean MMPI-2 profiles by occupational group. (Source: Dahlstrom & Tellegen, 1992. Reprinted by permission.)

TABLE I-5

Ethnicity of Subjects in the MMPI-A Normative Sample

Site	Boys		Girls	
	N	%	*N*	%
White	616	76.5	619	75.9
Black	100	12.4	100	12.3
Asian	23	2.9	23	2.8
American Indian	21	2.6	26	3.2
Hispanic	18	2.2	16	2.0
Other	20	2.5	21	2.6
None reported	7	0.9	10	1.2
TOTAL	805		815	

Note: From Williams et al. (1992). Reprinted by permission.

TABLE I-6

Age Distribution of the MMPI-A Normative Sample

Age	Boys[a]		Girls[b]	
	N	%	*N*	%
14	193	24.0	174	21.3
15	207	25.8	231	28.3
16	228	28.3	202	24.8
17	135	16.7	163	20.0
18	42	5.2	45	5.5
TOTAL	805		815	

Note: From Williams et al. (1992). Reprinted by permission.
[a]M = 15.54; SD = 1.17
[b]M = 15.60; SD = 1.18

TABLE I-7

Grade Level Distribution of the MMPI-A Normative Sample

	Boys		Girls	
Grade	***N***	**%**	***N***	**%**
7	5	0.6	3	0.4
8	57	7.1	64	7.9
9	212	26.3	204	25.0
10	238	29.6	235	28.8
11	206	25.6	184	22.6
12	87	10.8	124	15.2
None reported	0	0.0	1	0.1
TOTAL	805		815	

Note: From Williams et al. (1992). Reprinted by permission.

TABLE I-8

Father's Occupation Reported by the Adolescent Normative Sample

	Boys		Girls	
Occupation	***N***	**%**	***N***	**%**
High-level professional	139	17.4	125	15.3
Professional	269	33.4	267	32.8
Managerial	112	13.9	105	12.9
Skilled labor	68	8.4	70	8.6
Unskilled labor	23	2.9	23	2.8
Homemaker	1	0.1	3	0.4
Unemployed	6	0.7	8	1.0
Retired	12	1.5	17	2.1
Other	157	19.5	174	21.3
None reported	18	2.2	23	2.8
TOTAL	805		815	

Note: From Butcher et al. (1992). Reprinted by permission.

TABLE I-9

Mother's Occupation Reported by the Adolescent Normative Sample

	Boys		Girls	
Occupation	***N***	**%**	***N***	**%**
High-level professional	28	3.5	22	2.5
Professional	231	28.7	248	30.4
Managerial	194	24.1	193	23.7
Skilled labor	51	6.3	34	4.2
Unskilled labor	38	4.7	22	2.7
Homemaker	139	17.3	130	16.0
Unemployed	15	1.9	16	2.0
Retired	3	0.4	0	0.0
Other	92	11.4	120	14.8
None reported	14	1.7	30	3.7
TOTAL	805		815	

Note: From Butcher et al. (1992). Reprinted by permission.

TABLE I-10

Father's Education Reported by the Adolescent Normative Sample

	Boys		Girls	
Education	***N***	**%**	***N***	**%**
Grade school	17	2.1	15	1.8
Some high school	59	7.3	88	10.8
High school graduate	173	21.5	191	23.4
Some college	114	14.2	108	13.3
College graduate	272	33.8	262	32.1
Graduate school	152	18.9	122	15.0
None reported	18	2.2	29	3.6
TOTAL	805		815	

Note: From Butcher et al. (1992). Reprinted by permission.

TABLE I-11

Mother's Education Reported by the Adolescent Normative Sample

	Boys		Girls	
Education	***N***	**%**	***N***	**%**
Grade school	9	1.1	11	1.3
Some high school	38	4.7	54	6.6
High school graduate	250	31.1	230	28.2
Some college	145	18.0	183	22.5
College graduate	260	32.3	244	30.0
Graduate school	91	11.3	68	8.3
None reported	12	1.5	25	3.1
TOTAL	805		815	

Note: From Butcher et al. (1992). Reprinted by permission.

TABLE I-12

Geographic Distribution of Individuals in the MMPI-A Normative Sample

	Boys		Girls	
Site	***N***	**%**	***N***	**%**
Minnesota	201	25.0	300	36.8
New York	168	20.9	0	0.0
North Carolina	119	14.8	84	10.3
Ohio	101	12.5	109	13.4
California	99	12.3	127	15.6
Virginia	82	10.2	127	15.6
Pennsylvania	34	4.2	55	6.7
Washington State[a]	1	0.1	13	1.6
TOTAL	805		815	

Note: From Williams et al. (1992). Reprinted by permission.
[a]The data obtained from the American Indian Reservation (Muckleshoot) represent the entire population of testable children in the school. *Other American Indian boys were obtained in regular school settings.*

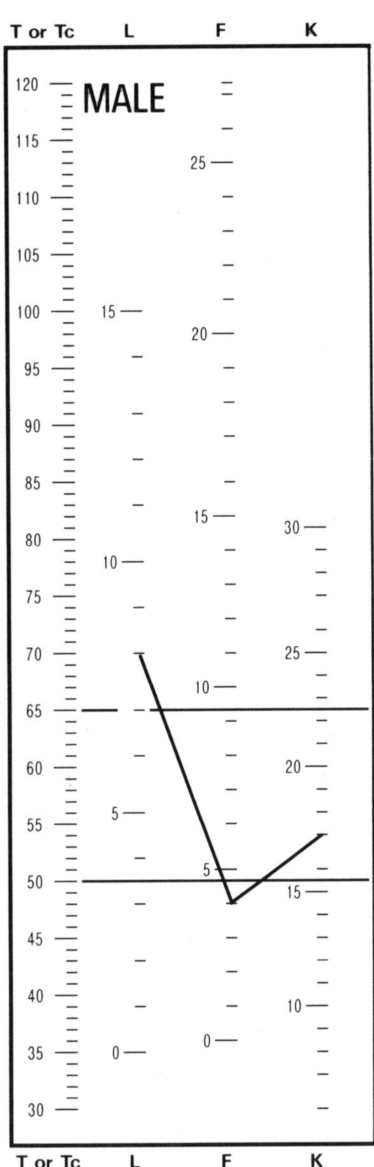

FIGURE I-25. Invalid *L* scale pattern. Elevated *L* scale pattern suggests a likely invalid test performance as a result of an overly virtuous self-report response style.

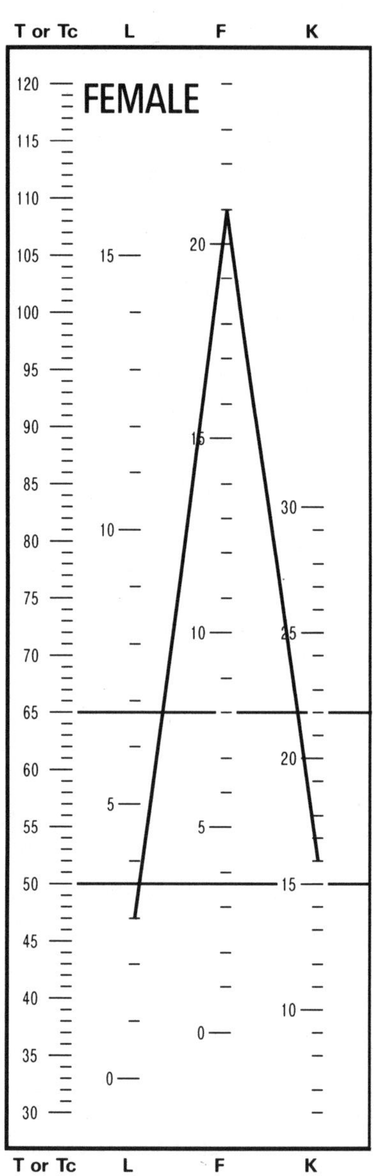

FIGURE I-26. Invalid *F* scale pattern. Elevated *F* scale pattern suggests a likely invalid test performance as a result of symptom exaggeration or malingering of psychological symptoms.

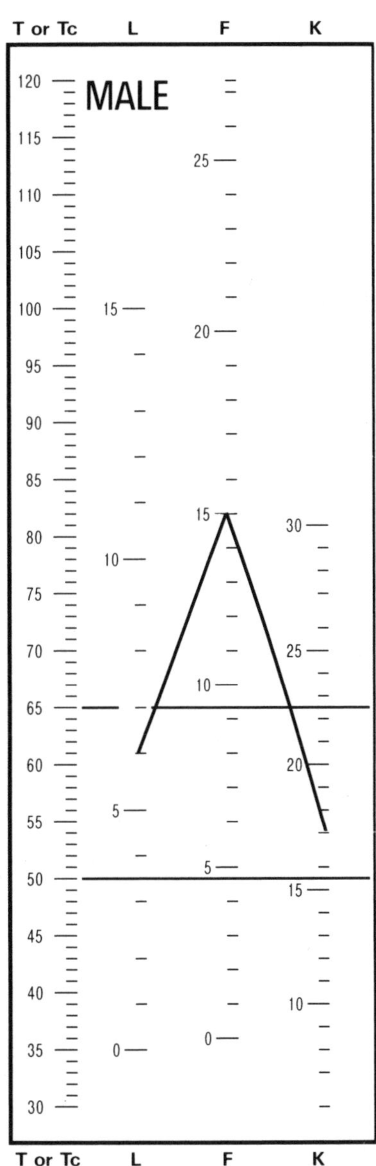

FIGURE I-27. Exaggerated but valid *F* scale pattern. Elevated *F* scale pattern suggests some symptom exaggeration in the context of an overall valid response record.

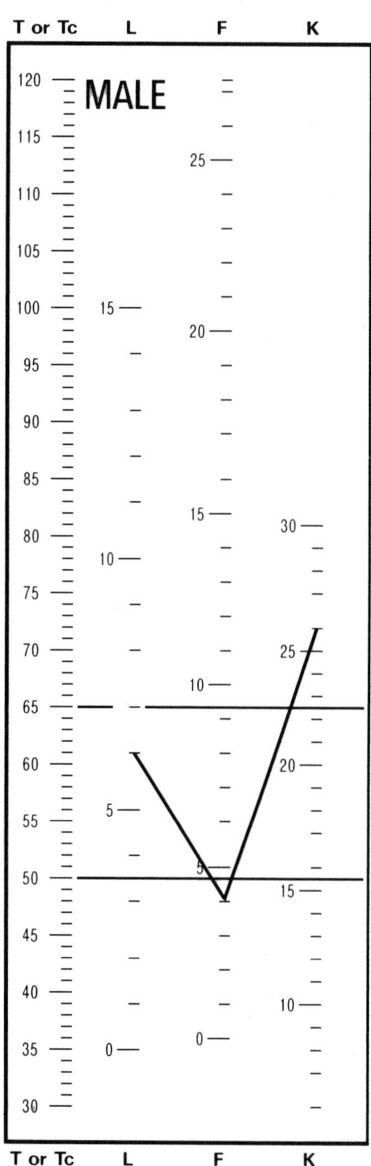

FIGURE I-28. Invalid *K* scale pattern. Elevated *K* scale pattern suggests a likely invalid test performance as a result of an overly defensive response style designed to present themselves in an overly positive light.

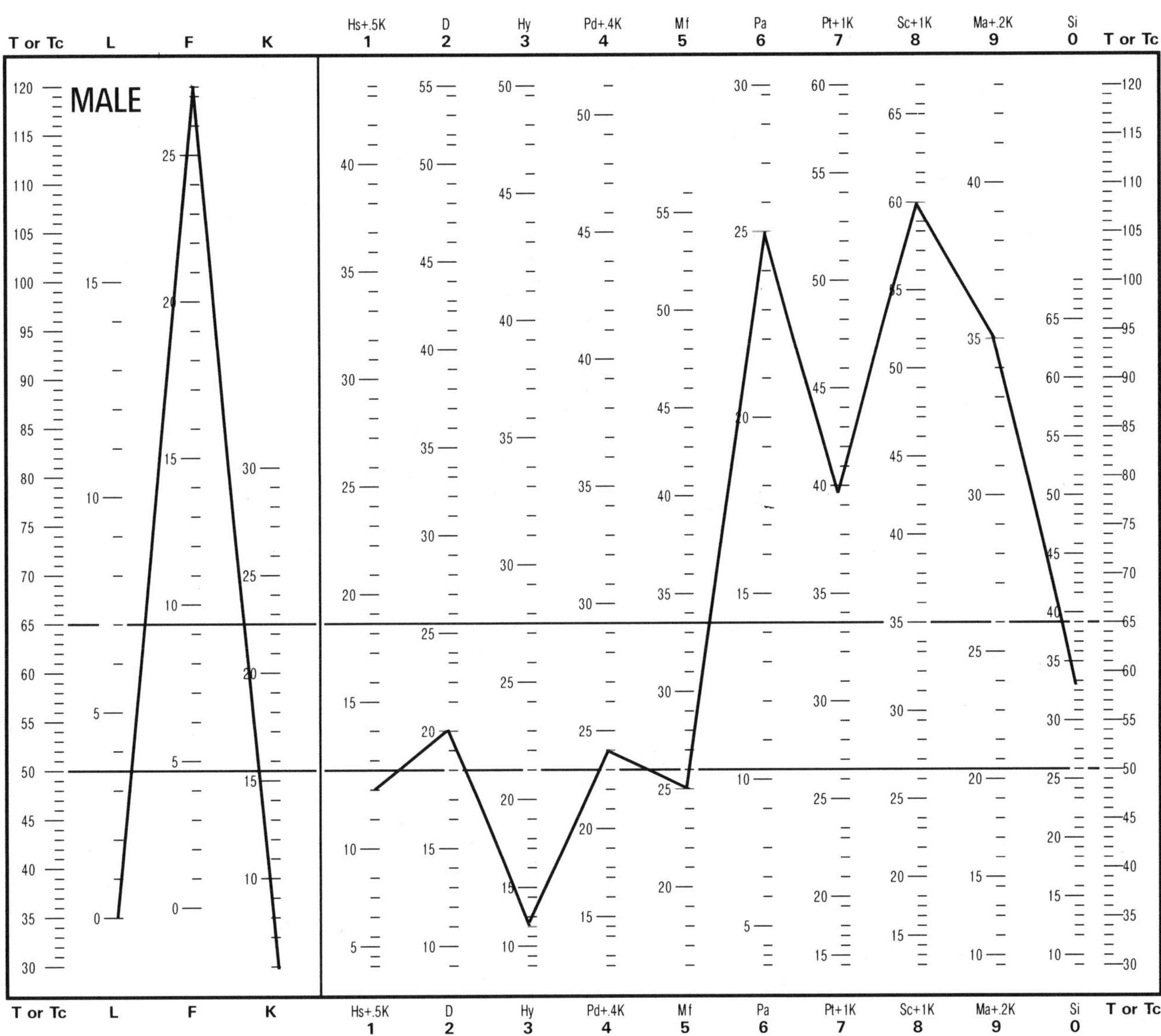

FIGURE I-29. All-true response pattern. Individuals who respond to the MMPI-2 in an all-true manner produce an invalid, uninterpretable profile.

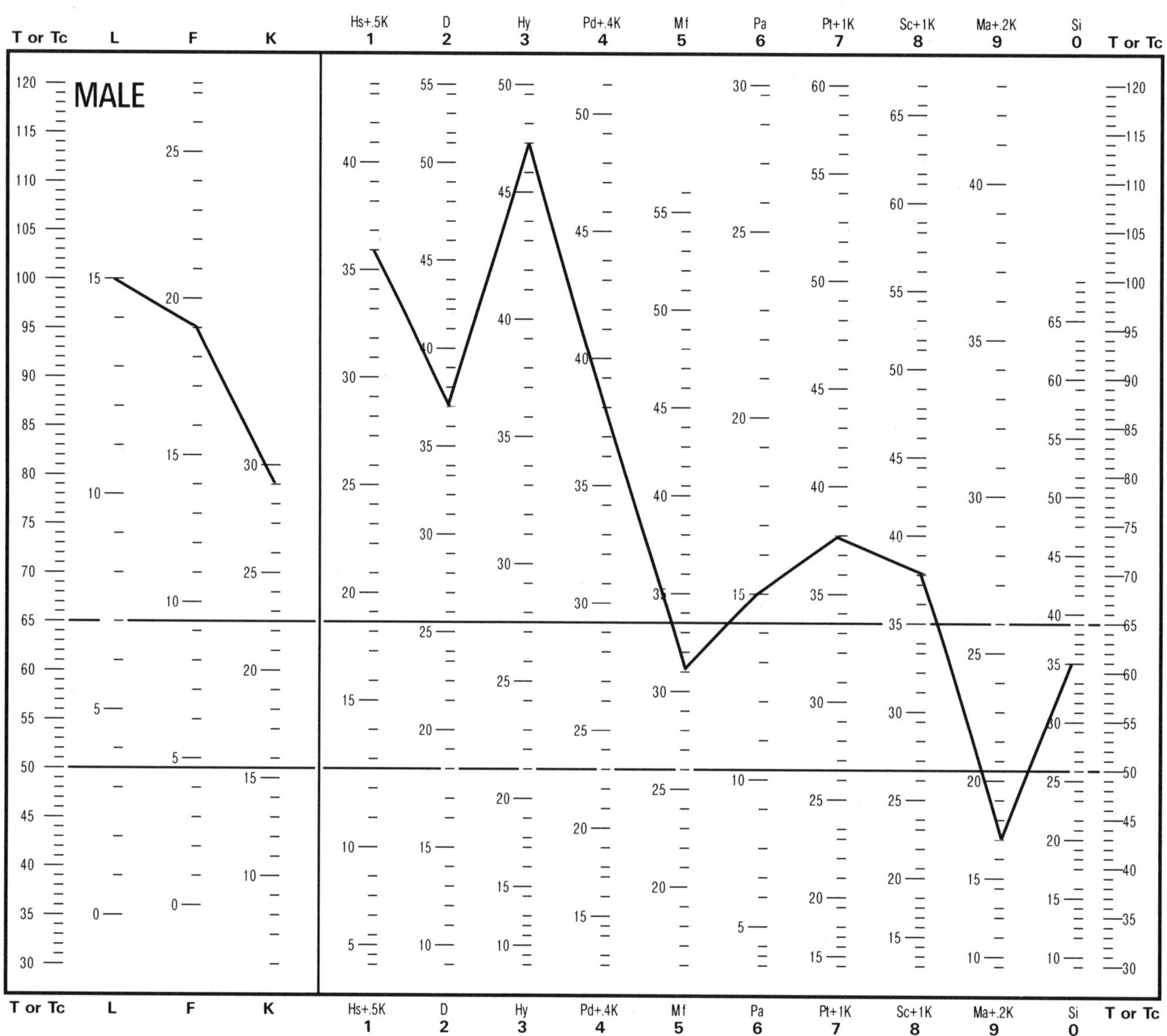

FIGURE I-30. All-false response pattern. Individuals who respond to the MMPI-2 in an all-false manner produce an invalid, uninterpretable profile.

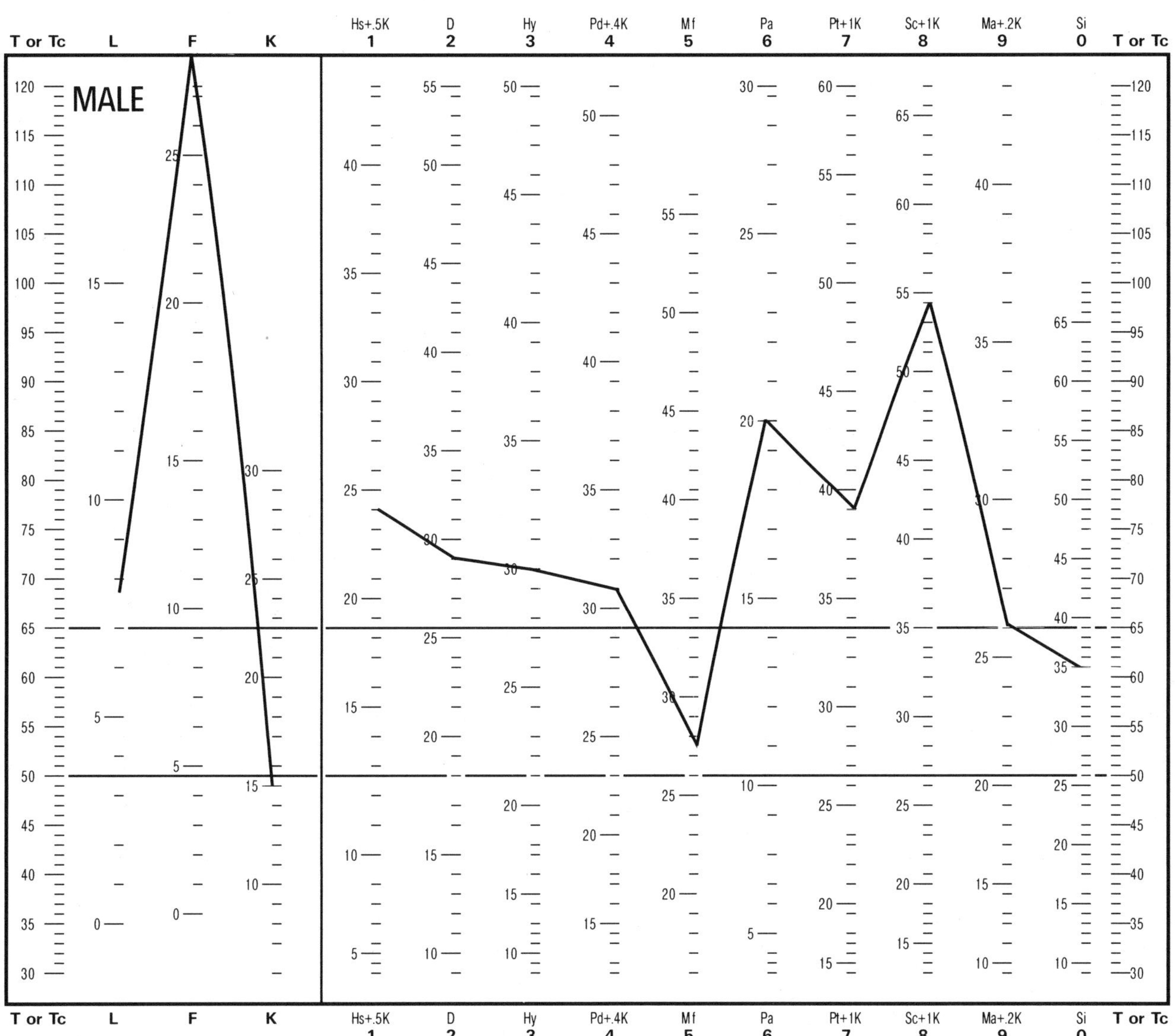

FIGURE I-31. Random response pattern. Individuals who respond to the MMPI-2 in a random manner produce a similar invalid, uninterpretable profile.

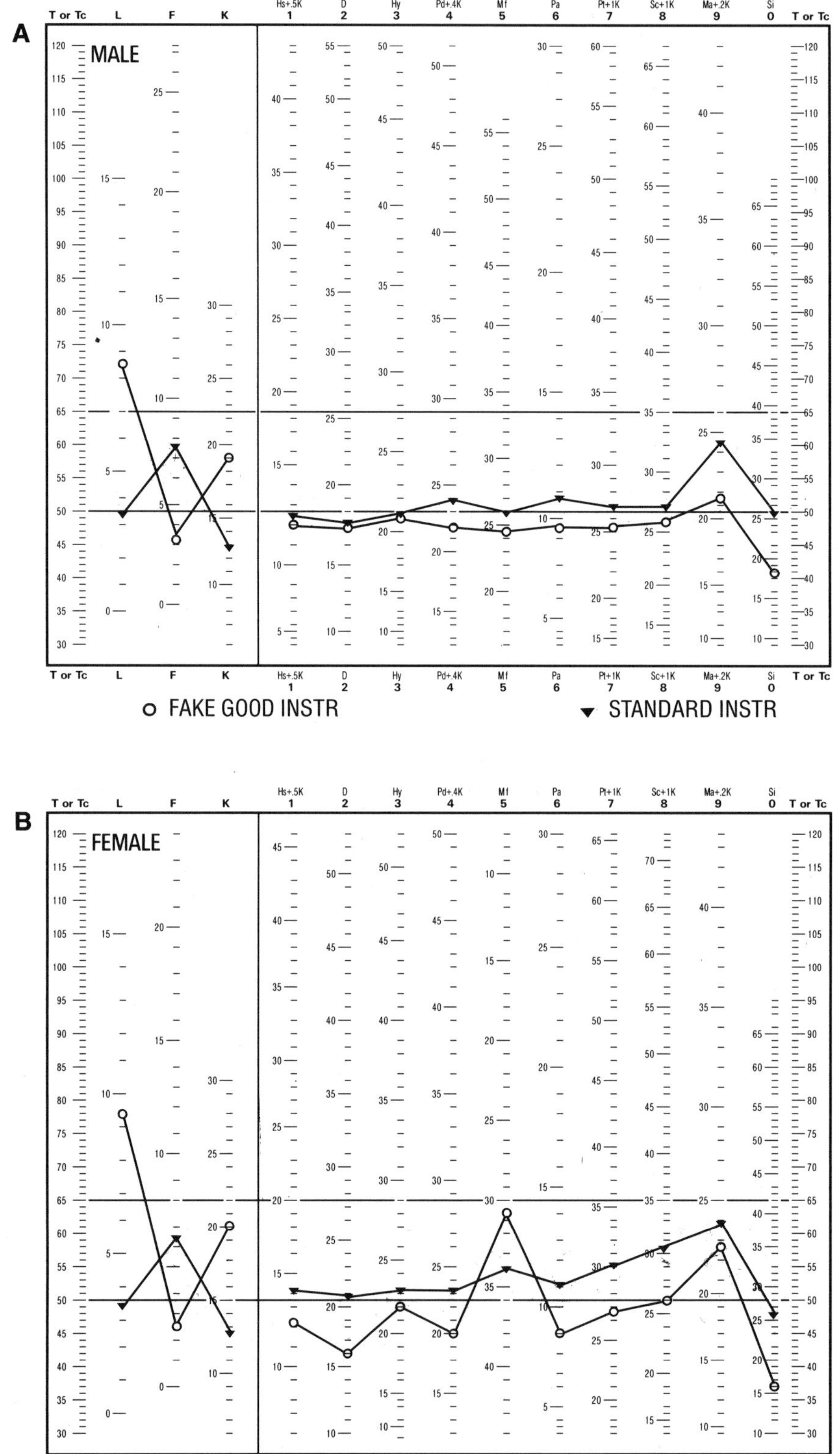

FIGURE I-32. Mean profiles for standard and fake good instructions, (*A*) men and (*B*) women. (Source: Graham, Watts, & Timbrook, 1991)

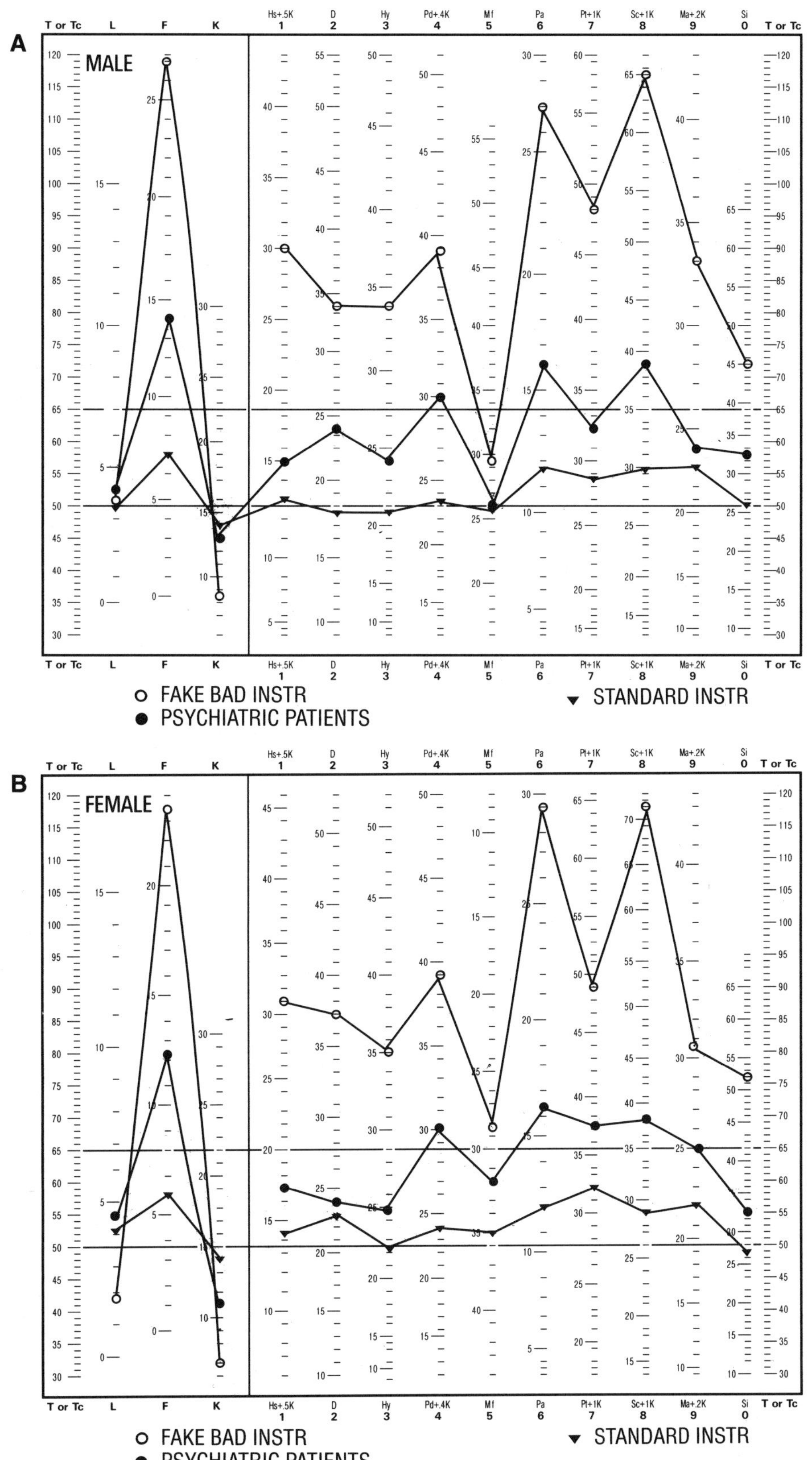

FIGURE I-33. Mean profiles for standard instructions, fake bad instructions, and psychiatric patients, (*A*) men and (*B*) women. (Source: Graham, Watts, & Timbrook, 1991)

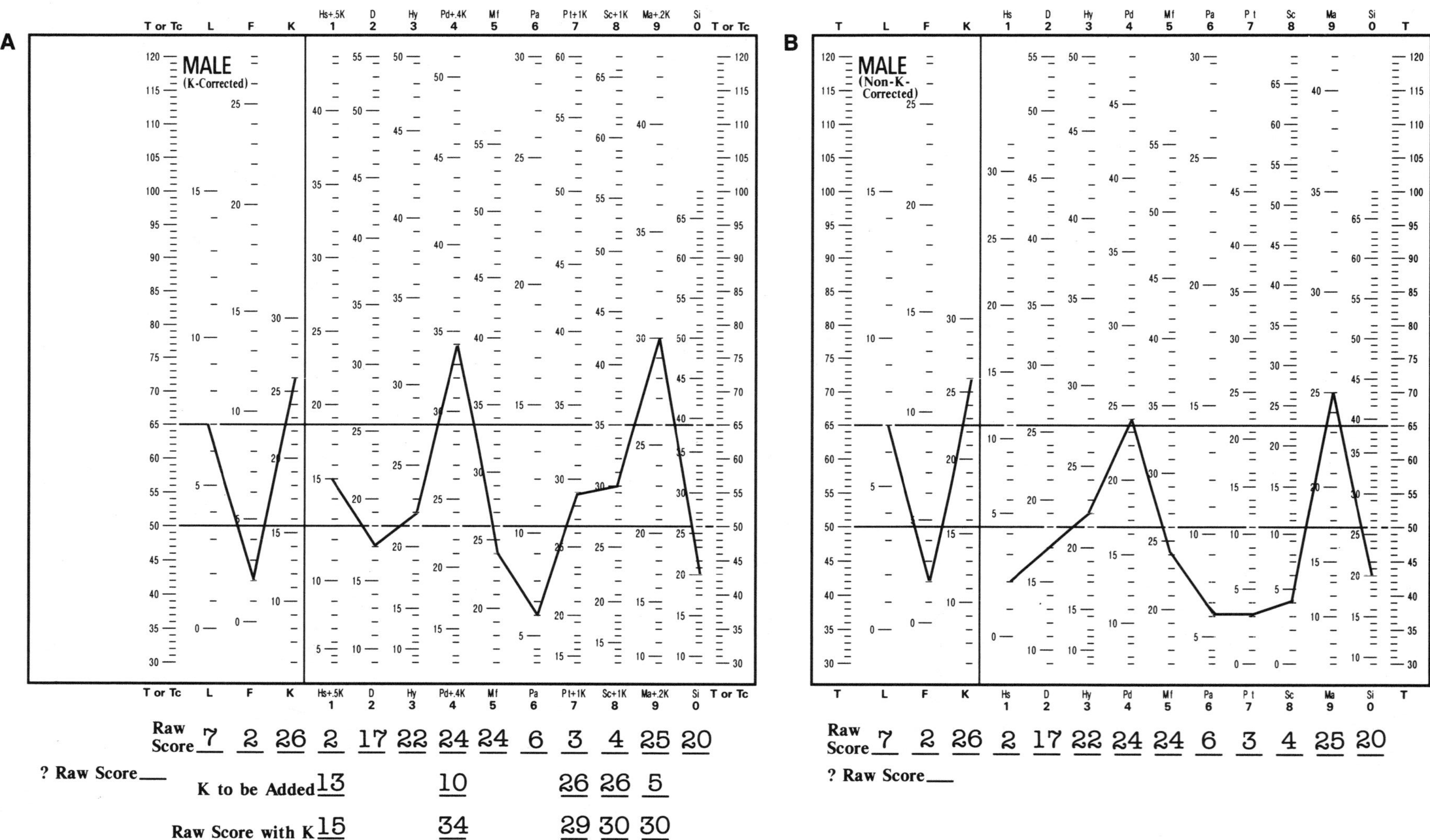

FIGURE I-34. Forensic case plotted on both (*A*) K-corrected and (*B*) non-K-corrected MMPI-2 profiles. (see Figure 6-7). Test taker is 41-year-old divorced salesman.

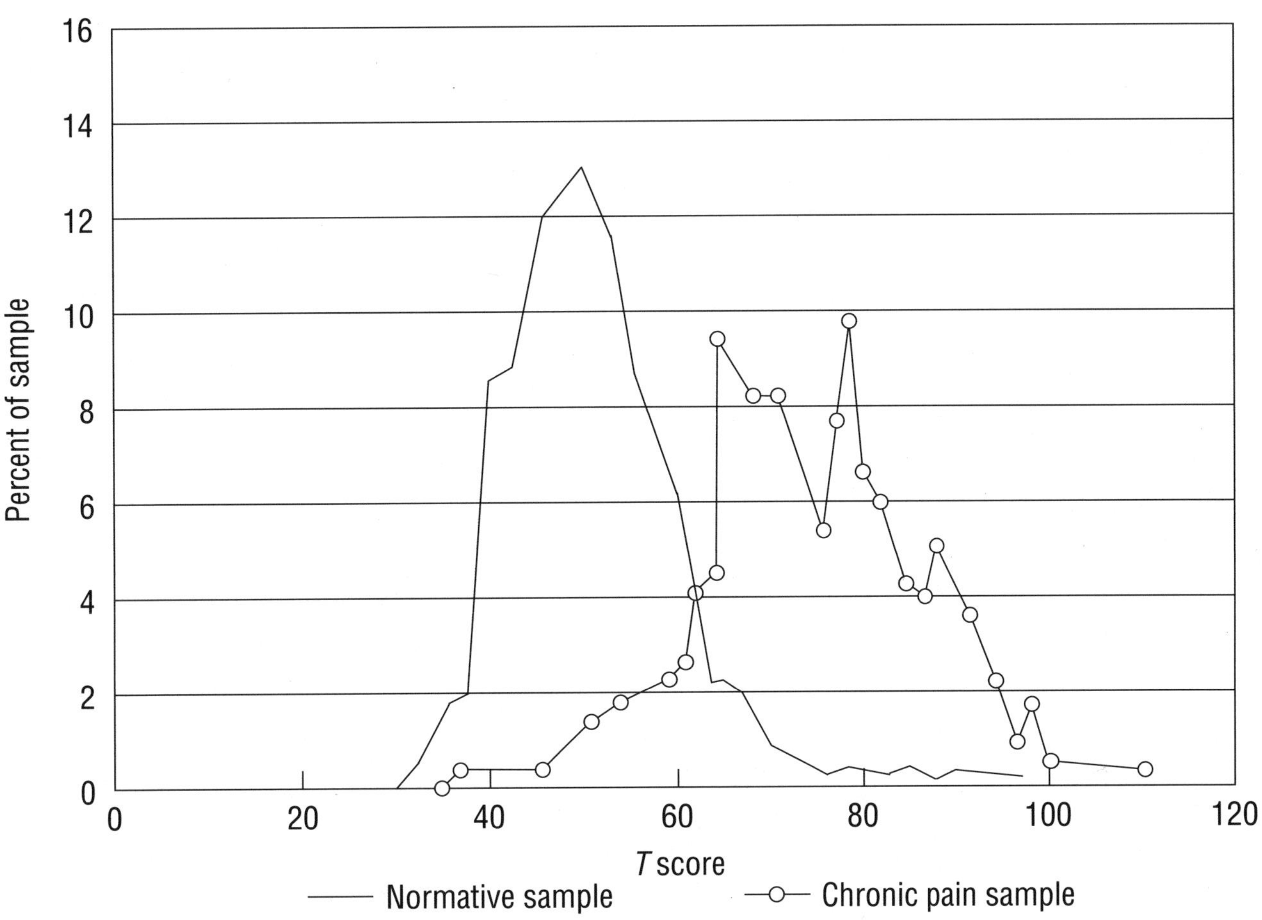

FIGURE I-35. Comparison of frequency distributions of chronic pain patients (men) with the MMPI-2 normative sample on the *Hs* scale. (Source: L. S. Keller & Butcher, 1991. Reprinted by permission.)

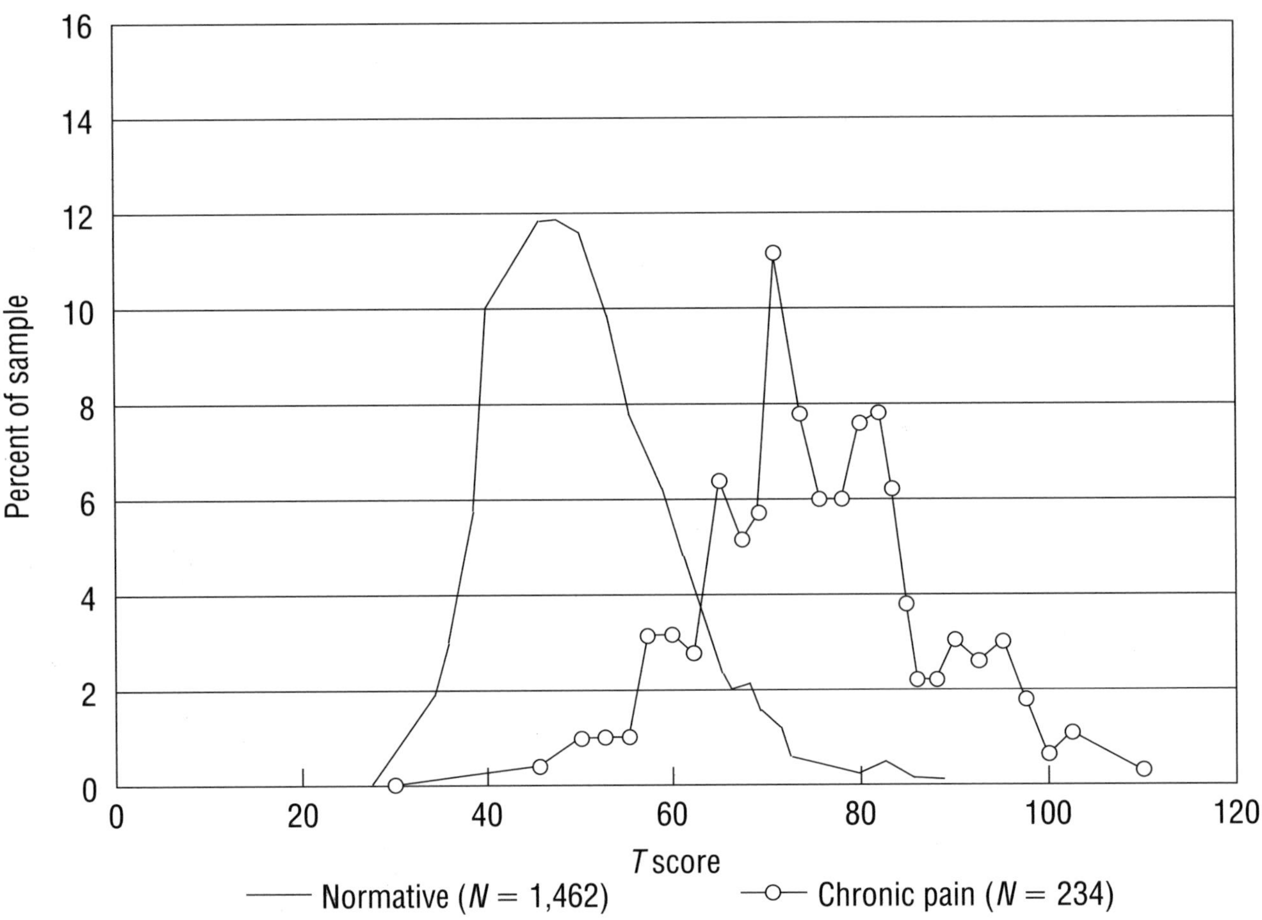

FIGURE I-36. Comparison of frequency distributions of chronic pain patients (women) with the MMPI-2 normative sample on the *Hs* scale. (Source: L. S. Keller & Butcher, 1991. Reprinted by permission.)

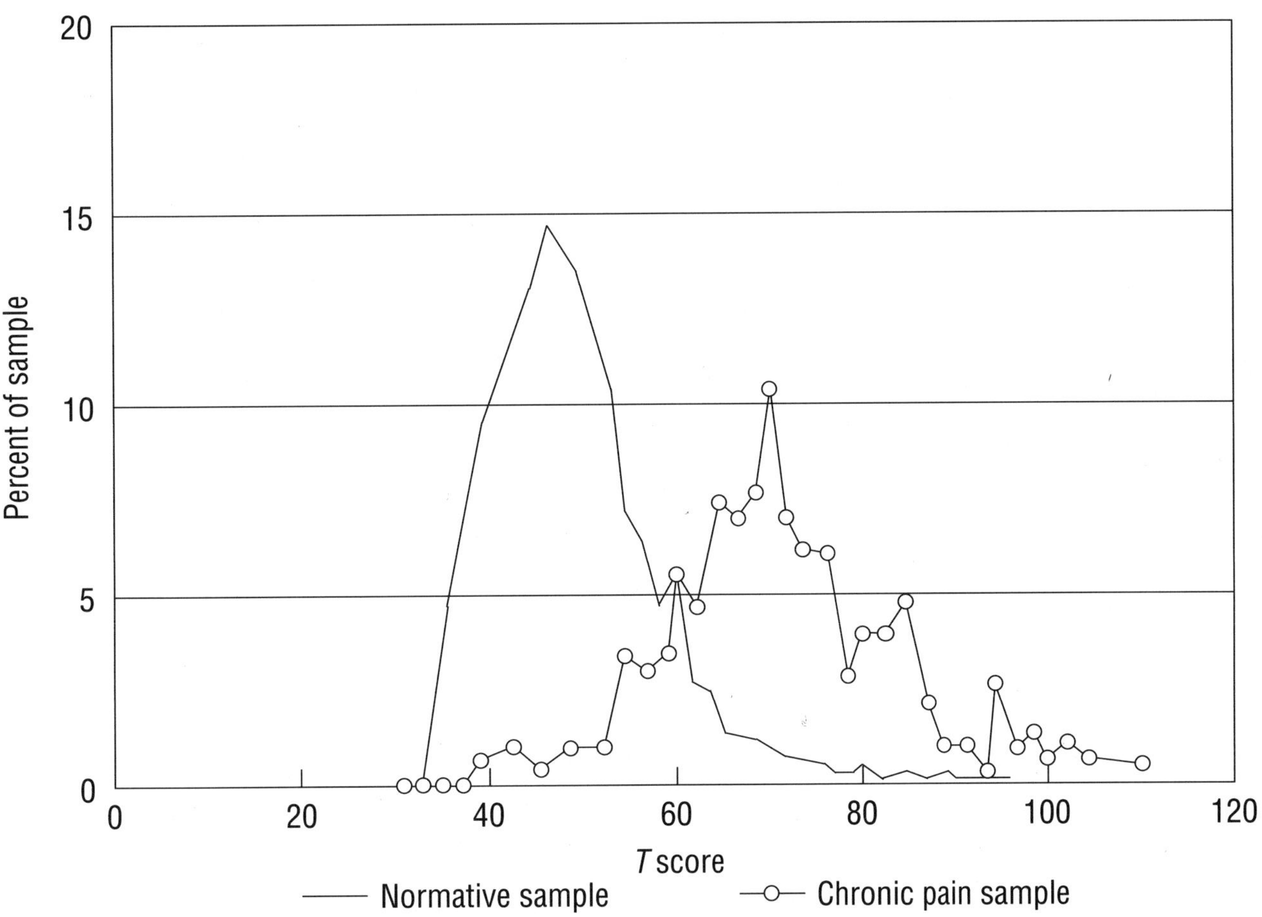

FIGURE I-37. Comparison of frequency distributions of chronic pain patients (men) with the MMPI-2 normative sample on the *Hea* scale, illustrating differential validity of the *Hea* content scale. (Source: L. S. Keller & Butcher, 1991. Reprinted by permission.)

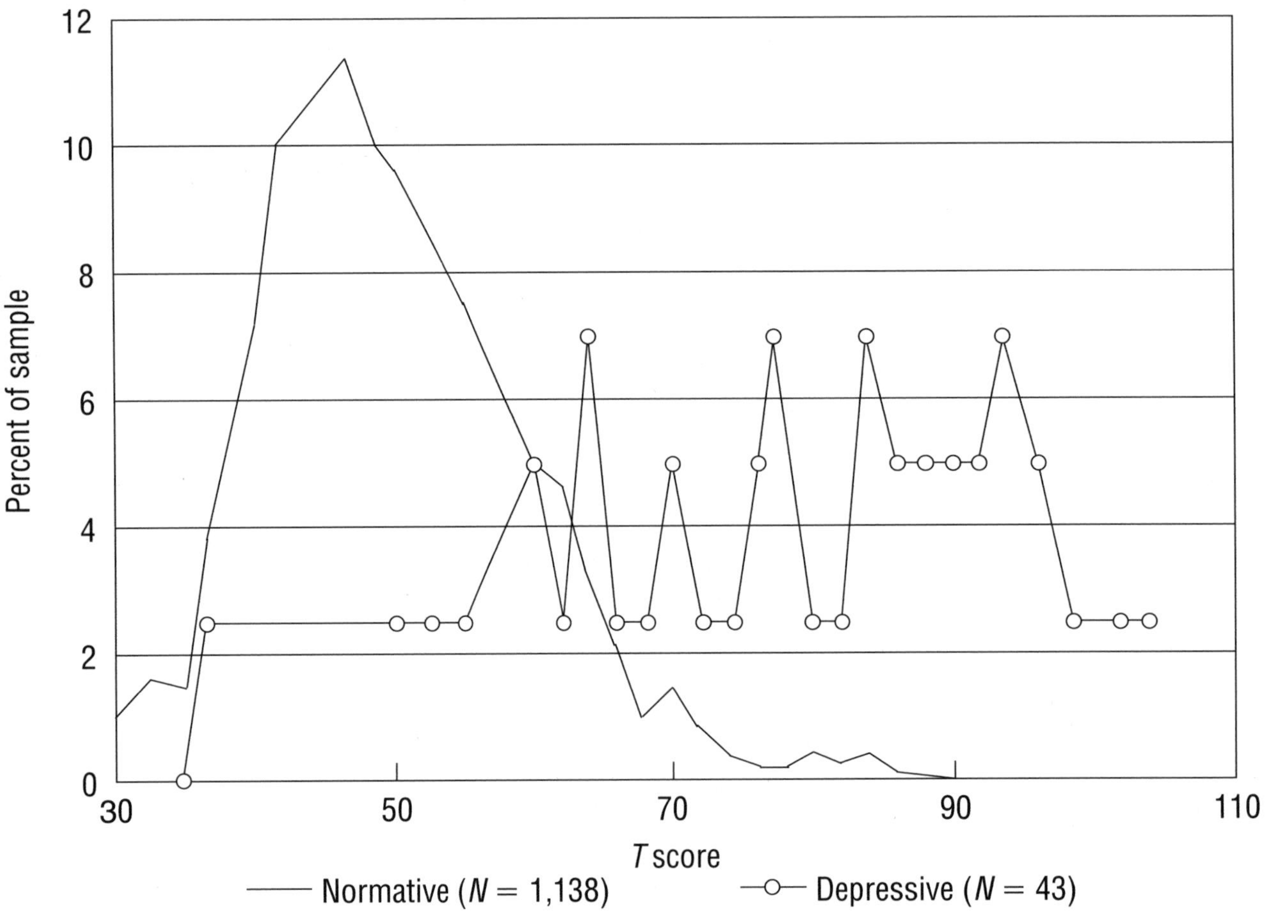

FIGURE I-38. Comparison of frequency distributions of inpatient depressed patients (men) with the MMPI-2 normative sample on the *D* scale. (Source: Graham & Butcher, 1988. Adapted by permission.)

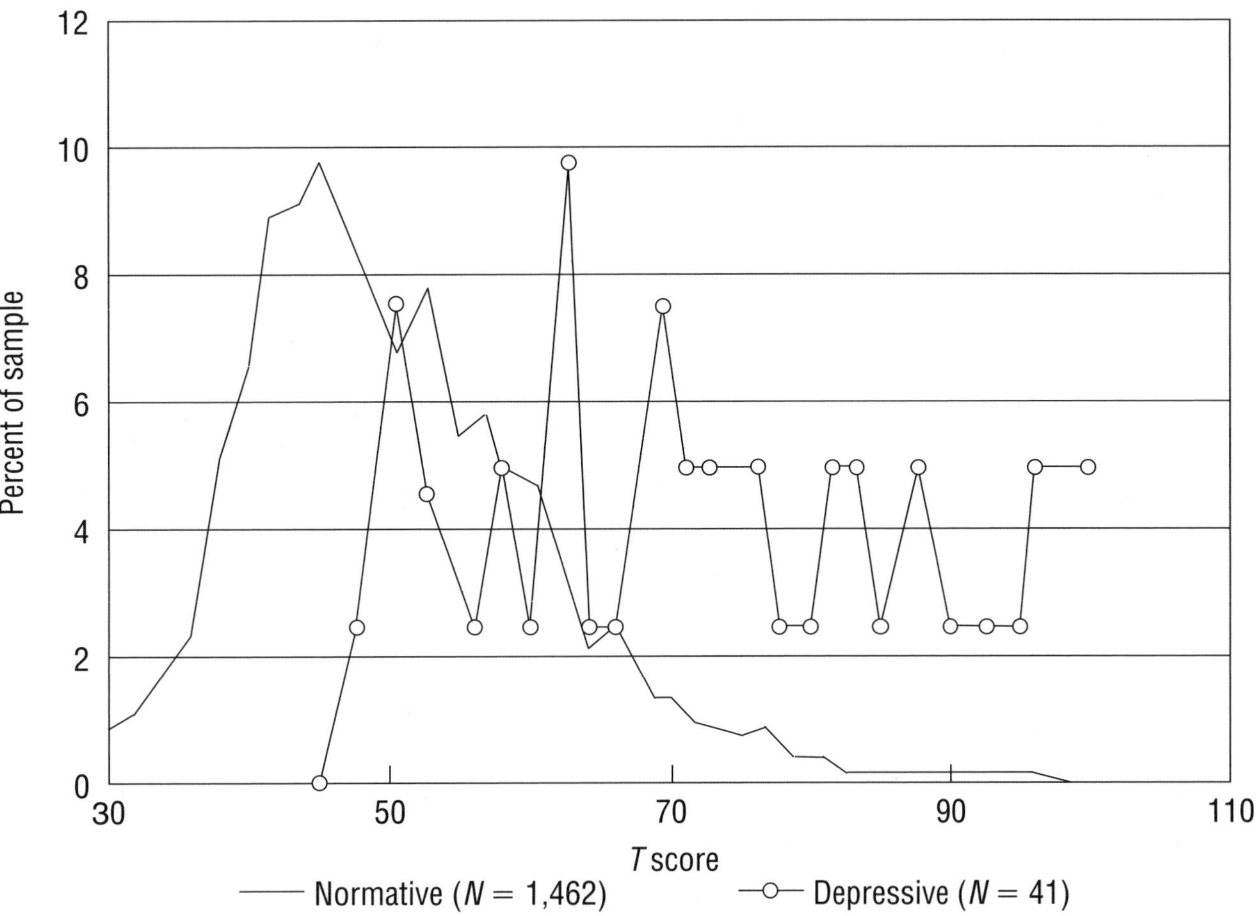

FIGURE I-39. Comparison of frequency distributions of inpatient depressed patients (women) with the MMPI-2 normative sample on the *D* scale. (Source: Graham & Butcher, 1988. Adapted by permission.)

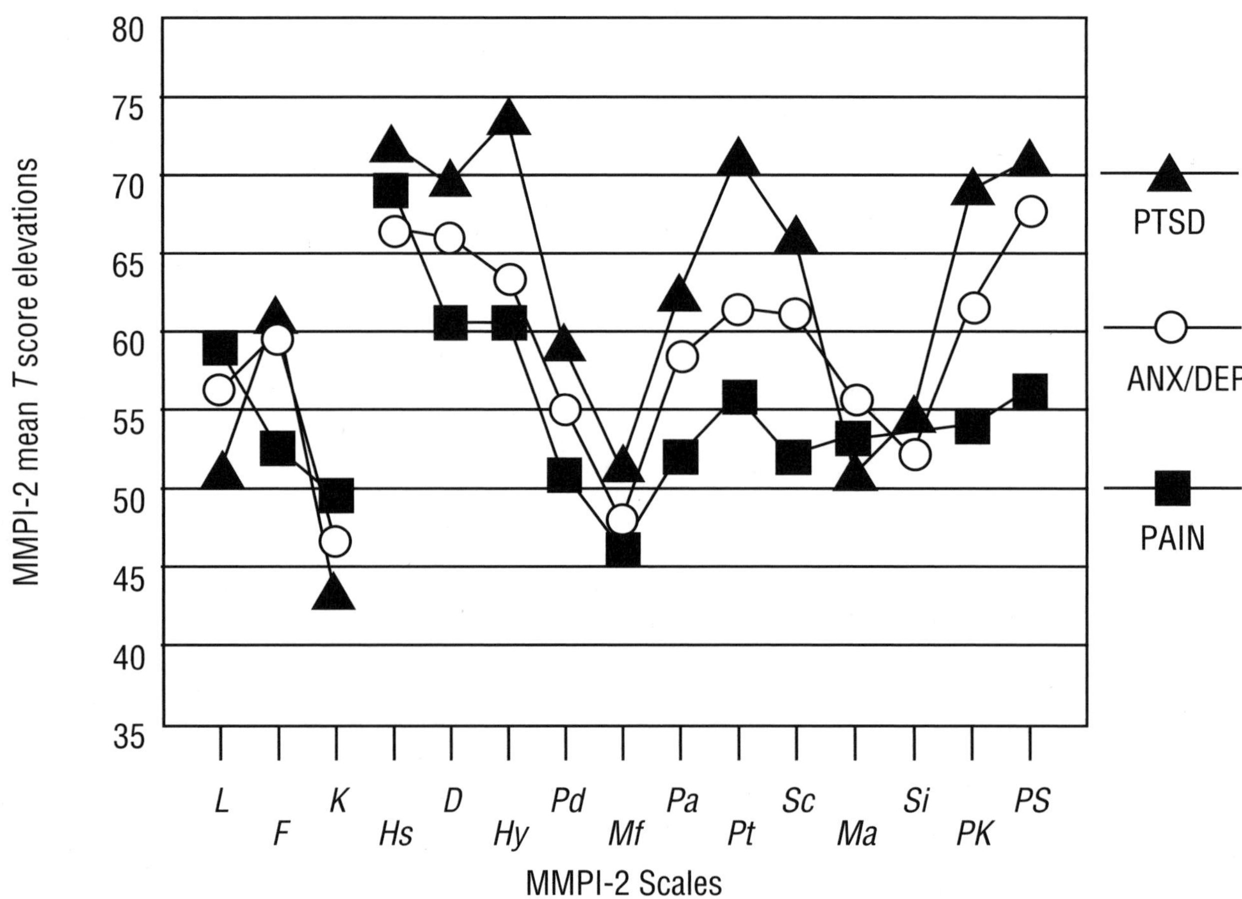

FIGURE I-40. Mean MMPI-2 clinical profiles for PTSD, anxiety/depression, and chronic pain samples. (Source: Flamer & Birch, 1992. Adapted by permission.)

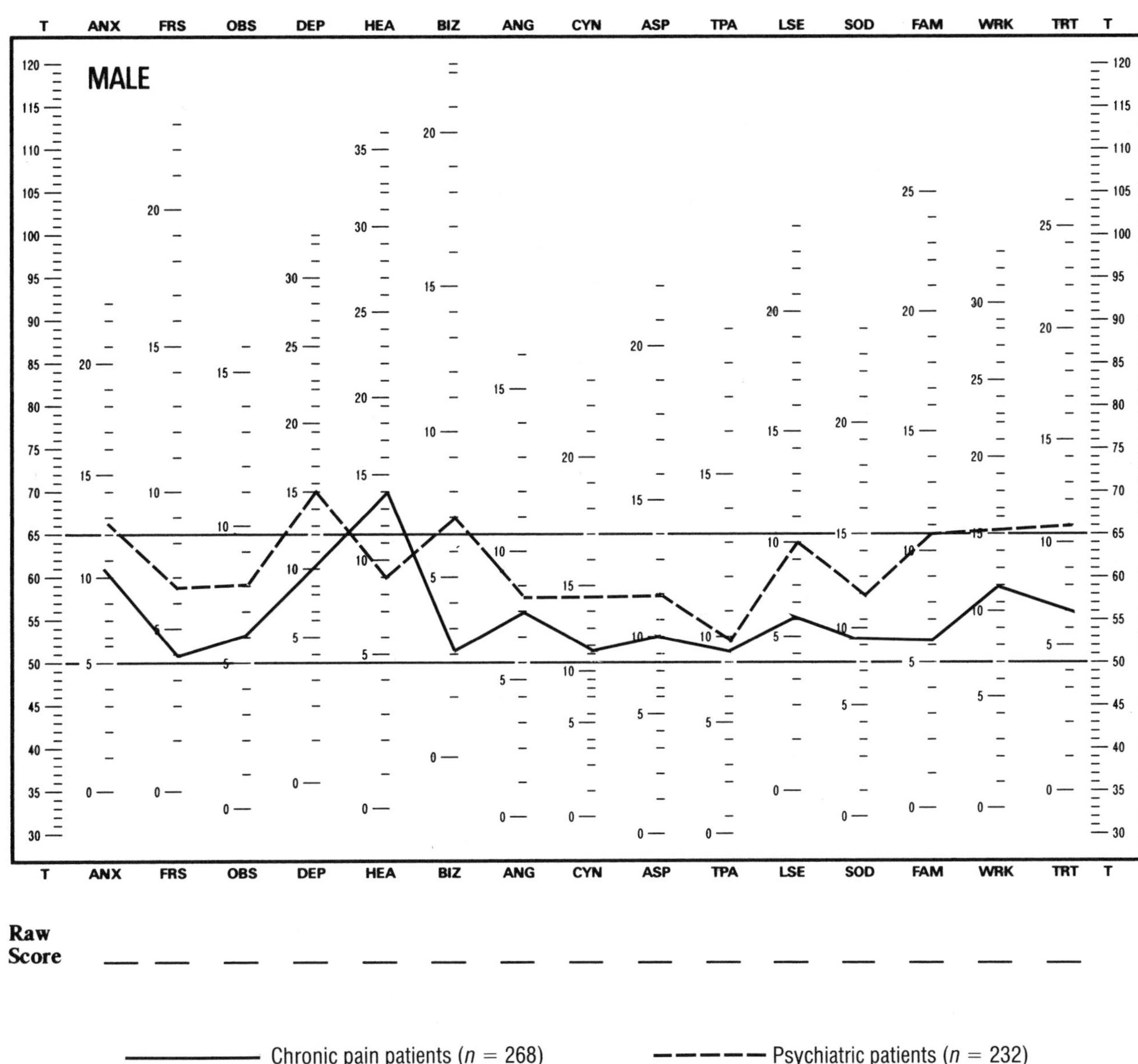

FIGURE I-41. Mean MMPI-2 content scale profiles contrasting men from a chronic pain treatment program with psychiatric inpatients, illustrating differential validity of the content scales. (Source: L. S. Keller & Butcher, 1991. Reprinted by permission.)

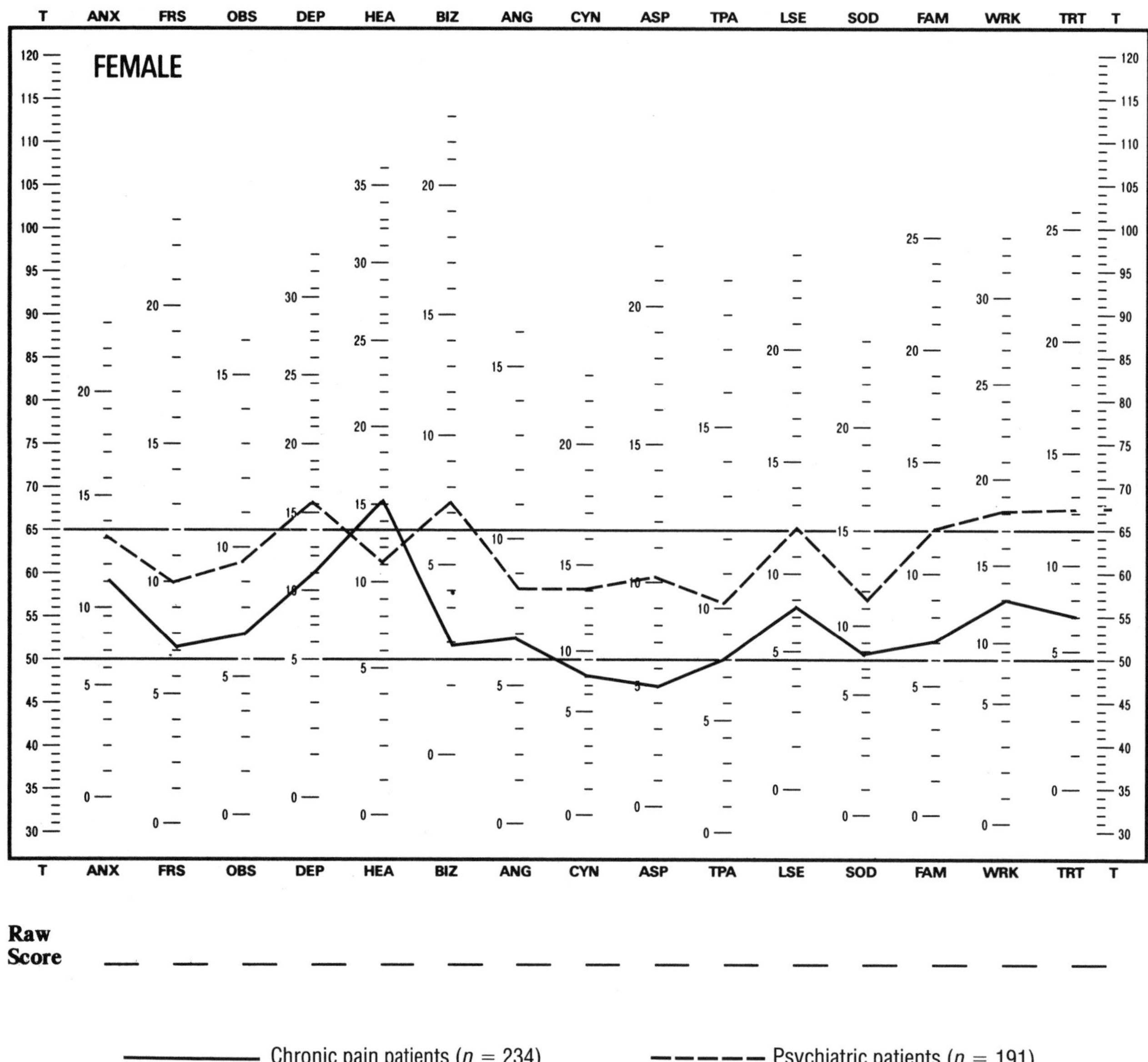

FIGURE I-42. Mean MMPI-2 content scale profiles contrasting women from a chronic pain treatment program with psychiatric inpatients, illustrating differential validity of the content scales. (Source: L. S. Keller & Butcher, 1991. Reprinted by permission.)

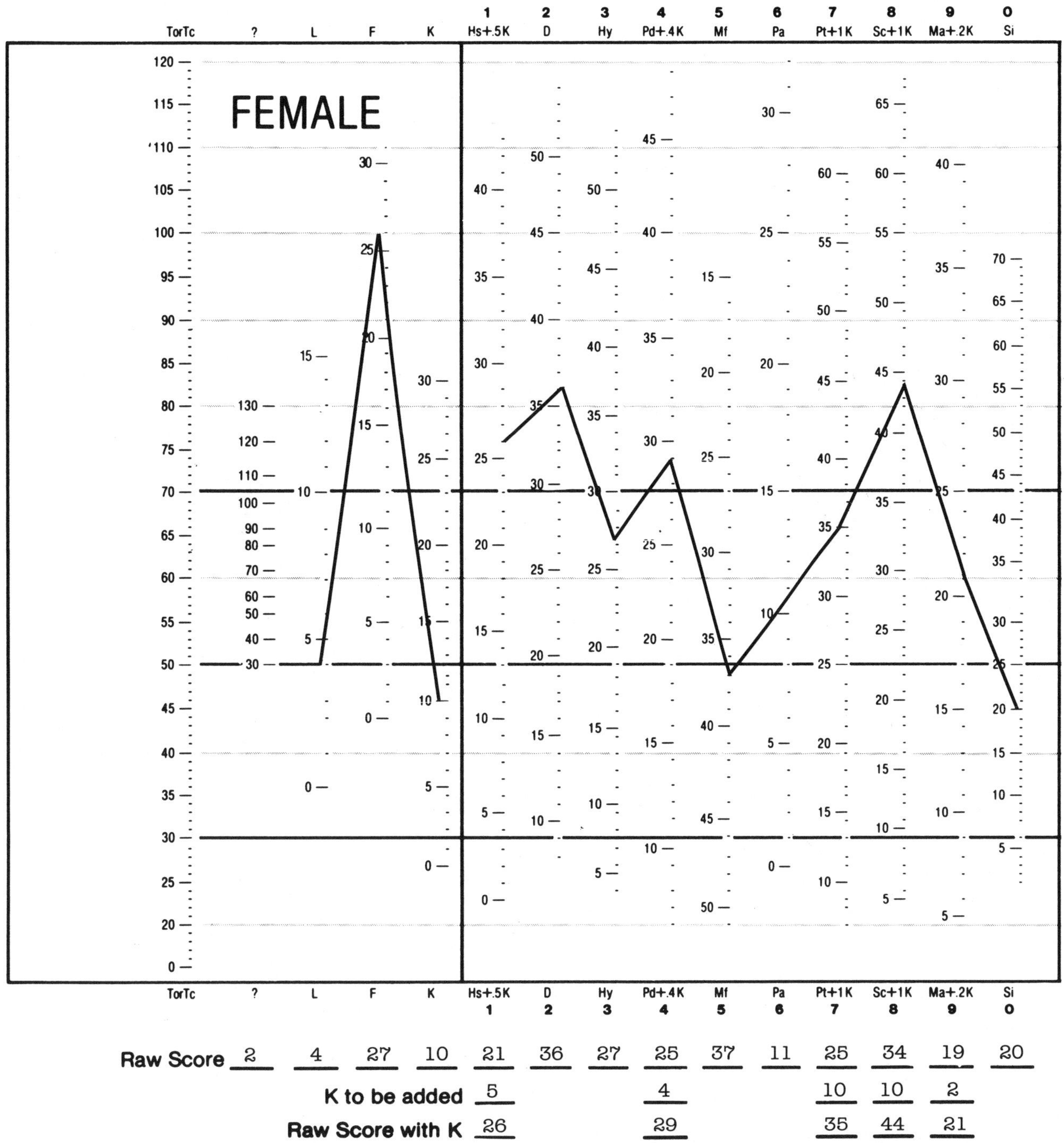

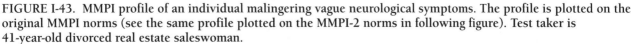

FIGURE I-43. MMPI profile of an individual malingering vague neurological symptoms. The profile is plotted on the original MMPI norms (see the same profile plotted on the MMPI-2 norms in following figure). Test taker is 41-year-old divorced real estate saleswoman.

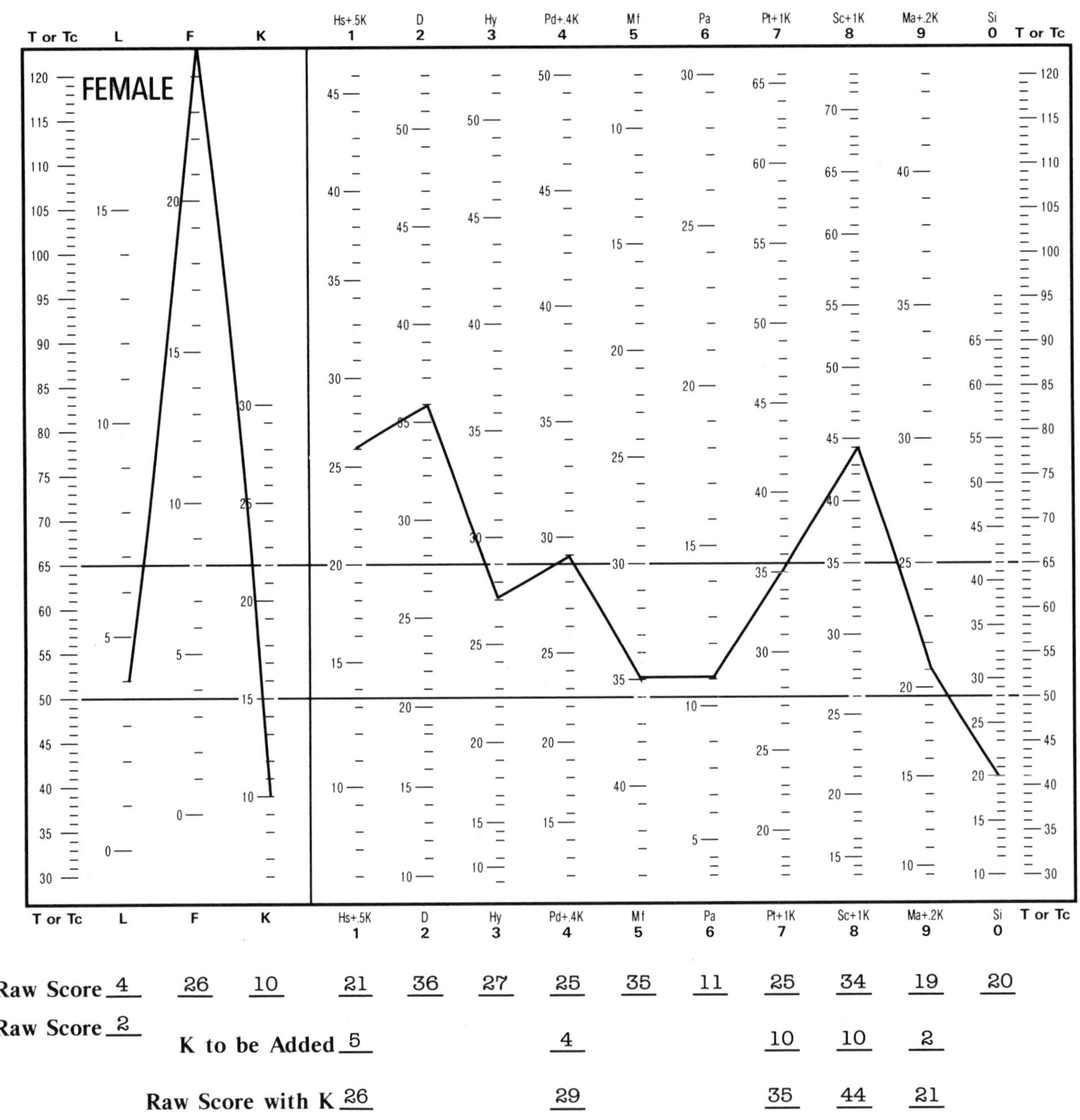

FIGURE I-44. MMPI-2 profile of an individual malingering vague neurological symptoms. The profile is plotted on the MMPI-2 norms (see the same profile plotted on the original MMPI norms in previous figure).

APPENDIX J

Ethical Principles of Psychologists and Code of Conduct

CONTENTS

INTRODUCTION

The American Psychological Association's (APA's) Ethical Principles of Psychologists and Code of Conduct (hereinafter referred to as the Ethics Code) consists of an Introduction, a Preamble, six General Principles (A–F), and specific Ethical Standards. The Introduction discusses the intent, organization, procedural considerations, and scope of application of the Ethics Code. The Preamble and General Principles are *aspirational* goals to guide psychologists toward the highest ideals of psychology. Although the Preamble and General Principles are not themselves enforceable rules, they should be considered by psychologists in arriving at an ethical course of action and may be considered by ethics bodies in interpreting the Ethical Standards. The Ethical Standards set forth *enforceable* rules for conduct as psychologists. Most of the Ethical Standards are written broadly, in order to apply to psychologists in varied roles, although the application of an Ethical Standard may vary depending on the context. The Ethical Standards are not exhaustive. The fact that a given conduct is not specifically addressed by the Ethics Code does not mean that it is necessarily either ethical or unethical.

Membership in the APA commits members to adhere to the APA Ethics Code and to the rules and procedures used to implement it. Psychologists and students, whether or not they are APA members, should be aware that the Ethics Code may be applied to them by state psychology boards, courts, or other public bodies.

This Ethics Code applies only to psychologists' work-related activities, that is, activities that are part of the psychologists' scientific and professional functions or that are psychological in nature. It includes the clinical or counseling practice of psychology, research, teaching, supervision of trainees, development of assessment instruments, conducting assessments, educational counseling, organizational consulting, social intervention, administration, and other activities as well. These work-related activities can be distinguished from the purely private conduct of a psychologist, which ordinarily is not within the purview of the Ethics Code.

The Ethics Code is intended to provide standards of professional conduct that can be applied by the APA and by other bodies that choose to adopt them. Whether or not a psychologist has violated the Ethics Code does not by itself determine whether he or she is legally liable in a court action, whether a contract is enforceable, or whether other legal consequences occur. These results are based on legal rather than ethical rules. However, compliance with or violation of the Ethics Code may be admissible as evidence in some legal proceedings, depending on the circumstances.

In the process of making decisions regarding their professional behavior, psychologists must consider this Ethics Code, in addition to applicable laws and psychology board regulations. If the Ethics Code establishes a higher standard of conduct than is required by law, psychologists must meet the higher ethical standard. If the Ethics Code standard appears to conflict with the requirements of law, then psychologists make known their commitment to the Ethics Code and take steps to resolve the conflict in a responsible manner. If neither law nor the Ethics Code resolves an issue, psychologists should consider other professional materials[1] and the dictates of their own conscience, as well as seek consultation with others within the field when this is practical.

The procedures for filing, investigating, and resolving complaints of unethical conduct are described in the current Rules and Procedures of the APA Ethics Committee. The actions that APA may take for violations of the Ethics Code include actions such as reprimand, censure, termination of APA membership, and referral of the matter to other bodies. Complainants who seek remedies such as monetary damages in alleging ethical violations by a psychologist must resort to private negotiation, administrative bodies, or the courts. Actions that violate the Ethics Code may lead to the imposition of sanctions on a psychologist by bodies other than APA, including

[1]Professional materials that are most helpful in this regard are guidelines and standards that have been adopted or endorsed by professional psychological organizations. Such guidelines and standards, whether adopted by the American Psychological Association (APA) or its Divisions, are not enforceable as such by this Ethics Code, but are of educative value to psychologists, courts, and professional bodies. Such materials include, but are not limited to, the APA's *General Guidelines for Providers of Psychological Services* (1987), *Specialty Guidelines for the Delivery of Services by Clinical Psychologists, Counseling Psychologists, Industrial/Organizational Psychologists, and School Psychologists* (1981), *Guidelines for Computer Based Tests and Interpretations* (1987), *Standards for Educational and Psychological Testing* (1985), *Ethical Principles in the Conduct of Research With Human Participants* (1982), *Guidelines for Ethical Conduct in the Care and Use of Animals* (1986), *Guidelines for Providers of Psychological Services to Ethnic, Linguistic, and Culturally Diverse Populations* (1990), and *Publication Manual of the American Psychological Association* (3rd ed., 1983). Materials not adopted by APA as a whole include the APA Division 41 (Forensic Psychology)/American Psychology–Law Society's *Specialty Guidelines for Forensic Psychologists* (1991).

This version of the APA Ethics Code was adopted by the American Psychological Association's Council of Representatives during its meeting, August 13 and 16, 1992, and is effective beginning December 1, 1992. Inquiries concerning the substance or interpretation of the APA Ethics Code should be addressed to the Director, Office of Ethics, American Psychological Association, 750 First Street, NE, Washington, DC 20002-4242.

This Code will be used to adjudicate complaints brought concerning alleged conduct occurring on or after the effective date. Complaints regarding conduct occurring prior to the effective date will be adjudicated on the basis of the version of the Code that was in effect at the time the conduct occurred, except that no provisions repealed in June 1989 will be enforced even if an earlier version contains the provision. The Ethics Code will undergo continuing review and study for future revisions; comments on the Code may be sent to the above address.

The APA has previously published its Ethical Standards as follows:

American Psychological Association. (1953). *Ethical standards of psychologists.* Washington, DC: Author.

American Psychological Association. (1958). Standards of ethical behavior for psychologists. *American Psychologist, 13,* 268–271.

American Psychological Association. (1963). Ethical standards of psychologists. *American Psychologist, 18,* 56–60.

American Psychological Association. (1968). Ethical standards of psychologists. *American Psychologist, 23,* 357–361.

American Psychological Association. (1977, March). Ethical standards of psychologists. *APA Monitor,* pp. 22–23.

American Psychological Association. (1979). *Ethical standards of psychologists.* Washington, DC: Author.

American Psychological Association. (1981). Ethical principles of psychologists. *American Psychologist, 36,* 633–638.

American Psychological Association. (1990). Ethical principles of psychologists (Amended June 2, 1989). *American Psychologist, 45,* 390–395.

Request copies of the APA's Ethical Principles of Psychologists and Code of Conduct from the APA Order Department, 750 First Street, NE, Washington, DC 20002-4242, or phone (202) 336-5510.

state psychological associations, other professional groups, psychology boards, other state or federal agencies, and payors for health services. In addition to actions for violation of the Ethics Code, the APA Bylaws provide that APA may take action against a member after his or her conviction of a felony, expulsion or suspension from an affiliated state psychological association, or suspension or loss of licensure.

PREAMBLE

Psychologists work to develop a valid and reliable body of scientific knowledge based on research. They may apply that knowledge to human behavior in a variety of contexts. In doing so, they perform many roles, such as researcher, educator, diagnostician, therapist, supervisor, consultant, administrator, social interventionist, and expert witness. Their goal is to broaden knowledge of behavior and, where appropriate, to apply it pragmatically to improve the condition of both the individual and society. Psychologists respect the central importance of freedom of inquiry and expression in research, teaching, and publication. They also strive to help the public in developing informed judgments and choices concerning human behavior. This Ethics Code provides a common set of values upon which psychologists build their professional and scientific work.

This Code is intended to provide both the general principles and the decision rules to cover most situations encountered by psychologists. It has as its primary goal the welfare and protection of the individuals and groups with whom psychologists work. It is the individual responsibility of each psychologist to aspire to the highest possible standards of conduct. Psychologists respect and protect human and civil rights, and do not knowingly participate in or condone unfair discriminatory practices.

The development of a dynamic set of ethical standards for a psychologist's work-related conduct requires a personal commitment to a lifelong effort to act ethically; to encourage ethical behavior by students, supervisees, employees, and colleagues, as appropriate; and to consult with others, as needed, concerning ethical problems. Each psychologist supplements, but does not violate, the Ethics Code's values and rules on the basis of guidance drawn from personal values, culture, and experience.

GENERAL PRINCIPLES

Principle A: Competence

Psychologists strive to maintain high standards of competence in their work. They recognize the boundaries of their particular competencies and the limitations of their expertise. They provide only those services and use only those techniques for which they are qualified by education, training, or experience. Psychologists are cognizant of the fact that the competencies required in serving, teaching, and/or studying groups of people vary with the distinctive characteristics of those groups. In those areas in which recognized professional standards do not yet exist, psychologists exercise careful judgment and take appropriate precautions to protect the welfare of those with whom they work. They maintain knowledge of relevant scientific and professional information related to the services they render, and they recognize the need for ongoing education. Psychologists make appropriate use of scientific, professional, technical, and administrative resources.

Principle B: Integrity

Psychologists seek to promote integrity in the science, teaching, and practice of psychology. In these activities psychologists are honest, fair, and respectful of others. In describing or reporting their qualifications, services, products, fees, research, or teaching, they do not make statements that are false, misleading, or deceptive. Psychologists strive to be aware of their own belief systems, values, needs, and limitations and the effect of these on their work. To the extent feasible, they attempt to clarify for relevant parties the roles they are performing and to function appropriately in accordance with those roles. Psychologists avoid improper and potentially harmful dual relationships.

Principle C: Professional and Scientific Responsibility

Psychologists uphold professional standards of conduct, clarify their professional roles and obligations, accept appropriate responsibility for their behavior, and adapt their methods to the needs of different populations. Psychologists consult with, refer to, or cooperate with other professionals and institutions to the extent needed to serve the best interests of their patients, clients, or other recipients of their services. Psychologists' moral standards and conduct are personal matters to the same degree as is true for any other person, except as psychologists' conduct may compromise their professional responsibilities or reduce the public's trust in psychology and psychologists. Psychologists are concerned about the ethical compliance of their colleagues' scientific and professional conduct. When appropriate, they consult with colleagues in order to prevent or avoid unethical conduct.

Principle D: Respect for People's Rights and Dignity

Psychologists accord appropriate respect to the fundamental rights, dignity, and worth of all people. They respect the rights of individuals to privacy, confidentiality, self-determination, and autonomy, mindful that legal and other obligations may lead to inconsistency and conflict with the exercise of these rights. Psychologists are aware of cultural, individual, and role differences, including those due to age, gender, race, ethnicity, national origin, religion, sexual orientation, disability, language, and socioeconomic status. Psychologists try to eliminate the effect on their work of biases based on those factors, and they do not knowingly participate in or condone unfair discriminatory practices.

Principle E: Concern for Others' Welfare

Psychologists seek to contribute to the welfare of those with whom they interact professionally. In their professional actions, psychologists weigh the welfare and rights of their patients or clients, students, supervisees, human research participants, and other affected persons, and the welfare of animal subjects of research. When conflicts occur among psychologists' obligations or concerns, they attempt to resolve these conflicts and to perform their roles in a responsible fashion that avoids or minimizes harm. Psychologists are sensitive to real and ascribed differences in power between themselves and others, and they do not exploit or mislead other people during or after professional relationships.

Principle F: Social Responsibility

Psychologists are aware of their professional and scientific responsibilities to the community and the society in which they work and live. They apply and make public their knowledge of psychology in order to contribute to human welfare. Psychologists are concerned about and work to mitigate the causes of human suffering. When undertaking research, they strive to advance human welfare and the science of psychology. Psychologists try to avoid misuse of their work. Psychologists comply with the law and encourage the development of law and social policy that serve the interests of their patients and clients and the public. They are encouraged to contribute a portion of their professional time for little or no personal advantage.

ETHICAL STANDARDS

1. General Standards

These General Standards are potentially applicable to the professional and scientific activities of all psychologists.

1.01 Applicability of the Ethics Code

The activity of a psychologist subject to the Ethics Code may be reviewed under these Ethical Standards only if the activity is part of his or her work-related functions or the activity is psychological in nature. Personal activities having no connection to or effect on psychological roles are not subject to the Ethics Code.

1.02 Relationship of Ethics and Law

If psychologists' ethical responsibilities conflict with law, psychologists make known their commitment to the Ethics Code and take steps to resolve the conflict in a responsible manner.

1.03 Professional and Scientific Relationship

Psychologists provide diagnostic, therapeutic, teaching, research, supervisory, consultative, or other psychological services only in the context of a defined professional or scientific relationship or role. (See also Standards 2.01, Evaluation, Diagnosis, and Interventions in Professional Context, and 7.02, Forensic Assessments.)

1.04 Boundaries of Competence

(a) Psychologists provide services, teach, and conduct research only within the boundaries of their competence, based on their education, training, supervised experience, or appropriate professional experience.

(b) Psychologists provide services, teach, or conduct research in new areas or involving new techniques only after first undertaking appropriate study, training, supervision, and/or consultation from persons who are competent in those areas or techniques.

(c) In those emerging areas in which generally recognized standards for preparatory training do not yet exist, psychologists nevertheless take reasonable steps to ensure the competence of their work and to protect patients, clients, students, research participants, and others from harm.

1.05 Maintaining Expertise

Psychologists who engage in assessment, therapy, teaching, research, organizational consulting, or other professional activities maintain a reasonable level of awareness of current scientific and professional information in their fields of activity, and undertake ongoing efforts to maintain competence in the skills they use.

1.06 Basis for Scientific and Professional Judgments

Psychologists rely on scientifically and professionally derived knowledge when making scientific or professional judgments or when engaging in scholarly or professional endeavors.

1.07 Describing the Nature and Results of Psychological Services

(a) When psychologists provide assessment, evaluation, treatment, counseling, supervision, teaching, consultation, research, or other psychological services to an individual, a group, or an organization, they provide, using language that is reasonably understandable to the recipient of those services, appropriate information beforehand about the nature of such services and appropriate information later about results and conclusions. (See also Standard 2.09, Explaining Assessment Results.)

(b) If psychologists will be precluded by law or by organizational roles from providing such information to particular individuals or groups, they so inform those individuals or groups at the outset of the service.

1.08 Human Differences

Where differences of age, gender, race, ethnicity, national origin, religion, sexual orientation, disability, language, or socioeconomic status significantly affect psychologists' work concerning particular individuals or groups, psychologists obtain the training, experience, consultation, or supervision necessary to ensure the competence of their services, or they make appropriate referrals.

1.09 Respecting Others

In their work-related activities, psychologists respect the rights of others to hold values, attitudes, and opinions that differ from their own.

1.10 Nondiscrimination

In their work-related activities, psychologists do not engage in unfair discrimination based on age, gender, race, ethnicity, national origin, religion, sexual orientation, disability, socioeconomic status, or any basis proscribed by law.

1.11 Sexual Harassment

(a) Psychologists do not engage in sexual harassment. Sexual harassment is sexual solicitation, physical advances, or verbal or nonverbal conduct that is sexual in nature, that occurs in connection with the psychologists's activities or roles as a psychologist, and that either: (1) is unwelcome, is offensive, or creates a hostile workplace environment, and the psychologist knows or is told this; or (2) is sufficiently severe or intense to be abusive to a reasonable person in the context. Sexual harassment can consist of a single intense or severe act or of multiple persistent or pervasive acts.

(b) Psychologists accord sexual-harassment complainants and respondents dignity and respect. Psychologists do not participate in denying a person academic admittance or advancement, employment, tenure, or promotion, based solely upon their having made, or their being the subject of, sexual-harassment charges. This does not preclude taking action based upon the outcome of such proceedings or consideration of other appropriate information.

1.12 Other Harassment

Psychologists do not knowingly engage in behavior that is harassing or demeaning to persons with whom they interact in their work based on factors such as those persons' age, gender, race, ethnicity, national origin, religion, sexual orientation, disability, language, or socioeconomic status.

1.13 Personal Problems and Conflicts

(a) Psychologists recognize that their personal problems and conflicts may interfere with their effectiveness. Accordingly, they refrain from undertaking an activity when they know or should know that their personal problems are likely to lead to harm to a patient, client, colleague, student, research participant, or other person to whom they may owe a professional or scientific obligation.

(b) In addition, psychologists have an obligation to be alert to signs of, and to obtain assistance for, their personal problems at an early stage, in order to prevent significantly impaired performance.

(c) When psychologists become aware of personal problems that may interfere with their performing work-related duties adequately, they take appropriate measures, such as obtaining professional consultation or assistance, and determine whether they should limit, suspend, or terminate their work-related duties.

1.14 Avoiding Harm

Psychologists take reasonable steps to avoid harming their patients or clients, research participants, students, and others with whom they work, and to minimize harm where it is foreseeable and unavoidable.

1.15 Misuse of Psychologists' Influence

Because psychologists' scientific and professional judgments and actions may affect the lives of others, they are alert to and guard against personal, financial, social, organizational, or political factors that might lead to misuse of their influence.

1.16 Misuse of Psychologists' Work

(a) Psychologists do not participate in activities in which it appears likely that their skills or data will be misused by others, unless corrective mechanisms are available. (See also Standard 7.04, Truthfulness and Candor.)

(b) If psychologists learn of misuse or misrepresentation of their work, they take reasonable steps to correct or minimize the misuse or misrepresentation.

1.17 Multiple Relationships

(a) In many communities and situations, it may not be feasible or reasonable for psychologists to avoid social or other nonprofessional contacts with persons such as patients, clients, students, supervisees, or research participants. Psychologists must always be sensitive to the potential harmful effects of other contacts on their work and on those persons with whom they deal. A psychologist refrains from entering into or promising another personal, scientific, professional, financial, or other relationship with such persons if it appears likely that such a relationship reasonably might impair the psychologist's objectivity or otherwise interfere with the psychologist's effectively performing his or her functions as a psychologist, or might harm or exploit the other party.

(b) Likewise, whenever feasible, a psychologist refrains from taking on professional or scientific obligations when preexisting relationships would create a risk of such harm.

(c) If a psychologist finds that, due to unforeseen factors, a potentially harmful multiple relationship has arisen, the psychologist attempts to resolve it with due regard for the best interests of the affected person and maximal compliance with the Ethics Code.

1.18 Barter (With Patients or Clients)

Psychologists ordinarily refrain from accepting goods, services, or other nonmonetary remuneration from patients or clients in return for psychological services because such arrangements create inherent potential for conflicts, exploitation, and distortion of the professional relationship. A psychologist may participate in bartering only if (1) it is not clinically contraindicated, and (2) the relationship is not exploitative. (See also Standards 1.17, Multiple Relationships, and 1.25, Fees and Financial Arrangements.)

1.19 Exploitative Relationships

(a) Psychologists do not exploit persons over whom they have supervisory, evaluative, or other authority such as students, supervisees, employees, research participants, and clients or patients. (See also Standards 4.05–4.07 regarding sexual involvement with clients or patients.)

(b) Psychologists do not engage in sexual relationships with students or supervisees in training over whom the psychologist has evaluative or direct authority, because such relationships are so likely to impair judgment or be exploitative.

1.20 Consultations and Referrals

(a) Psychologists arrange for appropriate consultations and referrals based principally on the best interests of their patients or clients, with appropriate consent, and subject to other relevant considerations, including applicable law and contractual obligations. (See also Standards 5.01, Discussing the Limits of Confidentiality, and 5.06, Consultations.)

(b) When indicated and professionally appropriate, psychologists cooperate with other professionals in order to serve their patients or clients effectively and appropriately.

(c) Psychologists' referral practices are consistent with law.

1.21 Third-Party Requests for Services

(a) When a psychologist agrees to provide services to a person or entity at the request of a third party, the psychologist clarifies to the extent feasible, at the outset of the service, the nature of the relationship with each party. This clarification includes the role of the psychologist (such as therapist, organizational consultant, diagnostician, or expert witness), the probable uses of the services provided or the information obtained, and the fact that there may be limits to confidentiality.

(b) If there is a foreseeable risk of the psychologist's being called upon to perform conflicting roles because of the involvement of a third party, the psychologist clarifies the nature and direction of his or her responsibilities, keeps all parties appropriately informed as matters develop, and resolves the situation in accordance with this Ethics Code.

1.22 Delegation to and Supervision of Subordinates

(a) Psychologists delegate to their employees, supervisees, and research assistants only those responsibilities that such persons can reasonably be expected to perform competently, on the basis of their education, training, or experience, either independently or with the level of supervision being provided.

(b) Psychologists provide proper training and supervision to their employees or supervisees and take reasonable steps to see that such persons perform services responsibly, competently, and ethically.

(c) If institutional policies, procedures, or practices prevent fulfillment of this obligation, psychologists attempt to modify their role or to correct the situation to the extent feasible.

1.23 Documentation of Professional and Scientific Work

(a) Psychologists appropriately document their professional and scientific work in order to facilitate provision of services later by them or by other professionals, to ensure accountability, and to meet other requirements of institutions or the law.

(b) When psychologists have reason to believe that records of their professional services will be used in legal proceedings involving recipients of or participants in their work, they have a responsibility to create and maintain documentation in the kind of detail and quality that would be consistent with reasonable scrutiny in an adjudicative forum. (See also Standard 7.01, Professionalism, under Forensic Activities.)

1.24 Records and Data

Psychologists create, maintain, disseminate, store, retain, and dispose of records and data relating to their research, practice, and other work in accordance with law and in a manner that permits compliance with the requirements of this Ethics Code. (See also Standard 5.04, Maintenance of Records.)

1.25 Fees and Financial Arrangements

(a) As early as is feasible in a professional or scientific relationship, the psychologist and the patient, client, or other appropriate recipient of psychological services reach an agreement specifying the compensation and the billing arrangements.

(b) Psychologists do not exploit recipients of services or payors with respect to fees.

(c) Psychologists' fee practices are consistent with law.

(d) Psychologists do not misrepresent their fees.

(e) If limitations to services can be anticipated because of limitations in financing, this is discussed with the patient, client, or other appropriate recipient of services as early as is feasible. (See also Standard 4.08, Interruption of Services.)

(f) If the patient, client, or other recipient of services does not pay for services as agreed, and if the psychologist wishes to use collection agencies or legal measures to collect the fees, the psychologist first informs the person that such measures will be taken and provides that person an opportunity to make prompt payment. (See also Standard 5.11, Withholding Records for Nonpayment.)

1.26 Accuracy in Reports to Payors and Funding Sources

In their reports to payors for services or sources of research funding, psychologists accurately state the nature of the research or service provided, the fees or charges, and where applicable, the identity of the provider, the findings, and the diagnosis. (See also Standard 5.05, Disclosures.)

1.27 Referrals and Fees

When a psychologist pays, receives payment from, or divides fees with another professional other than in an employer–employee relationship, the payment to each is based on the services (clinical, consultative, administrative, or other) provided and is not based on the referral itself.

2. Evaluation, Assessment, or Intervention

2.01 Evaluation, Diagnosis, and Interventions in Professional Context

(a) Psychologists perform evaluations, diagnostic services, or interventions only within the context of a defined professional relationship. (See also Standard 1.03, Professional and Scientific Relationship.)

(b) Psychologists' assessments, recommendations, reports, and psychological diagnostic or evaluative statements are based on information and techniques (including personal interviews of the individual when appropriate) sufficient to provide appropriate substantiation for their findings. (See also Standard 7.02, Forensic Assessments.)

2.02 Competence and Appropriate Use of Assessments and Interventions

(a) Psychologists who develop, administer, score, interpret, or use psychological assessment techniques, interviews, tests, or instruments do so in a manner and for purposes that are appropriate in light of the research on or evidence of the usefulness and proper application of the techniques.

(b) Psychologists refrain from misuse of assessment techniques, interventions, results, and interpretations and take reasonable steps to prevent others from misusing the information these techniques provide. This includes refraining from releasing raw test results or raw data to persons, other than to patients or clients as appropriate, who are not qualified to use such information. (See also Standards 1.02, Relationship of Ethics and Law, and 1.04, Boundaries of Competence.)

2.03 Test Construction

Psychologists who develop and conduct research with tests and other assessment techniques use scientific procedures and current professional knowledge for test design, standardization, validation, reduction or elimination of bias, and recommendations for use.

2.04 Use of Assessment in General and With Special Populations

(a) Psychologists who perform interventions or administer, score, interpret, or use assessment techniques are familiar with the reliability, validation, and related standardization or outcome studies of, and proper applications and uses of, the techniques they use.

(b) Psychologists recognize limits to the certainty with which diagnoses, judgments, or predictions can be made about individuals.

(c) Psychologists attempt to identify situations in which particular interventions or assessment techniques or norms may not be applicable or may require adjustment in administration or interpretation because of factors such as individuals' gender, age, race, ethnicity, national origin, religion, sexual orientation, disability, language, or socioeconomic status.

2.05 Interpreting Assessment Results

When interpreting assessment results, including automated interpretations, psychologists take into account the various test factors and characteristics of the person being assessed that might affect psychologists' judgments or reduce the accuracy of their interpretations. They indicate any significant reservations they have about the accuracy or limitations of their interpretations.

2.06 Unqualified Persons

Psychologists do not promote the use of psychological assessment techniques by unqualified persons. (See also Standard 1.22, Delegation to and Supervision of Subordinates.)

2.07 Obsolete Tests and Outdated Test Results

(a) Psychologists do not base their assessment or intervention decisions or recommendations on data or test results that are outdated for the current purpose.

(b) Similarly, psychologists do not base such decisions or recommendations on tests and measures that are obsolete and not useful for the current purpose.

2.08 Test Scoring and Interpretation Services

(a) Psychologists who offer assessment or scoring procedures to other professionals accurately describe the purpose, norms, validity, reliability, and applications of the procedures and any special qualifications applicable to their use.

(b) Psychologists select scoring and interpretation services (including automated services) on the basis of evidence of the validity of the program and procedures as well as on other appropriate considerations.

(c) Psychologists retain appropriate responsibility for the appropriate application, interpretation, and use of assessment instruments, whether they score and interpret such tests themselves or use automated or other services.

2.09 Explaining Assessment Results

Unless the nature of the relationship is clearly explained to the person being assessed in advance and precludes provision of an explanation of results (such as in some organizational consulting, preemployment or security screenings, and forensic evaluations), psychologists ensure that an explanation of the results is provided using language that is reasonably understandable to the person assessed or to another legally authorized person on behalf of the client. Regardless of whether the scoring and interpretation are done by the psychologist, by assistants, or by automated or other outside services, psychologists take reasonable steps to ensure that appropriate explanations of results are given.

2.10 Maintaining Test Security

Psychologists make reasonable efforts to maintain the integrity and security of tests and other assessment techniques consistent with law, contractual obligations, and in a manner that permits compliance with the requirements of this Ethics Code. (See also Standard 1.02, Relationship of Ethics and Law.)

3. Advertising and Other Public Statements

3.01 Definition of Public Statements

Psychologists comply with this Ethics Code in public statements relating to their professional services, products, or publications or to the field of psychology. Public statements include but are not limited to paid or unpaid advertising, brochures, printed matter, directory listings, personal resumes or curricula vitae, interviews or comments for use in media, statements in legal proceedings, lectures and public oral presentations, and published materials.

3.02 Statements by Others

(a) Psychologists who engage others to create or place public statements that promote their professional practice, products, or activities retain professional responsibility for such statements.

(b) In addition, psychologists make reasonable efforts to prevent others whom they do not control (such as employers, publishers, sponsors, organizational clients, and representatives of the print or broadcast media) from making deceptive statements concerning psychologists' practice or professional or scientific activities.

(c) If psychologists learn of deceptive statements about their work made by others, psychologists make reasonable efforts to correct such statements.

(d) Psychologists do not compensate employees of press, radio, television, or other communication media in return for publicity in a news item.

(e) A paid advertisement relating to the psychologist's activities must be identified as such, unless it is already apparent from the context.

3.03 Avoidance of False or Deceptive Statements

(a) Psychologists do not make public statements that are false, deceptive, misleading, or fraudulent, either because of what they state, convey, or suggest or because of what they omit, concerning their research, practice, or other work activities or those of persons or organizations with which they are affiliated. As examples (and not in limitation) of this standard, psychologists do not make false or deceptive statements concerning (1) their training, experience, or competence; (2) their academic degrees; (3) their credentials; (4) their institutional or association affiliations; (5) their services; (6) the scientific or clinical basis for, or results or degree or success of, their services; (7) their fees; or (8) their publications or research findings. (See also Standards 6.15, Deception in Research, and 6.18, Providing Participants With Information About the Study.)

(b) Psychologists claim as credentials for their psychological work, only degrees that (1) were earned from a regionally accredited educational institution or (2) were the basis for psychology licensure by the state in which they practice.

3.04 Media Presentations

When psychologists provide advice or comment by means of public lectures, demonstrations, radio or television programs, prerecorded tapes, printed articles, mailed material, or other media, they take reasonable precautions to ensure that (1) the statements are based on appropriate psychological literature and practice, (2) the statements are otherwise consistent with this Ethics Code, and (3) the recipients of the information are not encouraged to infer that a relationship has been established with them personally.

3.05 Testimonials

Psychologists do not solicit testimonials from current psychotherapy clients or patients or other persons who because of their particular circumstances are vulnerable to undue influence.

3.06 In-Person Solicitation

Psychologists do not engage, directly or through agents, in uninvited in-person solicitation of business from actual or potential psychotherapy patients or clients or other persons who because of their particular circumstances are vulnerable to undue influence. However, this does not preclude attempting to implement appropriate collateral contacts with significant others for the purpose of benefiting an already engaged therapy patient.

4. Therapy

4.01 Structuring the Relationship

(a) Psychologists discuss with clients or patients as early as is feasible in the therapeutic relationship appropriate issues, such as the nature and anticipated course of therapy, fees, and confidentiality. (See also Standards 1.25, Fees and Financial Arrangements, and 5.01, Discussing the Limits of Confidentiality.)

(b) When the psychologist's work with clients or patients will be supervised, the above discussion includes that fact, and the name of the supervisor, when the supervisor has legal responsibility for the case.

(c) When the therapist is a student intern, the client or patient is informed of that fact.

(d) Psychologists make reasonable efforts to answer patients' questions and to avoid apparent misunderstandings about therapy. Whenever possible, psychologists provide oral and/or written information, using language that is reasonably understandable to the patient or client.

4.02 Informed Consent to Therapy

(a) Psychologists obtain appropriate informed consent to therapy or related procedures, using language that is reasonably understandable to participants. The content of informed consent will vary depending on many circumstances; however, informed consent generally implies that the person (1) has the capacity to consent, (2) has been informed of significant information concerning the procedure, (3) has freely and without undue influence expressed consent, and (4) consent has been appropriately documented.

(b) When persons are legally incapable of giving informed consent, psychologists obtain informed permission from a legally authorized person, if such substitute consent is permitted by law.

(c) In addition, psychologists (1) inform those persons who are legally incapable of giving informed consent about the proposed interventions in a manner commensurate with the persons' psychological capacities, (2) seek their assent to those interventions, and (3) consider such persons' preferences and best interests.

4.03 Couple and Family Relationships

(a) When a psychologist agrees to provide services to several persons who have a relationship (such as husband and wife or parents and children), the psychologist attempts to clarify at the outset (1) which of the individuals are patients or clients and (2) the relationship the psychologist will have with each person. This clarification includes the role of the psychologist and the probable uses of the services provided or the information obtained. (See also Standard 5.01, Discussing the Limits of Confidentiality.)

(b) As soon as it becomes apparent that the psychologist may be called on to perform potentially conflicting roles (such as marital counselor to husband and wife, and then witness for one party in a divorce proceeding), the psychologist attempts to clarify and adjust, or withdraw from, roles appropriately. (See also Standard 7.03, Clarification of Role, under Forensic Activities.)

4.04 Providing Mental Health Services to Those Served by Others

In deciding whether to offer or provide services to those already receiving mental health services elsewhere, psychologists carefully consider the treatment issues and the potential patient's or client's welfare. The psychologist discusses these issues with the patient or client, or another legally authorized person on behalf of the client, in order to minimize the risk of confusion and conflict, consults with the other service providers when appropriate, and proceeds with caution and sensitivity to the therapeutic issues.

4.05 Sexual Intimacies With Current Patients or Clients

Psychologists do not engage in sexual intimacies with current patients or clients.

4.06 Therapy With Former Sexual Partners

Psychologists do not accept as therapy patients or clients persons with whom they have engaged in sexual intimacies.

4.07 Sexual Intimacies With Former Therapy Patients

(a) Psychologists do not engage in sexual intimacies with a former therapy patient or client for at least two years after cessation or termination of professional services.

(b) Because sexual intimacies with a former therapy patient or client are so frequently harmful to the patient or client, and because such intimacies undermine public confidence in the psychology profession and thereby deter the public's use of needed services, psychologists do not engage in sexual intimacies with former therapy patients and clients even after a two-year interval except in the most unusual circumstances. The psychologist who engages in such activity after the two years following cessation or termination of treatment bears the burden of demonstrating that there has been no exploitation, in light of all relevant factors, including (1) the amount of time that has passed since therapy terminated, (2) the nature and duration of the therapy, (3) the circumstances of termination, (4) the patient's or client's personal history, (5) the patient's or client's current mental status, (6) the likelihood of adverse impact on the patient or client and others, and (7) any statements or actions made by the therapist during the course of therapy suggesting or inviting the possibility of a posttermination sexual or romantic relationship with the patient or client. (See also Standard 1.17, Multiple Relationships.)

4.08 Interruption of Services

(a) Psychologists make reasonable efforts to plan for facilitating care in the event that psychological services are interrupted by factors such as the psychologist's illness, death, unavailability, or relocation or by the client's relocation or financial limitations. (See also Standard 5.09, Preserving Records and Data.)

(b) When entering into employment or contractual relationships, psychologists provide for orderly and appropriate resolution of responsibility for patient or client care in the event that the employment or contractual relationship ends, with paramount consideration given to the welfare of the patient or client.

4.09 Terminating the Professional Relationship

(a) Psychologists do not abandon patients or clients. (See also Standard 1.25e, under Fees and Financial Arrangements.)

(b) Psychologists terminate a professional relationship when it becomes reasonably clear that the patient or client no longer needs the service, is not benefiting, or is being harmed by continued service.

(c) Prior to termination for whatever reason, except where precluded by the patient's or client's conduct, the psychologist discusses the patient's or client's views and needs, provides appropriate pretermination counseling, suggests alternative service providers as appropriate, and takes other reasonable steps to facilitate transfer of responsibility to another provider if the patient or client needs one immediately.

5. Privacy and Confidentiality

These Standards are potentially applicable to the professional and scientific activities of all psychologists.

5.01 Discussing the Limits of Confidentiality

(a) Psychologists discuss with persons and organizations with whom they establish a scientific or professional relationship (including, to the extent feasible, minors and their legal representatives) (1) the relevant limitations on confidentiality, including limitations where applicable in group, marital, and family therapy or in organizational consulting, and (2) the foreseeable uses of the information generated through their services.

(b) Unless it is not feasible or is contraindicated, the discussion of confidentiality occurs at the outset of the relationship and thereafter as new circumstances may warrant.

(c) Permisison for electronic recording of interviews is secured from clients and patients.

5.02 Maintaining Confidentiality

Psychologists have a primary obligation and take reasonable precautions to respect the confidentiality rights of those with whom they work or consult, recognizing that confidentiality may be established by law, institutional rules, or professional or scientific relationships. (See also Standard 6.26, Professional Reviewers.)

5.03 Minimizing Intrusions on Privacy

(a) In order to minimize intrusions on privacy, psychologists include in written and oral reports, consultations, and the like, only information germane to the purpose for which the communication is made.

(b) Psychologists discuss confidential information obtained in clinical or consulting relationships, or evaluative data concerning patients, individual or organizational clients, students, research participants, supervisees, and employees, only for appropriate scientific or professional purposes and only with persons clearly concerned with such matters.

5.04 Maintenance of Records

Psychologists maintain appropriate confidentiality in creating, storing, accessing, transferring, and disposing of records under their control, whether these are written, automated, or in any other medium. Psychologists maintain and dispose of records in accordance with law and in a manner that permits compliance with the requirements of this Ethics Code.

5.05 Disclosures

(a) Psychologists disclose confidential information without the consent of the individual only as mandated by law, or where permitted by law for a valid purpose, such as (1) to provide needed professional services to the patient or the individual or organizational client, (2) to obtain appropriate professional consultations, (3) to protect the patient or client or others from harm, or (4) to obtain payment for services, in which instance disclosure is limited to the minimum that is necessary to achieve the purpose.

(b) Psychologists also may disclose confidential information with the appropriate consent of the patient or the individual or organizational client (or of another legally authorized person on behalf of the patient or client), unless prohibited by law.

5.06 Consultations

When consulting with colleagues, (1) psychologists do not share confidential information that reasonably could lead to the identification of a patient, client, research participant, or other person or organization with whom they have a confidential relationship unless they have obtained the prior consent of the person or organization or the disclosure cannot be avoided, and (2) they share information only to the extent necessary to achieve the purposes of the consultation. (See also Standard 5.02, Maintaining Confidentiality.)

5.07 Confidential Information in Databases

(a) If confidential information concerning recipients of psychological services is to be entered into databases or systems of records available to persons whose access has not been consented to by the recipient, then psychologists use coding or other techniques to avoid the inclusion of personal identifiers.

(b) If a research protocol approved by an institutional review board or similar body requires the inclusion of personal identifiers, such identifiers are deleted before the information is made accessible to persons other than those of whom the subject was advised.

(c) If such deletion is not feasible, then before psychologists transfer such data to others or review such data collected by others, they take reasonable steps to determine that appropriate consent of personally identifiable individuals has been obtained.

5.08 Use of Confidential Information for Didactic or Other Purposes

(a) Psychologists do not disclose in their writings, lectures, or other public media, confidential, personally identifiable information concerning their patients, individual or organizational clients, students, research participants, or other recipients of their services that they obtained during the course of their work, unless the person or organization has consented in writing or unless there is other ethical or legal authorization for doing so.

(b) Ordinarily, in such scientific and professional presentations, psychologists disguise confidential information concerning such persons or organizations so that they are not individually identifiable to others and so that discussions do not cause harm to subjects who might identify themselves.

5.09 Preserving Records and Data

A psychologist makes plans in advance so that confidentiality of records and data is protected in the event of the psychologist's death, incapacity, or withdrawal from the position or practice.

5.10 Ownership of Records and Data

Recognizing that ownership of records and data is governed by legal principles, psychologists take reasonable and lawful steps so that records and data remain available to the extent needed to serve the best interests of patients, individual or organizational clients, research participants, or appropriate others.

5.11 Withholding Records for Nonpayment

Psychologists may not withhold records under their control that are requested and imminently needed for a patient's or client's treatment solely because payment has not been received, except as otherwise provided by law.

6. Teaching, Training Supervision, Research, and Publishing

6.01 Design of Education and Training Programs

Psychologists who are responsible for education and training programs seek to ensure that the programs are competently designed, provide the proper experiences, and meet the requirements for licensure, certification, or other goals for which claims are made by the program.

6.02 Descriptions of Education and Training Programs

(a) Psychologists responsible for education and training programs seek to ensure that there is a current and accurate description of the program content, training goals and objectives, and requirements that must be met for satisfactory completion of the program. This information must be made readily available to all interested parties.

(b) Psychologists seek to ensure that statements concerning their course outlines are accurate and not misleading, particularly regarding the subject matter to be covered, bases for evaluating progress, and the nature of course experiences. (See also Standard 3.03, Avoidance of False or Deceptive Statements.)

(c) To the degree to which they exercise control, psychologists responsible for announcements, catalogs, brochures, or advertisements describing workshops, seminars, or other non-degree-granting educational programs ensure that they accurately describe the audience for which the program is intended, the educational objectives, the presenters, and the fees involved.

6.03 Accuracy and Objectivity in Teaching

(a) When engaged in teaching or training, psychologists present psychological information accurately and with a reasonable degree of objectivity.

(b) When engaged in teaching or training, psychologists recognize the power they hold over students or supervisees and therefore make reasonable efforts to avoid engaging in conduct that is personally demeaning to students or supervisees. (See also Standards 1.09, Respecting Others, and 1.12, Other Harassment.)

6.04 Limitation on Teaching

Psychologists do not teach the use of techniques or procedures that require specialized training, licensure, or expertise, including but not limited to hypnosis, biofeedback, and projective techniques, to individuals who lack the prerequisite training, legal scope of practice, or expertise.

6.05 Assessing Student and Supervisee Performance

(a) In academic and supervisory relationships, psychologists establish an appropriate process for providing feedback to students and supervisees.

(b) Psychologists evaluate students and supervisees on the basis of their actual performance on relevant and established program requirements.

6.06 Planning Research

(a) Psychologists design, conduct, and report research in accordance with recognized standards of scientific competence and ethical research.

(b) Psychologists plan their research so as to minimize the possibility that results will be misleading.

(c) In planning research, psychologists consider its ethical acceptability under the Ethics Code. If an ethical issue is unclear, psychologists seek to resolve the issue through consultation with institutional review boards, animal care and use committees, peer consultations, or other proper mechanisms.

(d) Psychologists take reasonable steps to implement appropriate protections for the rights and welfare of human participants, other persons affected by the research, and the welfare of animal subjects.

6.07 Responsibility

(a) Psychologists conduct research competently and with due concern for the dignity and welfare of the participants.

(b) Psychologists are responsible for the ethical conduct of research conducted by them or by others under their supervision or control.

(c) Researchers and assistants are permitted to perform only those tasks for which they are appropriately trained and prepared.

(d) As part of the process of development and implementation of research projects, psychologists consult those with expertise concerning any special population under investigation or most likely to be affected.

6.08 Compliance With Law and Standards

Psychologists plan and conduct research in a manner consistent with federal and state law and regulations, as well as professional standards governing the conduct of research, and particularly those standards governing research with human participants and animal subjects.

6.09 Institutional Approval

Psychologists obtain from host institutions or organizations appropriate approval prior to conducting research, and they provide accurate information about their research proposals. They conduct the research in accordance with the approved research protocol.

6.10 Research Responsibilities

Prior to conducting research (except research involving only anonymous surveys, naturalistic observations, or similar research), psychologists enter into an agreement with participants that clarifies the nature of the research and the responsibilities of each party.

6.11 Informed Consent to Research

(a) Psychologists use language that is reasonably understandable to research participants in obtaining their appropriate informed consent (except as provided in Standard 6.12, Dispensing With Informed Consent). Such informed consent is appropriately documented.

(b) Using language that is reasonably understandable to participants, psychologists inform participants of the nature of the research; they inform participants that they are free to participate or to decline to participate or to withdraw from the research; they explain the foreseeable consequences of declining or withdrawing; they inform participants of significant factors that may be expected to influence their willingness to participate (such as risks, discomfort, adverse effects, or limitations on confidentiality, except as provided in Standard 6.15, Deception in Research); and they explain other aspects about which the prospective participants inquire.

(c) When psychologists conduct research with individuals such as students or subordinates, psychologists take special care to protect the prospective participants from adverse consequences of declining or withdrawing from participation.

(d) When research participation is a course requirement or opportunity for extra credit, the prospective participant is given the choice of equitable alternative activities.

(e) For persons who are legally incapable of giving informed consent, psychologists nevertheless (1) provide an appropriate explanation, (2) obtain the participant's assent, and (3) obtain appropriate permission from a legally authorized person, if such substitute consent is permitted by law.

6.12 Dispensing With Informed Consent

Before determining that planned research (such as research involving only anonymous questionnaires, naturalistic observations, or certain kinds of archival research) does not require the informed consent of research participants, psychologists consider applicable regulations and institutional review board requirements, and they consult with colleagues as appropriate.

6.13 Informed Consent in Research Filming or Recording

Psychologists obtain informed consent from research participants prior to filming or recording them in any form, unless the research involves simply naturalistic observations in public places and it is not anticipated that the recording will be used in a manner that could cause personal identification or harm.

6.14 Offering Inducements for Research Participants

(a) In offering professional services as an inducement to obtain research participants, psychologists make clear the nature of the services, as well as the risks, obligations, and limitations. (See also Standard 1.18, Barter [With Patients or Clients].)

(b) Psychologists do not offer excessive or inappropriate financial or other inducements to obtain research participants, particularly when it might tend to coerce participation.

6.15 Deception in Research

(a) Psychologists do not conduct a study involving deception unless they have determined that the use of deceptive techniques is justified by the study's prospective scientific, educational, or applied value and that equally effective alternative procedures that do not use deception are not feasible.

(b) Psychologists never deceive research participants about significant aspects that would affect their willingness to participate, such as physical risks, discomfort, or unpleasant emotional experiences.

(c) Any other deception that is an integral feature of the design and conduct of an experiment must be explained to participants as early as is feasible, preferably at the conclusion of their participation, but no later than at the conclusion of the research. (See also Standard 6.18, Providing Participants With Information About the Study.)

6.16 Sharing and Utilizing Data

Psychologists inform research participants of their anticipated sharing or further use of personally identifiable research data and of the possibility of unanticipated future uses.

6.17 Minimizing Invasiveness

In conducting research, psychologists interfere with the participants or milieu from which data are collected only in a manner that is warranted by an appropriate research design and that is consistent with psychologists' roles as scientific investigators.

6.18 Providing Participants With Information About the Study

(a) Psychologists provide a prompt opportunity for participants to obtain appropriate information about the nature, results, and conclusions of the research, and psychologists attempt to correct any misconceptions that participants may have.

(b) If scientific or humane values justify delaying or withholding this information, psychologists take reasonable measures to reduce the risk of harm.

6.19 Honoring Commitments

Psychologists take reasonable measures to honor all commitments they have made to research participants.

6.20 Care and Use of Animals in Research

(a) Psychologists who conduct research involving animals treat them humanely.

(b) Psychologists acquire, care for, use, and dispose of animals in compliance with current federal, state, and local laws and regulations, and with professional standards.

(c) Psychologists trained in research methods and experienced in the care of laboratory animals supervise all procedures involving animals and are responsible for ensuring appropriate consideration of their comfort, health, and humane treatment.

(d) Psychologists ensure that all individuals using animals under their supervision have received instruction in research methods and in the care, maintenance, and handling of the species being used, to the extent appropriate to their role.

(e) Responsibilities and activities of individuals assisting in a research project are consistent with their respective competencies.

(f) Psychologists make reasonable efforts to minimize the discomfort, infection, illness, and pain of animal subjects.

(g) A procedure subjecting animals to pain, stress, or privation is used only when an alternative procedure is unavailable and the goal is justified by its prospective scientific, educational, or applied value.

(h) Surgical procedures are performed under appropriate anesthesia; techniques to avoid infection and minimize pain are followed during and after surgery.

(i) When it is appropriate that the animal's life be terminated, it is done rapidly, with an effort to minimize pain, and in accordance with accepted procedures.

6.21 Reporting of Results

(a) Psychologists do not fabricate data or falsify results in their publications.

(b) If psychologists discover significant errors in their published data, they take reasonable steps to correct such errors in a correction, retraction, erratum, or other appropriate publication means.

6.22 Plagiarism

Psychologists do not present substantial portions of elements of another's work or data as their own, even if the other work or data source is cited occasionally.

6.23 Publication Credit

(a) Psychologists take responsibility and credit, including authorship credit, only for work they have actually performed or to which they have contributed.

(b) Principal authorship and other publication credits accurately reflect the relative scientific or professional contributions of the individuals involved, regardless of their relative status. Mere possession of an institutional position, such as Department Chair, does not justify authorship credit. Minor contributions to the research or to the writing for publications are appropriately acknowledged, such as in footnotes or in an introductory statement.

(c) A student is usually listed as principal author on any multiple-authored article that is substantially based on the student's dissertation or thesis.

6.24 Duplicate Publication of Data

Psychologists do not publish, as original data, data that have been previously published. This does not preclude republishing data when they are accompanied by proper acknowledgment.

6.25 Sharing Data

After research results are published, psychologists do not withhold the data on which their conclusions are based from other competent professionals who seek to verify the substantive claims through reanalysis and who intend to use such data only for that purpose, provided that the confidentiality of the participants can be protected and unless legal rights concerning proprietary data preclude their release.

6.26 Professional Reviewers

Psychologists who review material submitted for publication, grant, or other research proposal review respect the confidentiality of and the proprietary rights in such information of those who submitted it.

7. Forensic Activities

7.01 Professionalism

Psychologists who perform forensic functions, such as assessments, interviews, consultations, reports, or expert testimony, must comply with all other provisions of this Ethics Code to the extent that they apply to such activities. In addition, psychologists base their forensic work on appropriate knowledge of and competence in the areas underlying such work, including specialized knowledge concerning special populations. (See also Standards 1.06, Basis for Scientific and Professional Judgments; 1.08, Human Differences; 1.15, Misuse of Psychologists' Influence; and 1.23, Documentation of Professional and Scientific Work.)

7.02 Forensic Assessments

(a) Psychologists' forensic assessments, recommendations, and reports are based on information and techniques (including personal interviews of the individual, when appropriate) sufficient to provide appropriate substantiation for their findings. (See also Standards 1.03, Professional and Scientific Relationship; 1.23, Documentation of Professional and Scientific Work; 2.01, Evaluation, Diagnosis, and Interventions in Professional Context; and 2.05, Interpreting Assessment Results.)

(b) Except as noted in (c), below, psychologists provide written or oral forensic reports or testimony of the psychological characteristics of an individual only after they have conducted an examination of the individual adequate to support their statements or conclusions.

(c) When, despite reasonable efforts, such an examination is not feasible, psychologists clarify the impact of their limited information on the reliability and validity of their reports and testimony, and they appropriately limit the nature and extent of their conclusions or recommendations.

7.03 Clarification of Role

In most circumstances, psychologists avoid performing multiple and potentially conflicting roles in forensic matters. When psychologists may be called on to serve in more than one role in a legal proceeding—for example, as consultant or expert for one party or for the court and as a fact witness—they clarify role expectations and the extent of confidentiality in advance to the extent feasible, and thereafter as changes occur, in order to avoid compromising their professional judgment and objectivity and in order to avoid misleading others regarding their role.

7.04 Truthfulness and Candor

(a) In forensic testimony and reports, psychologists testify truthfully, honestly, and candidly and, consistent with applicable legal procedures, describe fairly the bases for their testimony and conclusions.

(b) Whenever necessary to avoid misleading, psychologists acknowledge the limits of their data or conclusions.

7.05 Prior Relationships

A prior professional relationship with a party does not preclude psychologists from testifying as fact witnesses or from testifying to their services to the extent permitted by applicable law. Psychologists appropriately take into account ways in which the prior relationship might affect their professional objectivity or opinions and disclose the potential conflict to the relevant parties.

7.06 Compliance With Law and Rules

In performing forensic roles, psychologists are reasonably familiar with the rules governing their roles. Psychologists are aware of the occasionally competing demands placed upon them by these principles and the requirements of the court system, and attempt to resolve these conflicts by making known their commitment to this Ethics Code and taking steps to resolve the conflict in a responsible manner. (See also Standard 1.02, Relationship of Ethics and Law.)

8. Resolving Ethical Issues

8.01 Familiarity With Ethics Code

Psychologists have an obligation to be familiar with this Ethics Code, other applicable ethics codes, and their application to psychologists' work. Lack of awareness or misunderstanding of an ethical standard is not itself a defense to a charge of unethical conduct.

8.02 Confronting Ethical Issues

When a psychologist is uncertain whether a particular situation or course of action would violate this Ethics Code, the psychologist ordinarily consults with other psychologists knowledgeable about ethical issues, with state or national psychology ethics committees, or with other appropriate authorities in order to choose a proper response.

8.03 Conflicts Between Ethics and Organizational Demands

If the demands of an organization with which psychologists are affiliated conflict with this Ethics Code, psychologists clarify the nature of the conflict, make known their commitment to the Ethics Code, and to the extent feasible, seek to resolve the conflict in a way that permits the fullest adherence to the Ethics Code.

8.04 Informal Resolution of Ethical Violations

When psychologists believe that there may have been an ethical violation by another psychologist, they attempt to resolve the issue by bringing it to the attention of that individual if an informal resolution appears appropriate and the intervention does not violate any confidentiality rights that may be involved.

8.05 Reporting Ethical Violations

If an apparent ethical violation is not appropriate for informal resolution under Standard 8.04 or is not resolved properly in that fashion, psychologists take further action appropriate to the situation, unless such action conflicts with confidentiality rights in ways that cannot be resolved. Such action might include referral to state or national committees on professional ethics or to state licensing boards.

8.06 Cooperating With Ethics Committees

Psychologists cooperate in ethics investigations, proceedings, and resulting requirements of the APA or any affiliated state psychological association to which they belong. In doing so, they make reasonable efforts to resolve any issues as to confidentiality. Failure to cooperate is itself an ethics violation.

8.07 Improper Complaints

Psychologists do not file or encourage the filing of ethics complaints that are frivolous and are intended to harm the respondent rather than to protect the public.

Glossary

In this Glossary, we have attempted to provide a quick guide to some of the technical terms and abbreviations relevant to forensic evaluations and expert testimony. It is by no means comprehensive and does not purport to provide detailed, technical definitions accompanied by qualifications and proper context. The attorney reading a report of psychological and neuropsychological assessment, studying published psychological research relevant to a trial, or listening to deposition or trial testimony by an expert witness may need a convenient and easily used source to look up technical terms. Similarly, a clinician who specializes in the MMPI and who has not previously testified in court may wish, during preparation, to review terms relevant to some of the other major testing instruments and may find it useful to become familiar with some of the terms used in judicial proceedings (such as forms of objection). Numerous large volumes have been published over the years devoted exclusively to listing and defining psychological or legal terms; in making the difficult decisions regarding which terms to include in this relatively brief list, we have inevitably used our own experience concerning which terms are most likely to arise in cases involving a version of the MMPI and to be unknown to attorneys or witnesses.

A final note: There is a lack of consistency in the literature of neuropsychology in regard to the use of terms that differ according to whether the prefix is *a-* or *dys-* (e.g., agraphia, dysgraphia). In the list that follows, we have used the *a-* prefix to denote a complete lack or absence of the function and the *dys-* prefix to denote a partial (not complete) impairment of function.

ABREACTION A term usually used within a psychoanalytic or psychodynamic framework in which the individual lets out or expresses strong emotions that had been held in or repressed.

ACALCULIA Lack of ability to recognize and use numbers due to organic impairment (see DYSCALCULIA).

ACTING OUT A term usually used within a psychoanalytic or psychodynamic framework to denote a defense in which the individual expresses painful or "unacceptable" emotions through behavior as a way to keep them unconscious (or out of awareness).

ACTUARIAL APPROACH Application of probability statistics to human behavior, as in insurance mortality tables.

ACUTE POSTTRAUMATIC STRESS DISORDER A disorder in which symptoms develop within 6 months of an extremely stressful or traumatic experience.

ADAPTIVE TESTING An approach to test administration using the rapid computational capability of the computer. A different set of items is administered for each person depending upon the person's previous responses. Rather than administering all items for each person, the items are "tailor-made" for each individual.

ADMISSIBLE EVIDENCE Information that can be communicated or displayed to the trier of fact (e.g., judge or jury); certain information (e.g., hearsay or privileged) may be inadmissible under the applicable laws of evidence.

AFFECT Feelings or emotion.

AGGRAVATED ASSAULT An attack on another person in which, according to criteria enacted under state statute, serious bodily injury is inflicted or a deadly weapon is used.

AGNOSIA A state or condition in which the individual lacks knowledge in the relevant area (as in the adjective *agnostic*).

AGRAPHIA Lack of ability to write the letters of the alphabet due to organic impairment (see DYSGRAPHIA).

ALIENATION Loss or lack of a relationship with others.

ALPHA ERROR See TYPE I ERROR.

AMERICAN PSYCHOLOGICAL ASSOCIATION (APA; this abbreviation is also commonly used for the American Psychiatric Association) Holding its first meeting in 1892, and ratifying its constitution in 1984, the APA incorporated in 1925 (see Fernberger, 1932). The largest association of psychologists in the United States, with 114,000 members and affiliates, APA publishes approximately 20 scientific and professional journals (the first in 1925), including *American Psychologist*, the official or archival journal, *Behavioral Neuroscience*, *Journal of Abnormal Psychology*, *Journal of Consulting and Clinical Psychology*, *Journal of Personality and Social Psychology*, *Professional Psychology: Research and Practice*, and *Psychological Assessment,* as well as books.

AMERICAN BOARD OF FORENSIC PSYCHIATRY This board provides advanced certification as an expert witness to psychiatrists who have previously been certified by the American Board of Psychiatry and Neurology.

AMERICAN BOARD OF PROFESSIONAL PSYCHOLOGY (ABPP) This organization, incorporated originally in 1947 as the American Board of Examiners in Professional Psychology, grants diplomas to psychologists in six areas of practice: clinical psychology, clinical neuropsychology, counseling psychology, forensic psychology, industrial/organizational psychology, and school psychology. "The Board encourages the pursuit of excellence via its program of certification at an advanced professional level. The ABPP diploma signifies, to the public and to the profession, the highest recognition of competence as judged by one's professional peers" (American Board of Professional Psychology, 1984, p. 1).

AMERICAN PSYCHIATRIC ASSOCIATION (APA; this abbreviation is also commonly used for American Psychological Association) The American Psychiatric Association is the largest voluntary association of psychiatrists in the United States. Founded in 1844, the association publishes a variety of journals (e.g., *The American Journal of Psychiatry*, which is the official or archival journal, and *Journal of Hospital and Community Psychiatry*) and books.

AMERICAN PSYCHOLOGICAL SOCIETY (APS) "The American Psychological Society was founded in 1988 as an independent, multipurpose organization to advance the discipline of psychology, to preserve the scientific base of psychology, to promote public understanding of psychological science and its application, to enhance the quality of graduate education, and to encourage the 'giving away' of psychology in the public interest" (APS, 1990, p. 311; see also Holden, 1988). APS publishes two journals: *Psychological Science* and *Current Directions in Psychological Science*.

AMICUS CURIAE Literally a "friend of the court," this term generally refers to someone who is not a party to a case who offers a brief bearing on the case. For example, both the American Psychological Association and the American Psychiatric Association have provided briefs in cases in which an individual's ability to accurately predict whether a convicted murderer was likely to kill again was at issue.

ANALYSAND Term for a patient in psychoanalysis.

ANG Abbreviation for the anger content scale on the MMPI-2 (see chapter 2 and appendix D).

ANHEDONIA Impairment of the ability to experience pleasure or to engage in pleasurable activities.

ANTISOCIAL PERSONALITY Personality disorder involving a marked lack of ethical or moral development.

ANX Abbreviation for the anxiety content scale on the MMPI-2 (see chapter 2 and appendix D).

APHASIA Lack of ability to recognize or produce words (i.e., to process language; see DYSPHASIA).

APHONIA Lack of ability to make vocal sounds due to organic impairment (i.e., loss of voice; see DYSPHONIA).

APPELLANT An individual who appeals a decision of the court.

ARITHMETIC SUBTEST A verbal subtest of the WAIS-R.

ASKED AND ANSWERED A form of objection during a trial in which the attorney who is not currently questioning a witness asserts that the attorney who *is* currently questioning a witness is posing a question that has already been adequately answered by the witness.

ASP Abbreviation for the antisocial practices content scale on the MMPI-2 (see chapter 2 and appendix D).

ATAXIA Lack of ability to coordinate voluntary movements.

ATTEST A legal term denoting that an individual swears or otherwise affirms that certain information is true and accurate (e.g., an expert witness attests that an MMPI-2 has been incorrectly scored).

AUTOMATED ASSESSMENT Psychological test interpretation by electronic computer or some other mechanical procedures.

AVERSION THERAPY A term usually used within a behavioral or cognitive–behavioral framework to denote treatment in which an unwanted, punishing, or aversive stimulus is used to eliminate unwanted behaviors.

BATTERY An unlawful touching, beating, or physical violence done to another without consent.

BEHAVIOR MODIFICATION An intervention to change behavior based upon altering contingencies of reinforcement according to the principles of operant (or Skinnerian) conditioning.

BEHAVIOR THERAPY An intervention based on the laws of learning (e.g., classical or operant conditioning).

BEHAVIORAL ASSESSMENT A technique to determine the functional relationships between an individual's behavior and environmental stimuli.

BEHAVIORISM A framework in which the study of people (or animals) focuses primarily or exclusively on observable behavior.

BENDER-GESTALT (or BENDER VISUAL MOTOR GESTALT TEST) A test for neuropsychological impairment in which the individual is asked to copy nine geometric forms (see Bender, 1938; Lacks, 1984).

BENTON VISUAL RETENTION TEST A test for neuropsychological impairment focusing on visual memory; it takes about 5 or 10 minutes to administer and is appropriate for ages 8 and above.

BETA ERROR See TYPE II ERROR.

BETWEEN-SUBJECTS RESEARCH A study in which different but comparable groups of people (generally in which participants have been randomly assigned to the different groups) receive different interventions (e.g., behavior modification, dynamic therapy, and medication) or levels of interventions. Results are obtained by comparing (and contrasting) the (possible) effects of the values, forms, or levels of the variable as manifested in the differences between (groups of) subjects (see WITHIN-SUBJECTS RESEARCH).

BEYOND THE SCOPE A form of objection during a trial in which the attorney who is not currently questioning a witness asserts that the attorney who *is* currently questioning a witness is posing a legally impermissible cross-examination question because it goes beyond the scope of the material covered during direct examination.

BIMODAL DISTRIBUTION A statistical term indicating a distribution in which there are two values (or scores) that are tied in terms of being most frequent; thus the distribution has two modes (i.e., is bimodal); (see MODE; see also chapter 8).

BIZ Abbreviation for the bizarre mentation content scale on the MMPI-2 (see chapter 2 and appendix D).

BLOCK DESIGN SUBTEST A performance subtest of the WAIS-R.

BONA FIDE In good faith, without fraud or deceit.

BOOKLET CATEGORY TEST An altered form (making the test easier to administer) of the Category Test, one of the tests included in the Halstead-Reitan Neuropsychological Test Battery.

BRIEF A document prepared by counsel as a statement of the case, defining issues, presenting arguments, and citing authorities on the matter.

CANNOT SAY An MMPI validity scale (see chapters 2, 6, and 8) of the total number of unanswered items.

CATEGORY TEST One of the tests included in the Halstead-Reitan Neuropsychological Test Battery.

CATHEXIS The investment of psychological energy into a specific person, thing, or activity.

CENTRAL NERVOUS SYSTEM The portion of the nervous system that includes the brain and spinal cord.

CENTRAL TENDENCY A statistical term indicating the average; measures of central tendency include the mean, the median, and the mode (see MEAN, MEDIAN, and MODE; see also chapter 8).

CHARACTER DISORDER See PERSONALITY DISORDER.

CIVIL COMMITMENT A legal process in which an individual can be confined (e.g., in a mental hospital) against his or her will due to a mental, emotional, or behavioral disorder that meets certain criteria (e.g., the individual is assessed as constituting an immediate threat to self or others or is assessed as gravely disabled).

CLANG ASSOCIATIONS Language characterized by a sequence of words and phrases determined not so much by logical expression as by the similarity of word sounds and associations (e.g., "Two plus two. Too much. Let out the clutch. Clutch my heart. I'm heart of hearing. See my ear-ring? Ringing in my ears. Clinging to my tears.")

CLIENT-CENTERED THERAPY Predominantly originated and developed by psychologist Carl Rogers, this intervention is nondirective, tends to involve statements by the therapist that reflect (e.g., summarize or restate) what the client has just expressed, and focuses on trust, accurate empathy, and acceptance.

COGNITION Thinking or the processes involved in thinking; the intellectual processes by which a person takes in and processes information (e.g., intellectual learning, judging, planning, and reasoning).

COGNITIVE BEHAVIOR MODIFICATION Behavior modification (an intervention to change behavior based upon altering contingencies of reinforcement according to the principles of operant conditioning) that also focuses on cognitive processes as mediating factors.

COGNITIVE THERAPY An intervention that focuses on altering negative, self-defeating, and distorted thought processes.

COMPREHENSION SUBTEST A verbal subtest of the WAIS-R.

CONCRETE THINKING Impaired ability to engage in abstract thought.

CONFABULATION Inventing information to hide the fact that the individual cannot remember (e.g., an individual suffering from the early stages of Alzheimer's disease, asked what she had for breakfast but unable to remember, might make up what seems to her to be a plausible answer).

CONTINUANCE Postponement of an action or a session, hearing, trial, or other proceeding to a subsequent time.

CONTRAST ERROR A term of assessment or research denoting a tendency to erroneously inflate perceived differences (e.g., in assessing individuals or characteristics) because of (comparison to or contrast with) previous ratings.

CONTROL GROUP A comparison group used in research that attempts to assess the effect(s) of one or more independent variables (e.g., to assess the efficacy of client-centered therapy for depression, depressed individuals might be randomly assigned to two groups, one of which receives client-centered therapy, the other, as the control group, receives educational instruction about depression).

CORRELATION COEFFICIENT A statistic indicating the degree to which two variables are related (i.e., to which they co-vary, or vary together). The coefficient falls somewhere on the continuum running from −1 (perfectly negatively correlated) to 0 (no relationship whatsoever) to 1 (perfectly positively correlated) (see chapter 8).

COUNTERTRANSFERENCE This term has been defined in a variety of (sometimes inconsistent) ways, but generally refers to the therapist experiencing (sometimes on an unconscious level) feelings that are stirred up or elicited by the patient.

CYN Abbreviation for the cynicism content scale on the MMPI-2 (see chapter 2 and appendix D).

D Abbreviation for the depression clinical scale (i.e., Scale 2) on the MMPI (see chapter 2 and appendix D).

DECOMPENSATION Deterioration of an individual's personality, condition, or functioning.

DEFENSE MECHANISMS A term usually used within a psychoanalytic or psychodynamic framework to denote strategies by which an individual wards off awareness of unpleasant, frightening, or anxiety-inducing thoughts or experiences; these strategies are carried out on an unconscious level (i.e., the individual is not aware of them).

DELUSION A rigid belief not consistent with reality and maintained in spite of strong evidence to the contrary.

DEMENTIA Substantial loss of mental or cognitive abilities.

DEMUR To allege in a legal proceeding that the facts as charged, even if true, do not form an adequate legal basis for the case to go forth.

DEP Abbreviation for the depression content scale on the MMPI-2 (see chapter 2 and appendix D).

DEPENDENT VARIABLE A research term indicating the measure which, according to the hypothesis, will reflect changes in the independent variable (i.e., changes in the dependent variable are dependent upon the presence or absence or changes in the independent variable).

DEPERSONALIZATION A state in which the individual feels that his or her self or body is somehow unreal, unfamiliar, "different," or strange.

DEPOSITION A legal term indicating part of the pretrial discovery process in which an attorney may take the testimony—under oath—of a witness prior to the trial (see chapters 5 and 8).

DEREALIZATION A state in which the individual feels that the surroundings are somehow unreal, unfamiliar, "different," or strange.

DESCRIPTIVE STATISTICS Statistics that apply only to cases that have actually been counted or otherwise measured (e.g., the number of words in this book and the average number of letters in the words in this book); in descriptive statistics, no attempt is made to draw inferences about wider population than has actually been counted or measured (e.g., in the example above, no attempt would be made to use the number and length of words in this book to generalize about other books; see INFERENTIAL STATISTICS).

DESENSITIZATION A term usually used within the behavioral or cognitive–behavioral framework to refer to a process in which repeated exposure to a stimulus may tend to reduce the occurrence of a response (or the response's intensity) to the stimulus (e.g., in cognitive–behavioral therapy, an individual who has been traumatized by an event may be guided to experience much milder versions of the event in his or her imagination until the effects of the trauma are diminished).

DIAGNOSTIC AND STATISTICAL MANUAL OF MENTAL DISORDERS (DSM) One of the classification systems by which mental, emotional, or behavior disorders have been defined, described, and labeled. Published by the American Psychiatric Association, the first edition, influenced by Adolf Meyer's view of personality, appeared in 1952. After the second edition (1968), the manual adopted a new multiaxial system of diagnosis (American Psychiatric Association, 1980, 1987): Axis I presents clinical disorders or syndromes (as well as treatment issues that do not constitute mental disorders and some supplementary codes); Axis II presents personality and developmental disorders; Axis III presents physical disorders; Axis IV indicates the level of psychosocial stress; and Axis V indicates the best level of functioning the individual has experienced during the past year. The DSM includes a "cautionary statement" that there is no implication that categories meet legal criteria for various diseases, disorders, or disabilities. The "cautionary statement" further states that the "clinical and scientific considerations" of this classification system "may not be wholly relevant to legal judgments" (1987, p. xxix).

DICHOTOMOUS VARIABLE A statistical term denoting a scale that is divided into two mutually exclusive categories (e.g., a nominal scale that divides individuals into boys and girls; an age scale that divides all survey participants into those who are under 45 and all those who are 45 or older).

DIGIT SPAN A verbal subtest of the WAIS-R as well as of the mental status examination and other assessment approaches.

DIGIT SYMBOL SUBTEST A performance subtest of the WAIS-R.

DISCOVERY A legal term indicating the process that occurs before the trial commences in which attorneys are able to obtain documents, information, and testimony from opposition parties, expert witnesses, and others.

DOUBLE JEOPARDY A prohibition against a second prosecution or punishment for the same offense, as defined through common law, state constitutions, and the Fifth Amendment to the United States Constitution.

DYSCALCULIA Impaired ability to recognize and use numbers due to organic impairment (see ACALCULIA).

DYSGRAPHIA Impaired ability to write the letters of the alphabet due to organic impairment (see AGRAPHIA).

DYSKINESIA Impaired ability to produce voluntary movements (as in the side-effect Tardive Dyskinesia sometimes produced by antipsychotic medications).

DYSLEXIA Impaired ability to read due to organic impairment.

DYSPHASIA Impaired ability to recognize or produce words (i.e., to process language; see APHASIA).

DYSPHONIA Impaired ability to make vocal sounds due to organic impairment (i.e., loss of voice; see APHONIA).

DYSPRAXIA Impaired ability to conduct voluntary, coordinated, intentional movements, actions, or expressions.

ECHOLALIA A condition in which the individual constantly (and perhaps exclusively) mimics or repeats what others are saying.

ECHOPRAXIA A condition in which the individual mimics or repeats the behaviors of those around him or her.

EGO PSYCHOLOGY A branch, development, or revision of psychoanalytic theory focusing on the processes of the ego rather than the id; the relative emphasis is on the person's attempts to cope with reality rather than to express unconscious wishes and themes.

EXISTENTIAL PSYCHOLOGY OR THERAPY A framework for psychology or therapy in which the focus is the individual's immediate human experience rather than observable behaviors, cognitive processes, or unconscious motives.

EXPERT WITNESS Testifying person who may render an opinion based on specialized knowledge or skill if proper foundation is laid under F.R.E. Rule 702 and F.R.E. Rule 703 (see discussion of *Kenosha Liquor Company v. Heublein, Inc.* in chapter 8; see also percipient or lay witness).

F SCALE An MMPI validity scale (see chapters 2, 6, and 8) created to measure exaggeration of symptoms.

FACTOR ANALYSIS A statistical technique employed in research to reduce a large array of measurements or data down to supposedly more concise and fundamental dimensions.

FALSE NEGATIVE An error in assessment in which a test falsely indicates that the individual does not have a particular condition (that the test was designed to identify) when in fact the person does have the condition (see FALSE POSITIVE, SENSITIVITY, and SPECIFICITY).

FALSE POSITIVE An error in assessment in which a test falsely indicates that the individual has a particular condition (that the test was designed to identify) when in fact the person does not have the condition (see FALSE NEGATIVE, SENSITIVITY, and SPECIFICITY).

FAM Abbreviation for the family problems content scale on the MMPI-2 (see chapter 2 and appendix D).

FELONY A serious crime for which a person can be sentenced to long-term penitentiary incarceration or death.

FINGER OSCILLATION TEST One of the tests included in the Halstead-Reitan Neuropsychological Test Battery. Also known as the finger tapping test.

FRS Abbreviation for the fears content scale on the MMPI-2 (see chapter 2 and appendix D).

FUNCTIONAL DISORDER A form of psychopathological distress or dysfunction for which a physiological cause is neither known nor presumed.

FUNCTIONAL PSYCHOSES Severe mental disorders that are attributed primarily to psychological causes such as stress.

GESTALT THERAPY A form of therapy focusing on integrating behavior, thinking, and feeling.

GRIP STRENGTH One of the tests included in the Halstead-Reitan Neuropsychological Test Battery.

HABEAS CORPUS The name given to a variety of writs designed to bring a party before a court or judge. Whenever the words are used alone, the primary function of the writ is to release the party from unlawful imprisonment.

HALSTEAD IMPAIRMENT INDEX A number from 0.0 (none of the scores suggesting brain damage) to 1.0 (all seven scores suggesting brain damage) representing the proportion of seven (originally 10) Halstead-Reitan Neuropsychology tests on which the individual scored in the range characteristic of neuropsychologically damaged individuals.

HAPTIC Relating to touch.

HEA Abbreviation for the health concerns content scale on the MMPI-2 (see chapter 2 and appendix D).

HEARSAY A form of objection during a trial in which the attorney who is not currently questioning a witness asserts that the attorney who *is* currently questioning a witness is eliciting (or that the witness is providing) testimony that is inadmissible because it is based on information that was overheard.

HEARSAY RULE A rule of evidence to exclude statements made out of court when offered to prove the truth of the matter asserted.

Hs Abbreviation for the hypochondriasis clinical scale (i.e., Scale 1) on the MMPI (see chapter 2 and appendix D), measuring somatic concerns.

Hy Abbreviation for the hysteria clinical scale (i.e., Scale 3) on the MMPI (see chapter 2 and appendix D).

I.Q. An abbreviation for Intelligence Quotient; generally, the relation of mental age to chronological age, or the person's likely ranking in the population.

IMPLOSIVE THERAPY An intervention within the behavioral or cognitive–behavioral framework in which an "implosion" (sometimes termed "flooding") of anxiety or fear is evoked in an effort to desensitize an individual to a specific stimulus.

INCIDENCE A statistical term that refers to the number of *new* cases of a particular event or phenomenon within a specified period of time (see PREVALENCE).

INDEPENDENT VARIABLE A research term indicating a factor that, according to the hypothesis, will cause a change in at least one other (dependent) variable in the study; the independent variable is often presented at different levels while other factors are held constant.

INFERENTIAL STATISTICS Statistical techniques allowing inferences to be made about a larger population based upon counts and measurements of a (presumably representative) sample or subset of that population (see DESCRIPTIVE STATISTICS).

INFORMATION A verbal subtest of the WAIS-R.

IRRELEVANT A form of objection during a trial in which the attorney who is not currently questioning a witness asserts that the attorney who *is* currently questioning a witness is posing a question that is irrelevant to the case.

K SCALE An MMPI validity scale (see chapters 2, 6, and 8) created to measure test defensiveness.

KELLY-FRYE TEST A case law standard that expert testimony, to be admissible, must be generally accepted by the relevant scientific or professional community (see chapter 3).

KURTOSIS A statistical term describing the degree to which scores or measurements are clustered closely around or are spread far from the mean.

L SCALE (Lie Scale) An MMPI validity scale (see chapters 2, 6, and 8) created to measure the tendency to claim excessive virtue.

LAMBDA A statistical term indicating the degree to which two dichotomous variables are related or associated; also a variable used in the Rorschach Comprehensive System (Exner, 1991).

LAW OF EFFECT A term generally used within the behavioral or cognitive–behavioral framework to denote the phenomenon by which behaviors that are followed by pleasing consequences (positive reinforcers) tend to be repeated while behaviors that are followed by aversive consequences are less likely to be repeated.

LEADING A form of objection during a trial in which the attorney who is not currently questioning a witness asserts that the attorney who *is* currently questioning a witness is posing a question that is legally improper because it indicates to a witness how to respond (e.g., "When you saw the defendant that night did you think to yourself, 'This must be the man who killed the shopkeeper?' ").

LEARNED HELPLESSNESS A phenomenon in which the individual erroneously "learns" (perhaps from one or more traumatic situations in which his or her behavior produced no significant result) that his or her behaviors have little or no relationship to consequences.

LESION Damage of tissue (e.g., a lesion in the brain).

LINEAR *T* SCORES A statistical term (see *T* SCORES, in which the mean of the distribution is 50 and the standard deviation is 10); the type of scaling used by the original MMPI (see chapters 2 and 8).

LSE Abbreviation for the low self-esteem content scale on the MMPI-2 (see chapter 2 and appendix D).

LURIA-NEBRASKA A neuropsychological assessment battery.

Ma Abbreviation for the hypomania clinical scale (i.e., Scale 9) on the MMPI (see chapter 2 and appendix D).

MATERIAL EVIDENCE The quality of evidence that tends to influence the trier of fact because of its logical connection with the issue.

MEAN An arithmetic average in which the scores (or other numbers) are added and then the resulting sum is divided by the number of scores.

MEDIAN A statistical term indicating that score or measurement that divides all the scores or measurements into two equal groups: those falling below the median and those falling above the median (see chapter 8).

MEGARGEE FELONY CLASSIFICATION RULES An MMPI-based classification system designed to group felons' MMPI profiles into similar personality clusters (see chapter 2).

MENTAL STATUS EXAMINATION A generic term (i.e., numerous articles, texts, and guidebooks present different outlines for conducting the examination) that describes a structured observation and interview technique in which the examiner evaluates a comprehensive set of characteristics (e.g., appearance, orientation, attention, concentration, memory, and insight) related to the individual's current mental status.

Mf Abbreviation for the masculinity–femininity scale (i.e., Scale 5) on the basic MMPI profile (see chapter 2 and appendix D).

MILLON CLINICAL MULTIAXIAL INVENTORY (MCMI AND MCMI-II) A rationally derived scale that assesses individuals according to Millon's (e.g., 1969, 1981, 1987) conceptualization of clinical and personality disorders. As the title of the scale indicates, it focuses on clinical (rather than nonclinical) assessment.

MISDEMEANOR An offense that is not a felony and is punishable by a fine or short period of incarceration generally in a facility other than a penitentiary.

MODE A statistical term indicating the most frequently occurring score or measurement in a distribution (see chapter 8).

MOTION IN LIMINE A written request made to the presiding judge before or after the beginning of a jury trial for a protective order against prejudicial statements.

NATIONAL ASSOCIATION OF SOCIAL WORKERS (NASW) This voluntary professional association emerged in 1955 when seven previously established social work associations merged into NASW.

NO FOUNDATION A form of objection during a trial in which the attorney who is not currently questioning a witness asserts that the attorney who *is* currently questioning a witness is posing a question that is legally impermissible because no foundation has been provided for this area of testimony.

NONDIRECTIVE THERAPY See CLIENT-CENTERED THERAPY.

NORM-REFERENCED TESTS Those that compare test takers with each other. Grading on a "curve" is an example of norm-referenced tests.

NULL HYPOTHESIS In experimental research, the hypothesis that the independent or experimental variable exerts no effect so that there will be no statistically significant difference in outcome between the experimental group(s) and the control group(s).

OBJECT ASSEMBLY SUBTEST A performance subtest of the WAIS-R.

OBJECT RELATIONS THEORY A psychoanalytic view that the development of the ego (self) and social relationships are based upon or strongly influenced by the infant's attachment to the significant people (generally the parents).

OBS Abbreviation for the obsessiveness content scale on the MMPI-2 (see chapter 2 and appendix D).

OPERANT CONDITIONING The influence on behavior by the positive or negative reinforcements that follow the behavior (see BEHAVIOR MODIFICATION).

Pa Abbreviation for the paranoia clinical scale (i.e., Scale 6) on the MMPI (see chapter 2 and appendix D).

PARAPRAXIS An incident in which a person says or does something that is different from what he or she intends to say or do, resulting in an error of which the person may be unaware. An example is a "Freudian slip."

PATHOGNOMONIC SYMPTOM OR SIGN A sufficient indicant for assigning a particular diagnosis or classification (e.g., complete lack of brain activity is a pathognomic sign of death).

Pd Abbreviation for the psychopathic deviate clinical scale (i.e., Scale 4) on the MMPI (see chapter 2 and appendix D).

PERCENTILE RANK Tells what proportion of the group falls below a particular point.

PERCENTILE SCORE The rank from the bottom of a scale is expressed in percentage form.

PERCIPIENT OR LAY WITNESS Testifying person who does not posses any expertise in the matters about which he or she testifies (used in contrast to expert witness).

PERSONALITY DISORDER A group of maladaptive behavioral syndromes originating in the developmental years (usually considered learning-based disorders) and not characterized by neurotic or psychotic symptoms.

PICTURE ARRANGEMENT SUBTEST A performance subtest of the WAIS-R.

PICTURE COMPLETION SUBTEST A performance subtest of the WAIS-R.

PRACTICE EFFECTS A phenomenon in which the validity of a test may be affected because an individual has previously taken the test (e.g., the test is now familiar).

PREPONDERANCE OF EVIDENCE A standard of proof in which the evidence presented to the court appears more convincing than the evidence provided by the opposition. The evidence, as a whole, shows that the fact sought to be proved is more probable than not.

PREVALENCE A statistical term that refers to the total number of cases of a particular event or phenomenon within a specified time (see also INCIDENCE).

PROFILE A method of displaying test scores to provide a visual comparison of relative performance on similar scales.

PROJECTIVE TEST An assessment instrument in which the test materials (e.g., Rorschach cards, TAT pictures) contain some stimulus ambiguity; the individual's responses are hypothesized to reveal personality attributes.

PSYCHOPHYSIOLOGIC (PSYCHOSOMATIC) DISORDERS Physical disorders in which psychological factors are considered to play a major causative role.

Pt Abbreviation for the psychasthenia clinical scale (i.e., Scale 7) on the MMPI, created to measure anxiety (see chapter 2 and appendix D).

RANDOM SAMPLE A subgroup selected from a larger group (termed the population) in such a way that each member of the larger group has an equal probability of being chosen.

RATIONAL SCALE DEVELOPMENT Developing scales based on the content of the items by simply grouping items according to their explicit meaning.

RATIONAL–EMOTIVE THERAPY Predominantly originated and developed by psychologist Albert Ellis, this therapy attempts to identify and correct errors in thinking and misconnections between thinking and feeling.

REASONABLE DOUBT A doubt that would cause a reasonably prudent person to hesitate to act in matters of importance.

RECIDIVISM A return to a previous form of undesirable behavior after a course of intervention (see chapter 8).

REITAN-INDIANA APHASIA SCREENING TEST One of the tests included in the Halstead-Reitan Neuropsychological Test Battery.

REITAN-KLOVE LATERAL DOMINANCE EXAMINATION One of the tests included in the Halstead-Reitan Neuropsychological Test Battery.

REITAN-KLOVE SENSORY-PERCEPTION EXAMINATION One of the tests included in the Halstead-Reitan Neuropsychological Test Battery.

REITAN-KLOVE TACTILE FORM RECOGNITION TEST One of the tests included in the Halstead-Reitan Neuropsychological Test Battery.

RELIABILITY The degree to which a test or other form of measurement is consistent in producing the same result every time it is used to assess or measure a particular person who has not changed significantly between testings (see chapter 8).

REPLICATION Research that attempts to repeat previous research (either identically or with specific changes) to see if the original results are reliable.

RES IPSA LOQUITUR Literally from the Latin: The thing speaks for itself. In legal proceedings, the res ipsa loquitur principle of evidence or inference indicates that, under certain circumstances, the mere existence of an event may establish culpability.

RESPONSE RATE A statistical term indicating the percentage of those invited to participate in a study who actually participated in the study (e.g., If surveys were mailed out to 200 randomly selected individuals and 150 individuals completed and returned the survey form, the response rate would be 75%).

ROGERIAN THERAPY See CLIENT-CENTERED THERAPY.

RORSCHACH A projective technique in which the individual is shown 10 symmetrical "inkblots" in specific sequence and is asked to describe each blot and the specific attributes of the card that, according to the individual, make up or determine what the individual sees in the card.

Sc Abbreviation for the schizophrenia clinical scale (i.e., Scale 8) on the MMPI (see chapter 2 and appendix D).

SCALE A systematic framework for assigning names or measurements; for definitions of nominal, ordinal, interval, and ratio scales, see chapter 8.

SEASHORE RHYTHM One of the tests originally developed as part of the Seashore Tests of Musical Talent and now included in the Halstead-Reitan Neuropsychological Test Battery.

SELF-REPORT QUESTIONNAIRE A questionnaire or inventory designed to obtain self-descriptions from an individual.

SENSITIVITY If a psychological test has been validated to identify a certain condition, the sensitivity refers to the proportion of tested individuals who test positive who actually have the condition (see SPECIFICITY, FALSE POSITIVE, and FALSE NEGATIVE).

SENTENCE COMPLETION TEST A projective test appearing in many forms; the basic procedure involves presenting an individual with a word or phrase that begins a sentence and asking the individual to complete the sentence immediately.

SEQUELAE Distress, dysfunction, symptoms, and other consequences that linger in the aftermath of a trauma, disease, or disorder.

SERIAL SEVENS The individual is asked to count by sevens either forward (e.g., 7, 14, 21) or backward (100, 93, 86).

Si Abbreviation for the social introversion clinical scale (i.e., Scale 0) on the MMPI (see chapter 2 and appendix D).

SIGNIFICANT DIFFERENCE In inferential statistics, a difference that is unlikely to be due to chance (see TYPE I and TYPE II ERRORS).

SIMILARITIES SUBTEST A verbal subtest of the WAIS-R.

SKEWNESS A statistical term indicating the degree to which measurements fall in a symmetrical (i.e., not skewed) or asymmetrical (i.e., skewed) pattern around the mean.

SOCIAL APPROVAL OR SOCIAL DESIRABILITY BIAS The potential tendency for an individual participating in research or assessment to provide answers that would be perceived as socially approved or socially desirable.

SOCIOTHERAPY Intervention focusing on an individual's social or interpersonal relationships and functioning.

SOD Abbreviation for the social discomfort content scale on the MMPI-2 (see chapter 2 and appendix D).

SOMATIC Relating to the body (e.g., headaches and abdominal pain would be characterized as somatic complaints).

SPECIFICITY If a psychological test has been validated to identify a certain condition, the specificity refers to the proportion of tested individuals who test negative who actually do not have the condition (see SENSITIVITY, FALSE POSITIVE, and FALSE NEGATIVE).

SPEECH SOUNDS PERCEPTION TEST One of the tests included in the Halstead-Reitan Neuropsychological Test Battery.

STANDARD DEVIATION A statistical measure of the spread or dispersion of scores (or other measures) around the mean; the square root of the variance (see chapter 8).

STANDARD SCORE A score (e.g., on a standardized psychological test) that is calculated in terms of standard deviations from the statistical mean of scores.

STANFORD-BINET A standardized test of the intellectual abilities of children.

SUBPOENA DUCES TECUM Literally translated from the Latin: Under penalty, bring forth [this material] with you. A legal document requiring the individual to produce certain materials (see chapter 5).

SYNDROME A group or pattern of symptoms, sequelae, or characteristics of a disorder.

***T* SCORES** Scores falling along a distribution in which the mean is 50 and the standard deviation is 10 (see chapters 2 and 8).

TACTILE Relating to touch.

TACTUAL PERFORMANCE TEST One of the tests included in the Halstead-Reitan Neuropsychological Test Battery.

TELEPROCESSING A computer-based data processing procedure by which psychological tests are processed, scored, and interpreted through telephone link-up with a central processing center.

TEST "A systematic procedure for observing behavior and describing it on a numerical scale, or in terms of categories" (Cronbach, 1990, p. 706).

TEST USER QUALIFICATIONS Guidelines established by a professional organization (e.g., the American Psychological Association) specifying the level of training and experience required for different tests.

THEMATIC APPERCEPTION TEST A projective technique developed by psychologist Henry Murray (see Murray & Staff of the Harvard Psychological Clinic, 1943) in which an individual is shown a sequence of pictures and is asked to make up a story that goes with each picture.

TINNITUS A condition in which the individual hears noise (e.g., static, roaring, ringing) in the absence of an external stimulus for the noise.

TORT A legal term denoting a "wrong" for which the injured party may sue in civil court for damages in order to "be made whole."

TPA Abbreviation for the Type-A personality content scale on the MMPI-2 (see chapter 2 and appendix D).

TR (or T-R) Abbreviation for test-retest variation, a form of test reliability usually expressed as a correlation; changes in test scores for an individual test taker may reflect the imperfect reliability of the test (generally chance or error variance), an actual change in the individual's condition, or the possibility that the individual is intentionally or unconsciously distorting responses but is not doing so in a consistent manner.

TRAIL MAKING TEST One of the tests included in the Halstead-Reitan Neuropsychological Test Battery.

TRANSACTIONAL ANALYSIS A form of therapy focusing on three aspects of the self: parent, child, and adult.

TRANSFERENCE A phenomenon in which a patient "transfers" to or projects onto the therapist feelings from an earlier relationship (e.g., the child's relationship to a parent); the process is initially unconscious.

TRIN Abbreviation for the true response inconsistency scale, one of the validity scales of the MMPI-2 (see chapter 6 and appendix D).

TRT Abbreviation for the negative treatment indicators content scale on the MMPI-2 (see chapter 2 and appendix D).

TYPE I ERROR A research term indicating that a decision (in interpreting results) was made that there was an actual (i.e., not due to chance) difference or finding when in reality there was no such actual difference or finding; also known as alpha error.

TYPE II ERROR A research term indicating that a decision (in interpreting results) was made that there was no actual (i.e., not due to chance) difference or finding when in reality there *was* such actual difference or finding; also known as beta error.

UNIFORM T-SCORES A statistical term (see *T* SCORES); the type of scaling used by the MMPI-2 and MMPI-A resulting in comparable percentile values for a given *T* score across various clinical or content scales (see chapters 2 and 8).

VALIDITY The degree to which a test or other form of measurement actually assesses or measures what it is designed to assess or measure (see chapters 6 and 8).

VARIABLE A characteristic, attribute, or measurement that has at least two levels or categories. "Work" may be a variable that can be divided into "paid" and "unpaid" (i.e., two levels), although it is also possible to define work as variable with many more levels or categories (e.g., work as "hard," "medium," or "light" as experienced or defined by the individual doing the work).

VARIANCE A statistical measure of the spread or dispersion of scores (or other measures) around the mean; the square of the standard deviation (see chapter 8).

VERBAL TEST A test in which the person's ability to understand and use words and concepts is important in making the required responses.

VOCABULARY SUBTEST A verbal subtest of the WAIS-R and other tests.

VOIR DIRE A process by which attorneys and judges question potential jurors to determine whether they are appropriate (e.g., lack bias) to serve as jurors in a specific trial.

VRIN Abbreviation for the variable response inconsistency scale, one of the validity scales of the MMPI-2 (see chapter 6 and appendix D).

WAIS-R Wechsler Adult Intelligence Scale–Revised is comprised of six verbal/numerical (Verbal) and five perceptual/motor (Performance) subtests and is the 1981 revision of the 1955 WAIS (see WECHSLER-BELLEVUE).

WECHSLER MEMORY SCALE The original (WMS) and revised (WMS-R) versions contain subtests assessing such aspects of memory as forward and backward digit span, logical memory, visual reproduction, and associate learning.

WECHSLER-BELLEVUE SCALE A test (comprised of 11 subtests) divided into two main parts (Verbal and Performance) developed in the 1930s as a general intelligence test and later revised into the Wechsler Adult Intelligence Scale.

WESTERN APHASIA BATTERY A set of subtests that yield an AQ (aphasia quotient) and a CQ (cortical quotient), a more general measure of cognitive functioning.

WISCONSIN CARD SORTING TEST An untimed test focusing on perseverative and abstract thinking used to help identify neuropsychological impairment.

WITHIN-SUBJECTS RESEARCH A study in which each participant receives (generally in sequence) the different interventions or different levels of the intervention. The (possible) effects of the different values, forms, or levels of the variable are compared and contrasted in terms of (or within) each subject (see BETWEEN-SUBJECTS RESEARCH).

WORK PRODUCT A legal term denoting preparation conducted by an attorney (and in some instances consultants and others who work for the attorney) that, depending on circumstances and applicable law, are not subject to pretrail discovery by opposing counsel.

WRK Abbreviation for the work interference content scale on the MMPI-2 (see chapter 2 and appendix D).

***Z* SCORES** Standardized scores falling along a distribution in which the mean is 0 and the standard deviation is 1.

References

Abeles, N. (1982). Proceedings of the American Psychological Association, Incorporated, for the year 1981. Minutes of the annual meeting of the Council of Representatives. *American Psychologist*, *37*, 632–666.

Acorn, D. A., Hamilton, D. L., & Sherman, S. J. (1988). Generalization of biased perceptions of groups based on illusory correlations. *Social Cognition*, 6, 345–372.

Adams, K. B., & Putnam, S. (1992, May). *Use of the MMPI-2 in neuropsychological evaluations*. Workshop conducted at the 27th Annual Symposium on Recent Developments in the Use of the MMPI (MMPI-2), Minneapolis, MN.

Adams, T. C. (1976). Some MMPI differences between first and multiple admissions with a state prison population. *Journal of Clinical Psychology*, *32*, 555–558.

Adelman, R. M., & Howard, A. (1984). Expert testimony on malingering: The admissibility of clinical procedures for the detection of deception. *Behavioral Sciences & the Law*, *2*, 5–19.

American Bar Association. (1989). *American Bar Association criminal justice mental health standards*. Washington, DC: Author.

American Board of Professional Psychology. (1984). *Policies and procedures for the creation of diplomates in professional psychology*. Columbia, MO: Author.

American Psychiatric Association. (1952). *Diagnostic and statistical manual, mental disorders* (1st ed.). Washington, DC: Author.

American Psychiatric Association. (1968). *Diagnostic and statistical manual of mental disorders* (2nd ed.). Washington, DC: Author.

American Psychiatric Association. (1980). *Diagnostic and statistical manual of mental disorders* (3rd ed.). Washington, DC: Author.

American Psychiatric Association. (1987). *Diagnostic and statistical manual of mental disorders* (3rd ed., rev.). Washington, DC: Author.

American Psychological Association. (1981). Specialty guidelines for the delivery of services by clinical (counseling, industrial/organizational, and school) psychologists. *American Psychologist*, *36*, 639–681.

American Psychological Association. (1982). *Ethical principles in the conduct of research with human participants*. Washington, DC: Author.

American Psychological Association. (1983). *Publication manual of the American Psychological Association* (3rd ed.). Washington, DC: Author.

American Psychological Association. (1986a). *Accreditation handbook*. Washington, DC: Author.

American Psychological Association. (1986b). *Guidelines for computer-based tests and interpretations*. Washington, DC: Author.

American Psychological Association. (1987a). *Casebook on ethical principles of psychologists*. Washington, DC: Author.

American Psychological Association. (1987b). *General guidelines for providers of psychological services*. Washington, DC: Author.

American Psychological Association. (1987c). Model Act for state licensure of psychologists. *American Psychologist*, *42*, 696–703.

American Psychological Association. (1992). Ethical principles of psychologists and code of conduct. *American Psychologist*, *47*, 1597–1611.

American Psychological Association Insurance Trust. (1990). *Bulletin: Sexual misconduct and professional liability claims*. Washington, DC: Author.

American Psychological Society. (1990). American Psychological Society. *Psychological Science*, *1*, 311.

Anastasi, A. (1988). *Psychological testing* (6th ed.). New York: Macmillan.

Anderson, W., & Holcomb, W. (1983). Accused murderers: Five MMPI personality types. *Journal of Clinical Psychology*, *39*, 761–768.

Annas, G. J. (1991). Mengele's birthmark: The Nuremberg Code in United States courts. *Journal of Contemporary Health Law and Policy*, *7*, 17–45.

Annas, G. J., & Grodin, M. A. (1991). Forcing drugs on U.S. soldiers violates Nuremberg Code. *Los Angeles Daily Journal*, *103*(23), 6.

Annas, G., & Grodin, M. (1992). *The Nazi doctors and the Nuremberg Code: Human rights in human experimentation*. New York: Oxford University Press.

Anthony, N. (1971). Comparison of clients' standard, exaggerated, and matching MMPI profiles. *Journal of Consulting and Clinical Psychology*, *38*, 100–103.

APA-accredited predoctoral internships for doctoral training in psychology: 1990. (1990). *American Psychologist*, *45*, 1346–1359.

APA-accredited programs in professional psychology: 1990. (1990). *American Psychologist*, *45*, 1360–1367.

Archer, R. P. (1989). Use of the MMPI with adolescents in forensic settings. *Forensic Reports*, *2*, 65–87.

Arkes, H. R., Saville, P. D., Wortmann, R. L., & Harkness, A. R. (1981). Hindsight bias among physicians weighing the likelihood of diagnoses. *Journal of Applied Psychology*, *66*, 252–254.

Arnold, P. D. (1970). *Recurring MMPI two-point codes of marriage counselors and "normal" couples with implications for interpreting marital interaction behavior*. Unpublished doctoral dissertation, University of Minnesota, Minneapolis.

Asch, S. E. (1956). Studies of independence and conformity: I. A minority of one against a unanimous majority. *Psychological Monographs*, *70*(9, Whole No. 416).

Baer, R. (1981). *Homosexuality and American psychiatry*. New York: Basic Books.

Baer, R. A., Wetter, M. W., & Berry, D. T. (1992). Detection of underreporting of psychopathology on the MMPI: A meta-analysis. *Clinical Psychology Review*, *12*, 509–525.

Bakan, P. (1978). Two streams of consciousness: A typological approach. In K. S. Pope & J. L. Singer (Eds.), *The stream of consciousness: Scientific investigations into the flow of human experience* (pp. 159–184). New York: Plenum Press.

Bank, S. C., & Poythress, N. G. (1982). The elements of persuasion in expert testimony. *Journal of Psychiatry & Law*, 173–204.

Barber, T. X. (1976). *Pitfalls in human research*. Elmsford, NY: Pergamon Press.

Barnard, C. P., & Jenson, G. (1984). Child custody evaluations: A rational process for an emotion-laden event. *American Journal of Family Therapy*, *12*(2), 61–67.

Barrett, R. K. (1973). *Relationship of emotional disorder to marital maladjustment and disruption*. Unpublished doctoral dissertation, Kent State University, Kent, OH.

Barry, J. R., Anderson, H. E., & Thomas, O. R. (1967). MMPI characteristics of alcoholic males who are well and poorly adjusted to marriage. *Journal of Clinical Psychology*, *23*, 355–360.

Barton, W. A. (1990). *Recovering for psychological injuries* (2nd ed.). Washington, DC: ATLA Press.

Bates, C. M., & Brodsky, A. M. (1989). *Sex in the therapy hour: A case of professional incest*. New York: Guilford Press.

Bazelon, D. L. (1974). Psychiatrists and the adversary process. *Scientific American*, *230*, 18–23.

Beecher, H. K. (1963). Ethics and experimental therapy. *Journal of the American Medical Association*, *186*, 858–859.

Beecher, H. K. (1966). Ethics and clinical research. *New England Journal of Medicine*, *274*, 1354–1360.

Bell, B. E., & Loftus, E. F. (1985). Vivid persuasion in the courtroom. *Journal of Personality Assessment*, *49*, 659–664.

Bell, D. E., Raiffa, H., & Tversky, A. (1988). *Decision making: Descriptive, normative, and prescriptive interactions*. Cambridge, England: Cambridge University Press.

Bellack, A. S., Herson, M., & Kazdin, A. E. (Eds.). (1990). *International handbook of behavior modification and therapy* (2nd ed.). New York: Plenum Press.

Belli, M. M., & Carlova, J. (1986). *Belli for your malpractice defense*. Oradell, NJ: Medical Economics Books.

Ben-Porath, Y. S., & Butcher, J. N. (1989a). Psychometric stability of rewritten MMPI items. *Journal of Personality Assessment*, *53*, 645–653.

Ben-Porath, Y. S., & Butcher, J. N. (1989b). The comparability of MMPI and MMPI-2 scales and profiles. *Psychological Assessment: A Journal of Consulting and Clinical Psychology*, *1*, 345–347.

Ben-Porath, Y. S., Butcher, J. N., & Graham, J. R. (1991). Contribution of the MMPI-2 scales to the differential diagnosis of schizophrenia and major depression. *Psychological Assessment: A Journal of Consulting and Clinical Psychology*, *3*, 634–640.

Ben-Porath, Y. S., & Tellegen, A. (1992). Continuity and changes in MMPI-2 validity indicators: Points of clarification. *MMPI-2 News & Profiles*, *3*(2), 6–8.

Bender, L. (1938). A visual motor gestalt test and its clinical use. *Research Monographs of the American Orthopsychiatric Association*, *3*.

Beniak, T., Heck, D., & Erdahl, P. E. (1992, May). *Intractable epilepsy: MMPI and MMPI-2 profiles*. Paper presented at the 27th Annual Symposium on Recent Developments in the Use of the MMPI (MMPI-2), Minneapolis, MN.

Berry, D. T., Baer, R. A., & Harris, M. J. (1991). Detection of malingering on the MMPI: A meta-analysis. *Clinical Psychology Review*, *11*, 585–591.

Berry, D. T., Wetter, M. W., Baer, R. A., Larsen, L., Clark, C., & Monroe, K. (1992). MMPI-2 random responding indices: Validation using a self-report methodology. *Psychological Assessment: A Journal of Consulting and Clinical Psychology*, *4*, 340–345.

Berry, D. T., Wetter, M. W., Baer, R. A., Widiger, T. A., Sumpter, J. C., Reynolds, S. K., & Hallam, R. A. (1991). Detection of random responding on the MMPI-2: Utility of *F*, Back *F*, and *VRIN* scales. *Psychological Assessment: A Journal of Consulting and Clinical Psychology*, *3*, 418–423.

Black, J. B., & Bower, G. H. (1979). Episodes as chunks in narrative memory. *Journal of Verbal Learning and Verbal Behavior*, *18*, 309–318.

Blackburn, R. (1968). Personality in relation to extreme aggression in psychiatric offenders. *British Journal of Psychiatry*, *114*, 821–828.

Blake, D. D., Penk, W. E., Mori, D. L., Kleespies, P. M., Walsh, S. S., & Keane, T. M. (1992). Validity and clinical scale comparisons between the MMPI and MMPI-2 with psychiatric patients. *Psychological Reports*, *70*, 323–332.

Blau, T. H. (1984a). Psychological tests in the courtroom. *Professional Psychology*, *15*, 176–186.

Blau, T. H. (1984b). *The psychologist as expert witness*. New York: Wiley-Interscience.

Block, J. (1965). *The challenge of response sets: Unconfounding meaning, acquiescence, and social desirability in the MMPI*. New York: Appleton-Century-Crofts.

Block, N. J., & Dworkin, G. (Eds.). (1976). *The I.Q. controversy*. New York: Random House.

Bloom, W. (1977). Relevant MMPI norms for young Air Force trainees. *Journal of Personality Assessment*, *5*, 505–510.

Bloomquist, M. L., & Harris, W. G. (1984). Measuring family functioning with the MMPI: A reliability and concurrent validity study of three MMPI family scales. *Journal of Clinical Psychology*, *40*, 1209–1214.

Board of Professional Affairs, [APA] Committee on Professional Standards. (1987). General guidelines for providers of psychological services. *American Psychologist*, *42*, 712–723.

Bobb, P. (1992, March). *Ultimate advocacy course: Art of persuasion*. Workshop presented by the Association of Trial Lawyers of America, Washington, DC.

Boehnert, C. E. (1987). Characteristics of those evaluated for insanity. *Journal of Psychiatry and Law*, *15*, 229–246.

Bohn, M. J. (1979). Management classification for young adult inmates. *Federal Probation*, *43*, 53–59.

Booth, R. J., & Howell, R. J. (1980). Classification of prison inmates with the MMPI: An extension and validation of the Megargee typology. *Criminal Justice and Behavior*, *7*, 407–422.

Bower, G. H., & Clark, M. C. (1969). Narrative stories as mediators for serial learning. *Psychonomic Science*, *14*, 181–182.

Bower, G. H., & Morrow, D. G. (1990). Mental models in narrative comprehension. *Science*, *247*, 44–48.

Bowler, R. M., Rauch, S. S., Becker, C. H., Hawes, A., & Cone, J. D. (1989). Three patterns of MMPI profiles following neurotoxin exposure. *American Journal of Forensic Psychology*, *7*, 15–31.

Brauer, B. A., (1992). The signer effect on MMPI performance of deaf respondents. *Journal of Personality Assessment*, *58*, 380–388.

Briere, J., & Zaidi, L. Y. (1989). Sexual abuse histories and sequelae in female psychiatric emergency room patients. *American Journal of Psychiatry*, *146*, 1602–1606.

Brodsky, S. L. (1989). Advocacy in the guise of scientific objectivity: An examination of Faust and Ziskin. *Computers in Human Behavior*, *5*, 261–264.

Brodsky, S. L. (1991). *Testifying in court: Guidelines and maxims for the expert witness*. Washington, DC: American Psychological Association.

Brooten, K. E., & Chapman, S. (1987). *Malpractice: A guide to avoidance and treatment*. New York: Grune & Stratton.

Brown, L. S. (1988, August). *Taking account of gender and sexuality issues in clinical assessment*. Paper presented at the 96th Annual Convention of the American Psychological Association, Atlanta, GA.

Brown, L. S. (1991). Antiracism as an ethical imperative: An example from feminist therapy. *Ethics & Behavior*, *1*, 113–128.

Brown, L. S., & Root, M. P. P. (Eds.). (1990). *Diversity and complexity in feminist therapy*. New York: Haworth.

Brown, R., & Smith, A. (1989). Perceptions of and by minority groups: The case of women in academia. *European Journal of Social Psychology*, *19*, 61–75.

Brownfain, J. J. (1971). The APA professional liability insurance program. *American Psychologist*, *26*, 648–652.

Brozek, J. H., & Schiele, B. (1948). Clinical significance of the Minnesota Multiphasic *F* scale evaluated in experimental neurosis. *American Journal of Psychiatry*, *105*, 259–266.

Buechley, R., & Ball, H. (1952). A new test of "validity" for the group MMPI. *Journal of Consulting Psychology*, *16*, 299–301.

Burgess, J. A. (1984). Principles and techniques of cross-examination. In B. G. Warschaw (Ed.), *The trial masters: A handbook of strategies and techniques that win cases* (pp. 249–255). Englewood Cliffs, NJ: Prentice-Hall.

Burish, T. G., & Houston, B. K. (1976). Construct validity of the Lie scale as a measure of defensiveness. *Journal of Clinical Psychology*, *32*, 310–314.

Burke, E. L. (1992). Intelligence testing and neuropsychological assessment. In H. H. Goldman (Ed.), *Review of general psychiatry* (3rd ed. pp. 126–130). Norwalk, CT: Appleton & Lange.

Butcher, J. N. (Ed.). (1972). *Objective personality assessment: Changing perspectives*. San Diego, CA: Academic Press.

Butcher, J. N. (1985). Current developments in MMPI use: An international perspective. In J. N. Butcher & C. D. Spielberger (Eds.), *Advances in personality assessment* (Vol. 4, pp. 83–94). Hillsdale, NJ: Erlbaum.

Butcher, J. N. (1987a) (Ed.). *Computerized psychological assessment*. New York: Basic Books.

Butcher, J. N. (March, 1987b). *Use of the MMPI in personnel screening*. Paper presented at the 22nd Annual Symposium on Recent Developments in the Use of the MMPI, Seattle, WA.

Butcher, J. N. (1990a). Education level and MMPI-2 measured psychopathology: A case of negligible influence. *MMPI-2 News & Profiles*, *1*(2), 2.

Butcher, J. N. (1990b). *Use of the MMPI-2 in treatment planning*. New York: Oxford University Press.

Butcher, J. N. (1990c). What interpretive changes do the educational differences between the original MMPI and MMPI-2 normative samples require? *MMPI-2 News and Profiles*, *1*(1), 2.

Butcher, J. N. (1992a). *Clinical applications of the MMPI-2*. Workshop presented at MMPI/MMPI-2/MMPI-A Workshops & Symposia, University of Minnesota, Minneapolis.

Butcher, J. N. (1992b). Comparison of the original MMPI, MMPI-2, and MMPI-A. In *Topics in MMPI-2 and MMPI-A interpretation*. Workshop presented at MMPI/MMPI-2/MMPI-A Workshops & Symposia, University of Minnesota, Minneapolis.

Butcher, J. N. (1992c). [Psychological assessment of airline pilot applicants: Validity and clinical scores.] Unpublished raw data.

Butcher, J. N., Aldwin, C., Levenson, M., Ben-Porath, Y. S., Spiro, A., & Bosse', R. (1991). Personality and aging: A study of the MMPI-2 among elderly men. *Psychology of Aging*, *6*, 361–370.

Butcher, J. N., Dahlstrom, W. G., Graham, J. R., Tellegen, A., & Kaemmer, B. (1989). *Minnesota Multiphasic Personality Inventory-2 (MMPI-2): Manual for administration and scoring*. Minneapolis: University of Minnesota Press.

Butcher, J. N., Egli, E. A., Shiota, N. K., & Ben-Porath, Y. S. (1988). *Psychological interventions with refugees*. Rockville, MD: National Institute of Mental Health.

Butcher, J. N., Graham, J. R., Dahlstrom, W. G., & Bowman, E. (1990). The MMPI-2 with college students. *Journal of Personality Assessment*, *54*, 1–15.

Butcher, J. N., Graham, J. R., Williams, C. L., & Ben-Porath, Y. S. (1989). *Development and use of the MMPI-2 content scales*. Minneapolis: University of Minnesota Press.

Butcher, J. N., & Harlow, T. (1987). Psychological assessment in personal injury cases. In A. Hess, & I. Weiner (Eds.), *Handbook of forensic psychology* (pp. 128–154). New York: Wiley.

Butcher, J. N., & Hostetler, K. (1990). Abbreviating MMPI item administration: Past problems and prospects for MMPI-2. *Psychological Assessment: A Journal of Consulting and Clinical Psychology*, *2*, 12–21.

Butcher, J. N., Jeffrey, T., Cayton, T. G., Colligan, S., DeVore, J., & Minnegawa, R. (1990). A study of active duty military personnel with the MMPI-2. *Military Psychology*, 2, 47–61.

Butcher, J. N., & Owen, P. (1978). Survey of personality inventories: Recent research developments and contemporary issues. In B. Wolman (Ed.), *Handbook of clinical diagnosis* (pp. 475–546). New York: Plenum Press.

Butcher, J. N., & Pancheri, P. (1976). *Handbook of cross-national MMPI research*. Minneapolis: University of Minnesota Press.

Butcher, J. N., & Pope, K. S. (1990). MMPI-2: A practical guide to psychometric, clinical, and ethical issues. *Independent Practitioner, 10(1)*, 33–40.

Butcher, J. N., & Pope, K. S. (1992). The research base, psychometric properties, and clinical uses of the MMPI-2 and MMPI-A. *Canadian Psychology*, *33*, 61–78.

Butcher, J. N., & Tellegen, A. (1966). Objections to MMPI items. *Journal of Consulting Psychology*, *30*, 527–534.

Butcher, J. N., & Williams, C. L. (1992a). *Essentials of MMPI-2 and MMPI-A interpretation*. Minneapolis: University of Minnesota Press.

Butcher, J. N., & Williams, C. L. (1992b). *User's guide to the Minnesota Report: Adolescent Clinical System*. Minneapolis, MN: National Computer Systems.

Butcher, J. N., Williams, C. L., Graham, J. R., Archer, R., Tellegen, A., Ben-Porath, Y. S., & Kaemmer, B. (1992). *MMPI-A manual for administration, scoring, and interpretation*. Minneapolis: University of Minnesota Press.

Cairns, D., Mooney, V., & Crane, P. (1984). Spinal pain rehabilitation: Inpatient and outpatient treatment results and development of predictors for outcome. *Spine*, *9*, 91–95.

California Department of Consumer Affairs. (1990). *Professional therapy never includes sex*. Sacramento, CA: Board of Psychology.

Callanan, K., & O'Connor, T. (1988). *Staff comments and recommendations regarding the report of the Senate Task Force on Psychotherapist and Patient Sexual Relations*. Sacramento, CA: Board of Behavioral Science Examiners and Psychology Examining Committee.

Carlson, S. (1990). The victim/perpetrator: Turning points in therapy. In M. Hunter (Ed.), *The sexually abused male: Vol. 2. Application of treatment strategies* (pp. 249–266). Lexington, MA: Lexington Books.

Carson, R. C., & Butcher, J. N. (1992). *Abnormal psychology and modern life* (9th ed.). New York: HarperCollins.

Cartwright, R. E. (1984). Winning psychological principles in summation. In B. G. Warshaw (Ed.), *The trial masters: A handbook of strategies and tactics that win cases* (pp. 338–349). Englewood Cliffs, NJ: Prentice-Hall.

Chandler, M. J., Greenspan, S., & Barenboim, C. (1973). Judgments of intentionality of response to videotapes and verbally presented moral dilemmas: The medium is the message. *Child Development*, *44*, 315–320.

Chanowitz, B., & Langer, E. J. (1981). Premature cognitive commitment. *Journal of Personality and Social Psychology*, *41*, 1051–1063.

Chapman, L. J., & Chapman, J. P. (1962). Genesis of popular but erroneous psychodiagnostic observations. *Journal of Abnormal Psychology*, *72*, 193–204.

Chapman, L. J., & Chapman, J. P. (1969). Illusory correlation as an obstacle to the use of valid psychodiagnostic signs. *Journal of Abnormal Psychology*, *74*, 271–280.

Charles, S. C., & Kennedy, E. (1985). *Defendant*. New York: Free Press.

Cheung, F. M., & Song, W. Z. (1989). A review on the clinical applications of the Chinese MMPI. *Psychological Assessment: A Journal of Consulting and Clinical Psychology*, *1*, 230–237.

Cheung, F. M., Song, W. Z., & Butcher, J. N. (1991). An infrequency scale for the Chinese MMPI. *Psychological Assessment: A Journal of Consulting and Clinical Psychology*, *3*, 648–653.

Cheung, F. M., Zhao, J., & Wu, C. (1992). Chinese MMPI profiles among neurotic patients. *Psychological Assessment*, *4*, 214–218.

Chojenackie, J. T., Walsh, W. B. (1992). The consistency of scores and configural patterns between MMPI and MMPI-2. *Journal of Personality Assessment*, *59*, 276–289.

Chorover, S. L. (1979). *From genesis to genocide: The meaning of human nature and the power of behavior control*. Cambridge, MA: MIT Press.

Clark, L. A. (1985). A consolidated version of the MMPI in Japan. In J. N. Butcher & C. D. Spielberger (Eds.), *Advances in personality assessment* (Vol. 4, pp. 95–130). Hillsdale, NJ: Erlbaum.

Clopton, J. R., & Neuringer, C. (1977). MMPI Cannot Say scores: Normative data and degree of profile distortion. *Journal of Personality Assessment*, *41*, 511–513.

Cocks, G. (1985). *Psychotherapy in the Third Reich: The Goring Institute*. New York: Oxford University Press.

Cofer, C. N., Chance, J., & Judson, A. J. (1949). A study of malingering on the MMPI. *Journal of Psychology*, *27*, 491–499.

Colby, F. (1989). Usefulness of the *K* correction in MMPI profiles of patients and nonpatients. *Psychological Assessment: A Journal of Consulting and Clinical Psychology*, *1*, 142–145.

Cole, M., & Bruner, J. S. (1972). Cultural differences and inferences about psychological processes. *American Psychologist*, *26*, 867–876.

Coles, R. (1973a, February 22). Shrinking history (Part I). *New York Times Review of Books*, pp. 15–21.

Coles, R. (1973b, March 8). Shrinking history (Part II). *New York Times Review of Books*, pp. 20, 25–29.

Colligan, R. C., Osborne, D., Swenson, W. M., & Offord, K. P. (1983). *The MMPI: A contemporary normative study*. New York: Praeger.

Committee on Ethical Guidelines for Forensic Psychologists. (1991). Specialty guidelines for forensic psychologists. *Law and Human Behavior*, *15*, 655–665.

Committee on Professional Standards [of the American Psychological Association]. (1984). Casebook for providers of psychological services. *American Psychologist*, *39*, 663–668.

Conger, J. J. (1976). Proceedings of the American Psychological Association, Incorporated, for the year 1975: Minutes of the annual meeting of the Council of Representatives, August 29 and September 2, 1975, Chicago, Illinois, and January 23–25, 1976, Washington, DC. *American Psychologist*, *31*, 406–434.

Conger, J. J. (1977). Proceedings of the American Psychological Association, Incorporated, for the year 1976: Minutes of the annual meeting of the Council of Representatives, September 2 and 5, 1976, Washington, DC and January 28–30, 1977, Washington, DC. *American Psychologist*, *32*, 408–438.

Conley, J. M., O'Barr, W. M., & Lind, E. A. (1978). The power of language: Presentational style in the courtroom. *Duke Law Journal*, *6*, 1375–1399.

Cookerly, J. R. (1974). The reduction of psychopathology as measured by the MMPI clinical scales in three forms of marriage counseling. *Journal of Marriage and Family*, *36*, 332.

Costanzo, M., & Costanzo, S. (1992). Jury decision making in the capital penalty phase: Legal assumptions, empirical findings, and a research agenda. *Law and Human Behavior*, *16*, 185–202.

Couric, E. (1988). *The trial lawyers*. New York: St. Martin's Press.

Coyle, W. C., & Heap, R. F. (1965). Interpreting the MMPI *L* scale. *Psychological Reports*, *17*, 722.

Craddick, R. A. (1962). Selection of psychopathic from non-psychopathic prisoners within a Canadian prison. *Psychological Reports*, *10*, 495–499.

Cronbach, L. J. (1960). *Essentials of psychological testing*. New York: Harper & Row.

Cronbach, L. J. (1990). *Essentials of psychological testing* (5th ed.). New York: HarperCollins.

Dahlstrom, W. G. (1980). Altered versions of the MMPI. In W. G. Dahlstrom & L. E. Dahlstrom (Eds.), *Basic readings on the MMPI: A new selection on personality measurement* (pp. 386–393). Minneapolis: University of Minnesota Press.

Dahlstrom, W. G., (1992). Comparability of two-point high-point code patterns from original MMPI norms to MMPI-2 norms for the restandardization sample. *Journal of Personality Assessment*, *59*, 153–164.

Dahlstrom, W. G., & Dahlstrom, L. E. (Eds.). (1980). *Basic readings on the MMPI: A new selection on personality measurement.* Minneapolis, MN: University of Minnesota Press.

Dahlstrom, W. G., Lachar, D., & Dahlstrom, L. (1986). *MMPI patterns of American minorities.* Minneapolis: University of Minnesota Press.

Dahlstrom, W. G., Panton, J. H., Bain, K. P., & Dahlstrom, L. E. (1986). Utility of the Megargee-Bohn MMPI typological assignments: Study with a sample of death row inmates. *Criminal Justice and Behavior*, *13*, 5–17.

Dahlstrom, W. G., & Tellegen, A. (1992). *Socioeconomic status and the MMPI-2: The relation of MMPI-2 patterns of education and occupation*. Supplement to *MMPI-2: Manual for scoring and interpretation*. Minneapolis, MN: University of Minnesota Press.

Dahlstrom, W. G., Welsh, G. S., & Dahlstrom, L. E. (1972). *An MMPI handbook* (Vol. I). Minneapolis: University of Minnesota Press.

Dahlstrom, W. G., Welsh, G. S., & Dahlstrom, L. (1975). *An MMPI handbook: Volume II. Research applications*. Minneapolis: University of Minnesota Press.

Dalby, J. T. (1988). Detecting faking in the pretrial psychological assessment. *American Journal of Forensic Psychology*, *6*, 49–55.

Davison, G. C., & Neale, J. M. (1990). *Abnormal psychology: An experimental clinical approach* (5th ed.). New York: Wiley.

Dawes, R. M. (1988a). *Rational choice in an uncertain world.* San Diego, CA: Harcourt Brace Jovanovich.

Dawes, R. M. (1988b). You can't systematize human judgment: Dyslexia. In J. Dowie & A. Alstein (Eds.), *Professional judgment: A reader in clinical decision making* (pp. 150–162). Cambridge, England: Cambridge University Press.

Dawes, R. M., (1989). Experience and validity of clinical judgment: The illusory correlation. *Behavioral Sciences & the Law*, *7*, 457–467.

Dawes, R. M., Faust, D., & Meehl, P. E. (1989). Clinical versus actuarial judgment. *Science*, *243*, 1668–1674.

Deed, M. L. (1991). Court-ordered child custody evaluations: Helping or victimizing vulnerable families. *Psychotherapy*, *28*, 76–84.

Denmark, F., Russo, N. F., Frieze, I. H., & Sechzer, J. A. (1988). Guidelines for avoiding sexism in research. *American Psychologist*, *43*, 582–585.

Dershowitz, A. M. (1982). *The best defense*. New York: Random House.

Dickman, S., & Sechrest, L. (1985). Research on memory and clinical practice. In G. Stricker & R. H. Keisner (Eds.), *From research to clinical practice: Implications of social and developmental research for psychotherapy* (pp. 15–44). New York: Plenum Press.

Didion, J. (1979). *The white album*. New York: Simon & Schuster.

Dowling, J. F., & Graham, J. R. (1976). Illusory correlation and the MMPI. *Journal of Personality Assessment*, *40*, 531–538.

Drasgow, J., & Dreher, R. (1965). Predicting client readiness for training and placement in vocational rehabilitation. *Rehabilitation Counseling Bulletin*, *8*, 94–98.

Duthie, B., & McIvor, D. (1990). A new system for cluster-coding child molester MMPI profile types. *Criminal Justice and Behavior*, *17*, 199–214.

Dworkin, A. (1987). *Intercourse*. New York: Free Press.

Dzioba, R. B., & Doxey, N. C. (1984). A prospective investigation into the orthopaedic and psychologic predictors of outcome of first lumbar surgery following industrial injury. *Spine*, *9*, 614–623.

Eberly, R. E., Harkness, A. R., & Engdahl, B. E. (1991). An adaptational view of trauma response as illustrated by the prisoner of war experience. *Journal of Traumatic Stress*, *4*, 363–380.

Edinger, J. D. (1979). Cross-validation of the Megargee MMPI typology for prisoners. *Journal of Consulting and Clinical Psychology*, *47*, 234–242.

Edinger, J. D., Reuterfors, D., & Logue, P. E. (1982). Cross-validation of the Megargee MMPI typology: A study of specialized inmate populations. *Criminal Justice and Behavior*, *9*, 184–203.

Edwards, A. (1957). *The social desirability variable in personality assessment and research*. New York: Dryden Press.

Egeland, B., Erickson, M., Butcher, J. N., & Ben-Porath, Y. S. (1991). MMPI-2 profiles of women at risk for child abuse. *Journal of Personality Assessment*, *57*, 254–263.

Elwork, A. (1992). Psycholegal treatment and intervention: The next challenge. *Law & Human Behavior*, *16*, 175–183.

Elwork, A., & Sales, B. D. (1985). Jury instructions. In S. Kassin & L. Wrightsman (Eds.), *The psychology of evidence and trial procedure* (pp. 280–297). Beverly Hills, CA: Sage.

Elwork, A., Sales, B. D., & Alfini, J. J. (1977). Juridic decisions: In ignorance of the law or in light of it? *Law and Human Behavior*, *1*, 163–189.

Elwork, A., Sales, B. D., & Alfini, J. J. (1982). *Making jury instructions understandable*. Charlottesville, VA: The Michie Company.

Emery, O. B., & Csikszentmihalyi, M. (1981). The specialization effects of cultural role models in ontogenetic development. *Child Psychiatry and Human Development*, *12*, 3–18.

Epstein, L., & Feiner, A. H. (Eds.). (1979). *Countertransference*. New York: Aronson.

Erdberg, S. P. (1970). MMPI differences associated with sex, race, and residence in a southern sample (Doctoral dissertation, University of Alabama, 1969). *Dissertation Abstracts International, 30,* 5236B.

Erdberg, S. P. (1988, August). *How clinicians can achieve competence in testing procedures*. Paper presented at the 96th Annual Convention of the American Psychological Association, Atlanta, GA.

Erickson, B., Lind, E. A., Johnson, B. C., & O'Barr, W. M. (1978). Speech style and impression formation in a court setting: The effects of "powerful" and "powerless" speech. *Journal of Experimental Social Psychology*, *14*, 266–279.

Erickson, W., Luxenberg, M., Walbeck, N., & Seely, R. (1987). The frequency of MMPI two-point code types among sex offenders. *Journal of Consulting and Clinical Psychology*, *55*, 566–570.

Evans, J. (1989). *Bias in human reasoning: Causes and consequences*. Hillsdale, NJ: Erlbaum.

Exner, J. E. (1991). *The Rorschach: A comprehensive system* (Vol. 2; 2nd ed.). New York: Wiley.

Exner, J., McDowell, E., Pabst, J., Stackman, W., & Kirk, L. (1963). On the detection of willful falsification in the MMPI. *Journal of Consulting Psychology*, *27*, 91–94.

Eyde, L., Kowal, D., & Fishburne, F. J. (1991). In T. B. Gutkin, & S. L. Wise (Eds.), *The computer & the decision-making process* (pp. 75–123). Hillsdale, NJ: Erlbaum.

Fairbank, J. A., Keane, T. M., & Malloy, P. F. (1983). Some preliminary data on the psychological characteristics of Vietnam veterans with posttraumatic stress disorders. *Journal of Consulting and Clinical Psychology, 51,* 912–919.

Fairbank, J. A., McCaffrey, R., & Keane, T. M. (1985). Psychometric detection of fabricated symptoms of posttraumatic stress disorder. *American Journal of Psychiatry, 142,* 501–503.

Faschingbauer, T. R. (1979). The future of the MMPI. In C. S. Newmark (Ed.), *MMPI: Clinical and research trends.* New York: Praeger.

Faust, D., & Ziskin, J. (1988). The expert witness in psychology and psychiatry. *Science, 241,* 31–35.

Fernberger, S. W. (1932). The American Psychological Association: A historical summary, 1892–1930. *Psychological Bulletin, 29,* 1–89.

Fersch, E. A. (1980). Ethical issues for psychologists in court settings. In J. Monahan (Ed.), *Who is the client? The ethics of psychological intervention in the criminal justice system* (pp. 43–62). Washington, DC: American Psychological Association.

Finn, S., & Butcher, J. N. (1991). Clinical objective personality assessment. In M. Hersen, A. E. Kazdin, & A. S. Bellack (Eds.), *The clinical psychology handbook* (2nd ed.; pp. 362–373). New York: Pergamon.

Finn, S., & Tonsager, M. (1992). Therapeutic effects of providing MMPI-2 test feedback to college students awaiting therapy. *Psychological Assessment, 4,* 278–287.

Fischer, C. T. (1985). *Individualized psychological assessment.* Belmont, CA: Brooks/Cole.

Fischoff, B. (1982). For those condemned to study the past: Heuristics and biases in hindsight. In D. Kahneman, P. Slovic, & A. Tversky (Eds.), *Judgment under uncertainty: Heuristics and biases* (pp. 335–351). Cambridge, England: Cambridge University Press.

Fjordbak, T. (1985). Clinical correlates of high *L* scale elevations among forensic patients. *Journal of Personality Assessment, 49,* 252–255.

Flamer, S., & Birch, W. (1992, May). *Differential diagnosis of post traumatic stress disorder in injured workers; evaluating the MMPI-2.* Paper presented at the 27th Annual Symposium on Recent Developments in the Use of the MMPI (MMPI-2), Minneapolis, MN.

Flynn, R., & Salomone, P. R. (1977). Performance of the MMPI in predicting rehabilitation outcome: A discriminant analysis, double cross-validation assessment. *Rehabilitation Literature, 38,* 12–15.

Forgac, G. E., & Michaels, E. J. (1982). Personality characteristics of two types of male exhibitionists. *Journal of Abnormal Psychology, 91,* 287–293.

Fowler, R. D. (1969). Automated interpretation of personality test data. In J. N. Butcher (Ed.), *MMPI research developments and clinical applications* (pp. 105–125). New York: McGraw-Hill.

Fowler, R. D. (1987). Developing a computer-based test interpretation system. In J. N. Butcher (Ed.), *Computerized psychological assessment* (pp. 50–63). New York: Basic Books.

Fowler, R. D., & Butcher, J. N. (1986). Critique of Matarazzo's views on computerized testing: All sigma and no meaning. *American Psychologist, 41,* 94–96.

Fox, R. E. (1989). Proceedings of the American Psychological Association, Incorporated, for the year 1988. Minutes of the annual meeting of the Council of Representatives. *American Psychologist, 44,* 996–1028.

Freeman, L., & Roy, J. (1976). *Betrayal.* New York: Stein & Day.

Fromm, E., & Pope, K. S. (1990). Countertransference in hypnotherapy and hypnoanalysis. *Independent Practitioner, 10*(3), 48–50.

Gallagher, H. G. (1990). *By trust betrayed: Patients, physicians, and the license to kill in the Third Reich.* New York: Henry Holt.

Gallucci, N. (1984). Prediction of dissimulation on the MMPI in a clinical field setting. *Journal of Consulting and Clinical Psychology, 52,* 917–918.

Gambrill, E. (1990). *Critical thinking in clinical practice.* San Francisco: Jossey-Bass.

Garb, H. N. (1984). The incremental validity of information used in personality assessment. *Clinical Psychology Review, 4,* 641–655.

Garb, H. N. (1988). Comment on "The Study of Clinical Judgment: An Ecological Approach." *Clinical Psychology Review, 8,* 441–444.

Garb, H. N. (1992a). The debate over the use of computer-based test reports. *The Clinical Psychologist, 45,* 95–100.

Garb, H. N. (1992b). The *trained* psychologist as expert witness. *Clinical Psychology Review, 12,* 451–467.

Garcia, C., & Levenson, H. (1975). Differences between Blacks' and Whites' expectation of control by chance and powerful others. *Psychological Reports*, *37*, 563–566.

Gardner, M. (1963). In the name of science. In. S. Rapport & H. Wright (Eds.), *Science: Method and meaning* (pp. 31–43). New York: New York University Library of Science.

Garetz, F., & Anderson, R. A. (1973). Patterns of professional activities of psychiatrists: A follow-up of 100 psychiatric residents. *American Journal of Psychiatry*, *130*, 981–984.

Gass, C. S. (1991). MMPI-2 interpretation and closed head injury: A correction factor. *Psychological Assessment: A Journal of Consulting and Clinical Psychology*, *3*, 27–31.

Gass, C. S. (1992). MMPI-2 interpretation of patients with cerebrovascular disease: A correction factor. *Archives of Neuropsychology*, *7*, 17–27.

Gass, C., & Brown, M. C. (1992). Neuropsychological test feedback to patients with brain dysfunction. *Psychological Assessment*, *4*, 272–277.

Geisinger, K. F. (1992). The metamorphosis of test validation. *Educational Psychologist*, *27*, 197–222.

Geller, J. D. (1988). Bias in the evaluation of patients for psychotherapy. In L. Comas-Diaz & E. E. H. Griffith (Eds.), *Clinical guidelines in cross-cultural mental health* (pp. 112–134). New York: Wiley-Interscience.

Gendreau, P. M., Irvine, M., & Knight, S. (1973). Evaluating response set styles on the MMPI with prisoners faking good adjustment and maladjustment. *Canadian Journal of Abnormal Psychology*, *82*, 139–140.

Gibbs, J. T., & Huang, L. N. (1989). *Children of color: Psychological interventions and minority youth*. San Francisco: Jossey-Bass.

Gilberstadt, H. (1969). Construction and application of MMPI codebooks. In J. N. Butcher (Ed.), *MMPI research developments and clinical applications* (pp. 55–70). New York: McGraw-Hill.

Gilbert, D. H., & Lester, J. T. (1970). *The relationship of certain personality and demographic variables to success in vocational rehabilitation* (Research report from the Orthopedic Hospital). Los Angeles, CA.

Goldstein, M. J., Baker, B. L., & Jamison, K. R. (1980). *Abnormal psychology*. Boston: Little, Brown.

Gossett, T. F. (1975). *Race: The history of an idea in America*. Dallas, TX: Southern Methodist University Press.

Gough, H. G. (1947). Simulated patterns on the MMPI. *Journal of Abnormal and Social Psychology*, *42*, 215–225.

Gough, H. G. (1950). The *F* minus *K* dissimulation index for the MMPI. *Journal of Consulting Psychology*, *14*, 408–413.

Gould, S. J. (1981). *The mismeasure of man*. New York: Norton.

Gould, S. J. (1987). *An urchin in the storm: Essays about books and ideas*. New York: Norton.

Graham, J. R. (1977). *The MMPI: A practical guide* (1st ed.). New York: Oxford University Press.

Graham, J. R. (1987). *The MMPI: A practical guide* (2nd ed.). New York: Oxford University Press.

Graham, J. R. (1988, August). *Establishing validity of the revised form of the MMPI*. Symposium presentation at the 96th Annual Convention of the American Psychological Association, Atlanta, GA.

Graham, J. R. (1990). *MMPI-2: Assessing personality and psychopathology*. New York: Oxford University Press.

Graham, J. R. (1992). *Forensic assessment case*. Workshop presented at MMPI/MMPI-2/MMPI-A Workshops & Symposia, University of Minnesota, Minneapolis.

Graham, J. R., & Butcher, J. N. (1988, March). *Differentiating schizophrenic and major affective disorders with the revised form of the MMPI*. Paper presented at the 23rd Annual Symposium on Recent Developments in the Use of the MMPI, St. Petersburg, FL.

Graham, J. R., Timbrook, R., Ben-Porath, Y. S., & Butcher, J. N. (1991). Code-type congruence between MMPI and MMPI-2: Separating fact from artifact. *Journal of Personality Assessment*, *57*, 205–215.

Graham, J. R., Watts, D., & Timbrook, R. (1991). Detecting fake-good and fake-bad MMPI-2 profiles. *Journal of Personality Assessment*, *57*, 264–277.

Greene, R. L. (1979). Response consistency on the MMPI: The T-R Index. *Journal of Personality Assessment*, *43*, 69–71.

Greene, R. L. (1980). *The MMPI: An interpretive manual*. New York: Grune & Stratton.

Greene, R. L. (1982). Some reflections on "MMPI short forms: A literature review." *Journal of Personality Assessment*, *46*, 486–487.

Greene, R. L. (1987). Ethnicity and MMPI performance: A review. *Journal of Consulting and Clinical Psychology*, *55*, 497–512.

Greene, R. L. (1991). *The MMPI-2/MMPI: An interpretive manual*. Needham Heights, MA: Allyn & Bacon.

Greenfield, P. (1983/1984). Cognitive impact of the media. *Imagination, Cognition & Personality: Consciousness in Theory, Research, and Clinical Practice*, *3*, 3–16.

Grisso, T. (1986). Psychological assessment in legal contexts. In W. J. Curran, A. L. McGarry, & S. A. Shah (Eds.), *Forensic psychiatry and psychology: Perspectives and standards for interdisciplinary practice* (pp. 103–128). Philadelphia, PA: W. B. Saunders.

Gross, Z. (1977, August). *Erotic contact as a source of emotional learning in psychotherapy*. Paper presented at the 85th Annual Convention of the American Psychological Association, San Francisco, CA.

Grossman, L. S., & Cavanaugh, J. L. (1989). Do sex offenders minimize psychiatric symptoms? *Journal of Forensic Sciences, 34*, 881–886.

Grossman, L. S., Haywood, T. W., Ostrov, E., Wasliw, O., & Cavanaugh, J. L. (1990). Sensitivity of MMPI validity indicators to motivational factors in psychological evaluations of police officers. *Journal of Personality Assessment, 55*, 549–561.

Grossman, L. S., & Wasyliw, O. E. (1988). A psychometric study of stereotypes: Assessment of malingering in a criminal forensic group. *Journal of Personality Assessment, 52*, 549–563.

Grow, R., McVaugh, W., & Eno, T. (1980). Faking and the MMPI. *Journal of Clinical Psychology, 36*, 910–917.

Grutman, R., & Thomas, B. *Lawyers and thieves*. New York: Simon & Schuster.

Guthrie, H. (1976). *Even the rat was white: A historical view of psychology*. New York: Harper & Row.

Gynther, M. D. (1972). White norms and black MMPIs: A prescription for discrimination? *Psychological Bulletin, 78*, 386–402.

Gynther, M. D., Altman, H., & Warbin, R. (1973). Interpretation of uninterpretable MMPI profiles. *Journal of Consulting and Clinical Psychology, 40*, 78–83.

Gynther, M. D., Fowler, R. D., & Erdberg, S. P. (1971). False positives galore: The application of standard MMPI criteria to a rural, isolated, Negro sample. *Journal of Clinical Psychology, 27*, 234–237.

Gynther, M. D., & Gynther, R. A. (1976). Personality inventories. In I. B. Weiner (Ed.), *Clinical methods in psychology* (pp. 187–279). New York: Wiley.

Habush, R. L. (1984). Maximizing damages through trial techniques. *Trial, 20*, 68–72.

Hafner, A. J., Butcher, J. N., Hall, M., & Quast, W. (1969). Parent pathology and childhood disorders: A review of MMPI findings. In J. N. Butcher (Ed.), *MMPI: Research developments and clinical applications* (pp. 181–190). New York: McGraw-Hill.

Hall, G. C., Graham, J., & Shepherd, J. (1991). Three methods of developing MMPI taxonomies of sexual offenders. *Journal of Personality Assessment, 56*, 2–16.

Hall, G. C., Maiuro, R., Vitaliano, P., & Proctor, W. (1986). The utility of the MMPI with men who have sexually assaulted children. *Journal of Consulting and Clinical Psychology, 54*, 111–112.

Hall, G. C., Shepherd, J. B., & Mudrak, P. (1992). MMPI taxonomies of child sexual and nonsexual offenders: A cross-validation and extension. *Journal of Personality Assessment, 58*, 127–137.

Hanson, R. W., Moss, C. S., Hosford, R. E., & Johnson, M. E. (1983). Predicting inmate penitentiary adjustment: An assessment of four classificatory methods. *Criminal Justice and Behavior, 10*, 293–309.

Hart, R. R., McNeill, J. W., Lutz, D. J., & Adkins, T. G. (1986). Clinical comparability of the standard MMPI and the MMPI-168. *Professional Psychology: Research and Practice, 17*, 269–272.

Hartshorne, H., & May, M. A. (1928). *Studies in deceit*. New York: Macmillan.

Hastie, R. (1986). Notes on the psychologist as expert witness. *Law and Human Behavior, 10*, 79–82.

Hathaway, S. R. (1965). Personality inventories. In B. Wolman (Ed.), *Handbook of clinical psychology* (pp. 451–476). New York: McGraw-Hill.

Hathaway, S. R., & McKinley, J. C. (1940). A multiphasic personality schedule (Minnesota): I. Construction of the schedule. *Journal of Psychology, 10*, 249–254.

Hathaway, S. R., & McKinley, J. C. (1943). *Manual for administering and scoring the MMPI*. Minneapolis: University of Minnesota Press.

Hawk, G., & Cornell, D. (1989). MMPI profiles of malingerers diagnosed in pretrial forensic evaluations. *Journal of Clinical Psychology, 45*, 673–678.

Haynes, S. N. (1991). Behavioral assessment. In M. Hersen, A. E. Kazdin, & A. S. Bellack (Eds.), *The clinical psychology handbook* (2nd ed., pp. 430–464). Elmsford, NY: Pergamon Press.

Heaton, R. K., Chelune, G. J., & Lehman, R. A. W., Jr. (1978). Using neuropsychological and personality tests to assess the likelihood of patient employment. *Journal of Nervous and Mental Disease, 166*, 408–416.

Heaton, R. K., Smith, H. H., Lehman, R. A. W., Jr., & Vogt, A. T. (1978). Prospects for faking believable deficits on neuropsychological testing. *Journal of Consulting and Clinical Psychology, 46*, 892–900.

Heilbrun, K. (1992). The role of psychological testing in forensic assessment. *Law and Human Behavior, 16,* 257–272.

Heilbrun, K., Bennett, W. S., White, A. J., & Kelly, J. (1990). An MMPI-based empirical model of malingering and deception. *Behavioral Sciences & the Law, 8,* 45–53.

Heimann, P. (1950). On countertransference. *International Journal of Psychoanalysis, 31,* 81–84.

Helmes, E., & McLaughlin, J. D. (1983). A comparison of three MMPI short forms: Limited clinical utility in classification. *Journal of Consulting and Clinical Psychology, 51,* 786–787.

Herek, G. M. (1989). Hate crimes against lesbians and gay men: Issues for research and policy. *American Psychologist, 44,* 948–955.

Herkov, M. J., Archer, R., & Gordon, R. A. (1991). MMPI response sets among adolescents: An evaluation of the limitations of the subtle–obvious subscales. *Psychological Assessment: A Journal of Consulting and Clinical Psychology, 3,* 424–426.

Herman, J. L., (1992). *Trauma and recovery.* New York: Basic Books.

Herman, J. L., Perry, J. C., & van der Kolk, B. A. (1989). Childhood trauma in borderline personality disorder. *American Journal of Psychiatry, 146,* 490–495.

Herrnstein, R. J. (1973). *IQ in the meritocracy.* Boston: Little, Brown.

Hess, H. (1992). Affective response in group therapy process and outcome. *Psychotherapie Psychosomatik Medizinische Psychologie, 42,* 120–126.

Hjemboe, S., Almagor, M., & Butcher, J. N. (1992). Empirical assessment of marital distress: The Marital Distress Scale (MDS) for the MMPI-2. In C. D. Spielberger & J. N. Butcher (Eds.), *Advances in personality assessment* (Vol. 9; pp. 141–152). Hillsdale, NJ: Erlbaum.

Hjemboe, S., & Butcher, J. N. (1991). Couples in marital distress: A study of demographic and personality factors as measured by the MMPI-2. *Journal of Personality Assessment, 57,* 216–237.

Hoffman, N. G., & Butcher, J. N. (1975). Clinical limitation of three Minnesota Multiphasic Personality Inventory short forms. *Journal of Consulting and Clinical Psychology, 43,* 32–39.

Holcolmb, W., Adams, N., & Ponder, H. (1985). The development and cross-validation of an MMPI typology of murderers. *Journal of Personality Assessment, 49,* 240–244.

Holcomb, W. R., Adams, W. P., Ponder, H. M., & Anderson, W. (1984). Cognitive and behavioral predictors of MMPI scores in pretrial psychological evaluations of murderers. *Journal of Clinical Psychology, 40,* 592–597.

Holden, C. (1988). Research psychologists break with APA. *Science, 241,* 1036.

Howell, D. C. (1992). *Statistical methods for psychology* (3rd ed.). Boston: PWS Kent.

Huber, P. W. (1991). *Galileo's revenge: Junk science in the courtroom.* New York: Basic Books.

Hunt, H. F. (1948). The effect of deliberate deception on MMPI performance. *Journal of Consulting Psychology, 12,* 396–402.

Hunt, H. F., Carp, W. A., Cass, A., Winder, L., & Kantor, R. E. (1947). A study of the differential diagnostic efficiency of the MMPI. *Journal of Consulting Psychology. 12,* 331–336.

Hunter, J. A., Childers, S. E., & Esmaili, H. (1990). An examination of variables differentiating clinical subtypes of incestuous child molesters. *International Journal of Offender Therapy & Comparative Criminology, 34,* 95–104.

Hutton, H. E., Minor, M. H., Blades, J. R., & Langfeldt, V. C. (1992). Ethnic differences on the MMPI Overcontrolled-Hostility scale. *Journal of Personality Assessment, 58,* 260–268.

Hyer, L., Leach, P., Boudewyns, P. A., & Davis, H. (1991). Hidden PTSD in substance abuse inpatients among Vietnam veterans. *Journal of Substance Abuse Treatment, 8,* 213–219.

Hyman, G. J., Robb, S., & Burrows, G. D. (1991). The relationship between three multidimensional locus of control scales. *Educational and Psychological Measurement, 51,* 403–412.

Imwinkelried, E. J. (1982). *The methods of attacking scientific evidence.* Charlottesville, VA: The Michie Company.

Jackson, D. (1971). The dynamics of structured personality tests: 1971. *Psychological Review, 78,* 229–248.

Jackson, D., & Messick, S. (1962). Response styles and the assessment of psychopathology. In S. Messick & J. Ross (Eds.), *Measurement of personality and cognition* (pp. 129–155). New York: Wiley.

Janis, I. L. (1972). *Victims of groupthink.* Boston: Houghton Mifflin.

Janis, I. L. (1982). *Stress, attitudes, and decisions.* New York: Praeger.

Janis, I. L., & Mann, L. (1979). *Decision making: A psychological analysis of conflict, choice, & commitment*. New York: Free Press.

Jansen, D. G., & Bonk, E. C. (1973). MMPI characteristics of clergymen in counseling training and their relationship to supervisors and peers' ratings of counseling effectiveness. *Psychological Reports, 33*, 695–698.

Jemelka, R. P., Weigand, G. A., Walker, E. A., & Trupin, E. W. (1992). Computerized offender assessment: Validation study. *Psychological Assessment: A Journal of Consulting and Clinical Psychology, 4*, 138–144.

Jenkins, J. A. (1989). *The litigators*. New York: Doubleday.

Jensen, A. R. (1972). *Genetics and education*. New York: Harper & Row.

Johnson, D. L., Simmons, J. G., & Gordon, B. C. (1983). Temporal consistency of the Meyer-Megargee inmate typology. *Criminal Justice and Behavior, 10*, 263–268.

Jones, B. P., & Butters, N. (1991). Neuropsychological assessment. In M. Hersen, A. E. Kazdin, & A. S. Bellack (Eds.), *The clinical psychology handbook* (2nd ed., pp. 406–429). New York: Pergamon Press.

Jones, E. E., & Korchin, S. J. (Eds.). (1982). *Minority mental health*. New York: Praeger.

Jones, J. H. (1981). *Bad blood: The Tuskegee syphilis experiment—A tragedy of race and medicine*. New York: Free Press.

Jones, J. M. (1990a, September 14). Promoting diversity in an individualistic society. Keynote address presented at the Great Lakes College Association Conference on Multiculturalism Transforming the 21st Century: Overcoming the Challenges and Preparing for the Future, Holland, MI.

Jones, J. M. (1990b, August). Psychological approaches to race: What have they been and what should they be? Paper presented at the 98th Annual Convention of the American Psychological Association, Boston, MA.

Jordan, B. K., Schlenger, W. E., Hough, R. L., Kukla, R. A., Fairbank, J. A., Marmar, C. R., & Weiss, D. S. (1991). Lifetime and current prevalence of specific psychiatric disorders among Vietnam veterans and controls. *Archives of General Psychiatry, 48*, 207–215.

Julien, A. (1984). The opening statement. In B. G. Warshaw (Ed.), *The trial masters: A handbook of strategies and tactics that win cases* (pp. 139–147). Englewood Cliffs, NJ: Prentice-Hall.

Kahneman, D., Slovic, P., & Tversky, A. (Eds.). (1982). *Judgment under uncertainty: Heuristics and biases*. Cambridge, England: Cambridge University Press.

Kalichman, S. C. (1990). Affective and personality characteristics of MMPI profile subgroups of incacerated rapists. *Archives of Sexual Behavior, 19*, 443–459.

Kalichman, S. C. (1991). Psychopathology and personality characteristics of criminal sex offenders as a function of victim age. *Archives of Sexual Behavior, 20*, 187–197.

Kalichman, S. C., Craig, M. E., Shealy, L., Taylor, J., Szymanowski, D., & McKee, G. (1989). An empirically derived typology of adult rapists based on the MMPI: A cross-validation study. *Journal of Psychology & Human Sexuality, 2*, 165–182.

Kalichman, S. C., & Henderson, M. C. (1991). MMPI profile subtypes of nonincarcerated child molesters. *Criminal Justice and Behavior, 18*, 379–396.

Kalichman, S. C., Shealy, L., & Craig, M. E. (1990). The use of the MMPI in predicting treatment participation among incarcerated adult rapists. *Journal of Psychology & Human Sexuality, 3*, 105–119.

Kalichman, S. C., Szymanowski, D., McKee, G., Taylor, J., & Craig, M. E. (1989). Cluster analytically derived MMPI profile subgroups of incarcerated adult rapists. *Journal of Clinical Psychology, 45*, 149–155.

Kassin, S. M., Williams, L. N., & Saunders, C. L. (1990). Dirty tricks of cross-examination: The influence of conjectural evidence on the jury. *Law and Human Behavior, 14*, 373–384.

Kazdin, A. E. (1978a). Covert modeling: The therapeutic application of imagined rehearsal. In J. L. Singer & K. S. Pope (Eds.), *The power of human imagination: New methods in psychotherapy* (pp. 255–278). New York: Plenum Press.

Kazdin, A. E. (1978b). *History of behavior modification: Experimental foundations of contemporary research*. Baltimore: University Park Press.

Keane, T. M., Malloy, P. F., & Fairbank, J. A. (1984). Empirical development of an MMPI subscale for the assessment of combat-related posttraumatic stress disorder. *Journal of Consulting and Clinical Psychology, 52*, 888–891.

Keane, T. M., Wolfe, J., & Taylor, K. L. (1987). Post-traumatic stress disorder: Evidence for diagnostic validity and methods of psychological assessment. *Journal of Clinical Psychology, 43*, 32–43.

Kelin, W. G., & Bloom, L. J. (1986). Child custody evaluation practices: A survey of experienced professionals. *Professional Psychology: Research and Practice, 17*, 338–346.

Keller, L. S., & Butcher, J. N. (1991). *Assessment of chronic pain patients with the MMPI-2*. Minneapolis: University of Minnesota Press.

Keller, R. A., Wigdor, B. T., & Lundell, F. W. (1973). Adjustment of welfare recipients and applicants: Investigation of some relevant factors. *Canadian Psychiatric Association Journal, 18*, 511–517.

Kelven, H., & Zeisel, H. (1966). *The American jury*. Boston: Little, Brown.

Kendall, P. C., & Hollon, S. D. (Eds.). (1982). *Cognitive-behavioral interventions: Assessment methods*. San Diego, CA: Academic Press.

Kenderdine, S. K., Phillips, E. J., & Scurfield, R. M. (1992). Comparison of the MMPI-PTSD subscale with PTSD and substance abuse patient populations. *Journal of Clinical Psychology, 48*, 136–139.

Kennedy, R. D. (1983). *California expert witness guide*. Berkeley, CA: California Continuing Education of the Bar.

Kennedy, R. D., & Martin, J. C. (1987). *California expert witness guide: Supplement*. Berkeley, CA: California Continuing Education of the Bar.

Kennedy, T. D. (1986). Trends in inmate classification: A status report of two computerized psychometric approaches. *Criminal Justice and Behavior, 13*, 165–184.

Kernberg, O. F. (1975). *Borderline conditions and pathological narcissism*. Northvale, NJ: Jason Aronson.

Kimble, G. A., Garmezy, N., & Zigler, E. (1974). *Principles of general psychology* (4th ed.). New York: Ronald Press.

King, H. F., Carroll, J. L., & Fuller, G. B. (1977). Comparison of nonpsychiatric Blacks and Whites on the MMPI. *Journal of Clinical Psychology, 33*, 725–728.

Klawans, H. L. (1991). *Trials of an expert witness: Tales of clinical neurology and the law*. Boston: Little, Brown.

Korgeski, G. P., & Leon, G. R. (1983). Correlates of self-reported and objectively determined exposure to Agent Orange. *American Journal of Psychiatry, 140*, 1443–1449.

Kubiszyn, T. (1984, August). *The MMPI, litigation, and back pain treatment: A curvilinear relationship*. Paper presented at the 92nd Annual Convention of the American Psychological Association, Toronto, Ontario, Canada.

Kuperman, S. K., & Golden, C. J. (1979). Predicting pain treatment results by personality variables in organic and functional patients. *Journal of Clinical Psychology, 35*, 832–837.

Kurlychek, R. T., & Jordan, L. (1980). MMPI profiles and code types of responsible and non-responsible criminal defendants. *Journal of Clinical Psychology, 36*, 590–593.

Lachar, D. (1974). The prediction of early USAF freshman cadet adaptation with the MMPI. *Journal of Counseling Psychology, 21*, 404–408.

Lachar, D. (1979). How much of a good thing is enough?: A review of T. A. Fashingbauer & C. A. Newmark's *Short forms of the MMPI*. *Contemporary Psychology, 24*, 116–117.

Lachar, D., & Sharp, J. R. (1979). Use of parent's MMPIs in the research and evaluation of children: A review of the literature and some new data. In J. N. Butcher (Ed.), *New directions in MMPI research* (pp. 203–240). Minneapolis: University of Minnesota Press.

Lacks, P. (1984). *Bender Gestalt screening for brain dysfunction*. New York: Wiley.

Lahey, B. B., Russo, M. F., Walker, J. L., & Piacentini, J. C. (1989). Personality characteristics of mothers of children with disruptive behavior disorders. *Journal of Consulting and Clinical Psychology, 57*, 512–515.

Lakoff, R. T. (1990). *Talking power: The politics of language*. New York: Basic Books.

LaMarca, G. A. (1984). How to prepare and present effective opening statements. In B. G. Warshaw (Ed.), *The trial masters: A handbook of strategies and tactics that win cases* (pp. 148–157). Englewood Cliffs, NJ: Prentice-Hall.

Land, H. M. (1968). Child abuse: Differential diagnosis, differential treatment. *Child Welfare, 65*, 33–44.

Landberg, G. (1982). Proposed model for the intervention of the mental health specialist in the resolution of difficult child custody disputes. *Journal of Preventive Psychiatry, 1*, 309–318.

Langer, E. J. (1989). *Mindfulness*. Reading, MA: Addison-Wesley.

Langer, E. J., & Abelson, R. P. (1974). A patient by any other name . . . : Clinician group difference in labeling bias. *Journal of Consulting and Clinical Psychology, 42*, 4–9.

Langer, E. J., & Piper, A. I. (1987). The prevention of mindlessness. *Journal of Personality and Social Psychology, 53*, 280–287.

Lee, H. B., Cheung, F. M., Man, H., & Hsu, S. Y. (1992). Psychological characteristics of Chinese low back pain patients: An exploratory study. *Psychology & Health, 6*, 119–128.

Lees-Haley, P. R. (1989). Malingering post-traumatic stress disorder on the MMPI. *Forensic Reports, 2*, 89–91.

Lees-Haley, P. R. (1992). Psychodiagnostic test usage by forensic psychologists. *American Journal of Forensic Psychology, 10*, 25–30.

Lees-Haley, P. R., English, L. T., & Glenn, W. J. (1991). A Fake Bad Scale on the MMPI-2 for personal injury claimants. *Psychological Reports, 68*, 203–210.

Leon, G., Gillum, B., Gillum, R., & Gouze, M. (1979). Personality stability and change over a 30-year-period—middle age to old age. *Journal of Consulting and Clinical Psychology, 47*, 517–524.

Levenson, H. (1972). Distinctions within the concept of internal–external control: Development of a new scale [summary]. *Proceedings of the 80th Annual Convention of the American Psychological Association, 7*(Pt. 1), 261–262.

Levenson, H. (1973a). Multidimensional locus of control in psychiatric patients. *Journal of Consulting and Clinical Psychology, 41*, 397–404.

Levenson, H. (1973b). Perceived parental antecedents of internal, powerful others, and chance locus of control orientations. *Developmental Psychology, 9*, 260–265.

Levenson, H. (1973c, August). *Reliability and validity of the* I, P, *and* C *scales: A multidimensional view of locus of control.* Paper presented at the 81st Annual Convention of the American Psychological Association, Montreal, Quebec, Canada.

Levenson, H. (1974). Activism and powerful others: Distinctions within the concept of internal–external control. *Journal of Personality Assessment, 38*, 377–383.

Levenson, H. (1975). Additional dimensions of internal–external control. *Journal of Social Psychology, 97*, 303–304.

Levenson, H., Hirschfeld, M. L., & Hirschfeld, A. H. (1985). *Duration of chronic pain and the MMPI: Profiles of industrially-injured workers.* Paper presented at the 20th Symposium on Recent Developments in the Use of the MMPI, Honolulu, Hawaii.

Levenson, H., & Mahler, I. (1975). Attitudes toward others and components of internal–external locus of control. *Psychological Reports, 36*, 209–210.

Levenson, H., & Miller, J. (1976). Multidimensional locus of control in sociopolitical activists of conservative and liberal ideologies. *Journal of Personality and Social Psychology, 33*, 199–208.

Levenson, H., & Pope, K. S. (1992). Behavior therapy and cognitive therapy. In H. H. Goldman (Ed.), *Review of general psychiatry* (3rd ed., pp. 408–416). Norwalk, CT: Appleton & Lange.

Levin, F. G. (1984). Strategy for opening statement: A case study. In B. G. Warshaw (Ed.), *The trial masters: A handbook of strategies and tactics that win cases* (pp. 158–195). Englewood Cliffs, NJ: Prentice-Hall.

Levine, R. J. (1988). *Ethics and regulation of clinical research.* New Haven, CT: Yale University Press.

Lewis, A. (1991). *Make no law: The Sullivan case and the First Amendment.* New York: Random House.

Lewis, H. B. (1986). Is Freud an enemy of women's liberation? Some historical considerations. In T. Bernay & D. W. Cantor (Eds.), *The psychology of today's woman* (pp. 7–35). New York: Academic Press.

Lezak, M. D. (1983). *Neuropsychological assessment* (2nd ed.). New York: Oxford University Press.

Lifton, R. J. (1986). *The Nazi doctors: Medical killing and the psychology of genocide.* New York: Basic Books.

Litz, B. T., Penk, W., Walsh, S., Hyer, L., Blake, D. D., Marz, B., Keane, T. M., & Bitman, D. (1991). Similarities and differences between Minnesota Multiphasic Personality Inventory (MMPI) and MMPI-2 applications to the assessment of post-traumatic stress disorder. *Journal of Personality Assessment, 57*, 238–254.

Livermore, J., Malmquist, C., & Meehl, P. (1968). On justifications for civil commitment. *University of Pennsylvania Law Review, 117*, 75–96.

Loftus, E. F. (1986). Experimental psychologist as advocate or impartial educator. *Law and Human Behavior, 10*, 63–78.

Logsdon, S. A., Bourgeois, A. E., & Levenson, H. (1978). Locus of control, learned helplessness, and control of heart rate using biofeedback. *Journal of Personality Assessment, 42*, 538–544.

Loper, R. G., Robertson, J. M., & Swanson, E. O. (1968, November). College freshman MMPI norms over a fourteen year period. *Journal of College Student Personnel*, 404–407.

Louscher, P. K., Hosford, R. E., & Moss, C. S. (1983). Predicting dangerous behavior in a penitentiary using the Megargee typology. *Criminal Justice and Behavior, 10*, 269–284.

Lubin, B., Larsen, R. M., & Matarazzo, J. (1984). Patterns of psychological test usage in the United States: 1935–1982. *American Psychologist, 39*, 451–454.

Lueger, R. J., & Petzel, T. P. (1979). Illusory correlation in clinical judgment: Effects of amount of information to be processed. *Journal of Consulting and Clinical Psychology, 47*, 1120–1121.

Luginbuhl, J. (1992). Comprehension of judges' instructions in the penalty phase of a capital trial: Focus on mitigating circumstances. *Law and Human Behavior, 16*, 203–218.

Lund, S. N. (1975). *Personality and personal history factors of child abusing parents*. Unpublished doctoral dissertation, University of Minnesota, Minneapolis.

Lundy, R., Geselowitz, L., & Shertzer, C. (1985). Role-played and hypnotically induced simulation of psychopathology on the MMPI: A partial replication. *International Journal of Clinical and Experimental Hypnosis, 33*, 302–309.

Lyons, J. A., & Keane, T. M. (1992). Keane PTSD Scale: MMPI and MMPI-2 update. *Journal of Traumatic Stress, 5*, 111–117.

MacDonald, J. D. (1968). *No deadly drug*. New York: Doubleday.

MacDonald, J. M. (1976). *Psychiatry and the criminal: A guide to psychiatric examinations for the criminal courts*. Springfield, IL: Charles C Thomas.

Malyon, A. K. (1986a). *Brief follow-up to June 24, 1986, meeting with the American Psychiatric Association work group to revise DSM-III*. Unpublished manuscript.

Malyon, A. K. (1986b). *Presentation to the American Psychiatric Association work group to revise DSM-III*. Unpublished manuscript.

Manos, N. (1985). Adaptation of the MMPI in Greece: Translation, standardization, and cross-cultural comparison. In J. N. Butcher & C. D. Spielberger (Eds.), *Advances in personality assessment* (Vol. 4, pp. 159–208). Hillsdale, NJ: Erlbaum.

Manos, N., & Butcher, J. N. (1982). *MMPI: User's manual for the MMPI* (Greek). Thessaloniki, Greece: University Studio.

Marcus, E. H. (1983). Causation in psychiatry: Realities and speculations. *Medical Trial Technical Quarterly, 29*, 424–433.

Marcus, E. H. (1987). Defending mental injury claims: Cross-examining the plaintiff's expert witness. *Medical Trial Technique Quarterly, 33*, 430–439.

Martin, H. C. (1981/1982). The story underground. *Imagination, Cognition & Personality: Consciousness in Theory, Research, and Clinical Practice, 1*, 171–184.

Martin, J. C. (1985). *California expert witness guide: Supplement*. Berkeley, CA: California Continuing Education of the Bar.

Matarazzo, J. D. (1955). MMPI validity scores as a function of increasing levels of anxiety. *Journal of Consulting Psychology, 19*, 213–217.

Matarazzo, J. (1986). Computerized clinical psychological test interpretations: Unvalidated plus all mean and no sigma. *American Psychologist, 41*, 14–24.

Matz, P. A., Altepeter, T. S., & Perlman, B. (1992). MMPI-2 reliability with college students. *Journal of Clinical Psychology, 48*, 330–334.

Maxson, L. S., & Neuringer, C. (1970). Evaluating legal competency. *Journal of Genetic Psychology, 117*, 267–273.

Mays, V. M., & Comas-Diaz, L. (1988). Feminist therapy with ethnic minority populations: A closer look at Blacks and Hispanics. In M. A. Dutton-Douglas & L. E. A. Walker (Eds.), *Feminist psychotherapies: Integration of therapeutic and feminist systems* (pp. 228–251). Norwood, NJ: Ablex.

McAdoo, G., & Connolly, F. J. (1975). MMPIs of parents in dysfunctional families. *Journal of Consulting and Clinical Psychology, 43*, 270.

McCaffrey, R., & Bellamy-Campbell, R. (1989). Psychometric detection of fabricated symptoms of combat-related PTSD: A systematic replication. *Journal of Clinical Psychology, 45*, 76–79.

McCall, R. J. (1958). Face validity in the *D* scale of the MMPI. *Journal of Clinical Psychology, 14*, 77–80.

McCartney, J. (1966). Overt transference. *Journal of Sex Research, 2*, 227–237.

McCloskey, M., Egeth, H., & McKenna, J. (1986). The experimental psychologist in court: The ethics of expert testimony. *Law and Human Behavior, 10*, 1–13.

McConnell, J. V. (1974). *Understanding human behavior*. New York: Holt, Rinehart, & Winston.

McCord, J. (1978). A thirty-year follow-up of treatment effects. *American Psychologist, 33*, 284–289.

McCord, J., & McCord, W. (1959a). A follow-up report on the Cambridge-Somerville youth study. *Annals of the American Academy of Political and Social Science, 322*, 89–96.

McCord, W., & McCord, J. (1959b). *Origins of crime*. New York: Columbia University Press.

McCormick, R. A., Taber, J. I., & Kruedelbach, N. (1989). The relationship between attributional type and post-traumatic stress disorder in addicted patients. *Journal of Traumatic Stress, 2*, 477–487.

McDermott, J. F., Jr., Tseng, W., Char, W. F., & Fukunaga, C. S. (1978). Child custody decision making: The search for improvement. *American Academy of Child Psychiatry*, *17*, 104–116.

Mednick, M. T. (1989). On the politics of psychological constructs: Stop the bandwagon, I want to get off. *American Psychologist*, *44*, 1118–1123.

Meehan, A. M., & Janik, L. M. (1990). Illusory correlation and the maintenance of sex role stereotypes in children. *Sex Roles*, *22*, 83–95.

Meehl, P. E. (1954). *Clinical versus statistical predication*. Minneapolis: University of Minnesota Press.

Meehl, P. E., & Golden, R. (1982). Taxometric methods. In P. Kendall & J. Butcher (Eds.), *Handbook of research methods in clinical psychology* (pp. 127–181). New York: Wiley.

Meehl, P. E., & Hathaway, S. R. (1946). The *K* factor as a suppressor variable in the MMPI. *Journal of Applied Psychology*, *30*, 525–564.

Megargee, E. I. (1984). A new classification system for criminal offenders: VI. Differences among the types on the Adjective Checklist. *Criminal Justice and Behavior*, *11*, 349–376.

Megargee, E. I. (1992). *Impact of the revised MMPI (MMPI-2) on the Megargee MMPI-based Offender Classification System*. Report submitted to the National Institute of Justice. Washington, DC.

Megargee, E. I., & Bohn, M. J. (1977). A new classification system for criminal offenders: IV. Empirically determined characteristics of the ten types. *Criminal Justice and Behavior*, *4*, 149–210.

Megargee, E. I., & Bohn, M. J. (1979). *Classifying criminal offenders: A new system based on the MMPI*. Newbury Park, CA: Sage.

Megargee, E. I., Rivera, P., & Fly, J. T. (1991, March). *MMPI-2 and the Megargee Offender Classification System*. Paper presented at the 26th Annual Symposium on Recent Developments in the Use of the MMPI (MMPI-2), St Petersburg, FL.

Meichenbaum, D. (1977). *Cognitive-behavior modification: An integrative approach*. New York: Plenum Press.

Meier, P. (1982). *Damned liars and expert witnesses*. Paper presented at the Annual Meeting of the American Statistical Association.

Mendenhall, W., Wackerly, D. D., & Scheaffer, R. L. (1990). *Mathematical statistics with applications* (4th ed.). Boston: PWS Kent.

Meringoff, L. K. (1980). A story, a story. *Journal of Educational Psychology*, *72*, 240–249.

Messick, S. (1980). Test validity and the ethics of assessment. *American Psychologist*, *35*, 1012–1027.

Miller, M. O., & Sales, B. D. (1986). *Law and mental health professionals: Arizona*. Washington, DC: American Psychological Association.

Miller, R. D. (1990). Prearrangement forensic evaluation: The odyssey moves east of the Pecos. *Bulletin of the American Academy of Psychiatry and Law*, *18*, 311–321.

Millon, T. (1969). *Modern psychopathology: A biosocial approach to maladaptive learning and functioning*. Philadelphia, PA: W. B. Saunders.

Millon, T. (1981). *Disorders of personality: DSM-III: Axis II*. New York: Wiley.

Millon, T. (1987). *Manual for the Millon Clinical Multiaxial Inventory-II*. Minneapolis, MN: National Computer Systems.

Monahan, J. (Ed.). (1980). *Who is the client? The ethics of psychological intervention in the criminal justice system*. Washington, DC: American Psychological Association.

Moreland, K. (1987). Computerized psychological assessment: What's available. In J. N. Butcher (Ed.), *Computerized psychological assessment* (pp. 26–49). New York: Basic Books.

Morrow, D. G., Greenspan, S. L., & Bower, G. H. (1987). Accessibility and situation models in narrative comprehension. *Journal of Memory and Comprehension*, *26*, 165–187.

Moss, C. S., Johnson, M. E., & Hosford, R. E. (1984). An assessment of the Megargee typology in lifelong criminal violence. *Criminal Justice and Behavior*, *11*, 225–234.

Motiuk, L. L., Bonta, J., & Andrews, D. A. (1986). Classification in correctional halfway houses: The relative and incremental predictive criterion validities of the Megargee-MMPI and LSI systems. *Criminal Justice and Behavior*, *13*, 33–46.

Mrad, D. F., Kabacoff, R. I., & Duckro, P. (1983). Validation of the Megargee typology in a halfway house setting. *Criminal Justice and Behavior*, *10*, 252–262.

Muller-Hill, B. (1988). *Murderous science: Elimination by scientific selection of Jews, Gypsies, and others, Germany 1933–1945*. (G. Fraser, Trans.). New York: Oxford University Press.

Murray, H. A., & Staff of the Harvard Psychological Clinic. (1943). *Thematic Apperception Test manual*. Cambridge, MA: President and Fellows of Harvard College.

Murstein, B. I., & Glaudin, V. (1968). The use of the MMPI in the determination of marital adjustment. *Journal of Marriage and Family*, *30*, 651–655.

Nelson, L. (1987). Measuring depression in a clinical population using the MMPI. *Journal of Consulting and Clinical Psychology*, *55*, 788–790.

Nelson, L., & Cicchetti, D. (1991). Validity of the MMPI Depression Scale for outpatients. *Psychological Assessment: A Journal of Consulting and Clinical Psychology*, *3*, 55–59.

Newnan, O. S., Heaton, R. S., & Lehman, R. A. W. (1978). Neuropsychological and MMPI correlates of patient's future employment characteristics. *Perceptual and Motor Skills*, *46*, 635–642.

Nichols, B. L., & Czirr, R. (1986). Post-traumatic stress disorder: Hidden syndrome in elders. *Clinical Gerontologist*, *5*, 417–433.

Nizer, L. (1961). *My life in court*. Garden City, NY: Doubleday.

Noel, B., & Watterson, K. (1992). *You must be dreaming*. New York: Poseidon.

The Nuremberg Code. (1991). *Law, Medicine & Health Care*, *19*, 266.

O'Dell, J. W. (1972). P. T. Barnum explores the computer. *Journal of Consulting and Clinical Psychology*, *38*, 270–273.

Ollendick, D. G. (1984). Scores on three MMPI alcohol scales of parents who receive child custody. *Psychological Reports*, *55*, 337–338.

Ollendick, D. G., & Otto, B. J. (1983). MMPI characteristics of parents referred for child-custody studies. *Journal of Psychology*, *117*, 227–232.

Ollendick, D. G., Otto, B. J., & Heider, S. M. (1983). Marital MMPI characteristics: A test of Arnold's signs. *Journal of Clinical Psychology*, *39*, 240–245.

Osborne, D. (1971). An MMPI index of disturbed marital interaction. *Psychological Reports*, *29*, 851–854.

Ownby, R. L. (1987). *Psychological reports*. Brandon, VT: Clinical Psychological Publishing.

Pancoast, D. L., & Archer, R. (1989). Original adult MMPI norms in normal samples: A review with implications for future developments. *Journal of Personality Assessment*, *53*, 376–395.

Paolo, A., Ryan, J., & Smith, A. J. (1991). Reading difficulty of MMPI-2 subscales. *Journal of Clinical Psychology*, *47*, 529–532.

Parker, J. C., Doerfler, L. A., Tatten, H. A., & Hewett, J. E. (1983). Psychological factors that influence self-reported pain. *Journal of Clinical Psychology*, *39*, 22–25.

Parkison, S., & Fishburne, F. (1984). MMPI normative data for a male active duty Army population. In *Proceedings of Psychology in the Department of Defense, Ninth Symposium* (USAFA-TR-84-2, pp. 57–574). Colorado Springs, CO: USAF Academy Department of Behavioral Sciences.

Parwatikar, S. D., Holcomb, W. R., & Menninger, K. A. (1985). The detection of malingered amnesia in accused murderers. *Bulletin of the American Academy of Psychiatry and the Law*, *13*, 97–103.

Patterson, J. T. (1987). *The dread disease: Cancer and modern American culture*. Cambridge, MA: Harvard University Press.

Paulhus, D. L. (1986). Self deception and impression management in test responses. In A. Angleitner & J. Wiggins (Eds.), *Personality assessment via questionnaires* (pp. 143–165). Berlin: Springer-Verlag.

Paulos, J. A. (1988). *Innumeracy: Mathematical illiteracy and its consequences*. New York: Hill & Wang.

Paulson, M. J., Afifi, A., Chaleff, A., Thomason, M., & Lui, V. (1975). An MMPI scale for identifying at risk abusive parents. *Journal of Clinical Child Psychology*, *4*, 22–24.

Paulson, M. J., Afifi, A., Thomason, M., & Chaleff, A. (1974). The MMPI: A descriptive measure of psychopathology in abusive parents. *Journal of Clinical Psychology*, *30*, 387–390.

Paulson, M. J., Schwemer, G. T., & Bendel, R. B. (1976). Clinical applications of the *Pd*, *Ma*, and *O-H* scales to further understanding of abusive parents. *Journal of Clinical Psychology*, *32*, 558–564.

Pearson, C., & Pope, K. (1981/1982). Consciousness in the feminist novel. *Imagination, Cognition & Personality: Consciousness in Theory, Research, and Clinical Practice*, *1*, 185–192.

Pedersen, P. D., Draguns, J. G., Lonner, W. J., & Trimble, E. J. (Eds.). (1989). *Counseling across cultures* (3rd ed.). Honolulu: University of Hawaii Press.

Penk, W. E., Robinowitz, R., Dorsett, D., Black, J., Dolan, M. P., & Bell, W. (1989). Co-morbidity: Lessons learned about post-traumatic stress disorder (PTSD) from developing PTSD scales for the MMPI. *Journal of Clinical Psychology*, *45*, 709–717.

Pennington, N., & Hastie, R. (1981). Juror decision-making models: The generalization gap. *Psychological Bulletin*, *89*, 246–287.

Pennington, N., & Hastie, R. (1988). Explanation-based decision making: Effects of memory structure on judgment. *Journal of Experimental Psychology: Learning, Memory, and Cognition*, *14*, 521–533.

Pennington, N., & Hastie, R. (1991). A cognitive theory of juror decision making: The story model. *Cardozo Law Review, 13*, 5001–5039.

Pennington, N., & Hastie, R. (1992). Explaining the evidence: Tests of the story model for juror decision making. *Journal of Personality and Social Psychology, 62*, 189–206.

Peters, F. (1984). Cross-examination of the adverse medical expert: Keep the jury laughing. In B. G. Warshaw (Ed.), *The trial masters: A handbook of strategies and tactics that win cases* (pp. 287–304). New York: Prentice-Hall.

Physicians for Human Rights. (1991). *Medical testimony on victims of torture: A physician's guide to political asylum cases*. Boston, MA: Author.

Pollack, D. R., & Grainey, T. F. (1984). A comparison of MMPI profiles for state and private disability insurance applicants. *Journal of Personality Assessment, 48*, 121–125.

Pope, K. S. (1990a). Ethical and malpractice issues in hospital practice. *American Psychologist, 45*, 1066–1070.

Pope, K. S. (1990b). Therapist–patient sex as sex abuse: Six scientific, professional, and practical dilemmas in addressing victimization and rehabilitation. *Professional Psychology: Research and Practice, 21*, 227–239.

Pope, K. S. (1990c). Therapist–patient sexual involvement: A review of the research. *Clinical Psychology Review, 10*, 477–490.

Pope, K. S. (1992). Responsibilities in providing psychological test feedback to clients. *Psychological Assessment, 4*, 268–271.

Pope, K. S., & Bajt, T. R. (1988). When laws and values conflict: A dilemma for psychologists. *American Psychologist, 43*, 828.

Pope, K. S., & Bouhoutsos, J. C. (1986). *Sexual intimacy between therapists and patients*. New York: Praeger/Greenwood.

Pope, K. S., & Feldman-Summers, S. (1992). National survey of psychologists' sexual and physical abuse history and their evaluation of training and competence in these areas. *Professional Psychology: Research and Practice, 23*, 353–361.

Pope, K. S., & Garcia-Peltoniemi, R. E. (1991). Responding to victims of torture: Clinical issues, professional responsibilities, and useful resources. *Professional Psychology: Research and Practice, 22*, 269–276.

Pope, K. S., & Johnson, P. B. (1987). Psychological and psychiatric diagnosis: Theoretical foundations, empirical research, and clinical practice. In D. M. Levin (Ed.), *Pathologies of the modern self: Postmodern studies on narcissism, schizophrenia, and depression* (pp. 385–404). New York: New York University Press.

Pope, K. S., Sonne, J. L., & Holroyd, J. (1993). *Sexual feelings in psychotherapy: Explorations for therapists and therapists-in-training*. Washington, DC: American Psychological Association.

Pope, K. S., Tabachnick, B. G. (in press). Therapists' anger, hate, fear, and sexual feelings: National survey of therapists' responses, client characteristics, critical events, formal complaints, and training. *Professional Psychology: Research and Practice*.

Pope, K. S., Tabachnick, B. G., & Keith-Spiegel, P. (1987). Ethics of practice: The beliefs and behaviors of psychologists as therapists. *American Psychologist, 42*, 993–1006.

Pope, K. S., Tabachnick, B. G., & Keith-Spiegel, P. (1988). Good and poor practices in psychotherapy: A national survey of beliefs of psychologists. *Professional Psychology: Research and Practice, 19*, 547–552.

Pope, K. S., & Vasquez, M. J. T. (1991). *Ethics in psychotherapy and counseling: A practical guide for psychologists*. San Francisco: Jossey-Bass.

Pope, K. S., & Vetter, V. A. (1991). Prior therapist–patient sexual involvement among patients seen by psychologists. *Psychotherapy, 28*, 429–438.

Pope, K. S., & Vetter, V. A. (1992). Ethical dilemmas encountered by members of the American Psychological Association: A national survey. *American Psychologist, 47*, 397–411.

Powell, M., Illovsky, M., O'Leary, W. C., & Gazda, G. M. (1988). Life-skills training with hospitalized psychiatric patients. *International Journal of Group Psychotherapy, 38*, 109–117.

Proctor, R. N. (1988). *Racial hygiene: Medicine under the Nazis*. Cambridge, MA: Harvard University Press.

Putnam, S. H., Adams, K. M., & Butcher, J. N. (1992, May). *A comparative MMPI-2 study of three professional samples: Attorneys, insurance claims adjusters, and clergy*. Paper presented at the 27th Annual Symposium on Recent Developments in the Use of the MMPI/MMPI-2, Minneapolis, MN.

Rachman, S. (1989). The return of fear: Review and prospect. *Clinical Psychology Review, 9*, 147–168.

Rader, C. M. (1977). MMPI profile types of exposers, rapists, and assaulters in a court service population. *Journal of Consulting and Clinical Psychology, 45*, 61–69.

Raitz, A., Greene, E., Goodman, J., & Loftus, E. F. (1990). Determining damages: The influence of expert testimony on jurors' decision making. *Law and Human Behavior, 14,* 385–395.

Rathus, S. A., & Siegel, L. J. (1980). Crime and personality revisited. *Criminology, 18,* 245–251.

Redlich, F. C. (1977). The ethics of sex therapy. In W. H. Masters, V. E. Johnson, & R. D. Kolodny (Eds.), *Ethical issues in sex therapy and research* (pp. 143–157). Boston: Little, Brown.

Reitan, R. M., & Wolfson, D. (1985). *The Halstead-Reitan Neuropsychological Test Battery: Theory and clinical interpretation.* Tucson, AZ: Neuropsychology Press.

Repko, G. R., & Cooper, R. (1983). A study of the average worker's compensation case. *Journal of Clinical Psychology, 39,* 287–295.

Rice, M., Arnold, L., & Tate, D. (1983). Faking good and bad adjustment on the MMPI and overcontrolled-hostility in maximum security psychiatric patients. *Canadian Journal of Behavioral Sciences, 15,* 43–51.

Riskin, L. (1979). Sexual relations between psychotherapists and their patients: Toward research or restraint? *California Law Review, 67,* 1000–1027.

Rissetti, F., & Maltes, S. (1985). Use of the MMPI in Chile. In J. N. Butcher & C. D. Spielberger (Eds.), *Advances in personality assessment* (Vol. 4, pp. 209–257). Hillsdale, NJ: Erlbaum.

Roberts, A. H. (1984). The operant approach to the management of pain and excess disability. In A. D. Holzman & D. C. Turk (Eds.), *Pain management: A handbook of psychological treatment approaches* (pp. 10–30). New York: Pergamon Press.

Roberts, A. H., & Reinhardt, L. (1980). The behavioral management of chronic pain: Long-term follow-up with comparison groups. *Pain, 8,* 151–162.

Rogers, R. (1983). Malingering or random? A research note on obvious vs. subtle subscales of the MMPI. *Journal of Clinical Psychology, 39,* 257–258.

Rogers, R. (1984). Towards an empirical model of malingering and deception. *Behavioral Sciences & the Law, 2,* 93–111.

Rogers, R., Dolmetsch, R., & Cavanaugh, J. L. (1983). Identification of random responders on MMPI protocols. *Journal of Personality Assessment, 47,* 364–368.

Rogers, R., Gillis, J. R., McMain, S., & Dickens, S. E. (1988). Fitness evaluations: A retrospective study of clinical, criminal, and sociodemographic characteristics. *Canadian Journal of Behavioral Science, 20,* 192–200.

Rogers, R., Harris, M., & Thatcher, A. A. (1983). Identification of random responders on the MMPI: An actuarial approach. *Psychological Reports, 53,* 1171–1174.

Roman, D. D., & Gerbing, D. W. (1989). The mentally disordered criminal offender: A description based on demographic, clinical, and MMPI data. *Journal of Clinical Psychology, 45,* 983–990.

Roman, D. D., Tuley, M. R., Villanueva, M. R., & Mitchell, W. E. (1990). Evaluating MMPI validity in a forensic psychiatric population. *Criminal Justice and Behavior, 17,* 186–198.

Rosenbaum, R. (1991). *Travels with Dr. Death.* New York: Penguin Books.

Rosenthal, R. (1988). *Experimenter effects on behavioral research.* New York: Irvington.

Rosewater, L. B. (1985). Schizophrenic, borderline or battered? In L. B. Rosewater & L. E. Walker (Eds.), *Handbook on feminist therapy: Psychotherapy for women* (pp. 215–225). New York: Springer.

Rosewater, L. B. (1987). The clinical and courtroom application of battered women's personality assessments. In D. J. Sonkin (Ed.), *Domestic violence on trial* (pp. 86–94). New York: Springer.

Ross, S. (1988). *A first course in probability* (3rd ed.). New York: Macmillan.

Rothman, D. J. (1991). *Strangers at the bedside.* New York: Basic Books.

Rubenzer, S. (1991). Computerized testing and clinical judgment: Cause for concern. *The Clinical Psychologist, 44,* 63–66.

Sadoff, R. L. (1975). *Forensic psychiatry: A practical guide for lawyers and psychiatrists.* Springfield, IL: Charles C Thomas.

Saks, M. J. (1977). *Jury verdicts: The role of group size and social decision rule.* Lexington, MA: Lexington Books.

Saks, M. J. (1990). Expert witnesses, nonexpert witnesses, and nonwitness experts. *Law and Human Behavior, 14,* 291–314.

Salomone, P. R. (1972). Client motivation and rehabilitation counseling outcome. *Rehabilitation Counseling Bulletin, 16,* 11–20.

Savasir, I., & Erol, N. (1990). The Turkish MMPI: Translation, standardization, and validation. In J. N. Butcher & C. D. Spielberger (Eds.), *Advances in personality assessment* (Vol. 8, pp. 49–62). Hillsdale, NJ: Erlbaum.

Scarr, S. (1988). Race and gender as psychological variables: Social and ethical issues. *American Psychologist, 43,* 56–59.

Schafer, R. (1992). *Retelling a life*. New York: Basic Books.

Schaller, M., & Maass, A. (1989). Illusory correlation and social categorization: Toward an integration of motivational and cognitive factors in stereotype formation. *Journal of Personality and Social Psychology, 56*, 709–721.

Schank, R. C. (1980). Language and memory. *Cognitive Science, 4*, 243–284.

Schank, R. C. (1990). *Tell me a story: A new look at real and artificial memory*. New York: Scribner.

Schank, R. C., & Abelson, R. P. (1977). *Scripts, plans, goals, and understanding*. Hillsdale, NJ: Erlbaum.

Schank, R. C., Collins, G. C., & Hunter, L. E. (1986). Transcending inductive category formation in learning. *Behavioral and Brain Sciences, 9*, 639–651.

Scheaffer, R. L. (1990). *Introduction to probability and its applications*. Boston: PWS Kent.

Schiele, B. C., & Brozek, J. (1948). "Experimental neurosis" resulting from semistarvation in man. *Psychosomatic Medicine, 10*, 31–50.

Schlenger, W. E., & Kukla, R. A. (1987, August). *Performance of the Keane-Fairbank MMPI scale and other self-report measures in identifying post-traumatic stress disorder*. Paper presented at the 95th Annual Convention of the American Psychological Association, New York, NY.

Schlenger, W. E., Kukla, R. A., Fairbank, J. A., Hough, R. L., Jordan, B. K., Marmar, C. R., & Weiss, D. S. (1989). *The prevalence of post-traumatic stress disorder in the Vietnam generation: Findings from the National Vietnam Veterans Readjustment Study*. Report from Research Triangle Insitute, Research Triangle Park, NC.

Schmalz, B. J., Fehr, R. C., & Dalby, J. T. (1989). Distinguishing forensic, psychiatric and inmate groups with the MMPI. *American Journal of Forensic Psychology, 7*, 37–47.

Schmidt, H. O. (1948). Notes on the MMPI: The *K* factor. *Journal of Consulting Psychology, 12*, 337–342.

Schneider, L. J., & Cherry, P. (1976, September). MMPI patterns of college males from 1969–1973. *Journal of College Student Personnel*, 417–419.

Schneider, S.(1979). Disability payments for psychiatric patients: Is patient assessment affected? *Journal of Clinical Psychology, 35*, 259–264.

Schnelle, J. F. (1974). A brief report on invalidity of patient evaluations of behavior change. *Journal of Applied Behavior Analysis, 7*, 341–343.

Schretlen, D. (1988). The use of psychological tests to identify malingered symptoms of mental disorder. *Clinical Psychology Review, 8*, 451–476.

Schretlen, D. (1990). A limitation of using Wiener and Harmon obvious and subtle scales to detect faking on the MMPI. *Journal of Clinical Psychology, 46*, 1090–1095.

Schretlen, D., & Arkowitz, H. (1990). A psychological test battery to detect prison inmates who fake insanity or mental retardation. *Behavioral Sciences and the Law, 8*, 75–84.

Schretlen, D., Wilkins, S. S., Van Gorp, W. G., & Bobholz, J. H. (1992). Cross-validation of a psychological test battery to detect faked insanity. *Psychological Assessment, 4*, 77–83.

Scott, R., & Stone, D. (1986a). Measures of psychological disturbance in adolescent and adult victims of father–daughter incest. *Journal of Clinical Psychology, 42*, 251–269.

Scott, R., & Stone, D. (1986b). MMPI profile constellations in incest families. *Journal of Consulting and Clinical Psychology, 54*, 364–368.

Serrano, R. A. (1992, March 27). Expert says baton swings missed King; testimony purged. *Los Angeles Times*, pp. B3–B4.

Shafer, R. (1954). *Psychoanalytic interpretation in Rorschach testing: Theory and application*. New York: Grune & Stratton.

Shaffer, J. W. (1981). Using the MMPI to evaluate mental impairment in disability determination. In J. N. Butcher, G. Dahlstrom, M. Gynther, & W. Schofield (Eds.), *Clinical notes on the MMPI*. Nutley, NJ: Hoffman-La Roche Laboratories/NCS.

Shaffer, J. W., Nussbaum, K., & Little, J. M. (1972). MMPI profiles of disability insurance claimants. *American Journal of Psychiatry, 129*(4), 63–67.

Shapiro, D. L. (1984). *Psychological evaluation and expert testimony*. New York: Van Nostrand Reinhold.

Shapiro, D. L. (1991). *Forensic psychological assessment: An integrative approach*. Boston: Allyn & Bacon.

Shealy, L., Kalichman, S. C., Henderson, M. C., Szymanowski, D., & McKee, G. (1991). MMPI profile subtypes of incarcerated sex offenders against children. *Violence and Victims, 6*, 201–212.

Shepard, M. (1971). *The love treatment: Sexual intimacies between patients and psychotherapists*. New York: Wyden.

Shondrick, D. D., Ben-Porath, Y. S., & Stafford, K. (1992, May). *Forensic assessment with the MMPI-2: Characteristics of individuals undergoing court-ordered evaluations.* Paper presented at the 27th Annual Symposium on Recent Developments in the Use of the MMPI (MMPI-2), Minneapolis, MN.

Silver, R., & Sines, L. K. (1962). Diagnostic efficiency of the MMPI with and without *K* correction. *Journal of Clinical Psychology*, *18*, 312–314.

Simmons, J. G., Johnson, D. L., Gouvier, W. D., & Muzyczka, M. J. (1981). The Myer–Megargee inmate typology: Dynamic or unstable? *Criminal Justice and Behavior*, *8*, 49–54.

Singer, J. L. (1974). *Imagery and daydream methods in psychotherapy and behavior modification.* San Diego, CA: Academic Press.

Singer, J. L. (1980). The scientific basis of psychotherapeutic practice. *Psychotherapy: Theory, Research and Practice*, *17*, 372–383.

Singer, J. L., Sincoff, J. B., & Kolligian, J. (1989). Countertransference and cognition: Studying the psychotherapist's distortions as consequences of normal information processing. *Psychotherapy*, *26*, 344–355.

Smith, J. D., & Nelson, K. R. (1989). *The sterilization of Carrie Buck.* Far Hills, NJ: New Horizon Press.

Smith, V. L. (1991). Prototypes in the courtroom: Lay representations of legal concepts. *Journal of Personality and Social Psychology*, *61*, 857–872.

Smither, J. W., Collins, H., & Buda, R. (1989). When ratee satisfaction influences performance evaluations: A case of illusory correlation. *Journal of Applied Psychology*, *74*, 599–605.

Snibbe, J. R., Peterson, P. J., & Sosner, B. (1980). Study of psychological characteristics of a worker's compensation sample using the MMPI and the Millon Clinical Multiaxial Inventory. *Psychological Reports*, *47*, 959–966.

Snyder, D., & Regts, J. M. (1990). Personality correlates of marital satisfaction: A comparison of psychiatric, maritally distressed, and nonclinic samples. *Journal of Sex and Marital Therapy*, *16*, 34–43.

Sommers, R., & Sommers, B. A. (1983). Mystery in Milwaukee: Early intervention, IQ, and psychology textbooks. *American Psychologist*, *38*, 982–985.

Sonne, L., & Pope, K. S. (1991). Treating victims of therapist–patient sexual involvement. *Psychotherapy*, *28*, 174–187.

Spears, R., Van der Pligt, J., & Eisler, J. R. (1986). Generalizing the illusory correlation effect. *Journal of Personality and Social Psychology*, *51*, 1127–1134.

Spence, G. (1983). *Of murder and madness.* Garden City, NY: Doubleday.

Spence, G., & Polk, A. (1982). *Gunning for justice.* Garden City, NY: Doubleday.

Spiro, R. (1992). *Change and stability in the MMPI-2.* Manuscript submitted for publication.

Spring, F. L., & Foote, W. L. (1986). *Statement of principles relating to the responsibilities of attorneys and psychologists in their interprofessional relations: An interdisciplinary agreement between the New Mexico Bar Association and the New Mexico Psychological Association.* Adopted August 30, 1986, by the Board of Bar Commissioners of the State Bar of New Mexico and New Mexico Psychological Association.

Standards for educational and psychological testing. (1985). Washington, DC: American Psychological Association.

Stanton, W. (1960). *The leopard's spots: Scientific attitudes toward race in America 1815–59.* Chicago: University of Chicago Press.

Steinberg, E. R. (1982/1983). The stream-of-consciousness technique in the novel. *Imagination, Cognition & Personality: Consciousness in Theory, Research, and Clinical Practice*, *2*, 241–250.

Sternbach, R. A., Wolf, S. R., Murphy, R. W., & Akeson, W. H. (1973). Traits of pain patients: The low back "loser." *Psychosomatics*, *14*, 226–229.

Strassberg, D. S., Clutton, S., & Korboot, P. (1991). A descriptive and validity study of the Minnesota Multiphasic Personality Inventory-2 (MMPI-2) in an elderly Australian sample. *Journal of Psychopathology and Behavioral Assessment*, *13*, 301–312.

Strauss, M. E., Gynther, M. D., & Wallhermfechtel, J. (1974). Differential misdiagnosis of blacks and whites by the MMPI. *Journal of Personality Assessment*, *38*, 55–60.

Streiner, D. L., & Miller, H. R. (1986). Can a good short form of the MMPI ever be developed? *Journal of Clinical Psychology*, *42*, 109–113.

Stricker, G., Davis-Russell, E., Bourg, E., Duran, E., Hammong, W. R., McHolland, J., Polite, K., & Vaughn, B. E. (Eds.). (1990). *Toward ethnic diversification in psychology education and training.* Washington, DC: American Psychological Association.

Supplement to listing of APA-accredited doctoral and predoctoral internship training programs in psychology. (1991). *American Psychologist*, *46*, 770–772.

Sutker, P. B., Allain, A. N., & Geyer, S. (1978). Female criminal violence and differential MMPI characteristics. *Journal of Consulting and Clinical Psychology*, *46*, 1141–1143.

Sutker, P. B., Bugg, F., & Allain, A. N. (1991). Psychometric prediction of PTSD among POW survivors. *Psychological Assessment, 3*, 105–110.

Swan, R. J. (1957). Using the MMPI in marriage counseling. *Journal of Counseling Psychology, 4*, 239–244.

Sweetland, A. (1948). Hypnotic neurosis: Hypochondriasis and depression. *Journal of General Psychology, 39*, 91–105.

Taft, R. (1961). A psychological assessment of professional actors and related professions. *Genetic Psychology Monographs, 64*, 309–383.

Tallent, N. (1958). On individualizing the psychiatrist's clinical interpretation. *Journal of Clinical Psychology, 14*, 242–244.

Tallent, N. (1993). *Psychological report writing* (4th ed.). Englewood Cliffs, NJ: Prentice-Hall.

Tavris, C. (1992). *The mismeasure of woman*. New York: Simon & Schuster.

Tellegen, A., & Ben-Porath, Y. S. (1992a). *Code-type comparability of the MMPI and MMPI-2: Analysis of recent findings and criticisms.* Manuscript submitted for publication.

Tellegen, A., & Ben-Porath, Y. S. (1992b). The new uniform *T* scores for the MMPI-2: Rationale, derivation, and appraisal. *Psychological Assessment: A Journal of Clinical and Consulting Psychology, 4*, 145–155.

Therapist as sex partner better than "surrogate." (1976, June 1). *Ob. Gyn. News*, p. 11.

Thompson, W. C., & Schumann, E. L. (1987). Interpretation of statistical evidence in criminal trials: The prosecutor's fallacy and the defense attorney's fallacy. *Law and Human Behavior, 11*, 167–187.

Thomsen, J. L., Helwig-Larsen, K., & Rasmussen, O. V. (1984). Amnesty International and the forensic sciences. *American Journal of Forensic Medicine, 5*, 305–311.

Tierney, J. (1982). Doctor, is this man dangerous? Psychiatrists' predictions of criminal behavior are more often wrong than right. *Science, 82*, 28–31.

Timbrook, R., Graham, J. R., Keiller, S., & Watts, D. (1991, March). *Failure of the Weiner-Harmon subscales to discriminate between valid and invalid profiles.* Paper presented at the 26th Annual Symposium on Recent Developments in the Use of the MMPI (MMPI-2). St. Petersburg, FL.

Tversky, A., & Kahneman, D. (1973). Availability: A heuristic for judging frequency and probability. *Cognitive Psychology, 5*, 207–232.

Unger, R. K. (1979). *Female and male: Psychological perspectives.* New York: Harper & Row.

Van Cleve, E., Jemelka, R., & Trupin, E. (1991). Reliability of psychological test scores for offenders entering a state prison system. *Criminal Justice and Behavior, 18*, 159–165.

Villanueva, M. R., Roman, D. D., & Tuley, M. R. (1988). Determining forensic rehabilitation potential with the MMPI: Practical implications for residential treatment populations. *American Journal of Forensic Psychology, 6*, 27–35.

Vincent, K. R., Linsz, N. L., & Greene, M. I. (1966). The *L* scale of the MMPI as an index of falsification. *Journal of Consulting and Clinical Psychology, 22*, 214–215.

Wagenaar, W. A. (1988). The proper seat: A Bayesian discussion of the position of expert witness. *Law and Human Behavior, 12*, 499–510.

Walker, L. E. A. (1989). Psychology and violence against women. *American Psychologist, 44*, 695–702.

Walkup, B. (1984). Impeaching the expert. In B. G. Warshaw (Ed.), *The trial masters: A handbook of strategies and tactics that win cases* (pp. 272–286). Englewood Cliffs, NJ: Prentice-Hall.

Walter, M. J. (1982). Using the opponent's expert to prove your case. *Litigation, 8*, pp. 10–12, 59–60.

Walters, G. D. (1986). Correlates of the Megargee criminal classification system: A military correctional setting. *Criminal Justice and Behavior, 13*, 19–32.

Walters, G. D., White, T., & Greene, R. (1988). Use of the MMPI to identify malingering and exaggeration of psychiatric symptomatology in male prison inmates. *Journal of Consulting and Clinical Psychology, 56*, 111–117.

Warren, L. W., & Weiss, D. J. (1969). Relationship between disability type and measured personality characteristics. In *Proceedings of the 77th Annual Convention of the American Psychological Association* (Pt. II), pp. 773–774.

Warshaw, B. G. (Ed.). (1984). *The trial masters: A handbook of strategies and techniques that win cases.* New York: Prentice-Hall.

Waskow, I. E., & Parloff, M. B. (Eds.). (1975). *Psychotherapy change measures: Report of the Clinical Research Branch Outcome Measures Project.* Rockville, MD: National Institute of Mental Health.

Wasyliw, O. E., Grossman, L. S., Haywood, T. W., & Cavanaugh, J. L. (1988). The detection of malingering in criminal forensic groups: MMPI validity scales. *Journal of Personality Assessment, 52*, 321–333.

Weed, N., Ben-Porath, Y. S., & Butcher, J. N. (1990). Failure of the Wiener-Harmon Minnesota Multiphasic Personality Inventory (MMPI) subtle scales as predictors of psychopathology and as validity indicators. *Psychological Assessment: A Journal of Consulting and Clinical Psychology*, *2*, 281–285.

Weed, N. & Han, K. (May, 1992). *Is K correct?* Paper presented at the 27th Annual Symposium on Recent Developments in the Use of the MMPI, Minneapolis, MN.

Weiner, I. B. (1987). Writing forensic reports. In I. B. Weiner & A. Hess (Eds.), *Handbook of forensic psychology* (pp. 511–528). New York: Wiley.

Weiner, I. B. (1989). On competence and ethicality in psychodiagnostic assessment. *Journal of Personality Assessment*, *53*, 827–831.

Weissman, H. N. (1984). Psychological assessment and psycho-legal formulations in psychiatric traumatology. *Psychiatric Annals*, *14*, 517–529.

Wellman, F. L. (1936). *The art of cross-examination*. New York: Macmillan. (Originally published 1903)

West's California Codes: Evidence Code. (1986). St. Paul, MN: West Publishing Company.

Westermeyer, J., Williams, C., & Nguyen, N. (Eds.). (1992). *Refugee mental health and adjustment*. Washington, DC: US Government Printing Office.

Wetzler, S., & Marlowe, D. (1990). "Faking bad" on the MMPI, MMPI-2, and Millon-II. *Psychological Reports*, *67*, 1117–1118.

Wiener, D. N. (1948a). Personality characteristics of selected disability groups. In G. S. Welsh & W. G. Dahlstrom (Eds.), *Basic readings on the MMPI in psychology and medicine* (pp. 435–451). Minneapolis: University of Minnesota Press.

Wiener, D. N. (1948b). Subtle and obvious keys for the Minnesota Multiphasic Personality Inventory. *Journal of Consulting Psychology*, *12*, 164–170.

Wilcock, K. D. (1964). Neurotic differences between individualized and socialized criminals. *Journal of Consulting Psychology*, *28*, 141–145.

Wilcox, P., & Dawson, J. (1977). Role-played and hypnotically induced simulation of psychopathology on the MMPI. *Journal of Clinical Psychology*, *33*, 743–745.

Willcockson, J. C., Bolton, B., & Dana, R. H. (1983). A comparison of six MMPI short forms: Code type correspondence and indices of psychopathology. *Journal of Clinical Psychology*, *39*, 968–969.

Williams, C. L., & Butcher, J. N. (1989). An MMPI study of adolescents: I. Empirical validity of the standard scales. *Psychological Assessment: A Journal of Consulting and Clinical Psychology*, *1*, 251–259.

Williams, C. L., Butcher, J. N., Ben-Porath, Y. S., & Graham, J. R. (1992). *MMPI-A content scales: Assessing psychopathology in adolescents*. Minneapolis: University of Minnesota Press.

Williams, M. H. (1992). Exploitation and inference: Mapping the damage from therapist–patient sexual involvement. *American Psychologist*, *47*, 412–421.

Williams, R. D. (1988). Corporate policies for creation and retention of documents. In K. Ross & B. Wrubel (Eds.), *Product liability of manufacturers 1988: Prevention and defense* (pp. 529–596). New York: Practicing Law Institute.

Wilson, E. B. (1952). *An introduction to scientific research*. New York: McGraw-Hill.

Wilson, J. P., & Walker, A. J. (1990). Toward an MMPI trauma profile. *Journal of Traumatic Stress*, *3*, 151–168.

Wiltse, L. L., & Rocchio, P. H. (1975). Pre-operative psychological tests as predictors of success of chemonucleolysis and treatment of low back pain syndrome. *Journal of Bone and Joint Surgery*, *57*, 478–483.

Winkel, F. W. (1990). Crime reporting in newspapers: An exploratory study of the effects of ethnic references in crime news. *Social Behavior*, *5*, 87–101.

Wolf, S., Freinck, W. R., & Shaffer J. W. (1964). Comparability of complete oral and booklet forms of the MMPI. *Journal of Clinical Psychology*, *20*, 375–378.

Woody, R. H. (1977). Behavioral science criteria in custody determinations. *Journal of Marriage and Family Counseling*, *3*, 11–18.

Wright, L. (1970). Psychologic aspects of the battered child syndrome. *Southern Medical Bulletin*, *58*, 14–18.

Wright, L. (1976). The sick but slick syndrome as a personality component of parents of battered children. *Journal of Clinical Psychology*, *32*, 41–45.

Wrobel, T. A., Calovini, P. K., & Martin, T. O. (1991). Application of the Megargee MMPI typology to a population of defendants referred for psychiatric evaluation. *Criminal Justice and Behavior*, *18*, 397–405.

Wrobel, T. A., & Lachar, D. (1982). Validity of the Wiener subtle and obvious empirically derived psychological test items under faking conditions. *Journal of Consulting and Clinical Psychology*, *50*, 469–470.

Yates, J. F. (1990). *Judgment and decision making*. Englewood Cliffs, NJ: Prentice-Hall.

Young, R. K., & Veldman, D. J. (1981). *Introductory statistics for the behavioral sciences* (4th ed.). New York: Holt, Rinehart & Winston.

Younger, I. (1986a). *Credibility and cross-examination*. Hopkins, MN: Professional Education Group.

Younger, I. (1986b). *Expert witnesses*. Hopkins, MN: Professional Education Group.

Younger, I. (Ed.). (1986c). *Thomas Murphey's cross-examination of Dr. Carl A. Binger*. Hopkins, MN: Professional Education Group.

Zager, L. D. (1983). Response to Simmons and associates: Conclusions about the MMPI-based classification system's stability are premature. *Criminal Justice and Behavior, 10*, 310–315.

Zager, L. D. (1988). The MMPI-based criminal classification system: A review, current status, and future directions. *Criminal Justice and Behavior, 15*, 39–57.

Ziskin, J. (1969). *Coping with psychiatric and psychological testimony*. Marina Del Rey, CA: Law and Psychology Press.

Ziskin, J. (1981a). *Coping with psychiatric and psychological testimony* (Vols. 1–2, 3rd ed.). Marina Del Rey, CA: Law and Psychology Press.

Ziskin, J. (1981b). Use of the MMPI in forensic settings. In J. N. Butcher, W. G. Dahlstrom, M. D. Gynther, & W. Schofield (Eds.), *Clinical notes on the MMPI, 1*(Whole No. 19). Nutley, NJ: Hoffman-La Roche Laboratories/NCS.

Ziskin, J., & Faust, D. (1988). *Coping with psychiatric and psychological testimony* (Vols. 1–3, 4th ed.). Marina Del Rey, CA: Law and Psychology Press.

Index

About the Authors

Kenneth S. Pope, PhD, received advanced degrees from Harvard (where he studied as a Woodrow Wilson Fellow) and Yale, is a Diplomate in Clinical Psychology, and is a Fellow of the American Psychological Association (APA) and the American Psychological Society (APS). Having previously served as clinical director and psychology director in both private hospital and community mental health center settings, he is currently in independent practice. He taught courses in psychological and neuropsychological assessment, abnormal psychology, and related areas at the University of California, Los Angeles, where he served as a psychotherapy supervisor in the UCLA Psychology Clinic. He was elected and served as chair of the Ethics Committees of the APA and of the American Board of Professional Psychology. He received the Frances Mosseker Award for Fiction and the Belle Meyer Bromberg Award for Literature. His books include *Sexual Feelings in Psychotherapy: Explorations for Therapists and Therapists-in-Training* (with Janet Sonne and Jean Holroyd; APA, 1993); *Ethics in Psychotherapy and Counseling: A Practical Guide for Psychologists* (with Melba Vasquez; Jossey-Bass, 1991); *Sexual Intimacies Between Therapists and Patients* (with Jacqueline Bouhoutsos; Praeger, 1986); *On Love and Loving: Psychological Perspectives on the Nature and Experience of Romantic Love* (Jossey-Bass, 1980); *The Stream of Consciousness: Scientific Investigations into the Flow of Human Experience* (Plenum, 1978); and *The Power of Human Imagination: New Methods of Psychotherapy* (Plenum, 1978) (the latter two with Jerome L. Singer). A recipient of the LACPA Award for Outstanding Contribution to Psychology, and both the Silver Psi Award and the Distinguished Contributions to Psychology as a Profession Award from the California Psychological Association, he has served as an expert witness and consultant in both civil (malpractice) cases and licensing hearings.

James N. Butcher, PhD, received his BA in psychology from Guilford College, and his MA in experimental psychology and his PhD in clinical psychology from the University of North Carolina at Chapel Hill. Currently professor of psychology at the University of Minnesota and editor of the APA journal *Psychological Assessment,* he was recently awarded Doctor Honoris Causa by the Free University of Brussels. Maintaining active research programs in the areas of personality assessment, abnormal psychology, cross-cultural personality factors, and computer-based psychological assessment, he was selected by the University of Minnesota Press (who possesses the rights to the MMPI) to serve on the committee to revise and restandardize the MMPI. A consultant for airlines in the psychological screening of airline pilot applicants and also in developing and implementing disaster response programs for human problems following airline disasters, he organized and supervised psychological services following two recent airline disasters: Northwest Flight 255 and Aloha Airlines' Maui incident. Founder (in 1965) and organizer of the annual Symposium on Recent Developments in the Use of the MMPI, he also founded the International Conference on Personality Assessment. He is a member of the Board of Trustees of the Society for Personality Assessment and was elected to the Executive Committee of APA's Division of Measurement and Evaluation (Division 5). His most recent books include *Use of the MMPI-2 in Treatment Planning* (Oxford University Press, 1992); *A Practitioner's Guide to Computerized Psychological Assessment* (Basic Books, 1987); *Essentials of MMPI-2 and MMPI-A Interpretation* (with Carolyn L. Williams; University of Minnesota Press, 1992); *Abnormal Psychology and Modern Life* (9th ed.; with Robert C. Carson; HarperCollins, 1992); and *Handbook of Research Methods in Clinical Psychology* (with Philip C. Kendall; John Wiley & Sons, 1982). He consults and testifies as an expert witness in trials involving the MMPI.

JOYCE SEELEN received her BA in journalism from the University of Minnesota and her JD from the University of Denver School of Law. She practiced in Denver as a Colorado state public defender, after which she began a private practice that emphasizes representation of the victims of abuse by persons in positions of trust. An active litigator, she has tried several civil cases to jury verdict in excess of $1 million each. She is a partner in the Denver law firm of Holland, Seelen & Pagliuca, which emphasizes personal injury litigation and the defense of the criminally accused.